Preparing Quality Teachers

Advances in Clinical Practice

Preparing Quality Teachers

Advances in Clinical Practice

Editors

Drew Polly
University of North Carolina at Charlotte

Eva Garin
Bowie State University

INFORMATION AGE PUBLISHING, INC.
Charlotte, NC • www.infoagepub.com

Library of Congress Cataloging-in-Publication Data

CIP record for this book is available from the Library of Congress
http://www.loc.gov

ISBNs: 978-1-64802-868-7 (Paperback)

         978-1-64802-869-4 (Hardcover)

         978-1-64802-870-0 (ebook)

CONTENTS

SECTION II: RESIDENCIES AND ALTERNATIVE CERTIFICATION

SECTION III: INNOVATIVE PARTNERSHIPS

SECTION IV: OTHER INNOVATIVE IDEAS AND APPROACHES

FOREWORD

Section I: Diversity, Core Practices, and Dispositions

This section includes chapters that address the intersection of clinical practice with topics of diversity, core practices, and dispositions. This section opens with Chapter 1 where Candela, Register, Singer, Fisher, Smith-Sodey, Koscielski, and von der Heyde describe how they revamped their teacher education program to ensure that all teacher candidates gained worthwhile clinical practice experiences with PK–12 students with diverse ethnicities, races, and socioeconomic backgrounds. This clinical practice included work with community-based agencies that support children as well as time in classrooms. In Chapter 2 Sableski describes how an undergraduate certificate program focused on teaching students with dyslexia aligns to recommendations for clinical practice. The program focuses on developing a proper mindset about effective literacy instruction as well as specific knowledge and skills related to research-based practices to support students who have dyslexia.

In Chapters 3 through 5 authors describe how clinical practice helps prepare teacher candidates to enact core practices in classrooms. In Chapter 3 Shaughnessy, Selling, Garcia, and Ball examine what knowledge and skills teacher educators need to have to effectively prepare teacher candidates as well as how teacher educators can best learn these knowledge and skills. The authors situate their work in practice-based teacher education focused on the core practice of leading a group discussion in

Preparing Quality Teachers:
Advances in Clinical Practice, pp. xi–xv
Copyright © 2022 by Information Age Publishing
www.infoagepub.com
All rights of reproduction in any form reserved.

mathematics to discuss these topics. In Chapter 4 Hanley, Miller, Sorensen, and Rogan-Klyve describe a professional development workshop on clinical practice for teacher preparation programs focused on science, technology, engineering, and mathematics (STEM) education. The program focused on core practices and practice-based approaches to teacher education. In Chapter 5 Billings, Knapp, Sharpe, Swartz, Lynch, and Pinter share four vignettes about mediated field experiences where teacher candidates approximate and enact core teaching practices during clinical practice experiences in mathematics classrooms. Through these field experiences candidates develop their enactment of core teaching practices, mathematical knowledge for teaching, and work with concepts related to equity-based teaching while working with PK-12 students.

In Chapter 6 Wolfe and Newman explore the idea about what characteristics, knowledge, and skills that teachers feel are important for themselves as teachers and/or others as teacher leaders. The chapter includes data that includes a survey and interviews with select survey completers. The authors indicate a strong connection between teaching practice, teacher leadership, and teacher leadership engagement. In Chapter 7 Hands, Roselle, Kuhn, Cahill, and Hands discuss the complex process of examining teacher candidates' dispositions during clinical practice experiences. The authors contend that it is essential to engage candidates in reflective practice by self-assessing their own capacity for caring, engaging in authentic teacher-student relationships, committing to a culturally responsive and nurturing pedagogy. In Chapter 8 McCormack shared how an intentional partnership between a school and a university increased candidates' use of high-leverage core practices, differentiated culturally responsive instructional strategies, trauma-informed teaching practices, and social emotional learning knowledge and pedagogical skills

Section II: Residencies and Alternative Certification

This section includes chapters focused on clinical practice in the context of residencies and alternative certification. In Chapter 9 Cook, Eicher, and Martin describe the characteristics of their residency program, which is part of a combined bachelor's to master's degree pathway whereby students in any of our teacher preparation programs can begin graduate coursework as an undergraduate student. They also share data from mentor teachers and teacher candidates about residents' preparation to teach. In Chapter 10 Forte, Wilburne, and Swogger describe their design and implementation of a residency model for teacher candidates to complete clinical practice experiences in schools that have been labeled as high-need due to poor student achievement. The residency model helped to provide more authentic experiences than their previous traditional clinical model, and the residency model also helped to diversify the teacher workforce by attracting teacher candidates from demographic groups that are traditionally minoritized in teaching.

In Chapter 11 Ellerbrock describes how her university created a middle school teacher residency program focused on STEM education. This chapter includes a description of how university faculty have refined the program based on the data and the needs of the partnerships district. In Chapter 12 Audrain and Googins describe the concept of teacher academies located in secondary schools around the United States. They envision what these teacher academies could look like and how they could support teacher candidates with an intentional focus on clinical practice experiences. In Chapter 13 Rose and Sughrue share the findings of a study where they interviewed school leaders about their perceptions and understanding of the needs of teachers who were teaching with an alternative teacher certification. Administrators reported that they had high expectations for all teachers, including those with alternative certification, and that they identified very general supports that could benefit teachers with alternative certification.

In Chapter 14 Woods, Marshall, and Shetty consider various types of alternative pathways to teaching including summer pathways, postgraduate provisional pathways, career-switcher pathways, and distance learning pathways. The authors provide program outcome data and share that alternatively certified teachers perform as well if not better than teachers who were prepared through more traditional pathways. In Chapter 15 Henning, Mulvaney, Bragen, and George describe a program at their university where teacher candidates are paid by the school district while completing their internship. They have found that this program has led to teacher candidates having a better relationship with students

Section III: Innovative Partnerships

In Chapter 16 Strutchen, Conway, Mangram, Erickson, and Ratliff describe the design and implementation of a paired partnership model for teacher candidates. Clinical educators mentor and coach two teacher candidates during the intentionally-designed clinical practice experiences that were based on the Plan-Do-Study-Act model. In Chapter 17 Curcio, Braden, Compton-Lilly, Myers, and White describe how their educator preparation program aligns to multiple aspects of the AACTE Clinical Practice report with a focus on their school-embedded methods courses which take place in the buildings of their elementary Professional Development School partners. The chapter includes findings from a study of alumni who reported the benefits of the school-embedded methods courses on their preparation, including their strong sense of being ready to teach students whose background is different from their own.

In Chapter 18 Gibbs, Ohlson, Brown, Lester, Faulkner, Jackson, and Anderson describe the design and first-year outcomes of a partnership between multiple schools and a university. The partnership which included shared decision making with multiple Principals provided professional development of teacher candidates and mentor teachers, community outreach, and enhanced clinical experiences for teacher candidates. In Chapter 19 Good, Alston, Vintinner, Binns, Rock, and Putman describe how they revised their clinical practice experiences for their elementary education teacher candidates by forming intentional school partnerships, assigning multiple candidates to partner schools, and creating interdisciplinary experiences based on university faculty collaborating with one another. The chapter includes a description about how university faculty worked with clinical educators to create meaningful experiences for teacher candidates and the elementary school students in the partner schools.

In Chapter 20 Rees, Kaur, Ruberg, Maslowski, Bauhuis, Sjokvist, and Livingstone focus their process of establishing clinical practice settings through a democratic process that incorporated the input and opinions of teacher candidates, mentor teachers a clinical educators, university faculty, school administrators, and community organizations. The chapter includes the multiple voices and perspectives of these different stakeholders involved in the design and implementation of teacher candidates' clinical practice experiences. In Chapter 21 Hines, Glavey, Hanley, and Romualdo describe the relaunch of an Exceptional Education teacher preparation program that included community-embedded ongoing clinical experiences. They describe key components of the model as well as initial program outcomes, including feedback from teacher candidates. In Chapter 22 Shapiro and Kraus share the findings of a study that examined teacher candidates' perceptions of and experiences developing relationships during their clinical practice experiences. Teacher candidates reported that stronger relationships with their clinical educators led to more positive clinical experiences and a higher tendency to enact high-leverage practices.

Section IV: Other Innovative Ideas and Approaches

This section includes chapters that focus on other innovative ideas and approaches to clinical practice. In Chapter 23 Egelson and Hardesty propose ideas related to researching innovative clinical practice and research on teachers' and teacher candidates' self-reflection. The authors use a case study to show that a teacher candidate can reflect on their own clinical practice experiences and influence their development of their pedagogical and social practices. In Chapter 24 Sears, Brosnan, Castro-Minnehan, Clarke, and Stone describe how teacher candidates and clinical educators use the Apprenticeship Model for Learning during clinical practice experiences. Teacher candidates and clinical educators reported that aspects of the apprenticeship model led to powerful collaborative relationships that positively impacted students' learning.

In Chapter 25 Manuel, McIntyre, Reeves, and Curry share the findings of a study that compares data from a traditional teacher education program and a hybrid program that set up intensive clinical practice experiences. Data from clinical educators who hosted teacher candidates and faculty reported the hybrid model led to higher teacher candidate performance on various outcome measures such as use of teaching practices, unit planning, and lesson planning. In Chapter 26 Wagle, Eades-Baird, and Mahar describe the revision to the clinical model in a state-wide teacher preparation program that included placing teacher candidates in cohorts in clinical practice experiences, intentional work with clinical educators. The program also used micro-credentialing to recognize teacher candidates' development of important pedagogical skills.

In Chapter 27 Zelkowski, Yow, Waller, Edwards, Anthony, and Campbell describe their process of designing course modules for secondary mathematics teacher candidates that intentionally integrate course content with clinical practice experiences in secondary mathematics classrooms. The modules include multiple opportunities for teacher candidates to demonstrate their development of knowledge and skills related to teaching and feedback loops for clinical educators to inform university faculty about teacher candidates' development. Next, in Chapter 28 Baugher, Smith, and Haughey describe a teacher candidates' journey during their clinical experience. The authors use change theory, the learning zone model, and mindset theory in order to make sense of the clinical experience. In Chapter 29 Goodnough and Stordy describe the principles, content, structure, and features of a coherent program focused on primary/elementary Science, Technology, Engineering, and Mathematics (STEM) education at their university in Canada. The program integrates action research, service learning, and school-university partnerships in their teacher candidates' experiences. In Chapter 30 Bernauer advocates for the idea of guided entry into the teaching professions where clinical practice experiences and student teaching internship include more aspects similar to apprenticeships and mentoring relationships with clinical educators. The chapter includes examples and recommendations for teacher education programs on how to infuse more apprenticeship-like aspects into their teacher candidates' experiences.

PREFACE

CLINICAL PRACTICE IN EDUCATOR PREPARATION PROGRAMS

Challenges and Future Directions

Drew Polly
University of North Carolina at Charlotte

Eva Garin
Bowie State University

"Clinical practice is a model to prepare high-quality educators with and through a pedagogical skill set that provides articulated benefits for every participant, while being fully embedded in the PK–12 setting." —AACTE (2018, p. 6)

Educator preparation programs rely heavily on partnerships with school settings to provide clinical practice experiences to their current and future teachers (Badiali et al., 2021; Putman & Polly, 2021). In general, educator preparation programs have come under scrutiny regarding data from teacher candidates, data from student learning outcomes associated with teacher candidates, as well as the extent that these programs adequately prepare teacher candidates to teach PK–12 students who are different from

Preparing Quality Teachers:
Advances in Clinical Practice, pp. xvii–xxiii
Copyright © 2022 by Information Age Publishing
www.infoagepub.com
All rights of reproduction in any form reserved.

them in terms of socioeconomic status, race, ethnicity, and cultural background (Darling-Hammond, 2010, 2017; Howard & Milner, 2021; National Council for Accreditation of Teacher Education [NCATE], 2010; Siwatu et al., 2016). Recommendations have been made by national organizations (American Association of Colleges for Teacher Education [AACTE], 2018; National Association for Professional Development Schools [NAPDS], 2021) and scholars (e.g., Dresden & Thompson, 2021; Holmes Group, 1995; Goodlad, 1994; Zeichner, 2021; Zenkov et al., 2021) about ways to support clinical practice.

The purpose of this book is to showcase multiple ways that clinical practice has supported educator preparation as described by the Clinical Practice Commission Report (hereafter CPC Report) from AACTE. This book includes empirical, theoretical/conceptual, and anecdotal pieces that address aspects of teacher candidates' clinical practice experiences and provides recommendations and implications for clinical practice. These manuscripts provide evidence and well-developed ideas about the effective preparation of teachers through clinical practice that align to elements of the CPC Report. Further, they focus on improving candidates' capacity to develop specific pedagogies and pedagogical content knowledge, developing the dispositions and attitudes of teacher candidates, and preparing candidates to teach PK–12 students with backgrounds that are diverse or different from the teacher candidate. In the remainder of this introductory chapter, we aim to describe challenges and opportunities to clinical practice work with a focus on three areas: creating and maintaining mutually beneficial partnerships, determining priorities in clinical practice, and examining the impact of clinical practices.

CREATING AND MAINTAINING MUTUALLY BENEFICIAL PARTNERSHIPS

Educator preparation programs cannot operate in isolation and effectively prepare their teacher candidates to be effective in today's schools. Clinical practice is a nonnegotiable aspect of programs and the process of creating and maintaining mutually beneficial partnerships is of utmost importance for those who work in schools, departments, and colleges of education (Badiali et al., 2021). The phrase *mutually beneficial partnerships* has been advanced in the literature to describe formal agreements where both educator preparation programs and the P–12 schools who codevelop teacher candidates gain something from the partnership (NAPDS, 2008, 2021). In our opinion this focuses on two questions: How is the process of hosting teacher candidates for clinical practice beneficial to PK–12 schools? How are partnerships between PK–12 schools and educator preparation programs beneficial to the PK–12 school administrators, faculty, and staff?

From a staffing, hiring perspective PK–12 schools benefit from being able to form relationships with future teachers. In some cases, these mutually beneficial school-university partnerships help schools capture the attention of teacher candidates and create a teacher pipeline for teacher candidates to walk into a full-time teaching position in the same school and/or district where they completed their clinical practice experiences (Putman & Polly, 2021). Schools and districts also can leverage these partnerships to see these teacher candidates in action and get to know these candidates before they are ready to apply for full-time teaching positions.

Additionally, PK–12 schools can benefit with the opportunity for their faculty to engage in professional development co-led by university faculty (Burns & Baker, 2016; Dzielawa et al., 2020). Faculty in some cases have taken on the role of instructional coach or professor-in-residence to support PK–12 schoolteachers through planning meetings, professional development, and co-teaching lessons (Flores & Sigman, 2020; Polly, 2012, 2017; Polly et al., 2020).

Further studies are needed about ways to form these mutually beneficial partnerships that support clinical practice experiences for teacher candidates. Specific questions that require examination include:

- What are some frequently occurring characteristics of mutually beneficial school-university partnerships?
- What is the impact of these partnerships on PK–12 administrators, faculty, and teachers?
- When there are changes in the leadership and faculty from either educator preparation programs or the PK–12 school or school district how? And
- What are the contexts, factors and characteristics that contribute to effective long-lasting partnerships?

Lastly, there is a need to continue the conversation between partners about what mutually beneficial means to both educator preparation programs and PK–12 schools. As legislation mandating more and specific types of clinical practice experiences continue to increase, educator preparation programs and PK–12 schools need to regularly have conversations to make sure both entities are benefiting from the partnership.

DETERMINING PRIORITIES AND FOCUS IN CLINICAL PRACTICE

As both educator preparation programs and PK–12 schools consider how to best support teacher candidates with clinical practice experiences there is a need for both groups to consider what their priorities and focus is related to preparing future teachers. There are multiple things to consider.

First, educator preparation programs need to consider complexities of the cost and benefits of placing candidates in multiple schools for less time but providing experiences in a variety of settings (e.g., rural, suburban, and urban) and in schools with students coming from various backgrounds. On the other hand, is it beneficial to place candidates in fewer placements but have them spend more semesters and more time in those schools to become more of a part of the school culture?

Further, in response to the need for teacher candidates to participate in clinical practice experiences in schools in urban areas with students who are experiencing poverty, many states and educator preparation programs require at least one clinical practice experience in these settings. However, is an urban clinical placement as a junior where teacher candidates are just learning how to teach equivalent in the quality of experience as completing their full-time student teaching in such a setting?

For large educator preparation programs there is an additional need to determine how to prioritize placements of teacher candidates in all settings in schools that do not exhaust, wear out, or overburden schools.

PK–12 schools need to consider how to best support clinical educators who host and mentor teacher candidates. In order to be effective mentors, leaders of districts and PK–12 schools need to determine what teachers are interested in and possess the knowledge and skills related to mentoring teacher candidates. While being an effective teacher is certainly an important characteristic for clinical educators, effectiveness that is primarily measured by student learning outcomes and test scores is very short-sighted. There is a need to consider other factors such as potential clinical educators' teaching practices and their alignment to those practices emphasized by the educator preparation program, relationships with their students and their colleagues, and their knowledge and skills related to mentoring and coaching.

Intuitively there is a need for research related to the processes that both educator preparation programs and PK–12 schools to prioritize and focus on various aspects of clinical practice as well as what the influence of those processes and decisions have on PK–12 students, teacher candidates, clinical educators, and other participants in the partnership.

A CALL TO MORE BROADLY EXAMINE RESEARCH ON CLINICAL PRACTICE

As evident in the chapters in this book as well as recently published research on clinical practice, scholars are examining some important research questions and examining key issues related to teacher candidates' clinical practice experiences. However, there is a need for scholars to continue to extend the knowledge base related to clinical practice. Guskey (2000) offered a framework for evaluating and researching teacher learning that was intended to examine professional development efforts for inservice teachers, but is also applicable to educator preparation programs and clinical educators. Table 1.1 provides an overview of Guskey's framework as well as ways that it could relate directly to research around clinical practice.

Table 1 provides a framework, but scholars need to continue to look at ways to design studies that examine multiple facets of clinical practice. Too often educator preparation programs collect data for accreditation purposes that only encompass participants' reactions while faculty in educator preparation programs often collect data related to Level 3 about how teacher candidates are applying their knowledge and skills. Yet, there is a need to systematically examine how clinical practice and the specific experiences that candidates engage in contribute to and influence the teacher candidates' learning on course assignments, their teaching during clinical experiences, and their students' learning when they teach. As important as it is to innovate and think outside the box, there is a critical need to design and carry out research studies about how clinical practice and partnerships influence themselves, their clinical educators, and the students that they work with.

Table 1

Adaptation of Guskey's Framework to Examine Clinical Practice

Level	Possible Research Questions	Possible Data Sources
1: Participants' reactions	What were teacher candidates' and/or clinical educators' experiences during the clinical practice experience?	Survey/questionnaire Interviews or focus groups Written reflections
	What were PK–12 students' experiences during the clinical practice experience?	
2: Participants' learning	What was the influence of the clinical practice experience on teacher candidates' and/or clinical educators' knowledge and skills?	Written reflections Performance-based assessments

(Table continued on next page)

Table 1 (Continued)

Adaptation of Guskey's Framework to Examine Clinical Practice

Level	Possible Research Questions	Possible Data Sources
3: Participants' use of knowledge and skills	How did teacher candidates and/or clinical educators put to use their new knowledge and skills related to the clinical practice experience?	Interviews or focus groups Observations or videos of classroom teaching Lesson plans
4: Impact on organization(s)	How did the clinical practice experience influence decisions related to the educator preparation program and/or the PK–12 school	Survey/questionnaire Interviews or focus groups Documents from organizations

In closing, we hope that this book informs aspects of your own work, whether it is the creation or refinement of clinical practice experiences for teacher candidates in your context or for your inquiry and research efforts around topics related to clinical practice. Together, educator preparation programs and PK–12 schools must collaborate in order to mentor teacher candidates into the teachers that schools need.

REFERENCES

American Association of Colleges for Teacher Education (AACTE). (2018). *A pivot toward clinical practice, its lexicon, and the renewal of educator preparation.* https://aacte.org/professional-development-and-events/clinical- practice-commission-press-conference.

Badiali, B., Polly, D., Burns, R. W., & Garin, E. (2021). Cultivating change in clinical practice: Conclusions from the special issue. *Peabody Journal of Education, 96*(1), 112–116. https://doi.org/10.1080/0161956X.2020.1864251

Burns, R. W., & Baker, W. (2016). The boundary spanner in Professional Development Schools: In search of common nomenclature. *School-University Partnerships, 9*(2), 28–39.

Darling-Hammond, L. (2010). Teacher education and the American future. *Journal of Teacher Education, 61*(1–2), 35–47. https://doi.org/10.1177/0022487109348024

Darling-Hammond, L. (2017). Teacher education around the world: What can we learn from international practice? *European Journal of Teacher Education, 40*(3), 291–309.

Dresden, J., & Thompson, K. F. (2021). Looking closely at clinical practice: A clear-eyed vision for the future of teacher education. *Peabody Journal of Education*, *96*(1), 8–21. https://doi.org/10.1080/0161956X.2020.1864242

Dzielawa, S., Eberly, R., & Johnson, K. (2020). The power of PD in our PDS. *PDS Partners: Bridging Research to Practice*, *15*(2), 8–9.

Flores, B., & Sigman, K. (2020). Placements or partnerships? How an intern and university supervisor/liaison impacted practice, student learning, and overall university/school partnership. *PDS Partners: Bridging Research to Practice*, *15*(3), 3–6.

Goodlad, J. I. (1994). *Educational renewal: Better teachers, better schools.* Jossey-Bass.

Holmes Group. (1995). *Tomorrow's school of education: A report of the Holmes Group.*

Howard, T. C., & Milner, H. R. (2021). Teacher preparation for urban schools. *Handbook of Urban Education* (2nd ed.). Routledge.

National Association for Professional Development Schools. (2008). *What it means to be a professional development school.* The Executive Council and Board of Directors.

National Association for Professional Development Schools. (2021). *What it means to be a Professional Development School: The nine essentials* (2nd ed.). [Policy statement].

National Council for Accreditation of Teacher Education. (2010). *Transforming teacher education through clinical practice: A national strategy to prepare effective teachers* [Policy Statement].

Polly, D. (2012). Supporting mathematics instruction with an expert coaching model. *Mathematics Teacher Education and Development*, *14*(1), 78–93.

Polly, D. (2017). Providing school-based learning in elementary school mathematics: The case of a Professional Development School Partnership. *Teacher Development: An International Journal of Teachers' Professional Development*, *21*(5), 668–686. https://doi.org/10.1080/13664530.2017.1308427

Polly, D., Rock, T. C., Binns, I., & Zaionz, R. (2020). Tracking the path of a multifaceted Professional Development School partnership. In E. Garin & R. W. Burns & (Eds.), *The NAPDS nine essentials in action: Cases of Professional Development Schools* (pp. 79–86). Information Age Publishing.

Putman, S. M., & Polly, D. (2021). Examining the development and implementation of an embedded, multi-semester internship: Preliminary perceptions of teacher education candidates, clinical educators, and university faculty. *Peabody Journal of Education*, *96*(1), 99–111. https://doi.org/10.1080/01619 56X.2020.1864250

Siwatu, K. O., Chesnut, S. R., Aledjandro, A. Y., & Young, H. A. (2016). Examining preservice teachers' culturally responsive teaching self-efficacy doubts. *The Teacher Educator, 51*(4), 277–296. https://doi.org/10.1080/08878730.2016.1 192709

Zeichner, K. (2021). Critical and unresolved and understudied issues in clinical teacher education, *Peabody Journal of Education*, *96*(1), 1–7. https://doi.org/10 .1080/0161956X.2020.1864241

Zenkov, K., Lague, M., & Azevedo, P.C. (2020). *SEED "Seeds," "Stories of Injustice," and the equity ideals of our partnerships: A program in formation and pre-/in-service teachers as bridges to equity.* School-University Partnerships.

SECTION I

DIVERSITY, CORE PRACTICES, AND DISPOSITIONS

CHAPTER 1

ALL MEANS ALL

Adjusting the Lens on Field Experiences

**Amber G. Candela, April Regester, Nancy Robb Singer,
Jennifer Fisher, Julie Smith Sodey, Stephanie Koscielski,
and Nicolle von der Heyde**
University of Missouri–St. Louis

ABSTRACT

In this chapter we share how our institution chose to disrupt the traditional form of teacher preparation that can fail to adequately prepare teachers to educate *all* students who enter into their classroom. Our vision was to create a program that gave our teacher candidates unique and varied field experiences with diverse student populations. We intentionally designed early and mid-level field experiences to provide teacher candidates with the opportunity to actively participate within many different settings including community-based agencies and early school-based experiences. We discuss our specific situation and rationale for structuring each field experience and provide insight for others wishing to replicate.

Preparing Quality Teachers:
Advances in Clinical Practice, pp. 3–20
Copyright © 2022 by Information Age Publishing
www.infoagepub.com

Introduction

It is critical new teachers be prepared to educate each and every student in their classroom and meet the students' academic, social and cultural needs (Andrews et al., 2019). At our institution, a public land grant university in a large Midwestern city, we chose to disrupt the traditional form of teacher preparation that can fail to adequately prepare teachers to educate *all* students who enter into their classroom (American Association of Colleges for Teacher Education [AACTE], 2018; Feiman-Nemser, 2001). AACTE (2018) report on clinical practice states "Clinical practice is central to high-quality teacher preparation, and effective clinical partnerships are its foundation, supporting the continuous renewal of educator preparation as well as of experienced educators' development as professionals and leaders" (p. 44). Following this line, our vision was to create a program that gave our teacher candidates unique and varied clinical field experiences with diverse student populations. We recognize that children learn both inside and outside of school walls, so in addition to more traditional field experiences in schools, we intentionally partnered with community agencies in early and mid-level field experiences. This partnership taps the potential for teacher candidates to interact with children and their families in a variety of settings and expands the notion of clinical experience.

The U.S. Census Bureau (2014) projects that by 2043, the United States will become a "majority minority" and "plurality" nation, yet "student demographics are increasingly diverse and teacher workforces are racially and ethnically homogenous" (Andrews et al., 2019, p. 6). Given these statistics, it is increasingly essential that teacher candidates gain experience working with diverse groups of students (Johnson, 2002). The goal in our teacher preparation program is to provide teacher candidates embedded early field experiences—both in community agencies and in P–12 schools—to give them opportunities and experiences with diverse student populations. At our university, "diverse student populations" includes racially, culturally, linguistically, and economically diverse students as well as students with significant intellectual, developmental, and emotional disabilities. We strive to provide embedded experiences that include all of these diversities and also those that further our mantra that "all means all." That is, all children have the capacity to learn, and all deserve a well-prepared educator to help them achieve in the classroom and beyond.

The AACTE Clinical Practice Commission (2018) cautions, "without embedded clinical practice focusing on intentional pedagogical experiences in authentic educational settings, continuous renewal is unrealistic, and the ability to utilize high-leverage classroom practices is implausible" (p. 18). Field-based experiences in classrooms and community settings are essential for preparing teachers to teach students from different backgrounds, languages, and cultures than their own (Cochran-Smith, 1995; Coffey, 2010; Gallego, 2001; Oakes et al., 2002; Sleeter, 2008). It is the quality of the experience that has the most impact, not simply the amount of time spent working with students (Benedict et al., 2016; Coffey, 2010). With growing diversity and inclusive learning environments in U.S. schools, high-quality field experiences should occur early and throughout the teacher preparation program (Benedict et al., 2016; Coffey, 2010), provide varied experiences with students and community members outside of the formal classroom setting (Oakes et al., 2002; Sleeter, 2008), and provide deliberate practice-based learning opportunities for teacher candidates to connect coursework to instruction (Brownell et al., 2009; Forzani, 2014; Zeichner, 2010). We believe the sequence of our clinical experiences parallels the tenets outlined by the AACTE Clinical Practice Commission (2018) and provides our teacher candidates with high quality experiences in the field.

Impetus for Change

AACTE (2018) reminds us that local context matters and although teacher candidates at our university may be more diverse than many educator preparation programs, the majority of our candidates are still white (69%) and identify their sex as women (75%). Located in a large urban city, our university takes a strong stance in its mission as a land grant university to partner and operate as a change agent within the communities we serve. Between 2010–2019, 38% of our teacher certification graduates took jobs in high-need schools, defined by the U.S. Department of Education (n.d.) as schools that have 30% or more of their students living below the poverty line, have a high percentage of teachers who are not certified or teaching outside of their certification area, or have a high teacher turnover rate. More than 75% of our teacher candidates accepted teaching positions in the greater metropolitan area, many in the schools where they complete their culminating field experience. Like many urban communities, schools and school districts in our metro area continue to experience wide economic and social disparity. By design, we believe our targeted partnership with community agencies and schools reinforces to our candidates the systemic inequities among P–12 school settings while helping to break down assumptions and generalizations that may serve as barriers to academic and economic student success barriers. Our multipronged solution to increase and emphasize diversity in our field experiences at every level of our preparation program has resulted in early and continuous field experiences that include community agencies, school experiences, and a space for our teacher candidates to create their own research project in the field (Figure 1.1). Each of these experiences provides unique opportunities for deliberate exposure, for processing what candidates have experienced, and for skills practice. Facilitating early high-quality, community-based experiences in teacher preparation programs requires strategic partnerships that are mutually beneficial to community organizations as well as to teacher candidates (Benedict et al., 2016).

Figure 1.1

Progression of Clinical Experience Hours

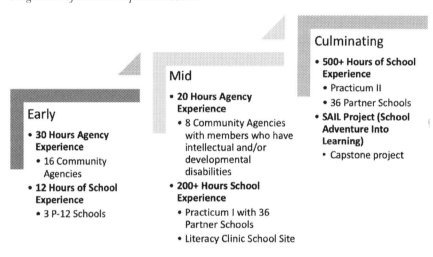

Early

- **30 Hours Agency Experience**
  - 16 Community Agencies
- **12 Hours of School Experience**
  - 3 P-12 Schools

Mid

- **20 Hours Agency Experience**
  - 8 Community Agencies with members who have intellectual and/or developmental disabilities
- **200+ Hours School Experience**
  - Practicum I with 36 Partner Schools
  - Literacy Clinic School Site

Culminating

- **500+ Hours of School Experience**
  - Practicum II
  - 36 Partner Schools
- **SAIL Project (School Adventure Into Learning)**
  - Capstone project

Our early redesign efforts were aided by our participation with the Collaboration for Effective Educator Development, Accountability, and Reform (CEEDAR) Center at the University of Florida which supported our work by providing guides, resources, and technical assistance to our institution. For three years, our college received funding for professional development, in-person training, and utilized targeted technical assistance tools that can be found on their website at https://ceedar.education.ufl.edu/. For three years, our college received funding for professional development, in-person training, and utilized targeted technical assistance tools that can be found on their website at https://ceedar.education.ufl.edu/. The work helped us seed curricular changes to include evidence-based practices and high-leverage practices which are scaffolded throughout the program from early clinical experience to the final practicum courses. In addition, we incorporated community based experiences that provided opportunities to engage with diverse communities that surround our campus and that serve the greater metro area. The modification of clinical practice experiences influenced curricular and program changes as well. As a result, the certifications for elementary education now also include certifications in other areas (Figure 1.2).

Figure 1.2

Certification Tracks for Elementary Education Majors

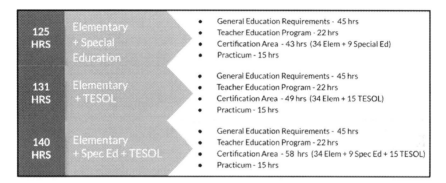

125 HRS	Elementary + Special Education	• General Education Requirements - 45 hrs • Teacher Education Program - 22 hrs • Certification Area - 43 hrs (34 Elem + 9 Special Ed) • Practicum - 15 hrs
131 HRS	Elementary + TESOL	• General Education Requirements - 45 hrs • Teacher Education Program - 22 hrs • Certification Area - 49 hrs (34 Elem + 15 TESOL) • Practicum - 15 hrs
140 HRS	Elementary + Spec Ed + TESOL	• General Education Requirements - 45 hrs • Teacher Education Program - 22 hrs • Certification Area - 58 hrs (34 Elem + 9 Spec Ed + 15 TESOL) • Practicum - 15 hrs

Preparing teachers for dual or multiple teaching certificates provided university faculty the opportunity and impetus to redesign the curriculum in *every* course—and specifically the content methods courses—while leveraging and reinforcing content through strategic field experiences. As we redesigned our clinical field experiences, we moved away from the one teacher candidate, one cooperating teacher, one classroom model to one where the teacher candidates have a variety of experiences within their school setting. While we try to give all teacher candidates experiences working with a diverse group of students, we are intentional that teacher candidates within the TESOL program are in schools with English Learners (ELs) and teacher candidates within the special education program are intentionally placed with a teacher who is providing special education services to students. The highlighted experiences presented here demonstrate and amplify the AACTE Clinical Practice Commission's skills proclamation in that each of these aspects "provide intentional pedagogical experiences in authentic educational settings" (AACTE, 2018, p. 18). Moreover, they demonstrate the importance of partnerships and provide sustainable infrastructure models so that the work may be sustained (AACTE, 2018).

Partnering With Community Agencies

We believe that clinical experience in a community agency setting benefits future educators in two important ways: (1) it introduces teacher candidates to a variety of options for education careers, providing broader professional choice and greater opportunity; and (2) it supports coursework with meaningful and engaging practice to work with P–12 students that enhances their capacities to build relationships and develop their understanding of family and community. We also believe partnering with community agencies aligns with the Partnership Proclamation Tenet 3 (AACTE, 2018) where "effective clinical partnerships allow for mutually beneficial outcomes for all stakeholder partners alongside a shared focus on improving success outcomes for P–12 students." The partnerships provide much-needed volunteer support for community partners while at the same time providing teacher candidates with experience working in locations and with children they may never have otherwise engaged, thus being mutually beneficial for all involved.

Our teacher candidates participate in two courses during their freshman and sophomore years—an early and mid-level field experience--that provide for extended time in community-based agencies. For each of these experiences teacher candidates attend a Community Agency Partnerships (CAP) fair. At this event, held twice each academic year, candidates attend presentations from 16 local agencies with whom we partner. These agencies provide academic and social services to P–12 students outside of the regular school day. In addition, a small number of the agencies provide services to adults of all ages who have intellectual or developmental disabilities. Candidates sign up for their selected agency in real time based on scheduling, (e.g., after school, weekend availability) and agency mission (e.g., tutoring, music enrichment, access to social activities, etc.). Teacher candidates complete their assigned hours (depending on the class) actively engaged with the agency organizers and the participants that agency serves. Explicit guidance is given to teacher candidates and agency partners to ensure that time spent with the agency goes beyond the observation only. Instead, teacher candidates actively support participants, lead enrichment activities, initiate supportive strategies, and at times mentor younger volunteers. Teacher candidates log their hours and complete relevant assignments analyzing their experiences and relating it to their future and current work as educators. The course they take in their sophomore year pairs teacher candidates with specific agencies that align best with associated objectives and learner outcomes, while providing access to the populations relevant to the course content (students with developmental and intellectual disabilities and their families).

Each semester after the CAP Fair, we hold a Community Agency Stakeholders' lunch meeting, where we are able to share ideas and collaborate with the agencies. This meeting includes the field experience office staff, key agency representatives, and instructors for the relevant courses. This meeting aligns to the fourth tenet of the AACTE Clinical

Practice Commission's Developmental Proclamation which states, "Ongoing assessment of an established partnership, including its effectiveness and impact, is necessary to ensure continued efficacy and sustainability" (2018, p. 28). At each meeting, updated information is provided to all agency representatives regarding two formal evaluations (midsemester and final). Survey measures, processes, and supports are reviewed as a collaborative team, and agency representatives provide extensive feedback that is then incorporated for mutual agreement. In addition, a shared understanding of the goals and objectives for all parties (agency, teacher candidates, instructors, etc.) is discussed, providing an opportunity for clarifications and expectations to be confirmed. Agency representatives and university staff/instructors communicate throughout the semester to address any questions, concerns, and/or successes. During these formal and informal opportunities for discussion, we identify specific ways to support the agencies (lack of support during summer activities) with needed volunteers (continued opportunity for candidates to practice skills during summer) to ensure reciprocity and benefits for all involved (university, teacher candidate and agency).

Feedback from past meetings indicates that many of our goals are achieved through this experience; our candidates move outside of their comfort zones, build relationships, experience the full scope of the agency's work and are open to learning and feedback. Occasionally, we also target feedback to judge the effectiveness of on-campus initiatives. For instance, when we made a concerted change to increase our candidates' understanding of learning strategies for emergent bilingual learners in our area, we engaged our community agency stakeholders in this effort. Through our discussions, we surfaced new opportunities for our candidates to work purposefully with the emergent bilingual agency members, thus developing candidates' skills and proficiency for teaching emergent bilinguals in their own classrooms.

Partnering With Schools

Our school partnerships align with the Partnership Tenet 2 (AACTE, 2018) which states that, "Effective clinical partnerships are gateways to developing reflective practice centered on preparing highly effective educators while simultaneously renewing teaching and learning in PK–12 classrooms" (p. 22). For our teacher candidates' early school experiences, they visit several P–12 schools in near proximity to campus. These school sites serve a diverse student population and the related challenges of inequitable educational environments. These early experiences are critical, specifically in support of the connected coursework which requires candidates to deeply consider the pursuit of teaching as their profession. Darling-Hammond (2006) calls for intense purposeful partnerships with schools as a critical component of effective teacher education programs, "It is impossible to teach people how to teach powerfully by asking them to imagine what they have never seen or to suggest they "do the opposite" of what they have observed in the classroom" (p. 308).

Later in their program, our teacher candidates complete their year-long culminating clinical experience in one of our 36 partner studio schools, representing urban, rural, and suburban school districts, and covering four large counties in eastern Missouri. As part of our elementary education certification program, many of our elementary education teacher candidates earn a secondary, or add-on, certificate in either special education or TESOL while simultaneously earning their primary area of certification. Therefore, we carefully select all of our studio schools with like-certified teachers and student populations to ensure an authentic and academically rich practicum experience. Once studio schools are selected, we begin our collaboration to develop the studio school model. In this model, teams of teacher candidates, clinical educators, teachers, and administrators work together to explore, envision, and enact innovative solutions that deepen learning and help raise P–12 student achievement. For grading and licensure purposes, the year-long experience is divided into Practicum I (first semester) and Practicum II (second semester). Practicum I candidates are onsite in a school two days a week. The following semester, candidates continue four days per week in the same studio school location to complete Practicum II. Each studio school hosts approximately five to eight teacher candidates who are supervised and mentored by a clinical educator, a university-employed supervisor who is onsite in each school one full day per week. While there, the clinical educator observes candidates and provides feedback, meets with P–12 mentor classroom teachers, and conducts collaborative exchanges which are targeted seminars that provide professional development around pedagogy, content, school engagement, and school policy. Examples of collaborative exchange topics include trauma-informed teaching, social-emotional considerations, school law, and global learning.

Early Clinical Experiences: Agencies and Schools

Our early clinical experiences include both agency and school experiences. As we shaped our clinical experiences for our teacher candidates, we wanted to make sure these experiences allowed our teacher candidates to experience multiple facets of what it means to educate the whole child. This aligns with the Skill Proclamation Tenet 1 (AACTE, 2018) which states that "university-based teacher educators, school-based teacher educators, and boundary-spanning teacher educators in successful clinical partnerships pioneer innovative roles and practices without the restrictions of traditional assumptions about educator preparation" (p. 18). So often we think of educator preparation as happening exclusively in school-based sites, but we wanted our teacher candidates to experience a variety of settings in the community which also support educating children.

For the first agency experience teacher candidates are connected with a wide range of youth-serving organizations and complete 30 hours in the field. Examples of these agencies range from Girls, Inc. (providing educational and cultural programs in safe environments) to Neighbor Works (an afterschool program based in a neighborhood community space). Our goal with this experience is for our candidates to interact with children who are not necessarily like themselves in their own neighborhoods and to foster and promote professional relationships, collaboration, and informal learning. In the university classroom component of this course, candidates explore their own cultural and linguistic identities and discuss how these lenses impact their own future P–12 students. Candidates learn explicitly about community programs and resources available to students and families who benefit from them while also providing a purposeful lens to be more conscious of the diversity around them.

A central focus of our teacher preparation program is creating opportunities to develop cultural competence and professional behaviors essential to the profession, which parallels the Mutual Benefit Proclamation (AACTE, 2018) Tenet 2: "School-and university-based teacher educators have a joint responsibility to foster teacher candidates' development of the dispositional characteristics necessary to be successful educators" (p. 34). With this in mind, an important aspect of reforming our program was to give our teacher candidates opportunities in schools in their freshman and sophomore year of their teacher preparation program. Like the agency experience, this early school-based experience targets specific cultural competencies and professional behaviors essential to the profession. This experience provides teacher candidates with an opportunity to gain perspective on the structure and challenges of today's classrooms. Currently, this early classroom experience totals a minimum 12 clock hours, which are scheduled over the course of several weeks and provide a P–12 view of today's public schools. Teacher candidates, regardless of intended certification area, are required to complete hours in elementary, middle school, and high school settings. The hours are primarily observational in nature but do allow for interaction with students, teachers, and administrators at the school sites.

The early classroom clinical experience is paired with foundational education coursework, providing a meaningful context in which to explore key concepts including communication, classroom management, identification of and meeting the needs of diverse populations, ethical and legal considerations, and educational philosophies that underlie American education. Faculty guide candidates through the structures of academic curriculum, school staffing, legal and ethical considerations, and professional expectations and behaviors that contribute to professional success.

The sites for early school-based clinical experiences are located geographically near our campus and serve diverse, high-need student populations. This placement is intentional and supports our teaching philosophy of preparing our candidates for a realistic view of today's classrooms. It also encourages the early development of professional self-efficacy, a critical skill of successfully teaching all students. By partnering the early clinical with foundational coursework, candidates are able to engage in purposeful discussions and activities that explore in greater depth the observed classroom challenges and successes. The experiences are supported by experienced faculty and supervision is structured in order to provide direct mentorship on candidate professional dispositions, exploration of bias, and the development of personal teaching philosophies. Throughout the clinical hours, candidates are asked to make specific observations around issues such as communication, student engagement, instructional objectives, and teacher/student relationships. The challenges of teaching as a lifelong profession is given serious consideration at this early level; candidates are engaged in discussions that require critical reflection on professional commitment.

Mid-Level Clinical Experiences: Agencies, Literacy Clinic, and Practicum 1

In our mid-level clinical experiences, teacher candidates have both community-based and school-based field experiences. These include a second community agency experience, a school-based experience completed in a literacy clinic setting, and Practicum I, the first semester of their year-long clinical experience requirement. Unlike the early agency experience that serves a wide range of community agency partners, the mid-level 20-hour field experience strategically partners with agencies that serve individuals with developmental and intellectual disabilities and their families. Examples of these agencies range from the Comprehensive Transition and Postsecondary Program (a postsecondary education program for students with intellectual and developmental disabilities) to Special Olympics (a program that promotes acceptance and inclusion of people with intellectual disabilities through year-round sports). This mid-level agency experience pairs with the dual certification aspect (e.g., elementary/

special education licensure) of our elementary and early childhood education programs. It also reinforces special education coursework as teacher candidates experience in action the concepts, interventions, and strategies that they learned about to support students in inclusive P–12 classrooms. For instance, while completing their mid-level agency experience, candidates have specific, targeted "look fors" (e.g., positive behavior supports, accommodations, modifications, etc.) that they reflect on and report on for class assignments. In addition to directly supporting children and adults with disabilities, candidates have an opportunity to interact with family members and caregivers to better understand their needs outside of the school environment (e.g., respite, access to leisure activities, adult services, etc.). It is especially important for future educators to understand how to build positive family partnerships, as this has been identified as a critical component for successful transition planning leading to positive post-school outcomes for young adults with disabilities (Test, 2016; Test et al., 2014; Turnbull et al., 2015).

As teacher education programs consider ways to best support the development of effective teachers, settings, and types of field experiences become critically important. School-based experiences help teacher education programs ensure varied, high quality field placements for their students, while extending support to practicing teachers with a shared goal of enhancing student learning (Ball & Cohen, 1999). The first mid-level school-based clinical experience for our early childhood and elementary teacher candidates is connected to literacy methods coursework. Building on an earlier methods course focused on literacy assessment, our candidates spend a full semester in an intensive theory to practice literacy clinic at a neighboring elementary school, working with second grade students in reading, writing, and word work. With a deliberate focus on the pedagogy of literacy assessment, this clinical experience parallels the Pedagogy Proclamation Tenet 1 with "The presence of strong, embedded pedagogical training is the hallmark of effective clinical educator preparation" (AACTE, 2018, p. 16). This two-course sequence develops candidates' understanding of the theories and pedagogies of accelerative literacy instruction situated within culturally responsive frameworks. In this clinic experience, candidates work one-on-one with an elementary student using observational assessment data to design and implement individualized instruction. Candidates benefit from embedding content work in a school setting with observation and coaching from university faculty; the emphasis is on sequencing instruction over a longer period of time. At the end of this experience, candidates write up the results of their work with students and share their findings with teachers and families, again, imparting the importance of fostering relationships between schools and home. This school-based field experience prepares candidates with the specific content and contextual knowledge needed to be responsive literacy teachers focused on student learning.

The second mid-level school experience correlates with Practicum I, the semester-long initial course that begins all teacher candidate's year-long practicum experience (comprised of Practicum I and Practicum II). Practicum I candidates are onsite in a school two full days per week while enrolled in a three-credit hour course. During Practicum I, teacher candidates are anchored with one mentor teacher; however, they also have the opportunity to be in several teachers' classrooms in their certification area. Teacher candidates who are in the Elementary Education/Special Education degree work in elementary classrooms as well as in special education settings—either class-within-a-class or a special education classroom. Likewise, teacher candidates who are in the Elementary Education/TESOL degree work with mentor teachers who have earned their TESOL endorsement and whose schools serve ELs. In our careful design of our Practicum I and II clinical experiences we wanted to address what Darling-Hammond (2006) identifies as far too common characteristics of many teacher education field experiences: "haphazard" and "loosely selected placements with little guidance about what happens in them and little connection to university work" (p. 308). Similarly, Darling-Hammond declares that powerful clinical placements "teach candidates to turn analysis into action by applying what they are learning" and such actions are "especially educative when they are followed by systematic reflection on student learning in relation to teaching and receive detailed feedback, with opportunities to retry and improve" (p. 308). The Practicum I experience also marks the beginning of candidates' intense, two-semester relationship with their assigned clinical educator; the clinical educator works closely with teams of candidates in studio schools (both Practicum I and II designations) to provide direct pedagogical instruction, observation, and mentorship. The clinical educator and teacher candidate relationship is specifically designed to support this systematic approach to developing effective teaching through the supported development and enactment of instructional components, direct observation, guided reflection, and feedback for future instruction.

Culminating Clinical Experiences: Practicum II and School Adventure Into Learning

For their culminating field experience, our teacher candidates remain in their studio schools for four days per week in Practicum II, continuing to build relationships, collaborate and plan with their mentor teachers. We have designed this to align with the Empowerment Tenet 2 (AACTE, 2018) where:

> The progression of embedded teaching and learning experiences, inherent to clinical practice, is essential to empowering teacher candidates to take active roles during their practicum experience as co-teachers in the classroom as well as professionals within the school and larger community. These experiences promote profession-and learner-ready efficacy once candidates matriculate to the classroom. (p. 31)

As the candidates have been embedded in their schools for the entire previous semester, they are ready to take a more active role during Practicum II. Teacher candidates co-teach or facilitate whole group instruction from the beginning of the semester. In order to give our teacher candidates opportunities to move theory to practice, as well as apply what they learned from their experiences throughout their teacher preparation program, candidates participate in a capstone experience: School Adventure into Learning (SAIL). The SAIL project provides a venue for groups of teacher candidates to create and enact an exploratory project of their choice within their school and/or neighboring community. Within this project, we endeavor to help our teacher candidates connect field experiences, community outreach, and creative exploration. Medwell and Wray (2014) support the notion that shared research experiences for teacher candidates are beneficial to the students they teach, the development of the candidates' reflective teaching practices, and the improvement of authentic understandings in classroom practice. SAIL projects are often small in scale, aiming to answer emerging lines of inquiry that our candidates develop at the start of their final practicum experience.

Like the early agency and field experiences mentioned above, SAIL projects often highlight the diverse experiences teacher candidates find in their final practicum experience. In alignment with the Development Proclamation Tenet 3 (AACTE, 2018) "While successful partnerships share some common stages and actions, each partnership possesses unique characteristics and requirements specific to its local context" (p. 28). The SAIL projects allow our teacher candidates to develop contextual responses which allow them to explore what is unique about their school community. Because our metropolitan area is home to many different types of schools with widely varied demographics, so too are the SAIL projects they choose to complete. These topics range from content focused projects such as *Exploring the Writing Process to Develop Independent Writers* and *Math Club,* to arts-based projects such as *Art with Heart Photography Club* and *Supporting STEAM.* Other projects have been based on cultural diversity, civic engagement and global learning with *Promoting Cultural Diversity and Raising Awareness of International Issues: The One World Club* and *Experimental School Study Abroad.* Finally, some teacher candidates focused on relationships and restorative practices with projects such as *Restorative Practices through Community Building* and *Effects of Teacher Empathy on Student Engagement.*

One example of a SAIL project evolved from an unexpected catalyst. In an effort to help her mentor teacher streamline an uninterrupted flow in the classroom, one teacher candidate explored the impact of procuring an ice machine for her studio school. The candidate noticed that many of her elementary students, when faced with minor playground bruises or headaches, sought ice packs from the nurse's office. This distraction interrupted class time, because there was a shortage of ice packs, and the nurse's office was a long walk from the classrooms. By seeking community donations and then using the donations to purchase an ice machine for the school, our teacher candidate made it possible for teachers to create makeshift ice packs and provide a larger number of them to students. The teacher candidate found that this significantly diminished classroom disruptions, especially right after recess, and improved the overall flow of the classroom. This teacher candidate considered the context of her school and its surrounding community, identified a localized hindrance to student learning, developed an exploratory project that had the potential to alleviate that hindrance, and analyzed the outcome of the project.

Another group of teacher candidates sought to determine whether or not hosting an after-school photography club would impact the interpersonal relationships they developed with their students. The group's findings indicated that their students not only enjoyed working with professional photography equipment, but that perceived levels of student responsibility increased when students were properly trained and trusted to handle quality art making equipment. The fourth graders began to expand their cross-curricular ideas about perspective, and the project culminated in a student-led art show. At least one friend or family member was present for each student at the show to celebrate the students' artwork. Our teacher candidates observed that their interpersonal relationships with the participating students grew more quickly and deeply than their relationships with students who did not participate in the photography club. Both of these projects sought to deepen our teacher candidates' understanding of how they could directly impact the school communities surrounding them.

At the end of their Practicum II selected teacher candidates are chosen to create presentations about their SAIL projects to be shared with their peer teacher candidates. All teacher candidates and their clinical educators attend, as well as university administrators, faculty, and staff. The gathering occurs in a university common space and presentation stations are set up throughout the large, open area. Community partners are welcome and encouraged to attend. Approximately ten teacher candidates, or groups of candidates, present the findings of their SAIL experiences as participants rotate through each presentation station. The teacher candidates often produce and project slide shows, complete with questions that guided the projects, photographs, and short videos. After approximately 10 minutes, viewers are encouraged to ask questions of their classmates in order to expand their own understanding of the project; accordingly, Medwell and Wray (2014) outline the importance of reflective practices in synthesizing the skills of teacher candidates. One teacher candidate summarized her experience by stating that SAIL became her passion project. The excitement she and her students shared for exploring new concepts together became a rallying point for enthusiasm, passion, and fun during the time she spent at her host school. The spark created by our teacher candidates' SAIL projects has often been cited as an overwhelmingly positive experience at the culmination of their practicum.

Suggestions for Replication

For readers who may wish to incorporate our models into their own teacher education programs, we have provided a list of recommendations and suggestions in order to aid in a smooth transition of our processes. First, we recommend that early and consistent field experiences be the standard for all teacher candidates. It is imperative that all teacher candidates be consistently involved in order to establish buy-in and maximize the best possible outcomes for everyone. Second, we recommend that these field experiences are tightly interwoven into courses that were specifically created for that purpose. This allows teacher candidates to cognitively "unpack" what they are experiencing in these early field placements. This is particularly useful for them in a group with other teacher candidates who are also having similar experiences.

Next, we recommend that any group who wishes to incorporate our models into their own prospective teacher programs maintain allegiance to the duality of experiences in the program. This means that we simultaneously maintain a curricular commitment to these principles, while also committing to practice what we preach. For example, our faculty collaborated on redesigning coursework to be inclusive for candidates in multiple certification programs rather than separate course sequences that include similar content (e.g., classroom management for elementary education and behavior management for special education combined into one course for all candidates). The reciprocal nature of this work demands that we hold ourselves and our partners equally accountable for building and maintaining the relationships we have developed over time. We both expect one another to set clear guidelines, commit to a consistent pattern of meeting throughout the field experience (benefitting both our students and their clients), and to maintain mutually respectful, professional practices with one another.

Last, we encourage groups to start small, beginning by partnering with a small number of committed, dependable agencies. Forging these relationships can be a delicate and timely process; this makes it advantageous to begin with dedicated, organized, and enthusiastic partners. It is essential to gain the feedback of these agencies, asking what their wants and needs are, particularly with regard to the relationships teacher candidates will build with them and their clients. One cannot assume that the needs of the agency are obvious. This essential feedback can guide the actions of university partners as they endeavor to match the needs of the agencies with the needs of the students. By maintaining flexibility and dedication to the process, we feel confident that teacher education programs can replicate, and build upon, our model.

Conclusion

We carefully designed field experiences that do not just satisfy requisite state mandates; rather, they get teacher candidates out into spaces they may not have ventured to meet all children and their families where they live, play, and learn. We also developed experiences to provide our teacher candidates more direct hours with students with disabilities and ELs to support candidates' understanding of how to reach each and every learner in their classroom. We provided carefully arranged placements so when our candidates experience these learners in the classroom, they are better prepared to engage them in high quality curricular experiences. In addition, we embedded specific opportunities for our candidates to practice true interagency collaboration, which is an integral component in the post-school success for students with disabilities. It is our hope that these authentic field experiences highlight and confront in real time—not just in a textbook or in a university classroom—issues of diversity and equity in our city and that all really does mean all. As Tenet 1 of the Central Proclamation (AACTE, 2018) states:

> Clinical practice serves as the central framework through which all teacher preparation programming is conceptualized and designed. In a preparation program where clinical practice is central, course work is designed and sequenced to support candidates' developing knowledge and skill. Candidates are observed through authentic practice in diverse learning environments. Course work complements and aligns with field experiences that grow in complexity and sophistication over time and enable candidates to develop the skills necessary to teach all learners. (p. 14)

While we revised our program to capture this and the subsequent tenets on high quality field experiences, we recognize that this work needs to be continually assessed and reframed to ensure our teacher candidates' clinical field experiences remain at the highest quality and are continually linking research to practice. Alsup (2006) explains that teacher education is where many future teachers begin to develop their professional identity. An implication of this work is in the development of our teacher candidates' professional identities and their belief of impact. These challenging yet productive clinical experiences provide our teacher candidates the opportunity to conceive themselves as successful future educators of *all* students. Through the implementation of highly supported and reflective clinical experiences, we anticipate great potential impact on longevity in the field for our teacher candidates. A next step for our program is to follow our teachers into the field to understand how these experiences have shaped their classroom teaching. Perhaps by promoting an asset, rather than deficit-based view of communities and teaching, teacher candidates will begin to recognize, value, and leverage cultural knowledge and community expertise. We can then frame conversations early in teachers' careers so that they, too, can work to influence policy and outcomes in support of renewed P–20 learning systems in which each and every learner has access to high quality learning experiences. All means all.

REFERENCES

Alsup, J. (2006). *Teacher identity discourses: Negotiating personal and professional spaces.* NCTE.

American Association of Colleges for Teacher Education (AACTE). (2018). *A pivot toward clinical practice, it's lexicon, and the renewal of educator preparation: A report of the AACTE Clinical Practice Commission.*

Andrews, D. J. C., Castro, E., Cho, C. L., Petchauer, E., Richmond, G., & Floden, R. (2019). Changing the narrative on diversifying the teaching workforce: A look at historical and contemporary factors that inform recruitment and retention of teachers of color. *Journal of Teacher Education, 70*(1), 6–12. https://doi.org/10.1177/0022487118812418

Ball, D. L., & Cohen, D. K. (1999). Developing practice, developing practitioners: Toward a practice-based theory of professional education. *Teaching as the learning profession: Handbook of policy and practice, 1*, 3–22.

Benedict, A., Holdheide, L., Brownell, M., & Foley, A. M. (2016). *Learning to teach: Practice-based preparation in teacher education* (Special Issues Brief). Center on Great Teachers and Leaders.

Brownell, M. T., Chard, D., Benedict, A. E., & Lignuagaris-Kraft, B. (2009). Teacher preparation and response to intervention frameworks. P. C. Pullen & M. J. Kennedy (Eds.), *Handbook of response to intervention and multi-tiered instruction.* Routledge.

Cochran-Smith, M. (1995). Color blindness and basket making are not the answers: Confronting the dilemmas of race, culture, and language diversity in teacher education. *American Educational Research Journal, 32*(3), 493–522. https://doi.org/10.3102/00028312032003493

Coffey, H. (2010). "They taught me": The benefits of early community-based field experiences in teacher education. *Teaching and Teacher Education, 26*(2), 335–342.

Darling-Hammond, L. (2006). Constructing 21st-century teacher education. *Journal of Teacher Education, 57(3)*, 300–314.

Feiman–Nemser, S. (2001). From preparation to practice: Designing a continuum to strengthen and sustain teaching. *Teachers College Record*, 103, 1013–1055.

Forzani, F. M. (2014). Understanding "core practices" and "practice-based" teacher education: Learning from the past. *Journal of Teacher Education, 65*(4), 357–368. https://doi.org/10.1177/0022487114533800

Gallego, M. A. (2001). Is experience the best teacher? The potential of coupling classroom and community-based field experiences. *Journal of Teacher Education, 52*(4), 312–325.

Johnson, L. (2002). "My eyes have been opened": White teachers and racial awareness. *Journal of Teacher Education, 53*, 153–216

Medwell, J., & Wray, D. (2014) Pre-service teachers undertaking classroom research: developing reflection and enquiry skills. *Journal of Education for Teaching, 40*(1), 65–77.

Oakes, J., Franke, M. L., Quartz, K. H., & Rogers, J. (2002). Research for high-quality urban teaching: Defining it, developing it, assessing it. *Journal of Teacher Education, 53*(3), 228–234.

Sleeter, C. (2008). Equity, democracy, and neoliberal assaults on teacher education. *Teaching and Teacher Education, 24*(8), 1947–1957.

Test, D. W. (2016). *Evidence-based practices and predictors in secondary transition: What we know and what we still need to know.* National Technical Assistance Center on Transition.

Test, D. W., Smith, L. E., & Carter, E. W. (2014). Equipping youth with autism spectrum disorders for adulthood: promoting rigor, relevance, and relationships. *Remedial and Special Education, 35*(2), 80–90. https://doi.org/10.1177/0741932513514857

Turnbull, A., Turnbull R., Erwin E., Soodak L., & Shogren K. (2015). *Families, professionals, and exceptionality: Positive outcomes through partnerships and trust.* Pearson.

U.S. Census Bureau. (2014). *2014 National population projections tables.* https://www.census.gov/data/tables/2014/demo/popproj/2014-summary-tables.html

U.S. Department of Education. (n.d). *Teacher quality enhancement grants, frequently asked questions.* https://www2.ed.gov/programs/heatqp/faq.html

Zeichner, K. (2010). Rethinking the connections between campus courses and field experiences in college-and university-based teacher education. *Journal of Teacher Education, 61*(1–2), 89–99.

CHAPTER 2

DEVELOPING A MINDSET

The Role of Clinical Practice in Preservice Teachers' Understandings About Dyslexia

Mary-Kate Sableski
University of Dayton

ABSTRACT

Teacher education programs must meet multiple stakeholders, ensuring preservice teachers are well prepared to become effective decision makers in the classroom. This chapter will describe how clinical practice, grounded in the AACTE Clinical Practice Commission Report, was integrated into an undergraduate Dyslexia Certificate program. This program was designed to help preservice teachers develop a mindset about effective literacy instruction to include in-depth understandings of a multiplicity of techniques for the teaching of reading, including specific understandings related to dyslexia. This chapter will provide a review of relevant literature on dyslexia and clinical practice in teacher education. Then, the program will be described, including how the clinical practice component was integrated into the coursework. Next, the results of a research study conducted during one semester of the clinical experience are discussed. Finally, implications for clinical practice and the preparation of effective teachers of reading are presented.

Preparing Quality Teachers:
Advances in Clinical Practice, pp. 21–40
Copyright © 2022 by Information Age Publishing
www.infoagepub.com
All rights of reproduction in any form reserved.

INTRODUCTION

As teacher educators, our goal is to prepare teachers who understand the complex nature of literacy instruction, and have ample "tools in the toolbox" to meet the needs of the students they will teach. Across the nation, legislation and state mandates surrounding school-based intervention for students with dyslexia prompted teacher educators to reexamine literacy curriculum to include specific research and methods for teaching students with dyslexia in teacher preparation programs (National Center on Improving Literacy, 2020). Specific instructional techniques are recommended as effective for students with dyslexia, including programs that are multisensory, systematic, and explicit (Brady & Moats, 1997; Shaywitz et al., 1992). Literacy coursework in teacher education programs is expected to meet accreditation standards put forth by CAEP and the International Literacy Association (Council for the Accreditation of Educator Preparation, 2013; International Literacy Association, 2016). The International Dyslexia Association, along with many states, has also issued standards for the integration of knowledge and practice concerning the support of students with dyslexia and other related reading difficulties, and began accrediting university programs in 2012. Teacher education programs are thus challenged to meet multiple stakeholders, ensuring that their preservice teachers are well prepared to become effective literacy decision makers in the classroom. Teacher education programs rely heavily on clinical practice to "prepare high-quality educators with and through a pedagogical skill set that provides articulated benefits for every participant, while being fully embedded in the PK–12 setting" (American Association of College Teacher Educators [AACTE], 2018, p. 6). The highly specific nature of multisensory teaching methods to support students with dyslexia makes this a pedagogical skill set that is effectively learned and practiced within the context of a clinical setting.

Ultimately, our goal as literacy teacher educators is to help our preservice teachers develop a mindset of flexibility, adaptation, and understanding of the complexity inherent to the act of reading. Further, we aim to prepare our preservice teachers to understand the ways in which a struggle with any component of the process can affect a developing reader. This chapter will describe how clinical practice was meaningfully integrated into an undergraduate Dyslexia Certificate program. This program was designed to help preservice teachers develop a mindset about effective literacy instruction to include in-depth understandings of a multiplicity of techniques for the teaching of reading, including specific understandings related to dyslexia.

REVIEW OF LITERATURE

Clinical Practice

In undergraduate teacher education courses, a variety of methods have been used to prepare students for the reality of teaching in P–12 classroom contexts. Video cases (Hughes et al., 2000; Mayall, 2010; Rowley & Hart, 1996), simulations (Montgomery & Brown, 1997), data analysis (Olah et al., 2010), active engagement strategies (L'Allier & Elish-Piper, 2007) and online discussion boards (Ajayi, 2010) surrounding articles and books on relevant topics give teacher candidates a window through which they can see and respond to classroom realities they will likely face in their eventual role as classroom teachers. In addition to the methods listed, field experiences allow teacher candidates to step through the window and into classrooms to observe and work alongside practicing teachers. Though field experiences provide teacher candidates with practical experiences to which they may "hook" their developing knowledge base regarding teaching and learning, these experiences are often minimally supervised by university instructors. To extend the potential of field experiences, teacher education programs can consider the intentional design of clinical practices and partnerships, grounded in recommendations from AACTE's Clinical Practice Commission. These recommendations provide a framework for teacher education programs to consider as they seek to implement clinical partnerships and practices grounded in research and best practices.

Effective clinical experiences for teacher candidates include a focus on P–12 student learning. This makes the clinical experiences mutually beneficial for all parties: teachers, students, and university programs (AACTE, 2018). Integration of clinical preparation throughout every facet of teacher education, including continuous evaluation of a teacher candidate's progress are critical components. The Clinical Practice Commission Report provides a framework for the implementation of clinical experiences across a teacher education program. Strategically designed clinical experiences support preparation of teachers who are content experts, collaborators, and problem solvers. Clinical experiences support candidate engagement in professional learning communities, a skill they will take with them into their first years of teaching. When clinical experiences incorporate rigorous selection of clinical educators from both higher education and PK–12 classrooms, teacher candidates learn from models who impart best practices. Clinical experiences can lead to the creation of powerful research agendas and systematic gathering and use of data to support continuous improvement in teacher preparation. Teacher preparation programs can work with PK–12 partners to establish strategic partnerships for powerful clinical preparation throughout their programs.

> The education of teachers in the United States needs to be turned upside down. To prepare effective teachers for 21st century classrooms, teacher education must shift away from a norm which emphasizes academic preparation and course work loosely linked to school- based experiences. Rather, it must move to programs that are fully grounded in clinical practice and interwoven with academic content and professional courses. (NCATE, 2010)

Ten central principles comprise the findings of the AACTE brief on clinical practice (AACTE, 2018). The goal of this commission was to bring together the research on clinical practice to provide some consistency across programs. Often, programs differ significantly in their definition and implementation of clinical practices (Goodlad, 1993). These principles address the centrality of clinical practices to the pedagogical skill development of future educators. They also address the quality of the partnership between schools and teacher preparation programs, including the principle of mutual benefits for both parties. Clinical practice, in other words, is more than simply placing teacher candidates in schools for observations. It also goes beyond holding class in a school; rather, effective clinical practices are comprehensive, collaborative, and intentional. Effective clinical practices take into account the developmental needs of the teacher candidate, as well as the benefits to the school and the P–12 students. In dyslexia discourse and legislation, there is a focus on how to bring effective methods for working with students with dyslexia into schools, by training teachers and teacher candidates to use these methods effectively in the classroom. Clinical practice, therefore, is at the heart of integrating methods for teaching students with dyslexia, into teacher preparation.

Dyslexia and Teacher Education

Reading is a complex act requiring the integration of multiple skills and strategies to be successful. In addition, reading is a skill that is required across disciplines. A struggle with reading, therefore, will have far-reaching consequences. The statistics pointing to the prevalence of reading difficulties as a cause of academic failure and underachievement are consequently not surprising (International Dyslexia Association, 2010). According to the International Dyslexia Association, "Between 15 and 20% of young students demonstrate significant weakness with language processes, including but not limited to phonological processing, that are the root cause of dyslexia and related learning difficulties" (p. 1). Dyslexia is defined by the International Dyslexia Association as a "language based disorder of learning to read and write originating from a core or basic problem with phonological processing intrinsic to the individual" (International Dyslexia Association, 2002). Research by the National Institute of Health (NIH) has identified that 20% of the population or 1:5 people have dyslexia. Despite this statistic, only 1 out of 10 cases will be eligible under special education laws for an Individualized Education Program (IEP) (Simon & Kule-Korgood, 2011).

Within the field of learning disabilities, there is great debate over the definition, identification, and treatment of dyslexia. Dyslexia can be described as operating on a continuum of severity, with those with mild forms of dyslexia often never receiving a diagnosis (International Dyslexia Association, 2010). As Stanovich (1996) identified, however, the existence of dyslexia along a continuum does not lessen the impact it has at whatever point the student operates. Adding to the complexity of identifying dyslexia in students is the variation in its definition across states and even school contexts. When students move from classroom to classroom, school to school, or district to district, their ability to qualify for individualized services may shift based on the way in which dyslexia is being identified and defined within the particular context.

This conflict in the literature surrounding how to define, identify and instruct students with dyslexia has been swirling for decades (Gunning, 2002; Lipson & Wixson, 2003; Snow et al., 1998). At present, the debate continues, as states work to identify consistent definitions, processes of diagnosis, and components to remediation and instruction. Defining dyslexia according to a dimensional model, rather than a categorical model, "has been embraced by most researchers, although not yet a majority of educators" (Snow et al., 1998, p. 91). According to the dimensional model, dyslexia is one component of reading disability, and is included at the lower end of a bell-shaped curve of reading ability (Shaywitz et al, 1992). Viewing reading difficulties in this way illustrates why identifying and diagnosing dyslexia is challenging. Using a categorical model, students are placed in categories based on the specific characteristics they present regarding their reading difficulties. The downside to this model is the inability to address the complex and layered needs students bring to classrooms. Each person with dyslexia will exhibit different characteristics than another, thus a nuanced and in-depth look at reading difficulty is required of classroom teachers to provide appropriate instruction for all of the students in their classrooms (International Dyslexia Association, 2010).

Regardless of the decisions made regarding the process of identifying and diagnosing dyslexia on a broad level, however, students remain in classrooms, struggling to learn to read in the traditional context and with existing programs. "Effective instruction includes artful teaching that transcends—and often makes up for—the constraints and limitations of specific instructional programs" (Snow et al., 1998, p. 314). Teachers who make decisions regarding their instruction based on individual student needs are the "difference makers" in classrooms (Pressley, 2002; Snow et al., 1998), not one single program. Teachers of reading need to understand the conceptual foundations of the reading process, develop deep knowledge of the structure of language, and have supervised practice in teaching reading (Brady & Moats, 1997; Santa et al, 2000; Snow et al., 1998). The Clinical Practice Commission Report (AACTE, 2018) refers to pedagogy as the "science of teaching," and the foundation on which teachers build credibility in decision making. Preparing teachers to take ownership of the decisions regarding the students who struggle with reading in their classrooms is a critical component to meeting the educational needs of all students.

The implications of the integration of research on dyslexia in teacher education courses are far-reaching, as the statistics regarding the pervasive nature of dyslexia in schools indicates. The major goal of the certificate program described in this chapter is to provide preservice teachers with the resources, experiences, and knowledge critical for instructing students with dyslexia within the regular classroom context. The research is clear that no one method will be the right match for all students (Gaskins, 2005; National Reading Panel [NPR], 2000), so preparing teachers who can effectively assess, evaluate, plan, and teach to meet the varied needs of the students in their classrooms is responsible practice. Additionally, there is a national conversation concerning dyslexia education in schools in response to increased policy and legislation across states. The Literacy Research Association Annual Conference in 2016 included multiple sessions and a research briefing on the topic of dyslexia and literacy education. The International Literacy Association issued two executive research briefs in responses to legislation and policy mandates across the country concerning dyslexia literacy education, to which the International Dyslexia Association responded. The International Literacy Association has an established historical relationship with teacher education programs, while the International Dyslexia Association is relatively new to the accrediting and teacher education contexts. This results in divergent perspectives, opinions, and responses to the body of work each group produces (Weir, 2018). Due to the significant variability in approaches to literacy instruction espoused by both groups, it is imperative that the integrity of teacher education programs maintains a focus on the students our future teachers will teach.

Effective Intervention Approaches

Research clearly demonstrates that there is no single most effective approach to teaching reading. Effective teachers make decisions daily to adjust and tweak instructional approaches to meet the changing needs of their students. Preservice teachers learn these critical decision-making schools through observation and active participation in carefully planned clinical practice opportunities throughout their teacher education programs (AACTE, 2018). Teaching decisions are made with knowledge of what research says about the nature and characteristics of effective reading instruction, including the purposeful integration of phonemic awareness, phonics, fluency, vocabulary, and comprehension instruction (NRP, 2000). In particular, there is some research that suggests that teachers who have knowledge of phonological awareness and phonics, including how a struggle with these concepts can affect overall reading ability, do positively impact student outcomes. Furthermore, teachers should not only be aware of, but also confident in implementing effective instructional techniques and programs that include explicit instruction in phonemic awareness and phonics (Martínez, 2011; Mesmer & Griffith, 2005; Hatcher et al., 1994).

One approach that has found success with students with dyslexia is a structured, multisensory method (Moats, 2017; Spear-Swerling, 2019). Foundational components to these approaches include phonological awareness, sound/symbol association, morphology, syntax, and semantics. Orton-Gillingham (Gillingham & Stillman, 2014) is the flagship method of this approach. Characteristics of Orton-Gillingham based approaches to reading intervention include a sequential, systematic, multisensory system of instructional strategies. A typical Orton-Gillingham based lesson includes phoneme drills, direct teaching of new phonemes, decoding, encoding, writing fluency, oral reading fluency, and comprehension. Orton Gillingham International (www.ortongillinghaminternational.org) is one approach to reading instruction and intervention grounded in these principles. Yoshimoto (2019) describes Orton-Gillingham as "a powerful instructional approach for teaching reading and spelling." Further, Yoshimoto identifies that Orton-Gillingham is clinical, diagnostic, and prescriptive, requiring specific training and high levels of knowledge from teachers. Thus, learning Orton-Gillngham pedagogy requires clinical approaches to practice and implementation of the techniques under supervision from a trained coach, a concept supported by the Clinical Practice Commission Report (AACTE, 2018). Orton-Gillingham International is intended for use by one-on-one tutors, small groups, and classroom teachers. The Scope and Sequence and lesson structure are modeled to teachers in a 30-hour training course. Teachers can begin using the materials right away in their classrooms, or can elect to complete further training to become certified at higher levels in the program.

Another method under the Orton-Gillingham "umbrella" is the Barton Approach, authored by Susan Barton (www.bartonreading.com). The Barton Approach can significantly improve spelling, reading, and writing skills in people of any age who struggle with reading or spelling. The Barton System is designed for intense intervention for students who struggle to learn to read, despite being taught phonics. It is scientifically research based, and reflects best practices for students with dyslexia, according to the website. The Barton System is based on a specific sequence of instruction, starting with the very beginning levels of phonemic awareness. Since it is described as an "intensive" intervention, the Baron System is intended for one-on-one instruction or small groups. Lessons are to be taught with fidelity, using the lesson structure, prompts, and sequence taught to tutors through the specialized year-long training program.

As mentioned previously, significant debate swirls in regards to how best to provide intervention to struggling readers. Another approach to reading intervention is Reading Recovery, an intervention program designed by Marie Clay (1994).

> Reading Recovery is a highly effective short-term intervention of one-to-one tutoring for low-achieving first graders. The intervention is most effective when it is available to all students who need it and is used as a supplement to good classroom teaching. (Reading Recovery, 2020)

Following a structured and intensive training program, teachers implement Reading Recovery lessons to struggling first-grade students on a short-term, 12- to 20-week basis. Since it is designed to supplement effective classroom teaching, Reading Recovery lessons occur during the school day as an intervention. Reading Recovery lessons include distinct components, including reading of familiar books, working with letters and sounds, writing a story or sentence, assembling a cut-up story or sentence, and reading a new book. Reading Recovery is grounded in *An Observation Survey* (Clay, 2019), a multifaceted assessment that identifies students' areas of need in reading words, writing vocabulary, hearing and recording sounds in words, reading fluency (running record), letter identification, and concepts about print. Once students can perform on grade level on these tasks, or after 20 weeks of intervention, Reading Recovery is discontinued. If the student is not on grade level, different interventions are implemented.

Each of these interventions has been explored in research and widely implemented in schools and tutoring contexts. They also represent different perspectives on what makes an effective reading intervention, and are at times at odds with one another (Stahl, 1998). Further, Reading Recovery was designed as a school-based intervention, while Orton-Gillingham originated as a one-to-one intervention by a private tutor. As the demand for more effective interventions for students with dyslexia grows in schools, there is a need to implement this intervention within the school day, delivered by a trained, knowledgeable teacher.

These interventions have in common the need for intensive, clinical training and experience on the part of the teacher or tutor. Becoming adept at implementing these methods in a classroom is best supported through intensive, purposeful clinical practice opportunities embedded in K–12 schools (AACTE, 2018). If the interventions are not implemented with fidelity, their effectiveness at improving reading performance in struggling students would be compromised (Spear-Swerling, 2019). Examining these interventions demonstrates the need for deep knowledge and extensive clinical practice in order to implement them effectively and help a student progress.

Building on the knowledge of how dyslexia discourse and legislation influences teacher education programs, as well as research around effective intervention approaches for students with dyslexia, this study examined how one program purposefully integrated instruction on dyslexia to help preservice teachers develop a mindset towards effective classroom-based literacy instruction, in consideration of the needs of all of their students. Clinical practice was a primary vehicle for helping the preservice teachers take on the knowledge, skills, and dispositions required to provide effective interventions for students with dyslexia in their future classrooms

CONTEXT

The university in which this study took place is a midsized, Midwestern university. The state in which the university is located requires 12 hours of coursework in the teaching of reading for teacher candidates, as well as the integration of the Knowledge and Practice Standards for Dyslexia (International Dyslexia Association, 2017) throughout the coursework. To extend this requirement, we chose to design a Dyslexia Certificate program at both the undergraduate and graduate levels. Through these certificate programs, preservice and in-service teachers take additional coursework in advanced phonics and multisensory instruction, and complete a practicum experience focused on implementing these methods in a one-to-one, clinical setting. This coursework extends the existing requirement for 12 semester hours of reading core courses, including one course focused specifically on phonics instruction.

In the Fall semester of their junior year, candidates took a classroom-based course focused on advanced phonics and multisensory instruction techniques. During this semester, the candidates learned critical content surrounding phonics, dyslexia, and multisensory instruction. A focus of the content for this course was also on the specific techniques that would be used the following semester in the practicum course. Multisensory techniques from the Yoshimoto and Barton programs were modeled and practiced, as well as key components of *An Observation Survey* (Clay, 2019), the assessment utilized in the Reading Recovery program. The purpose of learning this range of techniques and perspectives was so that the candidates would be able to implement critical methods during the clinical practicum experience the following semester.

In the Spring term, the candidates put this content into practice in the practicum course. The practicum class met at a partner elementary school two times per week for the spring semester. The elementary school and the university have a long-standing relationship. The school is located on the university campus, and opens its doors to multiple groups of preservice teachers throughout the academic year. Following AACTE Clinical Practice guidelines, there is an emphasis on this relationship being mutually beneficial to both parties. The university faculty also work with teachers in the school to be sure the instruction provided in the clinical experiences reflects the instructional strategies used in the classrooms. Multisensory instruction for students with dyslexia was not widely used throughout the school at the time of this study. Instructional approaches varied from classroom to classroom, but guided reading (Fountas & Pinnell, 2001), writer's workshop (Atwell, 1998; Calkins, 2020), and other techniques characteristic of a "balanced literacy" (Tompkins, 2016) approach were common. Thus, the lesson plan format the teacher candidates implemented reflected primarily multisensory, structured literacy techniques, while also incorporating methods consistent with the classroom instruction. The lesson plan will be explained in a later section.

Preservice teachers administered multisensory lesson plans in a one-to-one tutoring context to identified students. Students were identified through assessment data and consultation with both classroom teachers and the reading specialist. Since the focus of the clinical experience was to train preservice teachers in specific instructional methods for students with dyslexia, the goal was to identify students who struggled with reading, even after being taught phonics. Thus, we focused on second-grade students, who did not respond to the interventions provided in first grade. Though this intervention was not Reading Recovery, the reading specialist provided small group and one-to-one interventions throughout the first-grade year focused on phonics, reading fluency, and comprehension. In addition, our state's context includes a third-grade reading benchmark, so working with second-grade students would provide a mutual benefit to the school.

Data included pre and post scores on the Gates-McGinitie Reading Test and the Benchmark Literacy Assessment (Fountas & Pinnell, 2010) to measure the growth of P–12 student participants. These data were compared using quantitative methods, including statistical comparison of pre- and posttest score data across a control and treatment group.

A second data source included the lesson plan format utilized in the instructional sessions. Content analysis identified the instructional methods, strategies, and activities utilized throughout the practicum sessions. Finally, written reflections documented the participants' developing understandings about best practice instruction for students with dyslexia through the practicum experience. These data were coded for emerging themes and patterns using grounded theory and thematic coding to identify the dominant themes.

Sample/Location

The sample includes 22 preservice teachers enrolled in the undergraduate Dyslexia Certificate program. Students elected to pursue the Dyslexia Certificate beyond their required program of study. This study specifically took place during the Practicum course, in which the preservice teachers tutored a student struggling with reading at a partner elementary school. The university has an established relationship with this school, due to its close proximity to the university and willingness to provide clinical and field placements for our undergraduate students. This relationship developed over several years of continued partnership through other clinical placements, including student teaching, classroom observations, and professional development initiatives. The practicum course is supervised by a university instructor, trained in multisensory, structured literacy methods.

In addition, the sample includes a control and treatment group of P–12 students at the partner elementary school. A partnership with the school P–12 students were purposefully selected for the treatment group from the second-grade class based on a demonstrated struggle with reading skills. Students were evaluated utilizing multiple measures, including scores on the Gates-McGintite Reading Test, Benchmark Literacy Assessment, and teacher recommendations. Fifteen students were purposefully selected by the instructor of the Dyslexia Practicum course using these criteria. The control group consisted of the remaining second-grade students who were not identified for the tutoring program. Institutional Review Board approval was received for this study, and all participants provided consent to participate in the study.

Treatment

The treatment was provided to the selected P–12 student participants in the form of the multisensory lesson plan, delivered in an intensive one-to-one tutoring context. Preservice teachers visited the elementary school two times per week, and provided targeted instruction for 40 minutes each time. The tutoring was supervised by the course instructor, who also provided input and guidance on instructional methods and strategies.

P–12 students who were not selected for the tutoring based on their Gates-McGinitie scores, teacher assessment data, and teacher recommendation did not receive the targeted instruction, and comprised the control group. These students received the regular planned classroom instruction. The Gates-McGinitie was administered to the entire second-grade class at the end of the semester, and pre- and posttest scores of both groups were compared to determine the differential rate of change in scores between the treatment and control groups.

The treatment consisted of a specific multisensory lesson plan developed for the practicum course. The lesson plan was designed specifically for the practicum course, based on the essential components of multisensory instruction the participants learned about during the previous semester. The lesson included seven distinct components (see Table 2.1). The components of the lesson plan are grounded in the principles of Orton-Gillingham (Parts 1 through 5), as well as reflective of the instruction provided in the regular classroom (Parts 6 & 7).

In the coursework component of the Dyslexia Certificate, students learn about the principles of explicit, systematic, structured, multisensory instruction, and study multiple programs to understand how these components are implemented in instruction. The lesson plan provides opportunities for students to practice the components in a supervised practicum experience, where they receive specific feedback from the university instructor on the techniques they use to implement these components.

Table 2.1

Lesson Plan Components

Part 1: O-G Card Deck
Part 2: Arch/Building Words
Part 3: New Instruction
Part 4: Dictation
Part 5: Learned Words
Part 6: Writing Vocabulary
Part 7: Comprehension Graphic Organizer

Method of Analysis

The data for the study were analyzed utilizing quantitative and qualitative methods. The second-grade student test scores were compared pre- and posttreatment to determine the differential rates of growth in reading skills of the treatment and control groups. The lesson plan submissions and reflections from the preservice teachers were analyzed utilizing the constant comparative method, in which the data is analyzed as it is collected. Thematic coding and content analysis identified emerging themes and patterns across the data set.

FINDINGS

The analysis of the data informed the development of a knowledge base surrounding best practice instruction for students with dyslexia in schools, as well as an understanding of the developing knowledge base of university students who participate in a practicum experience in a partner elementary school. The findings included P–12 student data, measuring the impact of the practicum experience on P–12 student learning, as well as preservice teacher qualitative data, describing the impact of the practicum experience on preservice teacher learning about effective instruction for struggling readers, specifically those with dyslexia or other phonological based reading difficulties.

Second Grade Student Data

The Gates McGinitie Reading Test was administered to all of the second-grade students prior to the intervention and after the intervention was complete. The pretest demonstrated that 36% of the second-grade students were below grade level on the Gates McGinitie Reading Test when it was administered in January before the intervention. After the intervention, all of the students were at or above grade level. This group comprised the treatment group, as their assessment data indicated a demonstrated need for literacy intervention to bring their performance to grade level.

The Benchmark Literacy Assessment (Fountas & Pinnell, 2010) was also administered to the second-grade students before and after the intervention took place. Eighteen percent of the second-grade students, who were selected for the treatment group, were below grade level according to the Benchmark Literacy Assessment. Each of these students demonstrated grade level proficiency according to the measures of this assessment at the end of the intervention. Specifically, these students demonstrated a minimum change of five text levels, and a maximum change of six text levels, bringing each of them to grade level standards according to this assessment. The Benchmark Literacy Assessment guidelines state that second-grade students should be reading at a Level M at the beginning of the year. All seven of these students were reading below a Level M prior to the intervention, and at the end of the intervention, each of these students was at or above a Level M text level (see Table 2.2).

The quantitative data demonstrated that the treatment group did improve their literacy skills, as demonstrated by the improvement in their scores on the Gates-McGinitie Reading Test and the Benchmark Literacy Assessment. There are several limitations on this data, central to which is the external factors that could have influenced the assessment data. The target and control groups were all receiving regular classroom literacy instruction, which likely would add to the students' growth as readers. The treatment group was comprised of students identified as struggling with reading based on their scores on the assessments, as well as teacher observation and recommendation, so their improvement could be attributed to the additional intervention, but it also could be a result of classroom instruction or typical academic development. For these reasons, it is important to look at the data from an additional perspective.

Preservice Teachers

The preservice teacher participants used the lesson plan format as the treatment throughout the semester. They also submitted periodic written reflections on student progress to document their work with the student for the classroom teacher. These lesson plans and written reflections comprised

Table 2.2

Students With Most Significant Change in Benchmark Text Levels, Pre- and Postintervention

Student	Preintervention	Postintervention	Change
1	L	R	6
2	J	N	5
3	M	Q	5
4	J	N	5
5	I	M	5
6	I	M	5
7	H	M	6

the data sources for the preservice teachers. Through these data sources, the preservice teachers developed in their knowledge and skills concerning effective literacy instruction for struggling readers.

The preservice teachers noticed and addressed aspects of phonics, phonemic awareness, using the specific language of the multisensory programs they learned about in class. The practicum in which this study took place followed a semester of coursework in advanced phonics and multisensory instruction. Building on this knowledge base, the preservice teachers were expected to use the lesson plan structure to deliver instruction. Their written reflections on these lesson plans demonstrated the use of academic language associated with multisensory instruction as an integral component to their understanding of both student progress and effective instruction. For example, one participant stated,

> On the pretest, Kingston struggled to identify the sounds within a word. He could identify each letter's sound individually but when they were blended into a word he struggled. I taught Kingston how to fingerspell in order to help him separate the words. On the posttest if he thought he got a letter mixed up, I saw him fingerspell the word to himself to help correctly identify the sounds. In addition, on the pretest, Kingston struggled to identify diagraphs, the concept of two letters making one sound was extremely confusing to him. After working with our Yoshimoto cards he began to understand the concept. He fingerspelled the word to help him identify all of the sounds in the word and was able to self-correct to correctly apply rules that we had worked with that helped him to spell the word. (Kelsey, May 1, 2017)

In this quote, the preservice teacher specifically referred to specific phonics components, including blends, diagraphs, and self-correction to describe the performance of the student. The clinical context created an opportunity for her to apply the content of the course to an actual student.

The preservice teachers' written reflections and lesson plans also demonstrated their understanding of specific effective instructional strategies that were successful for their particular students. An analysis of the lesson plans demonstrates that the teachers utilized the technique of finger spelling predominantly when helping their students make progress in their encoding abilities. One candidate stated,

> If the words matched up, she would ask for the next word but if her written word and the spoken word did not match she would keep finger spelling until she found the correct spelling. I believe that this technique Miriam developed during my time with her increased her quality of spelling and especially on longer and more difficult words.

Finger spelling was a specific technique taught in the classroom portion of the course. The preservice teachers used this technique during each lesson with their students, appropriating it for their own teaching toolkits.

Finally, the preservice teachers were asked to take responsibility for their students' progress throughout the semester. Through the bi-weekly reflections they wrote to the classroom teacher, the preservice teachers documented the strategies they used, and their observations of the students' progress towards their goals. One preservice teacher observed, "She is a hard worker and I can see that she is trying her best ... I am adding more words to help her practice this and we will continue to finger spell." This statement, through the ownership the preservice teacher claimed for the observation of the student's efforts, demonstrates how the clinical experience offered the preservice teachers the opportunity to "think like a teacher." The university instructor read the reflections before they were presented to the classroom teachers, providing a layer of supervision and accountability needed at this point in the preservice teachers' development.

DISCUSSION AND IMPLICATIONS

This study has the potential to provide teachers with requisite knowledge and skills for working with students with dyslexia in their classrooms through the clinical partnership. Further, the partnership described in this study has the potential to increase awareness of the complexity of dyslexia as a language-based learning disability and the continuum on which it exists, including best practice methods for instruction. The clinical practice model employed in this program is a resource to university programs and members of the community seeking information and support for students with dyslexia.

Although the topic of this study focuses on the clinical practice model employed in the Dyslexia Certificate program, the results of this study also inform curriculum mapping decisions for other program areas. Three of our undergraduate licensure programs have been aligned with the International Dyslexia Association's Knowledge and Practice Standards for Teachers of Reading (2010), a process that involved a close look at textbook selections, syllabi, course activities, and curriculum mapping. This led faculty to purposeful conversations about reflective and culturally responsive practices for meeting the needs of students with dyslexia. Faculty not only revised coursework to prepare teachers who can meet the needs of students with dyslexia, but in so doing opened lines of communication with candidates who themselves experienced dyslexia in their educational careers. This subtle program change impacted the development of teacher candidates who possess knowledge, skills and dispositions with sensitivity to social justice and global awareness, and supports the recommendations from the Clinical Practice Commission Report to include research-based skill development as part of innovative clinical practice experiences. This research study informs continued program development in core reading courses for undergraduate and graduate students to continue to prepare all teachers to meet the needs of students with dyslexia in their classrooms, relying on the clinical practice model as the backbone of our teacher preparation, and without the assumptions of traditional models of teacher preparation (AACTE, 2018).

In addition, explicit partnerships with community stakeholders mutually benefit both the teacher education program and the community. Our Dyslexia Certificate team, comprised of faculty members in our department, has made multiple site visits to K–8 schools practicing exemplary methods for instructing students with dyslexia, community-based centers providing tutoring to students with dyslexia, and elementary schools seeking support for students with dyslexia in their schools. Through these collaborative interactions, lines of dialogue are opened, allowing the Dyslexia Certificate program to not only serve the moral imperative of preparing teachers who can meet the educational needs of all students, but also provide a resource to schools and the community seeking support and intervention for the students they serve. One component of this research study includes the partnership between the Department of Teacher Education and a local elementary school, a partnership which can inform the development of continued sustained partnerships at other levels of the teacher preparation program. As the Clinical Practice Commission report identified, clinical partnerships are the backbone of effective clinical practice. These partnerships take time and commitment from both parties to establish and mature, and this study pointed to the critical need for establishing these partnerships to support

The specific lesson plan structure the preservice teachers learned, and applied in the clinical setting, included elements of systematic, multisensory instruction. Although the preservice teachers were not trained in a specific program, they learned the foundational components of multisensory instruction to be able to use the methods in their future classrooms. Due to the specific nature of these methods, learning and applying them in a clinical context supported their ability to acquire these teaching skills. The Clinical Practice Commission report specifically recommends the application of clinical practice to support the development of specific pedagogical skills, "the science of teaching" (AACTE, 2018). Further, the preservice teachers took on an active role in their own learning and development through their participation in this clinical partnership, supporting the recommendation of the Clinical Practice Commission report to us clinical partnerships in developmentally appropriate ways.

CONCLUSION

Effective preparation of preservice teachers must involve meaningful, integrated clinical experiences. The AACTE Clinical Practice Commission report provided specific recommendations for these clinical practices and partnerships, which this study echoed. When considering the preparation of preservice teachers to implement specific methods for students with dyslexia in the classroom, the need for hands-on, supervised experiences with P–12 students is paramount. In the Dyslexia Certificate program described in this chapter, preservice teachers combined traditional classroom learning with a supervised practicum experience in a partner school, resulting in the adoption of high leverage strategies for students with dyslexia. As these preservice teachers enter their first years of teaching, they will be able to draw upon additional tools in the toolbox to reach the students in their classes. Follow-up research will follow the preservice teachers into their teaching positions to document whether or not they use the methods in their classrooms. Ultimately, the goal of this Dyslexia Certificate program is to utilize clinical practice to mutually benefit the students and teachers in the partner school, while also providing hands-on practice and supervision to preservice teachers as they adopt a mindset to implement specific, high-leverage strategies for working with students with dyslexia.

REFERENCES

American Association of College Teacher Educators. (2018). *A pivot towards clinical practice, its lexicon, and the renewal of educator preparation.* https://aacte.org/resources/research-reports-and-briefs/clinical-practice-commission-report/.

Ajayi, L. (2010). How asynchronous discussion boards mediate learning literacy methods courses to enrich alternative-licensed teachers' learning experiences. *Journal of Research on Technology in Education, 43*(1), 1–28.

Atwell, N. (1998). *In the middle: New understandings about writing, reading, and learning.* Boynton/Cook.

Brady, S., & Moats, L. (1997). *Informed instruction for reading success: Foundations for teacher preparation.* International Dyslexia Association.

Calkins, L. (2020). *Teaching writing.* Heinemann.

Clay, M. M. (1994). *Reading recovery: A guidebook for teachers in training.* Heinemann.

Council for the Accreditation of Educator Preparation. (2013). *2013 CAEP Standards.* http://caepnet.org/~/media/Files/caep/standards/caep-standards-one-pager-0219.pdf?la=en

Fountas, I. C., & Pinnell, G. S. (2010). *Fountas & Pinnell benchmark assessment system.* Heinemann.

Fountas, I. C., Pinnell, G. S., & Le Verrier, R. (2001). *Guided reading.* Heinemann.

Gaskins, I. W. (2005). *Success with struggling readers: The Benchmark School approach*. Guilford Press.

Gillingham, A., & Stillman, B. (2014). *The Gillingham manual: Remedial training for children with specific disability in reading, spelling, and penmanship* (8th ed.). Educators Publishing Service.

Goodlad, J. I. (1993). School-university partnerships and partner schools. *Educational policy*, 7(1), 24–39.

Gunning, T. G. (2002). *Assessing and correcting reading and writing difficulties*. Allyn and Bacon.

Hatcher, P. J., Hulme, C., & Ellis, A. W. (1994). Ameliorating early reading failure by integrating the teaching of reading and phonological skills: The phonological linkage hypothesis. *Child Development*, 65(1), 41–57.

Hughes. J. E., Packard, B., & Pearson. P. O. (2000). Pre-service teachers' perceptions of using hypermedia and video to examine the nature of literacy instruction. *Journal of Literacy Research, 32*(4), 599–629.

International Dyslexia Association. (2002). *Fact sheet: Definition of dyslexia*. Retrieved from May 16, 2014. https://dyslexiaida.org/dyslexia-basics-2/

International Dyslexia Association. (2010). *Knowledge and practice standards for teachers of reading*. https://www.readingrockets.org/sites/default/files/IDA%20 Knowledge%20and%20Practice%20Standards%20for%20Teaching%20 of%20Reading.pdf

International Dyslexia Association. (2017). *Standards for the preparation of literacy professionals 2017*. https://literacyworldwide.org/get-resources/standards/ standards-2017

International Literacy Association. (2016). *Dyslexia: A response to the International Dyslexia Association* [Research Advisory Addendum].

L'Allier, S. K., & Elish-Piper, L. (2007). "Walking the walk" with teacher education candidates: Strategies for promoting active engagement with assigned readings. *Journal Of Adolescent & Adult Literacy, 50*(5), 338–353.

Lipson, M. Y., & Wixson, K. K. (2003). *Assessment and instruction of reading and writing difficulty: An interactive approach*. Allyn & Bacon.

Martínez, A. M. M. (2011). Explicit and differentiated phonics instruction as a tool to improve literacy skills for children learning English as a foreign language. *GIST Education and Learning Research Journal, 5*, 25–49.

Mayall, H. (2010). Integrating video case studies into a literacy methods course. *International Journal of Instructional Media*, 37(1), 33

Mesmer, H. A. E., & Griffith, P. L. (2005). Everybody's selling it—But just what is explicit, systematic phonics instruction? *The Reading Teacher*, 59(4), 366–376.

Moats, L. C. (2017). Can prevailing approaches to reading instruction accomplish the goals of RTI? *Perspectives on Language and Literacy, 43*, 15–22.

Montgomery, K., & Brown, S. (1997). Simulations: Using experiential learning to add relevancy and meaning to introductory courses. *Innovative Higher Education, 21*(3), 217.

National Center on Improving Literacy. (2020). https://improvingliteracy.org/

National Reading Panel (U.S.), National Institute of Child Health, Human Development (U.S.), National Reading Excellence Initiative, National Institute for Literacy (U.S.), United States. Public Health Service, & United States Department of Health. (2000). *Report of the National Reading Panel: Teaching children to read: An evidence-based assessment of the scientific research literature on reading and its implications for reading instruction: Reports of the subgroups.* National Institute of Child Health and Human Development, National Institutes of Health.

NCATE. (2010). *Transforming teacher education through clinical practice: Report of the Blue Ribbon Panel on clinical preparation and improved partnerships for student learning.* National Council for Accreditation of Teacher Education.

Olah, L., Lawrence, N. R., & Riggan, M. (2010). Learning to learn from benchmark assessment data: How teachers analyze results. *Peabody Journal of Education*, *85*(2), 226–245.

Pressley, M. (2002). Effective beginning reading instruction. *Journal of Literacy Research*, *34*(2), 165–188.

Reading Recovery. (2020). *Basic facts.* https://readingrecovery.org/reading-recovery/teaching-children/basic-facts/

Rowley, J. B., & Hart, P. M. (1996). How video cases can promote reflective dialogue. *Educational Leadership*, *53*(6), 28–29.

Santa, C. M., Williams, C. K., Ogle, D., Farstrup, A. E., Au, K. H., Baker, B. M., Edwards, P. A., Klein, A. F., Kurek, G. M., Larson, D. L., Paratore, J. R., Rog, L. L., & Shanahan, T. (2000). Excellent reading teachers: A position statement of the International Reading Association. *Journal of Adolescent & Adult Literacy*, *44*(2), 193–199.

Shaywitz, S. E., Escobar, M. D., Shaywitz, B. A., Fletcher, J. M., & Makuch, R. (1992). Evidence that dyslexia may represent the lower tail of a normal distribution of reading ability. *New England Journal of Medicine*, *326*(3), 145–150.

Simon, J. A., & Kule-Korgood, M. (2011). Rights of individuals with dyslexia and other disabilities. In J. R. Birsh (Ed.), *Multisensory teaching of basic language skills* (pp. 685–698). Paul H. Brookes.

Snow, C. E., Burns, M. S., & Griffin, P. (Eds.). (1998). *Preventing reading difficulties in young children.* National Academies Press.

Spear-Swerling, L. (2019). Structured literacy and typical literacy practices: Understanding differences to create instructional opportunities. *Teaching Exceptional Children*, *51*(3), 201–211.

Stahl, S. A. (1998). Teaching children with reading problems to decode: Phonics and not "not-phonics" instruction. *Reading & Writing Quarterly: Overcoming Learning Difficulties*, *14*(2), 165–188. https://doi.org/10.1080/1057356980140203

Stanovich, K. E. (1996). Toward a more inclusive definition of dyslexia. *Dyslexia*, *2*(3), 154–216.

Tompkins, G. (2016). *Literacy for the 21st century: A balanced approach* (7th ed.). Pearson.

Yoshimoto, R. (2019). *What makes OG unique and effective.* https://www.ortongillinghamin-ternational.org/post/what-makes-og-unique-and-effective#:~:text=OG%20is%20a%20powerful%20instructional%20approach%20for%20teaching%20reading%20and%20spelling.&text=For%20the%20teachers%20and%20tutors,is%20financially%20or%20fiscally%20sound

CHAPTER 3

LEARNING TO TEACH TEACHING

What Capabilities and Knowledge Do Mathematics Teacher Educators Need and (How) Can We Support Their Development?

Meghan Shaughnessy
Boston University

Sarah Kate Selling
Stanford University

Nicole Garcia and Deborah Loewenberg Ball
University of Michigan

ABSTRACT

This chapter details out the capabilities and knowledge needed by teacher educators to effectively prepare teacher candidates for a teaching career. The chapter is framed by two questions: (1) what knowledge and skills are required by teacher educators engaged in practice-based teacher education and (2) what structures help to support novice teacher educators' learning of this knowledge and these skills? The authors use the context of leading a group discussion in mathematics to examine these two questions.

Preparing Quality Teachers:
Advances in Clinical Practice, pp. 41–68
Copyright © 2022 by Information Age Publishing
www.infoagepub.com

41

INTRODUCTION

In her mathematics methods class, Dr. Washington[1] asks her teacher candidates to work in groups to consider a scenario that might arise in teaching a third-grade mathematics lesson. She explains that children have solved the problem 59 + 36 mentally and are now discussing their strategies. Dr. Washington asks the class to consider one student's strategy, "I changed 59 to 60 because it is easier to add. Then I added 60 plus 36. Six tens plus three tens is nine and then there are six ones. Then I had to add one more. So it is 97." Dr. Washington has her teacher candidates restate the strategy as she knows that it is important that her teacher candidates develop skill with attending to the details of what children say. She then asks them to consider whether the strategy is mathematically valid. The strategy is illustrated in Figure 3.1.

Teacher candidates discuss the mathematical validity of the strategy with a partner. Then, Dr. Washington elicits ideas from the class. One teacher candidate says, "Well, the student's answer is wrong." Other teacher candidates in the class nod their heads in agreement. Dr. Washington asks the class to consider the method itself, "What is the student trying to do? What works in the method?" Another teacher candidate shares that the student is adjusting one of the addends to get a "friendlier" number, but they make a mistake with the adjusting. The class begins to discuss the student's strategy of changing the 59 to 60 and how that means that one needs to be subtracted from the final answer instead of adding a one. Dr. Washington

Figure 3.1

A Student's Strategy for Adding 59 + 36 Mentally

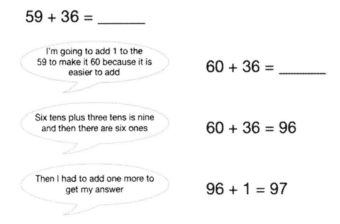

presses the class to explain both why the student's strategy does not work mathematically and how the strategy could be revised to be a valid strategy. She wants them to learn ways of responding to students' ideas, conscious that this can have significant impact on children's mathematical identities and how they are positioned in class.

Later, Dr. Washington shifts the focus of the conversation back to the third-grade discussion. She asks the teacher candidates to imagine that they are the classroom teacher and narrates the situation that she wants them to consider. She begins by telling them about a student who often volunteers to share in whole group but who often has incorrect answers. She continues:

> You are concerned about how this student is being positioned in the class as being "bad at math." The strategy has been shared in whole group. What moves might you make in this particular situation? What would you do to validate the thinking of this student? What would be your next steps with this compensation strategy, both for this student and the class?

With this framing, the teacher candidates work in small groups to consider ways they might respond. After several minutes, she calls the class back together and asks for a group to share their next moves in this situation and their reasoning for selecting those particular moves, "We'll all listen closely and try to consider the moves and their implications for the student who shared their thinking and the class."

What stands out about this short segment? What is Dr. Washington doing—and not doing? We see that the teacher candidates' own mathematical grasp of the task is settled at the beginning. Further, Dr. Washington has created a space for them to practice responding to a real problem of practice—a student presenting a strategy that does not work in general. The task she presents differentiates their own understanding of the mathematics from the knowledge and skill they will need in teaching. Dr. Washington could just explain the strategy to her teacher candidates, and the moves that she would make in this particular situation. Instead, she structures the work so that the teacher candidates have to make sense of the student's work and develop strategies to use in this situation. She knows that too often teacher candidates learn *about* teaching, or learn content they will have to teach, or learn about typical misconceptions that students might have, but stop short of practicing what they would do. And so, she designs tasks rooted in problems of practice that combine opportunities to work on mathematics, children's typical patterns of thinking, and decision making and talking as a teacher.

The activities that Dr. Washington is doing with her candidates in the course complements and is aligned with their clinical experiences. The methods course is linked to teaching opportunities that candidates will have in the coming days. After this class, each teacher candidate in Dr. Washington's class will be leading a discussion in their clinical placement. The classrooms are K–6 classrooms and Dr. Washington has provided a task that uses mental computation appropriate for each grade level. The teachers in the clinical placements have collaborated with Dr. Washington and others in the program to design a robust set of teaching experiences for teacher candidates where the aim is to support the learning of both teacher candidates and K–12 students.

Nevertheless, what can get overlooked is the complexity of the work that Dr. Washington is doing. Dr. Washington is doing specific work to help teacher candidates learn to integrate attention to content together with explicit efforts to disrupt patterns of inequities. This sort of work is fundamental to robust clinical partnerships that support the learning of both teacher candidates and K–12 students. Yet, when building clinical partnerships, it is easy to overlook the demands on the university-based teacher educator. Too often it is assumed that being a skilled K–12 teacher is sufficient for helping teacher candidates learn teaching practice. We argue in this chapter that the work done by Dr. Washington demands knowledge and skills that overlap with and yet different from the work required to teach children. The work that Dr. Washington is doing cannot be taken for granted, nor can the knowledge and skills required to carry out that work. This chapter focuses on the knowledge and skills that teacher educators themselves need to take advantage of the emphasis on clinical partnerships.

In this chapter, we focus on the work that Dr. Washington is doing with a specific focus on the knowledge and skills needed to teach methods courses that support and complement clinical partnerships. We ask—what is involved in learning to teach practice in ways that are not instantly con- verted to "academic," or propositional, knowledge? How, for example, would a teacher educator teach teacher candidates to *do* the actual work of leading discussions or eliciting children's thinking—not just teach them *about* these instructional practices? The work of teacher education is com- plex. Even if teacher educators are able to enact a teaching practice such as leading mathematics discussions with K–12 children, teaching teach- ers involves being able to decompose teaching practice (Grossman et al., 2009) (i.e., identifying and talking about specific skills and techniques for carrying out the practice) and support teacher candidates' learning of these practices. This is different from being able to engage in the teaching practice with children oneself successfully. We propose specific capabilities and knowledge needed for the work of teaching with a particular focus on the teaching of methods courses that support clinical partnerships. We also analyze strategies that we have developed to support teacher educators to develop these resources. Drawing on our experience as teacher educators, our argument rests on an analysis of the recurrent challenges of trying to teach teaching. The elements and framework that we propose can be extended and refined through empirical studies in a variety of settings.

The Work of Teacher Education

The work of teacher educators is broad, and in this chapter, we focus on the teaching of courses in the context of practice-based teacher education. In recent years, scholars and teacher educators have called for teacher preparation to focus more directly on the practice of teaching (Ball & Forzani, 2009; Grossman et al., 2009; Grossman et al., 2018; Lampert & Graziani, 2009). They emphasize that teacher candidates need opportunities to learn to do key aspects of the work of teaching, rather than just talking about teaching or analyzing others' teaching. This call has spurred important changes in the design and implementation of teacher education. For example, in some teacher education programs, course content has shifted to the teaching of specific "high-leverage practices" (Ball et al., 2009; Davis & Boerst, 2014; Ghousseini, 2015; Grossman et al., 2018; McDonald et al., 2013). Teacher education pedagogy is also shifting to incorporate "pedagogies of enactment" (Grossman et al., 2009), which include "approximations of practice," such as coached rehearsals (Kazemi et al., 2015), simulations ((Self & Stengel, 2020; Shaughnessy & Boerst, 2018) and scaffolded mini-lessons (Davis, 2020; Schutz et al., 2018).

Preparing teachers is something that people do; it is not merely something to know. Teacher educators must use knowledge flexibly and fluently as they interact with teacher candidates, with the aim of helping teacher candidates become proficient with teaching. We extend the conceptualization of teaching practice as interactions among teachers, students, content, and the environment presented by Cohen et al. (2003) to focus on interactions among teacher educators, teacher candidates and content. The "content" in this case is the practice of K–12 teaching. The work of teacher education occurs within broader environments that both shape and are shaped by the instruction happening in teacher education. This view of instruction informs the identification of skills and knowledge that teacher educators need to enact practice-based teacher education. For example, teacher educators' knowledge of content, particularly teaching practice, must go beyond being able to enact teaching practices to include being able to identify and decompose such practices, talk about the practices and equitable ways of enacting them, and see different ways of enacting the practice, all of which must adhere to the articulation of the practice. Further, teacher educators may need specialized knowledge of mathematics content for teaching teachers (Superfine & Li, 2014). They also need knowledge of their teacher candidates, including the beliefs, knowledge, and skills that candidates bring to teacher education, the ways in which they are likely to interpret particular practices, and progressions of development with such practices. Further, because the environment matters for the work of teaching, teacher educators must consider environments beyond their own classrooms (e.g., clinical placements and mentor teachers with particular orientations to teaching and supporting teacher candidates' learning). Thus, teaching practice-based courses requires the integrated use of knowledge and skills in particular contexts of instruction.

What Is Known About the Preparation of Beginning Teacher Educators?

We focus on the preparation of university-based teacher educators who teach courses held at the university and in school sites. No system exists for preparing university-based teacher educators in the United States or in much of the world. Many university-based teacher educators in the U.S. feel underprepared for the work that they do. They report "happenstance in becoming engaged in teacher education" and a "lack of explicit development of teaching skills or pedagogies related to teacher educating" (Goodwin et al., 2014, p. 291). The transition from teacher to teacher educator is challenging for many (Swennen et al., 2009; Wood & Berg, 2010; Zeichner, 2005). Pedagogical strategies and skills are different from K–12 teaching because the work of teacher education is different from the work of K–12 teaching. Additional challenges include developing a professional identity as a teacher educator, learning new institutional roles and norms, and working with adult learners (Murray & Male, 2005).

This chapter focuses on two fundamental questions in the preparation of teacher educators. First, we ask what knowledge and skills are required by teacher educators engaged in practice-based teacher education? Given the increasing focus on teaching novices to *do* the work of teaching, we focus on practice-based teacher education (Ball & Forzani, 2009; Grossman et al., 2009; Grossman et al., 2018; Lampert & Graziani, 2009. We believe that focusing on the teaching of practice entails specialized skills and knowledge, and requires the development of particular kinds of skills and capabilities. A second question asks what structures help to support novice teacher educators' learning of such knowledge and skill? There is increasing interest in developing systems of mentorship and apprenticeship for novice teacher educators (Goodwin et al., 2014). In this chapter, we consider these questions in the case of an elementary mathematics methods course.

CONTEXT

Over the last decade, our university-based teacher education program in the United States has engaged in a collective redesign of its elementary teacher education program, centered on an effort to focus more directly on practices of teaching (see Davis & Boerst, 2014). As part of this effort, an instructional planning group has worked together to develop the mathematics methods course to center on four high-leverage mathematics teaching practices: (1) leading group discussions; (2) explaining content; (3) assessing children's knowledge and skills; and (4) planning instruction. The course develops teacher candidates' capabilities with these practices intertwined with mathematical knowledge for teaching. The group meets regularly to analyze particular enactments of the course and to improve its design and pedagogy. An additional important component is providing a context and structured opportunities for doctoral students to learn to teach teaching. Because of the intentionality of this work, it was an ideal site for examining what is involved in learning to teach practice-based method courses.

We examined the records of the planning group's work over five years, focusing on (a) recurrent topics and practices that comprised regular meetings; (b) challenges that instructors encountered, and (c) areas of redesign, revision, and development. We asked three questions: (1) what do teacher educators have to learn—or unlearn—as they develop their capabilities and knowledge to teach practice-based teacher education? (2) What teacher education pedagogies and content seem to present particular challenges? (3) How do specific structures of the planning group function to support teacher educators' development? The records of our meetings offered a rich context to notice patterns and themes, and to surface unseen affordances and challenges of teacher educators' learning.

In this chapter, we report on this analysis of the group work to identify the knowledge and skills needed by teacher educators to teach the course and the structures used to support beginning teacher educators in learning to teach a practice-based course. To provide a focus, we center the chapter on what is involved in teaching the practice of leading a group discussion.

A FOCUS ON LEADING A GROUP DISCUSSION

The practice of "leading a group discussion" has received considerable attention in teacher education (e.g., Boerst et al., 2011; Ghousseini, 2015; Lampert et al., 2013; Shaughnessy et al., 2019) for a number of reasons. First, the practice is interactive and highly dependent upon the ideas that children bring and contribute. This creates challenges for novices because it is not always possible to anticipate the thinking that is going to be shared. In turn, it means that leading a discussion requires adjusting plans in the moment in response to ideas that are being shared by the learners. Preparing novices to do such work is challenging for teacher educators. Second, the practice is highly interwoven with content, which creates demands for both novices and the teacher educators who are supporting their development. Third, leading mathematics discussion well is inconsistent with the inclination towards saying that many teacher candidates bring to teacher education. Fourth, although we focus on the case of learning to lead mathematics discussions, the practice of leading discussions happens across content areas. Looking at the case of leading mathematics discussions has the potential to inform thinking about the knowledge and skills that teacher educators need to teach novices to lead discussions across content areas.

In mathematics, discussions are important for supporting students in developing conceptual understanding (e.g., Michaels et al., 2008) and learning disciplinary norms and practices (e.g., Lampert, 2003; Yackel & Cobb, 1996). There is much for teacher candidates to learn about this work, including launching a discussion, eliciting and probing student thinking, orienting students to the thinking of others, making contributions, recording and representing content, and concluding a discussion. In addition, teacher candidates must learn to enact discussion-enabling practices (Boerst et al., 2009) such as selecting a task, anticipating student thinking, setting up the task, and monitoring student work as they work on the task individually or in groups. The work is complex, and we work on the practice across our methods course.

MATHEMATICS TEACHER EDUCATORS' KNOWLEDGE AND SKILLS FOR A PRACTICE-BASED APPROACH

Teaching beginning teachers to lead group discussions skillfully and attentively to the mathematical learning goals and equity is not easy. In this section, we analyze what was involved for the instructors in our group in doing this well. First, we consider the specialized knowledge and skill called for by the complex interactions of leading a content-focused group discussion. We then identify teacher education practices and pedagogies used to support teacher candidates' learning to teach to further name the skills needed by teacher educators.

Specialized Knowledge for Teaching Teachers: The Case of Leading a Group Discussion

To enact the type of practice-based approach to teaching "leading a group discussion" described earlier, we saw that teacher educators need to draw on different types of specialized knowledge, paralleling domains of mathematical knowledge for teaching (Ball et al., 2008), that is, common content knowledge, specialized content knowledge, knowledge of content and students, and knowledge of content and teaching. The "content" in this case was the work of mathematics instruction—specifically, the work of leading a group discussion. Figure 3.2 illustrates domains of content knowledge for teaching mathematics instruction, using a modified version of a representation developed by Ball et al. (2008) to illustrate the domains of mathematical knowledge for teaching.

Figure 3.2

Domains of Content Knowledge for Teaching Mathematics Instruction

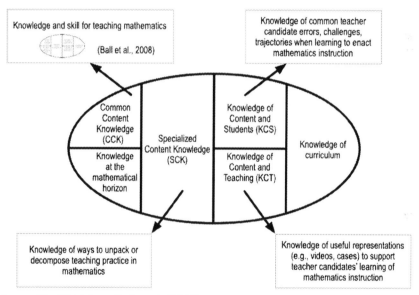

Source: Modified from Ball et al. (2008).

For teacher educators, we found that common content knowledge (CCK) could be viewed as the knowledge that mathematics teachers themselves hold regarding the teaching of the content to children. Consider the case of leading a discussion around different ways to represent the number 7 using Xs and Os (e.g., XXOOOOO and XXXXOOO are two ways), a type of task we use with our teacher candidates as they begin to lead discussions in K–1 clinical placements. Figure 3.3 shows the task, along with examples of possible student contributions that might emerge in kindergarten classrooms.

The common content knowledge for teaching teacher candidates to lead such a discussion includes the mathematical knowledge for teaching (MKT)

Figure 3.3

Making 7 with Xs and Os Task, Along With Possible Student Responses

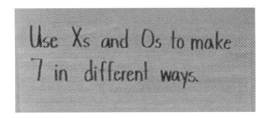

Student 1	Student 2	Student 3
X X X X O O O X X X O O O O X X O O O O O	X X X X O O O X O X O X O X	X O O X X O

that would allow teacher candidates to engage in this instructional practice. In relation to the task shown in Figure 3.3, our analyses revealed that this included knowing which key mathematical ideas are involved in this task (e.g., the importance of decomposing 7 in different ways such as $5 + 2$ and $3 + 4$ while preserving the quantity, commutativity), common student approaches, errors, or difficulties, and how different representations can be used to illustrate particular ideas. Other examples of common content knowledge for teacher educators that we identified include knowledge of the instructional practice itself, such as knowing particular talk moves to press for reasoning or to orient students to their peers' thinking (Chapin et al., 2013). In other words, teacher educators need the knowledge that they are helping teacher candidates learn; however, just as teachers need more than common content knowledge of mathematics (Ball et al., 2005; Ball et al., 2008; Ball & Hill, 2009), teacher educators also need more specialized knowledge for teaching mathematics instruction.

Teacher educators also need specialized content knowledge (SCK) for teaching mathematics teaching. Similar to specialized content knowledge for teaching mathematics, this type of teacher educator knowledge includes different ways to unpack or decompose instructional practices to support others in learning these practices. This knowledge is different from the knowledge needed to enact a particular teaching practice. For example, an elementary teacher might be skilled at leading mathematics discussions. However, they might not know how to name or break down the instructional work that they engage in to help others learn to lead discussions—for instance, the different ways that they could launch a discussion and the affordances/constraints of each of those approaches. This specialized content knowledge of teacher educators might also include understanding how different parts of an instructional practice function together to support student learning of mathematics.

Teacher educators also need a kind of "knowledge of content and students" (KCS)—in this case, knowledge of teacher candidates. This involves knowing how teacher candidates think, what they find challenging, as well as what they bring to learning teaching. For example, when our teacher candidates are learning to lead a discussion, we have found that they often engage in "filling in student thinking" (Shaughnessy & Boerst, 2018) rather than focusing on getting students to share their own thinking and reasoning. Additionally, they often struggle with how to respond when students share ideas that are not entirely correct (Bray, 2011; Son, 2013). For example, in the making seven with Xs and Os task, teacher candidates often find it challenging to respond when children focus on making patterns rather than making combinations that represent 7 (such as Student 2 in Figure 3.3), which is a common way that young children approach the task. We found that knowledge of content and teacher candidates also includes knowing what parts of an instructional practice can be difficult for teacher candidates—such as orienting students to the thinking of others.

Another type of specialized teacher educator knowledge can be described as "knowledge of content and teaching" (KCT). This includes knowing the types of tasks and representations that are useful in helping teacher candidates learn a particular part of mathematics instruction. In the case of leading a group discussion, we found that KCT includes knowing what types of mathematics tasks might be both "discussable" and accessible for teacher candidates to lead discussions around in their early attempts. KCT also includes knowing which mathematical content domains might be productive for teacher candidates, who are just beginning to learn this practice (e.g., leading a discussion about composing and decomposing numbers might be more accessible than one on the division of fractions). KCT also encompasses knowing the characteristics of video examples that might be useful in illustrating aspects of a practice. For example, we have found that using video examples in which students are less familiar with participating in discussions helps make more of the work visible.

These examples highlight that, while teacher educators need the same knowledge that skilled teachers need to engage in mathematics instruction, they also need an additional layer of knowledge that can be viewed through interactions inside an instructional triangle (Cohen et al., 2003) in which teacher candidates are the "students" and the "content" is mathematics instruction.

Skills for Teaching the Instructional Practice of Leading a Group Discussion

As we worked on identifying the specialized knowledge needed to teach novices to lead discussions with students, we saw that it was also important to identify the practices of teacher education that were being used to teach discussion leading. To illustrate some of these practices, we consider three pedagogies of practice used to support teacher candidates in learning to lead group discussions as well as a practice of teacher education, which has new demands inside of practice-based teacher education. These are not meant to be a comprehensive list of ways to support teacher candidates; rather, these serve as examples of the work that a practice-based approach demands on the part of the teacher educator and draws on the types of specialized knowledge illustrated in the previous section. In our description of each, we draw on prior research and describe how the practice or pedagogy was used to teach teacher candidates to lead discussions.

Modeling. In a practice-based approach to teacher education, "modeling by the teacher educator" is a key pedagogy (Loughran & Berry, 2005; McGrew et al., 2018; McDonald et al., 2013). This involves the teacher educator demonstrating the instructional practice through engagement in it and providing metacommentary to narrate and make visible the instructional work and decision making. Loughhan and Berry (2005) further highlight that

> modeling is not as simple as "just saying what one is doing," it involves a sensitivity to situations and a concentration on decision-making about what might be helpful to highlight (or not) in a given situation, and/or how to highlight a particular issue/concern/practice/thinking in a given situation. (p. 197)

Our analyses showed that to model the practice of leading a group discussion, a teacher educator might lead a discussion with teacher candidates about a mathematics task they worked on, while simultaneously making metacomments about the instructional work. For example, on the first day of our methods course, the teacher educator led a discussion about a mathematics task that involved finding all possible ways to represent two and two-thirds using pattern blocks, with the rhombus defined as the whole. During this discussion, the teacher educator made a metacomment about particular moves (such as physically moving around the classroom) to orient students to the thinking of peers:

> And, Alison, I'm going to have you turn. Try to turn and talk to everyone else. I know that this is one of those challenging things to do because you do want to turn- I think we all have this tendency to turn and talk to the

instructor, but I really want us to have this orientation to talking to each other. So, to help do that, I will try to move when we're doing this.

Here, the teacher engaged in orienting the teacher candidates to collective work and commented on her use and purpose of this move. We found that modeling, as a teacher educator pedagogy, requires that the teacher educator be able to engage productively in the practice of leading a discussion, drawing on the common content knowledge of teachers described above. However, this teacher educator pedagogy also requires new and different skills not required by teachers themselves. In this case, the skill of simultaneously engaging in a teaching practice while narrating and commenting on the instructional work involved. This additional layer involves skills such as deciding what to highlight (or not) about the instruction and how to describe the work in meaningful ways. These skills draw on the specialized knowledge described above; for example, when modeling the practice of leading a discussion, a teacher educator might decide what to highlight based on knowledge of common errors that teacher candidates tend to make when leading discussions (e.g., filling in thinking instead of asking questions) or what might be difficult or novel for teacher candidates (e.g., orienting students to the reasoning of others).

Using video representations of practice. Another key pedagogy of practice-based teacher education is using video representations of practice (Grossman et al., 2009; McDonald et al., 2013; Shaughnessy & Garcia, 2018; Star & Strickland, 2008; van Es et al., 2015). For the teacher educator, this involves work in a number of areas. First, the teacher educator must establish clear goals for what teacher candidates might be learning through watching through engaging with a video. These might include attending to children's thinking or noticing aspects of an instructional practice, such as orienting students to the thinking of others in a discussion. Teacher educators draw on these goals, as well as their specialized knowledge, to inform the selection of a video. Next, teacher educators must decide how to frame the video, including what aspects of the context are central to understanding the video and what might be unnecessary or distracting (Shaughnessy & Garcia, 2018).

In addition to deciding about the framing and context of the video representation, the teacher educator must decide what task the teacher candidates will work on through watching the video. For example, a teacher educator might ask teacher candidates to attend to what evidence of understanding of fractions is evident in a particular clip. Alternatively, a teacher educator might pause the video at strategic points and ask teacher candidates what they might be done next (Danielson et al., 2018; Shaughnessy & Garcia, 2018). These decisions about the use of the video are rooted in the instructional goal. Finally, using video representations of practice demands skills with facilitating discussion of the video and the activity in which the teacher candidates have engaged. This facilitation is different from leading a mathematics discussion with teacher candidates, as it involves addressing new problems of practice, such as how to respond to contributions from teacher candidates that may include problematic framings of students.

Rehearsal. Another pedagogy of practice that demands new work on the part of the teacher educator is facilitating coached rehearsals with teacher candidates (Kazemi et al., 2015). Consider the case of facilitating rehearsals of whole-class discussions. First is to articulate the instructional goals, including learning goals for the whole class (e.g., moves to probe student thinking) and for individuals (e.g., avoiding taking over the mathematical work for children). Because teacher candidates engage in leading a discussion in front of their peers, rehearsing discussions in a methods class also involves establishing norms and culture for working together on teaching practice. This adds new demands as the teacher educator invites teacher candidates to share their teaching publicly. For example, at the beginning of an activity focused on rehearsing different types of discussion conclusions, the teacher educator said:

> I've asked Katie to rehearse a conclusion for the discussion. And Katie's group was working on reinforcing productive discussion norms. So, we'll have Katie come to the front of the room. Katie, anyone that is seated in the front row right now can respond as one of your students if you need them to, but that said, for conclusion for a math discussion, you don't necessarily need to be calling on kids...It's more I'm just saying that as the heads up, okay? So, as Katie is practicing her conclusion right now, be watching the conclusion, be noticing what she's doing. I may stop her at points to ask some questions, and I may ask questions of her, I may ask questions of the entire group. So, there will be things for all of you to be considering. It's also possible, Katie, that I'm going to stop you at some particular point to just kind of underscore a particular thing that you did as being particularly important.

This framing of the activity established the roles and structures for the teacher candidates and also highlighted how rehearsals are opportunities for collective work on teaching.

Another set of skills is required for facilitating the coached rehearsals themselves. For example, the teacher educator must decide when to interrupt a rehearsing teacher candidate, what to comment on in the performance, and how to coach (e.g., asking a question, making a suggestion, commenting on what was productive). Decisions about these coaching moves are also guided by the teacher educator's learning goals for the teacher candidates. As they simultaneously analyze instruction in the moment and determine what might be most productive to coach on, providing feedback entails specialized knowledge. For example, in a rehearsal of setting up the making 7 with Xs and Os task, the teacher educator interrupted a rehearsing novice to suggest that, for kindergarteners, it would be important to have students participate in checking that XXXXOOX does represent 7 through counting. Additionally, teacher educators often played the role of a typical student in these rehearsals, offering contributions that are likely responses from students and constructing opportunities for teacher candidates to respond to common problems of practice (e.g., responding to a contribution that is not completely correct). For example, in a rehearsal of a set up for the making 7 with Xs and Os task, the teacher educator played the role of the student, saying, "Am I supposed to make patterns?" This requires additional skills on the part of the teacher educator to determine which student ideas to "play" in the discussion, when, and for what purposes.

Providing feedback on teacher candidate enactments. A teacher education practice used in our program to support teacher candidates to lead group discussions is the work of providing formative feedback on teacher candidates' enactments. Similar to the work involved in facilitating rehearsals, this practice involves determining which parts of a performance to provide feedback on and how. This rests on the teacher educators being able to recognize productive, problematic, or incomplete aspects of an enactment and draws significantly on the types of specialized knowledge described earlier. Additionally, teacher educators need to determine how to ground their feedback in particular rubrics or decompositions of practice. For example, in our methods course, our decomposition of leading a class discussion distinguishes between moves that elicit student contributions and moves that probe or follow-up with those contributions. Therefore, feedback on a discussion might need to draw on this language and distinction to focus a teacher candidate's attention on a particular area of strength or growth. For instance, a teacher educator might annotate a moment in a classroom discussion video, saying, "This was a strategic move to elicit another solution from a different student. Is there anything you could have asked to follow up about why this solution was different?" This work on the part of the teacher educator is different from giving feedback on teacher candidates' reflections about their practice, as it demands that the teacher educator interact with and directly give feedback on enactments of practice, rather than on teacher candidates' skill with analyzing and reflecting on their own practice.

Given the specialized content knowledge and pedagogies of practice required to teach a practice-based mathematics methods course, we sought to design and study supports that would enable novice teacher educators to build capacity while simultaneously supporting teacher candidates in learning to teach mathematics.

Structures for Supporting Teacher Educator Learning for a Practice-Based Approach

Our program has used a set of structures to build specialized knowledge and pedagogical skills demanded for the teaching of a practice-based methods course. We first describe the overarching organization of the work and then examine the structures used to support teacher educators.

Organizing the Work: Planning Group Participation

To teach the mathematics methods course, novice teacher educators participate in a "planning group," which takes the form of a professional learning community (Vescio et al., 2008) for both novice and experienced teacher educators. The group consists of four to five experienced teacher educators, many of whom are not currently teaching the course but are invested in either course development or teacher educator development, and three to four novice teacher educators, who are currently learning teacher education practice. About two-thirds of the group is also engaged in the study of teacher education. The group meets several times prior to the start of the course and then once per week throughout the duration of the course. The group is facilitated by a lead teacher educator, who is experienced and is also responsible for teaching one section of the course. All members of the group observe the lead teacher educator's teaching each week with an eye to identified areas of focus. Following the observation each week, members debrief the class with regard to the observation focus areas.

Four goals are central to the group's work. First, we seek to ensure that the course is designed and taught consistently to provide multiple cohorts of teacher candidates with learning opportunities that support their development as elementary mathematics teachers. Second, we provide opportunities for novice teacher educators to build specialized content knowledge and pedagogical knowledge and skill to ensure that all teacher candidates are receiving instruction that will allow them to engage in the mathematics teaching practices. Third, we use the observation of the lead instructor's teaching to adjust the plan or the materials for subsequent sections in response to what we learn from the first teaching of the shared plan. Fourth, the group serves as an ongoing opportunity for experienced and novice teacher educators to learn and think together about our own teacher education practice and the challenges and problems of practice encountered. This goal reflects a commitment to viewing the professional education of teacher educators as being continuous rather than occurring only before taking on the role of the teacher educator (Cochran-Smith,

2003) and the structure provides a designed space to support professional learning. We next provide an overview of the planning group organization.

Planning group organization. Prior to each meeting, the planning group members review detailed lesson plans and decompositions of practices involved in the upcoming class to prepare for the planning meeting. Each meeting is structured around three main activities: (1) debriefing the observed section, (2) building teacher educators' knowledge and skill related to the work of the upcoming class through structured activities, and (3) providing open space for both experienced and novice teacher educators to ask questions of the planning group and to work together to improve our collective practice.

The debrief provides teacher educators an opportunity to discuss both the common observation and the teaching of their own section. Following the debriefing, the teacher educators engage in work to prepare for the next class. Structures include: (1) framing and walking through particular activities, including providing space for discussion of questions that teacher educators may have about the lessons, (2) rehearsing sections of the lesson, and (3) discussing annotated videos. Each of these structures was designed to support novice teacher educators' content knowledge and development of skill with teacher education practices and pedagogies of practice, as well as offering opportunities for more experienced teacher educators to continue growing our own knowledge and skill. The focal and secondary uses of each of the structures shown in Table 3.1. Descriptions of structures that are specifically designed to support new teacher educators' understanding of and ability to engage in pedagogies of practice and teacher education practices follow.

Decompositions of practice. The decomposition of a teaching practice serves as an important support for teacher educators, particularly in the area of teaching the practice. The decomposition breaks the practice into component parts that can be named, represented, and taught to beginners, a critical part of the knowledge necessary for teacher educators. Figure 3.4 shows the decomposition that we use to detail the work of leading a mathematics discussion. Understanding the decomposition opens up the space for the planning group to discuss the purpose of each of the activities planned for class (e.g., supporting teacher candidates to learn to set up a task) as well as the content-pedagogy match for the activities (e.g., helping novice teacher educators to understand why we would choose to use a rehearsal for helping beginners to set up a mathematics task, but we would use a written task to practice anticipating student thinking).

Detailed lesson plans. The lesson plans include scaffolds to support teacher educators in the areas of specialized knowledge, pedagogies of practice, and teacher education practices. An excerpt from a lesson plan is shown in Table 3.2 to illustrate the level of detail provided. This plan

Table 3.1

Support Structures and Purposes for Teacher Educators' Learning

Structure to Support Teacher Educator Learning	Teacher Education Pedagogies & Practices				
	Modeling	*Video*	*Rehearsal*	*Feedback*	*Specialized Knowledge*
Decompositions of practices	Secondary		Secondary	Focal	Focal
Detailed lesson plans	Secondary	Focal	Secondary		Focal
Walk-throughs of activities including questions and discussion	Focal	Focal	Focal	Secondary	Focal
Teacher educator rehearsal	Focal		Focal		Focal
Annotated videos	Secondary		Secondary	Focal	Focal
Observation	Focal	Focal	Focal		Focal
Debrief	Secondary	Secondary	Secondary		Focal

supports teacher educators' knowledge of content and students by noting the areas in which teacher candidates may need support (i.e., interpreting the representation of practice as a model to be emulated rather than as an example to examine and adapt for specific contexts). Knowledge of content and teacher candidates (KCS) is also supported by comments about how teacher candidates might interpret the video examples (i.e., as a model to replicate).

Walk-throughs of activities, including questions and discussions. When teacher educators engage in work to prepare for the next class, the lead teacher educator frames the work for the next class by providing an overview of the goals for the teacher candidates, how these goals connect to past work, and how the goals connect to future work. For example, the goals of a class might include understanding the purpose of setting up a task, knowing the components and features of a strong set-up, and identifying particular teacher moves that can be used to set up a task. The teacher educator might name that these goals were identified because teacher candidates led a discussion in their clinical placement and in many instances, students were under-prepared to begin working on the mathematics task that was later going to be discussed (i.e., connection to past work) and teacher candidates are going to be leading another discussion in their

Table 3.2

Detailed Lesson Plan for Unpacking the Setting Up of a Mathematics Task

Activity/Goals	Detail	Notes

Unpacking the work of setting of a mathematics task
 	
• Understand the purpose of the set up
• Articulate components and features of effective set ups
• Identify particular teacher moves for establishing shared understanding of a task and establishing a work environment
	Explain that we will be working on the set up of mathematics task. A strong "set up" ensures that students are ready to work on the task independently. The goal is to make sure that the students understand the task, without the teacher doing much of the key work for them. Introduce the components and features of an effective task set-up:
	
	Components of effective set-ups:
	
	• Build a shared understanding of what the task is asking (without giving away the solutions or the methods)
	
	   o Have students read the task (or teacher reads it)
	   o Have a student say what they think the task is asking
	   o Work together to figure out what would count as an answer
	   o Ask a student to say how they are going to get started.
	   o Give directions to establish the work environment as needed, depending on routinized norms of the classroom
		We often find that we need to be explicit about how the practices that we are working on in the context of discussions are teaching practices that are important outside of leading a discussion. Might mention that being able to set up a task is crucial even if students are not going to discuss their work on the task.
		
		Throughout the course, we want to provide opportunities to see different images of discussions. There are many variables to consider here: grade-level of students, the teacher, the type of mathematics task being discussed. Because we are using this video to learn the components of a strong set-up, we selected a video containing many of the components of a strong set up. Furthermore, we selected a video in which the task has multiple solutions because teacher candidates will be leading discussions of this type during their next discussion.

(Table continues on next page)

Table 3.2 (Continued)

Detailed Lesson Plan for Unpacking the Setting Up of a Mathematics Task

Activity/Goals	Detail	Notes
	Features of effective set-ups: • Succinct • Clearly organized • Use language that is likely to be accessible to students • Task is publicly posted Show a video of a set-up in a classroom lesson. Teacher candidates should record what they notice the teacher doing during the set up with respect to the key components. They should also note whether the set up contains the all of the features of effective set-ups. *Caution*: Teacher candidates may be inclined to think that this is the "model" set up. Convey there are ways in which the set up could be improved and that context shapes what is viewed as an effective set-up. Pair/share Invite teacher candidates to comment in whole group. *Might pose question*: Are there things you might need to do in some cases, but not always? (e.g., distribute supplies; remind about routines for where to place complete work)	*Might consider bringing up the relative affordances and constraints of recording the conditions on the board v. underlining the conditions in the task. The first is likely more useful to use as a reference during class when supporting students in giving a verbal explanation. The second is likely to be useful for students as a strategy for identifying the conditions of a task on their own.*

Figure 3.4

Decomposition of Leading a Group Discussion

Discussion Enabling	Discussion Leading			
• Selecting a task	Framing	Orchestrating		Framing
• Identifying the mathematical point	• Launching	• Eliciting • Probing		• Concluding
• Anticipating student thinking		• Orienting • Making contributions		
• Setting up the task	Representing and recording content			
• Monitoring as students work on the task	Maintaining a focus on the mathematical point			

Note: Decompositions of practice change as we learn more about the enactment of practice and how teacher educators and candidates make sense of and use the decomposition. The most up-to-date versions of our decompositions are freely available through the TeachingWorks Resource Library at library.teachingworks. org.

clinical placement next week and the task that they are using will not be straight-forward for students to understand (connection to future work).

The lead teacher educator then walks the group through the activities. In doing so, the teacher educator articulates how the activities connect with the learning goals for teacher candidates, what should be highlighted for teacher candidates, and areas of caution (i.e., teacher candidates may interpret this video as a "model" set-up). Thus, walk-throughs serve to support the development of specialized content knowledge for teaching teachers as well as skill with practices and pedagogies of teacher education.

There are opportunities for teacher educators to ask questions throughout the walk-throughs of the lessons. Thus, space is provided for discussion of questions that teacher educators may have about the lessons. Some of these questions may be answered in the moment by an experienced teacher educator, but others may surface questions for the group to consider and potentially led to the refinement of the lesson. In this way, the "walk throughs" provide opportunities for teacher educators to develop specialized knowledge, as well as inform their developing skill with pedagogies and practices of teacher education, such as using video.

Teacher educator rehearsals. Teacher educator rehearsals are used in two different ways. To build skill with the teacher education pedagogy of modeling, we have novice teacher educators rehearse the modeling that will take place in front of the teacher candidates. One experienced teacher educator runs the rehearsal while other teacher educators participate in the role of teacher candidates. The experienced teacher educator pauses the rehearsal at strategic moments to support the novice teacher educators and the group as a whole in engaging in the metacognitive work of teacher educators. For instance, consider what should be highlighted (and how) for teacher candidates, at which moments metacomments should be made for teacher candidates, and how best to represent the connection between the mathematical notation and the representations. This collective work provides support for teacher educators in understanding the pedagogy as well as the pedagogical content knowledge and knowledge of content and students required to engage in the pedagogy with particular content.

We also rehearse the running of a rehearsal with teacher candidates. It is structured slightly differently, but provides many of the same supports. In a rehearsal of rehearsal, an experienced teacher educator serves as the teacher candidate who is engaging in the teaching practice, the novice teacher educator serves in the role of the teacher educator who is running the rehearsal with the teacher candidate, and another experienced teacher educator runs the rehearsal, giving feedback to the new teacher educator on their choices for pausing the rehearsal, the feedback they give to the teacher candidate, etc. In this case, the teacher educator serving in the role of the teacher candidate designs their performance to highlight common ways that teacher candidates approach setting up a task for discussion, including challenges with coordinating between representations and common language issues. For instance, to prepare teacher educators to lead a rehearsal of the "Make 7" task shown in Figure 3.3, novice teacher educators rehearsed the rehearsal in the planning group meetings. This design provides opportunities for teacher educators to develop their own KCS at the same time as developing their skill with the pedagogy of rehearsal.

Annotated videos. The work of providing feedback to teacher candidates involves not only the ability to identify key parts of the practice, but an ability to align feedback with both the decomposition of the practice that is being used with the teacher candidates and with the teacher candidates' progression of development expected at the time of the feedback. One way to support novice teacher educators with this work is through the use of annotated video. Our program uses the Edthena platform to facilitate the learning of teacher candidates about the interactive work of teaching. We are able to harness that same platform to support the work of novice teacher educators. We duplicate a small number of videos and have a "group" for the planning group on the Edthena platform, which also for the secure sharing of the videos and the annotations. Videos are annotated by experienced teacher educators to provide feedback to teacher candidates. The commenting interface allows a teacher educator to indicate the nature of a comment as a question, suggestion, strength, or note. Question comments are used to signal the need for a response from the teacher candidate. Suggestions are used to name ways that the teacher candidate could refine their practice. Strength comments are used to name aspects of the work that seem particularly useful or likely to be effective. Note comments convey information to the teacher candidate, including supporting the teacher candidate's developing content knowledge for teaching. These annotations serve as a critical resource for novice teacher educators.

Initially, novice teacher educators watch the videos with annotations in an attempt to notice and justify on what and how the teacher educator provided feedback to the teacher candidates. This initial experience supports new teacher educators in developing a sense of how to align feedback with the decomposition and how to choose what to give feedback on. Later, teacher educators watch videos without annotation then annotate the videos themselves as if they were giving feedback to the teacher candidates. Their annotation is then compared with the experienced teacher educator's annotation. Novice teacher educators (and other experienced teacher educators) are provided with opportunities to discuss decisions that experienced teacher educators made when providing feedback. These experiences with annotated videos support teacher educators in the provision of feedback to candidates on videos from their clinical experiences.

Observation. All members of the planning group attend the section of the course taught by the lead teacher educator. Common observation allows for a shared text which can be unpacked to study the work of teacher education. To support the observation, the lead teacher educator identifies particular foci. These foci might focus on teacher candidates' engagement in and learning from specific activities as well as the enactment of particular pedagogies of practice (i.e., focus on the pauses in the rehearsal and try to identify what each pause accomplished for the rehearsing teacher candidate and/or the larger group of teacher candidates). More generally, as they observe, teacher educators might be asked to consider how the pedagogies of practice used in a given lesson appear to support (or not support) teacher candidates' learning. This type of question brings to the fore the questions that teacher educators must consider when determining how to teach particular practices to teacher candidates as well as the key features of the pedagogies used.

Debrief. The 30-minute debrief provides teacher educators an opportunity to discuss both the common observation and the teaching of their own section. These debriefs are focused on questions designed by the lead teacher educator to highlight the key work of teacher educators in this context (i.e., the focus questions for the observation). Insights are recorded both collectively and individually. These insights both inform the sequence of work with these particular teacher candidates as well as the design of the course moving forward. In the case of refining a particular activity, sometimes it is possible to decide how to revise an activity for future iterations of the course. In other cases, we leave detailed notes about the questions and dilemmas that arose and revisit them in the planning of the next iteration of the course. These decisions about revision in the moment or in the future are often tied to the extent to which the adjustments needed for the particular activity is tied to the clinical experience. For example, if adjustments to content are suggested due to the content being covered in clinical experiences, the group might leave notes reflecting that rather than making a change since clinical experiences are often variable.

Summary. A set of structures are used to support teacher educators' learning. These include written artifacts (i.e., decomposition of practice, detailed lesson plans), planning meetings (walk-throughs, question sessions, rehearsals, debriefing of observations) and observations of the course being enacted by a lead instructor. Together, these constitute a system for supporting the development of novice teacher educators in learning to teach a practice-based mathematics methods course.

DISCUSSION

The knowledge and skills of university-based teacher educators are crucial for the success of clinical partnerships. Courses taught by university-based instructors must support teacher candidates in developing content knowledge for knowledge and pedagogical knowledge that is needed for teaching in clinical placements. Yet, the field is only beginning to identify the knowledge and skills needed by university-based teacher educators to teach methods courses in ways that connect with, leverage, and advance clinical partnerships. central. In this chapter, we focus on the work that Dr. Washington is doing with a specific focus on the knowledge and skills needed to teach methods courses that support clinical partnerships through the development of practice-based activities that tie to clinical enactments of practice. To identify the knowledge and skills needed by teacher educators to teach practice-based methods courses and structures to support its development, we focused our analysis on one teaching practice (leading a group discussion) in a particular course (elementary mathematics methods) in a particular context. As Cohen (2011) argues, "to teach is always to teach something" (p. 45), and we argue using the case of one teaching practice with particular content can shed light on the knowledge and skill that teacher educators need to support the learning of teacher candidates in practice-based teacher education and ways to support its development. Our analysis reveals both skills and knowledge needed by teacher educators as well as structures that we have found useful when supporting novice teacher educators' skills and knowledge development. As a field, we must plan deliberately for the development of novice teacher educators to realize the goals of practice-based teacher education. We see this as a needed goal both for doctoral preparation programs and teacher education programs as a doctoral program is only one pathway into the work of teacher education.

There are many productive questions that could be explored in future work. One question focuses on the degree to which the findings of this study generalize across other practice-based mathematics methods courses that focus on leading a group discussion—in other words, empirically testing the findings from this study. Are the knowledge and skills needed the same? Are the structures useful across contexts?

A second question is the degree to which the findings regarding the knowledge and skills needed to teach teacher candidates to lead discussions and structures to support the development of novice teacher educators' knowledge and skills for leading a discussion might generalize across multiple teaching practices that are taught in an elementary mathematics methods course. For instance, what knowledge and skills are needed to teach novices to elicit and interpret student thinking or to communicate with families about students' progress in mathematics class? Do the same set of structures function to support novice teacher educators' knowledge and skill? Relatedly, to what degree, does the set of structures extend across content areas and grade bands (e.g., secondary or early childhood).

A third question pertains to the development of experienced teacher educators who have not taught practice-focused courses. Although we focus on novice teacher educators in this chapter, because of the context of our work, we believe that experienced teacher educators who have not taught practice-focused courses need to develop additional skills to enact practice-based teacher education. Given the increasing focus on practice-based teacher education, teacher educators, researchers, and teacher education program administrators need ways to understand the supports and experiences teacher educators will need to learn to teach teacher candidates in new and different ways. For instance, what pedagogical shifts are challenging for experienced teacher educators? What types of knowledge do teacher educators who have not taught practice-focused courses need to develop?

A fourth question focuses on scale. The efforts reported in this chapter are situated within one practice-based teacher education program, which includes two sections of the described mathematics course. But, given the number of teacher educators entering the field each year as well as the number of teacher educators currently working and interested in learning to teach in practice-focused ways, what are ways in which capacity can be developed beyond efforts in individual teacher education programs.

As a field, we must put an increased focus on the preparation of teacher educators. This chapter offers an analysis of one teacher education program's attempt to do so. Importantly, this education of teacher educators takes place across a lifetime, and just as with teachers, teacher educators needed continued opportunities for professional development across their careers (Cochran-Smith, 2003).

REFERENCES

Ball, D. L., & Forzani, F. M. (2009). The work of teaching and the challenge for teacher education. *Journal of Teacher Education, 60*(5), 497–511.

Ball, D. L., Hill, H. C, & Bass, H. (2005). Knowing mathematics for teaching: Who knows mathematics well enough to teach third grade, and how can we decide? *American Educator, 30*(3), 14–17, 20–22, 43–46.

Ball, D. L., & Hill, H. (2009). The curious—and crucial—case of mathematical knowledge for teaching. *Phi Delta Kappan, 91*(2), 68–71.

Ball, D. L., Thames, M. H., & Phelps, G. (2008). Content knowledge for teaching: What makes it special? *Journal of Teacher Education, 59*(5), 389–407.

Ball, D. L., Sleep, L., Boerst, T., & Bass, H. (2009). Combining the development of practice and the practice of development in teacher education. *Elementary School Journal, 109*(5), 458–474.

Boerst, T., Sleep, L., Ball., D. L., & Bass, H. (2011). Preparing teachers to lead mathematics discussions. *Teachers College Record, 113*(12), 2844–2877.

Boerst, T., Moss, P., & Blunk, M. (2009). *Unpacking core teaching practices in elementary mathematics to support teacher learning and assessment.* Principal Investigators meeting for the National Science Foundation Discovery Research-K12 Program, Washington, DC.

Bray, W. S. (2011). A collective case study of the influence of teachers' beliefs and knowledge on error-handling practices during class discussion of mathematics. *Journal for Research in Mathematics Education, 42*(1), 2–38.

Chapin, S., O'Connor, C., & Anderson, N. (2013) *Classroom discussions in math: A teacher's guide for using talk moves to support the Common Core and more, Grades K–6* (3rd ed.). Math Solutions.

Cochran-Smith, M. (2003). Learning and unlearning: the education of TE. *Teaching and Teacher Education, 19*, 5–28.

Cohen, D. K. (2011). Learning to teach nothing in particular: A uniquely American educational dilemma. *American Educator, 34(4)*, 44–46, 54.

Cohen, D. K., Raudenbush, S., & Ball, D. L. (2003). Resources, instruction, and research. *Educational Evaluation and Policy Analysis, 25*(2), 119–142.

Danielson, K. A., Shaughnessy, M., & Jay, L. P. (2018). Use of representations in teacher education. In P. Grossman (Ed.), *Teaching core practices in teacher education* (pp. 15–33). Harvard Education Press.

Davis, E. A. (2020). Approximations of practice: Scaffolding for preservice teachers. In E. A. Davis, C. Zembal-Saul, & S. M. Kademian (Eds.), *Sense-making in elementary science: Supporting teacher learning* (pp. 97–112). Routledge.

Davis, E. A., & Boerst, T. (2014). *Designing elementary teacher education to prepare well-started beginners* (TeachingWorks Working Papers). TeachingWorks. http://www.teachingworks.org/research-data/workingpapers

Ghousseini, H. (2015). Core practices and problems of practice in learning to lead classroom discussions. *The Elementary School Journal, 115*(3), 334–357.

Goodwin, A. L., Smith, L., Souto-Manning, M., Cheruvu, R., Tan, M. Y., Reed, R., & Taveras, L. (2014). What should TEs know and be able to do? Perspectives from practicing TEs. *Journal of Teacher Education, 65*(4), 284–302.

Grossman, P., Compton, C., Igra, D., Ronfeldt, M., Shahan, E., & Williamson, P. (2009). Teaching practice: A cross-professional perspective. *Teachers College Record, 111*(9), 2055–2100.

Grossman, P., Kavanagh, S. S., & Dean, C. P. (2018). The turn towards practice-based teacher education: Introduction to the work of the Core Practice Consortium. In P. Grossman (Ed.), *Teaching core practices in teacher education* (pp. 1–14). Harvard Education Press.

Kazemi, E., Ghousseni, H., Cunard, A., & Turrou, A. C. (2015). Getting inside rehearsals: Insights from TEs to support work on complex practice. *Journal of Teacher Education, 67*(1), 18–31.

Lampert, M. (2003). *Teaching problems and the problems of teaching*. Yale University Press.

Lampert, M., Franke, M. L., Kazemi, E., Ghousscini, H., Turrou, A. C., Beasley, H., Cunard, A., & Crowe, K. (2013). Keeping it complex: Using rehearsals to support novice teacher learning of ambitious teaching. *Journal of Teacher Education, 64*(3), 226–243.

Lampert, M., & Graziani, F. (2009). Instructional activities as a tool for teachers' and TEs' learning. *The Elementary School Journal, 109*(5), 491–509.

Loughran, J., & Berry, A. (2005). Modelling by TEs. *Teaching and Teacher Education, 21*(2), 193–203. http://doi.org/10.1016/j.tate.2004.12.005

McDonald, M., Kazemi, E., & Kavanagh, S. (2013). Core practices and pedagogies of teacher education: A call for common language and collective activity. *Journal of Teacher Education, 64*(5), 378–386.

McGrew, S., Alstron, C. L., & Fogo, B. (2018). Modeling as an example of representation. In P. Grossman, *Teaching core practices in teacher education* (pp. 35–55). Harvard Education Press.

Michaels, S., O'Connor, C., & Resnick, L. B. (2008). Deliberative discourse idealized and realized: Accountable talk in the classroom and in civic life. *Studies in philosophy and education, 27*(4), 283–297.

Murray, J., & Male, T. (2005). Becoming a TE: Evidence from the field. *Teaching and Teacher Education, 21*, 125–142

Schutz, K., Grossman, P., & Shaughnessy, M. (2018). Approximations of practice in teacher education. In P. Grossman, *Teaching core practices in teacher education* (pp. 57–83). Harvard Education Press.

Self, E., & Stengel, B. S. (2020). *Toward anti-oppressive teaching: Designing and using simulated encounters*. Harvard Education Press.

Shaughnessy, M., & Boerst, T. (2018). Uncovering the skills that preservice teachers bring to teacher education: The practice of eliciting a student's thinking. *Journal of Teacher Education, 69*(1), 40–55.

Shaughnessy, M., & Garcia, N. (2018, April). *Using video to support the improvement of teaching practice* [Paper presentation]. The National Council of Supervisors of Mathematics Annual Meeting, Washington, DC.

Shaughnessy, M., Ghousseini, H., Kazemi, E., Franke, M., Kelley-Petersen, M., & Hartmann, E. (2019). An investigation of supporting teacher learning in the context of a common decomposition for leading mathematics discussions. *Teaching and Teacher Education, 80,* 167–179.

Son, J. W. (2013). How TCs interpret and respond to student errors: ratio and proportion in similar rectangles. *Educational Studies in Mathematics, 84*(1), 49–70.

Star, J. R., & Strickland, S. K. (2008). Learning to observe: Using video to improve preservice mathematics teachers' ability to notice. *Journal of Mathematics Teacher Education, 11*(2), 107–125.

Superfine, A. C., & Li, W. (2014). Exploring the mathematical knowledge needed for teaching teachers. *Journal of Teacher Education, 65*(4), 303–314.

Swennen, A., Shagrir, L., & Cooper, M. (2009). Becoming a TE: Voices of beginning TEs. In A. Swennen & M. Van der Klink (Eds.), *Becoming a TE: Theory and practice for practice educators* (pp. 90–102). Springer.

Van Es, E. A., Stockero, S. L., Sherin, M. G., Van Zoest, L. R., & Dyer, E. (2015). Making the most of teacher self-captured video. *Mathematics Teacher Educator, 4*(1), 6–19.

Vescio, V., Ross, D., & Adams, A. (2008). A review of research on the impact of professional learning communities on teaching practice and student learning. *Teaching and Teacher Education, 24*(1), 80–91.

Wood, D., & Berg, T. (2010). The rocky road: The journey from classroom teacher to TE. *Studying Teacher Education, 6*(1), 17–28.

Yackel, E., & Cobb, P. (1996). Sociomathematical norms, argumentation, and autonomy in mathematics. *Journal for Research in Mathematics Education, 27*(4), 458–477.

Zeichner, K. (2005). Becoming a TE: a personal perspective. *Teaching and Teacher Education, 21,* 117–124.

NOTE

1. Dr. Washingston is a pseudonym as are the names of teacher candidates used in the chapter.

CHAPTER 4

PREPARING UNIVERSITY FACULTY FOR CLINICALLY-ORIENTED, PRACTICE-BASED TEACHER EDUCATION

Dan Hanley
Western Washington University

Matthew Miller
Western Washington University

Jennifer Sorensen
Seattle University

Allyson Rogan-Klyve
Central Washington University

ABSTRACT

This chapter details the work of a group of teacher educators from three universities who developed and facilitated a day-long, in-person professional development (PD) workshop on clinical practice for science, technology, engineering, and mathematics (STEM) teacher preparation programs across

Preparing Quality Teachers:
Advances in Clinical Practice, pp. 69–93
Copyright © 2022 by Information Age Publishing
www.infoagepub.com

a state in the Pacific Northwest. The authors describe their synthesis of the clinical practice literature that led them to focus the PD on core practices and practice-based teacher education pedagogies, and they discuss how they operationalized those ideas through the PD for university-based teams of STEM education faculty. When considering potential pathways for improving STEM teacher education programs across the state, the PD providers adopted an incremental approach, or developmental progression, that initially focused on STEM teacher educators and their instructional practices, moved to programmatic and departmental discussions about priorities for preservice teachers' learning, and then deliberately expanded to consider the supporting school-university partnerships and systems.

INTRODUCTION

Preparing teachers who can support the learning of every student is a challenge for even the most skilled and experienced teacher educators. It requires teacher education programs to develop strong school partnerships and to support faculty as they engage preservice teachers in instructional practices that will support the learning of all P–12 students. A Report of the Blue Ribbon Panel on Clinical Preparation and Partnerships for Improved Student Learning from the National Council for Accreditation of Teacher Education (NCATE, 2010) noted that, "To prepare effective teachers for 21st century classrooms, teacher education must shift … to programs that are fully grounded in clinical practice and interwoven with academic content and professional courses" (p. ii). Subsequently, teacher education scholars like Darling-Hammond (2014) articulate the need for clinical practice, noting that

> one of the perennial dilemmas of teacher education is how to integrate theoretically based knowledge that has traditionally been taught in university classrooms with the experience-based knowledge that has traditionally been located in the practice of teachers and the realities of classrooms and schools. (p. 551)

More recently, the Clinical Practice Commission report by the American Association of Colleges for Teacher Education (AACTE, 2018) highlighted clinical practice and school-university partnerships as central to high-quality teacher preparation. The report provides 10 proclamations that focus on the need to support novice teachers' acquisition of pedagogies, skills, and dispositions in developmentally appropriate ways within clinically rich environments that leverage the mutual benefits of school partnerships and foster a shared vision and language of teaching and learning.

While *clinical practice* and *practice-based teacher preparation* are at the fore-front of reform efforts in teacher education, the terms can be amorphous, and the goals can be disparate. Forzani (2014) notes how some teacher preparation programs have focused their clinical practice efforts on cre-ating better school-university partnerships and systems to increase the amount of time preservice teachers (PSTs) spend in school settings. This includes teacher residency models and professional development schools that situate most of a PST's learning in P–12 classrooms. While these shifts toward greater opportunities for PSTs to work in proximity to P–12 stu-dents can be positive, they can also leave out important dimensions of teaching if they are the sole approach to reform. While PSTs might learn specific teaching practices because they intentionally observe or enact them in the field, their experiences in schools might also be less scaffolded and arbitrary. PSTs might move through their field experiences and stu-dent teaching without carefully structured opportunities to develop their knowledge and skills with well-defined, research-based practices, such as strategies to engage students in productive classroom discourse or diagnose common patterns of student thinking in subject-matter domains. Forzani describes how such clinical work, when focused more exclusively on time and experience in school placements, can be "practice-based" in the sense that PSTs spend a lot of time observing and teaching in P–12 classrooms that is "not necessarily directed at acquiring skill at specific practices" that support P–12 students' learning (p. 358). Similarly, an increasing number of scholars are drawing attention to the importance of providing PSTs with opportunities to develop their skills with key instructional practices through a guided approach that gradually releases responsibility to PSTs by first giving them opportunities to learn what the practices entail, and then enact the practices with their peers and/or small groups of P–12 students in controlled settings before having to apply practices responsively, in real-time, with P–12 students in schools (e.g., Ball et al., 2009; Grossman, 2018; Grossman et al., 2009c; Hollins, 2011; McDonald et al., 2013).

This chapter details the work of a group of teacher educators from three universities who developed and facilitated a day-long, in-person professional development (PD) workshop on clinical practice for science, technology, engineering, and mathematics (STEM) teacher preparation programs in Washington state. We describe our synthesis of the clini-cal practice literature that led us to focus the PD on core practices and practice-based teacher education pedagogies, and we discuss how we operationalized those ideas through the PD for university-based teams of education faculty. When considering potential pathways for improv-ing teacher education programs in our state, we adopted an incremental approach, or developmental progression, that initially focused on teacher educators and their instructional practices, moved to programmatic and departmental discussions about priorities for PSTs' learning, and then deliberately expanded to consider the supporting school-university partnerships and systems. This does not mean that school partners should not participate in programmatic discussions about the desired knowledge and skills for PSTs. Rather, when initiating reforms with finite resources (i.e., time and money), the question becomes: How can we effectively and expeditiously initiate change in areas that directly impact the learning experiences of PSTs, while working on broader systemic reforms at the program, department, and community levels?

Since teacher education faculty at many institutions have significant influence over their course content and pedagogies, our group began by working with teams of STEM education faculty from teacher preparation programs across our state. Our goal was to help faculty improve the learning experiences of their PSTs through the lenses of core practices and practice-based pedagogies. This focus on core practices and practice-based pedagogies was intended to foster a "common lexicon for clinical educator preparation" (AACTE, 2018, p. 39) between education faculty within institutions and across our statewide network of teacher preparation programs. We also believed that by having a clear, shared vision and language for high-quality teaching, university teacher educators could focus their conversations with school partners to help maximize the affordances offered by clinical placements for PSTs.

The 10 Clinical Practice Commission (CPC) proclamations address crucial elements of clinically-oriented teacher preparation, including developing PSTs' skills with high-leverage P–12 teaching practices and improving school-university partnerships. The research synthesis and corresponding professional development for teacher education faculty described in this chapter provide a promising pathway for supporting teacher preparation programs as they engage in the reform efforts advocated by the CPC report.

CONTEXT FOR THIS WORK

The Next Generation Science, Technology, Engineering, and Mathematics (NextGen STEM) Teacher Preparation project is an ambitious, multi-institutional collaboration formed in 2016 to transform STEM teacher preparation state-wide. Faculty, staff, and administrators from more than a dozen colleges and universities that graduate over 90% of the teacher candidates in Washington state are participating in the project, along with staff from several government agencies, nongovernment organizations, and nonprofits. With the state's adoption of the Next Generation Science Standards (NGSS Lead States, 2013) and Common Core State Standards for

Mathematics (National Governors Center for Best Practices and Council of Chief State School Officers, 2010), P–12 science and math teachers must teach according to rigorous standards using student-centered pedagogies. Teachers are now asked to draw upon deep content knowledge to elicit and build on students' initial ideas, to engage students in science, engineering, and mathematical practices in authentic and culturally relevant ways, and to build students' understanding of disciplinary and cross-cutting concepts. These new demands on in-service teachers require those in higher education who prepare future STEM teachers to examine how their programs are preparing PSTs to use effective student-centered and culturally responsive pedagogies.

The NextGen STEM Teacher Preparation project addresses these challenges through collaborative inter-institutional working groups, where faculty and staff from various institutions across the state work together to create and share models, resources, and strategies for improving teacher preparation. Then, institution-based implementation teams work to incorporate these models, resources, and strategies into their STEM teacher preparation programs. The project structure and theory of change is informed by Kania and Kramer's (2011, 2013) "collective impact" model, which espouses that building strong, effective collaborations amongst a diverse set of education experts and practitioners will lead to more significant improvements in teacher preparation programs than possible when individuals and institutions work independently.

One of the interinstitutional working groups created to support the university-based implementation teams across the state was the Clinical Practice (CP) working group that included four teacher educators from three universities. The group's charge was to review the literature in clinical practice to identify research-based frameworks, models, and strategies that the group could share with teacher educators around the state. While some prominent researchers in the field of teacher education are recommending residency models for clinical practice (Guha et al., 2016), the CP working group took into consideration the wide variety of teacher preparation programs across the state, their community contexts, and their capacity for change. Therefore, the group decided not to promote a specific program or model for clinical practice, but rather examined the clinical practice literature to identify the types of activities and interactions that support PSTs as they learn to teach.

CONCEPTUAL FRAMEWORK

As we reviewed the clinical practice literature to identify the key learning experiences that support the development of PSTs, we began by examining how the current math and science standards require P–12 teachers and students to teach and learn in new ways. These, in turn, require PSTs to develop their skills with student-centered instructional strategies, and requires teacher preparation programs to improve how they support the development of PSTs' effective enactment of these instructional strategies. Our synthesis of the literature resulted in a four-tiered model that became our guiding theoretical framework. Figure 4.1 presents this conceptual framework for teacher preparation that begins with the need to develop a shared vision of 21st century student learning and, as a consequence, a vision of teaching as a *professional* practice. Expanding out and up from those central ideas, the framework emphasizes components that contribute to the professional growth of new teachers through practice-based teacher preparation focused on core practices, and finally, the articulation of teacher education pedagogies to support novices as they learn to enact core practices to support P–12 students' learning.

Shared Visions of Learning and Teaching. Improvements in teacher education often derive from the goal of improving P–12 student learning. As Windschitl (2009) argues, educators need to work differently to help students develop "21st century skills," including systems thinking and nonroutine problem-solving. The complexity of our expectations for student learning is evident in the recent national standards for mathematics and science, which require P–12 students to develop rigorous disciplinary understandings and procedural knowledge, as well as the knowledge and skills to engage in the professional practices employed by scientists,

Figure 4.1

Nested Framework for Practice-Based Teacher Preparation

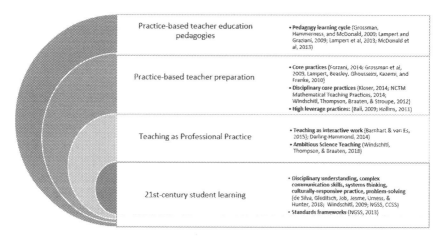

mathematicians, and engineers (NGSS Lead States, 2013). Windschitl et al. (2008) suggest that these robust learning goals are best achieved through discourse-driven and content-rich inquiry, which places students at the center of learning. In addition, there is an increased focus on culturally responsive instruction with an emphasis on engaging students' cultural assets (de Silva et al., 2018). The consequence of this evolution in thinking about student learning is that the 21st century classroom will look different by using student-centered pedagogies within P–12 classroom communities. This new vision of student learning requires a shift toward viewing teaching as professional practice, originating from the standards, but derived from students' ideas and questions, which requires more complex, responsive, and improvisational practices (Forzani, 2014). This positions teachers as interactive decision-makers (Grossman et al., 2009a) who are engaged in practical, intellectual work to elicit and respond in real time to students' ideas and questions (Feiman-Nemser, 2001).

Practice-Based Teacher Preparation. The new vision for P–12 teaching and learning articulated by the ambitious standards frameworks creates a need for teacher educators to rethink the learning activities and environments that provide PSTs with opportunities to develop their knowledge and skills with student-centered instructional strategies. Forzani (2014) notes how recent efforts to design and study teacher education have focused on several important ideas. One is that instruction should be aimed at ambitious learning goals that are grounded in the expectation that all P–12 students will develop high-level thinking, reasoning, and problem-solving skills. Second, the type of teaching that will help students learn content for these purposes is a partially improvisational practice, contingent on the ideas and contributions that are offered in the classroom, and that PSTs must learn to manage the uncertainty that arises as a result. Finally, this dual emphasis on ambitious learning and the need for sophisticated teaching to support it requires teacher preparation programs to provide PSTs with more opportunities to develop their skills with research-based, student-centered instructional strategies, and not solely relegate practice-based experiences to "clinical" school settings. Instead, programs can ground PSTs' learning in a set of pedagogies that are central to teaching, namely "core practices" or similarly, "high-leverage practices" (CPC, 2020; Grossman, 2018; TeachingWorks, 2020a).

Core practices for teaching are instructional practices that are paramount in supporting P–12 students' learning. They consist of strategies, routines, and moves that can be unpacked and learned by novice teachers (Grossman, 2018). Their enactment occurs "within the complexities of teaching and thus cannot be decontextualized from the histories and policies of schooling, where teaching occurs, or who students are. Core practices must be grounded in principles for high quality, equity-centered instruction in teacher preparation" (CPC, 2020). The central goal of learning core practices is "to improve learning opportunities available to all students, and especially those from low-income backgrounds and minority groups" (Grossman, 2018, p. 4).

In recent years, researchers have assembled core practices into both general and disciplinary frameworks to inform teacher educators about the essential pedagogical skills that novice teachers need to develop to effectively lead classroom activities and discussions centered on P–12 students' background knowledge and respond to students' ideas and problem-solving strategies in ways that move their thinking forward. Grossman et al. (2009) note that existing sets of core practices all share the following elements:

- Practices that occur with high frequency in teaching;
- Practices that novices can enact in classrooms across different curricula or instructional approaches;
- Practices that novices can actually begin to master;
- Practices that allow novices to learn more about students and about teaching;
- Practices that preserve the integrity and complexity of teaching; and
- Practices that are research-based and have the potential to improve student achievement. (p. 277)

Conversely, core practices are not a checklist of competencies, techniques divorced from principles and theory, teacher behaviors that fall farther away from a teacher's central instructional mission (e.g., taking attendance, administering standardized tests, etc.), or practices that students learn very little from, such as "using curriculum without adapting it to the current understanding of students, having students memorize lists of facts, or providing written or oral feedback to students in the form of "correct" or "incorrect" (Windschitl et al., 2012, p. 882). Furthermore, core practices are not synonymous with the NGSS or the CCSS in mathematics, since those standards focus more on what P–12 students should be able to know and do, and provide less specificity on how teachers can create productive classroom interactions (Windschitl et al., 2012). Such standards "provide teachers little guidance about how and when to enact teaching practices that are core to helping students achieve these goals" (Kloser, 2014, p. 1185).

There are several prominent sets of general and disciplinary core practices. Examples of general core practices include the 19 high-leverage practices developed by the TeachingWorks group (2020a) at the University of Michigan and the nine core practices that guide the University of Washington's Teacher Education by Design program (University of Washington, 2020a). Both of these general core practices include strategies, such as facilitating small or whole group discussions, modeling content and strategies, and checking for student understanding. In science, a delphi-panel study conducted by Kloser (2014) identified 10 core practices, while Windschitl et al. (2012) have identified four disciplinary core practices, namely planning engagement with important science ideas, eliciting students' ideas, supporting on-going changes in student thinking, and pressing students for evidence-based explanations. In mathematics, the National Council of Teachers of Mathematics have articulated eight effective mathematics teaching practices (Nabb et al., 2018) that include strategies like facilitating meaningful mathematical discourse, helping students use and make connections between mathematical representations, and supporting students' productive struggle in learning mathematics.

This emphasis on core practices in the teacher education literature has begun to move the field away from a focus on the clinical structures and systems that place PSTs in closer proximity to P–12 learners and toward a focus on contexts that will help PSTs develop their skills with research-based instructional practices that improve students' learning. Rather than an exclusive focus on enacting practices in P–12 classrooms, the process of learning core practices happens in a boundary-spanning cycle that includes teaching opportunities with students in classrooms and other structured learning experiences that may or may not include direct work with students. The learning cycle includes opportunities to represent, decompose, and approximate core practices. This focus on developing PSTs' knowledge and skills with core practices emphasizes the need to thoughtfully construct PSTs' learning experiences across university and clinical settings.

A pedagogical framework for teacher preparation. While core practices provide a framework of the instructional strategies that support P–12 students' learning, they do not constitute a curriculum or set of pedagogies for teacher preparation. Teacher preparation programs need to create opportunities for PSTs to engage in and enact these practices (Ball et al., 2009). Grossman et al. (2009a) developed a helpful framework for providing PSTs with opportunities to learn about, experience, and enact practices through the processes of *representation, decomposition, and approximation*.

Representations make practices visible to novices during their professional education. They can include opportunities such as stories told by practitioners, written narratives and case studies, videos of teaching practices, and live observations of teachers through instructional rounds. For example, Chazan and Herbst (2012) describe their work regarding the use of *representations*, where video and other pedagogies are employed to make practices visible to PSTs and engage them in a constructive process of proposing potential teaching strategies without the "need it now" pressures when teaching students in classroom settings.

The process of *decomposition* involves breaking down the work of teaching into disaggregated parts to make specific components of practice explicit (Grossman et al., 2009b). *Decompositions* help develop PSTs' ability to conduct focused observations and interpret what is observed. For example, *decomposing* the general core practice of "teaching toward a clear learning goal" might focus PSTs on certain components necessary for creating and communicating the learning goal to students, which might include considering students' funds of knowledge, identifying the targeted disciplinary standards, backwards designing activities that lead to the learning target, and facilitating students' understanding and ownership of the learning goal.

Approximations provide PSTs with opportunities to simulate and enact elements of practice with a high degree of support and under conditions of reduced complexity. *Approximations* of practice are not meant to be substitutes for "real" teaching. Instead, they offer novices "opportunities to try out parts of teaching in lower-stakes, supportive settings where they can receive feedback from teacher educators and peers on their performance" (TeachingWorks, 2020b). *Approximations* of practice can take the form of rehearsals or "bounded" enactments of practice with additional scaffolding and supports to resemble teaching in authentic classroom contexts. They require PSTs to engage in practice that is related, but not identical, to the work of in-service teachers, and can include pedagogies such as microteaching, coached and "fishbowl" rehearsals, teaching individual or small groups of students (versus the whole class), and co-teaching. Teacher education should engage PSTs in approximations of practice that provide them with opportunities to learn about, analyze, and enact core practices with scaffolding and support.

A pedagogical cycle for learning core practices. It is not enough for teacher educators to simply introduce core practices, and their potential to support P–12 students' learning, to PSTs. McDonald et al. (2013) suggest, "If we continue to develop and identify core practices for K–12 teaching without simultaneously considering how we will prepare teachers to enact those practices, implementation will fall short of leveraging the majority of teacher educators" (p. 381). Extending the work focused on representations, decompositions, and approximations of practice, McDonald et al. (2013) created a pedagogical cycle (Figure 4.2) for developing PSTs' knowledge and skills with core practices.

The cycle operationalizes pedagogies of enactment through the intentional and strategic use of practice-based pedagogies that move through a process of: (a) learning about the core practices, (b) preparing for the practices, (c) enacting the practices, and d) analyzing the enactment

Figure 4.2

Cycle for Collectively Learning to Engage in an Authentic and Ambitious Instructional Activity

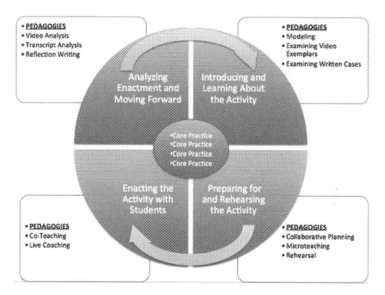

Source: Reprinted from "Core Practices and Pedagogies of Teacher Education: A Call for a Common Language and Collective Activity" by McDonald, M., Kazemi, E., and Kavanagh, S. 2013. *Journal of Teacher Education, 64*(5), 382.

and the next instructional steps. Some practice-based teacher education pedagogies in the cycle include examining video exemplars, rehearsals, co-teaching, and transcript analysis. Using these pedagogies with a focus on specific core practices and sequencing the pedagogies in an intentionally scaffolded cycle can provide teacher educators with a cohesive structure for engaging PSTs in a practice-focused stance toward learning to teach.

PROFESSIONAL DEVELOPMENT WORKSHOP FOR TEACHER EDUCATORS

To increase teacher educators' knowledge and skills with research-based teacher preparation practices across our multi-institutional network, the Clinical Practice Working Group first examined the research on clinical practice in Year 1, developed goals and accompanying PD activities in Year 2, and recruited eight university-based teams of teacher educators to participate in the PD in Year 3. These teams primarily consisted of education faculty in math and science, who were housed in both Education and STEM departments. We employed a backwards-design process (Wiggins & McTighe, 2005) to center the PD on the big ideas from our literature review. We decided to develop and facilitate a PD series for teacher educators that would begin with a day-long workshop on core practices and practice-based teacher education pedagogies, which they could incorporate into their courses and instruction. Subsequent PD would build on this work to help university teams analyze and improve their systems and structures for school-university partnerships (e.g., Burns et al., 2016).

Researchers have noted that there are a dearth of professional learning opportunities for teacher educators to improve their systems and practices for preparing PSTs (Lunenberg & Willemse, 2006; Smith, 2003; Swennen & Bates, 2010). While teacher educators are sometimes privy to theory and research about what *should* happen to support stronger clinical practice, they seldom have opportunities to learn *how* to do this, particularly in collaboration with colleagues across different teacher preparation programs. As the Core Practice Consortium suggests,

> The field of teacher education is in the midst of a major shift—from a primary focus on the knowledge needed for teaching to an increased focus on teachers' use of that knowledge in practice. However, there are too few opportunities for teacher educators who work across institutions, disciplines, and perspectives to grapple with what practice-based teacher education might look like and how best to prepare novice teachers to engage P–12 students in equitable and meaningful subject matter learning. (CPC, 2020)

Our efforts to engage universities across a state network to support the development of PSTs' skills with core practices was a purposeful attempt to improve STEM teacher preparation statewide in line with the research on the foci and pedagogies that matter most, while recognizing and honoring the different contexts, histories, and priorities of each of the participating teacher preparation programs.

Teacher preparation programs around the state vary in the extent to which their PSTs engage in clinical experiences in P–12 settings and their opportunities to enact core instructional practices in authentic contexts. Based on our understanding of our own teacher preparation programs, we believed that programs around the state would have different desired end points of how clinically oriented they wanted their programs to become. Therefore, the clinical practice working group decided to take a "guided facilitation" approach to the PD by having teacher educators in university-based teams: (1) analyze the extent to which their programs currently included core practices and practice-based pedagogies, (2) envision what they would like their programs to look like in 5–10 years with respect to core practices and practice-based pedagogies, and (3) draft some initial steps for how their programs could progress from where they are now to where they would like to go. We used the McDonald et al. (2013) cycle that identified categories of practice-based teacher education pedagogies centered around core practices as the organizational framework for the workshop. The methods used to engage participants in the day-long, in-person workshop included direct instruction, structured discussions, introductions to tools and support materials, and work time for the university-based teams. The learning goals focused on introducing and engaging the teacher educators in:

1. The research on, and case for, practice-based teacher preparation,
2. Core practices that PSTs could learn and enact to support pre-K–12 students' learning,
3. A pedagogical cycle for teacher educators to create cohesive, transferable learning experiences for PSTs, and
4. Specific pedagogies to support different quadrants of the pedagogical cycle.

Teacher educators participated in the PD activities to address these goals and worked in their university-based implementation teams (ITs) to develop an action plan to document how they could put this new learning to work in the service of their programs, PSTs, and the P–12 students with whom they work.

At the workshop, the facilitators first made the case for practice-based teacher education by presenting and discussing the supporting research. Then, faculty participants developed and extended their knowledge of core practices by examining the similarities and differences between several prominent sets of core practices and discussed the role core practices could have in improving the coherence of learning experiences for PSTs. We organized faculty into mixed groups (i.e., table groups with faculty from other universities across the state) to allow participants to get to know other teacher educators. In small groups, participants first analyzed two sets of general core practices (TeachingWorks, 2020a; University of Washington, 2020a), and then compared sets of science and math core practices (Kloser, 2014; University of Washington, 2020b; Windschilt et al., 2012). Participants discussed how the sets of core practices varied in number, specificity, and by discipline. Faculty members also discussed the benefits and challenges to anchoring a teacher education program around core practices for PSTs. We then regrouped faculty back into their university teams where they discussed the questions below and recorded their responses in a preformatted Google document (Appendix A: IT Action Plan Template),

Figure 4.3

PD Model to Support Clinical and Core Practices

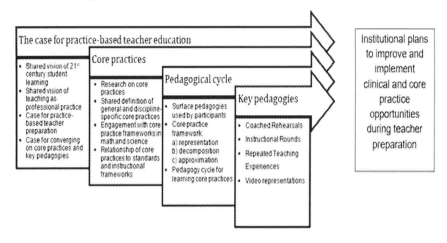

which anyone on the team could add to or edit synchronously and asynchronously in the future. The National Research Council (Atkin et al., 2001) framework for formative assessment formed the basis for the guiding questions in the IT Action Plan Template.

- **Where are you now?** To what extent is your teacher education program anchored around a set of core instructional practices for preservice teachers?
- **Where would you like to go?** In what ways would your teacher education program like to incorporate core practices into your program (within specific courses, throughout the program, etc.)?
- **How will you get there?** What are some anticipated supports? What are some anticipated constraints? Who should be included in this work? How will you allocate time for this work?

To end the three-hour morning session on core practices, we emphasized that the activity was not intended to have university teams identify and adopt a particular set of core practices for their program. Instead, the power of this activity came from discussing, and even debating, the most important skills for PSTs to develop. These ongoing discussions enabled the teams of teacher educators to begin to develop a shared language of practice and a vision for necessary reforms.

While the morning of the workshop focused on *what* was important for PSTs to learn, the afternoon focused on *how* teacher educators could develop PSTs' skills with core practices through practice-based pedagogies. Faculty participants read and discussed a section of McDonald et al. (2013) article to learn about the cycle for collectively learning to teach. Then, workshop facilitators presented a set of "pedagogical briefs," or written summaries, of some key, yet lesser-known practice-based teacher education pedagogies (see Appendix B for example). We highlighted specific pedagogies because they were not represented on the McDonald et al. learning cycle (2013), were particularly impactful, and were less prevalent in teacher education. Furthermore, we wanted participants to leave the workshop with concrete tools and pedagogies they could implement in their courses. The pedagogies we presented and discussed included:

a.   **Coached rehearsals:** Coached rehearsals typically occur in the context of a methods course in which a teacher educator is working with a group of PSTs to develop expertise enacting a particular core practice or set of core practices. PSTs practice a lesson or lesson segment, typically one that they are going to teach soon to P–12 students, in front of peers to receive in the moment feedback and support from a teacher educator.

b.   **Repeated teaching:** Repeated teaching rounds are a type of rehearsal that enables PSTs to enact core practices multiple times with different groups of students. The teacher educator alternately acts as an observer and coach, leading debriefing discussions in between each rehearsal, posing questions to stimulate PSTs' reflection of the instructional decisions they made, and helping PSTs consider pedagogical alternatives for the next round of teaching. While "one-shot" opportunities to teach a lesson are the norm in teacher education, there is widespread recognition that repeated practice is particularly beneficial for novices.

c.   **Instructional rounds:** Instructional rounds are unique in that the learning of the *observers* is central, not the teachers being observed. Rounds begin with a "pre-brief" during which the purpose and focus of the observations are established in relation to a specific instructional practice. Then PSTs in teams conduct observations of teaching and learning in one or more classrooms and collect data related to that instructional practice. Protocols guide subsequent analysis and reflection to identify the next instructional steps.

d.   **Video extensions:** With video extensions, PSTs watch a video-recorded lesson and "pick up" where the teacher left off in the lesson (at a selected stopping point). This is different from discussing a video after it has been viewed from beginning to end, as PSTs get the opportunity to stop, discuss, and consider the appropriate next steps to support P–12 students' learning (see Appendix B for a full example of a pedagogy brief).

For the final hour of the workshop, we employed the National Research Council assessment framework again and invited the university teams to discuss, debate, and develop action plans for improving the use of practice-based pedagogies in their programs. With their preliminary action plans in hand, teams returned to their campuses to consider their next steps. Appendix A includes the action planning template used by the university teams.

Next Steps for Implementation Teams. In the action plans and post-PD surveys, participants indicated a desire to continue to engage in the reform work focused on core practices and practice-based teacher education pedagogies. For example, prior to the PD, one of the university teams had identified four general core practices to guide their Masters in Elementary Teaching program and had begun to engage PSTs with the core practices. Through new learning and facilitated discussions at the workshop, the team identified the need to further discuss how core practices differed across disciplines, and wanted to engage faculty, clinical supervisors, and mentor teachers across all of their campuses in discussions to develop a shared vision and language around their four core practices. The team members also wanted to develop systems for PSTs to engage in core practices through the pedagogical learning cycle (McDonald et al,, 2013), particularly by improving their use of video and incorporating instructional rounds into practicum courses. Another university team returned to their campus and started to examine core practices across STEM disciplines in an effort to respond to the National Science Teaching Association's recommendation that elementary science teachers be prepared to teach life science, physical science, Earth science, computer science, and engineering.

Next Steps for Professional Development. At the beginning of this chapter, we noted our incremental approach, or developmental progression, to sequence and structure our reform work with university teams of teacher educators across the state to improve teacher preparation programs in ways that address the proclamations and tenets in the CPC report. Instead of approaching all of the proclamations simultaneously, there was value in first focusing on developing a "common lexicon" (AACTE, 2018, p. 39) within our teacher preparation programs as we worked to engage cooperating teachers, clinical supervisors, principals, and school communities.

Now that we have developed a common lexicon of core practices and pedagogies across the statewide network and begun to create some structural reforms to our teacher preparation programs, the clinical practice working group is extending this work to address issues of school-university partnerships. This encapsulates another proclamation of the CPC report, which notes that effective clinical partnerships are "gateways to … preparing highly effective educators" (p. 22) and should be developed for mutually beneficial outcomes for all stakeholders. We are currently examining the literature to identify the research-based components of effective school-university partnerships. Some "core ingredients" of effective partnerships include designating professional learning sites with articulated agreements, co-developing a shared, comprehensive mission dedicated to equity for improved P–12 student learning, engaging in shared governance with dedicated resources, active engagement in the school and local community, and committing to the professional learning of all stakeholders (Burns et al., 2016). Building off of our initial workshop, upcoming state-wide PD on school-university partnerships will: (1) link the research on effective partnerships to core practices and practice-based teacher education pedagogies, (2) develop participants' knowledge of research-based components of effective school-university partnerships, and (3) support university teams' examination of their current school-university partnerships in light of the research base as they (4) develop and implement an action plan.

CONCLUSION

Throughout this chapter, we have made a case for core practices and practice-based teacher education pedagogies as an important initial step for teacher preparation programs to take on the road to making their programs more clinically oriented. The proclamations and tenets embedded in the CPC report highlight the need to provide opportunities for PSTs to learn powerful praxis in mutually beneficial clinical partnerships with schools that meet the needs of PSTs, school partners, and P–12 students. Additionally, we argue that "clinical practice" does not solely entail situating PSTs and their learning in P–12 schools and classrooms. It is equally important to anchor teacher preparation programs around a set of core practices and prepare education faculty to employ pedagogies that provide PSTs with scaffolded opportunities to develop their skills with core practices. The PD approach described in this chapter provides a promising roadmap for manageable, incremental reforms that can help education faculty develop a shared vision and language for teacher preparation in order to help their programs and partnering schools work together to develop PSTs who can skillfully enact instructional practices that benefit P–12 student learning.

REFERENCES

American Association of College for Teacher Education [AACTE]. (2018). *A pivot toward clinical practice, its lexicon, and the renewal of educator preparation.* https://aacte.org/professional-development-and-events/clinical-practice-commission-press-conference

Atkin, J., Black, P., Comfot, K., Ray, C., & Wood, R. (2001). *Classroom assessment and the national science education standards.* National Academy Press.

Ball, D., Sleep, L., Boerst, T., & Bass, H. (2009). Combining the development of practice and the practice of development in teacher education. *Elementary School Journal, 109*(5), 458–474.

Burns, R., Jacobs, J., Baker, W., & Donahue, D. (2016). Making muffins: Identifying core ingredients of school-university partnerships. *School-University Partnerships, 9*, 81.

Chazan, D., & Herbst, P. (2012). Animations of classroom interaction: Expanding the bounddaries of video records of practice. *Teachers College Record, 114*(3), 1–34.

CPC. (2020). Core practices consortium. https://www.corepracticeconsortium.com/

Darling-Hammond, L. (2014). Strengthening clinical preparation: The holy grail of teacher education. *Peabody Journal of Education, 89*(4), 547–561. https://doi.org/10.1080/0161956x.2014.939009

de Silva, R. M., Gleditsch, R., Job, C., Jesme, S., Urness, B., & Hunter, C. (2018). Gloria Ladson-Billings: Igniting student learning through teacher engagement in "culturally relevant pedagogy". *Multicultural Education, 25*(3–4), 23.

Feiman-Nemser, S. (2001). From preparation to practice: Designing a continuum to strengthen and sustain teaching. *Teachers College Record, 103*(6), 1013–1055.

Forzani, F. (2014). Understanding "core practices" and "practice-based" teacher education: Learning from the past. *Journal of Teacher Education, 65*(4), 357–368.

Grossman, P. (Ed.). (2018). *Teaching core practices in teacher education.* Harvard Education Press.

Grossman, P., Compton, C., Igra, D., M., R., Shahan, E., & Williamson, P. (2009a). Teaching practice: A cross-professional perspective. *Teachers College Record, 111*(9), 2055–2100.

Grossman, P., Compton, C., Igra, D., Ronfeldt, M., Shahan, E., & Williamson, P. (2009b). Teaching practice: A cross-professional perspective. *Teachers College Record, 111*(9), 2055–2100.

Grossman, P., Hammerness, K., & McDonald, M. (2009). Redefining teaching, re-imagining teacher education. *Teachers and Teaching, 15*(2), 273–289. doi:10.1080/13540600902875340

Guha, R., Hyler, M., & Darling-Hammond, L. (2016). *The teacher residency: An innovative model for preparing teachers.* https://learningpolicyinstitute.org/product/teacher-residency

Hollins, E. R. (2011). Teacher preparation for quality teaching. *Journal of Teacher Education, 62*(4), 395–407. https://doi.org/10.1177/0022487111409415

Kania, J., & Kramer, M. (2011). *Collective impact.* Stanford Social Innovation Review.

Kania, J., & Kramer, M. (2013, Winter). Embracing emergence: How collective impact addresses complexity. *Stanford Social Innovation Review*. https://ssir.org/articles/entry/social_progress_through_collective_impact#

Kloser, M. (2014). Identifying a core set of science teaching practices: A delphi expert panel approach. *Journal of Research in Science Teaching, 51*(9), 1185–1217. https://doi.org/10.1002/tea.21171

Lunenberg, M., & Willemse, M. (2006). Research and professional development of teacher educators. *European Journal of Teacher Education, 29*(1), 81–98. https://doi.org/10.1080/02619760500478621

McDonald, M., Kazemi, E., & Kavanagh, S. S. (2013). Core practices and pedagogies of teacher education: A call for a common language and collective activity. *Journal of Teacher Education, 64*(5), 378–386. https://doi.org/10.1177/0022487113493807

Nabb, K., Hofacker, E., Ernie, K., & Ahrendt, S. (2018). Using the 5 practices in mathematics teaching *Mathematics Teacher, 111*(5), 366–373.

National Council for Accreditation of Teacher Education. (2010). *Transforming teacher education through clinical practice: A national strategy to prepare effective teachers*. http://www.highered.nysed.gov/pdf/NCATECR.pdf

National Governors Center for Best Practices and Council of Chief State School Officers. (2010). *The common core state standards initiative*. http://www.corestandards.org/

NGSS Lead States. (2013). *Next generation science standards: For states, by states*. The National Academies Press.

Smith, K. (2003). So, what about the professional development of teacher educators? *European Journal of Teacher Education, 26*(2), 201–215. https://doi.org/10.1080/0261976032000088738

Swennen, A., & Bates, T. (2010). The professional development of teacher educators. *Professional Development in Education, 36*(1–2), 1–7. https://doi.org/10.1080/19415250903457653

TeachingWorks. (2020a). *High leverage practices*. http://www.teachingworks.org/work-of-teaching/high-leverage-practices

TeachingWorks. (2020b). *What are pedagogies of approximation?* https://library.teachingworks.org/curriculum-resources/pedagogies/using-approximations-to-practice-practice/

University of Washington. (2020a). *Teacher education by design*. https://coetedd-wpengine.netdna-ssl.com/wp-content/uploads/2017/09/core_practice_primer.pdf

University of Washington. (2020b). *Teacher education by design*. https://tedd.org/mathematics/

Wiggins, G., & McTighe, J. (2005). *Understanding by design*. Association for Supervision and Curriculum Development.

Windschitl, M. (2009). *Cultivating 21st century skills in science learners: How systems of teacher preparation and professional development will have to evolve* [Paper presentation]. The National Academies of Science Workshop on 21st Century Skills, Washington DC. http://www7.nationalacademies.org/bose/WindschitlPresentation.pdf

Windschitl, M., Thompson, J., & Braaten, M. (2008). How novice science teachers appropriate epistemic discourses around model-based inquiry for use in classrooms. *Cognition and Instruction, 26*(3), 310–378. https://doi.org/10.1080/07370000802177193

Windschitl, M., Thompson, J., Braaten, M., & Stroupe, D. (2012). Proposing a core set of instructional practices and tools for teachers of science. *Science Education, 96*(5), 878–903.

APPENDIX A

NextGen Implementation Team Action Planning Template: Clinical Practice

Institution: _____

Teacher Education Program: _____

	Where are you now?	Where would you like to go?	How will you get there?
Core Practices	*To what extent is your teacher education program anchored around a set of core instructional practices for preservice teachers (PSTs)?*	*In what ways would your teacher education program like to incorporate core practices for PSTs into your program (within specific courses, throughout the program, etc.)?*	*– What are some anticipated supports?* *– What are some anticipated constraints?* *– Who should be included in this work?* *– How will you allocate time for this work?*
Practice-based Teacher Education Pedagogies	*What opportunities do PSTs have to build their instructional skills in core practices across courses and the teacher education program (i.e., opportunities to learn about, rehearse, enact, and analyze enactment of core practices)?*	*In what ways would your teacher education program like to develop PSTs' skills with core practices? What structure and sequence would give PSTs' opportunities to learn about, rehearse, enact, and analyze their enactment of core practices?*	*– What are some anticipated supports?* *– What are some anticipated constraints?* *– Who should be included in this work?* *– How will you allocate time for this work?*

Other Commitments:

TIMELINE FOR ACTION PLANNING:		
Quarter	Tasks	Meetings/Work Time
Spring 2019		
Summer 2019		
Fall 2019		
Winter 2020		
Spring 2020		

APPENDIX B

Example of a Pedagogy Brief: Instructional Rounds

Core Practice Pedagogy: Instructional Rounds

(Appendix B continued on next page)

| **What?** |
| What Is This Pedagogy? |

Increasingly, schools are implementing a new form of professional learning activity known as "rounds"—also referred to in the literature as Teacher Rounds, Instructional Rounds, Teaching Rounds, or Education Rounds (City et al., 2009). Like clinical rounds in medicine, rounds engage teachers in communities of practice, supporting critical reflection and mutual learning. They help educators look closely at what is happening in classrooms in a systematic, purposeful, and focused way. While more commonly used with practicing teachers, there is emerging evidence of the benefits of rounds as a socializing practice for prospective teachers (Roegman & Riehl, 2015).

Though there are several variations, rounds generally begin with a "pre-brief" during which the purpose and focus of observations is set in relation to a problem of practice. Teachers then conduct observations of teaching and learning in one or more classrooms as teams, collecting data related to the problem of practice. This is followed by reflection and debriefing guided by protocols, which aid in identifying next steps and application to future practice.

While the use of observation is not new to teacher education and is often used as a feedback mechanism for teacher candidates, rounds are unique in that the learning of the *observers* is central, not the one being observed.

| **Why?** |
| Why employ this pedagogy to support PSTs' understanding & use of core practices? |

An apprenticeship of observation (Lortie, 1975) is insufficient preparation to teach. Similarly, merely sitting in the classroom observing how experienced teachers teach does not necessarily help PSTs learn to teach (Ben-Peretz & Rumney, 1991) as observing cooperating teachers does not always lead to analysis, reflection, and growth (McIntyre, Byrd, & Foxx, 1996). One of the well-documented problems of learning from observations of teaching is knowing what to look for, or how to interpret what is observed (Feiman-Nemser & Buchmann, 1985). During traditional classroom observations, novices may not know what to attend to in looking at interactions between students and teachers. In fact, research on expertise suggests that part of what differentiates novices from experts is their ability to see and discern details in the classroom (Bransford et al., 2000). By decomposing complex practices, professional educators can help students learn first to attend to, and then to enact, the essential elements of a practice.

For in-service teachers, rounds have resulted in significant positive effects on teaching quality (sustained 6 months later) as well as positive effects on teacher morale (Gore et al., 2017). For beginning teachers, rounds have promoted greater confidence, stronger professional relationships, a clearer vision of their goals and direction for their work, a deeper commitment to good teaching, and a feeling of being able to speak and contribute to the profession (Gore & Bowe, 2015). When used in teacher education, rounds have helped highlight gaps in PSTs' understandings of how, when, and why to use specific instructional strategies and supported their development of tools and dispositions to study teaching in and with a community of learners (Reagan et al., 2015). This, in turn, can enhance the instruction PSTs receive face-to-face in the teacher education classroom (Scherff & Singer, 2012) by challenging PST's assumptions about students, helping them develop broader understandings of teaching contexts, and examine common problems of practice (Williamson & Hodder, 2015).

In terms of practice-based teacher education, the implementation of Instructional Rounds affords opportunities for PSTs to make focused and purposeful observations and to analyze multiple examples (representations) of enactment of a core practice and consider variations in the use of the practice within different classroom and lesson contexts, as well as within different grade levels. Through this, they can develop a more robust understanding of a practice, and the challenges they might encounter in enacting that practice.

Where?
In what context do you implement this pedagogy?

Rounds may be flexibly implemented in a variety of teacher education courses in which there is an existing practicum component or may be integrated as an activity in courses that do not include practicum experiences. PSTs need an opportunity to visit multiple classrooms in a single session to complete rounds.

How?
How do you engage PSTs in this pedagogy?

In the classroom: Begin with a pre-briefing in which you discuss the selected core practice that PSTs will observe in classrooms. Set the purpose and ground rules for rounds and introduce any specific note-taking protocols for to students. Note: Conducting a video-based practice round with students to familiarize themselves with data collection and analysis protocols can be helpful. Having students first observe the video and describe what they see, *then* provide them the lens of the core practice to re-observe the video and note differences in what they notice can be powerful in helping PSTs understand how to make more targeted observations that allow for rich analysis.

At the school site(s): At the appointed time, teams of 3–5 PSTs visit a classroom as non-participant observers, taking observational notes in relation to the problem of practice.

Back in the classroom: Working in their groups, PSTs should compare observations and denote any patterns—discussing these in terms of what they illuminate about how to implement the core practice, how it impacts student learning, and potential challenges in implementing the practice successfully. PSTs can share these analyses in a Gallery Walk format, followed by a whole-class sense-making discussion.

Next steps: Considering the implications of what they learn through rounds for their own implementation of the core practice is important. Implementing rounds prior to another task (such as engaging in lesson development and/or enactment) can provide opportunities for PSTs to strategize ways to enhance their enactment of the core practice.

Key Considerations

- Implementing rounds places little demand on classroom teachers, who do not need to prepare for the visit or interact directly with teachers.
- Rounds are not intended to showcase exemplary teaching, which places a greater burden on the teacher educator during the debriefing process.
- Some PSTs struggle to make nonjudgmental observations when participating in rounds initially. Conducting a video-based practice round in-class beforehand may help.
- The term "problem of practice" has a negative connotation to some PSTs (conveying the idea of looking for problems, possibly contributing to the above difficulty) and so focusing instead on a 'core practice' and, after observing, the difficulties associated with implementing the practice may be more beneficial.
- Your class size and size of small groups (3–5) will determine the number of classrooms needed.

(Appendix B continued on next page)

Key Considerations (Continued)
• Rounds are a collaborative process, so forming collaborative groups that function well is critical.
• Visiting 3 classrooms for 20-minute intervals appears sufficient for collecting data about a specific practice.
• It may be difficult to find instructional time slots in the school schedule that coincide to university class meeting times or that provide examples of teaching a particular discipline.
• Observing recess, lunch, choice/free time or seat work may be relevant for some problems of practice, but do not necessarily lend themselves to examining core teaching practices.
Rounds can be a powerful socializing process for PSTs; however, if not carefully implemented, rounds can confirm or reinforce PST's shallow understandings of teaching practice, rather than pushing them to consider teaching and learning more deeply. The organization and framing of rounds will constrain what PSTs are able to "see" and learn in terms of the complexities of practice.
Classroom Vignette
This quarter, the 12 PSTs in a residency-model teacher preparation program at Lincoln Middle School are working on the practice of helping students *construct and interpret models*. Four PSTs have just entered Riley's classroom as she is in the middle of showing students a graph of CO_2 emissions data over time. Dr. Johnston has asked the observing PSTs to notice three things: 1) What does Riley do to elicit students' thinking about what the graph means? 2) What does Riley do to model her thought process as she interprets the graph for students? 3) How do the students then apply their understanding to a novel question? While standing quietly at the back of the classroom, the PSTs take notes as they watch the students predict future CO_2 levels and what factors might impact them. After 20 minutes, Dr. Johnston and the PSTs thank the students and Riley for letting them observe, and they move on to Jorge's classroom. Jorge's students have just finished an activity using Slinkys to mimic electromagnetic radiation, and he is asking them what they observed about the wavelength, frequency, and amplitude of their "waves." The observing PSTs use the same three questions to focus their attention on how Jorge elicits students' thinking about the Slinkys' behavior, how he models his thought process about the relationship between wavelength and frequency, and how the students demonstrate their understanding of wave characteristics. During this time, another PST team observed two other classrooms with master teacher Mrs. Hooper. After lunch, the entire cohort gathers with Dr. Johnston and Mrs. Hooper in the conference room for a debriefing session. Dr. Johnston gives everyone sticky notes and asks them to describe what they observed, then post their descriptive "evidence" on poster paper that corresponds with the three focus questions. The PSTs then break up into small teams and work on sorting the evidence on one poster sheet into themes before labeling each theme. The small teams then do a gallery walk of the three poster sheets and look for patterns in the collected evidence. After this, Mrs. Hooper leads the cohort through a whole-group discussion of the patterns they identified. It takes some gentle reminders to keep the PSTs away from diagnosing "problems" and instead focused on the students' learning experience. To close the debrief, the PSTs suggest strategies and supports that would help students demonstrate their proficiency with interpreting models. Then, everyone shares something they learned or would like to try in their classroom.

Resources/References
Ben-Peretz, M., & Rumney, S. (1991). Professional thinking in guided practice. *Teaching and Teacher Education*, 7(5–6), 517–530.
Bransford, J. D., Brown, A. L., & Cocking, R. R. (2000). *How people learn.* National Academy Press.
City, E. A. (2011). Learning from instructional rounds. *Educational Leadership*, 69(2), 36–41.
City, E. A., Elmore, R. F., Fiarman, S. E., & Teitel, L. (2009). *Instructional rounds in education.* Harvard Education Press.
Feiman-Nemser, S., & Buchman, M. (1985). Pitfalls of experience in teacher preparation. *Teachers College Record*, 87(1), 53–65.
Fowler-Finn, T. (2013). *Leading instructional rounds in education: A facilitator's guide.* Harvard Education Press.
Goodwin, A. L., Del Prete, T., Reagan, E. M., & Roegman, R. (2015). A closer look at the practice and impact of "rounds." *International Journal of Educational Research*, 73, 37–43.
Gore, J. M., & Bowe, J. M. (2015). Interrupting attrition? Re-shaping the transition from preservice to inservice teaching through Quality Teaching Rounds. *International Journal of Educational Research*, 73, 77–88.
Gore, J., Lloyd, A., Smith, M., Bowe, J., Ellis, H., & Lubans, D. (2017). Effects of professional development on the quality of teaching: Results from a randomised controlled trial of Quality Teaching Rounds. *Teaching and Teacher Education*, 68, 99–113.
McIntyre, D. J., Byrd, D. M., & Foxx, S. M. (1996). Field and laboratory experiences. *Handbook of Research On Teacher Education*, 2, 171–193.
Reagan, E. M., Chen, C., Roegman, R., & Zuckerman, K. G. (2015). Round and round: Examining teaching residents' participation in and reflections on education rounds. *International Journal of Educational Research*, 73, 65–76.
Roegman, R., & Riehl, C. (2015). Playing doctor with teacher preparation: An examination of rounds as a socializing practice for preservice teachers. *International Journal of Educational Research*, 73, 89–99.
Scherff, L., & Singer, N. R. (2012). The preservice teachers are watching: Framing and reframing the field experience. *Teaching and Teacher Education*, 28(2), 263–272.
Teitel, L. (2013). *School-based instructional rounds: Improving teaching and learning across classrooms.* Harvard Education Press.
Williamson, P., & Hodder, L. (2015). Unpacking practice with clinical instructional rounds in the San Francisco Teacher Residency program. *International Journal of Educational Research*, 73, 53–64
This material is based upon work supported by the National Science Foundation's Division of Undergraduate Education under grant no. 1625566.

CHAPTER 5

CORE PRACTICES AND BEYOND

How Equity-Based Practices Emerged in Mediated Field Experiences

Esther M. H. Billings
Grand Valley State University

Melinda C. Knapp
Oregon State University-Cascades

Charlotte J. D. Sharpe
Syracuse University

Barbara A. Swartz
West Chester University

Sararose D. Lynch
Slippery Rock University

Holly Henderson Pinter
Western Carolina University

Preparing Quality Teachers:
Advances in Clinical Practice, pp. 95–127
Copyright © 2022 by Information Age Publishing
www.infoagepub.com

ABSTRACT

Researchers and educators increasingly agree that teacher preparation programs should integrate theory and practice via pedagogies where learning occurs *in and through the act of practice*, rather than learning *about* the practice. In this chapter we explore the use of "mediated field experience" (MFE), a hybrid space situating course and field work, where teacher candidates (TCs) are provided structured opportunities to engage in the phases of McDonald et al.'s (2013) learning cycle in order to approximate and enact core teaching practices in mathematics classrooms, at PK–12 partner schools, and integrate realities of the classroom with teaching theory. We share four vignettes, across four different institutions and teacher preparation courses, to illustrate ways the mathematics university-based teacher educator (UTE) "mediates" the implementation of each phase of the learning cycle in order to build TCs' understanding and capacity to enact core practices while simultaneously providing opportunity to explore issues of equity. This work describes ways MFEs provide real-time experiences for TCs in a rich and complex PK–12 classroom setting to: learn with and from children, develop and hone skills with different teaching practices, deepen mathematical knowledge for teaching, connect theory and practice, and explore issues of equity as they arise in the praxis of teaching.

Clinical practice is central to high-quality teacher preparation, and effective clinical partnerships are its foundation, supporting the continuous renewal of educator preparation as well as of experienced educators' development as professionals and leaders. The benefits of clinical practice accrue to all involved, from PK–12 students to the university- and school-based teacher educators as well as the aspiring and novice educators for whom they serve as mentors, models, and guides. To fully realize these benefits, educators must take the lead in advancing and sustaining high-quality clinical practice.

—American Association of Colleges for Teacher Education [AACTE] (2018, p. 44).

A call to situate teachers' learning within practice came more than twenty years ago (Ball & Cohen, 1999). As Ball and Forzani (2009) state, "[P]ractice must be at the core of teachers' preparation and that this entails close and detailed attention to the work of teaching and the development of ways to train people to do that work effectively" (p. 497). Researchers and educators increasingly agree that teacher preparation programs should integrate theory and practice via pedagogies where learning occurs *in and through the act of practice*, rather than learning *about* the practice (e.g., AACTE, 2018; Grossman et al., 2009; Hiebert & Morris, 2012; McDonald et al., 2013; National Council for Accreditation of Teacher Education [NCATE], 2010). The *AACTE Clinical Practice Commission Report* (AACTE, 2018) describes this learning as *clinical practice*, identifying it as central to high-quality teacher preparation, and highlights the need for authentic practice, where coursework complements and aligns with field experiences. This report defines *clinical practice* as:

> Teacher candidates work in authentic educational settings and engage[ment] in the pedagogical work of the profession of teaching closely integrated with educator preparation course work and supported by a formal school-university partnership. Clinical practice is a specific form of what is traditionally known as field work. (p. 11)

Yet, the question of specific ways educators might structure clinical practice into teacher preparation coursework persists.

LITERATURE REVIEW

Mediated Field Experiences

Our response to designing *clinical practice* experiences consistent with AACTE's (2018) vision in mathematics teacher preparation draws upon Horn and Campbell's (2015) idea of "mediated field experience" (MFE), a hybrid space situating course and field work. Within a MFE, teacher candidates (TCs) are provided structured opportunities and support to apply knowledge of teaching in specific situations within authentic classrooms (at PK–12 partner schools), and integrate realities of the classroom with teaching theory. The mathematics university-based teacher educator (UTE) "mediates" the implementation, providing scaffolding support and feedback throughout. Their role is critical: UTEs carefully structure learning experiences with input from the PK–12 partner teacher. Throughout the MFE, the UTE helps TCs apply theoretical knowledge to notice and make sense of particular features of teaching practice that produce unexpected results (Campbell & Dunleavy, 2016). MFEs integrate university coursework content with fieldwork in a way that develops TCs' knowledge and understanding of the interplay between the two and embodies AACTE's (2018) vision of clinical practice. Defining characteristics of MFEs include: exploring core teaching practices (within a particular disciplinary context), establishing and nurturing partnerships with local PK–12 schools, and situating the experience in local classrooms (Billings & Swartz, 2021) allowing for opportunities to understand challenges of practice in situ (see Figure 5.1) Furthermore, mathematics UTEs design MFEs based on research, especially related to core practices and teaching/learning mathematics, and pedagogical preparation is embedded within the MFE. The UTE facilitates and models reflective practice as they provide feedback and lead TCs to reflect on their experiences. Because MFEs are developed within a mutually beneficial partnership and the needs of the local school and teacher preparation program are placed on equal footing, the MFEs evolve based on current needs and challenges of both stakeholders.

Core Teaching Practices and Learning Cycle

Growing research and recommendations within the teacher educator community focuses teacher preparation around "core" or "high-leverage" teaching practices (e.g., AACTE, 2018; Ball & Forzani, 2009; Grossman et al., 2009; McDonald et al., 2013; National Council of Teachers of Mathematics [NCTM], 2014). Core teaching practices, for example, elicit and use evidence of students' thinking, are research-based, and cut across grade levels and subject areas. They afford opportunities to learn about students and teaching and are of such a nature that novice teachers can realistically enact and begin to master them (Grossman et al., 2009). A core-practice approach in teacher preparation involves organizing coursework and fieldwork around teaching practices while simultaneously providing TCs ample opportunities to enact these teaching practices via "pedagogies of enactment" (Grossman et al., 2009). McDonald et al. (2013) propose a

Figure 5.1

Design Principles of Mediated Field Experiences

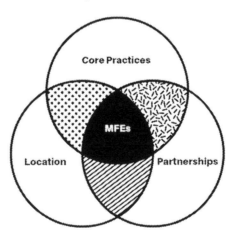

Source: Sharpe et al. (submitted).

learning cycle through which TCs approximate and enact teaching practices, offering different pedagogies of enactment to utilize (see Figure 5.2). This learning cycle involves four components: introducing and learning about an activity (including envisioning the teaching practice), preparing for enacting teaching practices through the activity, enacting the practice(s) with students, and analyzing and reflecting upon these enactments. This learning cycle provides a core-practice focus and framework for our construction of MFEs.

Core-Surround of Core Practices

Though core teaching practices are used as an organizing framework for supporting TCs' learning both on campus and in MFEs, we join Dutro and Cartun (2016) in distinguishing between *core* and *surround*, which is "only seen as surround because it is in relation to what we designate as core" (p. 120). We agree that this binary "holds potential to open a productive space for inquiry and conversations" (p. 120) about experiences that compel us to make this distinction.

Figure 5.2

Learning Cycle

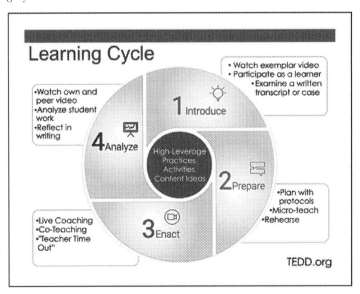

Source: McDonald et al. (2013, p. 382).

In MFEs, we regularly encounter such experiences—when activities designed to focus TCs' development of core practices end up creating spaces for conversations about "the uncertainty associated with teaching and learning" (Shulman, 2005, as cited in AACTE, 2018, p. 37). In multiple studies documenting the role of MFEs in supporting TCs' learning (Dutro & Cartun, 2016; Horn & Campbell, 2015; Laman et al., 2018; Rust & Cantwell, 2018; Zavala, 2017), all focus on how MFEs, even those organized around specific teaching practices, created rich opportunities for TCs to explore this *surround*. For example, though *facilitating writers' workshops* was the explicit practice-based focus of the elementary literacy methods course described in Laman et al.'s (2018) study, the authors found that working in an authentic setting with live coaching generated opportunities for TCs to recognize and problematize their deficit orientations toward young students of color. Similarly, MFE coach Zavala (2017) described how *her* position gave her new insights into how her bilingual TCs were gaining facility with core practices (e.g., eliciting and connecting student thinking through talk moves), but needed additional support to connect these practices to problematic patterns in classroom discourse:

> Miguel [the host teacher] and I observed that the different ways that the fifth graders contributed during [TC-facilitated] mathematics discussions fell into a predictable pattern: most of the time, White students explained *how a strategy worked* and *why it worked,* and Latino students did more *repeating someone's idea* or being asked to *agree or disagree with an idea* as prompted by the teacher.... While the specific tools for more equitable talk were used by the [bilingual TCs], they were not necessarily used with the intention of eliciting qualitatively different contributions from different populations of students. ([Emphasis original] p. 60)

These examples illustrate how MFEs create rich opportunities for UTEs and TCs to develop and *trouble* core practices. For this reason, we see MFEs as an important model for clinical practice in which UTEs and TCs can "attend to specific moves of teaching *and* all that bursts and spills from our efforts to define and enact them" (Dutro & Cartun, 2016, p. 120). In this next section, we discuss equitable teaching practices in mathematics which MFEs have allowed us to explore in our own classrooms. We frame these as aspects of the "surround" which complement and lend nuance to moments of uncertainty in teaching—even in moments designed to be about particular core practices.

Equitable Mathematics Teaching

Access and equity in mathematics classrooms rests on beliefs and practices that empower all students to participate meaningfully in learning mathematics and achieve outcomes in mathematics that are not predicted by or correlated with student characteristics (Gutiérrez, 2002). Support for access and equity requires, but is not limited to, high expectations, access to high-quality mathematics curriculum and instruction, adequate time for students to learn, appropriate emphasis on differentiated processes that broaden students' productive engagement with mathematics, and human and material resources (NCTM, 2014).

Equitable mathematics classrooms should provide every student with access to meaningful mathematics through leveraging students' strengths, drawing on students as resources of knowledge, and challenging spaces of marginality (Aguirre et al., 2013). Such math communities are collaborative, positioning every student to make sense of mathematics and develop positive mathematics identities (Huinker & Bill, 2017).

An obstacle to access and equity in schools are the differential opportunities to learn high quality grade-level mathematics content (Jackson et al., 2013; Phelps et al., 2012; Walker, 2003). This often occurs as a result of tracking—separating students academically on the basis of presumed ability—an unquestioned or commonly tolerated policy that is found in over 85% of U.S. schools and limits participation and achievement for students (Biafora & Ansalone, 2008).

Furthermore, inequalities in achievement are often perceived as the result of a hierarchy of competence. When students with more learning opportunities show higher achievement than students provided fewer opportunities, they are perceived as "more capable" or having more aptitude. This manner of talking about achievement gaps without mentioning opportunity gaps that cause them "invites a focus on deficit models to "explain" low performance in terms of factors such as cultural differences, poverty, low levels of parental education, and so on" (Flores, 2007, p. 40).

Recent scholarship on teaching elementary mathematics reveals the importance of helping children develop identities in which they powerfully use mathematics in their lives (Aguirre & Zavala, 2013; Aguirre et al., 2013). Relatedly, mathematics teacher preparation recommendations call for the development of TCs' personal mathematical identities and to "use teaching practices that provide access, support, and challenge in learning rigorous mathematics to advance the learning of every student" (Association of Mathematics Teacher Educators [AMTE], 2017, p. 13).

In *Catalyzing Change in Early Childhood and Elementary Mathematics: Initiating Critical Conversations* (NCTM, 2020) the authors suggest that education stakeholders need to challenge unjust structures and examine beliefs about who is capable of doing and understanding mathematics in order to disrupt existing inequitable policies and practices. Additionally, Kavanaugh and Danielson (2019) note scholars have argued that justice-oriented UTEs have ignored TC development (Zeichner, 2012) and should continue to resist practice-based pedagogical reforms because focusing on practice necessarily pushes justice to the periphery" (Anderson, 2019; Horn & Kane, 2019; Philip et al., 2019). This argument is based on the lack of explicit attention given to justice in the scholarship on practice-based teacher education and speaks to the field's need for investigations into conditions under which practice-based methods can provide novices "opportunities to experience the complexities of power that permeate learning of teaching practices" (Dutro & Cartun, 2016, p. 119). Feeling our way into critical questions about power and grappling with these questions in practice is the goal. "What counts as core to practice includes what cuts us to the core and what we do in light of moving into rather than away from that space" (Dutro & Cartun, 2016, p. 127).

We take up Kavanaugh's and Danielson's (2019) challenge that critical practice in teacher education should prepare teachers who are at once *ready* to enact high-quality instruction, and *intentional* as social change agents. Kavanaugh (2017) asks how we might reconceptualize core practices in teacher education in a way that does not mean turning away from justice, but instead means applying social justice frameworks to the rigorous study of practice. We believe MFEs provide opportunities to examine historical patterns and day-to-day routines of schooling that create and maintain inequalities (i.e., tracking) by orienting TCs to Aguirre et al. (2013) mathematics equity-based practices framework. These practices, stated below, highlight ways to strengthen mathematical learning and cultivate positive student mathematical identities:

- **Go deep with mathematics.** Develop students' conceptual understanding, procedural fluency, and problem solving and reasoning.
- **Leverage multiple mathematics competencies**. Use students' different mathematical strengths as a resource for learning.
- **Affirm mathematics learners' identities**. Promote student participation and value different ways of contributing.
- **Challenge spaces of marginality.** Embrace student competencies, value multiple mathematical contributions, and position students as sources of expertise.
- **Draw on multiple resources of knowledge**. Tap students' knowledge and experiences as resources for mathematics learning.

Through MFEs, we see both the benefits and possibilities of taking on manageable pieces of instruction with small groups of children while also helping TCs to attend to equity-oriented teacher practices and learn from real-time teaching dilemmas (Ghousseini, 2009; Zeichner, 2012).

MEDIATED FIELD EXPERIENCE CONTEXT

Our project group is comprised of mathematics UTEs. We began our collaboration at a 2015 National Science Foundation conference, and it is ongoing; additional colleagues have since joined in the work. Together we engage in reflective practice (Loughran, 2002) about our own work as UTEs and consider ways MFEs are impacting and developing our TCs' learning and development in teaching.

Across institutions, we have implemented MFEs in coursework at various stages of our teacher preparation programs and within a variety of educational settings: three at public universities and three at private colleges with student enrollments ranging from 1,200–25,000. We facilitate MFEs with both undergraduate and graduate TCs in the following types of mathematics courses: content, integrated pedagogy-content, and methods at both elementary and secondary levels.

As mathematics UTEs, we organize TCs' learning in our courses around developing the core teaching practices outlined in *Principles to Action* (NCTM, 2014); Huinker and Bill's (2017) graphic (see Figure 5.3) convey relationships and interconnections among these practices. We examine all or some subset of these practices depending on the course. In all respective programs, we center our MFEs on core practices focused on classroom discourse and specifically, elicit and use evidence of student thinking.

Our MFE design is research-based and follows McDonald et al.'s (2013) learning cycle (see Figure 5.2). Teaching practices are examined in university coursework and modeled by the UTE and/or partner PK–12 teacher. UTEs accompany TCs into partner classroom settings to prepare, enact, and reflect on teaching in shared classroom spaces. After introducing a mathematical concept set within a particular teaching practice, typically in the context of university coursework, TCs work in pairs or small groups as they participate in the next three segments of the learning cycle. They prepare, often rehearsing, an activity they will then enact with PK–12 learners in a partner classroom. After the enactment, the TCs debrief the classroom experiences with their UTE (and in some cases with partner teachers), in both small and whole-group discussions to synthesize learning that emerged through the experience, reflect on decisions made, and consider overall implications for teaching and learning.

As UTEs, we experience the tension of how to scaffold TCs' learning, so they become attuned to equity within the mathematics classroom and develop skills necessary to enact equitable teaching practices, reasoning this learning needs to be incremental. In order for TCs to deeply understand the equity-based practices and develop dispositions that support access and equity for students, they first need to listen and pay careful attention to what students are saying and doing, ask relevant questions that

Figure 5.3

Relationships Among Mathematics Teaching Practices

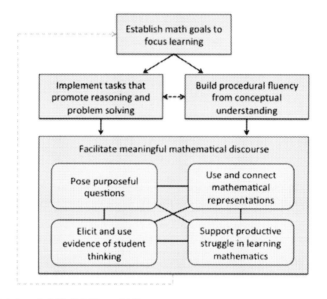

Source: Huinker & Bill (2017, p. 245).

attend to the ways students are reasoning, and successfully get students to share their thinking. As these core practices are successfully enacted by TCs, they are "ready" to notice, think about, and begin enacting more nuanced practices, such as Aguirre et al.'s (2013) mathematics equity-based practices that we see as "surrounding" the core.

VIGNETTES

We present vignettes from four of our programs to create a vivid picture of what a MFE might look like at different stages of the learning cycle. (Pseudonyms have been assigned to the TCs and children.) We first focus on the prepare, enact, and debrief components and then present one integrated case to highlight the interconnectedness and flow of the learning cycle embedded in the MFE. These vignettes illustrate ways that MFEs hone TCs' awareness and implementation of core teaching practices while simultaneously providing in situ opportunities to highlight and immerse TCs in equitable teaching practices and expand TCs' understanding of equity in the mathematics classroom.

Prepare

It was the seventh and final MFE in two local fourth grade classrooms for TCs in their third year enrolled in a 300-level elementary mathematics content course exploring fractions and focused on the core practices of: elicit and use evidence of student thinking and use and connect mathematical representations. This was the first semester the UTE had partnered with the fourth grade teachers, after working with second grade teachers in this school the previous four semesters. Partnerships with local teachers were developed through multiple meetings to collaboratively plan for the learning experiences in which all participants would engage. All but two of the TCs enrolled in the course were Caucasian; four male and 12 female. Each pair of TCs worked with the same assigned group of fourth graders for the entire MFE.

The TCs were planning a lesson targeting the concepts of fair sharing with fractions, which would revisit third grade content involving the construction and equivalence of fractions and not introduce any new 4th grade content. The UTE had two learning goals: (1) elicit the thinking of the fourth graders to see what they remembered from third grade and learn how students were thinking about fractions; and (2) connect the representation of the set model when partitioning a set to the numeric/symbolic representation when naming the fraction of the set. The UTE had created a lesson outline to help structure the TCs' planning process. One pair of TCs in each fourth grade classroom would lead a choral count to open the lesson. As a class, they decided to collectively count by one-fourths as a way to activate students' prior knowledge about fractions, including terminology (e.g., numerator, equivalent, etc.). All TC pairs were required to plan how they would co-lead the choral count and identify questions to ask thinking about the particular children in their group. The TCs then had the choice to use and "act out" the book, *The Doorbell Rang* (Hutchins, 1986), or to create their own fair-sharing task. Since this visit took place just after Halloween, Melissa and Nate chose to develop a task around sharing Halloween candy.

The UTE circulated around the college classroom to support the TC-pairs in planning their lessons for their upcoming MFE visit. As she circled back to Melissa and Nate, she asked them to share their plans, including how they were planning to use the set model with their fair-sharing of Halloween candy. They explained they would have their fourth graders first start with 12 pieces of candy shared among the two people, three people, and four people; and then pose the same questions with 24 pieces of candy. Melissa and Nate stated, "we will have our students 'act out' this sharing and make the connections fractions."

The UTE listened as they explained their plans to ensure they had thought deeply through the lesson and the questions they intended to pose with the children. Because she wanted them to connect the physical representations with the symbolic representation, she asked the TCs to clarify exactly what they would record for their group, "so you are saying that six is the same as one-half?" and wrote $6 = \frac{1}{2}$ on the board. The TCs hesitated at first knowing this was not true but were unsure how to answer that question. They initially did not see how they were possibly presenting a misconception by not being explicit about how the fraction would describe the relationship between the share and the total. However, because the UTE was in the same room as them while planning their lesson, she could prompt and question them to identify the key fraction concepts and representations they would use in their lesson so they would be prepared to work with the children.

Melissa and Nate eventually settled on the context of sharing 24 pieces of candy with the help of the UTE. They purposefully chose 24 pieces of candy because it could be divided into a number of different equal groups that could be modeled using the people in their small group: there were 4 children in the group, one had band during our visits (so then they could divide the 24 by 3); they could include themselves in the sharing (24/6). They determined they would represent the fractions using a chart (see Figure 5.4). After the children acted out all of the fair-sharing scenarios and the TCs created the chart on their board to display for their group, they would ask the children what they noticed and wondered about the chart as a tool to help develop the children's understanding of the relationships between equivalent fractions and their notation.

The presence of the UTE during the planning was significant. Her questions revealed a partial understanding of the TCs' personal understanding of teaching/learning of fractions that she mediated so the TCs could both deepen understanding of the mathematics and help avoid presenting misconceptions about fractions. Given their initial responses, it is likely that Melissa and Nate would have been caught off guard by children's inquiries. The UTE's questions also served as a catalyst for the TCs to consider ways to both develop and represent a conceptual understanding of fractions as division through a fair-sharing relationship so the children might also *go deep with the mathematics*. This also served to develop the TCs' ability to use and connect mathematical representations as teachers. By encouraging Melissa and Nate to create a scenario that was both directly relevant to the children's context (why the divisor might vary) and mathematically significant (dividing 24 into equal shares using different divisors), the UTE highlighted the importance of *drawing on multiple resources of knowledge* by tapping into the children's school experiences. By purposefully preparing questions to elicit and elucidate the

Figure 5.4

TCs Planned Representation for Fraction Lesson

$\frac{24}{2} = 12$	$\frac{12}{24} = \frac{1}{2}$	Each gets one-half
$\frac{24}{3} = 8$	$\frac{8}{24} = \frac{1}{3}$	Each gets one-third
$\frac{24}{4} = 6$	$\frac{6}{24} = \frac{1}{4}$	Each gets one-fourth
$\frac{24}{6} = 4$	$\frac{4}{24} = \frac{1}{6}$	Each gets one-sixth
$\frac{24}{8} = 3$	$\frac{3}{24} = \frac{1}{8}$	Each gets one-eighth

children's current knowledge of fractions, all TCs in this course not only honed their eliciting thinking skills, but considered ways to leverage the children's current understanding of fractions when planning their lesson for the seventh MFE visit.

Enact

It was the third of 11 MFEs in a third-grade classroom for TCs enrolled in a 200-level integrated mathematics content and pedagogy course exploring numbers and operations and focused on the core practices of elicit and use evidence of student thinking and use and connect mathematical representations. TCs must be at least a sophomore to enroll in this course and the course is taken by TCs in their sophomore, junior or senior year; in this vignette all the TCs enrolled in the class were seniors. The UTE had partnered with the school for four years meeting regularly to collaborate with the third-grade teachers each semester to determine particular concepts to explore with the children in small groups in their classes during the MFE; this was the third semester of the MFE partnership with this classroom teacher. All of the TCs enrolled in the course were Caucasian females and self-selected partners for the MFE. Throughout the semester, each TC pair/triple worked with the same two groups of third graders, teaching their lesson twice.

This was the first week of solving story problems that reviewed second grade standards; the problem was to first be introduced without numbers so the children could make sense of the situation and underlying mathematical actions inherent in the subtraction problem before solving with numbers. The UTE provided learning goals: (1) the learners will share their thinking/strategies for solving story problems and think relationally and (2) the learners will carefully listen to and share their thinking with others, which corresponded to the learning goal that the UTE set for the TCs: elicit third graders' thinking by asking open-ended questions and facilitate active listening, sharing, and re-voicing of the strategies shared in small group discussions. The other TC goal was: record children's mathematical strategies/thinking with detail and accuracy.

Serena and Octavia were working with a racially diverse group of children (Black, Brown, and White), including some with specific learning disabilities in mathematics, but no details were shared with the TCs. Prior to the children arriving at their designated spot, Serena had written the stated lesson story problem on the whiteboard: "There are ___ blueberries in the bowl. I eat some for a treat. Now there are ___ left in the bowl. How many blueberries did I eat?" After engaging the children in conversation about their group norms, she verbally introduced the blueberry problem, embellishing the context and stating that she had bought some blueberries from the store, put them in a bowl, and then washed and ate some of them but there were still some blueberries left over. Serena then asked, "How did the story start?" After a child paraphrased the shared story problem, Serena followed up by asking, "Will there be more or less blueberries?" When none of the children immediately responded, Serena redirected the conversation: she added the numbers into the original problem (12/9) and restated it. Since the problem ended with "How many blueberries did I eat?" Serena noticed a child responding by counting out 12 of the available unifix and then connecting the cubes, making a stick. Instead of asking a question to clarify or extend this thinking or connect back to the problem, Serena changed the problem and then asked, what if we added 3 to the 12 would there be more or less blueberries? A strategy was shared and a discussion about how there would be 15 blueberries unfolded. At this point Serena and Octavia looked uncomfortable: the children weren't responding in ways they had anticipated to their more or less questions, only one child had sharing thinking, and the TCs had deviated from the original mathematical problem in the lesson as their questioning progressed.

The UTE asked the TCs permission to intervene (a previously developed norm), and when granted, redirected the children's attention back to the original story problem (with numbers) and invited the children to collectively act it out. Using the same color unifix cubes to represent the blueberries the UTE asked a number of questions to elicit their thinking about what was happening in the story such as "What happened first?" "What happened next"? "How do you know?" "Can you show me what that looks like (pretending the cubes were blueberries)"? All of the children actively participated, answered questions, and took turns, invited by the UTE, to act out each part of the story and when relevant, count out appropriate numbers of cubes, ultimately solving the problem using a modeling strategy with the cubes. After the UTE paraphrased the children's collective strategy, she stepped out of the role of teacher and back into the observer role. The TCs then asked questions and led a brief discussion about how the children could record their collective thinking as a math number sentence on the white board. Finally, they asked the children to reflect on the lesson by asking them how they had thought/acted like mathematicians today.

As the UTE debriefed with Serena and Octavia immediately after the lesson, both TCs reflected on the importance of using a mathematical representation (cubes) to model the problem. They also realized asking eliciting questions, coupled with acting out the story, highlighted the underlying decreasing action (eating from a bowl) and helped the children make sense of subtraction. Modeling with unifix cubes also provided concrete opportunities for all the children to participate and successfully solve the problem. Though course discussions and assigned readings had emphasized the importance of modeling as a fundamental for making sense of a story problem and the TCs had even prepared a model to use (unifix cubes), they found it challenging to incorporate the model into the lesson enactment in a way that leveraged the children's understanding. Serena stated in her written reflection, "It was clear that the [sic] modeling it out for them made it much easier for them to visualize and understand. One of them was able to count out the cubes to get the right answer. This shows me that next time we need to make sure that we model the story/word problem for both groups." In addition, the TCs reflected they found it helpful to see how the UTE had involved one of the children with a specific learning disability in mathematics in the discussion by having her count out cubes and participate in acting out the story: they had noticed she was still working to count accurately but hadn't yet known how to elicit or build on her thinking in a group setting.

A few weeks later the TCs excitedly approached the UTE after their lesson with this same group. They shared that all the children were working together to use the physical mathematical representation (unifix cubes), actively listening to each other, and initiating encouragement to the child who was still working on counting skills. As the MFEs continued and transitioned to exploring multiplication and division, the TCs continued to use one collective physical model to explore different strategies within the group discussion, choosing accessible models that provided opportunities for all children to engage with the lesson.

Following the enactment with immediate debriefing and analysis allowed TCs to make sense of the ways that their use of the teaching practices contributed to the children's mathematical engagement and learning. For this group of TCs, observing how the UTE intervened to incorporate the use of models and elicited ideas from students in a way to involve *all* the children in their particular group was a powerful learning opportunity that exemplified equitable mathematics teaching and impacted future MFEs. This intervention provided a concrete example of a way to *affirm each of the children's mathematical learner identities* and *challenge spaces of marginality* by taking an asset-approach to their children's knowledge and embracing and valuing each child's contributions. The use of physical models to make sense of story problems afforded an opportunity for the children *to go deeper* in their understanding of the meaning of the operations.

Analyze

It was the seventh of eight MFEs in a local fourth grade classroom for TCs who were taking their mathematics methods coursework in a graduate level initial licensure program. This was the first and only mathematics methods course that occurred during the second term of their graduate program, and coincided with their first term in their student teaching placement. While all eight NCTM (2014) effective teaching practices were studied, the course emphasized core practices related to communication: elicit and use evidence of student thinking, pose purposeful questions, and facilitate meaningful mathematical discourse. This was the second year the UTE had partnered with the fourth grade teacher, but she had been working with the teachers in this school because of partnerships she had developed. Twenty-two of the TCs enrolled in the course were Caucasian; three male and 19 female and were assigned to co-teach in groups of three to a group of three to five fourth graders throughout the term. Each TC was also assigned to one or two children within the group, called a math buddy. The "buddy" structure afforded opportunities for the fouth graders and TCs to cultivate a personal connection and each classroom visit incorporated informal time to talk with one another (Kazemi, 2018) in order to break down barriers so students would be more willing to share their mathematical ideas.

The UTE tasked the TC triples to plan a problem-solving task based on knowledge of their students and relevant math standards, and enact a lesson that would explicitly focus on the teaching practices of elicit and use evidence of student thinking and use and connect mathematical representations. James, the lead teacher, and Heidi and Rachel, TCs assigned with the roles of supporting the lead teacher and capturing notes during the lesson enactment, planned accordingly: continuing the storyline of Mr. Ant from their prior lesson, they co-created a multiplicative word problem involving the area needed in Mr. Ant's garden. The TCs used their analysis of the children' thinking from the previous weeks to anticipate their thinking, and plan appropriate questions and representations accordingly.

Immediately following the 45-minute small group lesson each of the TCs gave a 15-minute "exit task" interview, constructed so TCs could continue to build relationships, check in individually with their math buddies, capture evidence of their mathematical understanding, and ask follow-up questions to promote student reflection from that day's lesson. Additionally, the TCs brought evidence from their exit-task interview discussion, including their students' written work to share during the TCs' debrief discussion.

After the exit-task interview, Heidi pulled the UTE aside before heading back to their classroom to debrief important aspects of the lesson. The typical MFE debrief structure started with 20-minute-long TC-teaching trios debriefing about what occurred in their individual groups and was followed by a longer, whole-class debrief conversation (about 30–40 minutes) where the UTE would pose important ideas (mathematically or otherwise) for the whole class to consider and contribute to.

Heidi was clearly distressed and described that something had happened during the lesson, but she was not sure if she was "blowing things out of proportion." Heidi then stated she felt her co-teacher was treating her math buddy, Lara, differently than the other students during the lesson and seemed to be making assumptions about her ability based on her gender. Heidi later described it like this:

> There was an incident this week where language was used towards my student, Lara, that made me feel uncomfortable. My student was asked repeatedly if she was confused, or comments were made that her face looked "perplexed." None of these comments were made to the other group members even though the problem lent itself to group-wide confusion. My student was asked to "try" and restate what someone had said, even though this skill is nothing challenging for her. As I mentioned prior, Lara is an internal processor, and in groups I'd describe her as more of a quiet personality. Eventually, the other student group members themselves began to ask Lara if she was confused or if she needed them to explain the problem to her. I used a Teacher Time Out with the lead teacher halfway through the lesson and shared my concerns and asked for the language to include the whole group and not isolate any students.

After Heidi shared more of the particulars of the lesson and her concerns that the dynamics in the group where Lara was targeted and marginalized, the UTE asked Heidi if she was comfortable bringing this up for discussion during the teaching trio group debrief and later in the whole class debrief. Heidi gave her assent and UTE asserted she would participate in the debrief discussion and help frame the discussion as needed, seeing it as an opportunity to "mediate" this situation and give insights about what gendered inequity might look like.

The UTE participated during the trio debrief discussion to make sure it was executed in a way that allowed all TCs to learn from the situation and understand marginalization further. The UTE's goal was to build awareness as well as disrupt this type of student interaction in the future. After the teaching trio had processed this amongst their group, they agreed to bring this situation out to the whole class so that all of the TCs could learn from the situation and not repeat this in their teaching. Heidi stated, "In the debrief I spoke with my group members about the incident. The lead teacher was very apologetic and also stated that if he could teach the lesson again, he would have approached it very differently." During the debrief, all three TCs went on to discuss nuances embedded in the teaching episode and set future goals around how to equalize status and pay close attention to the words that we say and how we can position students equitably during mathematical discussions. All TCs recognized that this small group represented a "microcosm" of the larger classroom. The lead teacher, James later reflected:

> Today's lesson illustrated how I still need to grow as a math teacher. I sought to include Lara, our quietest member and only girl, by addressing her specifically to bring her into the conversation. I made a mistake though and started off my introduction by saying, "Lara, you look perplexed. Could you restate...." By calling attention to her confusion I made it appear she understood the problem less than the boys, both of whom were throwing out incorrect ideas *more loudly*. Next time I would simply have her revoice and restate, incorporating her into the conversation without making it appear her understanding was any less than the talkative students.

Heidi reflected about the lesson and the debrief discussion positively as well. She saw the day as valuable because she confronted the situation and ensured that her students' ideas would be valued in the future.

> I think this incident was a great learning experience for myself because I need to be confident and trust my instincts with these types of situations and be an advocate for my students when they are placed in this situation. It also served as a reminder to be careful with the language I am using and to make sure I am building students' math confidence and shaping their math narrative in a way that makes math fun and not to negatively affect their self-efficacy in any way (except the positive way!)

Both the UTE's structuring of the analyze/debrief stage of the MFE and her physical presence provided multiple opportunities for Heidi to process and highlight her reactions to the marginality she witnessed and then expand this learning to the entire class. Heidi's initial, individual analysis, when responding to the exit interview, provided time to process her "teacher time out" intervention, ways Lara's competencies had been overlooked, and how implicit bias relating to gender might have contributed to James's responses to Lara. The UTE affirmed this was a key equity issue that deserved further analysis, and she provided support while the TCs debriefed, both in their small group and with the whole class. By both naming and unpacking the nature and consequence of this implicit gender bias, the TCs recognized ways they fell short, including assumptions they were making, and determined specific ways they might concretely value each child's unique mathematical contributions in the future.

An additional analysis of this incident shows how important it is to know your students and affirm what they add to discussions. Heidi had more detailed knowledge of her math buddy than the lead teacher did. This likely impacted how James engaged with Lara. While it is likely James made some assumptions about Lara due to her gender, he also made some assumptions because she was "more shy and quiet" than the other students. Heidi described strengths of Lara as: "fluent in working out a problem in her head, internally. I can often see Lara solving or attempting to solve a problem as she intently looks at the problem and also whispers under her breath her thinking" and "GREAT at using pictures or visual representations to support, represent, or solve our math work together." In this MFE, careful attention to eliciting and using evidence of children's thinking during a group discussion provided an opportunity for these TCs to also explore equity-based practices, as they *noticed and challenged spaces of marginality* and *affirmed mathematical learner's identities* (or acknowledged ways they fell short of affirming), recognizing and valuing different competencies and ways of processing information in solving complex mathematical problems.

The Integrated Flow of the Learning Cycle

It was the second of six MFEs in two rural Title I third grade classrooms. TCs were enrolled in a 300-level elementary mathematics methods course for early childhood (PK–4th grade) and Special Education (PK–8). This was the first and only mathematics methods course for the TCs and it occurred two semesters before their student teaching internship. This was the second semester the UTE had partnered with the third-grade teacher, but she had been working with the third grade teachers in this school the previous two semesters. While all eight NCTM (2014) teaching practices were studied, the course emphasized core practices related to communication: elicit and use evidence of student thinking, pose purposeful questions, and facilitate meaningful discourse. Ten of the TCs enrolled in the course were Caucasian; two males and eight females worked in assigned partnerships for the MFE. In addition to assigning each TC-pair two different groups of four third graders to work with throughout the semester, each TC was also assigned two particular children within the group, called math buddies, so that relationships would be developed that could be used to leverage instruction. The TCs were asked to plan to facilitate a multi-digit addition number talk for their third-grade groups, using the following number string:

354+111

267+232

215+136

342+64

Their UTE had established a learning goal for the TCs: elicit and record the thinking of the third graders to learn how they were thinking about addition within 1,000 using strategies and algorithms based on place value. This learning goal drove instruction throughout all phases of the learning cycle.

To launch the instructional activity for the second MFE, and as part of the *Introduce* phase of the learning cycle, the UTE engaged the TCs as a whole class in the same number string the TCs would facilitate with their small groups, discussing inherent mathematical purpose and underlying relationships. When the TCs participated in class-wide co-planning in the *Prepare* phase, they established their mathematical learning goal for students in this number string routine was to "solve three-digit and three-digit addition problems by breaking each number into its place value" as recommended by the Number Talks resource (Parrish, 2010). As part of their preparation, each pair of TCs: (1) anticipated third grade math buddy thinking based on interactions from the previous week's diagnostic interviews, (2) discussed ways to record thinking/strategy use of their third-grade math buddy, and (3) rehearsed conducting the number string. The *Enact* phase for this visit followed a typical schedule: work with one class of third grade students during the last 20 minutes of their math class, immediately followed by working with another third-grade math class during the first 20 minutes of their math class. The standard practice at this elementary school was to form "ability-grouped" third grade academic (mathematics, language arts, social studies, and science) classes based on school identified reading levels, so the same group of students rotated together through all three academic classes. In the first class of third graders, the students were identified as achieving above grade level expectations in reading; the second class included students working at or below grade level expectations. The TCs were aware of these groupings, as the UTE used this language earlier in the semester as a launching point into a discussion about access and equity in elementary mathematics instruction.

During the first-class Ashley's partner, Brant, productively engaged the students in the number string. As lead teacher during the second class, Ashley found the third graders struggled to accurately solve the first problem in the number talk. She changed her questioning techniques and students continued giving incorrect responses. At this point Ashley started to change the number string, replacing three-digit numbers with two digits, but was paused by the UTE using a "teacher time out" (Gibbons et al., 2017): the UTE suggested that before changing the number string, Ashley should have the students solve the problem using a tool—such as a number line or base-10 blocks—and then leverage that representation using a "compare and connect" discussion structure (Kazemi & Hintz, 2014). Once Ashley posed the questions, supported by base-10 blocks, all third-grade math buddies could access the problem and engage in the number string.

During the *Analyze* phase, TCs debriefed individually and in a whole group discussion facilitated by the UTE. During the individual debrief, the TCs independently completed a debrief form, addressing the following prompts: (1) What did you learn about your buddies as learners of mathematics?; (2) What did you learn about yourself as a teacher of mathematics?; (3) What are your mathematical and pedagogical goals for next visit?; and (4) Set a goal for eliciting student thinking. After the independent reflection the TCs debriefed with their partner and then as a whole class. In Ashley and Brant's written reflections and during the discussions, they both noted simplifying the mathematical task. Ashley specifically shared that "students are more capable mathematical thinkers and doers than I realize." Brant shared the importance of providing access to tools for students, even if only some of them needed them. Both TCs noted the importance of changing the questioning process to provide access for student engagement but neither partner considered why this occurrence happened until prompted by the UTE. When the UTE posed the question, "Why did you consider changing the number string?" Ashley responded, "The students were struggling to correctly find the sum of the addends and ... well ... they are in second block so I thought this string was too hard for them." The UTE also incorporated discussion of Ashley and

Brant's experiences into the whole group debriefing; discussing in detail and making public how Ashley's prior knowledge of the ability groupings influenced her to act on implicit beliefs about students' mathematical capabilities during instruction.

Reflecting on this MFE, and prior to the third MFE, the UTE revised components of all phases of the learning cycle to productively address equitable teaching practices. The UTE shifted from typically focusing on broad examples of student thinking and representing student thinking during the *Introduce* phase, to encouraging the TCs to attend to student thinking, presenting misconceptions or non-typical types of thinking first, followed by typical types of student thinking, the representations of those thoughts. During the *Prepare* phase, in addition to anticipating student thinking and rehearsing the instructional activity, TCs needed to identify tools students might use during instruction, prepare specific questions to ask a student in response to a UTE posed misconception, and justify these recommendations based on their math buddies' strengths, identified during previous visits. During the *Enact* phase, TCs now had to conduct a TC time-out with their partner to discuss any plans to change the learning goal of the instructional activity. Furthermore, if a partner observed the other TC making implicit changes that impacted the learning goal, they had to call a quick time-out. During the *Analyze* phase, the final two reflection prompts changed to: (1) What misconception did a math buddy have and how did you address it in an asset-based manner? and (2) What did you notice about eliciting student thinking during this visit? What are your mathematical and/or pedagogical goals for eliciting student thinking during your next visit? The prompt changes supported TCs to think more specifically about ways to elicit and use evidence of student thinking.

Since Ashley was an Early Childhood and Special Education major, the UTE had assumed Ashley had the knowledge base, based on college-based classroom instruction, of how to provide accessible, conceptually based, rigorous mathematics instruction for all students. The structure of MFE afforded the opportunity and illuminated the need for the UTE to provide in the moment feedback for TCs that *challenged spaces of marginality* that ability-grouping labelling created. By modifying structural instructional aspects of the MFE based on this in-the moment observation of the MFE, the UTE provided scaffolded support to help TC facilitate instructional opportunities to *affirm all of the children mathematics learners' identities, draw upon the students' current knowledge as a resource for learning* and assign competence to all students throughout the learning cycle which ultimately provided opportunities for the children to *go deeper with the mathematics.*

CONCLUSIONS AND IMPLICATIONS

Many lessons can be extracted from our experiences across our varied institutions that have broad implications for MFEs as a clinical practice model for supporting TCs' learning. MFEs provide shared, real-time experiences in a rich and complex setting in PK–12 classrooms to: learn with and from children, develop, and hone skills with different teaching practices, deepen mathematical knowledge for teaching, connect theory and practice, and explore issues of equity as they arise in the praxis of teaching. See Table 5.1 for summary of the key takeaways and implications from these vignettes that we detail in the following sections.

Table 5.1

Summary of Key Takeaways and Implications

Illustrative Vignette in the Learning Cycle	Description of Learning Cycle Phase	"Core" Practice(s) Highlighted in Vignette	Key Takeaways From MFE Vignette	"Surrounding" Equity Mathematics Practice
Prepare	Prepare to enact the math activity with a focus on enacting component(s) of core teaching practices utilizing collaborative planning and/ or rehearsals.	Elicit and Use Evidence of Student Thinking Use and Connect Mathematical Representations	• UTE's questions served as a catalyst for the TCs to consider ways to both develop and represent a conceptual understanding of fractions. • UTE's focus for TCs to create a task for students with a relatable context to explore specific content (equivalent fractions), TCs drew upon children's school experiences and prior math knowledge.	Go deep with mathematics Draw on multiple resources of knowledge

(Table continued on next page)

Table 5.1 (Continued)

Summary of Key Takeaways and Implications

Illustrative Vignette in the Learning Cycle	Description of Learning Cycle Phase	"Core" Practice(s) Highlighted in Vignette	Key Takeaways From MFE Vignette	"Surrounding" Equity Mathematics Practice
Enact	Enact core teaching practice(s) via live teaching with PK-12 students in partner school classrooms, with TCs co-teaching in pairs/triples. Often TC partners taught the activity twice to two different groups of PK-12 students.	Elicit and Use Evidence of Student Thinking Use and Connect Mathematical Representations	• TCs' observation of how the UTE intervened to incorporate the use of physical models and elicit ideas from all of the children in the group, using an asset-based approach to the children's knowledge and embracing and valuing each child's contributions, provided a concrete example of ways to enact teaching and equity practices. • The use of physical models to make sense of story problems afforded an opportunity for the children to go deeper in their understanding of the meaning of the operations.	Affirm mathematics learners' identities; Challenge spaces of marginality Go deep with mathematics
Analysis	Analyze and reflect about teaching enactments in light of core teaching practice utilizing partner and whole class debriefs and written reflections	Elicit and Use Evidence of Student Thinking Pose Purposeful Questions Facilitate Meaningful Discourse	• TCs were more likely to advocate for students with whom they had built relationships and had direct knowledge of their many capabilities (mathematics and otherwise). • The way the UTE structured the debrief conversation and was physically present supported TC conversations that confronted implicit bias. • The UTE was able to name and unpack the nature of implicit gender bias and how TCs could recognize and avoid this in the future.	Affirm mathematics learners' identities Challenge spaces of marginality

(Table continued on next page)

Table 5.1 (Continued)

Summary of Key Takeaways and Implications

Illustrative Vignette in the Learning Cycle	Description of Learning Cycle Phase	"Core" Practice(s) Highlighted in Vignette	Key Takeaways From MFE Vignette	"Surrounding" Equity Mathematics Practice
			• Allowing TCs time to process and discuss their teaching episode provided space for topics related to equity to arise.	
Integrated Case (Introduce, Prepare, Enact, Analyze)	Introduce and learn about an activity (including envisioning the teaching practice), prepare for enacting teaching practices through the activity, enact the practice(s) with PK-12 students in partner schools, and analyze and reflect upon these enactments.	Elicit and Use Evidence of Student Thinking Pose Purposeful Questions Facilitate Meaningful Discourse	• UTE provided in the moment feedback during the enact phase that confronted assumptions created from ability-grouping labelling. • The prompts provided by the UTE focused TCs' reflection when analyzing their teaching and interactions with children. The UTE drew TCs' attention to understanding how simplifying the numbers would have kept the second group of students from accessing rich mathematical content. • By spending time anticipating student responses and rehearsing the number string, the UTE supported TCs in feeling prepared to lead the activity in their small groups. • The UTE intervened during the enactment by providing math tools as scaffolds for learners to achieve the original number string instead of reducing the complexity or simplifying the mathematics content.	Challenge spaces of marginality Go deep with mathematics Affirm mathematics learners' identities Leverage multiple mathematics competencies

UTE's Mediation Central to MFE

"Clinical practice intentionally connects course work and field work so that teacher candidates can experience, with support, the interplay between the two"

—AACTE (2018, p. 35).

Having the UTE mediate as TCs are working within the prepare, enact, and analyze phases of McDonald et al.'s (2013) learning cycle provides opportunities to actively confront the TCs' incomplete understanding of mathematics or teaching practice and support TCs as they build connections that integrate theory and practice. In several of the vignettes we see a disconnect for TCs between their university readings and learning compared to what happens in the elementary classroom. For example, in the prepare vignette, the UTE pushed for deeper thinking about fractions by providing real-time scaffolds to unpack the mathematics of the lesson and develop a plan that incorporated relevant mathematical representations and questions for eliciting children's thinking. During the enact vignette, the UTE's intervention allowed for application of key ideas from coursework as they used physical models and elicited the children's thinking. In the integrated vignette, the UTE's observation and intervention during the enact stage provided an opportunity to revisit and challenge spaces of marginality that ability-grouping labelling created; though considered in a course discussion, it was the examination of ability grouping, both in the moment and analysis in the whole debrief, that led to affirming all children as capable of learning.

Emergence and Examination of Equity Issues

"Teacher preparation curriculum necessarily reflects the developmental, conceptual, and experiential needs of the teacher candidates and is shaped by local conditions and opportunities inherent in the clinical education partnership sites—not the other way around"

—AACTE (2018, p. 31).

Though the shared focus of our MFEs "situates high-leverage practices at the core of candidate development while methodically preparing to use these practices within clinical sites" (AACTE, 2018, p. 18), and the core practices, elicit and use evidence of student thinking and use and connect mathematical representations, are common across our vignettes, equity-based practices also emerge in each. Our vignettes highlight how issues of equity commonly present themselves and we illustrate ways a UTE might choose to emphasize them, while supporting TCs to learn how to enact core practices for instruction

Building Personal/Mathematical Relationships With Students

Each of the UTEs in our vignettes structured their MFEs so TCs can make personal and mathematical connections with students. Throughout the MFEs, the UTEs provided scaffolded opportunities for TCs to elicit and notice their students' mathematical thinking so they could both plan for and, in-the-moment, use student thinking to make instructional decisions.

When TCs see inequities in practice with students with whom they have built relationships, they are more likely to advocate—just as we saw with Heidi advocating for her math buddy, Lara. When, like Ashley, they observe children solving problems they initially didn't think capable of, they learn ways to cultivate an asset- based stance towards children's learning and capacities. The role of the UTE as "mediator" is critical in such situations. They help frame such situations for TCs as they analyze their teaching sessions, support TCs in "seeing" issues related to equity, and can provide in-the-moment coaching and guidance about how to disrupt inequities while TCs are putting these ideas into action.

Knowledge of Mathematics Needed for Teaching Is Key to Enacting Equity Practices

The vignettes also emphasize how mathematics knowledge for teaching is central to mathematics equity practices (Aguirre et al., 2013) and to teach mathematics for understanding. In order to *go deep with mathematics*, the first equity-based principle, TCs must personally make sense of the mathematical ideas and skills they are teaching. In order to enact the core practices of elicit and use evidence of student thinking and use and connect mathematical representations, TCs must *go deep with mathematics*: TCs need content knowledge about how mathematical ideas build, ways to represent and connect ideas to reveal mathematical structure, and insight into common patterns of children's mathematical thinking in order to develop students' conceptual understanding, procedural fluency, and problem solving and reasoning. These MFEs provided opportunities and motivation for TCs to *go deep with mathematics*. In the prepare vignette, the UTE's mediated conversation with TCs challenged and extended ways to construct and represent fractions via fair-sharing; preparing questions and representation to have the children explore fractional contexts conceptually served to hone the TCs' facility with using representations and eliciting mathematical thinking while also deepening the TCs' mathematical knowledge. In both the integrated and enact vignettes, the use of physical models, coupled with asking relevant questions to elicit and build on the children's current thinking, provided a visualization of quantities and underlying operation (addition/subtraction) so the children could successfully solve the given problems. In the analyze vignette, James became aware of how his questioning and implicit bias limited Lara's opportunities to share her mathematical thinking.

Additional Mathematics Equity-Based Practices

Through the exploration of core practices, examination of the other four equitable teaching practices also emerged and then were specifically addressed during planning, enactment, or analysis in authentic ways. For example, in the prepare vignette, as the UTE pushed for deeper thinking about fractions and their representations, the planning process also allowed for authentic connection to the equity framework where TCs *leveraged children's mathematical competencies* related to fractions. During the enact vignette, the UTE's real-time intervention afforded an opportunity for the CTs and UTE to address *issues of marginality* as they *affirmed the children's mathematics identities* while also *leveraging different mathematics competencies*. In the analyze vignette, the real-time intervention was essential for TCs awareness and connection to their teaching practices of both elicit and use evidence of student thinking and use and connect mathematical representations. In this case, Heidi asserted and advocated that her child's mathematical identity be affirmed during the lesson. It was particularly helpful to have the UTE present to moderate this interaction as the TCs identified and confronted *issues* of *marginality* and ways they affirmed and failed to *affirm mathematical learner's identities by* valuing different approaches for processing information needed to solve complex mathematical problems. In the integrated vignette, the UTE's observation and intervention during the enact stage provided an opportunity to *challenge spaces of marginality* that ability-grouping labelling created both in the moment and by bringing this up in the whole debrief. She then modified instructional aspects of all aspects of the learning cycle in order to provide further scaffolded support to help TC facilitate instructional opportunities to assign competence to all students that led to *affirming all of the children's identities as mathematical learners*.

While the equity-based practices were not the primary focus of any of our MFEs, they did surround the core practices in multiple ways: as the TC approximate and implement core practices in authentic PK–12 settings, issues relating to equity arise within their particular context, and the UTE is poised to help TCs notice complexities and issues that arise contributing to or hindering equity.

MFE Flexibility and Course Sequencing

"While successful partnerships share some common stages and actions, each partnership possesses unique characteristics and requirements specific to its local context"

—AACTE (2018, p. 28).

One strength of the MFE model is its flexibility. While the authors in this chapter used MFEs in the context of elementary mathematics courses (both content and methods) others have used MFEs across various content areas (e.g., writing and literacy) and levels (elementary through high school). MFEs are flexible enough so UTEs can either embed instructional activities (e.g., choral counts, number strings), problem solving structures (e.g., numberless word problems) or full-length math lessons to support TCs in learning how to productively engage students in mathematical thinking and discussion.

The challenges to center on equity in our mathematics-focused courses are common: rigid syllabus requirements and lack of flexibility in course content. The path forward is clear—we can address equity-based issues within the context of our MFEs while focusing on the core practices in teaching: we can address equity as the "surround" and explicitly name equity practices while staying within the framework of our given standards.

Still, this causes us to consider what TCs are developmentally prepared to handle over the duration of a one-term course during their teacher preparation program. The flexibility of MFEs can support different programs and courses has important implications for MFE design: UTEs should consider the trajectory of TCs learning in their preparation program when developing the goals and learning activities of the MFE. If, for example, courses on systemic racism and historical injustice precede the MFE semester, then UTEs could draw on the readings and concepts from those courses in discussions about the partner school context and the disparities in educational opportunities that may exist for students there. Alternatively, if MFEs in content or methods courses precede these types of foundational courses, then UTEs facilitating MFEs could invite instructors to the partner school so that in later discussions, the school or classroom context from MFEs can be used as instructors frame educational challenges and improvement. These implications support the idea that UTEs and other university faculty should work *together* to carefully consider how local experiences of TCs might inform their development of equitable practices.

Future Directions

In this chapter, we share our experiences with MFEs as a rich clinical practice structure designed around core practices but came to realize these spaces afford opportunities to simultaneously address issues of equity within schools, with our PK–12 students, and with our TCs.

> It is through the development of knowledge and understanding of the practice setting and the ability to recognize and respond to such knowledge that the reflective practitioner becomes truly responsive to the needs, issues, and concerns that are so important in shaping practice. (Loughran, 2002, p. 42)

Further qualitative research is needed to understand ways TCs' learning would be impacted if the mathematics equity-based practices were the "core" rather than the "surround." How can UTEs better design MFEs to more explicitly include mathematics equity-based practices in developmentally appropriate ways for beginning teachers? And how might a focus on mathematics equity-based practices inform TCs' development of core teaching practices within an MFE context? In what ways does a focus on mathematics equity-based practices inform TCs'development of mathematical/pedagogical knowledge for teaching? How might the development of these teaching practices transfer into their teaching outside of the MFE context? It is our hope, by developing a clear vision of high-quality MFEs that include core practices *and* mathematics equity-based practices, we can support the field to better align teacher education pedagogy and instructional design that improves TCs' learning and implementation of both core practices *and* mathematics equity-based practices in their teaching when in the field.

REFERENCES

Aguirre, J. M., & Zavala, M. D. (2013). Making culturally responsive mathematics teaching explicit: A lesson analysis tool. *Pedagogies: An International Journal*, *8*(2), 163–190. https://doi.org/10.1080/1554480X.2013.768518

Aguirre, J., Mayfield-Ingram, K., & Martin, D. M. (2013). *The impact of identity in K–8 mathematics teaching: Rethinking equity-based practices*. National Council of Teachers of Mathematics.

American Association of Colleges for Teacher Education. (2018). *A pivot toward clinical practice, its lexicon, and the renewal of educator preparation: A report of the AACTE clinical practice commission*. https://aacte.org/programs-and-services/clinical-practice-commission/

Anderson, L. (2019). Private interests in a public profession. Teacher education and racial capitalism. *Teachers College Record, 121*(6), 1–38. https://www.tcrecord.org ID Number: 22729.

Association of Mathematics Teacher Educators. (2017). *Standards for preparing teachers of mathematics*. https://amte.net/standards

Ball, D.L. & Cohen, D.K. (1999). Developing practice, developing practitioners. In L. Darling-Hammond & S. Sykes (Eds.), *Teaching as the learning profession: Handbook of policy and practice* (pp. 3–32). Jossey-Bass Education Series.

Ball, D., & Forzani, F. (2009). The work of teaching and the challenge for teacher education. *Journal of Teacher Education, 60*(5), 497–511. https://doi.org/10.1177/0022487109348479

Biafora, F., & Ansalone, G. (2008). Perceptions and attitudes of school principals towards school tracking: Structural considerations of personal beliefs. *Education, 128*(4), 588–603. https://www.jstor.org/stable/41674742

Billings, E., & Swartz, B. (2021). Supporting preservice teachers' growth in eliciting and using evidence of student thinking: Show me narrative. *Mathematics Teacher Educator, 10*(1), 29–67.

Campbell, S. S., & Dunleavy, T. K. (2016). Connecting university coursework and practitioner knowledge through mediated field experiences. *Teacher Education Quarterly, 43*(3), 49–70. https://files.eric.ed.gov/fulltext/EJ1110331.pdf

Dutro, E. & Cartun, A. (2016). Cut to the core practices: Toward visceral disruptions of binaries in PRACTICE-based teacher education. *Teaching and Teacher Education, 58*, 119–128. https://doi.org/10.1016/j.tate.2016.05.001

Flores, A. (2007). Examining disparities in mathematics education: Achievement gap or opportunity gap? *The High School Journal, 91*(1), 29–42. https://muse.jhu.edu/issue/12050

Ghousseini, H. (2009). Designing opportunities to learn to lead classroom mathematics discussions in pre-service teacher education: Focusing on enactment. In D. Mewborn & H. Lee (Eds.), *Scholarly practices and inquiry in the preparation of mathematics teachers*, (pp. 203–218). AMTE. https://www.researchgate.net/publication/281651492_Designing_opportunities_to_learn_to_lead_classroom_mathematics_discussions_in_pre-service_teacher_education_Focusing_on_enactment

Gibbons, L. K., Kazemi, E., Hintz, A., & Hartmann, E. (2017). Teacher time out: Educators learning together in and through practice. *Journal of Mathematics Education Leadership, 18*(2), 28–46. https://coetedd-wpengine.netdna-ssl.com/wp-content/uploads/2017/05/JMEL-2017-Teacher-Time-Out.pdf

Grossman, P., Hammerness, K., & McDonald, M. (2009). Redefining teaching, reimagining teacher education. *Teachers and Teaching: Theory and Practice, 15*(2), 273–289. https://doi.org/10.1080/13540600902875340

Gutiérrez, R. (2002). Enabling the practice of mathematics teachers in context: Toward a new equity research agenda. *Mathematical Thinking and Learning, 4*(2-3), 145–187. https://doi.org/10.1207/S15327833MTL04023_4

Hiebert, J., & Morris, A. K. (2012). Teaching, rather than teachers, as a path toward improving classroom instruction. *Journal of Teacher Education, 63*(2), 92–102. https://doi.org/10.1177/0022487111428328

Horn, I. S., & Campbell, S. S. (2015). Developing pedagogical judgment in novice teachers: Mediated field experience as a pedagogy in teacher education. *Pedagogies*, 10, 149–176. https://doi.org/10.1080/1554480X.2015.1021350

Horn, I. S., & Kane, B. D. (2019). What we mean when we talk about teaching: The limits of professional language and possibilities for professionalizing discourse in teachers' conversations. *Teachers College Record, 121*(4), 4. https://eric.ed.gov/EJ1204001

Huinker, D., & Bill, V. (2017). *Taking action: Implementing effective mathematics teaching practices in K–5.* National Council of Teachers of Mathematics.

Hutchins, P. (1989). *The doorbell rang.* Mulberry Books.

Jackson, K., Garrison, A., Wilson, J., Gibbons, L., & Shahan, E. (2013). Exploring relationships between setting up complex tasks and opportunities to learn in concluding whole-class discussions in middle-grades mathematics instruction. *Journal for Research in Mathematics Education, 44*(4), 646–682. http://www.jstor.org/stable/10.5951/jresematheduc.44.4.0646

Laman, T. T., Davis, T. R., & Henderson, J. W. (2018). "My Hair has a Lot of Stories!": unpacking culturally sustaining writing pedagogies in an elementary mediated field experience for teacher candidates. *Action in Teacher Education, 40*(4), 374–390. https://doi.org/10.1080/01626620.2018.1503979

Loughran, J. J. (2002). Effective reflective practice: In search of meaning in learning about teaching. *Journal of Teacher Education, 53*, 33–43. https://doi.org/10.1177/0022487102053001004

Kavanaugh, S. S. (2017). Practicing social justice: Toward a practice-based approach to learning to teach for social justice. In R. Brandenburg, K. Glasswell, M. Jones, & J. Ryan (Eds.), *Reflective theory and practice in teacher education* (pp. 161–175). Springer.

Kavanaugh, S. S., & Danielson, K. A. (2019). Practicing justice, justifying practice: toward critical practice teacher education. *American Educational Research Journal, 57*(1), 69–105. https://doi.org/10.3102/0002831219848691

Kazemi, E., & Hintz, A. (2014). *Intentional talk: How to structure and lead productive mathematical discussions.* Stenhouse.

Kazemi, E. (2018). Teaching a mathematics methods course: Understanding learning from a situative perspective. In S. Kastberg & A. Tyminski (Eds.) *Building support for scholarly practices in mathematics methods* (pp. 49–65). Information Age Publishing.

McDonald, M., Kazemi, E., & Kavanagh, S.S., (2013). Core practices and pedagogies of teacher education: A call for a common language and collective activity. *Journal of Teacher Education*, 64(5), 378–386. https://doi.org/10.1177/0022487113493807

National Council for Accreditation of Teacher Education (NCATE) Blue Ribbon Panel on Clinical Preparation and Partnerships for Improved Student Learning. (2010). *Transforming teacher education through clinical practice: A national strategy to prepare effective teachers.* http://caepnet.org/~/media/Files/caep/accreditation-resources/blue-ribbon-panel.pdf

National Council of Teachers of Mathematics. (2020). *Catalyzing change in early childhood and elementary mathematics: Initiating critical conversations.*

National Council of Teachers of Mathematics (2014). *Principles to actions: Ensuring mathematical success for all.*

Parrish, S. (2010). *Number talks: Helping children build mental math and computation strategies.* Math Solutions

Phelps, G., Corey, D., DeMonte, J., Harrison, D., & Ball, D. (2012). How much English language arts and mathematics instruction do students receive? Investigating variation in instructional time. *Educational Policy*, *26*(5), 631–662. https://doi.org/10.1177/0895904811417580

Philip, T. M., Souto-Manning, M., Anderson, L., Horn, I., J. Carter Andrews, D., Stillman, J., & Varghese, M. (2019). Making justice peripheral by constructing practice as "core": How the increasing prominence of core practices challenges teacher education. *Journal of Teacher Education*, *70*(3), 251–264. https://doi.org/10.1177/0022487118798324

Rust, J., & Cantwell, D. (2018). No one fits in a box: Preservice Teachers' evolving perceptions of self and others. *Contemporary Issues in Technology and Teacher Education*, *18*(2), 313–342. https://citejournal.org/volume-18/issue-2-18/english-language-arts/no-one-fits-in-a-box-preservice-teachers-evolving-perceptions-of-self-and-others/

Sharpe, C., Swartz, B., & Knapp. M (submitted). *Mediated field experiences in teacher education.*

Shulman, L. S. (2005). Signature pedagogies in the professions. *Daedalus*, *134*(3), 52–59. https://www.jstor.org/stable/20027998

Walker, E. N. (2003). Who can do mathematics? In B. Vogeli & A. Karp (Eds.), *Activating mathematical talent* (pp. 15–27). Houghton Mifflin and NCSM.

Zavala, M. (2017). Bilingual pre-service teachers grapple with the academic and social role of language in mathematics discussions. *Issues in Teacher Education*, *26*(2), 49–66. https://files.eric.ed.gov/fulltext/EJ1148173.pdf

Zeichner, K. (2012). The turn once again toward practice-based teacher education. *Journal of teacher education*, *63*(5), 376–382. https://doi.org/10.1177/0022487112445789

CHAPTER 6

DEVELOPING TEACHER LEADERSHIP SKILLS IN PRESERVICE TEACHER EDUCATION

Zora Wolfe and Patricia Newman
Widener University

ABSTRACT

In many urban settings, we see recent teacher education graduates taking leadership roles in their schools within their first few years of teaching. However, these teachers note they are still interested in continuing to improve their teaching skills even as they become teacher leaders. By examining what teachers identify as the important knowledge and skills for them as teachers and as teacher leaders, we can focus on developing these areas in teacher candidates and beginning teachers, so they are prepared when they find themselves in expanded teacher-leader roles.

The question guiding this study was, "What skills and types of knowledge related to teacher practice and teacher leadership do teachers feel they possess as second-stage teachers?" More specifically, this study also explored the relationship between teachers' confidence in the skills and

Preparing Quality Teachers:
Advances in Clinical Practice, pp. 129–153

types of knowledge that are important for teacher practice, and their confidence in the skills and types of knowledge that are necessary for teacher leadership. This study was conducted utilizing a mixed-methods approach, with survey findings from 24 teachers complemented by interviews of eight selected teachers. The study confirmed connections between teacher practice, teacher leadership, and teacher leadership engagement that can be capitalized within professional learning communities and collaborative inquiry.

INTRODUCTION

In the current era of school reform, research acknowledges the power and importance of teacher leaders (e.g., Lieberman & Miller, 2004; Mangin, 2005; Nguyen et al., 2019; Wenner & Campbell, 2017; York-Barr & Duke, 2004). School leaders typically include formal leaders such as principals, department chairpersons, instructional coaches, or school committee members. However, utilizing leadership defined as "the exercise of significant and responsible influence" (Sirotnik, 1995, p. 236), teachers in the classroom also have the potential to lead positive change to improve teaching and learning in their schools (Harris, 2013; Supovitz et al., 2010). In addition, the definition of teacher leadership is beginning to broaden to include the understanding that it can be exercised outside of the formal hierarchy of leadership and, consequently, be more related to teachers' practice within classrooms (Boles & Troen, 1994; Danielson, 2007; Darling-Hammond et al., 1995).

However, in many schools, especially schools with high teacher turnover and therefore younger staffs, beginning teachers often are asked to fill both formal and informal leadership roles. Specifically in our context, we see recent graduates in urban schools often taking leadership roles in their schools within their first few years of teaching, consistent with the research showing high teacher turnover in urban settings (e.g., Carver-Thomas & Darling-Hammond, 2017; Papay et al., 2017). However, these teachers note that they are still interested in continuing to improve their teaching skills even as they become teacher leaders.

Among the more seasoned educators, there are some concerns that taking on leadership positions early in their career may "stunt the growth" of some teachers, preventing them from fully developing and inquiring into their teaching practice. What implications does this early leadership recruitment have on the teachers, and as a result, what skills should we promote and support in teacher candidates in order to help them continue to learn and grow in their teaching practice, even as they take on teacher leadership roles?

There is current research about teacher leadership, the roles of teacher leaders, and school- and district-level supports that promote teacher leadership, but little on the development of teacher leadership skills in teacher candidates and beginning teachers. In this study, we begin an exploration of this area by looking at the intersection of teacher practice and teacher leadership in alumni teachers. The teachers in this study are what Eros (2011) calls second-stage teachers since they have between 5–10 years of experience. As second stage teachers, they generally have moved beyond the "survival stage" of beginning teachers, and are moving towards developing a more student-centered focused pedagogy (Eros, 2011). These later years are a crucial period for teachers because they are developing their teaching practice and also examining their commitment to the profession (Berg et al., 2005). By examining the perspectives of second stage teachers, we are able to reflect on the necessary implications for clinical practice in preservice teacher candidates to prepare them in these future roles.

This area of research is important because if we can create a framework for teachers to begin their careers with an understanding of how they can be instructional leaders and have their practice reach beyond their classroom, we can begin to break down the potential isolation of teaching and help those teachers lead and work collaboratively to continue enhancing instructional practice and improving student learning. By examining what teachers identify as the important knowledge and skills for them as teachers and as teacher leaders, we can focus on developing these areas in teacher candidates and beginning teachers, so they are prepared when they find themselves in expanded teacher-leader roles.

TEACHER LEADERSHIP AND LEADERSHIP DEVELOPMENT

This study draws on several major bodies of literature on teacher leadership and teacher development. Underlying the research is an understanding of the emerging role of second-stage teachers who are also teacher leaders within their schools and an exploration of the skills necessary for teachers to fulfill their roles as teacher leaders. In particular, this study focuses on the intersection of teacher practice skills and teacher leadership skills.

The National Council for Accreditation of Teacher Education (NCATE) for accreditation of teacher preparation programs and 38 states have adopted the InTASC Model Standards for Beginning Teachers as a basis for describing what teachers should know and be able to do (Council of Chief State School Officers, 2011). The current standards are an update from the 1992 "Model Standards for Beginning Teacher Licensing and Development: A Resource for State Dialogue," and reflect the knowledge and skills required of all teachers. Representatives of the teaching profession, including National Board Certified teachers, teacher educators, and state education officials, drafted these standards and aligned the standards with research and empirical evidence from the field of education (Youngs, 2011).

The most recent InTASC Model Core Teaching Standards identified four areas of practice that are required of effective teachers: The Learner and Learning, Content Knowledge, Instructional Practice, and Professional Responsibility (Council of Chief State School Officers, 2011). Within the area of professional responsibility, a specific standard related to leadership and collaboration is defined. An assumption of the new teaching standards is that this new vision of teaching is required in order to transform our current educational system. Therefore, "integrated across the standards is teachers' responsibility for the learning of all students [and] the expectation that they will see themselves as leaders from the beginning of their career" (Council of Chief State School Officers, 2011, p. 5). Also, an implicit understanding is that these leadership opportunities arise as teachers participate in the more collaborative culture of teaching.

As we continue to consider the expanding role of teachers in leading progress in school reform, including improved student learning, the intersection between teaching and leadership becomes even more significant. Lieberman and Miller (2004) described this new vision of the teachers and the teaching profession:

> When teachers cast off the mantle of technical and managed worker and assume new roles as researchers, meaning makers, scholars, and inventors, they expand the vision of who they are and what they do. They come to view themselves and are viewed by others as intellectuals engaged in inquiry about teaching and learning. Central to this expanded vision of teaching is the idea that teachers are also leaders, educators who can make a difference in schools and schooling now and in the future. (p. 11)

As such, it is important to determine the types of skills that would support the development of teacher practice and teacher leadership.

However, the skills required to be an effective teacher leader who can teach and lead peers are distinct from the skills required of teachers generally (Stein & Nelson, 2003; Miles et al., 1988; Snell & Swanson, 2000). Specifically, in order to create a school culture that is continually improving, "school leaders must teach not only students but also each other" (Flaum, 2003). Several frameworks for the skills required of teacher leaders, including the Teacher Leadership Skills Framework (Center for Strengthening the Teaching Profession, 2009) and the Teacher Leader Model Standards (Teacher Leadership Exploratory Consortium, 2011) have emerged.

These teacher leader standards recognize that teachers have critical knowledge and expertise, and as a result, they should take on leadership roles in order to positively influence decisions related to teaching and learning. The standards create a framework for supporting teachers to take on greater leadership roles in their schools and in the broader education community.

The Teacher Leadership Skills Framework (2009) illustrated that teacher leadership can occur when teachers have (a) the knowledge, skills, and dispositions, and (b) the roles and opportunities for teacher leadership. They defined the categories of knowledge and skills as related to five main categories, two of which can be directly connected to collaborative inquiry: collaboration and knowledge of content and pedagogy. The Teacher Leader Model Standards (Teacher Leadership Exploratory Consortium, 2011) identified seven domains for teacher leadership, with four relating to collaborative inquiry: promoting professional learning, facilitating improvements in teaching and learning, using assessment and data, and improving outreach and collaboration. Embedded within these frameworks is the concept that developing the skills to collaborate with other teachers to engage in critical inquiry into one's own teaching practice is central to teacher leadership.

Within the professional development arena, there is a recognized need for a more systemic approach to developing leadership skills since teachers often learn those skills as they are put in leadership positions (Gehrke, 1991; Mathur et al., 2013; Sherrill, 1999). As the demand for teacher leaders increases across the spectrum of leadership roles, there is also a recognition that the expectations and competencies required of teacher leaders may vary depending on the type of leadership work they are doing and the career phases of the teacher they are leading (Sherrill, 1999). In addition, a developmental continuum of teacher leadership skills also exists, similar to the developmental continuum of teaching practice (Lambert et al., 1996). Although there is literature focusing on the local building and district level supports for teacher leaders (Mangin, 2007; Mathur et al., 2013; Muijs & Harris, 2007; Murphy et al., 2009; Roselle et al., 2020; Stoelinga, 2010; Thornton, 2010), there is less literature on how to systematically develop the skills of leadership in beginning teachers.

METHODOLOGY

The purpose of this study was to examine the relationships between teachers' confidence in their teaching practice, their teacher leadership, and the types of leadership activities they engaged in as teacher leaders, utilizing the primary research question: *What skills and types of knowledge related to teacher practice and teacher leadership do teachers feel they possess as second-stage teachers?* More specifically, this study also explored the relationship between teachers' confidence in the skills and types of knowledge that are important for *teacher practice,* and their confidence in the skills and types of knowledge that are necessary for *teacher leadership.* In addition, this study examined the extent to which engagement in different leadership activities was associated with confidence in teacher practices and teacher leadership skills, and the extent to which different types of teacher support correlated with confidence in skills and types of knowledge for teacher practice and teacher leadership.

This study was conducted utilizing a mixed-methods approach in order to gather a wide range and depth of data from the available research participants to respond to the research questions (Caruth, 2013; Creswell, 2012). Due to the fact that the teaching alumni of the program were spread across the country, a survey was used to determine the types and characteristics of teacher leadership roles the alumni were taking on (if any) and to measure their perception of their development as beginning teachers and teacher leaders to discover patterns related to the research question and the research literature. Survey findings were complemented by interviews of eight selected teachers to provide a richer description of the relationship between their development as teachers and teacher leaders and how they took on leadership roles.

Of the 24 alumni who completed the survey, all teachers were in secondary schools, with 70% teaching in public, non-charter schools, 13% teaching in public charter schools, and 17% teaching in private schools, with school sizes for all schools ranging from 100 to over 24,000 students. The respondents had been teaching from 5 to 10 years as certified teachers in their own classrooms, and of the group, 10 were male, and 14 were female.

Survey

The survey included questions about participants' teaching experience and school contexts (e.g., number of years teaching, type of school, school size, and department size) in order to determine characteristics of structures within their schools that related to the research questions, such as opportunities and time for teacher leadership. In addition, data was gathered about how the alumni had (or had not) taken on leadership roles in their schools based on a broad definition of leadership (e.g., making their practice public and taking on roles beyond those of positional authority); this data was used to determine their range of leadership enactment.

The survey also asked alumni to rate their confidence on their skills related to teacher practice, based on the InTASC Model Core Teaching Standards (Council of Chief State School Officers, 2011). The questions were all based on the essential knowledge and performance indicators for each of the ten InTASC teaching standards, and focused on the domains of "the learner and learning" (including learner development, learning differences, and learning environments), content (including content knowledge and application of content), instructional practice (including assessment, planning for instruction, and instructional strategies), and professional responsibility (including professional learning and ethical practice, and leadership and collaboration). Sample questions include, "How would you rate your current level of confidence in the following skills and types of knowledge? Assessing individual and group performance in order to design and modify instruction to meet learners' needs. Designing, adapting, and delivering instruction to address each student's diverse learning strengths and needs and creating opportunities for students to demonstrate their learning in different ways." (Each indicator was adapted directly from the InTASC Model Core Teaching Standards.) The teachers rated their level of confidence for each indicator for teacher practice on a 4-point Likert scale where the numbers corresponded to the ratings very low, low, high, very high.

The questions in the survey related to teacher leadership were based on the functions under each domain of the Teacher Leader Model Standards (Teacher Leadership Exploratory Consortium, 2011): fostering a collaborative culture, accessing and using research, promoting professional learning, facilitating improvements in instruction and student learning, promoting the use of assessments and data, improving outreach and collaboration with families and community, and advocating for student learning and the profession. Sample questions include, "How would you rate your current level of confidence in the following skills and types of knowledge? Utilizing group processes to help colleagues work collaboratively to solve problems, make decisions, manage conflict, and promote meaningful change." The teachers rated their level of confidence for each indicator for teacher leadership on a 4-point Likert scale where the numbers corresponded to the ratings very low, low, high, very high.

A Cronbach's-alpha analysis was conducted to determine the internal consistency of the survey questions for each of the domains in the teacher practice and teacher leadership scales (Cronback, 1951). Cronbach's alphas for the 73 teacher practice items and 36 teacher leadership items were .93 and .91, respectively. A correlational analysis was also conducted on the survey data to determine relationships between confidence in the skills and knowledge related to teacher leadership and teacher practice, as well as to identify areas that may support both teacher leadership and teacher practice.

Interviews

Using the survey data, teachers were also identified as having high or low confidence in their teaching practice, high or low confidence in their teacher leadership skills, and high or low levels of enactment of teacher leadership. Using these three criteria, one alumna representing each combination of the three measures was selected for an interview, for a total of eight interviews.

Interview protocols were refined to further examine the domains of teaching practice and teacher leadership skills identified in the survey, as well as to explore the types of leadership activities that teachers participate in. Semistructured interviews were conducted in a conversational style via telephone with the intent to deepen the understanding of the survey responses and to uncover additional information regarding the alumni's perceptions of teacher leadership and teacher development from their experiences. The interviews also were used to gather further details about how the interview subjects viewed their practices as teachers and teacher leaders. The interview transcripts were coded and analyzed, utilizing inductive thematic analysis (Fereday & Muir-Cochrane, 2006), to look for descriptions of teacher practice and teacher leadership, as well as identifying confirming or disconfirming evidence of their descriptions of teacher leadership and its relationship to teacher practice. Additional details about common skills, types of knowledge, and supports that promote growth and learning in novice teacher leaders were also explored.

FINDINGS

The teachers in this study provided a range of scores for describing their overall confidence in the skills and knowledge related to teacher practice, teacher leadership, and leadership engagement (Table 6.1). They reported high levels of confidence in the domains related to the skills and types of knowledge related to teacher practice, with small variations between the different domains. However, as might be expected for second-stage teachers, the participants in this study were not as confident in their skills and types of knowledge related to teacher leadership.

The survey data from teachers indicated overlaps in the skills and knowledge related to teacher practice and the skills and knowledge related to teacher leadership. Specifically, teachers' confidence in the skills and types of knowledge associated with professional learning and ethical practice (as described in the teacher practice domain) was positively correlated with their confidence in accessing and using research (from the teacher leadership domains), $r = .485, p = .022$. In addition, the teachers' confidence in

Table 6.1

Survey Descriptive Statistics

	Minimum	Maximum	Mean	Std. Deviation	Median
Teacher Practice	22.19	29.79	26.69	2.19	26.48
Teacher Leadership	11.90	21.20	17.26	2.12	17.02
Engagement	42	98	65.68	13.76	65.50

$N = 22$

their knowledge of learners was positively correlated with their confidence in the teacher leadership domain of promoting professional learning, $r = .548$, $p = .008$. These positive correlations, and the correlations that are not present, between teacher practice and teacher leadership indicate that the overlap between the knowledge and skills required for teacher practice and the ones required for teacher leadership is not clearly or easily defined.

The survey also indicates that the teachers' overall confidence in their teaching practice was significantly correlated with their overall confidence in engaging in various types of leadership activities ($r = .571$, $p = .005$). Specifically, their overall confidence in their teaching practice was positively correlated with their confidence in engaging in school or district curriculum work ($r = .657$, $p = .001$), participation in school change and improvement ($r = .705$, $p = .000$), and contributions to the profession ($r = .423$, $p = .050$). These results indicate that teachers who are generally confident in their teaching practice are more likely than their peers to be confident in teacher leadership domains that closely align with their work as teachers.

In the correlations between teachers' confidence in the skills and types of knowledge related to teacher leadership and their level and confidence in leadership engagement, there were notably fewer significant correlations. The teachers' overall confidence in the teacher leadership domains which was only significantly correlated with their engagement in leadership activities related to parent and community involvement ($r = .539$, $p = .010$). This may indicate that although teachers may be engaged in leadership activities, they may not be as confident in the skills and types of knowledge required for teacher leaders.

The interviews of selected teachers gave further insights into what the teachers felt were important for classroom teaching and teacher leadership, specifically, the importance of being able to build relationships, the importance of communication skills, having a positive affective disposition, and a bigger awareness of teaching beyond their classroom or own school. Interestingly, these ideas that were raised by the teachers were not specifically addressed within the teacher practice or teacher leadership standards that served as the framework for this study.

With regards to building relationships, one teacher shared that his strength as a teacher included, "having a good rapport with my students to the point where my classroom climate is one in which students are willing to take risks, they're willing to explain what they're actually thinking." He connected this skill to how his work with other teachers: "I'd say my strengths are finding that I've got a decent way to relate to even, you know, the teachers that don't want to change, the teachers that are sort of negative towards things."

In addition to relationship building, teachers also commented on the importance of communication skills in both their teaching and leadership practice. This communication includes the importance of listening and having a dialogue, such as when a teacher shared, "I work best when I have someone else to bounce ideas back and forth. It's in that banter, that rallying back and forth that I really come alive as a leader."

The positive affective dispositions that were identified by teachers included a "can-do" attitude ("I don't like, 'no, we can't do that' as an answer and so I will work, and work to death to try and find a way if we really make to make this change. There's gotta be a way."), and the ability to be flexible and adapt ("the key piece of that [being a good leader] would be able to rethink how to put those things together and take things apart and put them together in new ways and see how they would fit differently").

Having a greater awareness of teaching and leadership that extended beyond a teacher's own classroom and school was also another idea that emerged as important to teacher practice and leadership. One teacher shared how he gained confidence as a teacher leader:

> So some of that comes with just confidence in my own teaching and some of that comes with thinking that I really want to be a part of something. Whether it's that bigger education profession, or if it's my school that I believe in. I think to be a good teacher, you have to be committed to the students that are in your room and to be a good teacher leader, you have to be committed to education in general, whether that's your school or something bigger.

Finally, the interviewed teachers identified a number of supports that they feel would enhance their abilities as teacher leaders- most prominent were (1) time, (2) experience, and (3) opportunity. Unsurprisingly, many of the teachers felt that they were stretched too far to engage deeply in leadership activities, ("If I'm devoting time to these meeting each week and this time preparing for this professional development, certainly that time comes from somewhere. How much time can I really devote to some of those things?"). Some teachers also felt that they could not or should not lead until they had more experience in the classroom. One teacher acknowledged, "maybe there's more work I need to do before I'm going to be accepted to that [leadership] opportunity. I'm still really young in my career and I'm young, relatively young, chronologically." Wiht regards to opportunity, teachers indicated (1) if they had opportunities to lead they would do so, and (2) they wanted opportunities to practice leading, with one teacher sharing, "The more you are put in that role and really try to do your best at it, the more experience you're going to gain and the more confident you'll be and the better leader."

DISCUSSION AND IMPLICATIONS

In addition, the teachers' interviews provide additional insights into what can be done to support teachers to take on teacher leadership roles in their schools. Particularly, this study gave insights into how teachers can learn to lead, how leadership can enhance teaching, characteristics to consider in teacher recruitment, and the importance of teacher retention. These insights have implications for teacher preparation programs, school and district administrators, and other teacher mentorship and in-service programs.

Learning to Lead

As we encourage teachers to become teacher leaders, we see that it cannot be assumed that teachers who have strong teaching practice will be able to translate those skills to the realm of teacher leadership. As seen in this study, even though domains in teacher practice and teacher leadership have similar concepts, teachers' confidence in one domain of teacher practice, did not lead to similar confidence in the related domain of teacher leadership. This suggests that more explicit professional development related to teacher leadership skills is necessary. We can help make the similarities and differences between working with students and working with adults more explicit, and we can help teachers translate the inquiry and reflective work they do individually as teachers to a more collaborative process. Rather than isolating themselves as they continue to develop their own teaching practice, teachers can use the opportunity to bring in others as they utilize teacher leadership skills.

We also see that the language in the InTASC Model Core Teaching Standards and the Teacher Leader Model Standards are not prominent in the teachers' conversations about teaching practice and teacher leadership. Although the teachers spoke to some of the indicators described in the standards, these were not the focus of their interviews. This may indicate that teachers may need to be made more explicitly aware of the important skills and types of knowledge that are specified in the standards if we believe that these are the specific areas teachers need to develop. However, this may also indicate that these frameworks do not encompass all of the areas that teachers feel are important to their work as teachers and as teacher leaders. This is interesting as we consider the purpose of the standards and how and why they should be used to support teachers.

However, we suggest that at an early stage within a teacher preparation program, preservice teachers should be encouraged and directed to delve into the InTASC Model Core Teaching Standards and the Teacher Leader Model Standards. By doing so, teacher candidates can develop a frame of reference that encourages dialogue and comprehension surrounding areas that they feel are important to their work as future teacher leaders. For example, the InTASC Model Core Teaching Standards weave the idea of leadership throughout all of their standards, which give direction to teacher preparation programs regarding the knowledge, content, and dispositions teacher candidates need (Rogers & Scales, 2013). When these candidates become teachers, they will have already been adequately exposed to the standards and will feel better prepared to discuss and determine further support needed for teachers and teacher leaders.

This will also provide preservice teachers with a framework of qualities and dispositions that are necessary for a teacher leader to possess. Once candidates understand these qualities, they can spend time emulating and developing them within themselves, while still enrolled. Clinically rich preparation programs allow candidates to recognize the qualities within current teacher leaders, as well, furthering the development of in-school leadership characteristics. Practicing and learning how to be a teacher leader helps to create future teachers who are prepared to transition that role within a school setting. While enrolled, preservice teachers should be exposed to opportunities to practice leadership that will encourage them to grow as individuals and professionals (Chambers & Laverty, 2012).

Leadership Can Enhance Teaching

This study confirms that taking on some teacher leadership roles can also enhance teaching. As with the teachers in Fiarman's (2007) study, the teachers in this study felt that engaging in leadership opportunities helped to develop their understanding of good teaching practices. For example, teachers shared that when they engaged in teacher leadership activities, they were challenged to become better teachers themselves. They wanted to try new strategies, they got new ideas from other teachers, and they were challenged to reflect on their own practice.

However, not all teachers will take on leadership roles on their own. As this study showed, teachers who had high confidence in their teaching practice and their teacher leadership skills, did not necessarily engage often in teacher leadership activities. The existing norms and structures in their schools may not invite teacher leadership and some teachers may not feel that they have the opportunities to influence instructional change in their schools.

In order to encourage teachers to take on teacher leadership roles, we must give them opportunities and structures to practice leadership. Several of the teachers in this study shared that the opportunities they had to practice leadership skills prepared them to consider leadership roles with their schools. One teacher shared, "we did a mock teachers' meeting and as silly as that seemed from the outside, that was one of the more impactful things I did, listening to how people reflect on what I said." Two other teachers suggested that we could do even more to give more opportunities for teachers to practice leadership within the program.

As the program has shifted to promote teacher leadership even among preservice and beginning teachers, we are beginning to see teachers rise to the challenge and be excited to share their teaching practice with others. However, the notion of "sharing your teaching practice" as a form of teacher leadership is still something new. For many teachers, taking on teacher leadership only means taking on formal leadership roles or moving into administration.

Because of this limited view of leadership, we still need to help teachers conceptualize informal leadership as a form of teacher leadership. As one teacher shared, it is possible to take on leadership roles without becoming an administrator:

> a lot of times, teacher leadership seems like your pathway into administration. You know that's just what people do. So the idea that there are roles I can take and the reason to take them is not because I want to become an administrator, but because I want to change something.

This view of leadership empowers teachers to make changes in their school and gives them ownership of the work they do in their schools.

Even when schools do not have a culture that support teacher leadership, having a broader view of leadership can help. In one teacher's school, "it's not encouraged very much among the teachers to be a teacher leader for education." However, she says, "I try and lead by doing my job in my classroom and doing it well and hopefully that reputation of expecting a lot of things from my student gets out to the other teachers. Through that, that's the way I feel that I lead." Her attitude has led her to engage in teacher leadership by allowing other teachers into her classroom and encouraging other teachers to visit other classrooms as well. Even small steps such as these can help to lead a change and foster a culture of collaboration and inquiry in a school.

This notion can also be applicable to preservice teachers. During classwork, teacher candidates, with guidance from instructors, can discuss field experience and clinical practice, share commonalities, frustrations, fears, and successes within a supportive and inclusive university setting. When candidates learn to value each other from an early stage in their preparation, they will be better suited to continue to support and rely on each other in the future, when they are no longer fellow students, but instead, colleagues within education.

Preservice teachers who meet and spend time with practicing teachers and teacher leaders are exposed to the dispositions, characteristics, and qualities of a teacher leader. This also allows teacher candidates to become leaders within the university setting, where they can apply leadership dispositions during their classwork, extracurricular activities, while volunteering, completing field experiences, and interacting with other students. Colleges and universities should purposefully develop socially responsible leaders—a task that is the responsibility of all of the campus community, not just those teaching leadership courses or working with co-curricular leadership programs (Dugan & Komives, 2007).

Indicators for Teacher Recruitment

If we want to recruit teachers who have the potential to become teacher leaders who are able to foster positive change in schools, this study suggests some characteristics of potential candidates that may be good indicators of leadership potential. The teachers in this study discussed specific skills and dispositions they felt were important for both teacher practice and teacher leadership: being able to build relationships, strong communication skills, having a positive affective disposition, and a bigger awareness of teaching beyond the classroom or school.

These ideas align with other research around positive organizational behavior and leadership, indicating that even in beginning teacher recruitment, we should consider the research related to organizational leadership. Specifically, positive organizational behavior applies the ideas of positive psychology including a focus on positive behaviors related to confidence, self-efficacy, hope, optimism, and emotional intelligence as human resource strengths that can be utilized in organizations (Avey et al., 2008; Luthans & Church, 2002). Just as business leadership literature indicates that positive behaviors can support successful leadership (Avolio & Gardner, 2005, Houghton & Neck, 2002; Luthans, 2002; Peterson & Luthans, 2003), we can make a similar connection to teacher leadership.

These soft skills are also important to identify, support and foster at the preservice teaching level. Skills, such as communication skills, critical and structured thinking, creativity, negotiation skills, time management, integrity/honesty, self-esteem, work ethic, good manners, courtesy, and responsibility, complement hard skills and have a positive impact on students during and after college (Schulz, 2008). Teacher preparation programs should develop leadership potential in all participants, and empathy, collaboration, community, knowledge, and skills should be developed (Chambers & Laverty, 2012; Kaye 2004).

As we examine our criteria for teacher candidates, we need to consider how these ideas align with our admissions criteria. If we determine that these positive skills and dispositions are what we would like to see in our teachers, it would be important to determine indicators that would indicate that candidates have these traits and could apply them to their work as teachers, or that they have the potential to develop those skills and dispositions. Just as it is important to determine if candidates have the potential to develop the content knowledge needed for teaching, we should also utilize research related to leadership and positive organization behaviors that have determined indicators of traits and behaviors that would lead to future successful teacher leaders.

Importance of Teacher Retention

As the teachers in this study shared, the amount of time teachers have taught in the classroom is an important factor in how they felt they could act as teacher leaders. Not only is it important for teachers to remain in the classroom so they can develop their teaching skills, but the amount of time they have in their classroom helps to build relational trust and social capital for instructional influence of other teachers.

At the preservice teaching level, within clinical practice, teacher candidates should be exposed to a variety of school settings and grade bands to increase self-efficacy and career-choice validation. Additionally, robust clinical experiences include time spent with administrators, to gauge the characteristics they believe new teachers should possess and what constitutes a teacher becoming a leader within a school. This expands the traditional label of the mentor teacher. Goodwin et al. (2015) state that under resourced schools facing teacher shortages in areas such as special education and STEM subjects, critical areas that impact schools in their entirety, should allow mentor teachers to spend almost every day with preservice teachers, so their perspectives, practices, and roles can provide a clinically rich experience (p. 2).

Clinical practice provides vital time for preservice teachers to observe, explore, and execute lessons and units. Ingersoll et al. (2014) note that observation, viewing lesson plans, and allowing preservice teachers to witness the planning and preparation process before teaching provides essential representations of practice, proving to be helpful in preservice teachers' pedagogical confidence (p. 364). Teachers need to be able to practice and gain familiarity regulating a classroom. The earlier preservice teachers and new teachers gain confidence in front of the classroom and within a school environment, the sooner they can become teacher leaders within the field of education.

This aligns with other research that has shown that teachers who seek to influence their colleagues' teaching practice find resistance to their efforts because the "norms of autonomy, egalitarianism, and seniority continue to exert great influence among teachers" (Moore Johnson et al., 2008). It is important to recognize this reality is something teachers face as they try to enact teacher leadership in their settings. Understanding how social capital plays a role in the construction of instructional leadership can help support how changes to instruction and learning can happen in schools (Spillane et al., 2003). As such, it is important for schools to consider ways to design and support roles that consider the existing power and structures that may be counter to instructional reform. As the interviews showed, schools that have a culture that supports teacher inquiry and professional development are much more likely to have teachers who are willing and open to innovations brought through teacher leadership.

As a teacher mentor, I have found that explicitly sharing and discussing this reality of the norms they might find in their schools that would be counter to their ideas has been helpful. Our teachers are often excited and eager to share their new ideas with their colleagues and assume all teachers want to improve and try new strategies, so they are sometimes surprised by the resistance they find in their schools. I have told teachers who are attempting to lead instructional change in their schools to find allies within their schools who can support them in their efforts. Teachers have also found it helpful to recognize and respect the existing power and seniority structures in their schools, and to consider how to minimize the disruption to the norms as they try to influence change in their schools.

RECOMMENDATIONS

For schools and universities, it is important to support current and future teachers in taking leadership roles by creating a culture that supports collaboration and inquiry. Schools and teacher preparation programs need to provide opportunities and time for teachers and candidates to collaborate on meaningful things that will impact their practice. By providing these opportunities for them to lead, schools will also benefit as teachers improve on their teaching practice and candidates learn to lead prior to even practicing within the field. Schools and teacher preparation programs should consider how they can build professional learning communities that support collaborative inquiry into teachers' and candidates' practice. These successful communities will be able to provide opportunities for current and future teachers to engage in leadership as well as support their continued professional growth. This aligns with other research that emphasizes the importance of having opportunities to become part of professional communities (e.g., Freedman et al., 1999), and to engage in inquiry about their practice with their peers (Cochran-Smith & Lytle, 1999; Nieto, 2003).

Professional Learning Communities

The use of professional learning communities is one way to incorporate and encourage these practices that improve beginning teachers' teaching and learning skills (DuFour & Eaker, 1998; Thompson et al., 2004). True teacher learning can occur when teachers have opportunities within these professional learning communities to inquire, collaborate, and reflect on their teaching practice (Cochran-Smith & Lytle, 2009; Darling-Hammond & McLaughlin, 1995).

A professional learning community requires teachers to "work collaboratively on matters related to learning" (DuFour, 2004). DuFour (2004) further elaborates that these "collaborative conversations call on team members to make public what has traditionally been private—goals, strategies, materials, pacing, questions, concerns, and results." The intent of professional learning communities is that they are explicitly structured to help teachers improve their instructional practice. Bolam et al. (2005) provide the following definition: "An effective professional learning community has the capacity to promote and sustain the learning of all professionals in the school community with the collective purpose of enhancing student learning" (p. 145).

The structure of professional learning communities extends beyond simply a group of teachers meeting together after school. DuFour (2004) identifies the "big ideas" that are the core principles of professional learning communities: ensuing students learn, a culture of collaboration, and a focus on results. Wenger (1998) described three characteristics of a learning community: mutual engagement, a shared repertoire, and a joint enterprise. Grossman et al. (2001) provide a framework for describing the development of these communities. The framework includes a rubric that describes communities as beginning, evolving, or mature, along the four dimensions of formation of group identity and norms of interaction, navigating fault lines, negotiating the essential tension, and communal responsibility for individual growth. Using these frameworks, teacher leaders can play an important role in developing these productive communities.

These frameworks for professional learning communities can also be incorporated within teacher preparation programs. In the college setting, coursework can be mindful of DuFour's (2004) "big ideas" while also including key stakeholders within education to improve candidates' learning and application skills. Teacher candidates benefit from the community of learners' format because regardless of their academic level in their teacher preparation program, they work collaboratively to grow academically, emotionally, and professionally while also dealing with personal and institutional barriers (Flores et al., 2006; Flores et al., 2007). As previously stated, these qualities positively affect teachers, aiding in the transition to becoming teacher leaders. Teacher leaders can also benefit from possessing and valuing collaborative inquiry skills and structures.

Collaborative Inquiry

One of the common themes that arises in examining teacher leadership and teacher practice frameworks is collaborative inquiry. As communities become more mature, Grossman et al. (2001) noted that collaboration and critical inquiry should be present: "Members begin to accept the obligations of community membership, which include the obligation to press for clarification of ideas and to help colleagues articulate developing understandings" (p. 990). Collaborative inquiry is defined as "a process consisting of repeated episodes of reflection and action through which a group of peers strives to answer a question of importance to them" (Bray, 2000, p. 6). This process can occur in a range of informal teacher groups to larger networks of teachers across schools who are engaged in examining their own teaching practice together.

As seen in the teaching leadership frameworks, collaborative inquiry skills are important for teacher leaders. But the literature would argue that these skills are important for all teachers as they improve their teaching practice (Cochran-Smith & Lytle, 1999; Stigler & Hiebert, 1999). For example, in *The Teaching Gap*, Stigler and Hiebert (1999) highlight the process of Japanese lesson study, in which teachers have the opportunity to work collaboratively on lessons, and observe and analyze their teaching. As teachers engage in this type of work, they are required to critically examine student work and teaching pedagogies as they work to improve their lessons and increase student learning.

Collaborative inquiry provides a structure for professional development in schools and improving teaching practice (Bray, 2002). Through this process, teachers have the opportunity to frame questions, examine evidence, reflect on practice, and make sense of their work in the classroom (Weinbaum et al., 2004). The process allows teachers to identify key problems or issues that are relevant to their specific context, but in order for collaborative inquiry to occur, Weinbaum et al. (2004) identified some skills that are required of the teachers involved. These include the ability to appropriately identify important questions to investigation, knowledge of the use data for inquiry, and facilitation skills and structures for discussions. These skills parallel those that are identified as important for teacher leaders, as well.

Teacher preparation programs can nurture collaborative inquiry by creating opportunities for groups of students to engage in self-regulated learning activities supported by an instructor, to increase students' motivation and interest (Bell et al., 2010). In order for future teachers to be able to instruct a wide range of learners, they should have many opportunities to participate in active-learning, steer learning topics as much as possible, research and review educational frameworks, and work through dynamic tensions inherent in learning to teach (Hamre & Oyler, 2004). Learning should not, and does not, follow from imposition of the teacher's viewpoints on the students, but rather unfolds from reflective dialogue about ideas and experiences (Dewey, 1938; Freire, 1970; Hamre & Oyler, 2004). With that in mind, Hamre and Oyler (2004) believe that collaborative forums for candidates to come together in dialogue, sharing and grappling with their own critical reflections could unearth the passions, perspectives, experiences, and leadership qualities that they can then bring forth to the education profession and connect them to a larger educational conversation (p. 161).

Collaborative inquiry also closely corresponds to the practices of practitioner inquiry (Cochran-Smith & Lytle, 2009) and action research (Mills, 2000). These ideas of teacher research as a way to improve teacher practice, have been explored since the early 1950s (Corey, 1953). The implication of teacher research, that teachers and candidates could be involved in research and create their own learning, strengthens the idea that teachers can be leaders and influence change in teaching and learning.

SUGGESTIONS FOR FURTHER RESEARCH

This study was designed to explore the perspectives of teaching alumni with regards to their confidence in the skills and types of knowledge related to teacher practice and teacher leadership. This study gives a preliminary overview of how teachers see the skills and knowledge of teacher practice and teacher leadership overlap, and how teachers' engagement in different types of leadership activities were associated with their confidence in teacher practice and teacher leadership. However, as a preliminary study, there are many areas for further research and many additional questions that were raised.

Because of the particular population of teachers in this study, further studies with a more general population of teachers would be required to determine if similar responses would be found with other teachers. In addition, it would be interesting to determine if the findings in this study are applicable to teachers who have been in the classroom for a longer amount of time. Particularly, perhaps there is a developmental trajectory for the development of teacher leadership and the teachers in this study may have only represented a particular stage of development.

To deepen our understanding of teacher practice and teacher leadership, an extension of this study would be to look at teachers' actual practice. Although self-report and measures of confidence have been used as a proxy for actual practice, we can verify the findings and learn more through observing actual teacher practice in their classrooms, looking for evidence of teacher leadership in their schools, and interviewing supervisors and colleagues. Because of the broad definition of teacher leadership that is used in this study, actual observation may be able to uncover more nuanced instances of teacher leadership than what is typically understood as leadership or more formal positions of leadership.

Likewise, gaining additional information regarding teacher preparation programs' groundwork for fostering leadership within its teacher candidates and the impact that has on beginning teachers could also positively impact the repertoire of educational literature. The symbiotic relationship between collaborative inquiry and preservice teacher leaders could be also further explored. Concurrently, examining preservice teachers' first-hand experiences and perspectives surrounding what they believe helped to contribute to becoming teacher leaders and organizational leaders could provide context and a beginning framework for teacher preparation programs to model.

By providing new teachers with the opportunity to continue to grow and develop and to effect change, the image of teaching as a flat profession can be disrupted. As such, sustained teaching experience is important because developing an expertise in teaching takes time and therefore, training and keeping promising teachers in the profession needs to be a priority.

REFERENCES

Avey, J. B., Wernsing, T. S., & Luthans, F. (2008). Can positive employees help positive organizational change? Impact of psychological capital and emotions on relevant attitudes and behaviors. *The Journal of Applied Behavioral Science*, *44*(1), 48–70.

Avolio, B. J., & Gardner, W. L. (2005). Authentic leadership development: Getting to the root of positive forms of leadership. *The Leadership Quarterly*, *16*(3), 315–338.

Bell, T., Urhahne, D., Schanze, S., & Ploetzner, R. (2010). Collaborative inquiry learning: Models, tools, and challenges. *International Journal of Science Education*, *32*(3), 349–377.

Berg, J. H., Charner-Laird, M., Fiarman, S. E., Jones, A., Qazilbash, E. K., & Johnson, S. M. (2005, April). *Cracking the mold: How second-stage teachers experience their differentiated roles* [Paper presentation]. The American Educational Research Association annual conference, Montreal, Quebec, Canada.

Bolam, R., McMahon, A., Stoll, L., Thomas, S., & Wallace, M. (2005). *Creating and sustaining professional learning communities* (Research Report No. 637, General Teaching Council for England). Department for Education and Skills.

Boles, K., & Troen, V. (1994, April). *Teacher leadership in a professional development school* [Paper presentation]. The annual meeting of the American Educational Research Association, New Orleans, LA.

Bray, J. N. (2000). *Collaborative inquiry in practice: Action, reflection, and meaning making*. SAGE.

Bray, J. N. (2002). Uniting teacher learning: Collaborative inquiry for professional development. *New Directions for Adult and Continuing Education*, *2002*(94), 83–92.

Caruth, G. D. (2013). Demystifying mixed methods research design: A review of the literature. *Mevlana International Journal of Education*, *3*(2), 112–122.

Carver-Thomas, D., & Darling-Hammond, L. (2017). *Teacher turnover: Why it matters and what we can do about it*. Learning Policy Institute.

Center for Strengthening the Teaching Profession. (2009). *Teacher Leadership Skills Framework*. https://cstp-wa.org/teacher-leadership/teacher-leadership-skills-framework/

Chambers, D. J., & Laverty, S. (2012). Service-learning: A valuable component of pre-service teacher education. *Australian Journal of Teacher Education*, *37*(4).

Cochran-Smith, M., & Lytle, S. (2009). *Inquiry as stance: Practitioner research for the next generation*. Teachers College Press.

Corey, S. M. (1953). *Action research to improve school practice*. Bureau of Publication, Teachers College.

Council of Chief State School Officers. (2011, April). *Interstate Teacher Assessment and Support Consortium (InTASC) Model Core Teaching Standards: A resource for state dialogue*.

Creswell, J. W. (2012). *Educational research: Planning, conducting, and evaluating quantitative and qualitative research* (4th ed.). Pearson Education.

Cronbach, L. J. (1951). Coefficient alpha and the internal structure of tests. *Psychometrika, 16*(3), 297–334.

Danielson, C. (2007). The many faces of leadership. *Educational Leadership, 65*(1), 14–19.

Darling-Hammond, L., Bullmaster, M. L., & Cobb, V. L. (1995). Rethinking teacher leadership through professional development schools. *The Elementary School Journal, 96*(1, Special Issue: Teacher Leadership), 87–106.

Darling-Hammond, L., & McLaughlin, M. W. (1995). Policies that support professional development in an era of reform. *Phi Delta Kappan, 76*(8), 597–604.

Dewey, J. (1938). *Experience and education*. Collier Books.

DuFour, R. (2004, May). What is a professional learning community? *Educational Leadership, 61*(8), 6.

DuFour, R., & Eaker, R. (1998). *Professional learning communities at work: Best practices for enhancing student achievement*. National Educational Service.

Dugan, J. P., & Komives, D. R. (2007). *Developing leadership capacity in college students: Findings from a national study* (A Report from the Multi-Institutional Study of Leadership). National Clearinghouse for Leadership Programs.

Eros, J. (2011). The career cycle and the second stage of teaching: Implications for policy and professional development. *Arts Education Policy Review, 112*(2), 65–70.

Fereday, J., & Muir-Cochrane, E. (2006). Demonstrating rigor using thematic analysis: A hybrid approach of inductive and deductive coding and theme development. *International journal of qualitative methods, 5*(1), 80–92.

Fiarman, S. E. (2007, April). *It's hard to go back: Career decisions of second-stage teacher leaders* [Paper presentation]. The American Educational Research Association Annual Conference, Chicago, IL.

Flaum, S. (2003). When ideas lead, people follow. *Leader to Leader. 30*, 7–12.

Flores, B. B., Claeys, L., & Wallis, D. (2006). Academy for teacher excellence: Extending the dialogue in university and community college partnerships. *Journal of Learning Communities Research, 1*(1), 29–51.

Flores, B. B., Clark, E., Claeys, L., & Villarreal, A. (2007). Academy for teacher excellence: Recruiting, preparing, and retaining Latino teachers through learning communities. *Teacher Education Quarterly, 34*(4), 53–69.

Freedman, S. W., Simons, E. R., Kalnin, J. S., & Casareno, A., The M-Class Teams. (Eds.). (1999). *Inside city schools: Investigating literacy in multicultural classrooms*. Teachers College Press.

Freire, P. (1970). *Pedagogy of the oppressed* (M. B. Ramos, Trans.). Seabury.

Gehrke, N. (1991). *Developing teachers' leadership skills*. ERIC Digest Clearinghouse of Teacher Education. ED330691

Goodwin, L., Roegman, R. & Reagan, E. (2015). Is experience the best teacher? Extensive clinical practice and mentor teachers' perspective on effective teaching. *Urban Education, 51*(10), 1198–1225.

Grossman, P., Wineburg, S., & Woolworth, S. (2001). Toward a theory of teacher community. *Teachers College Record, 103*, 942–1012.

Hamre, B., & Oyler, C. (2004). Preparing teachers for inclusive classrooms: Learning from a collaborative inquiry group. *Journal of Teacher Education, 55*(154).

Harris, A. (2013). Teacher leadership and school improvement. In A. Harris, C. Day, D. Hopkins, M. Hadfield, A. Hargreaves, & C. Chapman (Eds.), *Effective leadership for school improvement* (pp. 82–93). Routledge.

Houghton, J. D., & Neck, C. P. (2002). The revised self-leadership questionnaire: Testing a hierarchical factor structure for self-leadership. *Journal of Managerial psychology, 17*(8), 672–691.

Ingersoll, C., Jenkins, J., & Lux, K. (2014). Teacher knowledge development in early field experiences. *Journal of Teaching in Physical Education, 33*(3), 363–382.

Kaye, C. (2004). *The complete guide to service learning*. Free Spirit.

Lambert, L., Collay, M., Dietz, M., Kent, K., & Richert, A. (1996). *Who will save our schools? Teachers as constructivist leaders*. Corwin Press.

Lieberman, A., & Miller, L. (2004). *Teacher leadership*. Jossey-Bass.

Luthans, F. (2002). The need for and meaning of positive organizational behavior. *Journal of Organizational Behavior, 23*(6), 695–706.

Luthans, F., & Church, A. H. (2002). Positive organizational behavior: Developing and managing psychological strengths [and executive commentary]. *The Academy of Management Executive, (1993–2005)*, 57–75.

Mangin, M. M. (2005). Distributed leadership and the culture of schools: Teacher leaders' strategies for gaining access to classrooms. *Journal of School Leadership, 15*(4), 456–484.

Mangin, M. M. (2007). Facilitating elementary principals' support for instructional teacher leadership. *Educational Administration Quarterly, 43*, 319–357.

Mathur, S. R., Gehrke, R., & Kim, S. H. (2013). Impact of a teacher mentorship program on mentors' and mentees' perceptions of classroom practices and the mentoring experience. *Assessment for Effective Intervention, 38*(3), 154–162.

Miles, M. B., Saxl, E. R., & Lieberman, A. (1988). What skills do educational "change agents" need? An empirical view. *Curriculum Inquiry, 18*(2), 157–193.

Mills, G. E. (2000). *Action research: A guide for the teacher researcher*. Merrill.

Moore Johnson, S., Donaldson, M., Kirkpatrick, C., Marinell, W., Steele, J., & Szczesiul, S. (2008). Angling for access, bartering for change: How second-stage teachers experience differentiated roles in schools. *The Teachers College Record, 110*(5), 1088–1114.

Muijs, D., & Harris A. (2007). Teacher leadership in (in)action: Three case studies in contrasting schools. *Educational Management Administration Leadership, 35*(1), 111–134.

Murphy, J., Smylie, M., Mayrowetz, D., & Louis, K. S. (2009). The role of the principal in fostering the development of distributed leadership. *School Leadership & Management, 29*(2), 181–214.

Nieto, S. (2003). *What keeps teachers going?* Teachers College Press.

Nguyen, D., Harris, A., & Ng, D. (2019). A review of the empirical research on teacher leadership (2003–2017). *Journal of Educational Administration, 58*(1) 60–80.

Papay, J. P., Bacher-Hicks, A., Page, L. C., & Marinell, W. H. (2017). The challenge of teacher retention in urban schools: Evidence of variation from a cross-site analysis. *Educational Researcher, 46*(8), 434–448.

Peterson, S. J., & Luthans, F. (2003). The positive impact and development of hopeful leaders. *Leadership & Organization Development Journal, 24*(1), 26–31.

Rogers, C., & Scales, R. (2013). Preservice teachers' perceptions of teacher leadership: Is it about compliance or understanding? *Issues in Teacher Education, 22*(2), 17–37.

Roselle, R., Hands, R. E., & Cahill, J. (2020). Daring greatly: School-university partnerships and the development of teacher leadership. *School-University Partnerships, 12*(4), 111–121

Schulz, B. (2008). The importance of soft skills: Education beyond academic knowledge. *Journal of Language and Communication, 2*(1), 146–154.

Sherrill, J. A. (1999). Preparing teachers for leadership roles in the 21st century. *Theory into Practice, 38*(1, Redefining Teacher Quality), 56–61.

Sirotnik, K. (1995). Curriculum overview and framework. In M. J. O'Hair & S. J. Odell (Eds.), *Educating teachers for leadership and change: Teacher education yearbook III (Teacher Education)* (pp. 235–242). SAGE.

Snell, J., & Swanson, J. (2000, April). *The essential knowledge and skills of teacher leaders: A search for a conceptual framework* [Paper presentation]. The American Educational Research Association Annual Conference, New Orleans, LA.

Spillane, J. P., Hallett, T., & Diamond, J. B. (2003). Forms of capital and the construction of leadership: Instructional leadership in urban elementary schools. *Sociology of Education, 78*(1), 1–17.

Stein, M. K., & Nelson, B. S. (2003). Leadership content knowledge. *Educational Evaluation and Policy Analysis, 25*(4, Special Issue on Educational Leadership), 423–448.

Stigler, J. W., & Hiebert, J. (1999). *The teaching gap.* Free Press.

Stoelinga, S. R. (2010). At the intersection of principal and teacher instructional leadership: The case of Donaldson Elementary. *Journal of Cases in Educational Leadership, 13*(2), 21–28.

Supovitz, J., Sirinides, P., & May, H. (2010). How principals and peers influence teaching and learning. *Educational Administration Quarterly, 46*(1), 31–56.

Teacher Leadership Exploratory Consortium. (2011). *Teacher leader model standards.*

Thompson, S. C., Gregg, L., & Niska, J. M. (2004). Professional learning communities, leadership, and student learning. *RMLE Online: Research in Middle Level Education, 28*(1), 15.

Thornton, H. J. (2010). Excellent teachers leading the way: How to cultivate teacher leadership. *Middle School Journal, 41*(4), 36–43.

Weinbaum, A., Allen, D., Blythe, T., Simon, K., Seidel, S., & Rubin, C. (2004). *Teaching as inquiry.* Teachers College Press.

Wenger, E. (1998). *Communities of practice: Learning, meaning, and identity.* Cambridge University Press.

Wenner, J. A., & Campbell, T. (2017). The theoretical and empirical basis of teacher leadership: A review of the literature. *Review of educational research, 87*(1), 134–171.

York-Barr, J., & Duke, K. (2004). What do we know about teacher leadership? Findings from two decades of scholarship. *Review of Educational Research, 74*(3), 255–316.

Youngs, P. (2011, April). *InTASC Model Core Teaching Standards: Research synthesis.* Council of Chief State School Officers.

CHAPTER 7

THE *IT* FACTOR

How Can We Help Teacher Candidates Identify and Improve Their Teaching Dispositions?

Robin E. Hands
University of Connecticut

René Roselle
Sacred Heart University

Andrea Kuhn
Glastonbury Public Schools

June Cahill
Hartford Public Schools

Luke D. Hands
Mansfield Public Schools

ABSTRACT

It is complicated and nuanced work to find ways to positively challenge the growth of a developing teacher and help them identify whether or not they have the dispositions to become an effective and professional educator. While rejecting the simplistic notion that teachers are "born not made," we also acknowledge that there are key dispositions necessary to and shared by

Preparing Quality Teachers:
Advances in Clinical Practice, pp. 155–182
Copyright © 2022 by Information Age Publishing
www.infoagepub.com

155

dynamic educators. Good teaching is easy to talk about and hard to define. It is recognizable when we see *It*. We recognize the *It* factor when we observe a teacher who has *It*, but how do we help teacher candidates recognize their own dispositional strengths and weaknesses? What are the most salient dispositions? How do we measure them? Can they be nurtured or taught? Although caring alone is not enough to constitute competent educational practice, it is an essential element of teacher effectiveness. Exposing teacher candidates to teaching dispositions and asking them to engage in reflective practice by self-assessing their own capacity for caring, engaging in authentic teacher-student relationships, committing to a culturally responsive and nurturing pedagogy, bringing their best professional self into the learning community, and so forth, may lead them one step closer to forming a critically compassionate intellectualism that will have substantive implications for their practice.

Teaching dispositions have been a topic of concern and consideration in teacher preparation programs for a long time (Whitsett et al., 2007). As early as 1933, John Dewey said, "knowledge of methods alone will not suffice; there must be the desire, the will to employ them. This desire is an affair of personal dispositions" (p. 30). The work of studying teacher dispositions has taken a broad and varied path from Comb et al.'s (1969) studies focusing on the idea that the perceptions to which a person is exposed over time shape behavior and dispositions, to the more recent work of Schussler and Knar (2013) that explores "why and how dispositions can operate as a mechanism for enhancing teacher candidates' moral sensibilities" (p. 71). Some questions shaping the conversation have been: We recognize the *It* factor when we observe a teacher who has *It*, but how do we help teacher candidates recognize their own dispositional strengths and weaknesses? What are the most salient dispositions? How do we measure them? Can they be nurtured or taught?

   Good teaching is easy to talk about and hard to define. It is recognizable when we see *It*. Educators are sensitive to the fact that teaching truly is a craft that requires time, experimentation, support, and modeling. Educators are uniquely required to maintain a growth mindset and always be looking to challenge themselves in order to innovate and improve. There are very few jobs that require, and expect, a first-day professional to have the same knowledge and ability as a 20-year veteran, yet this is often the burden placed on educators. It is complicated and nuanced work to find ways to positively challenge the growth of a developing teacher and help them identify whether or not they have the dispositions to become an effective and professional educator. While rejecting the simplistic notion that teachers are "born not made," we also acknowledge that there are key dispositions necessary to and shared by dynamic educators. The question remains, how do we develop and nurture this *It* factor? What tools, that do not fall within the typical scope of teacher evaluation, are necessary to measure growth and effectiveness? How do we quantify these qualities that seem to be so resistant to traditional forms of evaluation, and yet are so pivotal to the success and effectiveness of teaching? Creating a fluid teaching dispositions rubric that informs, rather than restricts, and that creates a common language that educators can use to identify and discuss these important soft skills was the goal of this action research project.

The InTASC Model Core Teaching Standards and Learning Progressions for Teachers (Council of Chief State School Officers, 2013) claims that "the relationship between teacher and learner that defines a teacher's practice moves along a continuum" (p. 13). One of the key assumptions is:

> Expertise in teaching is knowable and teachable. It can be described, supported by research, demonstrated, experienced, and known. While there is a foundational base of practice with developmental benchmarks along a continuum, not all parts of an individual's performance progress along a continuum at exactly the same pace. Rather, a teacher's particular configuration of performances, knowledge, and dispositions may vary with high performance in some areas and weaker performance in others. Certain professional experiences and supports may spark growth in particular areas and, conversely, changes in context may cause a temporary set-back in skill level until the new context is mastered. (p. 11)

The expectation in many teacher preparation programs is that candidates will have a variety of contexts in which they have to adapt and potentially relearn skills they appeared to have mastered somewhere else.

Claxton et al. (2016) state that "dispositions, like thinking interdependently, striving for accuracy, and thinking flexibly are crucial to a person's success in school and life" (p. 63) and that dispositions be included as explicit outcomes. Teachers need to be able to model dispositional characteristics in order to be able to coach students towards acquiring them. Dispositions needn't be mindless habits that one is born with or not. Claxton et al. claim that when facing a problematic situation,

> people can consciously choose to draw on powerful ways of thinking and acting—such as drawing on past knowledge. And as a person becomes more *disposed* to use a particular facet of practical intelligence, that disposition can grow and become more sophisticated. (p. 63)

Clinical practice experiences in teacher preparation are the most authentic and organic places for candidates to develop, practice and be coached in refining their dispositional flexibility and strength.

Advancements in Clinical Practice

In 2010, the National Council for Accreditation of Teacher Education (NCATE) Blue Ribbon Panel released a report called *Transforming Teacher Education Through Clinical Practice: A National Strategy to Prepare Effective Teachers*. The report emphasized the importance for clinical practice to reside at the center of all teacher preparation efforts, identified ten design principles to develop clinical practice programs and included recommendations for sweeping changes in the delivery, monitoring, evaluation, staffing, and oversight of teacher preparation. The Blue Ribbon Panel report was received in the field as confirmation of the need to have clinical practice at the center of teacher preparations, but did not provide a comprehensive process on how to operationalize or how to accomplish that charge in teacher education programs.

In 2015, the American Association of Colleges for Teacher Education (AACTE) formed the Clinical Practice Commission (CPC) to take up the Blue Ribbon Panel report and advance the work by clearly describing clinical practice, recommending a shared lexicon, and identifying exemplary models and pathways on how to enact effective clinical practice. The intention of the work was to be a useable framework for both PK–12 and university-based contexts. The commission was composed of representatives from a variety of PK–24 educational contexts. In 2018, AACTE's Clinical Practice Commission released a report titled *A Pivot Towards Clinical Practice, Its Lexicon, and the Renewal of Educator Preparation*. This comprehensive report offers a framework, guidance, and common lexicon to expand the operationalization of clinical educator preparation. Its 10 proclamations and tenets identify highly effective and evidence-based practices for embedding teacher preparation in the PK–12 environment.

The complete list of AACTE proclamations and tenets are in Appendix A. Many proclamations indirectly address the importance of developing and supporting dispositions, but none more clearly than proclamation eight. The 8th proclamation, or the Mutual Benefit (8) Proclamation, states: *Boundary-spanners, school-based teacher educators, and university-based teacher educators play necessary, vital, and synergistic roles in clinical educator preparation*. In particular, Tenet 2 contends that *School and university-based teacher educators have a joint responsibility to foster teacher candidates' development of the dispositional characteristics necessary to be successful educators*. Based on the recommendations of the AACTE report, it is the responsibility of school and university partnerships to work to ensure candidates are developing along a continuum that results in dispositional awareness and appropriate developmental progress.

Tenet 4 of the Mutual Benefit proclamation further exclaims that the *clinical coaching of candidates is a vital and intensive endeavor that requires strategic and coordinated support. The evaluation of teacher candidates is a shared responsibility among all teacher educators, involving regular and purposeful communication and meaningful, coordinated feedback about candidate progress.* The co-creation of the dispositions rubric tool is an example of how schools and universities can work together in the "preparation, support, and induction of new and aspiring educators, as well as an understanding of the shared responsibility for preparing future educators" (AACTE, 2018, p. 4).

Theoretical Framework

"Students don't care how much you know until they know how much you care."

This is a quote that has been attributed to many people over the years including President Theodore Roosevelt, John Maxwell, Earl Nightingale, and others. More recently, this concept of caring and creating a culture of care has been galvanized in the theoretical framework Cammarota and Romero (2006a) refer to as "*critically compassionate intellectualism* [Emphasis original] (CCI)—a trilogy of critical pedagogy, authentic caring, and social justice–oriented curriculum" (Rector-Aranda, 2018, p. 388). The framework was originally intended to be used with Latinx youth to help them "comprehend systemic oppressions affecting them and their communities, so that they could rise above these limitations and create better worlds for themselves and others" (Rector-Aranda, 2018, p. 388). However, Rector-Aranda (2018) contends that "we should expand frameworks such as CCI into teacher education" (p. 388).

A theoretical framework promoting compassion and caring is not a novel idea. In 1993, John Goodlad, Roger Soder and Kenneth Sirotnik created the *Moral Dimensions of Teaching* framework that included practicing a nurturing pedagogy with an emphasis on educators forming authentic, caring, compassionate relationships with students in an effort to nurture the well-being and learning of every student. The framework challenges educators to think as much about who they teach as what they teach and to be culturally responsive in ways that validate the experiences that students and their families bring to the classroom.

Although caring alone is not enough to constitute competent educational practice, it is an essential element of teacher effectiveness. We can teach our teacher candidates how to teach, but can we teach them how to care? Exposing them to teaching dispositions and asking them to engage in reflective practice by self-assessing their own capacity for caring, engaging in authentic teacher-student relationships, committing to a culturally responsive and nurturing pedagogy, bringing their best professional self into the learning community, and so forth, may lead them one step closer to forming a CCI that will have substantive implications for their practice.

The Challenge of Teaching Dispositions

The challenges of candidates presenting with a lack of dispositional readiness for engagement in clinic are many and have wide-sweeping ramifications for teacher effectiveness and P–12 learning. Rarely is a teacher candidate in jeopardy of being discontinued from a teacher preparation program because of a lack of content knowledge, typically it has more to do with dispositions essential for teaching. Soft skills (Kyllonen, 2013), or dispositions, are necessary to promote and sustain a teacher's ability to engage and empathize with students; respond with cultural awareness and sensitivity; collaborate with colleagues in applicable ways; act, dress and speak professionally while in the school setting; read and appropriately respond to social cues; and maintain a sense of humor, to name a few. We can teach our candidates to teach, but we cannot teach them to care, or can we? Although caring has to emanate from within their own set of core values, can those core values be encouraged or enhanced to align with their intentions to teach with effectiveness and empathy?

When teacher candidates struggle to perform in ways that demonstrate dispositional readiness for the classroom, they require support and coaching, much in the ways that AACTE has recommended. In order for this process to be authentic, the teacher candidate must first begin by identifying the teaching dispositions with which they struggle. Because of the nuanced nature of teaching dispositions, it can be difficult for teacher candidates to be fully self-aware of what challenges them and yet Schussler and Knar (2013) contend that, "In order to align candidates' intention with their perceptions and their practice, teacher education programs must provide opportunities for candidates to consider how their values and ideals translate into actions in specific contexts" (p. 84). More "boundary objects" or tools are needed that are constructed to assist school and university-based educators to support candidate growth. According to Moje et al. (2004), third space has been positioned in education research as a space in which to: (1) build bridges between marginalized discourses; (2) allow members to navigate across different discourse communities; and (3) create conversational spaces that bring competing discourses into dialogue with each other. The dispositions rubric that is at the center of this action research was created in the critical third space with colleagues from the field.

Given the multi-contextual and multi-organizational terrain of teacher education *and* the need to develop horizontal expertise, we argue that boundary objects are particularly critical tools to implemented practice-based teacher education. Boundary objects are concrete, material resources that reify lived experiences, practices, and thought, freezing them into representations (Graven, 2004). They must be malleable enough to address the various constraints and demands of local settings yet structured enough to maintain some common identity.

Boundary objects can facilitate communication across university and school-based teacher educators by serving as focal points around which connections can be made across settings. They can also serve to assist people to organize their work with preservice teachers in their respective settings (Anagnostopoulos et al., 2010; Cobb et al., 2003) and can coordinate work even when they are used differently and hold different meanings for people (Star & Griesemer, 1989). Even resistance to boundary objects among some groups can contribute to horizontal expertise as using the objects in their settings can prompt people to articulate, reexamine, and enact existing conceptions and practices more deliberately.

Boundary objects are essential to practice-based teacher education for several reasons. Identifying and developing a set of boundary objects that instructors and preservice teachers can use across various university courses and clinical placements can help create the *curricular coherency* that university-based teacher education currently lacks. They can also facilitate the creation of *horizontal expertise* (Engeström, 1996; Gutiérrez, 2008) across the university and school settings as well as across the different divisions within university teacher education. Boundary objects have the potential to create *stronger partnerships* with *shared ownership* over the preparation of future teachers, create a *common language* between stakeholders, and can serve to *simultaneously renew* (Goodlad, 1994) both settings.

The Action Plan Process

Engaging in a process that results in a supportive Action Plan for teacher candidates who struggle to experience success in their field placements, offers one way to provide a coaching mechanism in an effort to raise teacher candidate self-awareness. These plans are co-designed with the teacher candidate, the school-based teacher educator, the university supervisor, and the faculty advisor. Their purpose is to target specific behaviors and attitudes that need to improve in order for the teacher candidate to be successful. However, because the issues are rarely related to a content deficit, the conversations are often uncomfortable and amorphous, and the process is more intuitive than empirical.

After having one of these difficult conversations with a struggling teacher candidate, a school-based teacher educator was committed to working with the university to design a teaching dispositions rubric (Appendix C) that would begin to put the "*It*-factor" into words. The hope was to give the school and university a common language to use when attempting to identify areas of challenge in an effort to target specific attitudes and behaviors that need to improve in order for the teacher candidate to be successful. AACTE identifies the need for common language in proclamation number 9, The Common Language Proclamation. The proclamation describes *coalescing the language of teacher preparation and teaching around a common lexicon facilitates a shared understanding of and reference to the roles, responsibilities, and experiences essential to high-quality clinical preparation.*

In a case study that was designed to pilot the Teaching Dispositions Rubric, a struggling teacher candidate (Lisa) used the boundary object in an effort to self-assess her areas of strength and her need for improvement regarding dispositions essential to effective teaching. There were initial concerns at the outset of Lisa's placement. During her first few days, it was apparent that she had a difficult time relating to colleagues. Lisa interrupted conversations during team meetings, often to give unsolicited advice or input. She did not demonstrate active listening skills, and did not pick up on social cues when the professionals around the table were signaling their disinterest in her opinions. Her school-based teacher educator became frustrated that Lisa's behavior was causing difficulty during team meetings with colleagues, and so she spoke with her about her role as an active listener.

Additionally, Lisa had inappropriate conversations with students. For example, on one occasion she was showing off her expensive phone to a group of elementary students during snack time, telling them that she had to have the latest version due to her love of photography. When told by her school-based teacher educator that this was not an appropriate conversation to have with students, she became defensive.

Early on in the placement, it is typical for preservice teachers to observe the mentor teacher for a majority of the day. Lisa was disengaged during long periods of the day, sitting at the back table on her laptop. When her mentor teacher talked with her, Lisa stated she was working on some of her lessons that were due the following week. Similarly, when the teacher asked her to create a bulletin board as one of her first tasks, she spent the rest of the school day asking questions and planning for the bulletin board instead of being engaged in what was happening in the classroom with student learning.

As the school-based teacher educator became increasingly frustrated with these and other concerns, it became apparent that a larger conversation was needed. The many smaller conversations didn't seem to be making a difference, especially given that Lisa was often defensive. This was a perfect time to use the Teaching Dispositions Rubric to set expectations. Lisa used the rubric to self-assess. Then the school-based and university educators sat down with Lisa, together they examined the rubric and were able to give her specific examples of where her behaviors fell in order to create an action plan. At first Lisa was defensive, but the behaviors were spelled out on the rubric (Appendix C) along a continuum, so there was very little room for her to argue, and there was a common language with which to shape the conversation and identify learning targets in order to co-construct an action plan (Appendix B).

Establishing a Professional Learning Community

"Simultaneous inquiry" was the process used to pursue this problem of practice (Roselle et al., 2017). Simultaneous inquiry is derived from the concept of "simultaneous renewal" (Sirotnik & Goodlad, 1988), a term coined by the late John Goodlad as a way for universities and public schools to engage in life-giving partnerships that create a foundation for renewal. Hands & Rong (2014) contend that, "Partnerships between teacher preparation programs and public schools are essential in providing contextual experiences for teacher candidates. The schools serve as the clinical sites where the theories and practical applications are visible and active" (p. 454).

School and university-based teacher educators held regular meetings, in person and electronically, to explore the research on teaching dispositions, and to begin to create a tool that could be used with teacher candidates who require more support. The University of Maryland, Baltimore County, Spring Arbor University had created a teaching dispositions rubric that was used as a template in the initial rubric design. Other descriptors were taken from teaching dispositions rubrics generated by several different universities, and from the professional teacher evaluation tool used by a partner school district.

Once a rubric was created, it required field testing. The school-based teacher educator who had initiated the teaching dispositions rubric development process and was hosting a struggling teacher candidate, agreed to serve as a member of the professional learning community, along with a school principal, and another school-based educator who was also hosting a teacher candidate who was experiencing difficulty in the classroom. The group decided that the rubric could be used as part of an Action Plan process to help support teacher candidates. A meeting with each teacher candidate, the corresponding school-based teacher educator and the university's director of school/university partnerships ensued. The rubric was used by the teacher candidates as an exercise in self-assessment and to encourage a growth-mindset (Haimovitz & Dweck, 2017). The school-based teacher educators also filled out the rubric in order to calibrate with the one completed by their teacher candidate. Finally, the director of school/

university partnerships facilitated Action Plan conversations in which the teacher candidate and school-based teacher educators were encouraged to share their perspectives using the language and qualitative measures provided by the rubric. As a result, specific and measurable learning targets were formed in order to support the teacher candidates in the successful completion of their clinical placement.

Following several field tests like those described, the professional learning community made edits to the rubric. Some of the language was made more prescriptive, and in order to build in accountability, a place for comments and specific evidence was added to each section of the rubric. Currently, when an Action Plan is needed, the teacher candidate, the school-based teacher educator, and the university supervisor fill out the rubric, separately, and then meet with the director of school/university partnerships to review the rubric. Instead of this process being intuitive and resorting to vague phrases such as, "Smiling would go a long way toward helping you to connect with your students," or "I think your school-based teacher educator is looking for you to exhibit a teachable spirit," the team is able to point to a particular disposition and use common language to identify growth targets and set measurable goals.

At the conclusion of a recent Action Plan meeting, using the teaching dispositions rubric to engage in a difficult and sensitive conversation about the teacher candidate's areas of struggle, the teacher candidate remarked, "Thank you for having the courage to point these things out to me, because if you hadn't told me I was coming across like this, I would never have known, and I want to be the best teacher I can be." That teacher candidate has embraced the process of regularly reflecting on the teaching dispositions that she finds difficult to embody and through coaching and practice, she has been able to become more relatable with her students, more collaborative with her colleagues, and more confident regarding her own teaching practices. This confirmed the need for an instrument that can help teacher candidates to identify the teaching dispositions with which they struggle and to create an Action Plan that can provide them with the support and guidance necessary for growth.

Furthermore, the pragmatic reality is that the litigious society in which we reside necessitates an audit trail if a teacher candidate is not able to successfully complete a teacher preparation program. A college of education is not inexpensive and education majors are in a unique position, as the major requires a field experience in order to qualify for professional state licensure. The student teaching experience is typically the culminating experience, so if a student is not able to demonstrate successful practice in the classroom, s/he graduates with a four-year degree, but is not able to seek professional certification as an educator. Parents are understandably unhappy that they have invested in their child's education, only to be told that the student cannot be recommended for professional licensure. The rubric offers empirical data to use in navigating these difficult decisions and potentially contentious situations.

Currently the dispositions rubric has only been used with senior teacher candidates. There is utility to systematizing the use of the rubric with junior teacher candidates in an effort to introduce them to the language and help them to target specific areas of growth that they can address prior to their sustained student teaching experience. The goal is to build capacity to support students to become the most effective teacher educators they can be by being intentional and purposeful in identifying and supporting their dispositional growth. Like Claxton et al (2016), we believe "a school's culture will also benefit when students—and teachers—develop these kinds of attributes, which are as cognitively demanding as any technical 'skill'" (p. 64).

Implications for Clinical Practice in Teacher Education

Teaching effectiveness is directly related to teaching dispositions. When teacher candidates enter a teacher preparation program, they need to understand that their soft skillset will be just as important to their practice as their content knowledge. Because teaching is a relational practice, it requires trust, empathy, reflection, collaboration, and humor. However, people, in general, have blind spots—they do not always see themselves as others do. This is why it is important to create a common lexicon that can be used by teacher candidates as an exercise in self-examination and assessment, and by school and university-based teacher educators as a way to calibrate the teacher candidate's reflection in order to identify areas of strength and to set goals for growth. Putting words to the *It* factor and creating a boundary object to use as a tool for identifying areas in need of growth, paves the way for coaching teacher candidates to examine and expand their capacity for developing teaching dispositions that will effectively shape their practice. It is important to introduce the teaching dispositions early in the teacher preparation program so that preservice teachers have an opportunity to improve their soft skill set prior to doing their fulltime student teaching. "Genuine compassion and relational connection—creating contexts of mutuality, respect, and authentic care … and providing and modeling this for our teacher education students is an important part of helping them become caring and just teachers themselves" (Rector-Aranda, 2018, p. 397).

Using a boundary object to assess teaching dispositions also provides a measure of accountability and an audit trail for school and university-based teacher educators who must document and defend the decisions they make on behalf of teacher candidates. These decisions have widespread ramifications, for teacher candidates, but also for P–12 students who need to be protected from incompetent teaching practices. It is the job of the teacher preparation program to determine whether or not a teacher candidate is competent to practice and that cannot be truly ascertained without considering effective and appropriate teaching dispositions.

The means by which the Teaching Dispositions Rubric was created also has implications for clinic, as *simultaneous inquiry* provides a rich and authentic forum for school and university-based teacher educators to collaborate in order to enhance the quality and efficacy of teacher preparation programs. This model has the potential to draw on the strengths and expertise of both the public-school practitioner and the university scholar in an effort to improve clinical practice and to promote CCI and nurturing pedagogy.

REFERENCES

Anagnostopoulos, D., Sykes, G., McCrory, R., Cannata, M., & Frank, K. (2010). Dollars, distinction, or duty? The meaning of the National Board for Professional Teaching Standards for teachers' work and collegial relations. *American Journal of Education, 116*(3), 337–369. https://doi.org/10.1086/651412

American Association of Colleges of Teacher Education. (2018). *A pivot towards clinical practice, its lexicon, and the renewal of educator preparation: A report of the AACTE Clinical Practice Commission*.

Cammarota, J., & Romero, A. (2006). A critically compassionate intellectualism for Latina/o students: Raising voices above the silencing in our schools. *Multicultural Education, 14*(2), 16–23.

Claxton, G., Costa, A. L., & Kallick, B. (2016). Hard thinking about soft skills. *Educational Leadership, 73*(6), 60–64.

Combs, A., W., Soper, D. W., Goodling, C.T., Benton, J. A., Dickman, J. F., & Usher, R. H. (1969). *Florida studies in the helping profession* (Social Science Monograph #37). University of Florida Press.

Cobb, P., Confrey, J., diSessa, A., Lehrer, R., & Schauble, L. (2003). Design experiments in educational research. *Educational Researcher, 32*(1), 9–13.

Council of Chief State School Officers. (2013, April). Interstate Teacher Assessment and Support Consortium In *TASC Model Core Teaching Standards and Learning Progressions for Teachers 1.0: A Resource for Ongoing Teacher Development*.

Dewey, J. (1933). *How we think: A restatement of the relation of reflective thinking to the educative process*. D.C. Heath and Company.

Engeström Y. (1996). Developmental work research as educational research. *Nordisk Pedagogik: Journal of Nordic Educational Research, 16*(5), 131–143.

Goodlad, J. I. (1994). *Educational renewal: Better teachers, better schools*. Jossey-Bass.

Goodlad , R. Soder, & K. A. Sirotnik (Eds). (1993). *The moral dimensions of teaching*. Jossey-Bass.

Graven, M. (2004). Investigating mathematics teacher learning within an in-service community of practice: The centrality of confidence. *Educational Studies in Mathematics, 57*(2), 177–211.

Gutiérrez, K. D. (2008). Developing a sociocritical literacy in the third space. *Reading Research Quarterly, 43*(2), 148–164.

Haimovitz, K., & Dweck, C. S. (2017, Nov/Dec). The origins of children's growth and fixed mindsets: New research and a new proposal. *Child Development, 88*(6), 1849–1859.

Hands, R.E., & Rong, Y. (2014). Schools as clinics: Learning about practice in practice. *Peabody Journal of Education, 89*(4), 453–465.

Kyllonen, P. C. (2013, Nov/Dec). Soft skills for the workplace. *Change, 45*(6), 16–23.

Moje, E., Ciechanowski, K. M., Kramer, K., Ellis, L., Carrillo, R., & Collazo, T. (2004). Working toward third space in content area literacy: An examination of everyday funds of knowledge and discourse. *Reading Research Quarterly, 39*(1), 38–70.

Rector-Aranda, A. (2018). Critically compassionate intellectualism in teacher education: The contributions of relational–cultural theory. *Journal of Teacher Education, 70*(4), 388–400. https://doi.org/10.1177/0022487118786714

Roselle, R., Hands, R., Anagnostopoulos, D., Levine, T., Cahill, J., Kuhn, A., & Plis, C., (2017). Simultaneous inquiry: Renewing partnerships and people in professional development schools. *School-University Partnerships: The Journal of the National Association for Professional Development Schools, 10*(4), 74–82.

Schussler, D. L., & Knarr, L. (2013). Building awareness of dispositions: Enhancing moral sensibilities in teaching. *Journal of Moral Education, 42*(1), 71–87.

Sirotnik, K. A., & Goodlad, J. I. (1988). *School-university partnerships in action: Concepts, cases, and concerns.* Teachers College Press.

Star, S. L., & J. R. Griesemer. (1989). Institutional ecology, translations, and boundary objects: Amateurs and professionals in Berkeley's Museum of vertebrate zoology, 1907–1939. *Social Studies of Science, 19,* 387–420.

Whitsett, G., Roberso, T., Julian, K., & Beckham, L. (2007). First year teacher's reported levels of functioning on selected professional dispositions. *Education, 128*(1), 95–102.

APPENDIX A

Essential Proclamations and Tenets for Highly Effective Clinical Educator Preparation

1.

THE CENTRAL PROCLAMATION
Clinical practice is central to high-quality teacher preparation.

Clinical practice serves as the central framework through which all teacher preparation programming is conceptualized and designed. The process of learning to teach requires sustained and ongoing opportunities to engage in authentic performance within diverse learning environments, where course work complements and aligns with field experiences that grow in complexity and sophistication over time and enable candidates to develop the skills necessary to teach all learners.

2.

THE PEDAGOGY PROCLAMATION
As pedagogy is the science of teaching, the intentional integration of pedagogical training into an educator preparation program is the cornerstone of effective clinical practice.

The presence of strong, embedded pedagogical training is the hallmark of effective clinical educator preparation. Pedagogy serves as a guidepost for shared professional standards of best practices in teaching that in turn guide the development of clinical practice models.

3.

THE SKILLS PROCLAMATION
Clinical practice includes, supports, and complements the innovative and requisite skills, strategies, and tools that improve teacher preparation by using high-leverage practices as part of a commitment to continuous renewal for all learning sites.

University-based teacher educators, school-based teacher educators, and boundary-spanning teacher educators in successful clinical partnerships pioneer innovative roles and practices without the restrictions of traditional assumptions about educator preparation. Mechanisms for teacher preparation and professional teacher development are aligned, research based, and professionally embedded.

4.

THE PARTNERSHIP PROCLAMATION
Clinical partnerships are the foundation of highly effective clinical practice.

Clinical partnership, as distinct from clinical practice, is the vehicle by which the vision of renewing teacher preparation through clinical practice becomes operational. Effective clinical partnerships allow for mutually beneficial outcomes and are gateways to developing reflective practice while simultaneously renewing teaching and learning in PK-12 classrooms.

5.

THE INFRASTRUCTURE PROCLAMATION
Sustainable and shared infrastructure is required for successful clinical partnership.

Clear governance structures and sustainable funding models are key to establishing and maintaining successful clinical partnerships. Individual preparation programs and school districts have different needs and resources. The roles and responsibilities of both school and university partners must be clearly articulated and defined.

6.

THE DEVELOPMENTAL PROCLAMATION
Clinical partnerships are facilitated and supported through an understanding of the continuum of development and growth that typifies successful, mutually beneficial collaborations.

A metacognitive teaching progression is needed when establishing and growing clinical partnerships. This progression is nonlinear and requires diligent commitment by all partners. While successful partnerships share some common stages and actions, each partnership possesses unique characteristics specific to local contexts. Ongoing assessment of partnerships is necessary to ensure continued efficacy and sustainability.

7.

THE EMPOWERMENT PROCLAMATION
As emerging professionals, teacher candidates are essential contributors and collaborators within clinical programs and partnerships.

The needs and responsibilities of teacher candidates should be factored into the curricula and infrastructures of educator preparation programs and clinical partnerships. The progression of embedded teaching and learning experiences is essential to empowering teacher candidates to take active roles during their practicum experiences, as well as to be profession- and learner-ready once they matriculate into their own classrooms.

8.

THE MUTUAL BENEFIT PROCLAMATION
Boundary-spanners, school-based teacher educators, and university-based teacher educators play necessary, vital, and synergistic roles in clinical educator preparation.

Both school-based and university-based teacher educators must be highly qualified professionals who value one another's expertise. Both also must reconceptualize their roles to effectively model best teaching practice, engage candidates as coteachers, and integrate course work into school-based experiences. The clinical coaching of candidates is a vital and intensive endeavor that requires strategic and coordinated support.

9.

THE COMMON LANGUAGE PROCLAMATION
Coalescing the language of teacher preparation and teaching around a common lexicon facilitates a shared understanding of and reference to the roles, responsibilities, and experiences essential to high-quality clinical preparation.

Implementing a common lexicon for clinical educator preparation facilitates consistency in the preparation, support, and induction of new and aspiring educators, as well as an understanding of the shared responsibility for preparing future educators. A shared lexicon establishes a more unified profession and enables external stakeholders to better understand the aspirations and real-world practice of the teaching profession.

10.

THE EXPERTISE PROCLAMATION
Teaching is a profession requiring specialized knowledge and preparation. Educators are the pedagogical and content experts. It is through the assertion and application of this expertise that they can inform the process and vision for renewing educator preparation.

While external stakeholders play a role in the development of policies and regulations that affect educator preparation and licensure, educators themselves must take the lead to guide, shape, and define the parameters and renewal of their profession. Schools and universities must recognize and support the vital role that educators play in preparing the next generation of teachers by setting appropriate policies for tenure, promotion, and compensation. External stakeholders and policy makers are also vital allies in securing support for efficacious models through dedicated funding streams and other arrangements.

APPENDIX B

Lisa's Action Plan

September 26, 2019

To: Lisa, Intern
cc:René Roselle, PhD, Interim Director of Teacher Education Programs

From: Robin Hands, EdD, Director School-University Partnerships

SUBJECT: Action Plan to Support Lisa's Successful Completion of her Internship Experience

Background
This contract is a proactive effort to support success for Lisa in her master's year in the IB/M program and is not meant to be punitive.

Lisa is a master's level student who is participating in a yearlong internship experience at Hall Memorial Middle School in Willington, CT. In the first few weeks, Lisa has exhibited some challenges with regard to teaching dispositions. Her internship supervisor, the school principal, and her seminar leader, have all expressed some concern regarding Lisa's affect. Lisa has been asked to use a teaching dispositions rubric that will help to measure specific professional behaviors and attitudes necessary to be an effective teacher. She will use the rubric to self-assess and her internship supervisor has also been asked to use the rubric to indicate some areas of challenge for Lisa. These data will be referenced in the design of this Action Plan. The following dispositions have been identified and the attached rubric will be used to track Lisa's growth over time.

Action Plan
Areas Requiring Improvement as Identified on the Teaching Dispositions Rubric:
- Collegiality with colleagues and students—**emerging**—will practice displaying greater enthusiasm and confidence with adults and children—smile more, use humor, ask questions that show interest—take every opportunity to engage relationally
- Affect and Interpersonal Relationships with Students—**unacceptable**—will work toward demonstrating caring, kindness, patience, humor, and vulnerability—make relational connections
- Interpersonal Skills with Colleagues—**target**—but will focus more on asking questions of teachers with whom Lisa is working, i.e., *"I wonder if I could …?" "Is there any way I can support you?" "Is that helpful or is there something else I should do?"*

- Social Cues—**emerging**—will practice recognizing and reacting to a variety of situations using a nuanced approach, including tone of voice, choice of words, etc. —needs to demonstrate
  intuition and the ability to relate to and empathize with others—
  every context demands a different type of response—it will be
  important for Lisa to check in with the adults in her purview in
  order to gauge the appropriateness of her responses and self-
  regulate, accordingly
- Engagement—**emerging**—will practice scanning the room in
  the interest of student safety and classroom management—could
  set a vibration on her phone for 5–7 minute increments—think
  about body placement so that she can see students – maybe use
  a visual cue as a reminder to scan (i.e., green and red plastic
  cups turned upside down on the table when a small group needs
  help—red on top—and is fine—green on top)
- Responding to Feedback—**unacceptable**—will practice a verbal
  response that indicates that Lisa is hearing and considering feedback from her supervisor, the school administration, and teachers with whom she is interfacing, i.e., *"I hear what you are saying
  and I am going to think about how to apply it."*

Next Steps

Lisa will reflect on each of the identified dispositions on a regular basis and
discuss her progress and her challenges with Bill. The goal would be for
Lisa to move toward "Acceptable," in all areas, on the Teaching Dispositions Rubric.

Another meeting with Lisa, Bill, and Robin, needs to be planned for some
time during the first two weeks of November, in order to assess progress.

School Principal C will be observing and we can arrange for other observations, as needed or requested.

Lisa could videotape herself and reflect on her teaching. It might be helpful to process this with another person.

Lisa	October 3, 2019
Lisa, Intern	Date
Robin E. Hands	October 3, 2019
Robin Hands, Ed.D.,	Date
Director of School-University Partnerships	
Bill	October 3, 2019
Bill, Internship Supervisor	Date

APPENDIX C

Lisa's Teaching Dispositions Rubric

Teacher Candidate/Intern's Name: Lisa, Intern

Clinic/Cooperating Teacher/Internship Supervisor Name: Bill, Internship Supervisor

Other Participant's Name(s): Dr. Robin E. Hands, UConn, Director of School-University Partnerships

Date: September 26, 2019

This document was used to assess and target teaching dispositions that require attention and support in an Action Plan.

Demonstrates Professionalism					
	UNACCEPTABLE (Unaware or unwilling to admit there is a problem	EMERGING (Awareness, articulation, identification)	TARGET (Puts into practice, implements)	EXEMPLARY (Builds on reflection, makes changes to improve practice, expands, connects)	NOT OBSERVED
Attendance	Consistently absent or late for classes/meetings/obligations.	Occasionally absent or late for classes/meetings/obligations.	Rarely absent or late for classes/meetings/obligations.	Consistently present and on time for classes/meetings/obligations and is prepared with all necessary materials.	
Appearance	Consistently dresses and maintains an appearance that is inappropriate based on social setting and role.	Occasionally dresses and maintains an appearance that is inappropriate based on social setting and role.	Regularly dresses and maintains an appearance that is appropriate based on social setting and role.	Consistently dresses and maintains an appearance that surpasses what is expected based on social setting and role.	

(Appendix C continued on next page)

APPENDIX C (CONTINUED)

Demeanor	Loses composure frequently. Avoids personal responsibility for his/her emotions and behaviors, blaming others or outside circumstances for loss of emotional control.	Loses composure under stressful situations. Does not always accept personal responsibility for his/her actions.	Regularly maintains professional demeanor and composure. Accepts and reflects upon alternative methods of expressing emotions, making sincere amends for rare loss of control.	Consistently maintains composure and professional demeanor even in stressful situations. Is consistently positive, enthusiastic, and confident. Accepts complete responsibility for actions, employing effective conflict resolution strategies.	
Ethical Behavior	Displays a pattern of dishonesty or deceitful behavior. Deliberately lies for personal advantage. Betrays confidences. Does not treat others fairly and equitably. Does not exert reasonable effort to protect others from conditions that interfere with learning or are harmful in any way.	Is mostly truthful and honest in dealing with others, except in minor and isolated circumstances.	Is truthful and honest in dealing with others. Maintains confidentiality. Exibits consistent and equitable treatment of others. Exerts reasonable efforts to protect others from conditions that interfere with learning or are harmful in any way.	Has a reputation for always being truthful and honest in dealing with others. Always maintains confidentialtiy.	

Ethical Behavior		Inconsistently maintains confidentiality. Usually treats others fairly and equitably. Sometimes exerts reasonable effort to protect others from conditions that interfere with learning or are harmful in any way.		Demonstrates and advocates for equitable treatment of others. Initiates preventive measures to protect others from conditions that interfere with learning or are harmful in any other way.	
Collegiality with Colleagues and Students	Interaction with colleagues and students is minimal or inappropriate.	Interaction with colleagues and students is limited or occasionally inappropriate.	Interaction with colleagues and students is minimal or appropriate and engaging.	Interaction with colleagues and students is consistent, appropriate, positive, productive, and engaging.	

Comments:

Lisa will practice displaying greater enthusiasm and confidence with adults and children —smile more, use humor, ask questions that show interest—take every opportunity to engage relationally.

Specific Evidence:

	Creates a Positive Learning Environment				
	UNACCEPTABLE (Unaware or unwilling to admit there is a problem	**EMERGING** (Awareness, articulation, identification)	**TARGET** (Puts into practice, implements)	**EXEMPLARY** (Builds on reflection, makes changes to improve practice, expands, connects)	**NOT OBSERVED**

(Appendix C continued on next page)

APPENDIX C (CONTINUED)

Community Building	Does not foster a sense of belonging for students.	Attempts to foster a sense of belonging by allowing students to express thoughts and ideas, build relationships, practice collaboration, and take academic risks in an atmosphere of emotional safety.	Fosters a sense of belonging by allowing students to express thoughts and ideas, build relationships, practice collaboration, and take academic risks in an atmosphere of emotional safety.	Continuously fosters a sense of belonging by allowing students to express thoughts and ideas, build relationships, practice collaboration, and take academic risks in an atmosphere of emotional safety.	
Affect and Interpersonal Relationships with Students	Does not demonstrate caring. Does not smile often. Does not remain calm or model kindness, patience, or vulnerability. Does not admit mistakes.	Inconsistently demonstrates caring. Attempts to remain calm in most circumstances and occasionally models kindness, patience, and vulnerability. Is reluctant to admit mistakes.	Frequently demonstrates caring by maintaining a cheerful disposition with students and smiling often. Remains calm most of the time and takes opportunities to model kindness, patience, and vulnerability. Admits mistakes and models lifelong learning for students.	Actively demonstrates caring by maintaining a cheerful disposition with students and smiling often. Remains calm at all times and takes every opportunity to model kindness, patience, and vulnerability. Is willing to admit mistakes and models lifelong learning for students.	

| Classroom Management Strategies | Is not able to engage students in learning. Does not establish or maintains classroom procedures and rules. Does not follow through with consquences or employ classroom management strategies. | Seeks to engage students by challenging and respecting their varied readiness levels, interests and needs. Attempts to establish and maintains classroom procedures and rules. Occasionanly follows through with consquences. Attempts to employ strategies such as circulating the room, holding class meetings and offering student choice, etc. | Engages students by challenging and respecting their varied readiness levels, interests and needs. Establishes and maintains clear and consistent classroom procedures and rules. Follows through with consquences. Employs strategies such as circulating the room, holding class meetings and offering student choice, etc. | Regularly engages students by challenging and respecting their varied readiness levels, interests and needs. Establishes and maintains clear and consistent classroom procedures and rules. Consistently follows through with consquences. Regularly employs strategies such as circulating the room, holding class meetings and offering student choice, etc. | |

Comments:

Lisa will work toward demonstrating caring, kindness, patience, humor and vulnerability —making relational connections.

Specific evidence:

(Appendix C continued on next page)

APPENDIX C (CONTINUED)

Communicates Effectively					
	UNACCEPT-ABLE (Unaware or unwilling to admit there is a problem	**EMERG-ING** (Aware-ness, ar-ticulation, identifica-tion)	**TARGET** (Puts into practice, imple-ments)	**EXEMPLA-RY** (Builds on reflec-tion, makes changes to improve practice, expands, connects)	**NOT OB-SERVED**
Oral Com-munication	Oral communi-cation does not effectively con-vey meaning and is dimin-ished and/or compromised.	Oral com-munication detracts from con-veying meaning and is di-minished and/or compro-mised.	Oral com-munication effectively conveys meaning and is easily understood.	Oral com-munication is consistently clear, engag-ing, and pro-fessional.	
Written Communi-cation	Written com-munication contains abun-dant errors and does not con-vey meaning.	Written communi-cation con-tains mul-tiple errors that detract from con-veying meaning.	Written communica-tion con-tains mini-mal errors and conveys meaning.	Written com-munication is free from errors and conveys meaning in a powerful and professional way.	

Interpersonal Skills with Colleagues	Interactions with peers, colleagues, or school and university personnel are often negative, demeaning, sarcastic, combative, or inappropriate. Often treats others rudely or with disrespect. Does not listen and or contribute appropriately to conversations and discussions.	Interactions with peers, colleagues, or school and university personnel are sometimes negative, demeaning, sarcastic, combative, or inappropriate. Sometimes treats others rudely or with disrespect. Often does not listen or contribute appropriately to conversations and discussions.	Interactions with peers, colleagues, or school and university personnel are positive, appropriate, respectful, and courteous in both words and actions. Listens and contributes to conversations and discussions when appropriate.	Interactions with peers, colleagues, or school and university personnel are consistently positive and engaging in both words and actions. Actively listens and contributes when appropriate. Exudes courtesy and respect.	
Social Cues	Does not recognize social cues and react to them appropriately. Lacks intuition and ability to relate to and empathize with others.	Has some difficulty recognizing social cues and reacting appropriately. Has limited intuition and ability to relate to and empathize with others.	Recognizes social cues and reacts to them appropriately. Demonstrates intuition and the ability to relate to and empathize with others.	Is sensitive to social cues and reacts to them appropriately. Demonstrates intuition and the ability to empathize and relate to others. Demonstrates leadership qualities.	

(*Appendix C continued on next page*)

APPENDIX C (CONTINUED)

Comments:

Although "on target for **Interpersonal Skills with Colleagues**," Lisa will focus more on asking questions of teachers with whom she is working, i.e., *"I wonder if I could . . .?" "Is there any way I can support you?" "Is that helpful or is there something else I should do?"*

With regard to **Social Cues**, Lisa will practice recognizing and reacting to a variety of situations using a nuanced approach, including tone of voice, choice of words, etc. – needs to demonstrate intuition and the ability to relate to and empathize with others – every context demands a different type of response – it will be important for Lisa to check in with the adults in her purview in order to gauge the appropriateness of her responses and self-regulate, accordingly.

Specific evidence:

Self-Regulates Personal Learning					
	UNACCEPT-ABLE (Unaware or unwilling to admit there is a problem	**EMERG-ING (Aware-ness, ar-ticulation, identifica-tion)**	**TARGET (Puts into practice, imple-ments)**	**EXEMPLA-RY (Builds on reflec-tion, makes changes to improve practice, expands, connects)**	**NOT OB-SERVED**
Initiative	Is consistently passive and does not initi-ate activities or conversation.	Is often passive and seldom initiates activities or conversa-tion.	Actively looks for ways to be helpful and engages. Initiates activities or conversa-tions.	Creates op-portunities to be useful and active. Con-sistently initi-ates activities or conversa-tions.	
Completes Assign-ments	Frequently turns in as-signments late. Does not fol-low directions. Needs exten-sive support to understand and complete assignments.	Turns in some as-signments late. Needs extended time and or support to understand and com-plete as-signments.	Consistently submits assign-ments on time. Usu-ally follows directions and asks for clarification if needed.	Completes all assign-ments on time with minimal sup-port. Follows directions and exceeds expectations.	

Engage-ment	Consistently distracted or disengaged from the learning environment.	Occasion-ally dis-tracted or disengaged from the learning environment.	Regularly engages in and is at-tentive to the learning environment.	Consistently engages in and is at-tentive to the learning environment. Facilitates the engagement of others.	
Responding to Feedback	Resists con-structive feedback and suggestions or responds nega-tively. Does not follow through.	Occasion-ally takes suggestions and con-structive feedback, but may not always follow through. May resist some con-structive feedback or sugges-tions.	Takes con-structive feedback and sugges-tions from students, colleagues, and super-visors and uses them to improve.	Actively seeks out construc-tive feedback and sugges-tions from students, colleagues, and super-visors and uses them to continuously improve. Ex-udes a desire to learn.	
Self-Reflection	Fails to take responsibility for successes and mistakes; blames oth-ers. Does not reflect on per-formance or progress.	Takes re-sponsibil-ity for suc-cesses and mistakes, but fails to take steps to improve or correct. Occasion-ally reflects on perfor-mance or progress.	Takes re-sponsibility for success-es and mis-takes. Seeks to make improve-ments and regularly self-reflects on perfor-mance and progress.	Consistently self-reflects and adjusts to make improve-ments. Takes ownership of progress and performance and strives to meet exemplary standards.	

(Appendix C continued on next page)

APPENDIX C (CONTINUED)

Comments:

With regard to **Engagment**, Lisa will practice scanning the room in the interest of student safety and classroom management—could set a vibration on her phone for 5–7 minute increments—think about body placement so that she can see students—maybe use a visual cue as a reminder to scan (i.e., green and red plastic cups turned upside down on the table when a small group needs help red on top—and is fine—green on top).

With regard to **Responding to Feedback**, Lisa will practice a verbal response that indicates she is hearing and considering feedback from her supervisor, the school administration, and teachers with whom she is interfacing, i.e., *"I hear what you are saying and I am going to think about how to apply it."*

Specific evidence:

Respects Diversity					
	UNACCEPTABLE (Unaware or unwilling to admit there is a problem	**EMERGING (Awareness, articulation, identification)**	**TARGET (Puts into practice, implements)**	**EXEMPLARY (Builds on reflection, makes changes to improve practice, expands, connects)**	**NOT OBSERVED**
Communication and Respect	Communicates an inability or unwillingness to work with some students, colleagues, parents, other school or university personnel	Sometimes interacts with students, peers, colleagues, parents, or other school or university personnel in a negative, demeaning, sarcastic, or combative manner.	Appropriately interacts with students, peers, colleagues, parents, or other school or university personnel.	Works harmoniously and effortlessly with diverse individuals, including students and adults.	

Values Different Perspectives	Ridicules/rejects differing perspectives, lived experiences, and worldviews.	Does not consistently recognize, acknowledge, or value all individuals in a community of learners.	Values varied perspectives, lived experiences, and worldviews.	Values varied perspectives, lived experiences, and worldviews that are different from their own. Listens to and shows interest in the ideas and opinions of others. Seeks opportunities to include or show appreciation for those that are marginalized.	
Cultural Competence	Demonstrates resistance to examine implicit cultural assumptions, frames of reference, perspectives and biases within the ways in which knowledge is constructed.	Demonstrates reluctance to examine implicit cultural assumptions, frames of reference, perspectives and biases within the ways in which knowledge is constructed.	Demonstrates the ability to examine implicit cultural assumptions, frames of reference, perspectives and biases within the ways in which knowledge is constructed.	Demonstrates a commitment to examine implicit cultural assumptions, frames of reference, perspectives and biases within the ways in which knowledge is constructed. Recognizes and values the cultural wealth of marginalized individuals and their communities.	

(Appendix C continued on next page)

APPENDIX C (CONTINUED)

Expecta-tions for All Students	Accepts achievement gaps based on inclusion in specific groups.	Does not identify or utilize strategies to address achieve-ment gaps based on inclusion in specific groups.	Communi-cates high expecta-tions for all students.	Demon-strates a commitment to high expecta-tions for all students and addresses structural barriers that impede stu-dent perfor-mance.	
Comments:					
Specific evidence:					

Note: Neag School of Education, University of Connecticut

Annie Kuhn, Robin Hands, Rene Roselle, June Cahill draft March 2019

(Partially adapted from University of Maryland Baltimore County draft)

CHAPTER 8

MULTIDIMENSIONAL APPROACHES TO CLINICAL PRACTICE WITH SCHOOL AND UNIVERSITY PARTNERSHIPS

Virginia McCormack
Ohio Dominican University

ABSTRACT

This chapter examined clinical instructional practices and approaches through the development of school and university partnerships. The purpose was to accentuate building a pathway to partnership through the unification of competencies required, dispositions, knowledge, and collaborative clinical practices to create unique interactive ways in which to engage teacher candidates, students, teachers, university professors and administrators. The development of school and university partnerships provided unique ways in which teacher candidates engaged with a variety of learning tasks, assessments, and resources while in clinical practice environment with diverse students. The effectiveness of school and university partnerships for clinical practice increased high-leverage practices, differentiated culturally responsive instructional strategies, trauma-informed teaching practices, and social emotional learning knowledge and pedagogical skills. School and university partnerships developed advanced effective and scalable teacher supports,

Preparing Quality Teachers:
Advances in Clinical Practice, pp. 183–197
Copyright © 2022 by Information Age Publishing
www.infoagepub.com
All rights of reproduction in any form reserved.

resources, and tools while cultivating and improving knowledge, leadership, and accountability with other educational professionals in clinical practice.

SYNTHESIS OF LITERATURE RELATED TO SCHOOL AND UNIVERSITY PARTNERSHIPS

The face of clinical practice within school-university partnerships has expanded greatly over the years. Teacher education programs strive to provide authentic classroom experiences to prepare teacher candidates. Clinal field experiences provide a gateway to bridge theory and practice in a real-world context that allows teacher candidates to apply and test their knowledge, skills, and dispositions. Past practices were limited and often did not include a true relationship between schools and universities. Schools and universities functioned as separate planning and delivery systems with only the students as a common denominator. Innovative clinical practices of today are embodying many instructional practices that incorporate effective, evidence-based practices that school and university partnerships have designed to increase learning for all students.

The American Association of Colleges for Teacher Education Clinical Practice Commission Report (2018) presents three tenets:

> **Tenet 1:** Clinical partnership, as distinct from clinical practice, is the vehicle by which the vision of renewing teacher preparation through clinical practice becomes operational.
>
> **Tenet 2:** Elective clinical partnerships are gateways to developing reflective practice centered on preparing highly selective educators while simultaneously renewing teaching and learning in PK–12 classrooms.
>
> **Tenet 3**: Elective clinical partnerships allow for mutually beneficial outcomes for all stakeholder partners alongside a shared focus on improving success outcomes for PK–12 students.

These three tenets provide a strong foundation for school and university partnerships that serve as a directive moving forward to grow school and university partnerships.

A crucial factor of teacher preparation is clinical practice that furnishes opportunities for teacher candidates to examine, practice their skills, analyze student outcomes, and fine-tune teaching methods in educational environment (Burroughs et al., 2020). The predominant purpose of fostering partnerships was to combine varied viewpoints on teacher preparation and instructional practice communicated by all educational participating school and university partners cooperating teachers, administrators, supervisors, and university educators (Burroughs et al., 2020). Robinson et al. (2017) have delineated a collection of quality markers for developing clinical partnerships that are grounded composition and role phase, instructional cycle phase and implementation phase. Robinson et al. specify that quality markers include (a) shared vision; (b) institutional leadership; (c) communication and collaboration; (d) joint ownership and accountability for results; (e) system alignment, integration, and sustainability; and (f) responsiveness to local context.

Maheady et al. (2019) noted that school and university partnerships are vital to productive growth, application, and improvement of teacher education programs clinical practice opportunities. Clinical field experiences enable circumstances for teacher candidates to link theory with instructional practices. The teacher candidates have the opportunity to apply content knowledge, skills and dispositions in context to a realistic, educational setting. Within this authentic environment, teacher candidates must be able to plan, select resources, analyze data, reflect, and improve instructional practice. Ideally, teacher candidates acquire appropriate attitudes and dispositions, apply available instructional resources, and manage accountability stresses to emerge in student teaching with a strong foundation of content and field expertise (Scales et al., 2018).

School and university partnerships strive to endorse a means to balance the inequities in education related the poverty, unemployment and family income, homelessness, underserved population, and lack of problem-solving skills related to poor executive functioning skills and self-regulation in children and adults. This shared commitment offers opportunities for growth, collaboration, and leadership for all involved in the school-university partnership. The ultimate goal of the partnership is the steadfastness to improve teaching and learning by transforming clinical practice.

CONTEXT AND BACKGROUND OF WORK AROUND CLINICAL PRACTICE

The author recalls a teacher education professor saying, "Once upon a time ... the first occasion to participate in field work was during student teaching." It is hard to believe this statement this day in age when teacher preparation programs are providing field hours in almost every teacher education course and mandating at least 100 hours clinical field practice prior to student teaching. For many years, school and university partnerships were not very strong for a variety of reasons. Over the years, research and organizations have promoted the benefits of clinical field hours. The emphasis on developing school and university partnerships has grown in popularity and structure. These efforts for communication, active school research, advanced degrees for teachers and administrators and participation in clinical practice has shattered the old barriers that prevented effective school and university partnerships.

Accrediting bodies have developed policy and mandated certain practices for teacher preparation programs that impact school district policy related to partnerships. The Council for Accreditation of Educator Preparation presented Standard 2: Clinical Partnerships and Practice. The provider ensures that effective partnerships and high-quality clinical practice are central to preparation so that candidates develop the knowledge, skills, and professional dispositions necessary to demonstrate positive impact on all P–12 students' learning and development (Council for the Accreditation of Educator Preparation, 2019). It is most important for teacher education programs to maintain accreditation and Standard 2 provides the necessary guidance to move forward with school and university partnerships.

It is vital that teacher candidates develop the skills and strategies to ensure that students of all ability levels achieve success in the classroom (Cooper et al., 2008). Likewise, teacher candidates who are not prepared to be special educators often experience an engulfing need trying to understand the diagnostic terminologies on individual educational plans, various special needs categories, and they are besieged by the range of abilities that each special needs students exhibit (Gerber & Guay, 2006). Linking course work and field work in a combined pathway aids teacher candidates in developing a positive attitude and self-confidence, so the teacher candidates can facilitate success for all students in grades one to twelve. Preparing teacher candidates to improve the educational opportunities of all students, ranging from those who are academically challenged to those who are gifted is contingent upon the quality and opportunities in the teacher candidates' field experiences (Gentry, 2012).

Some school and university partnerships are implementing high-leverage practices to meet the needs of all students. High leverage practices are "A set of practices that are fundamental to support … student learning, and that can be taught, learned, and implemented by those entering the profession" (Windschitl et al., 2012). The Council for Exceptional Children (2016) developed criteria for high leverage practices that included concentrating on frequent effective instructional practice; evidence-based learning and engagement strategies; generally relevant and functional content area and pedagogy; and competent delivery is fundamental to effective teaching. The high leverage practices include authentic educational settings, that span video task analysis, case studies, trial delivery, and virtual simulations that is aligned to content and field experience (Brownell et al., 2019). The Council for Exceptional Children and the CEEDAR Center (2017) grouped the 22 elemental techniques and identified four main categories that high leverage practices can be assembled. The four categories include assessment, collaboration, instruction and social/emotional/behavioral. High Leverage Practices for Inclusive Classrooms (McLesky et al., 2019) targets Tier 1 and Tier 2 in a multi-support system that focus on general education students with mild disabilities.

Federal and state policies furnish guidance for instructional programs and practice for multilingual learners and English language learners. By reviewing and developing such policies allows for sustainable rigorous academic experiences and choices while maintaining cultural awareness and identity. Typically, multilingual learners and English language learners are taught through bilingual instruction, pullout tutoring, or Sheltered English instruction. Research has shown that there is no significant evidence that any one of these approaches are more beneficial. School and university partnerships provide teacher candidates with culturally responsive experiences in classrooms and after school tutoring sessions with multilingual learners and English language learners. These partnerships furnished opportunities for teacher candidates to build cultural competence skills of empathy, good will, curiosity about other cultures, providing sincere praise, keeping confidences, and constructive feedback (Howe & Lisi, 2019).

School and university partnership educators are grappling with a major well-being crisis with up to two-thirds of students who have encountered at least one form of serious juvenile trauma such as personal abuse, homelessness, domestic violence, natural disaster, or drive by shootings (Centers for Disease Control and Prevention, 2019). Research has shown that trauma-informed education is key to recognizing and responding to students with trauma stress within the classroom to improve general well-being and to increase academic learning. Teacher candidates participating in school and university partnerships become cognizant of the advantages and challenges of trauma-informed teaching practices. There are five primary principles for trauma-informed care: safety, trustworthiness, choice, collaboration, and empowerment, (Substance Abuse and Mental Health Services Administration, 2014). School districts are sourcing trauma-informed care links to the social emotional learning competencies in the classroom.

The Collaborative for Academic, Social, and Emotional Learning (2020) defined social-emotional knowledge, skills, and dispositions necessary to recognize and process emotions, establish, and accomplish assured purposes, understanding the feelings of others and feel compassion, ascertain, and preserve affirmative contacts and make conscientious determinations. According to the Collaborative for Academic, Social, and Emotional Learning, a framework categorizes five core skills:

- **Self-awareness:** The ability to accurately, recognize one's emotions and thoughts and their influence on behavior. This includes accurately assessing one's strengths and limitations and possessing a well-grounded sense of confidence and optimism.
- **Self-management:** The ability to regulate one's emotions, thoughts, and behaviors effectively in different situations. This includes managing stress, controlling impulses, motivating oneself, and setting and working toward achieving personal and academic goals.
- **Social awareness:** The ability to take the perspective of and empathize with others from diverse backgrounds and cultures, to understand social and ethical norms for behavior, and to recognize family, school, and community resources and supports.
- **Relationship skills:** The ability to establish and maintain healthy and rewarding relationships with diverse individuals and groups. This includes communicating clearly, listening actively, cooperating, resisting inappropriate social pressure, negotiating conflict constructively, and seeking and offering help when needed.
- **Responsible decision-making:** The ability to make constructive and respectful choices about personal behavior and social interactions based on consideration of ethical standards, safety concerns, social norms, the realistic evaluation of consequences of various actions, and the well-being of self and others.

By focusing learning tasks within the classroom on these five core skills, students who have experienced trauma will learn the language to express feelings, thoughts, and emotions and grow in the ability to express themselves. Students will gradually increase their ability to form new friendships within positive relationships and become more empathic and compassionate.

Many states and school districts are requiring new K–12 standards for social emotional learning to be developed and realized in the classroom. Local school districts and schools with teachers, administrators, school counselors, and education personnel will determine what type of training for educational personnel is necessary. Teachers and administrators will decide how to implement social emotional practices into regular learning tasks throughout the school day to best assist the students.

DESCRIPTION ABOUT APPROACHES TO INNOVATIVE CLINICAL PRACTICE

Establishing equity in education may seem an insurmountable challenge for some educators, parents, and communities. All of the constituents want to develop strategies for how to better aid students who are underserved by the schools. Therefore, school and university partnerships are multidimensional and have similar purposes in mind whereby, both desire to increase student knowledge, skills and dispositions by choosing the best approaches for teaching and learning. These partnerships begin with a vision that faculty and staff support. A needs assessment is generated by discussion and outlining strategic goals. Gathered data from a needs assessment leads to advice and a well-crafted action plan for the school and university partnership. Often, schools with lower socioeconomic status, few resources, students with nutrition deficiencies, transient students, and students coping with family members in prison seem to overwhelm the students' ability to improve academically. The action plan is an intentional field experience that incorporates knowledge, skills, diversity, trauma—informed teaching and social emotional learning training. The focus is on high quality field placements with targeted tasks, assessment, and reporting mechanisms. University professors and school-based teachers are able to model identify and monitor desired practice of skills and dispositions in the field placement.

High Leverage Practices Integrated Into Reading Support Tutoring—Urban Clinical Practice Partnership

Reading support-tutoring partnerships with a school and university builds a connection between research and practice that values potential opportunity for teacher candidates. Teacher candidates were presented with the high-leverage practices information in general, began to familiarize themselves with the 22 practices, and specifically delved into the use of explicit instruction. Prior to the reading tutoring clinical practice, teacher candidates discussed reading skill development and comprehension in class simulations connected with applying high-leverage practices. Teacher candidates invested time reflecting and conversing about high-leverage practices such as short-term and long-term goal setting in relation to the reading tutoring clinical practice partnership.

Teacher candidates in the urban low performing elementary schools to help students improve reading in the classroom. The field hours associated with the reading course gave the teacher candidates the opportunity to engage in tutoring and literacy teaching strategies. Teacher candidates had the opportunity to work in small groups with a child or with children who were having difficulty with reading and literacy and participate in reading and literacy instructional learning tasks. Options included the possibly of working with larger groups, conferencing with student writers, and reviewing student work and journals. The Reading Recovery teacher coordinated the reading materials consisting of leveled book, handouts, and computer assisted materials. The cooperating teachers provided some of the instructional materials that they wished the teacher candidates to use with a particular student or asked the teacher candidates in advance to find some teaching materials.

Additionally, teacher candidates facilitated a Study Island practice in reading and mathematics, so that the students were prepared to read the questions and select an answer on the computer for statewide standardized testing. The students needed time to adjust to reading a question on the computer and answering the question. Some students had a very short attention span while others became frustrated and uncooperative. Most of the students just thought about using a computer for fun such as playing video games. Using Study Island as an assessment tool provided the necessary experience to distinguish gaming versus testing.

Depending on the time of the year of the reading tutoring, students are being recognized, pre-referred for intervention, referred for special education evaluation, and being evaluated for special education. The multifactor evaluation is required to be completed in 60 days but may be delayed due to parents or legal guardian concerns. In the interim, teachers and teacher candidates are guided by using high leverage practices in the classroom for all students. These high leverage practices serve as a compendium to engage students in learning and ultimately improve student learning outcomes.

Differentiated Culturally Responsive Practice for Multilingual Learners and English Language Learners— African Charter School Partnership

Teacher education programs offer teacher candidates' opportunities for reflection and prepare the teacher candidates to differentiate instruction in ways that allow diverse learners to be successful in school. Some teacher education programs address this situation by transforming the clinical practicum curriculum and requirements while faculty and teacher candidates work with English language learners and multilingual learners. This is especially true when practice is linked with reflections on teachers' attitudes, beliefs, and comfort levels regarding everyday classroom dilemmas. A culturally responsive partnership gives the students the opportunity to work one-on-one with the same child who is having difficulty learning to read for the semester. Teacher candidates observe teaching strategies, engage in tutoring, and developing instructional materials, administer appropriate reading assessments, analyzing the results of the diagnostic assessments and suggest a prescribed a course of study to remediate the reading difficulties and remediate one or more identified reading problem areas. Multiple field experiences in diverse placements assist teacher candidates in examining their commitment to teaching, clarify goals and give the teacher candidates a more realistic picture of life in the classroom.

At the outset, the teacher candidates viewed a map of a countries in Africa, expanded their purview through a slide presentation that underscored the history, culture, geography, religion, language, economics, arts, cuisine, and clothing and lastly, the class discussed culturally responsive teaching. Subsequently, the teacher candidates participated in an orientation by the principal and English as a second language (ESL) teacher at the host school where the teacher candidates were attentive and asked pertinent questions. Third, there was observation and participation by teacher candidates embedded in the context of the classrooms and shared classroom experiences. This phase was followed by teacher candidate reflection, whereby a majority of their original assumptions were dismantled. The teacher candidates began to see things differently through interactions at the African charter school and arrived at a different interpretation that changed their knowledge, skills, and dispositions. Towards the end of the field placement, the teacher candidates completed a questionnaire regarding their individual level of knowledge, skills, and dispositions for culturally and linguistically diverse learners. The concluding phase was the collective debriefing session that ensued in reading class after the field experience was completed. By building on limited previous knowledge, skills, and dispositions, the professor encouraged the teacher candidates to launch a self-assessment, provided feedback to unanswered questions and encouraged the teacher candidates to put their words and beliefs into action to further meet the needs of diverse learners in the classroom. The teacher candidates explored their feelings and views of the field experience that was overflowing with successes and challenges in terms of preparing teacher candidates for diverse field experiences. The reflections and survey completion during the field experience and debriefing session at the end of the experience provided a framework for discussing the triumphs and tribulations of working in a diverse setting.

Teacher candidates are often anxious about the first culturally and linguistically diverse clinical partnership experience. Four findings appeared: (1) Teacher candidates were very worried about communicating with the African students; (2) Teacher candidates were surprised that many of the African students spoke English in varying degrees; (3) Teacher candidates indicated a greater understanding and appreciation for diversity and the challenges of meeting the needs of diverse learners; and (4) Teacher candidates felt untrained and unprepared to work with culturally and linguistically diverse learners.

There were three themes that emerged from the teacher candidates in the linguistic and cultural minority school and university partnership during a second diverse field experience: (1) Teacher candidates knew what to expect in terms of structure and discipline in the learning environment and felt more confident working with the culturally and linguistically diverse students; (2) Teacher candidates recognized students' diversity and differing approaches to cultural influences on learning; and (3)Teacher candidates gained knowledge of and skills in instructional strategies that focused more intently on scaffolding instruction in a culturally responsive classroom to help the teacher candidates successfully respond to linguistic and cultural differences in the classroom and promote academic achievement for all learners. Selected anecdotes were chosen and grouped by themes. The anecdotes most cited were used to give clues to the ways that the teacher candidate's thinking was changing with the new diverse field experiences.

Teacher candidates disclosed after multiple culturally and linguistically diverse field experiences suggested that: (a) Teacher candidates became more comfortable within a diverse field setting; (b) There are multiple ways to teach and learn; and (c) The process of using cultural response teaching strategies and reflection was helpful to refine and adapt teaching practices.

Venturing from the conventional field experience has provided an opportunity for the teacher candidates to expand their knowledge, skills, and dispositions in understanding the facets of English language learner's and multilingual learner's education and strengthen the teacher candidates' commitment to developing effective and suitable strategies for teaching English language learners and multilingual learners.

Social Emotional Learning and Trauma-Informed Teaching—Clinical Practice Partnership

The need is increasing for teacher candidates to have a better understanding of trauma-informed practices and social emotional learning strategies. Preparation for the teacher candidates begins prior to the field component by specifying content-based information related to social-emotional learning and trauma-informed education and teaching strategies. Social-emotional learning and trauma-informed practices guide teacher candidates to understand that children become very anxious if they are confronting both academic expectations and social-emotional needs or trauma in their lives. Using an array of content, methods, and social story media to teach social-emotional competencies will strengthen the abilities of the teacher candidates as they work to recognize and respond appropriately to unfavorable childhood occurrences and circumstances. The goal is for teacher candidates to internalize how to assist children in becoming more resilient by making necessary adjustments to the learning environment by removing triggers, presenting a range of interventions, and demonstrating how to process feelings so that the children do not become unregulated all while being taught content information.

Teacher candidates explored blogs, an infographic, and videos related to social emotional learning to personally view cueing and prompts related to content learning. Reflection question prompts are listed within an online module to have the teacher candidates reflection on: (a). How has your understanding of implementing social emotional learning in the literacy classroom changed after creating social emotional learning literacy instructions materials? and (b) How can social emotional learning address the needs of special education students and multilingual learners (MLLs) in the educational environment and classroom?

Experiences during a school and university partnership furnish a springboard for teacher candidates to reflect on their biases and lack of experience in various educational environments. Through the school-university partnerships field component, teacher candidates can determine what are the appropriate reactions the teacher candidates should have to the students in the classroom when situations arise with social-emotional or trauma issues. School-based teachers and university professors provide real-time feedback and coaching to candidates throughout the field component to create a more robust, safe learning environment that promotes learning, acceptance, and responsiveness to all students.

IMPLICATIONS REGARDING FUTURE WORK RELATED TO CLINICAL PRACTICE IN TEACHER EDUCATION

The trajectory for clinical practice with school-university partnerships in the teacher education is increasing. Accreditation bodies are mandating that universities create new school partnerships or strengthen existing partnerships to revitalize teacher education curriculum, the knowledge base of teacher candidates, and provide better accountability of clinical practice. The focus of school-university partnerships is the student learner, whether it be teacher candidates or children.

School- university partnerships are advantageous for all participants. Schools are eager to eliminate funding disparities. The partnership between schools and universities is a counterbalance for the lack of funding by having access to teacher candidates and instructional field mentoring. It is beneficial for everyone involved in the school and university, no matter what the result or learning outcome may be.

Impactful clinical practices are established through positive relationships. The benefits vary from a positive academic and social relationship with teacher candidates and a team coaching focus with school-based teachers and university professors. The central role of school-university partnerships is dynamic and grows through assimilation and engagement. School-based educators and teacher candidates are able to cooperate with each other and acquire expertise and experience to continue the momentum expanding knowledge, skills, and values.

High-leverage practices are for general education and special education teachers to use as a guidebook. Students with disabilities and struggling learners are able to scaffold their learning experiences based on these instructional evidence-based practices. School and university partnerships are able to communicate the targeted goals, implement, and analysis data collected to determine the learning outcomes related to improved academic successes. High-leverage practices are being introduced in teacher preparation classes and some high leverage practices are selected for more intense exploration and implementation. Universities are also creating dual licensure programs that prepare teacher candidates for the general education classroom and special education classrooms.

Culturally responsive practices support the premise that teacher candidate's comments, written responses, and dispositions change with exposure in a diverse field partnership and seem to be positively affected toward teaching in a culturally and linguistically diverse school. Tracing the shift through multiple culturally and linguistically diverse field experiences demonstrates how the teacher candidates' experiences informed their preparation and mind set. It is critical to have appropriate dispositions, perceptions, and professional development to teach effectively in diverse classrooms. Culturally and linguistically diverse field experiences attempt to furnish teacher candidates with the foundational knowledge and insight necessary to teach in highly diverse classrooms. Teacher candidates do recognize the importance of being prepared for diverse educational settings and communities, in which they must value cultural and linguistic differences. Therefore, it is important to examine the impact on teaching and learning and the implications for teacher preparation programs and professional development initiatives. This suggests a need to continue exploring and expanding culturally and linguistically diverse field placements as well as advocating for approaches that build on culturally responsive teaching and well-established pedagogical principle.

Social-emotional learning and trauma-informed teaching professional development opportunities are expanding. Educators are engaged in ways that will motivate them, teach new skills to the educators and the educators in turn, bring back these social emotional learning and trauma-informed practices to the classroom, and school. State Departments of Education and school districts are examining research and practice in order to create informed policy that will demonstrate commitment to the success of all students.

School and university partnerships cope with an array of challenges and impediments to the utilization of educational partnerships and professional reflection. In addition, school and university partnerships can be time-intensive for both the school personnel, administrators, teacher candidates, and university supervisors. However, amid the challenges and barriers, educators are witnessing an increase of sustained school and university partnerships in various educational settings. It is essential that teachers understand how to generate reflective learning opportunities using technologies to create optimal reflective learning environments.

The participants in school and university partnership gain valuable insights into thinking and learning through a multidimensional approach to clinical practice. One significant advantage of developing school and university partnerships appears to be a better alignment and measurement of clinical practices that needed improvement. The clinical practice partners were able to target certain concepts and approaches to increase learning. Additionally, the students responded well and gained confidence while interacting within the school and university partnerships. Teacher candidates, school personnel, university supervisors and administrators were able to give immediate feedback on how the students were progressing, discuss the data collected from clinical practice and implications for revision, and provide samples of reflection throughout the clinical practice with the school and university partnerships.

Clinical practice skill development requires repeated assessment of the evidence-based strategies, and mindfulness of clinical practice and desired learning outcomes. Formative and summative assessment is essential for the development of clinical practice with school and university partnerships because with these assessment methods, partnership participants can improve and support students' self-directed and shared learning through innovative clinical practice. As teacher educators, we need to provide timely feedback, so that teacher candidates and P–12 students' self-assessment will be fostered and P–12 students' learning will be supported during the whole process. Future practice ensuring school and university partnership enhanced reflective learning tasks and learning segments consistently provide teacher candidates and P–12 students with a reason and will to engage in and to support successful learning outcomes.

Moving forward there are numerous innovative practices that can be introduced and implemented. What the best approach for clinical practice should be determined by the school and university partnerships. To maximize the benefits of all constituents, time is needed to build relationships, develop policies, expand communication, and investigate the appropriateness of innovative practices that will transform school and university partnerships. Innovative clinical practices for school and university partnerships is just the beginning of emboldening measures along the pathway.

REFERENCES

Brownell, M., Benedict, A., Leko, M., Peyton, D., Pua, D., & Richards-Tutor, C. (2019). A continuum of pedagogies for preparing teachers to use high leverage practices. *Remedial and Special Education, 40*(6), 338–355. https://doi.org/10.1177/0741932518824990

Burroughs, G., Lewis, A., Battey, D., Curran, M., Hyland, H., & Ryan, S. (2020). From mediated fieldwork to co-constructed partnerships: A framework for guiding and reflecting on P–12 school-university partnerships. *Journal of Teacher Education 71*(1) 122–134. https://doi.org/10.1177/0022487119858992

The Collaborative for Academic, Social, and Emotional Learning. (2020). *Fundamentals of SEL.* https://casel.org/what-is-sel/

Centers for Disease Control and Prevention. (2019). *Adverse childhood experiences.* www.cdc.gov/violenceprevention/childabuseandneglect/acestudy/index.html

Cooper, J. E., Kurtts, S., Baber, C. R., & Vallecorsa, A. (2008). A model for examining teacher preparation curricula for inclusion. *Teacher Education Quarterly, 35*(4), 155–176.

Council for the Accreditation of Educator Preparation. (2019). *Standard 2-clinical partnerships and practice.* http://www.ncate.org/standards/standard-2

Council for Exceptional Children. (2016). *CEC's high-leverage practices in special education.* https://highleveragepractices.org/

Council for Exceptional Children & CEEDAR Center. (2017). *High-leverage practices in special education.*

Gentry, R. (2012). Clinical experiences for teacher candidates: Taking preparation beyond the four walls. *Research in Higher Education Journal, 15*, 1–13.

Gerber, B. L., & Guay, D. P. (2006). *Reaching and teaching students with special needs through art.* National Art Education Association.

Howe, W. A., & Lisi, P. L. (2019). *Becoming a multicultural educator: Developing awareness, gaining skills, and taking action* (3rd ed.). SAGE.

Maheady, L., Patti, A., Rafferty, A. & del Prado Hill, P. (2019). School-university partnerships: One institution's efforts to integrate and support teacher use of high-leverage practices. *Remedial and Special Education, 40*(6) 356–364. https://doi.org/10.1177/0741932518812689

McLesky, J. Maheady, L., Billingsley, B., Brownell, M., & Lewis, T. (Eds.). (2019). *High Leverage Practices for Inclusive Classroom.* Council for Exceptional Children.

Robinson, S., Nemr, G., Nicoll-Senft, J., Spear-Swerling, L., & Tralli, R. (2017, February). *Developing quality fieldwork: Experiences for teacher candidates.* Collaboration for Effective Educator Development, Accountability, and Reform Center, University of Florida.

Scales, R. Q., Wolsey, T. D., Lenski, S., Smetana, L., Yoder, K. K., Dobler, E., & Young, Grisham, D., & Young, J. R. (2017). Are we preparing or training teachers? Developing professional judgement in and beyond teacher preparation programs. *Journal of Teacher Education, 6*(1), 7–21.

Substance Abuse and Mental Health Services Administration. (2014). *SAMHSA's concept of trauma and guidance for a trauma-informed approach.* HHS Publication No. (SMA) 14-4884. Substance Abuse and Mental Health Services Administration.

Windschitl, M., Thompson, J., Braaten, M., & Stroupe, D. (2012). Proposing a core set of instructional practices and tools for teachers of science. *Science Education*, *96*(5), 878–903.

SECTION II

RESIDENCIES AND ALTERNATIVE CERTIFICATION

CHAPTER 9

EFFECTIVE CLINICAL PREPARATION THROUGH TEACHER RESIDENCY

Michelle Cook, Laura Eicher, and Leigh Martin
Clemson University

ABSTRACT

Clinical experiences play an essential role in preservice teacher development (American Association of Colleges for Teacher Education [AACTE], 2018; National Council for Accreditation of Teacher Education [NCATE], 2010). While there are many ways to centralize clinical practice within teacher preparation, teacher residency programs meet many of AACTE's Clinical Practice Commission's (CPC) proclamations. In this chapter, we discuss the ways that a university-district developed teacher residency program used the CPC's report to operationalize clinical practice and initial program findings.

TEACHER RESIDENCY AND CLINICAL PREPARATION

Teacher residency programs offer a different approach to traditional teacher preparation. They are district-serving teacher education programs that pair a rigorous, full-year classroom internship with coursework tightly

Preparing Quality Teachers:
Advances in Clinical Practice, pp. 201–221
Copyright © 2022 by Information Age Publishing
www.infoagepub.com

integrated with clinical practice (Guha et al., 2017). Within residency programs, high-quality mentor teachers are recruited and trained to co-design, co-teach, and co-reflect on instruction and assessment in an immersive and sustained environment, going beyond the typical student-teaching experience of one semester or less. A report by the National Education Association examining the merit of teacher residencies concluded that the best way to ensure that every teacher is profession-ready from the first day as a teacher-of-record is for preparation programs to incorporate teacher residencies (Coffman & Patterson, 2014).

Teacher residency programs are not new to the United States and for years have been known to support teacher recruitment and retention, especially when aligned to key characteristics of highly effective residency models: strong university-district partnerships, highly qualified resident candidates, a full year internship, coursework aligned to the internship, continual mentoring of residents as they begin teaching, and careful selection and preparation of clinical educators (Guha et al., 2016). Further, research suggests that these residency programs can have long-lasting effects for the PK-12 students the resident teaches during the residents' fourth and fifth years of teaching (Papay et al., 2012; Washburn-Moses, 2017). Nevertheless, enacting successful teacher residency programs proves challenging for colleges and universities. During the 2016–2017 academic year, Clemson University, with the collaboration and support of seven regional school districts, created a sustainable teacher residency program using the key characteristics outlined above and proclamations and tenants laid forth in the American Association of Colleges for Teacher Education's (AACTE) Clinical Practice Commission (CPC) report, as a guide. The program graduated its first class of residents in the spring of 2018 and the number of candidates who apply to the residency program each year is rising. This chapter will highlight the ways in which the teacher residency program aligns to the CPC's proclamations and tenets and preliminary program successes.

As defined by the CPC, "clinical practice is a model to prepare high-quality educators with and through a pedagogical skill set that provides articulated benefits for every participant, while being fully embedded in the PK–12 setting" (AACTE, 2018, p. 6). AACTE's CPC report goes on to list ten proclamations with supporting tenets and details designed to operationalize clinical practices. These proclamations and tenets highlight the importance of teacher preparation programs aligning coursework to candidates' field experiences (Central Proclamation), selecting and preparing highly qualified and skilled clinical educators (Skills Proclamation), providing pedagogical content knowledge and specific pedagogical feedback (Pedagogy Proclamation), establishing and maintaining university-district partnerships that progress through four developmental stages and benefit all constituents (Partnership, Developmental, Mutual Benefit, and Expertise Proclamations), creating sustainable funding structures (Infrastructure Proclamation), and factoring candidates' needs into program development and refinement (Empowerment Proclamation). Taken together, the proclamations provide a set of recommendations that teacher preparation programs should consider in an effort to prepare highly qualified educators.

During the summer of 2016, faculty from Clemson's College of Education met with representatives from seven regional school districts, to begin to set forth a framework for the teacher residency program. In those meetings, several topics rose to the surface as key areas of focus: establishing a rigorous selection and preparation process for residents, mentor teachers, and university supervisors; ensuring that residents' coursework was aligned to field experiences and district needs; conceptualizing a co-teaching model as a way to empower residents and mentor teachers; and seeking a way to measure residents' growth and accomplishments in a way that is valued by the school districts. As conversations continued to evolve and the program began to take shape, the CPC held a session at the annual AACTE conference and released the executive summary of the CPC report for review. It was during this time that the alignment between the CPC's proclamations and tenets and the design of the residency program became clear.

ONE MODEL FOR TEACHER RESIDENCY

In general, teacher residency programs are research-based, innovative approaches to recruiting, preparing, and retaining high quality teachers (Guha et al., 2016). Clemson's program is the first university-led teacher residency program in South Carolina and aligns with our college's strategic priority to develop innovative and responsive programs to address the teacher shortage. Our residency program is a combined bachelor's to master's degree pathway whereby students in any of our teacher preparation programs can begin graduate coursework as an undergraduate student. The degree programs eligible for participation are Early Childhood Education, Elementary Education, Middle Level Education, Secondary Education (English, Mathematics, Biology, Chemistry, Physics, and Social Studies) and Special Education. The program tightly pairs coursework with a rigorous, full-year clinical experience with a specially prepared mentor teacher. In our first three years, 100 students have participated in the teacher residency program (graduates and current students) and 97 teachers from our partner districts have been prepared as mentor teachers.

Teacher residencies are sometimes confused with other models of teacher preparation. Some programs place candidates with the same mentor teacher for an entire academic year, but candidates are not full time for the entire experience (i.e., one-semester part-time practicum and one-semester full-time student teaching). Other programs employ candidates as teachers-of-record while they are completing the requirements of the clinical experience. In teacher residency models, districts host teachers-in-training for a year-long, full-time experience. In our residency program, we create systemic change by aligning with district and school priorities and by focusing on the following goals: increase the recruitment, quality, and retention of teacher residents; increase the quality of instructional leadership and the retention of mentor teachers; and improve student learning outcomes by focusing on the preparation and retention of teacher residents and mentor teachers.

Teacher Residents

Teacher residents undergo a rigorous and extensive process to be selected for programs (Silva et al., 2014). The application process for our teacher residents begins in the spring of their junior year. To be selected for the program, the application process includes: completion of an application consisting of free-response questions that determine motivation, teaching interests, and dispositions; submission of two letters for support from recommenders who can attest to the applicant's ability to work with children, reviews of transcripts to meet minimum GPA and credit hour requirements; evaluation of results from dispositions survey from former university supervisors and cooperating teachers; and review and evaluation by faculty members and district partners. Once accepted, students who would have typically begun student teaching in the spring of their fourth year instead replace student teaching with graduate education courses taken together as a learning community. Coursework includes classroom learning environments, curriculum theory, cultural diversity, and action research along with a minimum two day per week clinical practicum.

In their fifth year, residents engage in a full-year clinical residency internship, under the guidance of a mentor teacher. In both semesters of the fifth year, residents take seminar courses and courses focused on developing and implementing action research. The approach to residency is different than traditional student teaching. Rather than gradually increasing responsibilities for a full teaching takeover like we do in student teaching internships, our residents begin the year co-designing, co-teaching, and co-reflecting on assessment data to make decisions. Because residents are immersed immediately, they have a deepened connection to the school context and community and are able to better analyze situations to make informed decisions about teaching (Williamson & Hodder, 2015). Residents spend approximately 1,235 hours in clinical internships, which is double the number of hours our traditional four-year students spend in clinical intern-ships. Residents plan and attend professional development and meetings and engage in every responsibility as a mentor teacher would. While co-teaching is a norm in our program, residents do have periods of time throughout the year when they take on demanding lead teacher roles.

The design of our residency program aligns with the CPC's recom-mendations— clinical practices and pedagogical training are central in our program (Central Proclamation and Pedagogy Proclamation). Like students in our traditional four-year programs, residents have multiple early field placements in diverse school settings (Central Proclamation, Tenet 5). Teaching is complex and to learn the practice of teaching, our residents take coursework designed to develop their knowledge and skills and apply that understanding in clinical placements which occur almost every semester of the program (Central Proclamation, Tenets 1 and 2). We are intentional in developing our expectations of how students will develop over time from the first field experience during their freshman year through their culminating residency (Central Proclamation, Tenet 3). In addition, field experiences and coursework throughout the program are designed to enhance both content knowledge and pedagogical deliv-ery expertise to strengthen resident preparation (Pedagogy Proclamation, Tenets 1 and 2).

Clinical Educators

The CPC report defines a "lexicon of practice" to allow for common understanding of terms used regarding clinical practice (AACTE, 2018, p. 11). A mentor teacher "serves as the primary school-based teacher educator for teacher candidates completing clinical practice of an intern-ship" (AACTE, 2018, p. 12). The CPC also refers to a mentor teacher as a school-based teacher educator. University-based teacher educators (and in our program are called university supervisors) are "boundary-spanning teacher educators who engage in evaluation, coaching, instruction, and partnership" (AACTE, 2018, p. 12). Mentor teachers and university super-visors are both clinical educators who play a critical role in the development of teacher residents in our program.

Mentor Teachers

Mentor teachers have demonstrated their instructional effectiveness in their schools and while they want to expand their knowledge, skills, and role in their school, they want to remain in the classroom as a teacher

(Steffy et al., 2000). Our partnering school districts want to invest in these teachers and their professional growth, and their retention is a top priority in our program. While there is some variation among our seven partnering districts on how mentor teachers are selected, districts use the same list of qualifications and expectations to identify potential mentor teachers. To be selected, mentor teachers must submit an application, a recommendation from a building administrator, and in some cases, participate in an interview with district leadership. It is a competitive process that identifies teachers in schools who have the dispositions and ability to be supportive mentors and coaches and increases the instructional leadership capacity in a building.

Mentor teachers are prepared to serve as primary mentors to teacher residents and their development is supported through coursework, institutes, and learning communities. This professional development for the mentor teacher is aligned with the research-based practices and the preparation of teacher residents (Skills Proclamation, Tenet 2). In the spring before they are matched with a teacher resident, they take a graduate course (45 contact hours with face-to-face and online components) on elements of instructional effectiveness. While our mentor teachers have been identified as effective in their buildings, this course reviews pedagogical practices that should be central in teaching and should guide the development of clinical practice (Pedagogy Proclamation, Tenets 1 and 2). Mentor teachers also participate in a summer institute which covers critical conversations and transformations as teachers, effective use of student assessment data, responsive teaching practices, and leadership for building instructional capacity. And finally, in the first semester with a teacher resident, they take a second graduate course (45 contact hours with face-to-face and online components) focused on curriculum, instruction, assessment, and learning from a mentor perspective. Mentor teachers are recruited and prepared to co-design instruction and co-teach. They use a variety of coaching strategies to provide insight into effective teaching methods, help teacher residents develop knowledge and skills, and continue data gathering to provide targeted support and feedback, all of which is learned in their graduate courses and summer institute.

University Supervisors

University supervisors balance supportive and evaluative roles in the formative development of residents. While the university supervisor role is often overlooked and misunderstood, we recognize that recruitment and preparation of university supervisors must be grounded in mentoring, coaching, and evaluating residents (Asplin & Marks, 2013; Bates et al., 2011). University supervisors are employed by Clemson University and using the CPC terminology are also known as university-based teacher educators. We recruit and prepare university supervisors to ensure their understanding of the residency program, resident expectations, and research-based coaching and mentoring skills. University supervisors are expected to attend six half-day seminars. The first two seminars are held during the summer before the university supervisor begins to work with the resident; the next four seminars are held during the academic year that they are supporting the resident. The seminars provide time and space for supervisors to learn about topics addressed as part of the mentor teacher coursework: (1) planning and implementing culturally responsive pedagogies; (2) engaging in effective mentoring practices; (3) providing supportive feedback connected to specific pedagogies; (4) facilitating effective, reliable, evaluation (trained to achieve strong inter-rater agreement); and (5) reading and discussing pertinent literature. During the half-day seminars, university supervisors increase their understanding of these topics and connect their learning to the supports they are currently offering to the resident and mentor teacher. Seminar topics and discussions help supervisors gain the confidence needed to support residents in different ways, specific to resident needs (Skills Proclamation, Tenet 1).

Our clinical educators, both school-based and university-based, are selected and must participate in the coursework, institutes, and/or seminars to support and mentor our teacher residents (Mutual Benefit Proclamation, Tenet 1). Collectively, they share responsibility to foster and evaluate the knowledge, skill, and dispositions necessary to be a successful educator (Mutual Benefit Proclamation, Tenet 2 and Expertise Proclamation, Tenet 2). School-based and university-based clinical educators are prepared to coach our residents, routinely share formative feedback with residents about their progress, have rich interactions in the "third space" where teacher preparation programs and PK–12 schools intersect, and share the responsibility to evaluate teacher candidates on a variety of assessments (Mutual Benefit Proclamation, Tenet 4). In this "third space," roles and responsibilities are negotiated and the customary boundaries among stakeholders are redefined (Klein et al, 2013).

Intentional Placements and Co-Teaching

The NCATE (2010) explains that programs built around clinical practice need to "support the development of complex teaching skills and ensure all teachers will know how to work closely with colleagues, students, and community" (p. ii). Through co-teaching during the clinical placement, the teacher residents in our program are engaged in collaboration with a co-teaching partner (the mentor teacher) that provides them opportunities to develop skills necessary to work with professional colleagues with a collective focus to improve student learning (Darragh et al., 2011) (Partnership Proclamation, Tenet 3; Empowerment Proclamation, Tenet 2). Working with a mentor teacher over time allows for teacher residents to collaborate with a more experienced partner, observe and practice effective instruction, engage in discourse about pedagogy, and develop a more complex understanding of students, teaching, and learning (Gardiner, 2011). Both the mentor teacher and teacher resident are expected to continuously reflect on their teaching practice, engage in collective learning, and generate ideas about teaching that could not have been developed by themselves (Solheim et al., 2018) (Skills Proclamation, Tenet 1). Mentor teachers are taught during their graduate coursework and the summer institute to engage in instructional coaching cycles with their teacher resident which includes engaging in cogenerative dialogues to brainstorm and share ideas on ways to improve student learning. During the summer institute, mentor teachers are trained on strategies to co-teach with their teacher resident. Mentor teachers and teacher residents are encouraged to implement various co-teaching approaches throughout their clinical placement including one teach/one assists, parallel teaching, station teaching, alternate teaching, and team teaching (Barger-Anderson et al., 2013; Cook & Friend, 1995). With one teach/one assists, one teacher takes the lead during instruction while the other teacher drifts around the room assisting students as needed. In parallel teaching, the class is divided equally into two parts with the mentor teacher and the teacher resident both responsible for teaching one group. Each provides instruction at the same time while decreasing the student/teacher ratio. In station teaching, the class is separated into smaller groups. The mentor teacher teaches half of the material to a group of students while the teacher resident teaches the other half of the material to another group of students. They then switch groups and repeat the instruction. In the alternate co-teaching model, one teacher provides instruction for the majority of the class while the other teacher instructs a smaller group of students in an alternative location. The team-teaching approach to co-teaching requires the mentor teacher and teacher resident to provide instruction at the same time to a whole group of students. Both teachers have equal sharing of the stage.

Co-teaching serves as professional development for both the mentor teacher and the teacher resident (Gallo-Fox & Scantlebury, 2016) as they engage in a community of practice. A community of practice includes the dimensions of mutual engagement, joint enterprise, and a shared repertoire (Wenger, 1998). As teacher residents participate as active participants in the social community in the context of their clinical placement, their participation shapes not only what they do but who they are (Wenger, 1998).

In order to ensure an effective co-teaching relationship, it is important to make intentional matches between teacher residents and mentor teachers (Beck & Kosnik, 2002; Koerner & Rust, 2002). In our program, we use a questionnaire to collect information about degree of flexibility, orientation towards tradition, need for guidance and structure, organization, and communication styles. Mentors and mentees who hold similar views or similar personality characteristics are more likely to give and receive feedback, be more understanding, and ensure the relationship continues to be stable (Rajuan et al., 2010). Systematically looking at these qualities is more likely to foster a more trusting co-teaching relationship and support the success of the internship experience (Barger-Anderson et al., 2013).

Multi-District Partnership

An essential program feature that matters in effective teacher preparation programs is a strong relationship among school and university partnerships (Darling-Hammond, 2006), and our teacher residency program would not be successful without strong partnerships with seven area school districts. Since the start of the program, we have collaborated with partner districts though a Steering Committee comprised of school district and university representatives. The Steering Committee has co-constructed all of the essential components of the program together (Partnership Proclamation, Tenet 1 and Infrastructure Proclamation, Tenet 1). We collaboratively recruit and select teacher residents and mentor teachers; select, develop, and align coursework, institutes, and callback meetings to address programmatic needs; intentionally match and place teacher residents with mentor teachers; and collect and interpret data to revise aspects of the program. The university has a Memorandum of Understanding with each school district to outline our mutually beneficial policies and operational procedures (Infrastructure Proclamation, Tenet 3). While engaging in the work of the Steering Committee, we keep in mind our mutually beneficial outcomes—better prepared new teachers, mentor teachers prepared to be instructional leaders in a building, teacher retention of both residents and mentor teachers, and improving PK–12 student learning by focusing on the development of mentor teachers and teacher residents and by having two teachers in a classroom for a year (Partnership Proclamation, Tenet 3).

As a Steering Committee, we have made many changes to the program since year one but continue to reflect on and are able to maintain our partnership as the program evolves (Developmental Proclamation, Tenets 2 and 4). As one example of how the work of the Steering Committee is evolving, we are incorporating induction support for our teacher residents once they are employed in our partner districts. We are providing professional development seminars and using mentor teachers who are not currently placed with a resident to support graduates from our residency programs during their induction years. The addition of induction support further validates the investment districts are making in the mentor teachers and demonstrates we are continuing to find mutually beneficial ways to address issues that affect all partners.

Many teacher residency programs begin with grant-funded support. As the grant expires, it can be difficult to sustain the program without having another source of funding and this financial investment often falls to school district partners (Gardiner & Salmon, 2014; Scheib et al., 2019). As the Steering Committee cocreated our model, we wanted to ensure our model of residency would be sustainable without external funding (Infrastructure Proclamation, Tenet 1). Our school districts agreed to make their financial investment in the mentor teachers selected. School districts fund the coursework, the summer institute, the substitute teachers required to offer professional development, and the stipend for mentor teachers who work with teacher residents (Expertise Proclamation, Tenet 5). The university funds a director who leads and manages all aspects of the program and all other costs associated with the program. The cost of the master's degree our residents earn is greatly reduced and now that the program is running smoothly and successful, we can begin to fund scholarships and/or living stipends for students from underrepresented groups or majors through donor gifts and possibly state-appropriated or grant funding (Expertise Proclamation, Tenet 4).

Our partnership with school districts can be described using the developmental stages outlined in the CPC report (AACTE, 2018) and CAEP's design team report (CAEP State Alliance Clinical Partnership Design Team, 2016). We have provided a summary in Table 9.1. During the *exploring and networking* stage, our initial meetings began with district superintendents and college leadership. As we moved further into developing the clinical practice partnership, other stakeholders in the districts and university who had a deeper understanding of specific context and components involved in program development, were included. During the *establishing* stage, we used our individual understandings of context together in a "third space" to develop our plans for implementing the residency program to have a robust clinical component. Currently, we are in the *refining* stage. As collaborators, we continue to nurture and support the partnership and collect and use data to continually improve. Finally, we are beginning to engage in the *extending* stage. We continue to have candid and honest communication and are looking for ways to grow our partnership. One example of our next step to extend our collaboration is the addition of induction support for our residents hired by the school districts which was mentioned earlier.

Table 9.1

The Developmental Proclamation: An Alignment of Clemson's Residency Program to the Continuum of Clinical Partnership Development and Growth

Continuum Phase	Actions
Exploring and Networking	Initial meetings began with district superintendents and college leadership and focused on developing a mutually beneficial partnership.
Establishing	Follow-up meetings included key district personnel, usually human resource directors, and key college staff (associate dean, field placement director, department chair, residency coordinator). Conversations focused on the recruitment and retention of teacher residents and clinical educators, resident and teacher coursework, and specific methods to be used to evaluate teacher residents. This group was identified as the Teacher Residency Steering Committee.
Refining	During the first two years, the Teacher Residency Steering Committee met monthly to continue to discuss all aspects of the residency program and to make program refinements: recruiting and retaining teacher residents and clinical educators and program curriculum.
Extending	The Teacher Residency Steering Committee meets each semester to continue to discuss all aspects of the residency program.

BENEFITS OF STRONG CLINICAL PREPARATION THROUGH TEACHER RESIDENCY

Teacher residency programs have been in place for more than a decade with about 50 successful, well-documented programs existing across the United States (Guha et al., 2017; Silva et al., 2014). The research support for teacher residency programs has demonstrated the ability of these programs to recruit and retain profession- and learner-ready teachers. In addition, research has indicated residents outperform their non-resident counterparts in terms of student achievement gains (Guha et al., 2016; 2017). We have summarized the research from residency programs in Table 9.2. The research shows teachers prepared in residency programs stay in the classroom longer and are better prepared to thrive in more challenging settings.

As we developed our teacher residency program, it was an important goal for us to have a strong-research base to support our decisions. We collect feedback from all of our participants—residents, mentor teachers,

Table 9.2

Teacher Residency—Retention and Student Achievement

Evidence Regarding Teacher Retention	
Memphis Teacher Residency (Tennessee Higher Education Commission, 2014)	Residents: 95% were teaching statewide in Year 3
	Nonresidents: 41% were teaching statewide in Year 3
Teacher Quality Preparation Grants (Silva et al., 2015)	Residents: 82% were teaching in the same district in Year 3 or 4
	Nonresidents: 72% were teaching in the same district in Year 3 or 4
Boston Teacher Residency (Papay et al., 2012)	Residents: 80% were teaching in Year 3; 75% were teaching in Year 5
	Nonresidents: 63% were teaching in Year 3; 51% were teaching in Year 5
San Francisco Teacher Residency (Guha et al., 2016)	Residents: 80% were teaching in Year 5
	Nonresidents from traditional programs: 38% were teaching in Year 5
	Nonresidents from Teach for America: 20% were teaching in Year 5
Evidence Regarding Student Achievement	
New Visions Hunter College Urban Teacher Residency (Sloan & Blazevski, 2015)	Residents outperformed those taught by other novice teachers on 16 out of 22 (73%) comparisons of NY State Regents exam
Boston Teacher Residency (Papay et al., 2012)	Residents had student achievement gains initially comparable with other novice teachers but by Year 4 or 5, residents outperformed other teachers by 7% of a standard deviation
Memphis Teacher Residency (Tennessee Higher Education Commission, 2014)	Residents had higher student achievement gains than other beginning teachers and larger gains than veteran teachers on most state standardized tests

university supervisors, school principals, district leaders, and faculty—to evaluate how our program is working and to make changes. Teacher residents and mentor teachers are surveyed at the beginning, middle, and end of the residency program regarding their graduate coursework and all aspects of the clinical placement such as the mentoring relationship, co-teaching implementation, and support from university supervisors. University supervisors, principals, and district leaders provide feedback annually. In addition to these surveys, we interview, conduct focus groups, collect artifacts, and observe classrooms to understand the needs and responsibilities of residents and mentor teachers, ensuring their feedback is central when we make changes (Empowerment Proclamation, Tenet 1). Now that our program is in implementation and improvement phases, it is equally important for us to collect data to support assertions that our program results in improved preparation for our residents, retention of our mentor teachers and residents, and has an impact on the learning outcomes of PK–12 students (Central Proclamation, Tenet 4). While we are in the early stages of data collection, we present our initial findings regarding the experiences of teacher residents' experiences in the program and their preparedness to teach compared to traditional student teachers, teacher residents' job placement and retention in the first year of teaching, the experiences of mentor teachers.

Teacher Residents' Experiences in the Program

On an exit survey at the end of their teacher preparation program, teacher residents were asked to rate statements on a scale of 1 (Strongly Disagree) to 5 (Strongly Agree) about their experiences in the teacher residency program. Residents rated their teacher preparation program higher than traditional student teachers on 82% of the survey questions including the amount of time spent in field placements, diverse experiences, intentional matching with mentor teachers, and purposeful classes. We have summarized some of the results in Table 9.3.

Table 9.3

Mean Ratings of Teacher Residents' Survey Responses

Survey Item	M
Spending the entire year in the classroom has greatly improved my ability to teach.	5.00
I expect that my first year of teaching will be much easier as a result of my teaching residency experiences.	4.95
I would recommend the residency program to other students.	4.95

Preparedness to Teach Compared to Traditional Student Teachers

Mentor teachers and university supervisors evaluate student teachers and teacher residents at the conclusion of their internship using the South Carolina Teaching Standards (SCTS) rubric found at https://ed.sc.gov/

educators/educator-effectiveness/south-carolina-teaching-standards-4-0/. The SCTS rubric contains 23 indicators focused on instruction, planning, environment, and professionalism. The rubric has four performance levels: exemplary (4), proficient (3), approaching proficient (2), and unsatisfactory (1). We compared the scores of our residents and student teachers, who have the same levels of preparation before their clinical internships, at the final point in their programs and found a statistically significant difference between the groups. We summarized the results in Table 9.4.

Table 9.4

Overall Mean SCTS Rubric Scores of Student Teachers and Teacher Residents

COE Teacher Preparation Program	M
Traditional Student Teaching Programs	3.33*
Teacher Residency Program	3.57*

* $p < 0.005$

We also compared scores on each of the four major dimensions of the SCTS Rubric—Instruction, Planning, Environment, and Professionalism. We found statistically significant differences between teacher residents and student teachers in three of the four dimensions. We summarized the results in Table 9.5. Our residents have more extensive clinical placements where they co-teach with mentor teachers and are seen as professionals in their schools and communities (Empowerment Proclamation, Tenet 2). As a result, they are better prepared in the areas of instruction (standard-based, presenting content, motivating students, lesson structure/pacing, questioning, providing feedback, etc.), environment (setting expectations, managing behavior, positive and respectful learning environments), and professionalism (growing professionally, reflection on teaching, school, and community involvement). With regard to planning, our residents and student teachers have similar preparation before their clinical internship. There is a heavy emphasis on planning our methods courses and this focus and proficiency of all of our students regarding planning could be why the difference among our residents and student teachers are not as great in this dimension.

Job Placement, Retention, and the First Year of Teaching

Our first cohort of residents graduated in spring of 2019. As of fall 2020, all but one, or 96% of the cohort, are employed as teachers. (One resident

Table 9.5

Mean Dimensional SCTS Rubric Scores of Student Teachers and Teacher Residents

COE Teacher Prep Program	Instruction	Planning	Environment	Professionalism
Traditional Student Teaching Programs	3.23	3.20	3.38	3.49
Teacher Residency Program	3.46*	3.39	3.66*	3.77*

*$p < 0.05$

is not employed as a teacher due to her military service obligation.) Of all of the residents who are now employed as teachers, 91% teach in South Carolina public schools. We surveyed our first cohort of graduates after their first semester of teaching to see how they were progressing in their first year. In addition to the induction mentoring they received, all of the residents employed as teachers indicated they remained in contact with their mentor teacher who offered them support (i.e., provided resources, offered advice) throughout their first semester of teaching. All of the residents returned to teaching for a second year, and 94% returned to the same school for their second year of employment.

We asked about the aspects of the teacher residency program that prepared them the most for their first semester of teaching, on a Likert scale of 1 (not well in preparing) to 5 (extremely well in preparing). Our results indicated the aspects that prepared residents the best for employment were co-teaching (4.4) and their relationship with their mentor teacher (4.8). Intentional matches and use of co-teaching models are the foundations of strong clinical practice in our program. The following quote from a former resident after her first semester of teaching summarizes how her preparation and relationship with her mentor teacher is critical to her success as a learner-ready and profession-ready first-year teacher.

> Being able to see the school year from start to finish was HUGE. I went into this year knowing exactly when I would start to feel a little burnt out. Since I went through this with my Master Teacher last year, I knew that this was not abnormal. I also knew what to expect in terms of student behavior. I knew that my planning around certain times of the year needed to be exceptionally strong because their behavior might not be as great. Last year I saw how the expectations that are set in the first few weeks of school set the tone for the entire year. I was purposeful in how I planned this

out because I knew how crucial it was. I knew exactly what management aspects I needed to plan for. If it wasn't for last year, I wouldn't have even thought of having a plan for passing out papers or keeping up with student absences. I also felt extremely prepared to take on any parent interactions. I know how to deal with upset parents and how to make them feel at ease. I understand that sometimes negative parent reactions are not a result of my teaching. Sometimes things happen that are out of my control and I am the easiest person to put blame on. My Master Teacher taught me to think about what they said but to also continue doing what I know is best for kids. However, parents have been impressed with how put together I appear to be as a first-year teacher. Finally, having the support of my Master Teacher has been wonderful. She helped me design a classroom that was practical rather than "cute." She helped me brainstorm different management strategies and how to deal with larger behavioral concerns. I love having a support system outside of my school.

We have also interviewed a subset of principals who had positive comments about the first-year teachers in their building. Principals indicated that based on the knowledge, skills, and dispositions of our graduates, our residents do not seem like first-year teachers. Some of the themes that emerged from interviews revealed that our residents are very proficient at standards-based instruction, are prepared to handle the individual learning and emotional needs of children and know how to differentiate instruction for diverse learners. They also indicated our graduates are well-rounded, are expected to have a positive impact on PK–12 student learning outcomes and are coachable.

Mentor Teachers

We are also interested in the impact of the program on mentor teachers. Mentor teachers were asked to rate statements on a scale of 1 (Strongly Disagree) to 5 (Strongly Agree) about their experiences in the teacher residency program. We have summarized some of the results in Table 9.6.

Next Steps

The data we are collecting has strengthened our partnerships and has allowed us to make continual program improvements. As the program becomes more established, we have agreements in place to collect data from our graduates hired in our partner districts. We will collect and compare PK–12 student achievement data from classrooms taught by former

Table 9.6

Mean Ratings of Mentor Teachers' Survey Responses

Survey Item	M
My teaching has become better as a result of having a teacher resident in my classroom.	4.84
The students in my classroom benefited as a result of my participation in the teacher residency program.	4.79
My participation in the teacher residency program has helped me to become more dedicated to the teaching profession.	4.63

teacher residents and those taught by former traditional student teachers. Likewise, we will compare teaching evaluations using the SCTS rubric during induction between our former teacher residents and traditional student teachers. Finally, we will collect teacher retention data for both our former teacher residents and our mentor teachers.

SUMMARY

Clinical experiences play an essential role in preservice teacher development (AACTE, 2018; NCATE, 2010). While there are many ways to centralize clinical practice within teacher preparation, teacher residency programs meet many of the CPC's proclamations. We provide a summary in Table 9.7 connecting the proclamations to features of our program. It is important that we prepare teachers with integrated academic content knowledge and pedagogical knowledge who know how to apply this knowledge in multiple and diverse school settings. Their progress should be continually monitored with a particular focus on PK–12 student learning. Our residents should work under the mentorship of clinical educators who participate in a rigorous selection process, professional development, and learning communities. And finally, PK–12 and universities should work within a "third space" to build strong relationships, co-develop and coimplement programs, and evaluate student progress and program features in an effort to better clinical experiences. These practices are the best way to ensure our preservice teachers are prepared for the classroom on day one as teacher of record (Coffman & Patterson, 2014).

Table 9.7

Summary of CPC's Report Proclamations (AACTE, 2018) and Features of Clemson's Teacher Residency Program

CPC Report Proclamation	Feature of Teacher Residency Program
The Central Proclamation	Faculty articulate what accomplished practice is and how to measure it by using in-service teacher evaluation tools as assessments and aligning coursework to clinical experiences.
	Residents engage in a culminating year-long clinical experience.
The Pedagogy Proclamation	Mentor teachers, university supervisors, and faculty provide specific pedagogical feedback to residents, specific to their teaching, during their culminating year-long clinical experience.
The Skills Proclamation	Mentor teachers and university supervisors take courses and attend seminars, specifically focused on innovative and research-based practices, allowing them to move beyond the traditional structures used to support teacher education candidates.
The Partnership Proclamation	A collaborative partnership, with identified mutually beneficial outcomes, between the college and school district partners form a firm foundation for the residency program.
The Infrastructure Proclamation	A clear governance structure was identified from the onset that created a sustainable funding structure.
The Developmental Proclamation	All partners continue to meet to monitor the progress of residents and mentor teachers and to make program adjustments. Some program components are school district-specific, allowing for consideration of local context.
The Empowerment Proclamation	Resident and teacher needs are assessed on a regular and on-going basis; feedback is carefully considered and used to make curricular and programmatic changes.
	Residents engage in co-teaching, beginning with students' first day in the classroom, empowering them from the onset.

(Table continued on next page)

Table 9.7 (Continued)

Summary of CPC's Report Proclamations (AACTE, 2018) and Features of Clemson's Teacher Residency Program

CPC Report Proclamation	Feature of Teacher Residency Program
The Mutual Benefit Proclamation	Clinical educators are highly qualified and work together to support, coach, and mentor the resident during their culminating year-long clinical experience. Clinical educators take graduate coursework and attend professional learning seminars focused on mentoring and coaching the resident.
The Common Language Proclamation	The college and school district partners collaboratively developed a common and shared understanding of the language used for the residency program. As much as possible, this language mirrors the clinical education lexicon in current literature.
The Expertise Proclamation	Clinical educators, residents, school district partners, and other external stakeholders play an active and critical part in shaping the residency program.

REFERENCES

American Association of Colleges for Teacher Education. (2018). *A pivot toward clinical practice, its lexicon, and the renewal of educator preparation: A report of the AACTE Clinical Practice Commission.* https://aacte.org/resources/research-reports-and-briefs/clinical-practice-commission-report/

Asplin, K. N. & Marks, M. J. (2013). Increasing the influence of university supervisors during student teaching. *The Professional Educator, 37*(1), 1–10.

Barger-Anderson, R., Isherwood, R. S., & Merhaut, J. (2013). Co-teaching. In *Strategic co-teaching in your school: Using the co-design model* (pp. 111–122). Brookes Publishing.

Bates, A. J., Drits, D., & Ramiriz, L. A. (2011). Self-awareness of supervisory stance: Influences on responsiveness toward student teacher learning. *Teacher Education Quarterly, 38*(3), 69–87.

Beck, C., & Kosnik, C. (2002). Components of a good practicum placement: Student teacher perceptions. *Teacher Education Quarterly, 29,* 81–98.

Coffman, A. N., & Patterson, R. (2014). *Teacher residencies: Redefining preparation through partnerships.* National Education Association.

Cook, L., & Friend, M. (1995). Co-teaching: Guidelines for creating effective practices. *Focus on Exceptional Children, 28*(3), 1–16.

Council for the Accreditation of Educator Preparation State Alliance Clinical Partnership Design Team. (2016, March 24). *Findings and outcomes: Framework for the development of clinical partnership practice [PowerPoint slides]. SlideShare.* https://www.towson.edu/coe/about/documents/caep/frameworkforthedevelopment.pdf

Darling-Hammond, L. (2006). Constructing the clinical experience: The glue for powerful preparation. In *Powerful teacher education: Lessons from exemplary programs* (pp. 152–185). Josey-Bass.

Darragh, J. J., Picanco, K. E., Tully, D., & Henning, A. S. (2011). When teachers collaborate, good things happen: Teacher candidate perspectives of the co-teach model for the student teaching internship. *The Journal of the Association of Independent Liberal Arts Colleges of Teacher Education, 8*(1), 83–109.

Gallo-Fox, J., & Scantlebury, K. (2016). Co-teaching as professional development for cooperating teachers. *Teaching and Teacher Education, 60,* 191–120.

Gardiner, W. (2011) Mentoring in an urban teacher residency: Mentors' perceptions of yearlong placements. *The New Educator, 7*(2), 153–171.

Gardiner, W., & Salmon, D. (2014). Bridging the theory-practice gap in an urban teacher residency: Two interventions and a cautionary note. *Journal of Urban Learning, Teaching, and Research, 10,* 87–100.

Guha, R., Hyler, M. E., & Darling-Hammond, L. (2017). American Educator. The teacher residency: A practical path to recruitment and retention. *American Educator, 41*(1), 31–44.

Guha, R., Hyler, M. E., & Darling-Hammond, L. (2016). *The teacher residency: An innovative model for teacher preparation.* Learning Policy Institute.

Klein, E. J., Taylor, M., Onore, C., Strom, K., & Abrams, L. (2013) Finding a third space in teacher education: creating an urban teacher residency, *Teaching Education, 24*(1), 27–57.

Koerner, M., & Rust, F. (2002). Exploring roles in student teaching placements. *Teacher Education Quarterly, 29,* 35–58.

National Council for Accreditation of Teacher Education. (2010). *Transforming teacher education through clinical practice: A national strategy to prepare effective teachers* (Report of the Blue Ribbon Panel on clinical preparation and partnerships for improved student learning). National Council for Accreditation of Teacher Education.

Papay, J. P., West, M. R., Fullerton, J. B., & Kane, T. J. (2012). Does an urban teacher residency increase student achievement? Early evidence from Boston. *American Educational Research Association, 34*(4), 413–434.

Rajuan, M., Beijaard, D., & Verloop, N. (2010) The match and mismatch between expectations of student teachers and cooperating teachers: exploring different opportunities for learning to teach in the mentor relationship. *Research Papers in Education, 25*(2), 201–223.

Scheib, C., Davis, C. B., & the National Center for Teacher Residencies. (2019). Scale and sustainability of residency programs. In C. A. Torrez & M. Krebs (Eds.), *The teacher residency model: Core components for high impact on student achievement* (pp. 223–236). Lexington Books

Silva, T., McKie, A., & Gleason, P. (2015). *New findings on the retention of novice teachers from teaching residency programs.* National Center for Education Evaluation and Regional Assistance, Institute of Education Sciences.

Silva, T., McKie, A., Knechtel, V., Gleason, P., & Makowsky, L. (2014). *Teaching residency programs: A multisite look at a new model to prepare teachers for high-need schools.* National Center for Education Evaluation and Regional Assistance, Institute for Education Sciences.

Sloan, K. & Blazevski, J. (2015). *New Visions Hunter College Urban Teacher Residency: Measures of success* (Summative Report). https://b.3cdn.net/nvps/d1725192f4cb60167f_qsm6vz3qx.pdf

Solheim, K., Roland, P., & Ertesvåg, S. K. (2018). Teachers' perceptions of their collective and individual learning regarding classroom interaction. *Educational Research, 60*(4), 459–477.

Steffy, B. E., Wolfe, M. P., Rasch, S. H., & Enz, B. J. (Eds.). (2000). *Life cycle of the career teacher.* Kappa Delta Phi & Corwin Press.

Tennessee Higher Education Commission. (2014). *2014 report card on the effectiveness of teacher training programs.* Tennessee Higher Education Commission, Tennessee Department of Education, State Board of Education.

Washburn-Moses, L. (2017). A national descriptive survey of teacher residency programs. *School-University Partnerships, 10*(2), 33–41.

Wenger, E. (1998). *Communities of practice: Learning, meaning, and identity.* Cambridge University Press.

Williamson, P., & Hodder, L. (2015). Unpacking practice with clinical instructional rounds in the San Francisco teacher residency program. *International Journal of Educational Research, 73*, 53–64.

CHAPTER 10

BUILDING A TEACHER RESIDENCY COLLABORATIVE

Mapping the Synergistic Activities to the Continuum of Clinical Partnership Development and Growth

Karin Sprow Forté, Jane M. Wilburne, and Michael J. Swogger
Pennsylvania State University–Harrisburg

ABSTRACT

Using the AACTE's 2018 Clinical Practice Commission Report as a guiding framework, the authors discuss their experiences in networking/exploring, establishing, refining, and extending a clinical-experience model from traditional student teaching to a residency model. The transition's primary goal was to prepare teacher candidates to teach in high-need schools, increase the diversity of the teacher workforce, and promote stronger partnerships between all stakeholders. Beginning with explaining the context and background of the preparation program and the challenges facing the partner school districts, the authors then address the initial stages of exploring and establishing a residency program and the significance of the collaborations with local stakeholders. The authors next share the areas of their residency model that required refinement to extend its effectiveness. Finally, we share implications for other programs considering a residency model for teacher preparation.

Preparing Quality Teachers:
Advances in Clinical Practice, pp. 223–240
Copyright © 2022 by Information Age Publishing
www.infoagepub.com

An effective workforce of teachers requires a rigorous preparation process to prepare candidates to meet the demands of today's classrooms (Carver-Thomas, 2018). Teacher education programs need to recruit candidates and prepare them to be profession-ready through coursework and clinical experiences (Bulger et al., 2015). The nature of these clinical experiences and the opportunities to make connections between the coursework and the clinical experiences are critical to ensure candidates learn research-based practices and have the opportunities to implement the practices in various settings and with diverse pre-K–12 students. The American Association of Colleges for Teacher Educators (AACTE) Clinical Practice Commission published a report that includes recommendations for the development, implementation, and practices for teacher preparation institutions to consider for productive and efficacious clinical experiences (AACTE, 2018). Specifically, they state teacher candidates need "sustained and ongoing opportunities to engage in authentic performance within diverse learning environments" (p. 14). Clinical practice should be a "non-negotiable component of every high-quality teacher preparation" (p. 14) with "intentional pedagogical experiences in authentic educational settings" (p. 18). This chapter shares insights and challenges one university faced to address this recommendation and how the Continuum of Clinical Partnerships Development and Growth (AACTE, 2013) guided their transition to a new clinical experience model (Mourlam et al., 2019).

BACKGROUND

Our campus is located in the northeastern part of the United States. It is surrounded by middle-, upper-middle-, and working-class suburbs and exurbs, with a significant number of rural communities and farm acreage. Over 15 individual school districts serve the surrounding region with student populations ranging from predominantly White rural and suburban to mostly non-White. Some school districts consist of relatively low levels of student poverty, as measured by the number of students receiving free and reduced lunches. In contrast, other school districts are high-poverty districts with anywhere between 25% to 80% of the students receiving free and reduced lunches.

The campus has roughly 5,000 undergraduate and graduate students from around the country and world. The Teacher Education program includes elementary (pre-K–4, Grades 4–8 math, social studies, and English language arts (ELA), and secondary (Grades 7–12) math, social studies, and ELA certifications. Post-baccalaureate certification in secondary math, social studies, English language arts, and special education, with reading specialist, English as a second language (ESL), instructional coaching, and principalship certification add-ons also available. Enrollment in our initial certification programs is currently around 45–50 elementary candidates and 50–55 secondary candidates over the junior and senior years (Semesters 5–8 of their college career). While the campus, as a whole, is one of the most diverse in the region, the demographics in the education programs remain stubbornly homogeneous, approximating the current race and gender demographics of teachers in the United States.

The teacher education faculty has expertise in literacy, mathematics education, social justice, culturally relevant practices, social and emotional learning, early childhood, learning theory, special education, science, and ESL, including inclusive translanguaging practices. The department faculty, along with faculty in social sciences and psychology, often work collaboratively integrating interdisciplinary activities and assignments into the education courses and clinical work. The faculty are also actively involved in visiting candidates during their field experiences, observing, and assessing candidates' instruction, providing feedback, and discussing field-to-practice course assignments.

Teacher candidates have the opportunity to complete their clinical experiences in high-need, suburban, and rural school districts. Both the elementary and secondary certification programs require candidates to engage in various clinical field experiences along with their requisite education and content-area coursework. Elementary teacher candidates participate in classrooms at a local Head Start program as part of their fifth-semester fieldwork. In their sixth semester, they participate in a more traditional classroom. These placements are introductory clinical experiences designed to acclimate the teacher candidates to the rigors of teaching while also enabling them to engage with students from different ages and socioeconomic and ethnic backgrounds. By the seventh semester, elementary teacher candidates participate in a field experience two days per week, often in the same classroom where they plan to conduct their student-teaching experience.

The secondary teacher candidates likewise participate in several different field experiences. In their fifth semester, secondary candidates are in the field two days each week for 10 weeks. This field experience is concurrent with taking a course in learning theory and instruction for secondary-age students, affording candidates to make theory-to-practice and practice-to-theory connections through narrative reflections and dialogue (Goh, 2019). The following semester, all secondary candidates must engage in two field experiences, with one experience associated with a special education course and another centering on social and cultural factors in education.

Like most teacher preparation programs, our teacher candidates' culminating clinical experience is student teaching, which occurs during the candidates' final semester of their program. Placements for both elementary and secondary candidates are typically in settings commensurate with their intended area of certification and often in school districts with mentor teachers with whom we have developed a strong working relationship.

CO-TEACHING

Another important component of our traditional student teaching program is St. Cloud University's co-teaching model for student teaching (Heck et al., 2010), which we implemented in 2014. The co-teaching model allows us to foster a more meaningful partnership between mentor teachers and teacher candidates and engages the teacher candidates in more active classroom planning and instruction.

The co-teaching model differs in both quality and effectiveness of the traditional student teaching model. Under the traditional model, teacher candidates enter their placement as novices and contribute little to classroom planning and instruction in the beginning weeks. Candidates observe the mentor teacher, get to know classroom, and school procedures, and engage in various support activities in the first few weeks. After the initial weeks, the teacher candidate begins teaching one lesson, perhaps with some level of independence in planning and assessment. The level of responsibility for planning and teaching typically increases incrementally by class or subject area, leading to full teacher responsibilities by the middle of the student teaching experience. As the semester winds down, the teacher candidate begins the gradual transfer of responsibility back to the mentor. The mentor teacher generally plays a supportive and observational role, offering the candidate formative feedback with limited classroom involvement.

The co-teaching model differs significantly from the traditional model. Co-teaching is defined as "[t]wo teachers (teacher candidate and [mentor] teacher) working together with groups of students; sharing the planning, organization, delivery, and assessment of instructions, as well as the physical space" (Heck et al., 2010, p. 7). Unlike the traditional approach, the teacher candidate works alongside the mentor teacher and is part of the classroom routine from the beginning as a co-teacher. Neither teacher "takes over" a class; instead, one can "take the lead" in planning and or teaching (p. 7). The mentor teacher incorporates the teacher candidate into the planning process, is open to new ideas, and considers ways to take advantage of a two-teacher classroom effectively. Fundamental to this planning process is a set of seven co-teaching strategies, on which both the mentor teacher and candidate have been trained before the start of the experience. These strategies include one teach-one observe and one teach-one assist; parallel teaching (two teachers implementing the same plan simultaneously to half the class); alternative/differentiated teaching (two teachers implementing different plans to deliver the same content); stations or centers; and team teaching. Our teacher candidates are still required to embrace full classroom leadership roles for at least two weeks of their experience, but at all other times, it is co-teaching that predominates.

The documented advantages to co-teaching in a clinical setting are numerous. Bacharach and Washut-Heck (2012) conducted extensive mixed-methods research focusing on St. Cloud University's co-teaching program for student teachers. For instance, mentor teachers overwhelmingly identified important benefits to the co-teaching model, including more help for high-need pupils, a robust mentor-candidate relationship, professional growth through the co-planning process, and a reinvigoration for teaching. Bacharach et al. (2010) indicated that:

> Since adopting the co-teaching model, St. Cloud State University now has more cooperating teachers willing to host candidates than available candidates in most licensure areas. Cooperating teachers recognize the "value-added" by hosting a teacher candidate using the co-teaching model. (pp. 17–18)

In other words, mentor teachers more eagerly host student teachers when using a co-teaching model.

Teacher candidates, too, cite important benefits, such as more teaching time, improved collaboration skills, improved classroom management skills, and more opportunities to ask questions and reflect with the mentor teacher, providing opportunities to meet individual learning needs. As Richmond et al. (2020) point out, while different relationships are essential to the development of teacher candidates, "perhaps none is more important than the role of the mentor teacher (MT) and that mentor's relationship with the teacher candidate (TC), whom she or he has committed to support" (p. 6). Additionally, 88% of the candidates surveyed reported higher confidence levels and a greater sense of professional status due to co-teaching (Bacharach & Washut-Heck, 2012). Wilburne and Ozman (2017) also found teacher candidates reported a greater sense of self-efficacy with the co-teaching model than those in the traditional student teaching model. While we recognized the benefits of the co-teaching model, we wanted to expand the clinical experience opportunities with our partner school districts.

CHALLENGES OF OUR HIGH-NEED
PARTNER SCHOOL DISTRICTS

Three school districts that surround our campus are categorized by the Pennsylvania Department of Education (2018) as high need because they

(1) have high rates of minority students or high percentages of students in poverty, or (2) can demonstrate chronic, multiple teacher shortages in special education, STEM subjects, or other state-identified or local shortage areas. Table 10.1 provides a summary of the school districts' student population rates.

Table 10.1

Partner High-Need School District Statistics

Partner High Need School District	% ESL Students	% Economically Disadvantaged	% Minoritized Groups
District A	7.7	47.9	51.6
District B	16.5	88.3	96.0
District C	5.0	79.9	84.9

Source: https://futurereadypa.org/Search/District#

The three school districts have an underrepresentation of teachers of color, with only 9% identified as persons of color compared to 58% of the students (Pennsylvania Department of Education, 2020). These districts also face the challenge of retaining teachers. They note that approximately 20% to 30% of their new teachers leave the teaching profession within the first five years. These statistics comport with data published from similar classifications of school districts (Darling-Hammond & Sykes, 2003; Ingersoll, 2003; Sutcher et al., 2016).

Promoting more diversity in the teacher workforce is essential to advance educational equity in all schools (Council of Chief State School Officers [CCSSO], 2018, p. 6). Our partner school district administrators have struggled with finding diverse applicants for teaching positions. They recognize that teachers of color "serve as role models, set high expectations, and support the academic growth of students of color" (Egalite et al., 2015). If they are to promote equity for each student in today's schools, these high-need school districts need to significantly increase the diversity of their teacher workforce.

CHALLENGES OF OUR CLINICAL EXPERIENCE MODEL

Our teacher preparation program struggled to encourage teacher candidates to select the high-need districts for their student-teaching placement. Placements often depended on the number of teacher candidates in any given semester and mentors' availability within those schools. Many candidates wanted to be placed near their home school districts or where they hoped to gain employment. However, we wanted them to experience enacting subject matter knowledge (Hill et al., 2008) in classrooms with culturally and linguistically diverse students.

While our program saw the benefits of implementing the co-teaching model, we realized that our traditional student teaching model focused more on what took place in individual classrooms and did not consider activities that would engage the candidates in the schools or their schools' surrounding communities. For our teacher candidates to learn how to be responsive to the needs of the diverse students, they needed to become knowledgeable about the broader social and community aspects of society that impact the learning environment in the high-need school districts (Hammond, 2015). Also, "while the U.S. student population becomes more ethnically, racially, and linguistically diverse, the demographic make-up of teacher candidates remains mostly White/Caucasian" (AACTE, 2013, p. 4). Since our teacher preparation program roughly reflects the overall teacher population in the United States, which is mostly White and female, we needed to recruit more diverse candidates into our program, especially historically underrepresented minority groups.

The above challenges facing both the university teacher preparation program and our local high-need school districts required collaborative problem solving. As a result of a series of meetings with school district administrators and university teacher education leaders, we decided to explore the implementation of an undergraduate residency program. The format and structure of a year-long residency program provided the best solution to (a) address the challenges facing our partner high-need school districts; (b) enhance our candidates' clinical experience to prepare them with the knowledge and skills needed to be a successful teacher in high-need schools, and; (c) recruit more diverse teacher candidates for teacher preparation programs.

THE EVOLUTION OF A RESIDENCY PROGRAM

To begin, we explored the research behind residency programs and how those programs meet the challenges of recruiting teachers in hard-to-staff subjects, increasing the diversity of the teaching workforce, and reducing the turnover among novice teachers in high-need districts (Guha et al., 2016; Guha et al., 2017; Hammerness et al., 2016; Le Maistre, 2000; Papay et al., 2012). A study by Roegman et al. (2017) indicates that as a result of participation in a residency program, "ninety-five percent of residents were retained in the profession after three years, whereas in the fifth year, 85%

of residents were still teaching—70% in the same urban partner district" (p. 446). We considered how a residency program aligns with the AACTE (2018) Clinical Practices Proclamation which states, "clinical practice must provide sustained and ongoing opportunities to engage in authentic performance in diverse learning environments and is an essential component of high-quality teacher preparation" (p. 14). We believed that a residency program would bolster our teacher preparation programs' theory-to-practice connections through the emphasis on sustained and embedded classroom-learning experiences, as well as planned school and community activities (DeMoss, 2016).

Designing an effective and sustainable residency program involved conversations and meetings with our school partners to be sure the program would also meet the unique needs of their students. Our collaborative work progressed through a cycle of developmental stages that included networking/exploring, establishing, refining, and extending (AACTE, 2018). These stages were "not necessarily linear, they were recursive and boundary spanning as our partnerships evolved" (p. 29). We highlight our work's progression with our clinical partners to implement a residency program as we moved through these four stages.

STAGE 1: NETWORKING AND EXPLORING AN UNDERGRADUATE RESIDENCY PROGRAM

Networking and exploring began by receiving a planning grant from PDE and then engaging the stakeholders in discussions to "develop a deep understanding of local contextual variables and how those factors would shape the partnership" (AACTE, 2018, p. 29). These discussions aimed to merge the diverse perspectives regarding teacher preparation and effective clinical experiences shared by cooperating teachers, school administrators, university supervisors, and university teacher educators (Burroughs et al., 2020). The initial discussions focused on considering the design and operation of an intensive residency clinical experience model to better prepare candidates for teaching in high-need schools. Teacher preparation programs are often criticized for a "lack of rigor and for focusing too much on educational theory and too little on classroom practice" (Dubin, 2017, para. 11). Our program focused on a theory-to-practice connection across courses (Hollins, 2011). However, we wanted to shift our emphasis to a program that was "fully grounded in clinical practice and interwoven with academic content and professional courses" (National Council for Accreditation of Teacher Education [NCATE], 2010, p. 9). The addition of a residency program would also promote "more confidence in the candidates' ability to provide quality instruction ... and better prepare them for the high-needs classroom" (Mentzer et al., 2019, p. 45).

The collaborative discussions led to the writing of several proposals for state-funded grants to plan and implement a teacher residency program in partnership with our three high-need school districts. Upon receiving funding first for a planning grant, we formed a Steering Committee that included a collective representation of partner school district administrators and educators, university representatives, teacher education faculty members, and community liaisons. The committee, composed of 30 individuals, met biweekly over one-year to identify key areas to consider and plan to transition to a residency program. In line with the AACTE Mutual Benefits Proclamation (2018), the planning focused on meeting the needs of the university teacher preparation program and the partner school districts, and how to address our state's teacher shortage needs both regionally and in content areas. The Steering Committee established four subcommittees focused on: (a) recruiting, selecting, and hiring residency candidates and mentor teachers; (b) co-teaching and professional development trainings; (c) competencies and credits; (d) and superintendent, administrators, and stakeholder needs and buy-in. Each subcommittee created a co-constructed action plan and presented it to the full committee for review and feedback. The Steering Committee agreed that a residency program is one way to address the district and teacher preparation program needs including retention, diversity, and incorporating the co-teaching model, all of which would be essential to the quality and impact of the clinical residency. The partnership component ensured that that residency program would be tailored to meet the district, university, teacher candidate, and community needs.

In the ongoing and iterative process, the partners continued to work together to identify their needs and develop detailed implementation plans that identify key personnel, develop necessary policies and procedures, and determine how resources will be shared" (AACTE, 2018, p. 29). They submitted a second grant proposal for an implementation grant that was funded through the state department of education program.

STAGE 2: ESTABLISHING AN UNDERGRADUATE RESIDENCY PROGRAM

The residency model began with an intensive clinical experience during semesters seven and eight of the teacher candidates' four-year academic degree plan. In the fall semester, residency candidates are in their field placement three days per week and on campus two days per week completing their education coursework. One change from the traditional student teaching model is the residency model requires the candidates to begin their placement before the university fall semester. This change allows the candidates to establish a relationship with their mentor teacher, assist in preparing the classroom for the school year, and participate in their host district's professional-development activities. The residency candidates follow their host school's calendar in the fall semester and return to the school immediately after the district's winter break. Unlike the traditional student teaching model, in which candidates complete their student teaching before their college graduation in May, the residency candidates continue their placements until the end of the host district's school year.

During this stage, the Residency Advisory Committee's formation replaced the Steering Committee in its co-construction role. The committee meets biannually to address the broader issues of the districts (e.g., retention, substitute teacher shortages) and the teacher preparation program (e.g., funding for supervisors and mentor teachers), and is exploring the expansion of the program to a fourth and fifth high-need school district.

One of the critical planning items was the diversification of the teacher candidate pool that would help increase the diversity of educators in pre-K–12 schools. Our pilot year began with 11 residency candidates, 9 elementary certification candidates, and 2 secondary certification candidates. Two of the 11 residency candidates were from minoritized groups, and all identified as female. Since the residency program required us to select candidates in the senior year of the teacher education program, we could not target recruitment for a broader pool of candidates. Recruitment efforts are focusing on the freshman and sophomore years, where undergraduate candidates have not declared a major. The pilot year provided us with an opportunity to identify actions to recruit and retain diverse teacher candidates in the program. Specific actions include tutoring for entrance-to-major tests, consistent monitoring and advising sessions, and planning for additional financial support.

As with any new program, there were challenges and unexpected outcomes. One challenge was the COVID-19 pandemic, which had an unpredictable impact on our candidates' experiences with the residency program. Despite the closing of schools, our residency candidates continued to work with their mentor teachers and provided instruction remotely to their students. The experience allowed the residency candidates an opportunity to demonstrate to their mentor teachers how to use various technologies effectively to promote students' learning. They also learned the need to be flexible and the importance of attending to their students' mental health and access to resources.

STAGE 3: REFINING THE RESIDENCY PROGRAM

During the refining phase, "all partners share responsibility for nurturing the partnership. Expectations for clear communication and meaningful collaboration support the collection and analysis of data for continuous improvement" (AACTE, 2018, p. 29). The Residency Advisory Committee identified three issues for refinement: increase and retain diverse teacher candidates, sequence, and align the teacher education curriculum, and enhance the mentor teachers' effectiveness.

Refinement Issue 1: Increase and Retain Diverse Teacher Candidates

Minoritized groups represent approximately 40% of the undergraduate enrollment on our campus. Among this year's entering freshman, 42% of minoritized students have no identified major. While recruiting students of color into our teacher education program has long been a priority, achieving this goal has been challenging. The shortage of non-White teacher candidates is a nationwide phenomenon not easily overcome. Carver-Thomas (2018) has identified several strategies institutions can implement to attract more potential teachers of color. One strategy is to foster more inclusive admission strategies. As such, we are working closely with the undergraduate advising center and the Office of Career Counseling to make connections with diverse students who have not declared a major. Another recruitment strategy is to consider the costs of participating in teacher education programs (Carver-Thomas, 2018). We are working on strategies to pay the fees associated with the required basic skills and certification testing to reduce the teacher candidates' financial burden. Grant funds currently support the residency candidates through stipends and scholarships to help defray the cost of attendance. We seek additional funding to continue the program beyond the grant, and we are working with our partner school districts on financial incentives for the candidates.

Finally, we are working with the partner districts to develop a Grow-Your-Own (GYO) program (Skinner et al., 2011) that specifically targets students of color from the partner schools to address the teacher retention and shortage issues. GYO programs align with the social justice and culturally relevant pedagogical foundations of our teacher preparation programs, as well as with our efforts to serve the high-need districts in our region. GYO programs can offer a promising and successful pipeline of teachers who will be more likely to "stay teaching in the community" (Valenzuela, 2017, p. 1). We hope to recruit from within the local middle and high schools and from the paraprofessional population and college graduates with nonteaching degrees to create various pathways and implement the needed support measures to prepare them for the teaching profession.

Refinement Issue 2: Sequencing and Aligning the Curriculum

The mentor teachers and residency candidates provided feedback regarding the need to revisit the undergraduate teacher preparation curriculum. The Steering Committee addressed the curricular alignment during the exploration phase. Candidates in the pilot program had difficulty balancing their coursework and field experience work in the fall semester. Several candidates said it was challenging to continually shift back and forth in their role as students and as teachers. As a result, teacher education faculty met to discuss ways to shift some courses around so fewer courses were required in the fall semester of the candidates' senior year.

First, we realigned the coursework sequence in the elementary education program to better meet the teacher candidates' expectations and clinical experience needs. Candidates in the residency program work with their mentor teacher in the pre-K–12 classrooms for a full semester (the seventh semester) earlier than the traditional student teaching program. Thus, we moved several methods classes to the seventh semester to be concurrent with the clinical experience. By communicating regularly with school administrators and mentor teachers, university-based educators who teach the methods courses align assignments more closely with the current classroom curriculum and practice. "This intentional planning also provides a vehicle to expand relationships, encourage reflection, and provide increased opportunities to make connections between theory and classroom practice (Stanulis, 1995), while modeling effective pedagogical practice" (AACTE, 2018, p. 37).

Second, we altered the seventh-semester schedule so the candidates would complete most of their coursework in the first half of the semester. This change provides them with more time in the second half of the semester to focus on their field experiences. Prescribed coursework and the suggested academic plans were reconfigured by frontloading more credits in the first three years so that pre-majors can begin to plan for residency from the outset.

Third, we included more emphasis on topics such as culturally relevant teaching, social justice, and teaching with technology in our elementary education courses. We added a course on culturally responsive pedagogy and poverty- and trauma-informed teaching to the secondary program curriculum. Candidates take the course during the fall semester of their senior year. This change will prepare candidates to make important theory-to-practice and practice-to-theory connections while they are in the field.

One challenge has been to maintain the rigor of the courses and align coursework with the progression of the candidates' pedagogical learning while they are in their clinical experience. We are also trying to avoid overloading the candidates during their seventh semester. We are hopeful that the refinements to the curriculum that we made will address those concerns and meet candidates' needs.

Refinement Issue 3: Mentor Matching and Professional Development

During the pilot year, we realized there was a need to refine the mentoring components of our residency program. As we have with every other aspect of the residency program, we worked with our partners to engage "school leaders and their instructional leadership team in productive partnerships to advance beginning teacher effectiveness and the learning of every student" (New Teacher Center, 2018, p. 3). The goal should be to build "collaborative, respectful, instructional-focused mentoring partnerships to foster beginning teacher ownership of continuous improvement of practice and advance every student's learning" (p. 3).

We presented the residency candidate applications to the school principals and administrators. They paired the applications with teachers who would be supportive and effective mentors. In some cases, teacher candidates who were not confident in their planning and instruction skills were paired with mentor teachers who struggled to build the candidate's confidence. An essential part of every relationship is each person's personality and interaction styles. "Mentors are expected not just to impart the technical aspects of teaching, but also to cultivate a certain disposition, an inquisitive and reflective mindset, and a constant focus on students' understanding" (National Center for Teacher Residencies, 2014, p. 15). To refine the matching process and avoid mismatches in the future, we revised the candidate application to include attitudinal and behavioral information so principals and administrators can better match candidates and mentors.

We also observed that some mentor teachers seemed to be better at mentoring candidates than others. A teacher who is considered an expert in terms of their effect on students' performance may not necessarily have the interpersonal skills to be an effective mentor. In some cases, mentor teachers were eager to participate in the residency to improve their own teaching practices. As one teacher stated in Dubin's (2017) study, " 'having someone in here watching me, I feel like I have to be more intentional in my moves.' And having to explain them has pushed her to improve" (para. 31). Our priority was to identify mentor teachers who continually seek to improve their practice and participate in ongoing professional development (Darling-Hammond, 1999). Thus, one criterion added to the mentor selection process was to identify teachers who expressed a desire to "deepen and maintain [their] own knowledge of rigorous content standards, social and emotional learning, learner variability, and culturally responsive pedagogy" (New Teacher Center, 2018, p. 3).

To help promote professional-learning opportunities for the mentor teachers, we developed a series of online mentoring modules on topics related to communication and coaching, culturally relevant pedagogy, families and communities, and co-planning and co-teaching. Our goal with this refinement is to build our mentor teachers' mentoring skills and their ability to coach the residency candidates, effectively observe candidates' instruction, and engage in critical and reflective conversations with our candidates on culturally responsive teaching (Gay, 2000). The plan is to have all new mentor teachers participate in these online mentor modules. These refinements hope to improve the mentor teacher-teacher candidate matching process and promote a stronger bidirectional learning relationship.

STAGE 4: EXTENDING THE RESIDENCY PROGRAM

The extending stage is characterized by "mutuality, interdependence, and reciprocity. All partners share responsibility for growing the partnership, and all partners view themselves as both learners and teachers" (AACTE, 2018, p. 29). Input from all partners is essential to assess the functionality and effectiveness of the residency program. The Residency Advisory Committee focused on what's working and what could be enhanced. In one meeting, we discussed the hiring of university supervisors for the full academic year. The university supervisor's role is to observe and assess teacher candidates in their clinical experience and provide feedback on their teaching competencies. In our pilot year, we hired supervisors to observe the residency candidates in both the fall and spring semesters. The goal was to track the residency candidates' progression of learning throughout the residency academic year and identify competencies that required more attention in the methods courses. As we plan for our program's sustainability, we recognize the need to be fiscally responsible and minimize expenses where possible. The Steering Committee agreed to have the school principals include informal observations of the teacher candidates in their walkthroughs and rely on the mentor teachers' formal observations for input on the candidates' performance in the fall semester. This interdependence on the initial observations of the residency candidates' performance ensures that all partners are working together to support the candidates' growth in implementing culturally relevant and highly effective practices and adjusting to the work of teaching. This approach allows for the residency candidates to hone their pedagogical skills before the university supervisor's formal observations are conducted in the spring semester.

In another meeting, the leadership team discussed the option of allowing the residency candidates to serve as substitute teachers for their mentor teachers. As school districts, especially those serving high-needs communities, struggle to find qualified substitute teachers (Mathewson, 2017), this agreement benefits both the candidate and the school district. Reflections from the residency candidates indicated they found the substitute-teaching experience valuable in their pedagogical learning, teaching confidence, and their ability to see themselves as classroom teachers. The candidates shared that the intensive experience in the classroom helped them understand each student's learning needs and the importance of promoting equity in the classroom. As school districts have critical needs, extending the program's operation must be considered to support the sustainability of the partnership (AACTE, 2018, p. 25).

IMPLICATIONS FOR PROGRAMS AND CONCLUSION

We have been working to ensure that "the benefits of clinical practice accrue to all involved, from pre-K–12 students to the university- and school-based teacher educators as well as the aspiring and novice educators for whom they serve as mentors, models, and guides" (AACTE, 2018, p. 44). Data collected (e.g., surveys, interviews) from both the candidates and mentor teachers during the residency experiences show enthusiasm for the teacher preparation model with benefits for all stakeholders, as well as the students in the pre-K–12 classroom.

The candidates' initial years of independent teaching will determine the overall effectiveness of the residency program. Assessments of their teaching performance will be obtained in future years through surveys, self-assessments, supervisor assessments, and interviews about their progress and how prepared they were due to their participation in the residency program. The teacher education programs will also monitor their time in their current positions and their long-term retention in teaching.

Using the AACTE framework for planning and implementing a residency model can prepare all stakeholders for any potential challenges. The recursiveness of the four stages is evident in the continual improvement process and the focus on establishing mutually beneficial clinical partnerships. The preparation of candidates in a residency program is the shared responsibility of both university teacher educators and school districts. Planning, implementing, and assessing the program's effectiveness and the residency candidates' experiences involves "regular and purposeful communication and productive feedback" (AACTE, 2018. p. 34). The shared commitment by all partners to identify, establish, and sustain high-quality and diverse candidates, relevant and concurrent coursework, candidates' learning, expert mentoring, funding, and resources to support and foster the efficacy of the residency program, is the essence of our success (AACTE, 2018).

ACKNOWLEDGEMENT

This project was made possible by the Innovative Teacher and Principal Residency Program Grants sponsored by the Pennsylvania Department of Education.

REFERENCES

AACTE Clinical Practice Commission. (2013). *The changing teacher preparation profession: A report from AACTE's professional education data system (PEDS)*.

AACTE Clinical Practice Commission. (2018). *A pivot toward clinical practice, its lexicon, and the renewal of educator preparation*. American Association of Colleges for Teacher Education. www.aacte.org

Bacharach, N. L., & Washut-Heck, T. (2012). Voices from the field: Multiple perspectives on a co-teaching in student teaching model. *Educational Renaissance, 1*(1), 49–69.

Bacharach, N. L., Heck, T. W., & Dahlberg, K. (2010). *Changing the face of student teaching through co-teaching*. St. Cloud State University, the Repository at St. Cloud State. *Teacher Development Faculty Publications, 1*, 1–32.

Bulger, S. M., Jones, E. M., Taliaferro, A. R., & Wayda, V. (2015). If you build it, they will come (or not): Going the distance in teacher candidate recruitment. *Quest, 67*, 73–92.

Burroughs, B., Lewis, A., Battey, D., Curran, M., Hyland, N. E., & Ryan, S. (2020). From mediated fieldwork to co-constructed partnerships: A framework for guiding and reflecting on P–12 school-university partnerships. *Journal of Teacher Education, 71*(1), 122–134.

Carver-Thomas, D. (2018, April). *Diversifying the teaching profession: How to recruit and retain teachers of color*. Learning Policy Institute. https://learningpolicyinstitute.org/product/ diversifying-teaching-profession

Council of Chief State School Officers (CCSSO). (2018). *A vision and guidance for a diverse and learner-ready teacher workforce*. www.ccsso.org

Darling-Hammond, L. (1999). Educating teachers for the next century: Rethinking practice and policy. In G. Griffin (Ed.), *The education of teachers*. University of Chicago Press.

Darling-Hammond, L., & Sykes, G. (2003). Wanted: A national teacher supply policy foreducation: The right way to meet the "highly qualified teacher" challenge. *EducationPolicy Analysis Archives, 11*(33). http://epaa.asu.edu/epaa/v11n33/

DeMoss, K. (2016). *For the public good: Quality preparation for every teacher*. Bank Street College of Education.

Dubin, J. (2017, Fall). Investing wisely in teacher preparation: A San Francisco residency program recruits and retains classroom talent. *AFT, A Union of Professionals* https://www.aft.org/ae/fall2017/dubin

Egalite, A. J., Kisida, B., & Winters, M. A. (2015). Representation in the classroom: The effect of own-race teachers on student achievement. *Economics of Education Review, 45*(1), 44–52.

Gay, G. (2000). *Culturally responsive teaching: Theory, research, and practice.* Teachers College Press.

Goh, P. S. C. (2019). Implementing narrative-pedagogical approaches in a teacher education classroom. *The Qualitative Report, 24*(7), 1731–1746.

Guha, R., Hyler, M. E., & Darling-Hammond, L. (2016, September). *The teacher residency: An innovative model for preparing teachers.* Learning Policy Institute.

Guha, R., Huyler, M. E., & Darling-Hammond, L. (2017). The teacher residency: A practical path to recruitment and retention. *American Educator*, 31–44.

Hammerness, K., Williamson, P., & Kosnick, C. (2016). Introduction to the special issues on urban teacher residencies: The trouble with "generic" teacher education. *Urban Education, 51*(10), 1155–1169.

Hammond, Z. (2015). *Culturally Responsive Teaching and the Brain.* Corwin.

Heck, T. H., Bacharach, N., Dahlberg, K., Ofstedal, K., Mann, B., Wellik, J., & Dank, M. (2010). *Mentoring teacher candidates through co-teaching: Collaboration that makes a difference.* Teacher Quality Enhancement Center, St. Cloud University.

Hill, H. C., Ball, D. L., & Schilling, S. G. (2008). Unpacking pedagogical content knowledge: Conceptualizing and measuring teachers' topic-specific knowledge. *Journal for Research in Mathematics Education, 39*(4), 372–400. https://www.jstor.org/stable/40539304

Hollins, E. R. (2011). Teacher preparation for quality teaching. *Journal of Teacher Education, 62*(4), 395–407.

Ingersoll, R. (2003). *Is there really a teacher shortage?* University of Pennsylvania Graduate School of Education. https://repository.upenn.edu/gse_pubs/133/

Le Maistre, C. (2000). Mentoring neophyte teachers: Lessons learned from experience. *McGill Journal of Education*, 83–87. Retrieved from https://search.proquest.com/docview/202720287/fulltextPDF/4BF66FF6CEE34DFFPQ/1?accountid=13158

Mathewson, T. G. (2017, Nov.). Sub shortage leaves schools scrambling. *The Education Digest, 83*(3), 24–29.

Mentzer, G. A., Czerniak, C. M., & Duckett, T. R. (2019). Comparison of two alternative approaches to quality STEM teacher preparation: Fast-track licensure and embedded residency programs. *School Science and Mathematics, 119*(1), 35–48.

Mourlam, J., De Jong, D., Shudak, N. J., & Baron, M. (2019). A phenomenological case study of teacher candidate experiences during a yearlong teacher residency program. *The Teacher Educator, 54*(4), 397–419.

National Center for Teacher Residencies. (2014). *Building effective teacher residencies* (Research Report). https://nctresidencies.org/wp-content/uploads/2014/11/NCTR-BETR-v2-Final.pdf

National Council for Accreditation of Teacher Education (NCATE). (2010). *Transforming teacher education through clinical practice: A national strategy to prepare effective teachers.*

New Teacher Center. (2018). *Mentor practice standards.* https://p.widencdn.net/ifn6g0/Mentor-Practice-Standards-2018

Papay, J. P., West, M. R., Fullerton, J. B., & Kane, T. J. (2012). Does an urban teacher residency increase student achievement? Early evidence from Boston. *Educational Evaluation and Policy Analysis, 34*(4), 413–434.

Pennsylvania Department of Education. (2018). *Guidelines for innovative teacher and principal residency programs.*

Richmond, G., Bartell, T. G., Floden, R. E., & Jones, N. D. (2020). How research sheds light on the pivotal role of mentors in teacher preparation. *Journal of Teacher Education, 71*(1), 6–8.

Roegman, R., Pratt. S., Goodwin, A. L., & Akin, S. (2017). Curriculum, social justice, and inquiry in the field: Investigating retention in an urban teacher residency. *Action in Teacher Education: The Journal of the Association of Teacher Educators, 39*(4), 432–452.

Skinner, E. A., Garreton, M. T., Schultz, B. D. (2011). *Grow your own teachers: Grassroots change for teacher education.* Teacher College Press.

Stanulis, R. V. (1995). Classroom teachers as mentors: Possibilities for participation in a professional development school context. *Teaching and Teacher Education, 11*(4), 331–344.

Sutcher, L., Darling-Hammond, L., & Carver-Thomas, D. (2016, September). *A coming change? Teacher supply, demand, and shortages in the U.S.* (Research Brief). Learning Policy Institute. https://files.eric.ed.gov/fulltext/ED606665.pdf

Valenzuela, A. (2017). *Grow your own educator programs: A review of the literature with an emphasis on equity-based approaches.* Intercultural Development Research Association, South.

Wilburne, J. M., & Ozman, C. (2017). Using co-teaching to grow novice teachers' self-efficacy. (Center for Schools and Communities Research Brief #9). Center for Schools and Communities.

CHAPTER 11

CLINICAL PRACTICE AT THE *HEART* OF TEACHER PREPARATION

Developing a STEM Middle School Residency Program

Cheryl R. Ellerbrock
University of South Florida

ABSTRACT

This chapter highlights a school-university partnership between the University of South Florida and one of the largest school districts in the nation who collaboratively developed, from the ground up, an undergraduate STEM middle school teacher residency program. The STEM middle school teacher residency program places clinical practice at the *heart* of the program. This chapter provides details on the context and background of the program, an overall description of the current iteration of the program, program refinement driven by data, program sustainability, and implications regarding future work related to clinical practice in teacher preparation based on lessons learned.

Preparing Quality Teachers:
Advances in Clinical Practice, pp. 241–267
Copyright © 2022 by Information Age Publishing
www.infoagepub.com
All rights of reproduction in any form reserved.

Context and Background

In spring 2007, I interviewed for and accepted a position as a middle grades and general secondary teacher educator at the University of South Florida (USF), my first faculty position straight out of my doctoral studies. I received my teacher educator training from a university well-grounded in the tenets of rich clinical practice in teacher preparation. As a recipient of such training, I assumed all institutes of higher education offering teacher preparation programs were organized and functioned under best clinical practices for preparing future teachers. During my onsite interview, I recall asking various questions about the types of clinical opportunities available at the secondary level, such as professional development school opportunities, professor in residence opportunities, and the like. Quite to my dismay, I was met with responses indicating this type of work was not currently part of secondary teacher preparation programs to the depths I was accustomed. Accepting the position, it was my desire to forge a path toward the establishment of strong clinical practice experiences for the teacher candidates (TCs) under my tutelage.

Fast forward to 2010 and the publication of the National Research Council's report on the study of teacher preparation programs (NRC, 2010) and the National Council for Accreditation of Teacher Education's [NCATE] Blue-Ribbon Panel report that challenged educational institutions to rethink and recreate teacher preparation programs around clinical practice (NCATE, 2010). Shortly after these publications, a senior colleague approached a small group of colleagues, myself included, about an opportunity to work with a private granting agency who sought to support STEM education for middle school students. At the time, multiple key reports indicated the performance of middle school mathematics and science students in the United States, while either not measurably different or slightly improving, still lagged behind other key countries internationally (i.e., TIMMS). We saw this as an opportunity to act on NRC and NCATE's reports while simultaneously supporting STEM teaching and learning at the middle level. In late 2011, we received a one-year planning grant and, in 2013, a multi-year implementation grant to reimagine clinical educator preparation and develop a STEM middle school teacher residency program in collaboration with our partner school district, one of the top ten largest school districts in the United States. Our school-university partnership was a collaboration between the university and the district's middle school education program and its high-quality middle school STEM teachers who we call school-based teacher educators. In this school-university partnership, the goal was to develop and implement a STEM middle school teacher residency program in partnership with the best school-based teacher educators the district has to offer in order to recruit, prepare, and retain highly effective STEM middle school teachers to support the diverse learners in our partner school district. Further, we had a long-term goal of creating a culture of change for other secondary teacher preparation programs at our institution, one where clinical practice resides at the heart of each program.

Grounded in a central principle that clinical practice and school-university partnerships are fundamental to high-quality teacher preparation (American Association of Colleges for Teacher Education [AACTE], 2018; Burroughs et al., 2020; NCATE, 2010) and that the most effective teacher is experience itself (Goodlad, 1984), we collaboratively reimagined how to best prepare middle school STEM TCs that resulted in the creation of a new clinical education program from the ground up versus modifying a currently existing program. Overhauling current practice, we strived for an interconnectedness between academic understanding and its application in the clinical setting alongside highly-skilled teacher educators—both university and school based (NCATE, 2010). The result was the creation of a STEM Middle School Residency Program that consists of two parallel programs—one in middle grades mathematics and another in middle grades science.

Extremely collaborative and nonhierarchical in nature (Zeichner, 2010), school-based teacher educators and district personnel along with university-based faculty across multiple colleges (college of education, college of engineering, college of arts and sciences) worked in teams in partnership to imagine and design this program, including a science content team, a mathematics content team, and a general education team that focused on middle grades and clinical practice. This program was designed to meet the needs of our partner school district with curriculum that focuses on the content and skills middle school mathematics and science teachers need to know deeply (Ball et al., 2008) along with a focus on teaching grounded in the developmental needs of young adolescents from diverse backgrounds (Association for Middle Level Education [AMLE], 2012; Bishop & Harrison, 2021; Caskey & Anfara, 2014; Horowitz et al., 2005) while affording flexibility so that customization is possible (AACTE, 2018). This mutually beneficial partnership provided an opportunity to foster high-quality clinical practice experiences at the middle level (Council for the Accreditation of Educator Preparation [CAEP], 2013) with the hope of retaining TCs in the partner school district upon graduation.

The school-university partnership has evolved as the development and implementation of this clinical education program grew. In its current state, eight of the nine essentials of professional development schools as outlined by the National Association for Professional Development Schools (NAPDS, 2021) are implemented to varying degrees, including a comprehensive mission (Essential 1), clinical preparation (Essential 2), professional learning and leading (Essential 3), reflection and innovation

(Essential 4), research and results (Essential 5), shared governance structures (Essential 7), boundary-spanning roles (Essential 8), and resources and recognition (Essential 9). Further, our partnership supports 6 of the 10 NCATE's (2010) design principles, including a shared vision of supporting young adolescent learning, integration of clinical preparation throughout the program, ongoing evaluation of both program and TC development, a predetermined and rigorous process for the selection of school and university-based teacher educators who participate in this program, an ongoing and systematized research process to support program and TC development, and the creation of a strategic partnership with a school district and school-based faculty at middle schools within the district to support strong clinical practice.

Burroughs et al.'s (2020) framework for partnerships breaks down partnership work into five categories (links to courses, role of university, role of school, decision making, and placement) and provides a range of implementation, including taking from schools (Level 1), borrowing from schools (Level 2), emerging partnership (Level 3), developing partnership (Level 4), co-constructed partnership (Level 5), and a learning community (Level 6). Based on Burroughs et al.'s framework, in its current iteration this school-university partnership primarily resembles a Level 4 partnership. However, in some categories, select aspects are beginning to resemble a co-constructed partnership (Level 5) while there are also instances when the partnership has interactions that resemble more of the borrowing from schools' level (Level 2). It is important to note that Burroughs et al. state a school-university partnership can be at more than one level at the same time and that fostering a partnership is ongoing and constantly in a state of flux. I find this to be especially true with our partnership. As the chapter unfolds, connections to NAPDS' essentials, NCATE's design principles, and Burroughs et al.'s levels of school-university partnerships will become evident.

Despite the aforementioned, lower than anticipated student enrollment has plagued this program, especially in science. Anticipating a total enrollment of 40 new TCs each year (20 TCs in middle school mathematics and 20 TCs middle school science), we have consistently fallen short of this goal as our largest cohort consisted of 23 TCs across middle school mathematics and science. To date, we have only been able to offer the middle grades science program on two occasions but have offered the middle school mathematics program since inception. Despite lower than anticipated enrollment, the reputation of this program is strong, and our graduates are successful in the field (e.g., high impact award winners, high scores on district evaluations, multiple school, and district awards). In the next section I will briefly provide a description of the program in its current state and, when appropriate, include information on science.

Description of Program

In USF's STEM Middle School Teacher Residency Program, clinical practice is at the *heart* of the program and is viewed as the "central element of learning to teach" (McDonald et al., 2014, p. 500). The sequence of coursework and even content itself is carefully considered and organized throughout the program to support clinical practice (NCATE, 2010). A common understanding of the types of knowledge, skills, and practices are foundational and designed to cut across coursework and clinical practice (Grossman et al., 2009). In this program, the focus is on "intentional pedagogical experiences in authentic educational settings" (AACTE, 2018, p. 18). Therefore, throughout this two-year program TCs experience continuous and ongoing clinical experiences in our partner school district in the form of clinically focused coursework and multiple scaffolded student-teaching experiences under the direct supervision of highly qualified school-based teacher educators and supervised by a highly trained university-based teacher educators.

Clinically Focused Coursework. Clinically focused courses were created for this program with the intent that coursework should place a strong emphasis on the exact knowledge middle school mathematics/science teachers need to know based on what they actually will teach in middle schools (Ball et al., 2008) while simultaneously considering the developmental characteristics and needs of the students under their care (AMLE, 2012; Bishop & Harrison, 20210). We took great care to ensure that coursework supported the continual development of TC's knowledge and teaching skills (AACTE, 2018). Because pedagogy and clinical practice should be foundational in any high-quality teacher preparation program (AACTE, 2018), the goal was for all coursework to complement and extend the teaching and learning that actually occurs in middle school classrooms to the greatest extent possible (AMLE, 2012). When both parallel programs were offered simultaneously, mathematics and science education TCs were organized into a large, combined cohort and took a majority of their coursework together as a large cohort.

All new content courses (mathematics/science) were created with a focus on providing TCs with "advanced experiences" with topics more elementary in nature such that the exact middle school content actually taught in middle schools reflected what TCs were learning rather than "elementary experiences" with more advanced content topics that may not be what they will actually teach at the middle level (Ball et al., 2008). The goal was to provide TCs with the specific content knowledge they actually need to teach middle school using the National (National Council of Teachers of Mathematics and National Science Teachers Association) and state standards as the backbone of these courses. Examples of application to the middle school mathematics and science teaching were infused throughout the curriculum.

What eventually became known as core program courses were created to provide a laser-like focus on young adolescents' developmental characteristics and needs, middle level content-specific methods, middle level classroom management, and clinical practice. Core program courses include two middle level education courses, two middle school mathematics and science methods courses, a classroom management course, and a clinical support course (practicum or residency seminar) offered with each clinical experience. Because teacher reflection is a practice that strengthens TCs' teaching, ongoing critical reflection became regular practice in each of these core program courses (NAPDS, 2021).

Two middle level education courses with rich clinical connections and field-embedded assignments were created (Middle Level education, Teaching the Young Adolescent Learner). These courses are designed to meet AMLE's (2012) Teacher Preparation Standards and include a curriculum that focuses on the characteristics of successful schools for young adolescents (Bishop & Harrison, 2021). An established secondary classroom management course was redesigned to focus on ways to implement a responsive middle level learning environment that supports the characteristics and needs of young adolescent learners. Two middle school methods courses (Middle School Mathematics Methods and Middle School Science Methods) were created to run in tandem with two practicum courses, offered in both fall and spring of TCs' first year in the program. Practicum 1 consists of a seminar and a clinical component where both school and university-based teacher educators share control of assisting TCs make meaning of teaching. The seminar affords opportunities for TCs to convert knowledge into clinical practice as they wrestle with important general education topics (e.g., planning, co-teaching, professionalism, relationship development, communication), helping to bridge the theory to practice disconnect (NCATE, 2010). Practicum 2 extends on Practicum 1 and also consists of a seminar with a clinical component. The residency experience consists of a yearlong clinical experience and a yearlong biweekly support seminar. Up until this program, there was not a yearlong residency internship in secondary education at my institution.

A capstone STEM Issues course was created in order to combine the various STEM disciplines together to explore STEM education topics in a comprehensive manner. TCs learn the engineering design process through the creation of integrated unit plans that mirror the types of plans school-based teacher educators in our partner district are expected to create. We also reimagined all our educational core courses (e.g., ESOL, Social Foundations) so content and assignments align as much as possible with TCs' clinical experiences along with the developmental age range of the middle school students our TCs will be teaching. Last, a few courses from the established secondary mathematics/science education programs were included with modifications made (e.g., Reading the Language of Math).

While it was our intent to have this program be an ongoing collaborative effort between the colleges of education, engineering, and arts and sciences, this has proven to be a bit more difficult than originally anticipated. Due to low student enrollment and staffing issues, many of the content courses in the college of arts and sciences have been modified from the original design and/or co-listed with other courses in order to meet enrollment numbers. Further, recently we were no longer able to have engineering faculty continue to offer the STEM Issues course due to workload issues and the college of education now offers the STEM Issues course with faculty support from the college of engineering. While these changes are certainly unfortunate and merit further discussion, for the sake of this chapter I mention these issues to shed light on the need for future discussions to focus on ways to support collaborative high-need but often low-enrollment teacher education programs across colleges.

Student-Teaching Experience. The student-teaching experience where TCs are "learning about practice *in* practice" (Darling-Hammond et al., 2005, p. 401) is the pinnacle component of high-quality teacher preparation programs (Clarke et al., 2014). Our TCs deserve an opportunity to learn about teaching and to learn about how to teach in rich, authentic student-teaching experiences that are located in multiple, diverse learning environments at each grade level represented in our partner school district (grades 6-8). Therefore, in this program it is a priority that TCs gain early and ongoing teaching experiences in the form of two practicum experiences and a yearlong internship so that, by the time they complete the program, TCs have gained teaching experiences in three different grade levels—one sixth, one seventh, and one eighth—at three different middle schools within our partner school district alongside the highest-quality school-based teacher educators the district has to offer. For example, a typical TC's clinical experience in this program may entail teaching eighth-grade mathematics at an urban Title 1 all girls magnet middle school for practicum one, sixth-grade mathematics at a suburban middle school for practicum two, and seventh-grade mathematics at a rural Title 1 middle school for the yearlong residency (see Table 11.1).

When the program first began, TCs in this program spent 1,156 hours in the field engaged in student teaching, including two semester-long early field clinical experiences (practica) in year one followed by a year-long internship (residency) in the final year. Originally, TCs began their clinical practice approximately six weeks into the start of the program, spending eight hours a week in the field for eight weeks (64 hours total). Placed at school sites in teaching pairs, in Practicum 1 TCs worked hand-in-hand

Table 11.1

Sample Clinical Experiences by Semester

Semester	School Demographics	Grades Taught
Year 1 Fall Semester Practicum 1	Urban, Title 1, All-Girls Magnet Middle School	8th Grade (Prealgebra & Algebra)
Year 1 Spring Semester Practicum 2	Suburban Middle School	6th Grade Math
Year 2 Fall-Spring Semesters Yearlong "Residency" Internship	Rural, Title 1 Middle School	7th Grade Math

with experienced and specially trained school-based teacher educators as they began to immerse themselves into the teaching craft. In Practicum 2 TCs spent 10 hours a week for 10 weeks (100 hours total) in the field with another partner at another school site with another school-based teacher educator teaching another grade level and were supported by a second practicum seminar course. The purpose of a practicum seminar is to support the TCs hands-on experience with middle grades teaching and the opportunity to connect what they learn in their university-based teacher preparation courses to practice and vice versa. Topics frequently covered include, but are not limited to: professional expectations, ethics and professional discourse, classroom management, higher level questioning, communication, integration of STEM, assessment, planning for instruction, unpacking standards, supporting the learning of all learners, and equity.

A university-based teacher educator coached the TC pair and worked collaboratively with the school-based teacher educator to support the supervision process throughout both practicum experiences. In the last year in the program, each TC engaged in 992 hours (124 days) of a yearlong residency where the TC took on the role of classroom teacher to the fullest extent possible. TCs and the school-based teacher educator co-planned and co-taught for most of the school year, which provided TCs with strong support and mentorship unlike the "sink-or-swim" model so frequently used in teacher preparation (Badiali & Titus, 2010). Based on evaluation data and feedback from partners, the clinical practice portion of the program has been radically updated and will be discussed later in the chapter.

This program is a partnership that necessitates a shared commitment between school and university-based teacher educators. Due to this commitment along with our middle school STEM focus, we strategically pair our TCs with a school-based teacher educator specially trained to work in the program based on who can offer the best learning opportunity for each TC (e.g., personality, strengths, common beliefs). The process for becoming a school-based teacher educator in this program is relatively straightforward. Reflective of a Level 4 developing partnership (Burroughs et al., 2020), middle school teachers are identified by the district as those who would be ideal school-based teacher educators using a set of collaboratively agreed upon tenets (e.g., characteristics of a high-quality mentor, teaching practice aligns with program and university goals; Grossman et al., 2009; McDonald et al., 2014; Zeichner, 2010) along with state-mandated criteria (i.e., at least three years teaching experience, meets evaluation criteria, clinical educator trained, holds appropriate certifications). As program coordinator, I reach out to each school-based principal to solicit feedback regarding the identified faculty and obtain their support. Only those supported by both the district middle school instructional leadership director, subject area supervisor, and site-based principal are invited by the university and school district to partner as a teacher educator in the program. If they agree, they then engage in a series of professional development experiences (outlined later in the chapter) and, upon completion, are added to the pool of individuals who are eligible to serve as school-based teacher educators in the program. The result is the establishment of a pool of school-based teacher educators (40 in middle school mathematics alone) who are recognized by the district as partners in this clinical education program. Many of these school-based teacher educators are at the same school site, which has afforded the opportunity to cluster our TCs and begin the establishment of a deeper, win-win school-university partnership with select schools.

Over time we were also able to purposefully select university-based teacher educators who serve as supervisors in the triad. At present, advanced doctoral students who are majoring in Curriculum and Instruction or Teacher Education in a STEM area who are specially trained by core program faculty and commit to work in the program for at least one academic year are serving as supervisors. A graduate student who trains to work in early field experiences will supervise TCs in both practicum experiences in year one of the program. Similarly, a graduate student who trains to work in the residency field experience will supervise the same TCs for their entire yearlong residency. These graduate students also teach a variety of courses in the program under the direct supervision of core program faculty as well as co-teach with core program faculty.

Supervision Process. The entire supervision process was created to place emphasis on field-based education and the connection between university-based and field-based education (Zeichner, 2010). First, we immersed ourselves in the literature on clinical practice in teacher preparation by holding regular meetings with program faculty where we met to discuss relevant articles. We then used the research-based best practices obtained from the literature to inform and guide the creation of the supervision process for this program. The result was the creation of a supervision process utilizing the triad approach to supervision, which consists of the university supervisor, school-based teacher educator, and the TC working collaboratively together. Over the years, the supervision process has evolved and grown as we have grown with our partner district but the triad approach to supervision remains a core component of the program.

As a triad, the school-based teacher educator, university-based teacher educator who serves as supervisor, and the TC work collaboratively together to create goals for the TC and identify the skills and strategies to focus on during the student-teaching experience. Regular opportunities for practice with feedback and coaching transpire throughout the clinical experience along with multiple formal observations.

All formal observations include the completion of a pre-observation form that aids the planning process and a post observation form that serves as a reflective exercise. Additionally, a pre-observation conference and a post-observation conference with all members of the triad is held for every formal observation. It is our intent for TCs to develop a reflective practice in an effort to support continual professional growth. As such, during the post conference, the triad engages in critical reflection of the TC's planning and preparation, classroom environment, instruction, and professional responsibilities all while holding an asset-oriented stance. All conversations are grounded in the need for ongoing continuous improvement for all members of the triad, not just the TC.

Faculty in this program believe that the triad reflects the overall quality of the clinical partnership (Sarnoff & Ellerbrock, 2020). Frequently members of the triad serve in more than one capacity in the clinical education program. Thus, their roles are "boundary-spanning in nature" (Burns & Baker, 2016, p. 28). For example, a university-based teacher educator who supervises TCs may also teach multiple courses in the program. Multiple school-based teacher educators co-teach with university school-based teacher educators on an ongoing basis, and some are even graduate students at the university. The flow of practices and even materials between school and university-based teacher educators enriches the connection to clinical practice in coursework and fieldwork.

Based on formal and informal feedback from members of our triads, we have found it critically imperative to explicitly define the roles of each member of the triad early on in the supervision process (AACTE, 2018), even when at times these roles blend and appear to be one in the same— that of teacher educator (Burroughs et al., 2020). The overall goal of the triad is to "work together to achieve the common goals of continuing their own professional growth and providing high-quality educational experiences for students" (Sarnoff & Ellerbrock, 2020, p. 3). Our school-based teacher educators understand it is their job to help guide TCs through the praxis of teaching (AACTE, 2018) and our university-based teacher educators understand it is their job to support TCs and the school-based teacher educator in an effort to support the learning of both TCs and middle school students. Essentially, in this program school and university-based teacher educators have a mutually shared responsibility to support one another in the process of supporting TCs understanding of teaching. The interconnected nature of the people who serve in the triad adds to its beauty and complexity.

Program Refinement Driven by Data

As stated in the Blue Ribbon report, impactful research is needed and can be used to support ongoing enhancements to teacher preparation (NCATE, 2010). As such, we have been and continue to research our practice and make program refinements based on findings from these studies. Since the program was implemented in 2013, we have collected biannual programmatic evaluation data conducted by an external reviewer. To date, there are over 1,700 pages of data from programmatic reviews that include findings and recommendations based on the data derived from surveys, individual interviews, and focus group interviews of all participating groups (i.e., district personnel, school-based teacher educators, TCs, graduates of the program, instructors, program coordinator, executive council). Further, in summer 2020, school and university-based teacher educators along with district personnel engaged in a collaborative self-study of the program where we analyzed aspects of the program (subject area content, STEM education, middle level education content, clinical practices) and made collaborative decisions regarding programmatic revisions and enhancements (e.g., increased emphasis on unpacking content standards, inclusion of a professionalism survey for all residency TCs).

This program has naturally brought forth multiple opportunities to research our practice which helped inform program refinement and contribute to the research base on clinical education. As of 2020, two book chapters (Ellerbrock et al., 2016; Ellerbrock & Vomvoridi-Ivanovic, 2019), one conference proceeding (Thomas et al., 2019), and three articles (Ellerbrock et al., 2018; Ellerbrock et al., 2019; Sarnoff & Ellerbrock, 2020) have been published along with 20 presentations delivered at national conferences on various aspects of this clinical education program. Multiple other works are in preparation or underway, including a grant proposal inspired by this project, a self-study on co-planning and co-teaching teacher preparation courses, and a longitudinal investigation on responsive middle level mathematics teaching.

These data mentioned above have tremendously helped to transform and enrich our program. While the focus on clinical practice remains a stronghold, much of the program has been modified and continues to be modified to meet the ever-changing needs of the teaching profession and our partner school district. In the following paragraphs, I will elaborate on the following areas of programmatic refinement driven by data: university-based teacher educators, courses and coursework, clinical practice, and professional development.

University-Based Teacher Educators. One would surmise that university-based teacher educators working in clinical education programs within a school-university partnership would be invested in clinical practice work. However, external programmatic evaluations (i.e., surveys, individual interviews, and focus group interviews of faculty, students, and school-based partners) suggest this has not consistently been the case in this program. Select faculty teaching in the program remained uncommitted to programmatic ideals, including the importance of clinical practice and the need to establish positive relationships with school-based partners. Developing positive relationships with school-based partners is critical to successful school-university partnerships (Zeichner, 2010). Based on feedback from invested parties, the responsibility for fostering such relationships begins with the university-based teacher educator.

Committed Program Faculty. As previously mentioned, it is imperative to have a group of dedicated university-based teacher educators who understand the purpose and ideals of a clinical education program and are willing to support programmatic aims. In all honesty, this is easier said than done. Because clinical work is messy and bears a large time commitment on behalf of all parties involved (Howell et al., 2016), some faculty may be hesitant to participate. Further, it has been my experience that many faculty simply do not understand clinical education and, therefore, think it is one thing when in reality it is really something very different. Unfortunately, this has been the case at various points in our program's history. Over the years, programmatic evaluation data clearly points to courses and faculty who were helping to advance the program and courses and faculty who were neither aligned with program ideals nor helping to enhance the program. With time and education of faculty and leadership on the aims and time committal associated with being involved in a clinical education program such as this one, faculty reassignments have been made and now there is a consistent group of core faculty and graduate teaching assistants under their direction who work in the program on an ongoing basis. Further, the work these faculty do in the program is becoming more understood by leadership and support for their efforts are improving as evidenced by, among other things, departmental leadership nominating this program for a 2020 university-based student success award, which this program was awarded.

Positive Relationships. Building and sustaining a school-university partnership requires relationships to be formed and then nurtured. Because this partnership is across multiple schools and includes a large number of school-based and district personnel, it became a priority to ensure that relationships remain at the center of our work. To this aim, core program faculty have purposefully attended to fostering positive and trusting relationships with district level personnel, school-based teacher educators, and site-based administrators in our partnership (Zeichner, 2010). For example, I have attended meetings with the district middle school director to brainstorm ways to work collaboratively to support middle school student success, attended district principal meetings to get to know school leadership and offer my services, worked with school-based teacher educators on an ongoing basis in an effort to support and enrich their teaching practice, shared research with faculty and administrators, worked with one of our school's to foster stronger relationships between and among teachers and students along with aid the establishment of responsive school organizational structures (i.e., interdisciplinary teaming), and collaborated with administrators on professional development. Efforts such as these were consistently noted in external programmatic evaluations as ways our program continues to nurture positive relationships with our partners and enrich the clinical partnership.

Courses and Coursework. From our first iteration to present day, there has been much change to the program's sequence and course schedule, structure of courses, course delivery methods, and course content. While some changes were not guided by programmatic data but forced upon the program due to variables outside of our control, such as the issue with content courses and the STEM Issues course previous mentioned, the following changes highlighted below were informed by evaluation reports and feedback from collaborators as ways to improve courses and coursework: the co-planning and co-teaching of core program courses, teaching coursework and class sessions in schools, and curriculum refinement and enhancement.

Co-Planned and Co-Taught Core Program Courses. One major change to coursework has been the rearrangement of the schedule in order for core program courses (three courses per semester) to be co-planned and co-taught by middle level faculty and middle level content area experts one day per week in a large block of time with multiple field embedded experiences. In its current state, Middle Level Education, Middle School Mathematics Methods 1, and Practicum 1 are the core program courses co-planned and co-taught in fall of year one. In spring of year one, Classroom Management, Middle School Mathematics Methods 2, and Practicum 2 are the core program courses co-planned and co-taught (see Appendix A for the current middle school mathematics program schedule). Curriculum is delivered in an integrated fashion to the fullest extent possible. For example, it is often difficult to determine where the content of one course stops and the content of another course begins. Major assignments are field embedded and combined with content from each course infused into the assignment. As the science of teaching is naturally integrated, the program models the integration of content versus having TCs go through a series of courses taught in isolation and removed from the clinical setting. Programmatic reports and other forms of programmatic feedback consistently state that this approach is perceived by all (TCs, school-based teacher educators, university-based teacher educators) to be very beneficial to TC learning. However, getting to this point took years. The program commenced like many other programs where each course was taught independent of one another, abet the practicum courses and residency seminar, without integrated assignments or rich clinical connections. Further, many TCs did not experience co-teaching firsthand prior to implementing this type of teaching method in their clinical experiences. In this co-plan and co-teach model, planning and delivery take more time than teaching in the more traditional manner, requiring a group of dedicated faculty members who are willing to put in the time and work together. However, the benefits are immense. As with other parts of this program, we are researching our co-plan and co-teach experience to learn from our practice.

Courses and Class Sessions Taught in Schools. As the program evolved and deeper school-based relationships were fostered, additional opportunities became available to enhance clinical connections in the form of courses and classes taught in schools, also known as mediated field placements (McDonald et al., 2014). University-based teacher educators believe their presence in schools spurs a deeper understanding of schooling that, in turn, can be reflected in coursework (Burrough et al, 2020) and fills in gaps between university coursework and clinical practice (Zeichner, 2010). As such, core program courses are taught at partner middle school sites by a group of university-based teacher educators or in partnership with school-based teacher educators. This practice had varied from year to year depending on scheduling and onsite availability. For example, during the 2016–2017 academic year our program was "housed" at a local middle school and all of the core program courses were cotaught onsite. We were provided our own university classroom and given an open invitation to fully immerse ourselves in the school setting. School-based teacher educators co-taught coursework with university-based teacher educators and university-based teacher educators taught with school-based teachers in middle school classrooms. TCs were immersed in middle school classrooms and with middle school students (e.g., co-teaching lessons with school-based teacher educators, shadowing and interviewing middle school students). They were witness to expert teachers who modeled best teaching practices. At the core, this experience was authentic and immersive, one where learning how to teach was intimately connected to the act of teaching (McDonald et al., 2014). While we lost our classroom due to an increase in school enrollment the following academic year, many of these immersive practices developed throughout our time onsite continue as part of our program to this day. Due to the extensive relationships built at the school site (as well as other partner middle schools), we now conduct class sessions at various partner middle schools throughout the district where these immerse practices are replicated. Therefore, it is not uncommon in these courses to meet at one middle school for multiple weeks in a row and then another middle school for multiple weeks thereafter.

Additionally, in the core program courses, one or more class sessions are conducted onsite at various middle schools that partner with this program to provide TCs with those authentic experiences to help bridge the connection between theory and practice. During these onsite sessions, we strategically prearrange purposeful classroom visits where TCs observe our school-based teacher educators teaching a lesson that match the content knowledge and pedagogical content knowledge taught in core program courses. After the classroom observation, we engage in a collaborative conversation with the school-based teacher educator about the lesson in an effort to support TCs understanding of the teaching practices observed (Burroughs et al., 2020; McDonald et al., 2014).

Curriculum Refinement and Enhancement. Regarding course content, as a program we are now at a place where we can place acute attention on deep curriculum refinement and enhancement. Therefore, for the 2019–2020 school year we shifted our programmatic evaluation to capture data on ways to modify and enrich our curriculum to better meet the needs of our students and partner district. Topics included TCs' knowledge of middle level mathematics content and their ability to teach this content to young adolescents in responsive ways during clinical experiences, understanding and implementation of responsive middle level mathematics teaching during clinical experiences, and understanding and implementation of STEM practices during clinical experiences. The aforementioned have been identified by university and school-based teacher educators as the "big ideas" of the program (Darling-Hammond et al., 2005) that have associated "high-leverage practices" TCs must be taught and able to implement in the clinical setting (McLeskey & Brownell, 2015; Windschitl et al., 2012). This information was used during the program-wide self-study mentioned earlier to make curricular refinements and enhancements.

Clinical Practice. To date, the clinical practice element is the most revised and enhanced aspect of this program. Primarily informed by collaborations between school-based teacher educators, TCs, and graduates of the program and secondarily through programmatic evaluations, the evolution of the clinical practice experience has resulted in a stronger alignment with CAEP standards (CAEP, 2013) and best practices in clinical educator preparation. The present iteration not only includes increased quantity of hours of clinical experiences but, more importantly, the quality of how those hours are spent (McDonald et al., 2014). Further, feedback exposed the need for a stronger clinical supervision process and a refined residency schedule.

Quantity and Quality of Clinical Experiences. TCs in this program now spend, at minimum, 1240 hours in the clinical setting throughout the program (up from 1,156 hours), 240 hours (up by 76 hours) in early field experiences, and 1,000 hours in the yearlong residency experience (up by 8 hours). For many of our TCs, they will graduate having spent well over 1,500 hours in the field working hand-in-hand with highly effective school-based teacher educators across an array of middle school settings and grade levels. Hours were increased and dates of clinical experiences modified based on data that suggest changes be made to the current clinical structure.

Feedback from our school-based teacher educators suggested the need for early field placements to move to a scaffolded experience, both in time and substance. Therefore, we moved from a 8-hour for 8 weeks structure in Practicum 1 where students completed those hours in any day and time combination they choose to a two half-day two days a week (4 hours each day, 8 hours a week) for 10 weeks in the field structure, resulting in an increase in 16 hours in Practicum 1. In Practicum 2, we moved from a 10-hour for 10 weeks structure to two full days a week (8 hours each day, 16 hours a week) for 10 weeks, resulting in an increase of 60 hours in Practicum 2.

In addition to quantity, the quality of the clinical experience in this program has been enriched. Scaffolded teaching tasks parallel this gradual increase in clinical hours to help support TCs' understanding of teaching. Each clinical experience (Practicum 1, Practicum 2, Residency) is accompanied by a list that consists of various teaching tasks organized into four categories (planning and preparation, the classroom environment, instruction, professional responsibilities). These tasks were collaboratively developed by school and university-based teacher educators, TCs, and graduates of the program. Each list builds on the prior and culminates in an extensive teaching portfolio that parallels the types of teaching tasks expected of a professional educator. For example, in Practicum 1, TCs complete a series of activities designed to familiarize them with the school,

school faculty, middle school students, content area teaching, teaching of other STEM content areas, teaching of non-STEM subjects, student supports, the educational system at large, and the overall teaching craft. In Practicum 2 they repeat similar tasks from Practicum 1 but at a different school and grade level plus they are asked to complete additional tasks. Examples include: teach a small groups of students, observe other areas of the school (e.g., cafeteria, hallways, media center, bus loop in morning or after school), teach lessons and reflect on these experiences, shadow an administrator, videotape a co-taught lesson and reflect on the lesson, and administer and evaluate a classroom level assessment. Residency includes an extensive list of tasks as teacher candidates assume primary responsibility for all teaching duties. Examples include: engage in a professional learning community, participate in a parent/guardian conference, and analyze the impact instruction had on student learning. Artifacts for each task are collected and organized into a digital teaching portfolio that TCs can use to show evidence of their teaching and growth in teaching over time.

Stronger Clinical Supervision Process. The supervision process itself has also evolved based on data from programmatic evaluations (data from school-based teacher educator, TC, and surveys and focus group interviews) and feedback from school-based teacher educators during programmatic meetings that all suggested the need for refinements to our supervision process (i.e., exposure to the program and district evaluation tool starting in the practica experience, increased coaching opportunities in practica and yearlong residency). In this program, early field experiences now center more on providing TCs with feedback on their acclimation to teaching, including strengths and focus areas in terms of planning, learning environment, instruction, and professionalism. As school and university-based teacher educators, we agreed that it is important to both informally and formally observe TCs in their early field experiences but that these formal observations serve as a coaching tool and not be evaluative in any way. The intent was to expose TCs to the evaluation tool and process used during residency that mirrors the district evaluation tool and process with relatively few adaptations and help them begin to think deeply about their teaching. Therefore, in the first practicum a university and school-based teacher educator together formally observe the TC at least twice and in the second practicum at least three times. Further, in Practicum 2, at least one lesson must be co-planned and co-taught in practicum pairs. This lesson is part of a larger collaborative project in PSTs' Practicum 2 course, Methods course, and Classroom Management course and involves the university-based teacher educators and school-based teacher educator to collaboratively work together to scaffold this process and provide feedback.

For residency, school and university-based teacher educators originally believed that more formal observations were necessary with informal coaching opportunities sprinkled throughout. However, as time passed, it was realized that the coaching experiences where the triad works on the areas needing development and supports and enriches TC's strengths is more meaningful than multiple formal observations. As a result, we dramatically changed the supervision cycle in residency from six times a year formal observation structure to four times a year (two per semester) and increased the number of informal observations and coaching sessions. We also added multiple videotaping and analysis assignments in an effort to help TCs critically reflect on their teaching practice.

Refined Residency Schedule. For residency, feedback from school-based teacher educators spoke of the desire to have TCs start their yearlong residency during preplanning versus starting at the beginning of the university's fall semester (a difference of approximately two weeks). This, along with our partner school district moving up their start date, resulted in adding one day (8 hours) to the residency experience and shifting the residency calendar up by two weeks. As a result, TCs now complete their yearlong residency around spring break each year. This shift in the residency calendar brought forth an opportunity for our partner district to hire our students as permanent substitutes to fill much needed middle school positions upon completion of their clinical hours. As a result, an early release from internship policy was created to accommodate this district need. Other areas of change to clinical practice include the need to calibrate our scoring of formal evaluations among school and university-based teacher educators, the need for a collaborative plan for how many different preparations TCs teach, how and when TCs assume co-teaching responsibilities for select classes, and how and when TCs take majority teaching responsibility and for what classes.

Professional Development. Over the years, professional development for school-based teacher educators and TCs has evolved. At the onset, in addition to the typical one time 20-hour teacher educator training required by the state, each year a program-specific two-day face-face training was held in the summer for all school-based teacher educators and TCs were we addressed topics such as supervising TCs, integrating STEM into middle school mathematics, coaching and evaluation, co-planning and co-teaching, and shifting mathematics instruction. Some years we hired individuals who specialized in desired topics to work with our school-based teacher educators and TCs during the summer orientation (e.g., co-planning and co-teaching in K–12 settings). However, as the years went by and feedback was received as a result of our biannual program evaluations, it became increasingly evident that the expertise needed to refine and enhance this program resides within those most intimately involved in the program.

As a result, we began to tap into our collective expertise—school-based teacher educators and their vast content knowledge and expertise implementing high-leverage practices; university-based teacher educators and graduate assistants who specialize in middle level mathematics education and teacher education; district level personnel with expertise in middle grades education, middle grades mathematics education, and STEM education; and our TCs themselves. Working in collaboration, we created a multi-phase research-based professional development program informed by clinical practice with topics intimately aligned with our current agreed upon understanding of the knowledge, skills, and practices TCs need to become high-quality middle school STEM educators and delivered by those partners with talents in each respective area (AACTE, 2018; Grossman et al., 2009).

We now hold a two-part program orientation (online and in person) for all school-based teacher educators who will be serving as school-based teacher educators in our program for the upcoming school year. The intent of the online orientation is to provide a detailed understanding of the program. All school-based teacher educators (both residency and practicum school-based teacher educators) engage in a series of online modules, including modules on the theoretical underpinnings of this program, program courses and clinical experiences, and the supervision process. Additionally, each summer we pool our expertise to create a series of online modules identified in programmatic evaluation reports as professional growth opportunities. Select topics previously identified as vital to enhancing program effectiveness include STEM teaching, effective questioning, differentiation, responsive middle level mathematics teaching, and data informed decision making.

Additionally, in mid-July of each year, school and university-based teacher educators who will be working with residency TCs during the upcoming school year attend a daylong face-to-face orientation. The first half of this orientation is typically college-wide and serves as a way to speak about clinical practice as a whole and make explicit connections between and among clinical best practices. The second half of the day is dedicated to program-specific needs. District personnel, school-based teacher educators, and university-based teacher educators work collaboratively to develop and deliver the afternoon orientation. During this time, residency school-based teacher educators interact with university-based teacher educators who work in the program. TCs who are entering their yearlong residency also attend the afternoon session, affording school-based teacher educators and TCs a chance to meet and plan for the upcoming school year. All attendees learn more about co-plan and co-teach models; discuss skills, strategies, and tools that help prepare high-quality teachers; and ask questions to ensure a successful clinical experience for all.

School-based teacher educators who work with our practicum TCs and the candidates themselves also attend an orientation session conducted in person in early fall for Practicum 1 and upon returning from winter break for Practicum 2. All the same topics are covered along with specific practica-related topics. School-based teacher educators earn district in-service points for their participation in all orientations (online and face-face). Additionally, we hold biannual touchpoint sessions where university and school-based teacher educators gather (face-face or virtual) and share with one another topics of shared interest. In past iterations, we have held these sessions in person and virtually in an online space. Last, we hold biannual touchpoint sessions where university and school-based teacher educators gather and discuss topics of mutual interest. This practice has been in place since the onset of the program and has proven to be valuable in gathering data on ways to enhance the program, including the clinical aspect of the program as well as university-based coursework.

Sustainability

As with any funded project, sustainability is paramount to the longevity of the project. This project is no different. To provide a bit of backstory, during the funded period the College of Education was under the leadership of six different deans and six different department chairs. The constant change in leadership made it extremely difficult to keep a project of this magnitude in operation and moving toward sustainability. Because this program is so fundamentally different from other programs that prepare secondary educators at my institution, some leaders struggled to understand why it required the amount of human and financial resources allocated under the grant in order to effectively develop, operate, and refine the program. Constant education and reeducation of college leadership on clinical practice and what I call "clinical *best* practice" was key. Even securing myself the role of program coordinator for this program was a challenge as typically academic program faculty (e.g., mathematics education) "own" and coordinate teacher preparation programs, which meant this program technically belonged to faculty in the respective academic areas. Being a middle school and general education faculty member, many did not see how such a faculty member could coordinate any such program even though I was principal investigator and project manager of the project. As a result, I spent much time educating colleagues on clinical practice and the importance of clinical education, the program itself and all its innerworkings, and my role in the vitality of the program. Over time, I was able to secure the role as program coordinator, which opened the door to efficient institutionalization of changes to the program based on recommendations from program evaluations, feedback from school-based partners, and so forth.

Due to the intensive focus on clinical practice (e.g., field supervision, relationship development), this clinical education program requires more resources than the traditional teacher preparation programs at my institution. Not unlike other Colleges of Education in the United States, my institution has been and continues to be in a state of reform as it wrestles with how to operate with decreased revenue. Within the current climate, attempting to sustain a program such as this one leads to a critical question, "How do you operate a costly and under enrolled yet successful clinical education program in the current climate of reform and having to do more with less?" Luckily, our college leadership understands the call for teacher education to transform its practice to be more clinical in nature. They hear the voices of our district partners, of our university-based teacher educators, and of our students and graduates. Through conversations and much education on the program, it is clear to all that we created an infrastructure for a clinical education program that has the potential to serve as a model for our secondary teacher preparation programs.

To date, the program has been sustained but not without fundamental modifications. For example, the grant included resources to secure a clinical instructor for the program, a boundary-spanning role (Burns & Baker, 2016; Burns et al., 2015), which quickly became the nucleus of the program in the early rendition and is noted as being a critical part of any school-university partnership (Burroughs et al., 2020). Unfortunately, the college simply could not afford to maintain this position. Our creative solution was to reallocate this workload to two faculty most invested in the program and graduate teaching assistants under their direction, one faculty and graduate assistant to work directly in the early field aspect of the program and another faculty and graduate assistant to work in the yearlong residency aspect of the program. These faculty are highly involved in the partnership as they are out in the schools, working side-by-side with school-based teacher educators and TCs on an ongoing basis (Burroughs et al., 2020). I currently serve as the faculty member for the yearlong residency portion of the program where I work in the field with the residency triads and lead the residency seminar, counting as one course in my workload assignment. As with what I surmise many who work in clinical education would say, working in clinical education is a labor of love, one that is not neatly and adequately represented on one's workload assignment or annual review. Nevertheless, with this change, we were able to maintain the other fundamental aspects of the program (e.g., rich clinical supervision, co-planned and co-taught classes) and sustain the program beyond the granting cycle. However, the question now is, "Can we keep it?"

Recently, USF finds itself facing major financial issues resulting in the need for the College of Education to re-imagine current practice. As such, the future of current teacher preparation programs in the College is uncertain. I share this for the purpose of reminding all of us that while you can design, implement, and sustain beyond a granting period a program that is, for all intents and purposes, well-aligned with best practice, meeting the needs of your clinical partners, and resulting in high-quality TCs, there are outside forces that are always at play which can steer your ship in another direction. I want to remind us that, as faculty committed to clinical practice, we must advocate for the fundamental tenets of our programs but also exhibit the flexibility necessary to work within the constraints placed upon us in order for our programs to remain, even if they continue in a modified form.

Implications Regarding Future Work Related to Clinical Practice in Teacher Preparation

Reflecting on the journey to establishing a STEM middle school residency program at USF, it is clear that we were, at times, charting relatively newly marked waterways. As a result, there are implications regarding future work related to clinical practice in teacher preparation learned as a result of engaging in this work that may help others as they navigate their way along the journey to establishing clinically rich teacher preparation programs. First, those involved in clinical practice work must possess an ongoing commitment to clinical practice. Second, it is necessary to immerse yourself in and, ultimately, research your practice in order to expand the research base and contribute to ongoing programmatic enhancement. Additionally, it is imperative that those involved in clinical practice continue to have opportunities to collaborate and foster professional and program development.

Ongoing Commitment to Clinical Practice. I often compare clinical practice to a living being—it grows and develops over time and needs constant nourishment in order to properly develop. Clinical practice takes on a personality of its own and, at times, may be misunderstood. It requires tender loving care and the belief that it can and will develop into something amazing with commitment and effort. This amount of commitment may be too much for some. It may be perceived to be easier to develop a teacher preparation program and then, year after year, roll out the same program with little to no modification. The template has been created and all that is needed is to simply go through the motions of enacting the program. However, with clinical educator programs, this is simply not possible. You can have a template, but the program is alive and evolving and requires those involved in the program to be flexible and innovative as things grow and evolve. Further, clinical practice work is messy and certainly not easily reflected in words on documents such as annual reviews and applications for promotion and tenure. To be involved in clinical practice work, faculty, both school and university based, need to be committed to the cause and understand they may have to work both hard *and* smart. For example, university-based faculty should highly consider how to bridge their teaching and service duties associated with clinical practice work with their research agenda so that the trilogy of higher education—teaching, research, and service—are able to be met through their clinical practice work.

Contributing to the Literature Base. Listed as one of the ten design principles to develop clinical practice programs by NCATE (2010), it is imperative that the field of education expand its research base on clinical practice in teacher education in an effort to drive continual advancement. More specifically, there is a great need to expand the body of knowledge on ways to establish strong clinical practices at the middle and secondary level along with exemplar case studies to support those institutions seeking to transform or create new programs. As stated by Darling-Hammond (as cited by Scherer, 2012), there appears to be a lack of conversation on high-quality teacher preparation programs. I found this to be especially true at the secondary education level. When establishing this program, my colleagues and I sought research on exemplar middle and secondary clinical education program models but relatively few examples were available. While research on clinical practice in elementary settings can be useful, when thinking about ways clinical practice can be instituted at the middle and secondary level, it is very beneficial to review literature relative to the age-range and grade levels the program intends to service. For those of us who work in clinical education, contributing to this growing body of literature is imperative and helps to champion our cause (for quality clinical education programs at the middle school, see Howell et al., 2016).

Continual Professional and Program Development. Through the experience of co-developing and, ultimately, coordinating this clinical educator program, I have learned the sheer importance of ongoing high-quality professional development. High-quality professional development is collaboratively developed, ongoing, and evolving. When all invested parties work toward improving their own professional practice, the ripple effect this improvement has on the development and enhancement of the teacher preparation program can be immense. When teacher preparation programs are studied and findings shared with invested parties, such findings can inform future professional development. The two—professional development and program development—go hand-in-hand with one another.

CONCLUSION

Planning and implementing a clinically based STEM middle school residency program has been no easy feat. Takeaways from this experience include an understanding that school-university partnerships and clinical practice is not for those who are uncommitted and unwilling to roll up their sleeves and get a bit messy. It is complex work. It takes time. It takes dedication. It takes compromise. Another takeaway is that faculty in clinical education must release themselves from the need to know everything and rest in the fact that, at times, you are more of a learner than expert. This is not work that can be done in isolation from your clinical partners. You have to trust your school and university-based colleagues and understand that together, in collaboration, you are stronger and wiser. Together you can develop a clinically rich program that meets the needs of both the higher education institution and the district/school with whom you partner. Another takeaway is that faculty must be prepared to advocate for clinical education programs to prepare teacher candidates. This type of work may not be perceived of high value to some in higher education and many do not understand its necessity. We must realize that this work *is* of high value for the field of education and, thus, merits our attention and time to develop strong clinical partnerships.

The STEM Middle School Residency program, now in its ninth year, has grown and blossomed into something that, at onset, I could have never imagined possible. Although this clinical education program is not perfect, and I would never claim that it is, we have come a long way since our initial cohort in 2013. Only through complete trust, respect, and dedication of all partners and the willingness to try something new and different, and possibly fail, were we able to transform the program into what it is today. I thank my colleagues, both school and university based, for their dedication to our school-university partnership and their persistence to the cause of rich clinical practice. Together, hand-in-hand as equal partners in this partnership we will continue to tackle college and programmatic-level issues and advance our clinical practice in an effort to provide TCs with the best clinical preparation possible. It is my hope that this program is able to endure the reimagining efforts our college is currently undergoing and that it contributes to these efforts in such a way that results in high quality clinical practice being placed at the *heart* of all teacher preparation programming at USF. There is much work ahead on the horizon.

REFERENCES

American Association of Colleges for Teacher Education. (2018). *Clinical practice commission report.* https://aacte.org/resources/research-reports-and-briefs/clinical-practice-commission-report/

Association for Middle Level Education. (2012). *AMLE Standards*. http://www.amle. org/AboutAMLE/ProfessionalPreparation/AMLEStandards.aspx

Badiali, B., & Titus, N. E. (2010). Co-teaching: Enhancing student learning through mentor-intern partnerships. *School-University Partnerships*, *4*(2), 74–80.

Ball, D. L., Thames, M. H., & Phelps, G. (2008). Content knowledge for teaching: What makes it special? *Journal of Teacher Education*, *59*, 389–407.

Bishop, P. A., & Harrison, L. M. (2021). *The successful middle school: This we believe*. Association for Middle Level Education.

Burns, R. W., & Baker, W. (2016). The boundary spanner in professional development schools: In search of common nomenclature. *School-University Partnerships*, *9*(2), 28–39.

Burns, R. W., Yendol-Hoppey, D., & Jacobs, J. (2015). High-quality teaching requires collaboration: How partnerships can create a true continuum of professional learning for educators. *The Educational Forum*, *79*(1), 53–67.

Burroughs, G., Lewis, A., Battey, D., Curran, M., Hyland, N. E., & Ryan, S. (2020). From mediated fieldwork to co-conconstructed partnerships: A framework for guiding and reflecting on P–12 school-university partnerships. *Journal of Teacher Education*, *71*(1), 122–134. https://doi.org/10.1177/0022487119858992992

Caskey, M. M., & Anfara, V. A., Jr. (2014, October). *Research summary: Developmental characteristics of young adolescents*. http://www.amle.org/BrowsebyTopic/WhatsNew/WNDet.aspx?ArtMID=888&ArticleID=455

Clarke, A., Triggs, V., & Nielson, W. (2014). Cooperating teacher participation in teacher education: A review of the literature. *Review of Educational Research*, *84*(2), 163–202. https://doi.org/10.3102/0034654313499618

Council for the Accreditation of Educator Preparation. (2013). 2013 *CAEP standards*. http://caepnet.org/standards/2013/introduction.

Darling-Hammond, L., Hammerness, K., Grossman, P., Rust, F., & Shulman, L. (2005). The design of teacher education programs. In L. Darling-Hammond & J. Bransford (Eds.), *Preparing teachers for a changing world* (pp. 390–441). Jossey-Bass.

Ellerbrock, C. R., Kersaint, G., Smith, J. J., & Kaskeski, R. (2016). Transforming teacher preparation for the transition years: A partnership-based STEM residency program. In P. B. Howell, J. Carpenter, & J. Jones (Eds.), *Clinical preparation at the middle level: Practices and possibilities* (pp. 33–58). Information Age Publishing.

Ellerbrock, C. R., & Vomvoridi-Ivanovic, E. (2019). A framework for responsive middle level mathematics teaching. In K. M. Brinegar, L. M. Harrison, & E. Hurd (Eds.), *The handbook of research in middle level education: Equity and cultural responsiveness in the middle grades* (pp. 45–68). Information Age Publishing.

Ellerbrock, C. R., Vomvoridi-Ivanovic, E., & Duran, J. (2018). Working Together: Preparing the next generation of highly qualified middle school STEM teachers. *The Clearing House*, *91*(3), 124–130. https://doi.org/10.1080/00098655.2018.1428458

Ellerbrock, C. R., & Vomvoridi-Ivanovic, E., Sarnoff, K., Jones, B., & Thomas, M. (2019). Collaborating to "Grow Our Own": The Helios STEM middle school residency program. *The Clearing House*, *92*(4–5), 119–124.

Goodlad, J. I. (1984). *A place called school*. McGraw-Hill.

Grossman, P., Hammerness, K., & McDonald, M. (2009). Redefining teaching, re-imagining teacher education. *Teachers & Teaching*, *15*(2), 273–289.

Horowitz, F. D., Darling-Hammond, L., Bransford, J., Comer, J., Rosebrock, K., Austin, K., & Rust, F. (2005). Educating teachers for developmentally appropriate practice. In L. Darling-Hammond & J. Bransford (Eds.), *Preparing teachers for a changing world* (pp. 88–125). Jossey-Bass.

Howell, R. B., Carpenter, J., & Jones, J. (2016). *Clinical preparation at the middle level: Practices and possibilities*. Information Age Publishing.

McDonald, M., Kazemi, E., Kelley-Peterson, E., Mikolasy, K., Thompson, J., Valencia, S., & Windschitl, M. (2014). Practice makes practice: Learning to teach in teacher education. *Peabody Journal of Education*, *89*(4), 500–515.

McLeskey, J., & Brownell, M. (2015, October). *High-leverage practices and teacher preparation in special education*. https://ceedar.education.ufl.edu/wp-content/uploads/2016/05/High-Leverage-Practices-and-Teacher-Preparation-in-Special-Education.pdf

National Association for Professional Development Schools. (2021). *What it means to be a professional development school: The nine essentials* (2nd ed.). https://3atjfr1bmy981egf6x3utg20-wpengine.netdna-ssl.com/wp-content/uploads/2021/03/What-it-Means-to-be-a-PDS-Second-Edition-2021.pdf

National Council for Accreditation of Teacher Education. (2010). *Transforming teacher education through clinical practice: A national strategy to prepare effective teachers*. http://www.highered.nysed.gov/pdf/NCATECR.pdf

National Research Council (2010). *Preparing teachers: Building evidence for sound policy*. Committee on the Study of Teacher Preparation Program in the United States. The National Academies Press.

Sarnoff, K., & Ellerbrock, C. R. (2020). Stronger together: A collaborative triad approach to middle school STEM teacher preparation. *School-University Partnerships*, *13*(1), 48–53.

Scherer, M. (2012, May). The challenges of supporting new teachers: A conversation with Linda Darling-Hammond. *Educational Leadership*, *69*(8), 18–23.

Thomas, S. W., Campbell, S. W., Subramanyam, M. D., & Ellerbrock, C. R. (2019). Contemporary STEM issues: Engineering training of pre-service teachers for middle school STEM curriculum development. *Proceedings of the ASEE Annual Conference & Exposition*, 1–10.

Windschitl, M., Thompson, J., Braaten, M., & Stroupe, D. (2012). Proposing a core set of instructional practices and tools for teachers of science. *Science Education*, *96*(5), 878–903.

Zeichner, K. (2010). Rethinking the connections between campus courses and field experiences in college- and university-based teacher education. *Journal of Teacher Education*, *61*(1), 89–99.

APPENDIX A

Term	Course	Hours
Semester 1 Fall	MAS 3205 Number Concepts Connections	3
	MTG 3207 Geometry Connections	3
	MAE 3224 Middle School Mathematics Methods I	3
	EDF 4430 Measurement for Teachers	3
	EDM 3403 Middle Level Education	3
	MAE 3941 Practicum I	2
	Semester 1 Total	**17**
Semester 2 Spring	STA 3027 Statistics and Probability Connections	3
	MAS 3108 Algebra Connections	3
	MAE 3225 Middle School Mathematics Methods Course II	3
	ESE 4322 Class Management for Diverse School and Society	3
	MAE 3942 Practicum II	2
	Semester 2 Total	**14**
Semester 3 Summer	EDF 3214 Human Development	3
	EDM 3620 Teaching the Young Adolescent Learner	3
	EEX 4070 Integrating Exceptional Students in General Education Settings	3
	RED 4333 Content Area Reading	3
	Semester 3 Total	**12**
Semester 4 Fall	MAE 4551 Reading in Mathematics	3
	TSL 4324 ESOL Competencies and Strategies	3
	MAE 4941 Internship I	6
	Semester 4 Total	**12**
Semester 5 Spring	EDM 4406 Contemporary Issues in STEM Education	3
	EDF 3604 Social Foundations of Education	3
	MAE 4942 Internship II	6
	Semester 5 Total	**12**
Totals	**Total After Admission**	**67**
	Total Before Admission	**53**
	Program Total	**120**

CHAPTER 12

BEYOND TEACHING TEDDY BEARS

Generating and Sustaining High School Students' Interest in the Teaching Profession Through Clinical Practice

R. Lennon Audrain
Harvard Graduate School of Education

Jody Googins
Xavier University

ABSTRACT

Precollegiate teacher academies have existed in high schools across the United States for over 65 years. Since their inception, field experiences have been a hallmark of this secondary course, providing opportunities for students to explore the teaching profession before they enter college. The goal of teacher academies has been to provide hands-on experiences that generate student interest in the teaching profession. This article presents a rationale centering clinical practice in teacher academies. We begin by giving an overarching history of teacher academies in the United States. Then, we unpack the historical and current practices in field experiences in teacher academies.

Preparing Quality Teachers:
Advances in Clinical Practice, pp. 269–284

Finally, utilizing the Association for Colleges of Teacher Education's Clinical Practice Commission and the *Educators Rising Standards*, we discuss what a teacher academy—centered on clinical practice—might look like, and what implications it holds for colleges of education, school districts, and the future of the educator workforce.

INTRODUCTION

We are facing a crisis in recruiting, training, and retaining individuals to the teaching profession (Robinson, 2017). This crisis is not new, however. Even in 1952, Indianapolis Public Schools' (IPS) Superintendent H. L. Shibler recognized this growing problem and how it might potentially impact the teaching workforce in his district. The district had a solution: it created a course—called the Teacher Academy, which would count for social studies credit—in high schools for juniors and seniors. Teacher Academy students, called teacher cadets, would go to a neighboring elementary school for one period a day to "cadet teach" (Guild, 1954). The aim of the program was—and remains to this day—to generate interest from high school students by providing them with vocational information and hands-on experiences in actual classrooms. IPS's Teacher Academy is just one recorded example of a high school course designed to Grow-Your-Own (GYO) teachers—a contemporary term for the various pathways, pipelines, or partnerships (Valenzuela, 2017) which exist, or could exist, to attract different types of individuals to the teaching profession. IPS's Teacher Academy was extremely successful at generating interest in the teaching profession in its first year; 94% ($n = 36$) of participants indicated that the program had helped them to decide to become teachers. Unfortunately, as with most educational interventions and programs in teacher education, longitudinal data is hard to track; there is no available information on what percentage of those participants who expressed interest in teaching actually completed teacher preparation programs or even returned to Indianapolis public schools to teach.

We titled this chapter "Beyond Teaching Teddy Bears" for a few reasons. First, it is a nostalgic reminder of the story many teachers share about their "first teaching experience"—what we could even go so far as to call their first attempt at approximating clinical practice: teaching their stuffed animals in their bedroom. Second, we want to remain cognizant of the fact that high school students often still have a youthful perspective and perception of the teaching profession, one that is energized by the potential of the profession. Lastly, it is important that we design experiences that move these precollegiate, teacher candidates (PCTCs) beyond those perspectives and perceptions, open their eyes to the complexities and possibilities of the profession, and give them clinical experiences—through which they can generate and sustain their interest in the profession—that allow them to confront those complexities.

We focus this chapter on how centering clinical practice experiences in teacher academies can be key to generating and sustaining high school student interest in the teaching profession. First, we explore the historical role and practices of field experiences in the teacher academy (TA). Then, we juxtapose those with modern roles and practices of field experiences in TAs. Finally, we devise a framework—drawing from the American Association of Colleges of Teacher Education's Clinical Practice Commission and the *Educators Rising standards*—for what clinical practice ought to look like in TAs. The first element of our framework is Teacher Academies and Partnerships, in which we discuss how partnerships provide TAs with a connection to the community to provide examples, and opportunities to engage in, innovative practice. The second element of our framework is Teacher Academies and Pedagogy, in which we acknowledge the theory-practice divide and suggest remedies to help bridge the gap. Finally, the third element of our framework is Teacher Academies and Politics and Position, in which we acknowledge the delicate accountability dance that TAs must perform in the political area to meet state and Career and Technical Education standards and the positional arena, acknowledging the role TAs play in delivering transformative experiences to future teachers which will, in turn, lead to transformative experiences for future students. In addition, we briefly explore the role of colleges of education and districts in supporting TAs, touching briefly on potential longitudinal outcomes of the TA course, such as matriculation to colleges of education and retention in the profession.

HISTORICAL CONTEXTS

1936: Club Beginnings

We must begin a historical perspective on Teacher Academies--as we know them today—by discussing Future Teachers of America (FTA), which was established in 1937 by the National Education Association (NEA). FTA was housed under NEA's Publication division and was a "movement" created to give "students in each highschool [sic] who look forward to teaching as a career" the opportunity to "get together as an informal group with some of the best teachers in the highschool [sic] to consider their common aims" (NEA, 1936, p. 287). FTA also existed at the collegiate level. Most high schools classified FTA as a club, including Laramie High

School in Wyoming and Walterboro High School in South Carolina, who are regarded as the "pioneers" of the FTA movement.

From its nativity, FTA claimed that the movement was not to increase the number of young people who entered teaching, but to encourage those students with the "aptitude" and "personal character" to enter the profession (NEA, 1936, p. 287). Some common FTA exercises included regular, formal, and informal meetings at the homes of teachers and students, annually leading the planning of the Horace Mann Centennial Celebration in October, and reading, reflecting on, and discussing the NEA leaflet, "Shall I Become a Teacher?" By 1953, there were 24,000 collegiate students and 35,000 high school students in FTA (Faust, 1953).

1950s: The Teacher Academy Course Emerges

We can trace the establishment of the first contemporary Teacher Academy to Elkhart Public Schools in Indiana back to 1946, though it was a one semester course where no credit was offered (McAllister, 1954). After TAs were established, the clubs and the course/program continued to work in tandem, offering engaging extracurricular opportunities for participants. Wilbur Young, Indiana state superintendent of public instruction at the time, and the Commission on the General Education of Indiana State Board of Education, both saw the Teacher Academy as a potential remedy to the teacher shortage and ratified that it could be a formal, credit-bearing course (Young, 1954, p. 62). Indiana public schools (IPS) established their Teacher Academy course in 1952 and offered credit in social studies (Guild, 1953; Frick, 1955).

Under the leadership of Herman Shibler, the superintendent of IPS, the Teacher Academy was a course which functioned as a "readiness program for teacher education" offered to juniors and seniors in high school as a chance to explore their "interest and aptitude in teaching" (Frick, 1955, p. 234). The central task of the course was the field-experience component where participants, called cadet teachers, were placed in a neighboring elementary school classroom for one of their scheduled periods each day. Cadet teachers would observe the classrooms, noting and inferring about the teacher's behaviors. Once the elementary teacher, cadet, and Teacher Academy instructor thought the cadet was ready, they would engage in activities that contributed to the life of the classroom, including mixing paints, preparing bulletin board materials, mounting pictures, umpiring baseball games, grading papers, conducting morning exercises, helping to lesson plan, and helping individual children and small groups (Guild, 1953, p. 80).

1950s–1980s: FTA Disbands, but TAs Continue to Exist

In 1955, FTA was passed from NEA's Publication division to the National Commission on Teacher Education and Professional Standards (NCTEPS) division. A working group was formed to develop an understanding of the current climate of FTA. The group produced the DeKalb Report, which made recommendations and asked questions about the difference in purpose between the high school clubs and college chapters (NEA, 1955). The committee reached a consensus that the purpose of the high school organizations seemed to be exploratory in nature and intended to help students discover whether teaching was a career interest to them. The collegiate chapters, on the other hand, were regarded as part of the total program of preparation of teachers, and thus, a collegiate organization should follow the pattern of the professional teacher organization. It was then that collegiate chapters split from Future Teachers of America, and the Student National Education Association was born. The National Education Association continued to intermittently publish about Future Teachers of America in the *NEA Journal* from 1958–1972; however, FTA functioned less and less in the 1970s and was officially disbanded in 1982 by Mark Lowe, the executive coordinator for FTA at the time, due to the teacher surplus. During this time, we know very little about what happened to FTA. We do know, though, that this was a formative time in the identity of Teacher Academies as a separate entity from the accompanying extracurricular organization.

1985–Today: (Re)building

In 1984, Terence Garner, assistant superintendent of the Office of Personnel Staffing for the Dade County Public Schools in Florida, and Murray Sisselman, president of the United Teachers of Dade, which Garner (1993) claims was the "country's only recognized bargaining agent for teachers and paraprofessionals" (p. 421), established Future Educators of America (FEA). In Dade County Public Schools, FEA was open to students in second through twelfth grade. The Florida State Legislature made FEA a state-level organization in August 1986.

In 1987, Jan Towslee, a former FTA member and president of her high school chapter, became president of the Association of Teacher Educators (ATE). She recognized the impending teacher shortage, as the 70s surplus of teachers had dissipated, and in 1989, ATE established Future Educators of America to carry on the legacy of FTA.

ATE could no longer sponsor FEA due to its rapid growth, so, in 1994, Phi Delta Kappa International assumed responsibility for it and became its parent organization. In 2005, Future Educators of America changed its name to Future Educators Association to encompass the international chapters. In 2010, the U.S. Department of Education Office of Vocational and Adult Education recognized FEA as a Career and Technical Student Organization (Gordon, 2014). In 2015, FEA rebranded as Educators Rising.

TEACHER ACADEMIES AS GROW-YOUR-OWN AND CAREER AND TECHNICAL EDUCATION

Teacher Academies and their professional organizations were not always in lockstep. TAs and programs like it, that is, "teacher cadet" programs and various GYO initiatives, did not always matriculate alongside a professional organization like FTA, FEA, or EdRising. Because of the Career Tech tag, many TAs are governed by individual state departments of education; participation in the club/professional organization is not mandated.

States like Ohio, for example, have created their own standards for the program, positioning TAs as Career Technical "Pathway Programs," alongside other career tech programs. "Pathway programs," located in career education initiatives across the state, are meant to "prepare students to combine broad knowledge, insight and understanding of business processes, academic attainment and workplace readiness with depth of knowledge and expertise in a technical area" (Ohio Department of Education, 2016, p. ii). All career technical programs in the state of Ohio have at least one shared learning outcome centered on "Business Operations/21st Century Skills." While many career technical programs in Ohio have an affiliated professional organization, Ohio does not mandate participation or alignment. This is true of TAs in Ohio. Educators Rising has a strong presence in the state of Ohio, but participation and alignment are not required by the Ohio Department of Education. Furthermore, data is not even available for how many TAs currently operate in the state of Ohio. A current estimation is that there are about 50 TAs in both high schools and career centers across the state (M. J. Kohl, personal communication, February 25, 2018). Nationally, there are roughly 152,000 students enrolled in TAs or programs like it (U.S. Department of Education, n.d).

The Educators Rising Standards

With the inception of Educators Rising in 2015, the organization recognized two things. First, many Teacher Academies and their Career and Technical Student Organization counterpart, EdRising, had historically functioned separately. Second, since each state had its own standards for the Teacher Academy, there was a need for a more unified, national understanding of what PCTCs should know and be able to do by the time they exit the Teacher Academy.

Through grant funding from the National Education Association, Educators Rising convened a committee of practitioners and educational leaders to develop the Educators Rising standards. The National Board for Professional Teaching Standards (NBPTS) was a key player in the standards' development; the protocols used in the development process and the framework for the standards themselves were derived from NBPTS.

The Educators Rising (2016) standards are built around the cyclical nature of teaching: planning, teaching, assessing, and reflecting. The standards "tell a story about the knowledge and skills that rising educators will acquire and the models they may observe in professional educators" (p. 3). The seven standards and their descriptions can be found in Table 12.1.

Table 12.1

The Educators Rising Standards

Standard	Description
Standard I: Understanding the Profession	Rising educators learn about the profession to explore career opportunities, develop skills they need, and make informed decisions about pathways to accomplished teaching.
Standard II: Learning About Students	Rising educators learn about themselves and their students for the purpose of building relationships and supporting student development.
Standard III: Building Content Knowledge	Rising educators learn how to build content knowledge for the purpose of creating relevant learning opportunities for their students.
Standard IV: Engaging in Responsive Planning	Rising educators learn how to respond to students' needs through thoughtful planning.
Standard V: Implementing Instruction	Rising educators learn effective instructional strategies to engage students and promote learning.
Standard VI: Using Assessments and Data	Rising educators learn to use assessments and interpret data for the purpose of making decisions that will advance teaching and learning.
Standard VII: Engaging in Reflective Practice	Rising educators learn how reflective practice enables them to advance student learning and grow professionally.

Source: Educators Rising (2016)

In many ways, the Educators Rising standards function in a similar way to the Five Core Propositions of NBPTS. While each state has its own standards and requirements for what it means to be a professional teacher, NBPTS are a national framework—an even higher "gold standard"—of what it means and looks like to be "an accomplished teacher." Likewise, although each state has their own standards for the Teacher Academy—built around the projected needs of each state's teacher workforce—the Educators Rising standards are a national framework for what a PCTC could or ought to know and be able to do at the completion of their program.

These standards are a right direction towards creating a common understanding of what a Teacher Academy student should know and be able to do by the time they complete the program. One missing element from the standards, however, is how clinical practice and clinical practice experiences center what happens in Teacher Academies. Direct naming of anything related to the word "clinical" only appears once when Educators Rising (2016) discusses the rising educator as a "transitional figure" who moves from "student (during coursework) to teacher (during clinical internships) while remaining a learner" (p. 5).

DEFINING CLINICAL PRACTICE

Two seminal works about clinical practice emerged in the 2010s. The National Council for Accreditation of Teacher Education's (NCATE) Blue Ribbon Panel released Transforming Teacher Education Through Clinical Practice: A National Strategy to Prepare Effective Teachers (2010) in which they promulgated that clinical practice should rest at the heart of teacher preparation. The panel created 10 guiding design principles for what elements effective clinical experiences should have. AACTE (2018) released their Clinical Practice Commision eight years later, in which they developed a conceptual framework, definition, and explanation of clinical practice with recommendations for implementation.

Clinical practice, according to AACTE (2018) is "a model to prepare high-quality educators with and through a pedagogical skill set that provides articulated benefits for every participant, while being fully embedded in the PK–12 setting" (p. 6). In addition, clinical practice "offers a lens through which to understand the problems of practice that currently face the profession" (p. 8). Opportunities to engage in clinical practice have traditionally been conducted at the postsecondary or collegiate level in teacher preparation programs (TPP). These opportunities fall under a variety of names—field experiences, internships, and student teaching to name a few. TPPs place a teacher candidate (TC) in authentic educational, clinical settings and engage the TC in the pedagogical work of the profession of teaching (p. 12). TCs work under the supervision of a mentor teacher (MT)—the TC's primary school-based teacher educator.

Clinical practice experiences are often referred to as "field experiences" or "internships" in TAs. While the names inherently do not suggest a difference in what happens in these experiences, it is important that TAs adapt the language as proclaimed by AACTE. This unifying language can "facilitate a shared understanding of and reference to the roles, responsibilities, and experiences essential to high-quality clinical preparation" (p. 38). If TAs adapt the language promulgated by AACTE—even so simply as to refer to "field experiences" and "internships" as "clinical practice experiences"—TAs can establish themselves as a cohesive point on the teacher education continuum. Additionally, TAs must take a critical lens to their curriculum, instruction, and assessment and really consider whether clinical practice is at the heart of their curriculum.

Synergizing AACTE's CPC + the Educators Rising Standards

We know that Teacher Academies have a longstanding history of providing students with field experience opportunities that, since their inception, have solidified PCTCs' desire to teach (Guild, 1953). By synergizing AACTE's Clinical Practice Commission (2018) and the Educators Rising (2016) standards, we can further their development and set them up on a trajectory to becoming an accomplished, highly skilled teacher through early access to clinical practice experiences.

In many ways, our chapter echoes AACTE's vision for the Clinical Practice Commission in that it is:

> operational rather than exhaustive. We make several recommendations that frame a definition of clinical practice, and we offer several model protocols. Because local context matters when considering how to best operationalize clinical practice, we avoid making sweeping national recommendations, other than the guiding statements provided. Ultimately, our best intentions for this paper are to bring about a common understanding of what comprises clinical practice. This is a framework to build, maintain, and sustain a clinical partnership, which joins the needs of a college or university and local PK–12 schools in the preparation of highly effective educators to meet the needs of all learners. (p. 4)

In the following sections, we propose three themes that frame our thinking about the intersections of the Clinical Practice Commission and Educators Rising standards: partnerships, pedagogy, and position. Throughout these three themes, we reconstruct the Commission and

Table 12.2

New Teacher Academy Terminology Aligned With AACTE's Clinical Practice Commission (2018)

Term	Prior Terms	Definition
Clinical [Practice] Setting	Placement	A "school or authentic education setting that works in partnership with" a Teacher Academy program to "provide clinical practice [experiences]" for precollegiate, preservice teachers.
Clinical Practice Experience	Internship, field experience	An experience in which a precollegiate, preservice teacher is approximating clinical practice. In addition to activities conducted in the clinical practice setting, this also includes approximations such as rehearsals.
Mentor Teacher	Host Teacher	The classroom teacher at the clinical practice setting to whom PCTCs are assigned during clinical practice experiences.
Precollegiate, Preservice Teacher (PCPST) or Precollegiate Teacher Candidate (PCTC)	Teacher cadet, Teacher Academy student	The student enrolled in a Teacher Academy. We use terminology that mirrors the term for a student enrolled in a teacher preparation program, using "precollegiate" as a marker to distinguish that they are not enrolled in a collegiate preparation program.
Teacher Academy Instructor	Class sponsor, Teacher Academy Teacher, Teacher Leader	The instructor of the Teacher Academy Course, considered to be a teacher educator.
Teacher Academy Course		The precollegiate course whose curriculum, instruction, and assessment is designed to generate and sustain interest in the teaching professional through clinical practice experiences. This term includes both Teacher Academies and Early Childhood Education coursework.
Teacher Academy Program		The program is the overarching organization at each high school that includes the Teacher Academy Course, potential Career and Technical Student Organization (CTSO) affiliation, clinical practice setting, and any additional partnerships that the program may have with institutions of higher education or others organizations.

Standards to form a new vision for Teacher Academies—one that is long overdue—drawing from our experiences working with Educators Rising and Teacher Academies. In addition, we stitch together a robust framework, using conceptual ideas and frameworks, such as critical pedagogy and culturally relevant practices, while maintaining our concentration on clinical practice.

Teacher Academies and Partnerships

Partnerships are the lifeblood of Teacher Academies. Partnerships for TAs provide PCTCs the opportunity to put the theory they learn in the TA classroom to practice in another space, one beyond their home classroom. We look towards the community for opportunities for our PCTCs to see education happening, a third space for the multitude of stakeholders, such as universities, community leaders, and businesses—all organizations and individuals who invest in education, to support, inform, and influence the praxis of the Teacher Academy. Furthermore, this chapter recognizes that each Teacher Academy is built and formed to the needs of its surrounding community, in true Grow-Your-Own programming fashion. This conceptualization provides the overarching elements that must be considered and/ or exist for a clinically oriented Teacher Academy while simultaneously provoking the reader to innovate in praxis.

Teacher Academies cannot, and do not, operate in isolation of other entities. In their most basic form, TAs are typically situated in a larger school building, which is situated in a school district, which is situated in a community. The inherent structure of a Teacher Academy is inclined towards partnerships, and intentionally cultivating these partnerships contributes to rich and engaging clinical practice experiences for PCTCs, thus expanding the long-term impact for PCTCs who choose to continue to study education in their postsecondary pursuits. It is the partnerships that TAs naturally form, and the partnerships they work to cultivate, that make them sustainable.

Post-secondary education programs work hard to form relationships with local school districts, hoping to place Teacher Candidates (TCs) in nurturing, engaging classrooms that bridge the theory to practice gap that is often present in the clinical practice experiences of TCs (Knight, 2015). While postsecondary institutions and local school districts' relationships must be instigated and nurtured overtly, TAs are already situated within schools. PCTCs are constantly observing teaching practice as it unfolds around them. The gap between theory and practice is reduced in TAs due to proximity, creating a succinct "third space" that nurtures "reflection and renewal" (Flessner, 2014, p. 2).

In addition to PCTCs constantly observing and reflecting on teaching practice in their home schools, the partnership with the school district as a whole encourages access to the clinical practice settings of all the schools in the district. Proximity, prior relationships, familiarity, and shared expectations of pedagogy strengthen the ability for the TA instructor and mentor teacher to design clinical practice experiences that can encourage PCTCs to use a critical lens examining the curriculum, instruction, and assessment happening in the setting. What happens in this relationship is what AACTE (2018) might call a mutual benefit. While PCTCs can be that extra set of hands and eyes that mentor teachers might need in the classroom, completing task-oriented practices, they can also engage in the critical consciousness that is desired from authentic clinical practice, all while utilizing the narrowed third space of reflection and renewal. An added benefit to multi-year TAs and the inherent partnerships with their home school and district is the formation of lasting and meaningful relationships between PCTCs and their TA Instructor and Mentor Teachers. This relationship, and partnership, is optimal for meaningful clinical practice experiences, as PCTCs matriculate and participate in through the TA program.

Teacher Academies and Pedagogy

The theory-practice divide has been an obstacle to high-quality teacher education (Knight, 2015). In Teacher Academies and the Teacher Academy course, this is no different. While many Teacher Academy curricula and standards afford a viable framework from which to derive a solid program, the reality is that, for many Teacher Academy instructors, the Teacher Academy accounts for a minimal portion of their teaching load.

When considering how to execute teacher education pedagogy at the collegiate level, many programs have turned to Pam Grossman and colleagues' (2009) practice-based teacher education (PBTE). She and her colleagues propose that there are three tenants to quality teacher preparation, which is echoed in AACTE's CPC. First, teacher candidates need to see good teaching practice in multiple representations, including videos and observation of highly effective teachers which include intricate explanations of the pedagogical reasoning teachers use to make instructional moves (Kavanagh et al., 2020). Second, teacher candidates need to be given ample opportunities to decompose teaching practice, breaking it up into smaller parts for analytical discussions. Third, teacher candidates should be given opportunities to approximate practice through rehearsals and in clinical settings, both under the guidance of university-based teacher educators and mentor teachers.

With multiple representations of high-quality teaching practice complemented by instruction in TAs, PCTCs begin to develop a vision for what professional practice looks like. In addition, representations, paired with powerful pedagogical reasoning, support PCTCs in learning about the interplay of knowledge and action (Kavanagh et al., 2020). With ample opportunities to examine represented practice, PCTCs should have equal opportunities to decompose teaching practice, or break it down into named parts. Decomposition of represented practice can allow PCTCs to cultivate a nuanced professional vision and language. PCTCs interpreting, categorizing, and gaining proficiency in describing and interpreting what they see contribute to this quality teacher preparation. While AACTE's CPC "common language" is a call for a lexicon of clinical preparation, it is equally important that PCTCs begin learning a lexicon of practice. By starting to use the lexicon of clinical practice in high school, PCTCs can begin to more fluently discuss and unpack clinical practice, allowing them to name-what-they-see.

There are a myriad of occasions within the Teacher Academy program to approximate practice. Clinical practice experiences, particularly those conducted in clinical school sites, is the most evident opportunity to approximate clinical practice. Additionally, rehearsals in the Teacher Academy course should be a common pedagogical activity, since it is an opportunity for PCTCs to "try out their craft in safe waters" (Kavanagh et al., 2020). Through partnerships with local institutions of higher education, these clinical practice experiences in some instances have even counted towards undergraduate clinical experience clock hours.

Grossman et al's (2009) practice-based teacher education has the potential to transform Teacher Academies. As TA Instructors are considering how to design meaningful experiences for PCTCs, building a Teacher Academy program with representations, decompositions, and approximations at heart can advance the teaching profession in multiple ways. Teacher Academies, by providing space for PCTCs to envision professional practice, align well with AACTE's CPC's Developmental Proclamation. PCTCs develop a facilitated and supported understanding of the continuum of developmental growth on their pathway to accomplished teaching and the Skills Proclamation because it "includes, supports, and complements the innovative and requisite skills, strategies, and tools that improve teacher preparation by using high-leverage practices as a part of a commitment to continuous renewal for all learning sites" (AACTE, 2018, pp.17,27).

Teacher Academies and Politics and Position

TAs are in schools and career technical campuses. They are often funded by individual school districts and/or state departments of education, while typically under the umbrella of CTE in most states. A professional organization like Educators Rising can serve different purposes for TAs.

Affiliation can add prestige to the program in the school through success in participation. It can allow PCTCs in the TAs to feel a sense of belonging and camaraderie. Oftentimes participation in an organization like Educators Rising leads to leadership opportunities for PCTCs who participate. They find themselves participating in competitions they would have never endeavored before, competitions that require them to go outside of their comfort zones and interact with peers and adults with whom they did not know previously. In this way, Educators Rising is/can be a primer for authentic clinical experiences, as it gives PCTCs experiences in new environments and within new contexts.

In the Educators Rising standards, there seems to be an emphasis on culturally responsive teaching (CRT) with the inclusion of Standards 2 and 4. Many TAs are also evolving to include standards that address the need for teachers to engage in a diverse population. Despite the prevalence of CRT in academia and in teacher preparation programs, it is not always a common practice in schools with veteran teachers. The hope is that ER and TAs are positioning young people to disrupt the current pedagogical practices in schools, practices that have persisted for generations (Educators Rising, 2016).

TAs have the potential to build a foundation of theory, and then extend that foundation to practice, enacting a theory to practice continuum that is necessary for PCTCs to disrupt the current systems, all while remaining in the high school classroom. EdRising standards emphasize that a PCTC can be a "transitional figure, moving from student (during coursework) to teacher (*during clinical internships) while remaining a learner" (Educators Rising, 2016, p. 5). For teacher candidates (TCs) at the collegiate level, there is often an additional pressure attached to the student teaching/clinical experience. When TCs are completing their clinical experience, they are at the end of a four-year degree, a four-year commitment to a career path. For some TCs, this is their first significant experience in a clinical situation. In addition to being immersed in the field, they are also at the end of a road, of sorts. There are high stakes attached to this ever-important clinical experience. For PCTCs, the clinical experiences are just the beginning. Clinical experience for PCTCs is an opportunity to experience the field in a way that is not high stakes, is not the end of a long journey. This positioning can empower PCTCs to be change-makers.

PCTCs are uniquely positioned to enter their field of study and, eventually, the teaching profession, with hours of experience more than a typical TC. The hours that PCTCs spend in clinical experiences aligns with the AACTE (2018) Empowerment proclamation, which pushes for "empowering teacher candidates to take active roles during their practicum experience as coteachers in the classroom as well as professionals within the school and larger community" (p. 31). PCTCs' experiences in both the clinical setting and with initiatives attached to their professional organization are leadership-building endeavors.

CONCLUSION

The Teacher Academy has the potential to be transformed by centering and framing clinical practice as the guiding foundation for all design. Through concentrating efforts on robustly developing partnerships, pedagogy, and politics and position, Teacher Academies can transform the way the United States has historically prepared teachers. By starting this in high school, we have the potential to create meaningful experiences that set 150,000 secondary students on a trajectory to becoming accomplished teachers. Future considerations include the creation of a set of standards for clinical practice in the Teacher Academy, more intentional efforts to build bridges between Teacher Academies and local institutions of higher education, and considering how these Teacher Academies might be conceptualized on the teacher education continuum.

REFERENCES

American Association of Colleges of Teacher Education [AACTE]. (2018). *A pivot towards clinical practice, its lexicon, and the renewal of educator preparation: A report of the AACTE Clinical Practice Commission*.

Educators Rising. (2016). *Educators rising standards*.

Faust, W. (1953). Future Teachers of America. *NEA Journal*, 291.

Flessner, R. (2014). Revising reflection: Utilizing third spaces in teacher education. *Scholarship and Professional Work—Education*, 37.

Frick, H. (1955). Future Teachers of America. *NEA Journal*, 234–235.

Garner, T. Future Educators of America. (1993). *Phi Delta Kappan, 74*(5), 421–422.

Gordon, H. R. D. (2014). *The history and growth of career and technical education in America* (4th ed.). Waveland Press.

Grossman, P., Hammerness, K., & McDonald, M. (2009). Redefining teaching, reimagining teacher education. *Teachers and Teaching: Theory and Practice, 15*(2), 273–289. https://doi.org/10.1080/13540600902875340

Guild, F.C. (1953). Cadet teaching—A step towards solving the teacher shortage. *Nation's Schools, 51*(5), 79–80.

Guild, F. C. (1954). Cadet teaching in the Indianapolis Public Schools. *The Teachers College Journal, XXV*(5), 66–67.

Kavanagh, S., Conrad, J., & Dagogo-Jack, S. (2020). From rote to reasoned: Examining the role of pedagogical reasoning in practice-based teacher education. *Teaching and Teacher Education*, 89.

Knight, R. (2015). Postgraduate student teachers' developing conceptions of the place of theory in learning to teach: "More Important to Me Now than When

I Started." *Journal of Education for Teaching*, *41*(2), 145–160. https://doi.org/1
0.1080/02607476.2015.1010874

McAllister, A. (1954). Cadet teaching in the Elkhart Public Schools. *The Teachers College Journal*, *XXV*(5), 62–66.

National Council for Accreditation of Teacher Education. (2010). *Transforming teacher education through clinical practice: A national strategy to compare effective educators.* http://caepnet.org/~/media/Files/caep/accreditation-resources/blue-ribbon panel.pdf

National Education Association. (1936). Future Teachers of America. *NEA Journal*, *25*(9), 287.

National Education Association. (1955). *National Commission on Teacher Education and Professional Standards* (Dekalb Conference Report).

Ohio Department of Education. (2016). *Ohio education and training: Career field technical content standards.* http://education.ohio.gov/getattachment/Topics/Career-Tech/Education-and-Training-Career-Field/6-13-16-Education-and-Training-Content-Standards-FINAL-1.pdf.aspx

Robinson, W. (2017). Teacher education: A historical overview. In D. Clandinin & J. Husu (Eds.), *The SAGE handbook of research in teacher education*. SAGE.

Transforming teacher education through clinical practice: A national strategy to prepare effective teachers. (2010). *Report of the Blue Ribbon Panel on Clinical Preparation and Partnerships for Improved Student Learning*. NCATE.

U.S. Department of Education. (n.d.). *Perkins Data Explorer.* https://perkins.ed.gov/pims/DataExplorer

Valenzuela, A. (2017). *Grow your own educator programs: A review of the literature with an emphasis on equity-based approaches*. Intercultural Development Research Center. https://files.eric.ed.gov/fulltext/ED582731.pdf

Young, W. (1954). Cadet teaching in Indiana. *The Teachers College Journal*, *XXV*(5), 62.

CHAPTER 13

DEVELOPING NOVICE ALTERNATIVE CERTIFIED TEACHERS

K–12 School Leaders' Knowledge

Amanda L. Rose and Jennifer A. Sughrue
Florida Gulf Coast University

ABSTRACT

Alternative certification routes gained popularity as a solution to the increasing teacher shortage in the United States in the 1980s. Concerns of teacher quality and retention arose due to the unique challenges these teachers face. The purpose of this study was to investigate school leaders' knowledge of the professional development needs of novice alternative certification teachers for the ultimate goal of increased student achievement. In this sequential-explanatory, mixed-methods study, assistant principals, and principals in one large, mixed urban and suburban and two rural southern Florida school districts were surveyed during the quantitative research phase. Three leaders were then interviewed during the qualitative research phase, which was based on a phenomenological approach. Data were also collected through field notes from interviews and relevant professional development documents from participating leaders. Leaders had some knowledge of the immediate

Preparing Quality Teachers:
Advances in Clinical Practice, pp. 285–310
Copyright © 2022 by Information Age Publishing
www.infoagepub.com

285

challenges of alternative certified teachers and factors for retention, yet their expectations for the novice alternative certified teacher's performance were too high. Although individualized opportunities existed on an informal basis, long-term, systematically implemented differentiated professional development programs were not available. With greater understanding of alternative certified teacher challenges, school leaders could implement targeted professional development opportunities, for the ultimate goal of assisting them in overcoming barriers.

Alternative teacher certification is an option for individuals who have a degree but not in an educational field and who want to serve as a classroom teacher (Kee, 2012; Woods, 2016). These individuals may be in the classroom while meeting condensed and expedited requirements for professional certification. Each state defines eligibility criteria for alternative certification, including coursework and clinical experiences, or lack thereof (Woods, 2016).

This expedited entrance into the classroom is one solution to the teacher shortage in the United States (Aragon, 2016) and is attractive to individuals who did not choose education as a first career or who delayed entering the workforce (Brantlinger & Smith, 2013). However, the accelerated nature of alternative certification programs has implications for school leaders, such as unique support needs for novice alternative certified teachers (Humphrey et al., 2008). Likewise, inconsistent quality of alternative certification programs creates challenges for school leaders (Koehler et al., 2013; Lewis-Spector, 2016) due to the lack of depth and breadth in completion requirements (National Council on Teacher Quality [NCTQ], 2018; Unruh & Holt, 2010) and the resulting impact on student achievement (Lewis-Spector, 2016). Moreover, these alternative certified teachers are often hired in hard-to-staff, rural and high-poverty communities in which the teacher shortage is excessive (Garcia & Weiss, 2019a, 2019b; Hohnstein, 2017; Zhang & Zeller, 2016).

Limited research exists on the level of knowledge school leaders have regarding the particular needs of alternative certified teachers and how they use that knowledge in supporting these teachers once they are employed in their schools. While existing literature includes an in-depth analysis of the reasons alternative certification teachers either persist or leave the profession, there is minimal discussion of the perspectives of school leaders in nurturing the professional development of alternative certification teachers (Brown & Militello, 2016). Additionally, no clear guidance on professional development programs exists to ensure success of these teachers in the classroom (Nagy & Wang, 2007). Therefore, because of the increasing numbers of alternative certification teachers around the United States (Lewis-Spector, 2016), further research is necessary to establish what educational leaders can do best to support these teachers and to promote quality teaching in the classroom.

A review of empirical literature on alternative certified teachers shows no researchers examining school leaders' knowledge of the unique challenges novice alternative certified teachers face and how those leaders used that knowledge to provide professional development to assist them in overcoming challenges. Ultimately, the purpose of this study was to help alternative certified teachers improve their effectiveness by gaining insight into school leader knowledge, thus increasing the likelihood they will remain in the profession (Darling-Hammond, 2010).

BACKGROUND

Educational leaders and policy makers created paths to alternative teacher certification in the 1980s in response to an increasing teacher shortage in certain subject areas and schools in the United States (Aragon, 2016; Lewis-Spector, 2016). Teachers who hold alternative certification are those who have an undergraduate degree in a noneducation field (Woods, 2016). Approximately one-third of teacher preparation programs in the United States are designated for alternative certification (U.S. Department of Education [USDOE], 2015). Enrollment in alternative teacher preparation programs increased approximately 12.8% from 2008–2009 to 2015–2016 (National Center for Education Statistics [NCES], as cited in Garcia & Weiss, 2019b). Florida is the third-highest producer of alternative certification teachers in the United States (USDOE, 2015). In 2015–2016, approximately 9,500 individuals were issued an alternative certification in Florida, compared to the approximately 6,500 individuals who earned professional certification through a traditional route in the academic year 2014–2015 (Florida Department of Education [FLDOE], 2017).

Although alternative certification program requirements vary by program and state (Ludlow, 2013), the ultimate shared goal of each program is to grant individuals accelerated access to teaching in the K–12 public school system, especially in subjects like math, science, and bilingual education in which the greatest teacher needs exist (Woods, 2016). Common topics of focus in these programs include: (a) racially, financially, linguistically, and cognitively diverse student populations; (b) psychology and youth development; (c) curriculum and instruction; (d) school sociology; and (e) standards-based instructional theory (Johnson et al., 2005; Koehler et al., 2013). However, the inclusion of clinical opportunities similar to traditional certification programs vary in alternative certification programs, ranging from nonexistent, to modified internship experiences, and on-the-job training with school-based mentors (Kelly et al., 2015; Unruh &

Holt, 2010; Woods, 2016). Nonetheless, perhaps the most notable difference between alternative and traditional certification is the lack of depth and understanding in pedagogy and educational practice that alternative certification candidates experience due to the expedited time frame in which these programs are able to be completed (NCTQ, 2018; Unruh & Holt, 2010). In reality, quality and skilled teaching develops over time in an authentic educational environment that nurtures teacher growth (American Association of Colleges for Teacher Education [AACTE], 2018).

Implications: Alternative Certification Teacher Quality, Needs, and Retention Rates

While alternative certification offered a promising reform effort that would place teachers in classrooms in which shortages exist, the quality of these teachers is arguable, as evident by the gaps and disagreements in existing literature regarding their quality (Boyd et al., 2011; Koehler et al., 2013). Although federal educational policy (Every Student Succeeds Act, 2015, Title II, § 9214(a)(2)) and education clauses in state constitutions grant states the ability to define the requirements for a teacher to be considered "effective," appropriate supports such as mentorships, professional development, and interactions with administrators at school sites are not available in many cases, resulting in these state-designated "effective" teachers potentially lacking quality and the ability to increase student achievement (Easley, 2006; Scribner & Heinen, 2009). Furthermore, this question of quality could potentially negatively impact the already existing cycle of educational inequities in the high-poverty and rural communities, where the teacher shortages are greatest and where a disproportionately high number of alternative certified teachers who are least equipped to fill the existing roles are employed (Garcia & Weiss, 2019a, 2019b; Lewis-Spector, 2016).

Additionally, the needs of these teachers are diverse and differ substantially from those credentialed on a traditional route (Humphrey et al., 2008). For instance, not only did alternative certified first-year teachers believe they were less prepared than those with traditional certification (Kee, 2012), they had a greater focus on basic survival functions, whereas traditionally certified individuals concentrated on more advanced pedagogical concerns, including lesson differentiation (Linek et al., 2012). Other specific challenges alternative certified teachers faced include: (a) meeting the needs of diverse student populations (Kelly et al., 2015); (b) instruction, pedagogy, and classroom management (Zhang & Zeller, 2016); (c) lesson planning (Casey et al., 2011; Linek et al., 2012); (d) assessment of learning; (e) increasing student motivation (Foote et al., 2011); (f) student emotional and academic issues (Nagy & Wang, 2007); (g) parent communication (Foote et al., 2011); (h) classroom technologies (Miller et al., 1998); and (i) collaborating with colleagues (Unruh & Holt, 2010). Although many alternative certification programs are designed on the basis that school personnel will support teachers in facets for which knowledge is limited (Foote et al., 2011), school administrators are not trained explicitly on meeting the specific needs of these teachers (Hayes-Jacobs, 2004).

With the aforementioned struggles, retention of alternative certification teachers is a concern (Foote et al., 2011). Van Overschelde and Wiggins (2019) found that alternatively certified individuals were less likely than traditionally certified teachers to persist in the profession. However, specific factors leading to the retention of alternative certified teachers include preparation (Zhang & Zeller, 2016) and the teacher's perceived impact on students (Carter & Keiler, 2009). Other considerations include school leadership (Kelly et al., 2015), school vision (Moscovici, 2009), professional culture and value (Easley, 2006, 2008), and the availability of resources to aid in success (Kelly et al., 2015). Conversely, causes of alternative certification teacher turnover include: (a) disillusionment with job placement such as course and student volume and workload (Unruh & Holt, 2010); (b) misunderstandings related to school law (Casey et al., 2011); (c) limited school-level supports, including interactions with leadership (Zhang & Zeller, 2016); (d) limited professional respect (Easley, 2008); (e) personal view of teaching as a temporary placement (Easley, 2006); and (f) low salary (Unruh & Holt, 2010).

Given the repetition of reasons in existing empirical literature why alternative certified teachers leave the profession, inadequate or insufficient support likely exists. While school leaders and certification program instructors share a mutual responsibility for meeting the needs of alternative certification teachers (Parfitt & Rose, 2018), the existence of aforementioned needs indicates follow up and ongoing professional development tailored to their specific needs are not normally available (Rose, 2019). The diverse skills and areas in need of improvement with which alternative certification teachers enter the profession indicate a rationale for professional development opportunities that are differentiated from those that traditionally certified and veteran teachers require (Darling-Hammond et al., 2005). Some characteristics of beneficial professional development opportunities include involvement of teachers in the planning, implementation, and evaluation stages of professional development; a focus relevant to and aligned with school goals and practical applications; ongoing administrative support; and time for learning, planning, implementing, and reflecting (Glickman et al., 2015). Beneficial professional development opportunities must also increase in complexity and sophistication to match the developing educator's growth over time (AACTE, 2018). These, among other factors, should be considered by building-level leaders to ensure the success of alternative certified teachers.

Florida Alternative Certification Requirements

In Florida, where the study takes place, an individual may begin as a classroom teacher with a professional certificate or license earned through a traditional route or a temporary certificate, which is used by alternative certified teachers while they complete additional requirements for the Florida Professional Educator's Certificate (FLDOE, 2019a). Although numerous routes to earning the Florida Professional Educator's Certificate exist when one holds a temporary certificate, standard requirements include passing scores on all applicable certification examinations; a bachelor's degree; and demonstration of understanding—as defined by the certification program—of the Florida Educator Accomplished Practices (FEAP) (FLDOE, 2019a, 2019b, 2019c). While most traditionally certified individuals also meet the same FEAP standards in their respective programs, many Florida colleges of education undergraduate programs also base graduation requirements on the Council for the Accreditation of Educator Preparation (CAEP) standards, which involve a more detailed and greater volume of mastery areas (CAEP, 2015), including clinical experiences, than do the FEAP standards solely.

Research Questions

The purpose of this study was to investigate school leaders' knowledge of developing and supporting novice alternative certification teachers, who are in their first three years in the profession. The findings should inform school leaders and higher education institution leaders about gaps that exist in professional development opportunities for alternative certified teachers to influence positively the quality of these teachers and their impact on student achievement. Through this study, the following research questions were addressed:

1. What is the school leaders' knowledge of the particular challenges that alternative certified teachers face in their first three years of classroom teaching?
2. In what ways are school leaders using their knowledge of these unique challenges to provide professional development for alternative certified teachers?

3. How do school leaders describe the influence of professional development on the classroom performance of alternative certified teachers?
4. What do school leaders perceive as barriers to providing targeted professional development for alternative certified teachers?

METHODS

A mixed-methods approach was appropriate for this study because it offered quantitative survey responses, in addition to qualitative responses from current school administrators that allowed an in-depth insight into the knowledge of these individuals regarding the unique needs of novice alternative certified teachers. In the first stage of the sequential-explanatory, mixed-methods design, a survey was distributed to collect quantitative data regarding the knowledge of current school administrators about the challenges and preparation alternative certified teachers face in Florida, as well as school leaders' implementation of professional development and support. During the second stage, qualitative interviews of school administrators were conducted to gain an in-depth understanding of principals' knowledge of the professional development needs of alternative certified teachers in Florida. Field notes from interactions with interview participants were recorded, and professional development documents also were collected from participating school districts and building-level leaders, so multiple points of data could be triangulated for the purpose of checking for accuracy (Creswell, 2012).

Sample

In survey research, a sample that is representative of the population is typically chosen so the results can be generalizable to the whole population (Creswell, 2012), hence the choice to conduct research with a stratified sample of one large, mixed, urban, and suburban (90,000 students) and two smaller, rural school districts (6,000 students and 1,200 students) in southern Florida that were representative of the leadership and alternative certified teacher populations in the state. These districts are referenced below as Mixed, Rural A, and Rural B. A simple random sample was collected, in which individuals at various locations had the same probability of being selected (Creswell, 2012).

School-level principals and assistant principals were appropriate individuals to participate because, in the school building, these administrators hold supervisory positions over alternative certified teachers and have the ability to influence their professional development and to provide support. The chosen districts were appropriate because of their accessibility. Also, the demographics of the mixed, urban, and suburban, larger school district made it representative of other similar-sized school districts in the state. Additionally, alternative certified teachers are frequently hired in rural school districts to fill teacher shortages (Garcia & Weiss, 2019a, 2019b; Hohnstein, 2017; Zhang & Zeller, 2016), so it was also appropriate to conduct research in two smaller, rural school districts. The survey was completed by 34 leaders (11.97%), including principals and assistant principals, out of a total of 284 individuals who were surveyed (Table 13.1). While the response rate was low, it is only one measure of study quality. The response rate was acceptable because additional data were collected from other sources to support the findings (Baruch & Holtom, 2008). Table 13.2 includes the demographic information of the survey respondents.

Table 13.1

Number of Individuals by Position

District	Principals	Assistant Principals
Rural A	3	4
Rural B	11	17
Mixed	82	167
Total	96	188

Table 13.2

Demographic Information for Survey Participants

	n	%
School District		
Rural A	7	20.6
Rural B	3	8.8
Mixed	23	67.7
No Response	1	2.9
Gender		
Female	20	58.8
Male	14	41.2
Ethnicity		
White	30	88.2
Black or African American	3	8.8

(Table continued on next page)

Table 13.2 (Continued)

Demographic Information for Survey Participants

	n	*%*
Ethnicity		
Hispanic or Latino	1	2.9
American Indian	0	0.0
Mixed Race	0	0.0
School Level		
Elementary School	13	38.2
Middle School	4	11.8
High School	11	32.4
Combination School	5	14.7
Age Range		
25 to 34 Years	3	8.8
35 to 44 Years	9	26.5
45 to 54 Years	15	44.1
55 to 64 Years	7	20.6
Years in Education		
3 to 10 Years	2	5.9
11 to 15 Years	5	14.7
16 to 20 Years	10	29.4
21 or More Years	17	50.0
Years as an Administrator		
0 to 3 Years	10	29.4
4 to 5 Years	6	17.6
6 to 10 Years	6	17.6
11 to 15 Years	7	20.6
16 to 20 Years	2	5.9
21 or More Years	3	8.8
Current Position		
Principal	16	47.1
Assistant Principal	17	50.0
No Response	1	2.9
Number of ACTs in the Building		
Unsure	3	8.8
0 to 5 Teachers	13	38.2

(Table continued on next page)

Table 13.2 (Continued)

Demographic Information for Survey Participants

	n	%
Number of ACTs in the Building		
6 to 10 Teachers	8	23.5
11 to 15 Teachers	3	8.8
16 to 20 Teachers	4	11.8
21 or More Teachers	3	8.8

In the second, qualitative phase of research, three leaders were interviewed. The criteria for selection of participation included the following:

1. Elementary, middle, and high school principals and assistant principals who volunteered for a follow-up interview after survey completion;
2. School leaders demonstrating a range of knowledge regarding the challenges of alternative certified teachers and varied levels of support offered; and
3. School leaders with at least three years in a building-level administrative role.

Table 13.3 includes the demographic information of the interview participants.

Table 13.3

Demographic Information for Interview Participants

Participant	Position	Age	Ethnicity
L-1	K–8 Principal	55 to 64	White
L-2	Secondary Assistant Principal	45 to 54	White
L-3	Secondary Assistant Principal	35 to 44	Black or African American

Data Collection and Analysis

Data were collected through an electronic survey, interviews, field notes, and other relevant documents from participating school district leaders. During the first stage of research, quantitative data were collected via an electronic survey. All survey items aside from participant demographic information required a response through a five-point Likert scale of "strongly disagree," (1) "disagree," "neither disagree or agree," "agree," or "strongly agree" (5) (Fink, 2013). Reliability of the survey instrument was examined through the internal consistency of the questions in which the coefficient alpha was calculated to estimate the consistency of scores on the instrument (Creswell, 2012). After the original authors of the survey validated the items, content experts including professors of measurement and educational leadership and practicing school administrators and novice alternative certified teachers, reviewed the surveys in their entirety prior to them being distributed to establish further content and construct validity and to assert the appropriateness of the instrument for its intended participants (Creswell, 2012).

The second stage of research consisted of interviews to collect qualitative data. A semistructured interview protocol was generated to focus on explaining results from the quantitative collection. The interview questions were open-ended and focused on the phenomenon of the professional development needs of alternative certification teachers (Creswell, 2013). The questions were reviewed by expert readers prior to conducting any interviews.

To analyze quantitative survey results, the Statistical Package for the Social Sciences (SPSS) software was employed for descriptive statistics and a multivariate analysis of variance (MANOVA). Mean scores were calculated for each item, revealing the level of agreement or knowledge school leaders had regarding the various needs of alternative certified teachers identified in existing literature. The MANOVA revealed whether any of the independent variables (age, gender, ethnicity, school level, position, number of years with experience, and type of school district) had any level of impact on the dependent variables (school leaders' knowledge of the challenges alternative certified teachers face in the first three years of teaching and the support they provided in light of that knowledge), further demonstrating the knowledge level of school leaders regarding the challenges of novice alternative certified teachers.

To collect qualitative data during interviews, participant responses were audio recorded, and field notes were logged as they responded to ensure accuracy in the interpretation of their responses. Once the interviews were transcribed, those who were interviewed were asked to verify the transcription to ensure the essence of their experience was properly conveyed. After collection and transcription of qualitative interview data, qualitative responses were coded into themes (Creswell, 2013). A conventional content analysis was used to allow codes to emerge directly from the interview data (Kumar, 2011). An overarching description of the phenomenon using the context from the previous stages of analysis was documented and reviewed by an external reviewer who had experience with both alternative certified teachers and administrative responsibilities, followed by participant confirmation of the emerging themes to ensure the intended was captured and explained accurately (Husserl, 2012).

Validity

The range of threats to internal, external, and content validity, as well as reliability through reflexivity, were considered. Threats to internal validity have the potential to compromise survey results if not accounted for properly (Creswell, 2012). In particular, selection was one threat to internal validity, whereas "people factors" such as smartness or familiarity with the subject could threaten the outcome of the study (Creswell, 2012, p. 304). Employing a random selection of principals and assistant principals in all three school districts minimized this threat (Creswell, 2012). Additionally, third-person, expert reviewers with experiences with alternative certified teachers and education leadership reviewed the research methods, data collection instruments, and results at various stages of the research process including before and after data collection to ensure content validity of the survey items and the reliability and validity of results (Creswell, 2012).

Qualitative data were validated through triangulation and member checking to account for verisimilitude and ensure accurate, rich, thick descriptions (Creswell, 2013). Triangulation involved the confirmation of evidence from multiple sources including surveys, interviews, field notes, and relevant professional development documents from districts to ensure the findings were valid (Creswell, 2013). For member checking, each interview participant was provided a copy of the interview transcription and the cause researchers' analysis of the results, so he or she was able to judge for accuracy, credibility, and verisimilitude (Creswell, 2013).

As a result of the lead author's professional practice as an alternative certified educator and instructional coach to teachers entering the profession through various preparation paths, she is acutely aware of the insufficient opportunities for differentiated professional development support for alternative certified teachers. Her interest in this research stems from a personal passion for coaching novice teachers and from a desire to improve student learning opportunities. To counter this researcher positionality, the belief that the experiences of the researcher will influence the presentation of the research (Temple & Young, 2004), peer revision took place through all stages of researching and reporting to assist in the evaluation and validation of the overall narrative and results. Likewise, the lead author's immersion in the reading and coding process provided for reflexivity and reliability of results (Creswell, 2013).

FINDINGS

Through a sequential-explanatory, mixed-methods design to determine school leaders' knowledge of the professional development needs of novice alternative certified teachers, findings were drawn from the leaders' perspectives in the four areas of inquiry: (a) school leader knowledge of the unique needs of alternative certified teachers, (b) how they used this knowledge to provide targeted professional development, (c) the influence of professional development on the classroom performance of alternative certified teachers, and (d) the barriers to providing targeted professional development to alternative certified teachers. These findings are discussed relative to the existing empirical literature on the unique needs of alternative certified teachers.

School Leader Knowledge

School leaders claimed to have some level of knowledge regarding alternative certification requirements and preparation. In alignment with existing literature (Carter & Keiler, 2009; Easley, 2008; Kelly et al., 2015; Nagy & Wang, 2007; Unruh & Holt, 2010; Zhang & Zeller, 2016), leaders acknowledged the following opportunities as beneficial for alternative certified teacher effectiveness and retention: (a) teacher administrator interactions, (b) colleague collaboration, (c) perceptions of value to the organization, (d) working with students with disabilities, (e) classroom management and student discipline, (f) building rapport with students, (g) student social and academic development, (h) curriculum, and (i) encouragement and moral support. The level of knowledge of school leaders was not supported or negated by researchers due to the fact that limited research exists on the level of knowledge school leaders have regarding the particular needs of alternative certified teachers and how they use that knowledge in developing alternative certified teachers once employed.

Further concern was expressed by the interview participants about the limited background and challenges that may arise due to the nonexistent clinical experience, which was consistent with the empirical literature on the subject (Adcock & Mahlios, 2005) and noted as an essential component of effective educator preparation (AACTE, 2018). Female assistant principal L-2 noted the lack of an internship experience for alternative certified teachers as a potential downfall that contributes to negative retention:

> I truly believe that everyone who wants a career in teaching needs to go
> through some sort of internship program or training. Until you are actually
> in a classroom teaching students you are responsible for, you have no clue
> what teaching is really like. You can understand curriculum, be strong in

the content knowledge and know strategies that will help you teach that content, but until you actually stand in front of a room full of kids and plan, teach, and learn on a day-to-day basis, your knowledge of the profession is shallow.

Additionally, as captured by Casey et al. (2011) and Linek et al. (2012), the requirements to complete certification coursework including some clinical opportunities while employed as a novice, full-time classroom teacher tended to overwhelm novice alternative certified teachers. Moreover, although not noted with as much importance in survey data, interviewees emphasized alternative certified teacher challenges with time management.

Low mean scores on responses to several survey questions regarding areas in which school leader support could positively influence alternative certified teachers' decisions to remain in the profession indicated that they did not assign much importance to professional development in the areas of: (a) students' cultural backgrounds ($M = 3.56$), (b) students from low-income backgrounds ($M = 3.68$), (c) student motivations ($M = 3.68$), (d) management of job-related stress ($M = 2.74$), and (e) parent interactions and involvement ($M = 3.18$) (Table 13.4). This is contrary to existing empirical literature in which alternative certified teachers indicated they did not have sufficient knowledge in these areas and how to address them in the classroom (Foote et al., 2011; Kelly et al., 2015; Miller et al., 1998; Unruh & Holt, 2010). These findings appear to be a clear indication that school leaders are unaware of the immediate challenges novice alternative certified teachers face when they enter the classroom. Conversely, L-2 noted that in the beginning of the alternative certified teacher's career, the school leaders did not give alternative certified teachers "anything more than what they need[ed] to know," and they were given "tools that will help them in their classrooms now … to make their teaching experience as positive and supportive as possible and help them maintain an academic focus in their classrooms."

In addition, school leaders must temper their expectations for these novice teachers. Leader interviewees identified the following as challenges for which novice alternative certified teachers were unprepared, as compared to traditionally prepared novice teachers: (a) pedagogy, (b) lack of ability to implement professional development in the classroom, (c) how to structure a classroom, (d) how to adapt curriculum to the level of student, and (e) how to incorporate cooperative groupings into instruction. Even as novice teachers, traditionally certified individuals engage in advanced arts of teaching, including instructional differentiation, whereas alternative certified teachers are focused on day-to-day survival tasks, such as preparing curriculum (Linek et al., 2012). As indicated by their interview responses, school leader participants came to realize novice alternative certified teachers were not well prepared in terms of pedagogy and classroom

Table 13.4

Descriptive Statistics: Select Survey Questions

#	Question	*n*	*M*	*SD*
3	I interact (e.g., discussions about curriculum, feedback on instruction) with alternative certified teachers on a regular basis.	34	4.03	.758
5	I support discussions about teaching and learning between more experienced teachers and alternative certified teachers on a regular basis.	33	4.18	.635
8	PD influences classroom performance of alternative certification teachers.	34	4.38	.551
10	I offer PD for alternative certified teachers for understanding students' cultural backgrounds.	34	3.56	.860
11	I offer PD for alternative certified teachers for working with students from low-income backgrounds.	34	3.68	.878
13	I offer PD for alternative certified teachers for specific classroom management problems, including student discipline.	34	4.15	.702
15	I offer PD for alternative certified teachers for student motivations for wanting to succeed.	34	3.68	.727
16	I offer PD for alternative certified teachers for handling job related stress.	34	2.74	.864
17	I offer PD for alternative certified teachers for working with parents.	34	3.18	.936

management and could not be expected to perform similarly to novice traditional certified teachers.

Expecting alternative certification teachers to have a similar level of pedagogical knowledge and skills early in their careers could result in additional stress on these teachers. Cleveland (2003) confirmed that such feelings of being overwhelmed or stressed can lead to teacher turnover. School leaders' unrealistic expectations or a lack of awareness of these areas of weakness result in the absence of appropriate supports and in the addition of stress on the teacher, both of which contribute to the alternative certified novice teacher leaving the profession.

Professional Development Support

School leaders perceived they (a) provided support through personal interaction with alternative certified teachers ($M = 4.03$) and (b) facilitated interactions between alternative certified and experienced teachers on a regular basis ($M = 4.18$), as well as offered opportunities specific to certain challenges such as classroom management ($M = 4.15$) (Table 13.4). However, little evidence emerged from the surveys and interviews that leaders systematically differentiated professional development opportunities specifically for alternative certified teachers. Darling-Hammond et al. (2005) emphasized the need for and benefits of differentiated professional development due to the differences in certification requirements and individual backgrounds. Furthermore, AACTE (2018) reported that differentiated teacher development is not only essential, but it also requires a partnership between the leader or mentor and the developing professional to assess individual needs and future action, which supports Foote et al.'s (2011) notion that development opportunities should be built based on the strengths of individuals. Nevertheless, differentiated professional development supports specific to novice alternative certified teachers were not the norm in practice across the three school districts in the study.

All three leader interviewees, however, indicated opportunities for one-on-one coaching and for all novice teachers to observe veteran teachers. Female principal L-1 emphasized the importance of "on-site mentors" and the "positive impact [the following] can make on student success":

> We do a lot of going in and observing highly effective teachers and their strategies and stuff. Professional development, I think, is necessary for them, to not only be told about what to do, but actually having somebody train them how to do, and then maybe even have practice or apply it while they are in their professional development.

Male assistant principal L-3 outlined the following approach to providing professional development to alternative certified teachers through one-on-one coaching. "The first step is to observe the teacher in the classroom, in the actual setting, and that kind of gives me an idea of the particulars that I need to coach that teacher." He also recommended "they observe other teachers ... especially those with that core group of students that they teach" as an opportunity for these teachers to develop (L-3). These practices align with Altan and Sağlamel's (2015) and AACTE's (2018) recommendations for supporting novice teachers.

These leader interviewees also recommended specific courses offered through the district to individual teachers based on what each needed. According to L-1, "When we see something that comes up that will help them be successful in their position, we will offer that professional development to them."

Therefore, these individualized opportunities offered to all novice teachers indicated some informal differentiated practices. Also, leaders in the large mixed school district (L-2, L-3) noted a formal, multiple-week summer professional development academy specifically for some alternative certified teachers employed in the district; however, a similar opportunity was not mentioned by the rural school district leader (L-1).

Overall, participants in this study specified varying implementation of informal differentiated practices in place of systematic differentiated professional development programs. These findings are in alignment with the existing literature that differentiated professional development specific to alternative certified teachers is not common practice, which adds to the evidence that such a need exists.

Influence of Professional Development on Classroom Performance

Through survey data, a majority of leaders noted the positive influence of professional development on classroom performance ($M = 4.38$) (Table 13.4), which was also a prominent theme in existing literature (Clarke & Hollingsworth, 2002; Glickman et al., 2015; Mtetwa & Thompson, 2000; Seyfarth & Seyfarth, 2008). Likewise, during interviews, all three leaders emphasized the positive impact of professional development opportunities on participating individuals. Among the specific benefits of professional development was the opportunity for teachers to increase their skill levels through personal application in the classroom. L-1 hoped professional development would "give them tools in their tool bag, to go back and improve something in areas they feel they are struggling in." L-2 similarly noted:

> A teacher with an alternative certification most often does not come with the tools and experiences an individual with a teaching certificate has ... professional development opportunities give these teachers what they can use now to help them teach all of their students the content they need to know using research-based best practices.

Educational researchers have agreed that successful professional development included follow-up support for application and implementation in the classroom (Glickman et al., 2015). L-3 noted that professional development "uplift[s] us as educators," which "transcends the same information to our students," naturally increasing achievement. This aligns with Steyn's (2011) research that self-motivation for continuous growth ultimately affects student achievement.

In addition to leaders widely accepting the importance of professional development, they also noted the necessity of differentiated professional development that is germane to their practice for teachers to benefit. Because teachers face different challenges based on their backgrounds and experiences, opportunities must be differentiated to meet these needs (Darling-Hammond et al., 2005; Tigchelaar et al., 2010). According to L-2, "To retain alternative certified teachers, you have to provide professional development opportunities that are specific to their needs, are relevant and meaningful, and teaches them something they can implement now." This notion of relevance and timeliness is also supported by Glickman et al. (2015). School leaders must be aware of teacher challenges, as well as the components of beneficial professional development including its practical application, time for implementation, and ongoing support and follow up (Glickman et al., 2015). Moreover, the leaders considered coaching or observing highly effective or veteran teachers as beneficial professional development, which is consistent with the empirical literature (AACTE, 2018; Linek et al., 2012; O'Connor et al., 2011).

While leader responses were overwhelmingly positive regarding the importance of professional development on classroom performance, a clearly defined, individualized plan for each teacher should also be implemented on greater scale to support increased performance. Hence, differentiated and consequential professional development, including follow-up would assist alternative certified teachers' ability to overcome challenges and improve their performance in the classroom. This, in turn, would have a positive influence on student outcomes.

Barriers to Providing Targeted Professional Development

School leaders often know what needs to be done, but are limited by what can be done, given the circumstances. Time, funding, and the availability of substitutes were cited by two of the leader interviewees as barriers to providing targeted professional development. L-1 indicated, "Funding is always the problem ... and to have substitutes, that is a whole other problem." Similarly, L-2 explained, "We are limited to the number of substitutes we can use each school year because of funding by the district, and each school receives a specific amount of money for this expense." A substitute would be needed to free the alternative certified teacher for training opportunities and for observing a veteran teacher's classroom during the school day. The benefits of observing veteran teachers on the development of the alternative certified teacher were confirmed by all three leader interviewees and by O'Connor et al. (2011). According to O'Connor et al., alternative certified teachers noted the helpful nature of observing veteran teachers and requested additional opportunities to experience this practice.

Thus, an appropriate allotment of funds and time for targeted professional development, including opportunities for alternative certified teachers to observe veteran teachers, must be a priority for school leaders to ensure a high quality of teaching in the classroom and to offset the high financial costs of alternative certified teacher turnover (Podolsky et al., 2016). Options to maximize resources as a compromise in overcoming barriers include the following: (a) strategic integration of relevant and timely professional development opportunities through preexisting teacher induction programs, (b) training and maintaining a highly knowledgeable school leadership team with the ability to diagnose and support teacher needs in a timely manner, and (c) assigning quality mentors who are devoted and well-equipped with experiences and knowledge to influence positively these teachers. Because retention and teacher quality are the responsibility of school leaders (Unruh & Holt, 2010), their ability to overcome barriers in a creative manner to provide targeted professional development is essential.

DISCUSSION AND IMPLICATIONS

Based on the findings, three implications for practice for how alternative certified teachers should be supported once employed as a classroom teacher were identified: (a) leader knowledge and expectations, (b) individualized support systems, and (c) differentiated and systematic support systems. These are relevant to both higher education and K–12 leaders.

Institutions of Higher Education Leaders and Faculty

Two important findings were (a) inadequate familiarity of school leaders with the immediate challenges faced by alternative certified teachers and (b) their limited knowledge of what they should do to retain novice teachers, particularly alternative certified teachers, as evidenced in the empirical literature (Boyd et al., 2011; Carter & Keiler, 2009; Casey et al., 2011; Easley, 2006, 2008; Foote et al., 2011; Humphrey et al., 2008; Kelly et al., 2015; Unruh & Holt, 2010; Zhang & Zeller, 2016). Based on the findings, leaders expected novice alternative certified teachers to perform similarly to novice traditional certified teachers, such as being able to differentiate instruction and incorporate cooperative learning groupings. Participants learned after hiring them that alternative certified teachers were not as prepared to engage in higher level pedagogical practices.

Ultimately, leader knowledge of alternative certified teacher challenges, of factors for retention, and of necessary supports for these teachers is essential for teacher growth and student achievement, because it is the responsibility of the leader to initiate relevant supports and facilitate classroom success for all teachers (Brown & Militello, 2016). Likewise, alternative certification pathways probably are going to continue to enjoy political support and, hence, continue to generate teachers who are not as well prepared for the classroom as they should be. Therefore, higher education institution leaders and faculty who are educating school leaders should integrate this information into the leader preparation curriculum and develop in-service training opportunities for leaders who are supporting alternative certified teachers, thus also strengthening the university-school partnership. Without opportunities for current and future leaders to increase their knowledge of how to support novice alternative certified teacher challenges, they will be unable to diminish the number of these teachers who will exit the profession, resulting in questionable retention rates, thus perpetuating the teacher shortage (Donitsa-Schmidt & Zuzovsky, 2016).

Additionally, because resources such as time and funding may not be available in each district to provide the individualized and ongoing professional development that novice alternative certified teachers need, a partnership should be established between school districts and local higher education institutions to ensure support is effective, lasting years into the teachers' careers (Parfitt & Rose, 2018). One of the participating school administrators confirmed the benefits of their established partnership with a local university for the development of alternative certified teachers. However, for such support to be successful, university faculty and public school leaders must use their knowledge of the needs of alternative certified teachers to differentiate topics and instruction to ensure opportunities result in teacher growth. Teachers do not learn in the same manner, at the same speed, nor do they necessarily need the same information on a generic topic (AACTE, 2018; Ng & Thomas, 2007).

District and School Leaders

A key finding was leaders' recognition of the need for relevant and timely professional development that fosters teacher growth, particularly for novice teachers. Leaders confirmed implementing informal individualized support systems, such as teacher mentors and opportunities to observe veteran teachers. In practice, these support systems are important to preparing novice teachers for classroom success and retention in the profession (AACTE, 2018). Additionally, implemented professional development must be based on the following pillars of effective professional development: practical application, time for implementation, and ongoing support and follow up (Glickman et al., 2015).

The findings clearly indicated a lack of systematically implemented differentiated professional development. With increased knowledge of the needs of novice alternative certified teachers, school leaders can establish appropriate expectations for alternative certified teachers in their first three years of teaching. Without such knowledge and appropriate expectations, leaders cannot provide the necessary support and applicable opportunities for alternative certified teachers to increase their effectiveness and their likelihood to remain in the profession.

Furthermore, school leaders rank among the most important influences on teacher practice (Brown & Militello, 2016). Therefore, school district and building-level leaders must work together to establish long-term systematic and appropriately differentiated professional development opportunities for all alternative certified teachers. As described in the interviews, a summer institute with follow-up support throughout the year was seemingly very beneficial for those teachers who participated. However, for it to meet the needs of all alternative certified teachers, the institute must target the whole group rather than a select few. Also, the program for alternative certified teachers must last throughout the first three years of the teachers' careers. Such long-term and systematically implemented, differentiated support systems must be the norm for school and district leaders employing these teachers. The expected outcomes would be better classroom performance, improved student results, and increased retention of novice alternative certified teachers (Lewis-Spector, 2016; Zhang & Zeller, 2016).

Limitations

The survey response rate was a limitation of the study; only 11.97% of leaders responded. Because the survey requests were sent to candidates through senior-level district administrators, only one reminder was permitted and sent approximately two weeks after the initial survey request. Reliance on district-level administrators to disseminate the survey potentially affected the number of responses gathered, thus limiting generalizability (Creswell, 2012). However, there is no single response rate that is defined as appropriate due to the unique nature of each study (Fink, 2013), and this rate was close to the lower end of Kumar's (2011) suggested response rate of 20–50% for survey research. The in-depth interviews, field notes, and district documents supplemented the survey results, which helped with establishing a better understanding of the problem under investigation.

Another limitation was that the number of minority leader respondents was low (8.8% Black or African American, 2.9% Hispanic or Latino, & 0.0% American Indian or Mixed Race) and not representative of the demographics of the districts. Furthermore, participants' self-reporting responses was a limitation because of the reliance on their honesty, self-awareness, and potential bias when responding (Stone et al., 1999). However, review of survey responses and interviews did not uncover any indications that respondents were hesitant or responded untruthfully.

To conclude, the purpose of this study was to investigate school leaders' knowledge of the professional development supports necessary for novice alternative certified teacher success in the classroom because school leaders have among the most important influences on teacher practice (Brown & Militello, 2016). Therefore, their knowledge of the best methods to support all teachers is essential for the future of education. School leaders must foster relevant, individualized, and differentiated opportunities for alternative certified teachers that result in meaningful improvement in practice, retention in the profession, and most importantly, student achievement.

REFERENCES

Adcock, P. K., & Mahlios, M. (2005, Fall). Nontraditional alternative teacher certification programs: Their purpose, design and participants. *Essays in Education, 15*, 60–70.

Altan, M. Z., & Sağlamel, H. (2015). Student teaching from the perspectives of cooperating teachers and pupils. *Cogent Education, 2*(1), 1–16. https://doi.org /10.1080/2331186X.2015.1086291

American Association of Colleges for Teacher Education. (2018). *Clinical practice commission report.* https://aacte.org/resources/research-reports-and-briefs/ clinical-practice-commission-report/

Aragon, S. (2016, May). Teacher shortages: What we know. *Education Commission of the States,* 1–12. https://www.ecs.org/wp-content/uploads/Teacher-Shortages-What-We-Know.pdf

Baruch, Y., & Holtom, B. C. (2008). Survey response rate levels and trends in organizational research. *Human Relations, 61*(8), 1139–1160. https://doi. org/10.1177/0018726708094863

Boyd, D., Grossman, P., Ing, M., Lankford, H., Loeb, S., O'Brien, R., & Wyckoff, J. (2011). The effectiveness and retention of teachers with prior career experience. *Economics of Education Review, 30*(6), 1229–1241. https://10.1016/j. econedurev.2011.08.004

Brantlinger, A., & Smith, B. (2013). Alternative teacher certification and the new professionalism: The pre-service preparation of mathematics teachers in the New York City Teaching Fellows program. *Teachers College Record, 115*(7), 1–44.

Brown, C., & Militello, M. (2016). Principal's perceptions of effective professional development in schools. *Journal of Educational Administration, 54*(6), 703–726. https://doi.org/10.1108/JEA-092014-0109

Carter, J. H., & Keiler, L. S. (2009). Alternatively certified teachers in urban small schools: Where policy reform meets the road. *The Urban Review, 41*(5), 437–460. https://doi.org/10.1007/s11256-008-0117-7

Casey, P., Dunlap, K., Brister, H., & Davidson, M. (2011). I only wish I'd known: Voices of novice alternatively certified special education teachers. *International Journal of Special Education, 26*(1), 182–190.

Clarke, D., & Hollingsworth, H. (2002). Elaborating a model of teacher professional growth. *Teaching and Teacher Education, 18*(8), 947–967. https://doi.org/10.1016/S0742-051X(02)00053-7

Cleveland, D. (2003). A semester in the life of alternatively certified teachers: Implications for alternative routes to teaching. *The High School Journal, 86*(3), 17–34.

Council for the Accreditation of Educator Preparation. (2015). *The CAEP standards*. http://caepnet.org/standards/introduction

Creswell, J. W. (2012). *Educational research: Planning, conducting, and evaluating quantitative and qualitative research* (5th ed.). Pearson Education.

Creswell, J. W. (2013). *Qualitative inquiry and research design: Choosing among five approaches* (3rd ed.). SAGE.

Darling-Hammond, L. (2010). Teacher education and the American future. *Journal of Teacher Education, 61*(1–2), 35–47. https://doi.org/10.1177/0022487109348024

Darling-Hammond, L., Holtzman, D. J., Gatlin, S. J., & Heilig, J. V. (2005). Does teacher preparation matter? Evidence about teacher certification, Teach for America, and teacher effectiveness. *Education Policy Analysis Archives, 13*(42), 1–51.

Donitsa-Schmidt, S., & Zuzovsky, R. (2016). Quantitative and qualitative teacher shortage and the turnover phenomenon. *International Journal of Educational Research, 77*, 83–91. https://doi.org/10.1016/j.ijer.2016.03.005

Easley, J. (2006). Alternative route urban teacher retention and implications for principals' moral leadership. *Educational Studies, 32*(3), 241–249. https://doi.org/10.1080/03055690600631176

Easley, J. (2008). Moral school building leadership: Investigating a praxis for alternative route teacher retention. *Journal of Educational Administration, 46*(1), 25–38. https://doi.org/10.1108/09578230810849790

Every Student Succeeds Act. (2015). Pub. L. No. 114-95.

Fink, A. (2013). *How to conduct surveys: A step-by-step guide*. SAGE.

Florida Department of Education. (2017). *Florida temporary educator's certificates: Report on preparation pathways to the professional certificate*. http://www.fldoe.org/core/fileparse.php/9960/urlt/FLTempRPPPC.pdf

Florida Department of Education. (2019a). *Certificate pathways & routes*. http://www.fldoe.org/teaching/certification/pathways-routes/

Florida Department of Education. (2019b). *General knowledge*. http://www.fldoe.org/teaching/certification/general-cert-requirements/general-knowledge.stml

Florida Department of Education. (2019c). *Subject area examinations*. http://www.fldoe.org/teaching/certification/certificate-subjects/certification-subject-examinations.stml

Foote, M. Q., Brantlinger, A., Haydar, H. N., Smith, B., & Gonzalez, L. (2011). Are we supporting teacher success: Insights from an alternative route mathematics teacher certification program for urban public schools. *Education and Urban Society, 43*(3), 396–425. https://doi.org/10.1177/0013124510380420

Garcia, E., & Weiss, E. (2019a). *The teacher shortage is real, large and growing, and worse than we thought: The first report in 'The perfect storm in the teacher labor market' series*. https://www.epi.org/publication/the-teacher-shortage-is-real-large-and-growing-and-worse-than-we-thought-the-first-report-in-the-perfect-storm-in-the-teacher-labor-market-series/

Garcia, E., & Weiss, E. (2019b). *U.S. schools struggle to hire and retain teachers: The second report in 'The perfect storm in the teacher labor market' series*. https://files.eric.cd.gov/fulltext/ED598209.pdf

Glickman, C. D., Gordon, S. P., & Ross-Gordon, J. M. (2015). *Supervision and instructional leadership: A developmental approach* (9th ed.). Allyn & Bacon.

Hayes-Jacobs, H. (2004). *Getting results with curriculum mapping*. ASCD.

Hohnstein, S. (2017). The rise of urban alternative teacher certification. *Teacher Education and Practice, 30*(1), 194–206.

Humphrey, D. C., Wechsler, M. E., & Hough, H. J. (2008). Characteristics of effective alternative teacher certification programs. *Teachers College Record, 110*(4), 1–63.

Husserl, E. (2012). *Ideas: General introduction to pure phenomenology*. Routledge.

Johnson, S. M., Birkeland, S. E., & Peske, H. G. (2005). Life in the fast track: How states seek to balance incentives and quality in alternative teacher certification programs. *Educational Policy, 19*(1), 63–89. https://doi.org/10.1177/0895904804270774

Kee, A. N. (2012). Feelings of preparedness among alternatively certified teachers: What is the role of program features? *Journal of Teacher Education, 63*(1), 23–38. https://doi.org/10.1177/0022487111421933

Kelly, A. M., Gningue, S. M., & Qian, G. (2015). First-year urban mathematics and science middle school teachers: Classroom challenges and reflective solutions. *Education and Urban Society, 47*(2), 132–159. https://doi.org/10.1177/0013124513489147

Koehler, A., Feldhaus, C. R., Fernandez, E., & Hundley, S. P. (2013). Alternative certification programs & pre-service teacher preparedness. *Journal of STEM Education: Innovations and Research, 14*(4), 45–55.

Kumar, R. (2011). *Research methodology: A step-by-step guide for beginners*. SAGE.

Lewis-Spector, J. (2016). State-level regulations for alternative routes to teacher certification in the U.S.: Are candidates being prepared to develop their students' literacy? *Literacy Practice & Research, 42*(1), 5–15.

Linek, W. M., Sampson, M. B., Haas, L., Sadler, D., Moore, L., & Nylan, M. C. (2012). The impact of teacher preparation: A study of alternative certification and traditionally prepared teachers in their first year of teaching. *Issues in Teacher Education, 21*(2), 67–82.

Ludlow, C. (2013). Alternative certification pathways: Filling a gap? *Education and Urban Society, 45*(4), 440–458. https://doi.org/10.1177/0013124511413916

Miller, J. W., McKenna, M. C., & McKenna, B. A. (1998). A comparison of alternatively and traditionally prepared teachers. *Journal of Teacher Education, 49*(3), 165–176. https://doi.org/10.1177/0022487198049003002

Moscovici, H. (2009). Science teacher retention in today's urban schools: A study of success and failure. *Urban Education, 44*(1), 88–105. https://doi.org/10.1177/0042085908318527

Mtetwa, D. K., & Thompson, J. J. (2000). Towards decentralised and more school-focused teacher preparation and professional development in Zimbabwe: The role of mentoring. *Journal of In-Service Education, 26*(2), 311–328. https://doi.org/10.1080/13674580000200119

Nagy, C. J., & Wang, N. (2007). The alternate route teachers' transition to the classroom: Preparation, support, and retention. *NASSP Bulletin, 91*(1), 98–113. https://doi.org/10.1177/0192636506299153

National Council on Teacher Quality. (2018). *2018 teacher prep review*. https://www.nctq.org/publications/2018-Teacher-Prep-Review

Ng, J., & Thomas, K. (2007). Cultivating the cream of the crop: A case study of urban teachers from an alternative teacher education program. *Action in Teacher Education, 29*(1), 3–19. https://doi.org/10.1080/01626620.2007.10463435

O'Connor, E. A., Malow, M. S., & Bisland, B. M. (2011). Mentorship and instruction received during training: Views of alternatively certified teachers. *Educational Review, 63*(2), 219–232. https://doi.org/10.1080/00131911.2010.537312

Parfitt, C. M., & Rose, A. L. (2018). Collaborating to meet the needs of alternative certification teachers using formative design. *Journal of Formative Design in Learning, 2*(1). https://doi.org/10.1007/s41686-018-0017-5

Podolsky, A., Kini, T., Bishop, J., & Darling-Hammond, L. (2016, September). *Solving the teacher shortage: How to attract and retain excellent educators* (Research Brief). Learning Policy Institute.

Rose, A. L. (2019). *Supporting alternative certification teachers' professional development needs in Florida: Knowledge of K–12 school leaders* (Publication No. 13808049) [Doctoral dissertation, Florida Gulf Coast University]. ProQuest Dissertations and Theses Global Publishing.

Scribner, J. P., & Heinen, E. (2009). Alternative teacher certification: A program theory analysis. *Teacher Education Quarterly, 36*(2), 179–197.

Seyfarth, J., & Seyfarth, J. (2008). *Human resource leadership for effective schools* (5th ed.). Pearson/Allyn and Bacon.

Steyn, G. M. (2011). Continuing professional development in South African schools: Staff perceptions and the role of principals. *Journal of Social Sciences, 28*(1), 43–53. http://www.krepublishers.com/02-Journals/JSS/JSS-28-0-000-11-Web/JSS-28-1-000-2011-Abst-PDF/JSS-28-1-043-11-1168-Steyn-G-M/JSS-28-1-043-11-1168-Steyn-G-M-Tt.pdf

Stone, A. A., Bachrach, C. A., Jobe, J. B., Kurtzman, H. S., & Cain, V. S. (Eds.). (1999). *The science of self-report: Implications for research and practice*. Psychology Press.

Temple, B., & Young, A. (2004). Qualitative research and translation dilemmas. *Qualitative Research, 4*(2), 161–178.

Tigchelaar, A., Brouwer, N., & Vermunt, J. D. (2010). Tailor-made: Towards a pedagogy for educating second-career teachers. *Educational Research Review, 5*(2), 164–183. https://doi.org/10.1016/j.edurev.2009.11.002

Unruh, L., & Holt, J. (2010). First-year teaching experiences: Are they different for traditionally versus alternatively certified teachers? *Action in Teacher Education, 32*(3), 3–14. https://doi.org/10.1080/01626620.2010.10463555

U.S. Department of Education, Office of Post-secondary Education. (2015). *Alternative teacher preparation programs: Alternative programs offer a different pathway to earn an initial teaching credential*. https://title2.ed.gov/Public/44110_Title_II_Issue_Brief_Altn_TPP.pdf

Van Overschelde, J. P., & Wiggins, A. Y. (2019) Teacher preparation pathways: Differences in program selection and teacher retention. *Action in Teacher Education*. https://doi.org/10.1080/01626620.2019.1656116

Woods, J. R. (2016, May). Mitigating teacher shortages: Alternative teacher certification. *Education Commission of the States*, 1–7. https://www.ecs.org/wp-content/uploads/Mitigating-Teacher-Shortages-Alternative-Certification.pdf

Zhang, G., & Zeller, N. (2016). A longitudinal investigation of the relationship between teacher preparation and teacher retention. *Teacher Education Quarterly, 43*(2), 73–92.

CHAPTER 14

CLINICAL EXPERIENCES AND PROGRAM OUTCOMES IN ALTERNATIVE LICENSURE PATHWAYS

Sarah W. Sharpe
Columbus State University

David T. Marshall and Parinita Shetty
Auburn University

ABSTRACT

Quality preservice clinical experiences are an important factor in determining how successful teachers will be in their early careers. With almost one-third of teachers being prepared through alternative teacher preparation pathways it is important to examine the nature of their clinical experiences. Alternative teacher preparation programs are nontraditional pathways of training that have an expedited structure and differ from traditional university-based programs in a few common components which include eligibility requirements, delivery of coursework, and clinical experiences. This chapter examines clinical teaching experiences in four types of alternative pathways to teaching, including: (1) summer practicum pathways, where participants receive summer training and experience in summer school teaching prior to

Preparing Quality Teachers:
Advances in Clinical Practice, pp. 311–334
Copyright © 2022 by Information Age Publishing
www.infoagepub.com

their first year of teaching; (2) postgraduate provisional pathways that gives participants an opportunity to earn a provisional license while completing their master's degree in education; (3) career-switcher pathways that supports participants who have made the decision to switch from noneducation related careers to a career in teaching, and (4) distance learning pathways that offer courses, workshops and mentorship in an online setting. We conclude with a discussion of program outcomes including student achievement, classroom management, and attrition. It was found that alternatively certified teachers perform at least as well as those who were prepared through traditional programs.

INTRODUCTION

An individual who wishes to pursue a career in teaching can do so through multiple pathways. Teacher preparation pathways can vary greatly from one another; however, some common features exist across programs (Fraser & Lefty, 2018; National Research Council, 2010; Zeichner, 2018). Almost all programs will have some type of pedagogical instruction for novice teachers, and almost all programs will have some form of a practicum or clinical experience that allows preservice teachers an opportunity to gain some classroom experience prior to being placed as teachers of record themselves (Krieg et al., 2020). Traditionally, those desiring to teach received training in a traditional preparation program[1] (Fraser & Lefty, 2018; Zeichner, 2018). While it should be recognized that experiences in traditional programs vary across settings, these programs tend to front-load and privilege university-based coursework in pedagogy, and they typically include a student teaching placement prior to graduation and licensure. Student teacher placements are typically 12- to 16-weeks long, and they afford preservice teachers the opportunity to gain valuable classroom experience prior to being placed as teachers of record (National Research Council, 2010).

As recent as three decades ago, the traditional pathway was the norm for teachers prior to their placement as teachers of record (Fraser & Lefty, 2018). Individuals who wished to pursue a career as a classroom teacher enrolled in a university-based program, took classes that armed them with educational theories and pedagogical strategies, completed student teaching, and found a job. However, today, as many as one-third of teachers are prepared through a nontraditional pathway (Zeichner, 2018). These alternative licensure programs (ALPs) are often not university based (Gastic, 2014). Programs vary in approach and across settings, but often feature a summer training program that includes between four and six weeks in the classroom prior to placement as a teacher of record. Many of these programs then provide additional supports after placement, which is not common in a traditional preparation program. Through their expedited structure, these programs tend to place greater emphasis on classroom experience than preservice coursework. Compared to peers who are prepared to teach through a traditional program, non-White and male participants are more likely to be represented in ALPs (National Center for Education Statistics, 2018; Van Overschelde & Wiggins, 2020). They are also more likely to teach in charter schools and in schools whose student enrollments are 90%+ non-White and 76%+ eligible for free or reduced-price lunch than their traditionally prepared peers are. See Table 14.1 for a comparison of teachers prepared in traditional and alternative pathways.

The National Council for Accreditation of Teacher Education (2010) has recommended that opportunities for quality clinical practice be a central part of teacher preparation. This recommendation is supported by ample research which demonstrates that when teachers have a quality practicum experience prior to becoming teachers of record, they are more likely to experience success during their first years in the classroom (Darling-Hammond, 2014; Gastic, 2014; Fraser & Lefty, 2018; Zeichner & Bier, 2012; Zeichner, 2018). This, of course, makes sense. For example, it is highly unlikely that Derek Jeter would have become a Hall of Fame baseball

Table 14.1

Traditionally and Alternatively Prepared Teacher Candidates

	Traditional	Alternative
Race/Ethnicity		
American Indian	**	**
Asian	2%	3%
Black	5%	13%
Hispanic	8%	15%
White	83%	66%
Two or more races	1%	2%
Gender		
Female	78%	68%
Male	22%	32%
School Characteristics		
90+% non-White	15%	25%
76+% FRL eligible	26%	32%
Charter school	5%	8%

Note: Figures represent 2015–16 national statistics (National Center for Education Statistics, 2018) ** less than 1% of teachers meet this criteria; FRL = students eligible for free or reduced-price lunch player had he only listened to lectures and read books about baseball prior to his first season with the New York Yankees. The National Research Council (2010) studied first- and second-year teachers in New York City and found that a quality field experience was the strongest predictor of improved student reading and math scores. Having the opportunity to gain classroom experience with a veteran teacher has additional benefits as well. Novice teachers inevitably make mistakes. Having the opportunity to reflect on and learn from these mistakes alongside an experienced teacher is a hallmark of a successful clinical experience (Marshall et al., 2021).

Alternative teacher preparation pathways have emerged for a myriad of reasons. A primary aim of ALPs is to train teachers for understaffed schools (Ludlow, 2013). Teacher labor markets vary by geography, but shortages often exist in rural and urban areas, especially where there is a concentration of poverty (Fuller & Pendola, 2020). School districts often have an inadequate supply of qualified special education teachers (Peyton et al., 2020), and several ALPs focus on filling this gap. Lohmann et al. (2019) studied an online ALP in Colorado and found that the program was successful at recruiting and preparing special education teachers. They found that the online and asynchronous nature of the program met the needs of individuals seeking to be teachers and living in more remote parts of the state. LaRon Scott (2019) found that ALPs in Virginia were successful at recruiting and preparing Black male special education teachers. This is particularly noteworthy given the overrepresentation of Black male students in special education (Garibaldi, 2009) and the underrepresentation of Black male special education teachers (Scott, 2016).

Some of the enthusiasm for alternative preparation models is born out of a critique of the traditional model. Indeed, entire books have been written over the decades critiquing traditional university-based teacher preparation programs (see Elsbree, 1939; Green, 2014; Koerner, 1965; Kramer, 2000; Sedlak, 1989; Smith, 1954 as examples of such volumes). It is not our intent here to comment on the efficacy of traditional teacher preparation; alternative preparation programs have their critics as well (e.g., Thomas, 2018). However, if one out of every three new teachers entering public school classrooms is prepared in an alternative pathway, it is important to understand the nature of the clinical experiences these teachers receive.

CLINICAL EXPERIENCE IN
ALTERNATIVE PATHWAYS TO TEACHING

Preparing high quality teachers requires alternative licensure programs to offer well-designed training with a combination of effective components

(Humphrey & Wechsler, 2007). Several ALPs mimic the overall structure of traditional licensure programs at colleges and universities; however, there are differences in the common components of accelerated alternative licensure programs from traditional programs. Some differences include eligibility requirements, delivery of coursework, and the length of clinical experience. We examine four types of alternative learning programs to better understand the structure of ALPs and participants' clinical experiences, though there is limited research on participants' perceptions of clinical experiences offered in ALPs. Generally, ALPs have similar structures; however, we found differences in programs in terms of their purpose and approach to preparing educators.

For most alternative licensure programs, there are eligibility requirements and an admission process the candidates must undergo before they are accepted into the program. Many of these programs have high standards, and they seek highly educated and talented candidates (Schonfeld & Feinman, 2012). Once the candidates have been admitted into the ALP, most programs require coursework, professional training, and a practicum before program participants are qualified to teach. Typically, the coursework and training focus on classroom management, curriculum, and teaching methods (Adcock & Mahlios, 2005; Zeichner & Schulte, 2001). The clinical practicum is the supervised experience candidates gain working with students in a classroom. This is important as it allows program participants the opportunity to work with students in a classroom setting with the support of a mentor, often an in-service teacher or a staff member of the program who has years of teaching experience.

Programs have different names for the participants in their program (e.g., fellows, corps members, preservice teachers, interns, and students). Here we generically refer to all ALP participants as *program participants*. Additionally, each program refers to participants' experiences in the classroom differently (i.e., clinical experience, student teaching, practicum, field experience); we refer to these as *clinical experiences*. We categorize ALPs in the following four pathways: (1) summer practicum pathway; (2) postgraduate provisional pathway; (3) career-switcher pathway; and (4) distance learning pathway. We describe each pathway in further detail, share examples and general program formats, and features of the clinical experience for each of the pathways. We recognize that the four typologies described here are not mutually exclusive; the ALPs have characteristics that overlap with more than one of these pathways.[2] However, we see discussing ALPs in terms of these four pathways as a useful endeavor. See Figure 14.1 for a visual depiction of the four typologies in contrast to traditional teacher preparation.

Figure 14.1

Comparison of Traditional and ALP Pathways

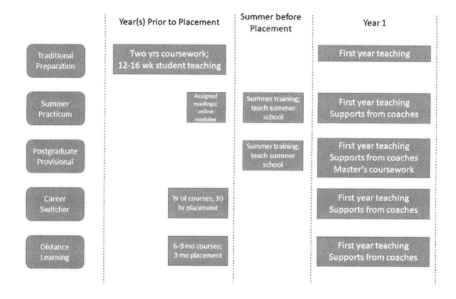

Summer Practicum Pathway

Summer practicum pathway ALPs are programs that conduct summer training and whose participants typically teach summer school immediately prior to participants' first year of teaching. Examples of this pathway option are Teach for America (TFA) and The New Teacher Project (TNTP). TFA is one of the largest alternative routes to teaching certification in the country, placing teachers in more than 50 communities across the United States. Their stated mission is to close the achievement gap by providing under-resourced schools with teachers who are committed to this mission (Humphrey & Wechsler, 2007). There are two main differences between this type of ALP and the traditional, university-based program. First, the coursework is offered through the program (in this case TFA) rather than a university. Second, participants are placed in the classroom sooner than they would in a typical, university-based program. Compared to other alternative pathways to teaching, summer practicum ALPs often attract candidates for their programs directly out of college. Many participants are in their early 20s, have less full-time, professional work experience, and have degrees that are often in disciplines other than education (Humphrey & Wechsler, 2007).

TFA candidates must have earned a bachelor's degree by the first day of training, have a minimum cumulative GPA of 2.5, and should be a United States citizen, or hold Deferred Action for Childhood Arrivals (DACA) status. Additionally, participants must exhibit characteristics that demonstrate their commitment to TFA's mission. TFA participants, also referred to as corps members, attend a five-week institute in the summer for rigorous, hands-on experience (Teach for America, 2020). TFA collaborates with the local schools, colleges, and departments of education on the coursework for program participants (Rooks, 2018). As a result, program participants' coursework is tailored to fit the needs of the specific region to which they are assigned. TFA staff, alumni, and corps members, as well as community partners run the summer training. The training also includes immersive practice with teaching and coaching. Participants co-teach with other members and receive feedback from TFA instructional staff and local, veteran teachers.

Program participants in TFA receive four weeks of clinical experience before their first year of teaching. Concurrent with their preservice teaching, they are also assigned readings, observe teachers, and are observed teaching, and have follow-up conversations with the observed teachers and observers (Humphrey & Wechsler, 2007). Heather Kern Lanier (2012) and Donna Foote (2008) have written firsthand accounts of their experiences as TFA alumni, and both describe the summer training and clinical experience as intense, with days that start early and end late. Each day participants focused on learning culturally relevant practices, pedagogical techniques, and other relevant knowledge while simultaneously learning from the struggles of their classroom practice with a mentor and from each other.

Postgraduate Provisional Pathway

Postgraduate provisional pathway options provide program participants an opportunity to earn a provisional license while completing their master's degree in education. This is an option for participants who did not earn a bachelor's degree in education, but in a different subject area. Often, these programs represent the inverse of a traditional preparation program. Traditional preparation programs begin with coursework, followed by a clinical experience, and then placement as a teacher of record. Conversely, postgraduate provisional pathways often begin with a summer practicum combined with instruction, followed by placement as a teacher with the participant taking coursework towards a master's degree while teaching. Examples of postgraduate provisional pathway programs include the New York City Teaching Fellows (NYCTF), the Alternative

Route to Licensure program at the University of Nevada in Las Vegas, and Alternate Route Teacher Licensure programs at The University of Southern Mississippi. NYCTF's mission is to fill teaching vacancies in New York City's low-performing, high-needs schools (O'Connor et al., 2011). This ALP is considered a regional program, where program participants are prepared specifically to teach in schools in New York City. Each state has requirements for teacher certification; therefore, NYCTF follows New York's guidelines. Since the program participants in NYCTF obtain their master's degree while in the program, the host college or university creates the curriculum for the postgraduate coursework, not the program (Humphrey and Wechsler, 2007).

NYCTF prefers candidates with a 3.0 GPA. If they have between a 2.5 to 3.0 GPA, they are still eligible, but must submit a GPA statement to provide context on their GPA (NYC Teaching Fellows, 2020). Participants in the program earn their master's degree while in the program. Their training begins in the summer and lasts approximately seven to eight weeks. The program's key components include a hands-on classroom experience, daily coaching conversations, skill-building sessions, and master's degree coursework. During the summer training, the fellows begin their master's degree coursework in teaching. Participants have reported that the coursework was not as beneficial for preparing them for classroom teaching (Costigan, 2004; Sipe & D'Angelo, 2006). Sipe and D'Angelo (2006) interviewed former participants in the NYCTF program to understand their experience with the program. According to one of the participants in Sipe and D'Angelo's case study, who quit after their two-year commitment, summer training was "overwhelming" and they felt as though "everything was thrown at them at once" (p. 16). However, compared to the overall attrition rate for ALPs, NYCTF's numbers were lower than the average (Sipe & D'Angelo, 2006).

Under the guidance of an experienced NYC teacher, participants teach each day in a NYC summer school classroom and receive constant feedback. Additionally, fellows are provided strategies that can be immediately implemented in their classroom. In regards to the summer teaching experience, Costigan (2004) collected and analyzed journal entries from participants in the program recording their thoughts throughout their summer training. Each of the participants took the same summer postgraduate degree courses, mentoring courses, and were assigned to either elementary or middle schools for their summer teaching. Before the summer teaching began, Costigan reported participants' feelings on wanting to befriend and mold students, hoping to make a change, and wanting to go towards a new direction in their lives through teaching. Once the summer teaching began, however, several of the participants experienced struggles, especially with classroom management. One participant in Costigan's study stated:

In my classroom. I am upset today. I have got to relax.... There are a few kids that I think are great. And two or three are going to be a problem. I just have to make sure that they stay a small problem. (p. 134)

One of the participants purchased a book on classroom management because she did not feel as though the coursework and mentoring provided during the summer training were efficient enough to prepare her for controlling and managing the classroom (Costigan, 2004). Fortunately, once the participants began their first year of teaching, some reported being naive at the start of the summer training and felt more comfortable teaching as the school year progressed.

Career-Switcher Pathway

Some ALPs are designed to support participants who have made the decision to switch from non-education-related careers to a career in teaching. Career Switcher Alternative Route to Licensure Program (CSALP), the Restricted License Program at Emporia State University, and Georgia Teacher Academy for Preparation and Pedagogy (GaTAPP) pathway are programs designed to prepare "career-switchers" to become highly qualified teachers. CSALP was created at Virginia Commonwealth University (VCU) and it was designed to attract those specialized in particular subject areas from various occupations to become "highly qualified" teachers in critical needs areas (Wilcox & Samaras, 2009). It provides mid-career professionals in other fields an opportunity to switch to a career in education and to teach in Virginia schools.

CSALP requires participants to have earned a bachelor's degree from a regionally accredited college or university and have at least three full years of full-time work experience (Virginia Commonwealth University [VCU], 2020). Before candidates are able to teach, they must pass the Praxis exam for the subject area(s) they want to teach. According to their website (VCU, 2020), in the first year, participants complete intensive, face-to-face course modules over two semesters (which take approximately 198 hours to complete). Additionally, participants interested in secondary education complete 30 hours of field experience in a secondary school setting. Participants interested in pre-K–12, will complete an additional 20 hours of field experience (50 total). Once participants successfully complete the course modules, they receive a Provisional Career Switcher license and are eligible for provisional employment for one year. The Virginia Department of Education (VDOE) website states:

> Intensive Level I preparation includes a minimum of 180 clock hours of instruction, including field experience. This phase includes, but is not limited to, curriculum and instruction (including instructional technology), reading in the content area, language acquisition, differentiation of instruction, classroom/behavior management, instructional design based on assessment data, human growth and development and other specific course work related to the Virginia Standards of Learning. (VDOE, 2021)

Level I requirements must be completed over the course of a year after which participants are awarded the Provisional Career Switcher License, which is active for one year. After receiving the Provisional Career Switcher License, participants are expected to seek and find employment in schools. If they are unable to do so during the first year of the life of the Provisional Career Switcher License, the license may be extended annually for up to two additional years upon the recommendation of an employing school division or accredited nonpublic school. Level II preparation begins during the first year of employment. In Level II, a minimum of five seminars are provided, and each participant is assigned a trained mentor to assist during their first year of employment. Level III is an additional year of preparation that is provided to participants, only if required, to address areas of improvement identified in the participants' professional improvement plan (VDOE, 2021). Participants are eligible to apply for a 10-year renewable license upon completion of the program.

Transitioning into the classroom is not as smooth and easy for many career switchers (Bullough & Knowles, 1990; Lee & Lamport, 2011). The demands of teaching are significantly different from other career fields and switching to a career in education requires a change in mindset. Wilcox and Samaras (2009) found that some challenges career switcher program participants faced during their clinical experience included the time demands and managing student behavior and students' needs. The participants Wilcox and Samaras interviewed shared the difficulties with managing the numerous responsibilities as a teacher (i.e., planning lessons, grading, and teaching), as well as difficulties with lesson pacing and covering all standards. Participants also shared that they appreciated the level of mentoring they received in the program.

Distance Learning Pathway

Distance learning pathways to alternative licensure offer courses, workshops, and mentorship in an online setting. Some of these programs are university-based; examples of this would include programs at Kansas State University, the University of Tennessee-Martin, and a special education-focused program at Virginia Commonwealth University. Other distance programs are independent of a higher education institution; examples of such programs are Teach Away and Teacher Ready. Participants typically choose distance learning for alternative licensure for a number of reasons. Geography is often one such reason. Many individuals either do not live near a university offering a face-to-face option, or find the time and expense associated with traveling back and forth to engage with face-to-face instruction to be a barrier (Arkorful & Abaidoo, 2015). Distance learning pathway programs afford individuals whose work schedules create barriers to enrolling in face-to-face coursework (Fekula, 2010). Others simply prefer the convenience of working from home on an asynchronous or synchronous schedule (Oblender & Glass, 2004; Schweizer et al., 2008; Simmons & Mebane, 2012).

Teach Away is an example of a distance-learning program that offers an accelerated, alternative route to teacher certification. Whereas traditional programs and the other ALPs we discuss require face-to-face training, online options for licensure, such as Teach Away, provide more flexibility for program participants. Program participants are able to create their own schedule as they complete the coursework. Eligibility requirements for admittance into the Teach Away program are to be eligible to work in the United States and to have a bachelor's degree in any subject area. On the Teach Away website (Teach Away, 2020), there were no specifications on GPA requirements for the online Teach Away Teacher Certification Program. Two states that offer teacher certification through Teach Away are Hawaii and Arizona (Teach Away, 2020). In Hawaii, participants must take 20 hours of online coursework per week for six months. In addition to the coursework, students must complete three months of clinical placement in Hawaii, which can be completed concurrently or consecutively with the coursework. Also, Hawaii requires participants studying to teach in Hawaii to take an online module on the Hawaiian history, culture, and language (Teach Away, 2020). Participants are placed in an online cohort (with up to 15 other participants) and assigned an online mentor.

In Arizona, participants take 360 hours of online coursework within six months and 450 hours (approximately 12 weeks) of clinical placement, which can be completed concurrently or consecutively. Students in the Arizona Teach Away program receive one-on-one guidance from experienced teachers. Participants studying to teach in Arizona must take part in a mandatory webinar on adjusting to life in Arizona personally and professionally (Teach Away, 2020). The four core modules of coursework for both states focus on understanding learner development, assessing student learning, planning instruction, and implementing instructional strategies.

The lengths of clinical placement for distance-learning pathways are similar to the lengths of placements in traditional licensure pathways. Distance licensure programs precede with online coursework and conclude with a semester of clinical placement (Fiechtl & Hager, 2019; Lohfink et al., 2011). The flexibility of how the coursework is completed is a factor that draws in participants. Schweizer et al. (2008) investigated the training, effectiveness, and perceptions of a distance-learning pathway to alternative licensure. Flexibility of the online program attracted some of the participants. One of the distance pathway participants from their investigation said, "As a working adult, I was looking for a program that fit into my schedule. An online program such as this one made the most sense to me and seemed doable in terms of my own life" (Schweizer et al., 2008). The participants of this online program were graded based on their lesson plans, reflective journals, case studies, and self-recorded lessons that were collected and evaluated throughout the program—the overall GPA of the participants was 3.95 out of 4.0. Overall, participants believed the course assignments, online discussions, student-to-instructor interactions, and student-to-student interactions were efficacious in terms of preparing them for their clinical experience.

Additionally, the participants were evaluated for their clinical teaching by their university supervisor and cooperating teacher (the primary teacher of record of the assigned classroom who also serves as a mentor for preservice teachers). Participants' evaluation scores on their clinical teaching demonstrate the effectiveness of the online program. Collectively, participants received a 3.55 score out of 4 from university supervisors and a 3.50 out of 4 from their cooperating teachers (3 being satisfactory and 4 being exemplary) (Schweizer et al., 2008). Moreover, the cooperating, mentor teachers appreciated the backgrounds the nontraditional students brought into the classrooms. For example, one participant had a background in business and the cooperating teacher felt the participant brought a great deal into the curriculum (Schweizer et al., 2008). Brigman and Petty (2013) found similar, positive results on participants' perceived preparedness following their completion of a distance learning alternative licensure program. In their study, Brigman and Petty found that participants who completed the online program felt prepared to have their own classroom. The researchers measured the participants' preparation using a survey to measure the following areas: general education, major background deficiency courses, academic concentration courses, professional education courses, clinical experiences, and student teaching. Other work has found that some participants have experienced frustrations with online teacher preparation. Fiechtl and Hager (2019), suggest some of the challenges participants may face are uploading documents and videos of their teaching to meet course requirements.

While there were classifications established for particular programs, it is important to mention there is some overlap between the programs and their approaches to alternative licensure. For example, though NYC

Teaching Fellows was categorized as a program that offers a postgraduate degree in the process, the website also shares it has an option for persons interested in changing their careers. Additionally, some programs that offer postgraduate coursework also provide options for distance learning. Other similarities among the programs are the support and mentorship available to the new teachers. Furthermore, the challenges faced during the first year of teaching for ALP participants are congruent with the challenges faced from traditional teacher preparation programs (i.e., classroom management, time demands, lesson pacing) (Williams, 2007). As with any first-year encounter in a new career, there will be several complications and challenges. See Table 14.2 for a table comparing the examples discussed above.

ALTERNATIVE LICENSURE PROGRAM OUTCOMES

The literature on ALP outcomes has explored these programs' efficacy in terms of student test scores, classroom management, and attrition; studies comparing alternatively certified and traditionally prepared teachers have produced mixed findings (Zeichner & Schulte, 2001).

Student Achievement

The literature exploring the extent to which student achievement differences exist between traditionally prepared and alternatively certified teachers is mixed. The State of Tennessee publishes an annual report entitled the Tennessee Teacher Preparation Report Card (Tennessee State Board of Education, 2017). As of this writing, the most recent report is from 2017 and it awards one of four ratings to each of the state's teacher preparation programs—Category 1–4. A Category 1 rating is the lowest rating a program can receive; a Category 4 rating is the highest rating awarded. Seven of the state's 39 teacher preparation programs received the highest rating. This included three traditional preparation programs such as the University of Tennessee. It also includes all four of the state's ALPs, including the Memphis Teacher Residency, Teach for America–Memphis, Teach for America–Nashville, and The New Teacher Project–Nashville. In other words, Tennessee ALPs outperformed all but three of the state's traditional preparation programs using the state's benchmarks for performance. Some scholars have been critical of Tennessee's system due to its reliance in part on value-added measures (Gulosino, 2018), which come with some psychometric limitations (Everson, 2017).

Gimbert et al. (2007) explored whether differences existed between traditionally prepared teachers and those who participated in an alterna-

Table 14.2

Comparison of ALP Pathway Examples

Program	Eligibility Requirements	Coursework and Training	Clinical Experience	First-Year of Full-Time Teach Teaching
Traditional, Undergraduate Licensure Programs	• 2.75 GPA • Minimum of 45 credit hours • Successful completion of teaching introductory course	• May begin in fall or spring semester • Duration of two to three semesters in conjunction with field experience	• One full year of supervised student teaching • Successfully complete a teaching portfolio	• No formal arrangement of support from traditional licensure program
Teach for America – Summer Practicum Pathway	• 2.50 GPA • Have a bachelor's degree • United States citizen or hold DACA status	• Assigned readings before the summer training begins • Five-day regional induction • Five to seven-week institute, which includes teaching summer school	• Observe teachers' lessons • Four to five weeks of supervised, summer school clinical experience • Debriefs on lessons taught and observed	• Access to support from TFA network and other program participants
NYC Teaching Fellows – Postgraduate Degree Pathway	• Preference for 3.0 GPA; required to submit explanation for 2.5 – 3.0 GPAs	• Begins coursework for master's degree (2–3 years for most participants) • Continue coursework through first year of teaching	• Daily teaching in NYC summer school with constant feedback (from mid-June to early August)	• Full-time teaching with mentorship support • Weekly and monthly visits from DOE mentor and university mentor
Career Switcher Alternative Route to Licensure Program – Career Switcher Pathways	• Have a bachelor's degree • Three full years of full-time work experience	• Two semesters of coursework (approximately 198 hours)	• 30 hours of practicum for secondary education; additional 20 hours of practicum for grades Pre-K – 12	• One-year provisional teaching license • Mentorship by a university and school mentor • Access to continue professional development

(Table continued on next page)

Table 14.2 (Continued)

Comparison of ALP Pathway Examples

Program	Eligibility Requirements	Coursework and Training	Clinical Experience	First-Year of Full-Time Teach Teaching
Teach Away in Hawaii – Distance Learning Pathways	• Eligible to work in the United States • Have a bachelor's degree in any subject area	• 20 hours of coursework per week online for 6 months • Online cohort and mentorship	• 3 months of practicum in Hawaii • Practicum may be completed while completing coursework and following coursework	• Access to discussion board for 6 months • Online workshops (free and discounted options) • May contact assigned specialist

tive teacher preparation pathway in Virginia. They compared students on district-level quarterly assessments, as well as on Algebra I standardized test scores. Overall, they found no difference between the two types of teachers; however, they did find that the students of alternatively certified teachers outperformed their traditionally prepared peers in statistics.

Penner (2019) examined the relationship between participation in TFA and student achievement across elementary, middle, and high school in North Carolina from the 1999-2000 academic year to 2010–2011. Findings demonstrate a positive relationship between TFA participation and student achievement in every subject and grade with the exception of elementary reading where no statistically significant difference existed between the two groups of teachers. Boyd et al. (2006) found that the students of TFA participants had small, positive differences in English and math standardized test scores; however, these differences disappeared over time. Overall, the literature suggests that teachers prepared through alternative licensure programs perform at least as well as traditionally prepared teachers in terms of student test scores, and in some cases have students who perform better on standardized tests than the students of their traditionally prepared peers.

Classroom Management

Novice teachers' experiences with classroom management seem to be similar for both traditionally prepared and alternatively certified teachers.

Indeed, classroom management has consistently been a challenge for new teachers (Dias-Lacy & Guirguis, 2017). Schonfeld and Feinman (2012), completed a study where beginning teachers in New York public schools wrote in a daily diary for two weeks regarding their teaching experiences. Seventy percent of the teachers in this study were alternatively certified. The results of the diaries showed that the alternatively certified teachers had more classroom management problems, received more threats from students, and had more difficulties with administrators. Some of the challenges encountered are similar to participants in most teacher preparation programs (traditional and nontraditional). One feature of postgraduate degree pathway programs that may contribute to challenges faced in first-year teaching is balancing postgraduate degree coursework and the typical challenges of first-year teaching.

Good et al. (2006) conducted a three-year study of first -year teaching practices, in the domains of assessment, classroom management, and implementation of instruction. They found that traditional preparation programs better prepared teachers for teaching at the elementary and middle school levels, whereas alternative preparation appeared to be a better fit for teachers in high school settings. In an observational study that examined differences in teaching practices between those educated in traditional and alternative certified programs and employed in Georgia public schools, the two groups did not significantly differ on the specific dimensions of instruction known to be causally related to learning (Miller et al., 1998). As such, the authors concluded that alternative certification did not lead to inferior practice among teachers evaluated three years into their careers (Miller et al., 1998). Miller et al. (1998) also conducted a qualitative study conducted to gain insight into teachers' perceptions of their teaching abilities, classroom management skills and feelings of adequacy of preparation at the beginning of their teaching preparation. They found that neither group of teachers felt particularly well prepared. Interestingly, traditionally certified teachers tried to explain this as a natural tendency to feel inadequate at the beginning of a career, whereas alternatively certified teachers felt that something was missing (Miller et al, 1998). Fenzel et al. (2014) investigated the perceived learning environments of individuals who participated in a summer practicum ALP. Among the 80 teachers included in their study, alternatively certified teachers reported "they spent more time in class disciplining students and indicated student behavior was more of a problem" than reported by the more experienced teachers (p. 26). Additionally, the inexperienced teachers shared lower levels of satisfaction, self-efficacy, and success in engaging unmotivated students.

Attrition

Teacher retention issues are often both a catalyst for and a critique of ALPs. Public schools in the United States experience approximately eight percent attrition annually, and this accounts for about 90% of the overall demand for new teachers (Darling-Hammond & Carver-Thomas, 2017). Teacher attrition is costly both in terms of financial and human capital for districts (Carver & Feiman-Nemser, 2009), and has been associated with lower levels of student achievement (Ingersoll & Strong, 2011). Although teacher retention is an issue nationwide, attrition levels are much higher in urban and rural areas (Jacobs, 2007; Lankford et al., 2002; Latterman & Steffes, 2017; Maranto & Shuls, 2013), and in high-poverty schools (Carlson, 2017; Song, 2006). More than one-third of rural schools struggle to fill positions in every subject (Latterman & Steffes, 2017) and almost three-fourths of teachers who begin their careers in urban districts will leave the profession within the first five years (Papay et al., 2017). This leaves districts with vacancies to fill, and graduates of these alternative teacher preparation programs are filling in the gaps in many of these hard-to-staff urban and rural schools.

In a longitudinal study conducted in North Carolina over the span of seven years, a comparison was made between the retention rates of teachers prepared in traditional certification programs, alternative licensure programs and lateral entry alternative licensure programs (where qualified individuals begin teaching while obtaining a license simultaneously). It was found that overall, teachers from lateral entry alternative programs had lower retention rates when compared to both traditional and alternative licensure programs. In year two and three, traditionally and alternatively certified teachers had similar retention rates, however, by year seven, traditionally certified teachers had higher retention rates than their alternatively certified peers (Zhang & Zeller, 2016). Kirby et al. (1989) surveyed 481 nontraditional teacher education program participants and traditional program graduates and found that graduates from nontraditional programs appeared to enter and remain in teaching at rates that are comparable to, and probably higher than those for traditionally prepared teachers are.

CONCLUDING THOUGHTS

There are general differences in alternative pathways to teaching in their purposes and approaches to preparing participants for teaching. For some programs, participants have two months of training with no formal mentorship during their first year of teaching, while others are prepared and continue to take courses during their teaching. Some programs specifically seek individuals of specialized interest and who have had prior careers, and other programs recruit participants directly from college with no full-time career experience but with a passion for social justice. Overall, each of the programs mentioned, in their own way, has a mission to reduce teacher vacancies by filling classrooms with highly motivated, educated, and qualified teachers. In terms of program outcomes, the literature is mixed. Overall, most studies have found that alternatively certified teachers have performed at least as well as those who were prepared through a traditional, university-based program. Given the shorter length of most ALPs and reduced costs, these findings are positive for ALPs. However, studies that focus on TFA are over-represented. Future studies should explore other ALPs and other types of ALPs to broaden our collective understanding of nontraditional teacher preparation pathways.

Quality preservice clinical experiences are an important part of teacher preparation, and perhaps the most important factor in determining how successful teachers will be in their early careers. The extent to which traditional preparation graduates and ALP graduates have similar outcomes is interesting, but perhaps not surprising when one exclusively considers the clinical teaching experience. Preston (2020) conducted a study that examined the different components of teacher preparation programs in North Carolina and found that student teachers spent less than half of their student teaching placements engaged in full-time teaching. In many cases, student teachers spent about the same amount of time (4–5 weeks) as alternatively prepared teachers teaching full time prior to being placed as teachers of record. Future research should continue to explore not just the length, but also the nature of clinical experiences.

Much of the work that exists in the literature focuses on student test scores. These are standardized across settings, and comparisons can easily be made using this measure of success. However, test scores alone do not capture all facets of teacher success (or lack thereof) and certainly do not adequately assess the efficacy of teacher preparation programs. In several states and school districts, additional factors are explored to measure more holistic notions of teacher success. There are evaluation systems, such as the Teacher Keys Effectiveness System (used in Georgia) and the National Board for Professional Teaching Standards, that have been created to analyze observations from teachers' instruction and other artifacts to measure teachers' success and effectiveness. Some of the standards used for evaluation are teachers' content knowledge, how they monitor students' learning and use assessments, and evidence of systematic reflection of instructional practices (Georgia Department of Education, 2020; National Board for Professional Teaching Standards, 2020). Marshall et al. (2021) explored markers of success for participants in a teacher residency program. They found that learning from mistakes, building relationships with colleagues and students, managing work-life balance, and developing teacher presence were indicative of a successful residency year. Additional work should explore how these items can be incorporated into our measures of success for ALP program participants.

REFERENCES

Adcock, P. K., & Mahlios, M. (2005). Nontraditional alternative teacher certification programs: Their purpose, design and participants. *Essays in Education, 15*(4), 1–11.

Arkorful, V., & Abaidoo, N. (2015). The role of e-learning, advantages and disadvantages of its adoption in higher education. *International Journal of Instructional Technology and Distance Learning, 12*(1), 29–42.

Boyd, D., Grossman, P., Lankford, H., Loeb, S., & Wyckoff, J. (2006). *How changes in entry requirements alter the teacher workforce and affect student achievement.* https://www.nber.org/papers/w11844

Brigman, M. J., & Petty, T. M. (2013). Perceptions of preparation of online alternative licensure teacher candidates. In R. Hartshorne, T. L. Heafner, & T. M. Petty (Eds.), *Teacher education programs and online learning tools: Innovations in teacher preparation* (pp. 38–58). IGI Global.

Bullough, R. V., & Knowles, J. G. (1990). Becoming a teacher: Struggles of a second career beginning teacher. *Qualitative Studies in Education, 3*(2), 101–112.

Carlson, D. (2017). *Teachers and crisis: Urban school reform and teachers' work culture.* Routledge.

Carver, C. L., & Feiman-Nemser, S. (2009). Using policy to improve teacher induction: Critical elements and missing pieces. *Educational Policy, 23*(2), 295–328. https://doi.org/10.1177/0895904807310036

Costigan, A. (2004). Finding a name for what they want: A study of New York City's Teaching Fellows. *Teaching and Teacher Education, 20*(2), 129–143. https://doi.org/10.1016/j.tate.2003.10.003

Darling-Hammond, L. (2014). Strengthening clinical preparation: The Holy Grail or teacher education. *Peabody Journal of Education, 89*(4), 547–561. https://doi.org/10.1080/0161956X.2014.939009

Darling-Hammond, L., & Carver-Thomas, D. (2017). *Teacher turnover: Why it matters and what we can do about it.* Learning Policy Institute.

Dias-Lacy, S. L., & Guirguis, R. V. (2017). Challenges for new teachers and ways of coping with them. *Journal of Education and Learning, 6*(3), 265–272. https://doi.org/10.5539.jel.v6n3p265

Elsbree, W. S. (1939). *The American teacher: Evolution of a profession in a democracy.* American Book.

Everson, K. C. (2017). Value-added modeling and educational accountability: Are we answering the real questions? *Review of Educational Research, 87*(1), 35–70. https://doi.org/10.3102/0034654316637199

Fekula, M. J. (2010). Perpetual enrollment online courses: Advantages, administration, and caveats. *Online Journal of Distance Learning Administration, 13*(1).

Fenzel, L. M., Dean, R. J., & Darden, G. (2014). Effective learning environments and the use of teaching fellows in alternative urban middle schools. *Journal of Education for Students Placed at Risk, 19*(1), 20–35. https://doi.org/10.1080/10824669.2014.924320

Fiechtl, B. J., & Hager, K. D. (2019). A statewide early childhood alternative teacher preparation program delivered via synchronous video conference. *Rural Special Education Quarterly, 38*(4), 210–216. https://doi.org/10.1177/8756870519860069

Foote, D. (2008). *Relentless pursuit: A year in the trenches with Teach for America*. Vintage Books.

Fraser, J. W., & Lefty, L. (2018). *Teaching teachers: Changing paths and enduring debates*. Johns Hopkins University Press.

Fuller, E., & Pendola, A. (2020). *K–12 teacher supply, demand, and shortages in Pennsylvania*. Center for Rural Pennsylvania. https://www.rural.palegislature.us/documents/reports/PA-Teacher-Supply-Demand-Shortages-2020.pdf

Garibaldi, A. M. (2009). The educational status of African American males in the 21st century. In H. F. Frierson, W. Pearson, & J. H. Wyche (Eds), *Diversity in higher education. Black American males in higher education: Diminishing proportions* (pp. 99–112). Emerald Group.

Gastic, B. (2014). Closing the opportunity gap: Preparing the next generation of effective teachers. In F. M. Hess & M.Q. McShane (Eds), *Teacher quality 2.0: Toward a new era in education reform* (pp. 91–108). Harvard Education Press.

Georgia Department of Education. (2020). *Teacher keys effectiveness system*. GADOE. https://www.gadoe.org/School-Improvement/Teacher-and-Leader-Effectiveness/Pages/Teacher-Keys-Effectiveness-System.aspx

Gimbert, B., Bol, L., & Wallace, D. (2007). The influence of teacher preparation on student achievement and the application of national standards by teachers of mathematics in urban secondary schools. *Education and Urban Society, 40*(1), 91–117. https://doi.org/10.1177/0013124507303993

Gulosino, C. (2018). Evaluating the Tennessee Higher Education Commission's report card on the value-added estimates of teacher preparation programs. *Educational Policy Analysis Archives, 26*(33), 1–45. https://doi.org/10.14507/epaa.26.2604

Good, T. L., McCaslin, M., Tsang, H. Y., Zhang, J., Wiley, C. R. H., Bozack, A. R., & Hester, W. (2006). How well do 1st-year teachers teach: Does type of preparation make a difference? *Journal of Teacher Education, 57*(4), 410–430. https://doi.org/10.1177/0022487106291566

Green, E. (2014). *Building a Better Teacher: How teaching works (and how to teach it to everyone)*. W. W Norton & Company.

Humphrey, D. C., & Wechsler, M. E. (2007). Insights into alternative certification: Initial findings from a national study. *Teachers College Record, 109*(3), 483–530.

Ingersoll, R. M., & Strong, M. (2011). The impact of induction and mentoring programs for beginning teachers. *Review of Educational Research, 81*(2), 201–233. https://doi.org/10.3102/0034654311403323

Jacobs, B. A. (2007). The challenges of staffing urban schools with effective teachers. *Future of Children, 17*(1), 129–153.

Kirby, S. N., Darling-Hammond, L., & Hudson, L. (1989). Nontraditional Recruits to Mathematics and Science Teaching. *Educational Evaluation and Policy Analysis, 11*(3), 301–323. https://doi.org/10.3102/01623737011003301

Koerner, J. D. (1965). *The miseducation of American teachers.* Pelican Press.

Kramer, R. (2000). *Ed school follies: The miseducation of America's teachers.* The Authors Guild Backprint.

Krieg, J. M., Goldhaber, D., & Theobald, R. (2020). Teacher candidate apprenticeships: Assessing the who and where of student teaching. *Journal of Teacher Education, 71*(2), 218–232. https://doi.org/10.1177/0022487119858983

Lanier, H. K. (2012). *Teaching in the terrordome: Two years in West Baltimore with Teach for America.* University of Missouri Press.

Lankford, H., Loeb, S., & Wyckoff, J. (2002). Teacher sorting and the plight of urban schools: A descriptive analysis. *Education Evaluation and Policy Analysis, 24*(1), 37–62.

Latterman, K., & Steffes, S. (2017). *Tackling teacher and principal shortages in rural areas.* National Conference of State Legislatures.

Lee, D., & Lamport, M. A. (2011). Non-traditional entrants to the profession of teaching: Motivations and experiences of second career educators. *Christian Perspectives in Education, 4*(2), 1–40. http://digitalcommons.liberty.edu/cpe/vol4/iss2/3

Lohfink, G., Morales, A., Shroyer, G., Yahnke, S., & Hernandez, C. (2011). A distance-delivered teacher education program for rural culturally and linguistically diverse teacher candidates. *The Rural Educator, 33*(1). https://doi.org/10.35608/ruraled.v33i1.420

Lohmann, M. J., White, B., & Johnson, K. A. (2019). Increasing the rural special education teacher pipeline through asynchronous online instruction: A program description of the Colorado Christian University alternative certification program. *Rural Special Education Quarterly, 38*(3), 151–161. https://doi.org/10.1177/8756870519860065

Ludlow, C. (2013). Alternative certification pathways: Filling a gap? *Education and Urban Society, 45*(4), 440–458. https://doi.org/10.1177/0013124511413916

Maranto, R., & Shuls, J.V. (2013). How do we get them on the farm? Efforts to improve rural teacher recruitment and retention in Arkansas. *The Rural Educator, 34*(1), 1–10.

Marshall, D. T., Scott, M. R., & Wan, G. (2021). Through failure and reflection: Conceptualizations of a successful teacher residency experience. *Action in Teacher Education. 43*(2), 160–175. https://doi.org/10.1080/01626620.2020.1765897

Miller, J. W., McKenna, M. C., & McKenna, B. A. (1998). A comparison of alternatively and traditionally prepared teachers. *Journal of Teacher Education, 49*(3), 165–176.

National Board for Professional Teaching Standards. (2020). *National board standards.* https://www.nbpts.org/standards-five-core-propositions/

National Center for Education Statistics. (2018). *Characteristics of public school teachers who completed alternative route to certification programs.* https://nces.ed.gov/programs/coe/indicator_tlc.asp

National Council for the Accreditation of Teacher Education. (2010). *Transforming teacher education through clinical practice: A national strategy to prepare effective teachers* (A report of the Blue Ribbon Panel on Clinical Preparation and Partnership for Improved Student Learning).

National Research Council. (2010). *Preparing teachers: Building evidence for sound policy.* Committee on the Study of Teacher Preparation Programs in the United States, Center for Education. Division of Behavioral and Social Sciences in Education. National Academies Press.

NYC Teaching Fellows. (2020). *Apply.* https://nycteachingfellows.org/eligibility

O'Connor, E. A., Malow, M. S., & Bisland, B. M. (2011). Mentorship and instruction received during training: Views of alternatively certified teachers. *Educational Review, 63*(2), 219–232. https://doi.org/10.1080/00131911.2010.537312

Oblender, T. E., & Glass, J. (2004). Five reasons to offer online courses. *Principal Leadership, 5*(2), 40–42.

Old Dominion University. (2020). *Career switcher program.* https://www.odu.edu/cepd/career-switcher

Papay, J. P., Bacher-Hicks, A., Page, L. C., & Marinell, W. H. (2017). The challenge of teacher retention in urban schools: Evidence of variation from a cross-site analysis. *Educational Researcher, 46*(8), 434–448. https://doi.org/10.3102/0013189X17735812

Penner, E. K. (2019). Teach For America and teacher quality: Increasing achievement over time. *Educational Policy.* https://doi.org/10.1177/0895904819843595

Peyton, D. J., Acosta, K., Harvey, A., Pua, D. J., Sindelar, P. T., Mason-Williams, L., Dewey, J., Fisher, T. L., & Crews, E. (2020). Special education teacher shortage: Differences between high and low shortage states. *Teacher Education and Special Education*, 1–19. https://doi.org/10.1177/0888406420906618

Preston, C. (2020). Learning to teach: Optimizing coursework and fieldwork requirements in traditional teacher preparation. In J. E. Carinci, S. J. Meyer, & C. Jackson (Eds), *Linking teacher preparation program design and implementation to outcomes for teachers and students* (pp. 33–61). Information Age Publishing.

Rooks, D. (2018). The unintended consequences of cohorts: How social relationships can influence the retention of rural teachers recruited by cohort-based alternative pathway programs. *Journal of Research in Rural Education, 33*(9), 1–22. https://doi.org/10.1018113/P8JRRE3309

Schonfeld, I. S., & Feinman, S. J. (2012). Difficulties of alternatively certified teachers. *Education and Urban Society, 44*(3), 215–246. https://doi.org/10.1177/0013124510392570

Schweizer, H., Hayslett, C., & Chaplock, S. (2008) Student satisfaction and performance in an online teacher certification program. *The Journal of Continuing Higher Education, 56*(2), 12–25. https://10.1080/07377366.2008.10400149

Scott, L. A. (2016). Where are all the Black male special education teachers? *Perspectives on Urban Education, 13*(1), 42–48.

Scott, L. A. (2019). Experience of Black male special education teachers: Are alternative licensure programs the desired route for recruitment and preparation? *Education and Urban Society, 51*(3), 332–350. https://doi.org/10.1177/0013124517719971

Sedlak, M. W. (1989). Let us go and buy a schoolmaster: Historical perspectives on the hiring of teachers in the United States. In M. Cochran-Smith, S. Feiman-Nemser, & D.J. McIntyre (Eds.), *American teachers: Histories of a profession at work* (pp. 257–291). MacMillan.

Simmons, S. C., & Mebane, D. J. (2012). NC teach and NC teach online: Viable alternative routes to teaching in North Carolina. *Action in Teacher Education, 27*(1), 45–52. https://doi.org/10.1080/01626620.2005.10463373

Sipe, P., & D'Angelo, A. (2006, February). *Why do fellows stick around? An inquiry into the retention of New York City Teaching Fellows* [Paper presentation]. The annual conference of the National Center for Alternative Certification (NCAC), San Diego, CA.

Smith, M. B. (1954). *The diminished mind: A study of planned mediocrity in our public schools.* Henry Regnery.

Song, K. H. (2006). Urban teachers' beliefs on teaching, learning, and students: A pilot study in the United States of America. *Education and Urban Society, 38*(4), 481–499. https://doi.org/10.1177/0013124506289030

Teach Away. (2020). *Alternative teacher certification programs.* https://www.teachaway.com/courses/teacher-certification

Teach for America. (2020). *Life in the corps.* https://www.teachforamerica.org/life-in-the-corps

Tennessee State Board of Education. (2017). *2017 Tennessee teacher preparation report card.* https://www.tn.gov/content/dam/tn/stateboardofeducation/documents/teacherprep/2017/2017_Tennessee_State_Report.pdf

Thomas, M. A. M. (2018). "Good intentions can only get you so far:" Critical reflections from Teach for America corps members placed in special education. *Education and Urban Society, 50*(5), 435–460. https://doi.org/10.1177/0013124517713604

Van Overschelde, J. P., & Wiggins, A. Y. (2020). Teacher preparation pathways: Differences in program selection and teacher retention. *Action in Teacher Education, 42*(4), 311–327. https://doi.org/10.1080/01626620.2019.1656116

Virginia Commonwealth University. (2020). *VCU SOE Pathways to Teaching: Career Switcher Program.* https://soe.vcu.edu/community/office-of-strategic-engagement/pathways-to-teaching/

Virginia Department of Education. (2021). *Career Switcher Program.* http://www.doe.virginia.gov/teaching/educator_preparation/career_switcher/index.shtml

Wilcox, D. R., & Samaras, A. P. (2009). Examining our career switching teachers' first year of teaching: Implications for alternative teacher education program design. *Teacher Education Quarterly, 36*(4), 173–191.

Williams, J. (2007). Becoming a teacher. In A. Berry, A. Clemans, & A. Kostogriz (Eds.), *Dimensions of professional learning: Professionalism, practice, and identity* (pp. 141–154). Sense.

Zeichner, K. M., & Schulte, A. K. (2001). What we know and don't know from peer-reviewed research about alternative teacher certification programs. *Journal of Teacher Education*, *52*(4), 266–282. https://doi.org/10.1177/0022487101052004002

Zeichner, K., & Bier, M. (2012). The turn toward practice and clinical experience in U.S. teacher education. *Beitrage zur Lehrerbildung*, *30*(2), 153–170.

Zeichner, K. M. (2018). *The struggle for the soul of teacher education.* Routledge.

Zhang, G., & Zeller, N. (2016). A longitudinal investigation of the relationship between teacher preparation and teacher retention. *Teacher Education Quarterly*, *43*(2), 73–92.

NOTES

1. For our purposes, we exclude teacher residency programs from our discussion of ALPs. We consider them distinct from both traditional preparation models and the alternative models described in this chapter.

2. One such example is the Career Switcher Program at Old Dominion University (2020), which delivers instruction 100% online.

CHAPTER 15

PAID PROFESSIONAL INTERNSHIPS

Designing a Curriculum for Clinical Experiences

John E. Henning
Tracy Mulvaney
Bernard F. Bragen, Jr.
Columbus State University

William O. George, III
Auburn University

ABSTRACT

The purpose of this study is to examine the experiences of undergraduate and graduate teacher candidates who have performed the roles of substitute teacher, paraprofessional, or tutor as part of a pilot program to create paid internships in teacher education. The program provides opportunities for teacher candidates to work additional time in schools, including additional time during the semester, during semester breaks, and during the months of May and June when K–12 schools are still in session in New Jersey. The

Preparing Quality Teachers:
Advances in Clinical Practice, pp. 335–354
Copyright © 2022 by Information Age Publishing
www.infoagepub.com

335

program is intended to replace part time work outside of education with work in P–12 school classrooms that better prepares teacher candidates for their teaching careers. As part of the program, teacher candidates perform functions traditionally given to substitute teachers, paraprofessionals, and tutors. In turn, monies from school budgets to compensate these positions are invested into the teacher residency program. Data was collected through interviews. The findings indicated that the primary benefit of working in paid positions was developing relationships and managing the classroom. The discussion addresses how substitute teaching, paraprofessional work, and tutoring can contribute to teacher candidate learning.

INTRODUCTION

In a previous study, the authors reported on a pilot program to compensate teacher candidates for their work in schools (Henning et al., 2018). The purpose of the program was to extend the length of clinical experiences to enable more development through practice in clinical settings. The funding to support the internships came primarily from existing school budgets with some supplementation from university sources, such as graduate assistantships. School budgets were utilized by placing teacher candidates in professional positions such as substitute teacher, paraprofessional, and tutor. These experiences were not intended to replace the existing, required clinical experiences, but rather to add additional time in schools while compensating teacher candidates for their work. Thus, during this program teacher candidates worked in schools during winter break, during the months of May and June (schools are in session during these months in New Jersey), and during days when they did not have class. Since most graduate classes are at night, these students had more opportunities than undergraduate students to work in schools during the semester.

Findings from this study showed that teacher candidates spent additional time in schools, valued the additional experience, and felt more confident in their teaching. They cited a greater breadth of experience, increased flexibility and proficiency in decision-making, a greater awareness of the classroom, and a greater self-reliance. Similarly, school administrators commented on the benefits for both schools and teacher candidates when utilizing preservice teachers in these roles.

However, much is still unknown about the specific skills needed to effectively perform the roles of substitute teacher, paraprofessional, and tutor. Clearly, none of these roles entails the same level of complexity as the role of teacher. So, it would not be appropriate to completely replace existing clinical experiences with substitute teaching, paraprofessional work, and tutoring. Yet these paid positions might incentivize teacher candidates to extend the length of their current clinical experiences in order to gain additional experience interacting with children. However, properly incorporating these roles into a teacher preparation program requires a greater understanding of what each contributes to the process of learning to teach. Any paid professional internship program must be careful not to exploit teacher candidates solely to serve the needs of school (e.g., to address teacher or substitute teacher shortages). Conversely, teacher preparation programs must also ensure their teacher candidates are properly prepared to undertake the professional responsibilities that these positions entail. Knowing more about the types of skills associated with the roles of substitute teacher, paraprofessional, and of tutor would help address these concerns.

The purpose of this case study is to examine the experiences of both undergraduate and graduate teacher candidates who have performed substitute teaching and paraprofessional roles as part of a pilot program to create paid internships for teacher candidates. The program provides opportunities for teacher candidates to work additional time in schools, including additional time during the semester, during semester breaks, and during the months of May and June when K–12 schools are still in session in New Jersey. The program is intended to replace part time work outside of education with work in P–12 school classrooms that better prepares teacher candidates for their teaching careers. Data was collected through fourteen interviews. The findings indicated that the primary benefit of working in paid positions was the additional experience interacting with students for the purpose of developing relationships and managing the classroom. The discussion addresses how substitute teaching, paraprofessional work, and tutoring can contribute to teacher candidate learning.

THEORETICAL FRAMEWORK

Currently, there is a world-wide trend to expand the clinical experiences of preservice teachers (Ronfeldt & Reininger, 2012). In the United States, there have been numerous calls to extend clinical experiences, two of the most notable being the National Council for the Accreditation of Teacher Education's Blue Ribbon Panel Report (NCATE, 2010) and the American Association of the Colleges of Teacher Education's (AACTE's) Clinical Practice Commission (CPC) proclamations (AACTE, 2018). The former recommended turning "teacher education upside" by implementing clinically-based teacher education. In a clinically-based program, practice is situated at the core of the preparation program, and coursework is organized to support those experiences (Henning, Gut, & Beam, 2019). The latter extended the work of the Blue Ribbon Panel through ten proclamations and tenants for strengthening clinical experiences. The work in this study reflects the national effort described by both the Blue Ribbon Panel Report and the CPC proclamations to expand and strengthen clinical experiences by putting clinical practice at the center of teacher preparation. Further, this study examines the "how" of enacting stronger clinical experiences as described by CPC recommendations that address developing teacher candidate skills and the partnership infrastructure, such as the Skills, Partnership, Empowerment, and Mutual Benefit Proclamations.

Teacher Development

The rationale for extending clinical experiences is well supported by theories of learning and learning to teach. Several giants in the field have described experience as foundational to learning, including Dewey's (1963) seminal work on the role of experience when learning, Piaget's (1952) theory that bodily action precedes mental capability, and Vygotsky (1986) who holds that social interactions are the precursor to thought. Succeeding researchers on experience have posited theories that are consistent with these foundational theories, including Kolb (1984): Concrete Experience, Reflective Observation, Abstract Conceptualization, and Active Experimentation; Lewin (1946): Plan, Do, Observe, and Reflect; and the new field of Improvement Science (Langley et al., 2009): Plan, Do, Study, Act (PDSA).

In each of these models, learning occurs through repeated cycles of learning followed by the internalization of the action as thought (Korthagen, 2001, 2010). Teacher candidates gradually move from gestalts, consisting of feeling and impressions, to more abstract schemas, which serve as mental representations that facilitate reflection and planning. As they gain familiarity with the context for their teaching, candidates gradually acquire an increasingly complex set of specific skills through recursive cycles of learning (Henning et al., 2019). The context for learning includes the time, place, students, activities, and dialogue that occur within the school setting (Borko & Putnam, 1996). The need for repeated cycles of learning provides support for placing teacher candidates in extended clinical experiences. Without the necessary experience, teacher candidates cannot gain the thinking skills needed to become an expert teacher. It may also explain why certain areas of teacher learning are more challenging than others. For example, differentiated instruction, assessment, and classroom management may require more extended clinical experiences to ensure enough cycles of experiential learning for teacher candidates to become profession ready.

Teacher Residency

The research on models of extended clinical experiences has been very encouraging thus far, for example, the research conducted on Teacher Residency programs. Teacher Residency programs are typically developed as a partnership between a school district and a university (Guha et al., 2017, 2018). They usually involve a more extensive clinical experience than a traditional or alternative program, often a one-year, full time teaching experience for teacher candidates at the graduate initial licensure level combined with a curriculum that is tightly integrated with clinical practice. To date, there are approximately 37 programs in the United States (Washburn-Moses, 2017). Early research indicates that teacher residencies attract more diverse teachers, increase teacher retention, and positively impact student achievement (Papay et al., 2012; Guha et al., 2017, 2018).

Sustainability

Despite the early success of Teacher Residency programs, the additional hours in clinical placements has put increasing financial pressure on teacher candidates, who often must work during college to pay their tuition and residential bills (DeMoss et al., 2017). These additional financial challenges can serve as a significant barrier to teaching for first generation students from lower socioeconomic backgrounds. Recently there has been a call for a more sustainable model of teacher residency program that would include paid residencies (Henning et al., 2018; DeMoss et al., 2017; The Sustainable Funding Project, 2016). Currently, paid internships for teacher candidates exist throughout the country. They are funded in various ways depending first on their purpose; which could include teacher shortages, increasing the number of stem teachers, and diversifying the profession and the available funds. The second determining factor is the availability of funds, which could include government funds, grants, local school districts, or university budgets (e.g., scholarships or graduate assistantships).

The paid internship program in this study seeks to utilize local school budgets as the primary source of funding for paid internships (Fallon, 2017). Funds for substitute teaching, paraprofessionals and tutors already exist in school budgets and could be utilized to support paid internships. These are likely sources of funds because schools need this work performed, because there are current statewide shortages in these positions, and because teacher candidates are better trained than many current staff members in those positions. Prospective applicants for these positions can receive their substitute license (which qualifies them for paraprofessional work as well) after they complete 60 credit hours of college in the state of

New Jersey. Thus, teacher candidates are eligible to serve in these roles near the end of their sophomore year.

Learning in Clinical Experiences

For professional roles such as substitute teachers, paraprofessionals, or tutors to become a legitimate part of a teacher education program, it is necessary to investigate how they can contribute to learning how to teach. Prior conceptions of teacher candidate learning have focused on learning in a classroom under the direction of a mentor teacher. Teacher candidates are encouraged to acquire the teaching skills associated with the InTASC standards or as described by high leverage or core teaching practices (Grossman et al., 2009; TeachingWorks, 2012). Each of these provides descriptions of the practice when it has been mastered. For beginners, it is helpful to show teacher candidates how these skills can be acquired through practice in an incremental fashion. A tool for guiding this approach is the *Developmental Curriculum for Clinical Experiences*, which describes a developmental sequence of tasks that eventually leads to the fully realized performance for each InTASC standard (Henning et al., 2016). Implicit in the use of the Development Curriculum is the understanding that teacher candidate development is dependent on opportunities to perform the tasks and skills delineated. Until the teacher candidate is in the classroom on a full time or continuous basis and unless the candidate is exposed to large group instruction, not all of the standards can be met.

The Developmental Curriculum was developed based on the assumption that the teacher candidate would be under the guidance of a mentor teacher, which is often not the case when serving in the role of paraprofessional or substitute teacher. Little has been written about these professional roles from a scholarly perspective regarding their use in a teacher preparation program. Most of the publications related to work as a paraprofessional or a substitute teacher consists of recommendations of how to be effective in the role, often by someone who has experience serving in the role. For example, substitute teachers are advised to know the schedule, to be prepared in case there are no lesson plans, and how to manage the classroom (Coron, 2017). Paraprofessionals and tutors are advised on how to work with individual students and small groups (Ashbaker & Morgan, 2013; Fisher et al., 2014).

METHODS

The purpose of this study was to investigate the experiences of teacher candidates performing the roles of substitute teachers, paraprofessionals, and tutors as part of their teacher preparation program. Fourteen teacher candidates who performed these roles as part of an extended clinical experience known as the Teacher Residency program, were interviewed about their experiences as a substitute teacher, paraprofessional, or a tutor. Participants were interviewed for approximately one hour. The interviews were recorded, transcribed, and coded into categories such as relationship, classroom management, teaching strategies, and differentiation. See below for a fuller description of the process and descriptions of the coding categories.

Participants

There were 14 participants in the study, including 13 women and 1 man. Eleven of the participants worked as substitute teachers, 4 worked as paraprofessionals or instructional assistants, and 1 worked as a tutor. One participant, Kara, worked as both a substitute teacher and a paraprofessional. Another, Teresa, worked both as a paraprofessional and a tutor. The number of substitute teaching days varied from 3 to 100 days. Teacher candidates worked as paraprofessionals from 1 to 5 days per week depending on their circumstances and the opportunity afforded by the school district. Graduate students tended to have more experience than undergraduates based on their more flexible schedule during school hours.

Four graduate students and 10 undergraduate students participated in the study. The four graduate students were part of the Master of Arts in Teaching (MAT) program. Of the 10 undergraduate students, 6 were seniors, 1 was a junior, 2 were sophomores, and one was a freshman. One was compensated as a tutor for working at a local private school. Three are classified as instructional assistants and received a small stipend for their work from the university. See Table 15.1 for a complete summary of the participants.

Program Description

The study took place in central New Jersey at a medium sized nondenominational, private university. Participants conducted their experiences in a variety of public and private schools throughout the local area. All the participants were part of the Teacher Residency program. To join the program, teacher candidates committed to extending their clinical experiences beyond the minimum requirements. The requirements included a full-time clinical internship during the last semester of the program, a minimum of a hundred hours during the semester immediately preceding, a 75-hour experience in a prior semester, and an initial 50-hour experience. As part of the teacher Residency program, teacher candidates could

Table 15.1

Participant Summary

	Participants	Days Per Week	Total Days of Subbing	Grade Levels	Days Per Week if Assisting	Level
Substitute Teaching						Graduate
1.	Kerry	1–2	40	HS		Graduate
2.	Kara	1–2	35	MS		Graduate
3.	Sally	1	10	El		Senior
4.	Janey	2	50	El/MS		Senior
5.	Anna	2	40	El		Senior
6.	Sophia	1	15	El/MS		Senior
7.	Danielle	3	100	K-12		Junior
8.	Kendra	1	12	MS		Freshman
9.	Joan	N/A	3	El		
Long-Term Substitute Teaching						Senior
1.	Alyssa	2–3	100	El/MS		Senior
2.	Meredith	3	100	K-12		
Pararprofessional Position						
1.	Andre	1–2	10	HS	5	Graduate
2.	Kara	1–2	35	MS	1-2	Graduate
3.	Teresa	N/A	N/A	El	4	Sophomore
4.	Amy	N/A	N/A	El	1	Freshman
Tutoring						
1.	Teresa	N/A	N/A	El	4	Tutor

extend their experience by working as a substitute teacher, a paraprofessional, or a tutor over winter break, during the months of May and June while New Jersey schools are still in session, and during days within semesters as allowed by their schedule.

Data Collection and Analysis

The data was collected during an approximately one-hour interview. The questions consisted of six groups of questions: demographic questions; questions about substitute teaching, paraprofessional experiences, and tutoring. The interviews were transcribed, analyzed, and coded. A description of the categories is given below and summarized in Table 15.2 in the next section.

Relationship—This category referred to any comment made by a teacher candidate concerning relationships with students or colleagues. However, comments related to student relationships far outnumbered those referring to colleagues.

> My best experience ... I felt that came with my experience as a substitute teacher—just getting to know the kids and getting to know how they— let's just say work—not their work ethic, but their expectations. In a way, it made me reflect on how I am in the classroom as a role model and the teacher for a day or the class period. So how they react off me, and how they understand, and how I need to implement the lessons to them.

Classroom Management—This category referred to any comment made by a teacher candidate concerning classroom management or managing students. When asked what was one of her most important lessons she learned from her experience, one teacher candidate replied as follows.

> Definitely classroom management is one of them and also I've learned that you have to have a good balance between being friends with your students and also being the teacher when you have to be the teacher.

Teaching Strategies—This category referred to any comment made by a teacher candidate concerning teaching strategies they used in the classroom.

> I did some vocab where I would read some sentences, and it would be fill-in-the-blank or true or false, and the students would have to interact and answer the questions. And then I was able to check their answers after they did their independent work. And then the ancient Egypt lesson: I read to the class, and they had to answer questions that I was asking.

Differentiation—This category referred to any comment made by a teacher candidate concerning differentiating instruction, understanding learning differences among students, or understanding individual students as learners.

> So, the teacher would leave a project, and they would all do it one way. But then the class in the middle of the day, I always did a little bit less with them or did things a little bit different. Just because they had more severe, like academic challenges—which was fun. We would do paper airplane contests. We were talking about physics and design and aerodynamic. And the first class had to do a lot of online research when they were designing their airplanes and do all this additional work. And there were two aides in

the middle of the day class, with the kids who had more challenges. And so, they kind of worked with me in that moment to figure out what parts of the assignment were really appropriate for them to be doing and what parts weren't. So, we focused on the lighter stuff with the making airplanes and what not.

Experience—This category referred to any comment made by a teacher candidate concerning the value of the clinical experience to their learning. Primarily, they commented on the value of the experience to their learning to teach, which they valued more than the compensation. In response to a question about the benefit if the Teacher Residency program, one candidate answered as follows.

> Gave me more experience, definitely more network. Because when I tell my wife, who is also a teacher, "Oh yeah, I'm having a meeting with the superintendent, she says, "I don't even know my superintendent." Now every time I see my superintendent, he's like, "Hey, how are you doing? How's the – how are the kids?" So, it's building a relationship. I have a good relationship with my principal as well. But yeah, mostly experience and networking on top of the salary I'm getting.

Preparation—This category referred to any comment made by a teacher candidate concerning the teacher's preparation of lessons for the substitute, their preparation of lessons for their classes, or the importance of preparation.

> I noticed that in order for me to deliver a good lesson is to prepare, and for me to get the know the material in order to teach it. I've also noticed that I need to work on trying to deliver or teach mathematical lessons a little bit better. For math, it's straightforward, so I think in the future, as a substitute teacher and a teacher, to figure out how to make the math lessons more engaging and interactive.

Reflection—This category referred to any comment made by a teacher candidate concerning their reflection on teaching. The comment below is a reflection on how serving as a professional will have an impact on her future teaching.

> Definitely thinking about if I had a paraprofessional in my room as a future teacher how I could implement that and how we could work together or if I'm ever in a co-teaching sort of situation.

Decision-making—This category referred to any comment made by teacher candidates concerning their decision making. Primarily, comments in this category referred to the need to make decisions quickly and their increased ability to do so.

> And it's fun to be the real teacher in the room and you have the whole lesson for the whole day and you really get to make those decisions that a real teacher would make. So, if students are struggling in math, you can kind of extend the math period and maybe start writing a little later.

Parents—This category referred to any comment made by a teacher candidate concerning their interactions with parents. For the most part, there were few interactions with partners from the role of substitute teacher, paraprofessional, or tutor.

> I find that parents tend to think of the substitute teacher as some student who doesn't know what they are doing. So, it's kind of nice to show them all that I know, and all that I'm doing with their child and to say that I'm not just a sub that they found somewhere. I'm a training teacher.

Flexibility—This category referred to teacher candidate comments concerning their increased flexibility due to the experience they acquired in the classroom. In response to a question that asked about the most important lesson she learned in substitute teaching; one teacher candidate gave the following answer:

> It's probably the flexibility aspect of it, like being adaptable. Just going off what I said before, you go in and you don't know anyone and there's no plan, you have to be on your feet and you have to have a positive mindset about it because that's where you are for a full day and there's going to be 20-something kids looking to you for the answers and you have to manage it.

Assessment—This category referred to teacher candidate comments concerning the assessment of students. Very few teacher candidate comments referred to assessment, and when they did, the reference was usually to formative assessment, as illustrated below.

> Usually, I ask the question and they'll respond, I do a lot of the talk and turn to a partner. And then just talk it out that way. Sometimes, there are exit slips, and they stand at the door and hand it to you on the way out. There's a lot of different things that can be done.

Communication—This category referred to teacher candidate comments concerning communication with students, as illustrated below.

The biggest stress was making sure you're not giving them false information and making sure that you're reading the sub plans correctly and how
the teacher intended it to be completed.

Other—This category refers to comments that do not fit into other categories. Each of these categories included 1% or less of the comments.
They include comments about communication, mentoring, achievement,
and training.

RESULTS

The results indicate that the types of comments made about substitute
teaching, paraprofessional work, and tutoring were often very similar. Each
of these roles elicited comments about relationship, classroom management, teaching strategies, differentiation, and decision-making. Therefore,
the first part of this section will report on the types, number, and percentage of the total comments made during the interviews. The second part
of the section will report on the differences we will report on the differences among the roles. These will include the difference among substitute
teaching, day-by-day, long-term subbing; paraprofessional work with a
small group, a small group in special education, or a single individual;
and tutoring.

Overall Comments

The types of comments were similar across both the substitute teaching and paraprofessional roles. In descending order, the highest number
of comments were made about relationships (99, 27% of the total), the
second highest about classroom management (87, 24%), and the third
highest about teaching strategies (69, 29%). There was a significant drop
off to the next five categories: differentiation (26, 7%), experience (17,
4%), preparation (21, 5%), reflection (11, 3%), and decision making
(10, 3%), Interaction with parents engendered 6 (2%) comments and flexibility (5, 1%). Notably only 5 comments were made about assessment. The
Other category included 6 comments (2%). See Table 15.2 for a complete
summary.

These data suggest that all three roles add to teacher candidate skill
sets related to relationship building, managing a classroom, and developing new teaching strategies. These data may also suggest that additional
time developing these skills would be beneficial to teacher candidates,
given that these experiences occurred in addition to the required clinical

Table 15.2

Summary of Participant Comments

	Categaory	All Partici-pants	Sub	Long-Term Sub	Paraprofes-sional	Tutor
		Number & Percentage				
1.	Relationship	99 (27%)	60 (25%)	6 (13%)	21 (45%)	12 (75%)
2.	Classroom Mgt	87 (24%)	66 (27%)	9 (20%)	11 (16%)	1 (8%)
3.	Teaching Strategies	69 (19%)	52 (22%)	4 (9%)	13 (17%)	–
4.	Differentiation	26 (7%)	19 (8%)	3 (6%)	4 (5%)	-
5.	Experience	17 (4%)	7 (3%)	4 (9%)	4 (6%)	2 (17%)
6.	Preparation	21 (5%)	10 (4%)	9 (20%)	2 (3%)	–
7.	Reflection	11 (3%)	6 (2%)	4 (9%)	1 (2%)	–
8.	Decision Making	10 (3%)	6 (2%)	2 (4%)	3 (4%)	–
9.	Parents	6 (2%)	3 (1%)	2 (4%)	1 (2%)	–
10.	Flexibility	5 (1%)	5 (2%)	–	–	–
11.	Assessment	5 (1%)	3 (1%)	–	1 (2%)	–
12.	Communication	4 (1%)	1 (–%)	3 (6%)	–	–
13.	Other	7 (2%)	3 (1%)	1 (2%)	2 (6%)	1 (8%)
14.	Total	367	241	47	63	16

experiences. There were also a limited number of similar comments across substitute teaching and paraprofessional work in decision-making, working with parents, decision making, and assessment. In the following sections we use the data to contrast differences among these roles.

Substitute Teaching

The data on substitute teaching can be divided into two types: day-to-day substitute teaching and long-term substitute teaching. Both involved large groups of students, and both provided an opportunity for the teacher candidate to be the sole decision-maker in the classroom. However, there was a noticeable difference in the number of comments made about preparation, which accounted for 20% of the comments about long term subbing and only 4% of the comments about day-to-day subbing. However, they differed in the continuity of the experience and subsequently in the skills learned.

Long-Term Substitute Teaching

The difference in the comments is probably dues to the greater continuity of experience for long-term substitute teachers, who are responsible for the organizing an orderly curricular sequence form day to day. This responsibility necessitated the need for increased preparation. For example, one candidate in a long-term substitute position commented nine times on the importance of preparation for teaching, including her daily preparation for three classes.

> I make three separate lessons a day because it's three different levels for Spanish, but there's a ton of different resources that you can use. There's an online textbook. There's no like actual hard copy textbook that we use, which was hard to comprehend at first because I've always used a textbook in Spanish class at least like just to lean back on if we need to look something up or to follow along and make sure that we're like on the right track with the units and the curriculum as part of the school district and the state. But there's like an online kind of textbook, and there's not too much reading. So, if you have to pull like reading from other places and implement it into the chapters of the online textbook.

Day-by-Day Substitute Teaching

In contrast, teacher candidates in day-today substitute positions were more likely to comment on the host teacher's preparation, as illustrated below.

> I think it's just hard when the teacher doesn't leave adequate plans. So, if you walk into the school at the beginning of the day, and they don't really explain where to find certain worksheets or how exactly they want things given out. I remember there was one time I was working in a 4th grade class, and they were doing a writing assignment and the plan said for the students to copy from their draft paper onto the final paper, but I had no idea where the final paper was. And I was looking everywhere I could.

The comments of teacher candidates about day-to-day substitute teaching was focused primarily on classroom interactions during real time. As a result, the increased engagement with students, teacher candidates became more independent and flexible, as expressed by one teacher candidate commented below.

> I got to lead a classroom. I don't get to do that in either of those other roles [two paraprofessional positions]. And you really get to be independent and you—it's such a different experience from the other two, also commented

on the opportunity to observe many different types of experience or the breadth of their experience.

Paraprofessional Work

Teacher candidates spoke most often about building relationships when discussing paraprofessional work (45%). That may be because during paraprofessional work teacher candidates worked with single individuals or small groups of students. The type of paraprofessional work varied according to eh nature of the experience.

Small Groups in a Class

This type of experience was more likely to involve a continuous experience than substitute teaching. However, the level of autonomy associated with small groups in a class was less than substitute teaching because the teacher candidate worked with a more trained, full time staff member who could provide directions. In the following example, Meredith felt disempowered to make decisions and thus was dependent on following the teacher's lead.

> I definitely didn't get to teach really. It was kind of more in the observation perspective of it where I was still there, and I was still standing in front of the classroom or moving around trying to help students, but I didn't really. I wasn't using my own voice and speaking to them. It was more just with them.

Small Groups With Special Needs Students

The purpose of some paraprofessional groups was to assist special needs children. This setting afforded an opportunity to learn differentiation strategies for teacher candidates. For example, Andre worked with special needs students as a paraprofessional. Through mentoring form his paraprofessional partner, he overcame his initial lack of experience with special education students and learned how to respond to each student as an individual. When asked what surprised him as a paraprofessional, Andre said:

> How much the other teachers of regular classes trust in the paraprofessional. Sometimes, they don't even know how to react to a student with autism. Sometimes it's misbehaving. Sometimes it's reacting in bad ways. And they don't know how to react. So, they just look at me like, "What should I do

now?" So, I, what I was surprised is that—how much they trust in the para-professional. How much help they need from the paraprofessional.

Individual Student

One of the students was hired as a paraprofessional responsible for a single special student. Often other teachers relied on the paraprofessional to use her insider knowledge to praise, to support, or to discipline the students. For example, she commented:

> I'd say the biggest [difference from her substitute teaching experience] was behavioral difficulties. Because one of the classrooms I followed had a student with a very bad behavioral difficulty, so my challenge was, how I am I going to diffuse this before he hurts himself and somebody else gets hurt? And that was my task, and I noticed other teachers would look to me. Whelp, it's your time to shine. Go, go do it.

Tutoring

One teacher candidate engaged in tutoring as part of the Teacher Residency program. A distinguishing feature of her comments about tutoring was the high number of comments associated with relationship and the absence of classroom management from her experience, as illustrated by the teacher candidate below.

> During tutoring, we weren't really in a classroom. We were kinda just in a little sectioned room where sometimes there was more than one tutor. So, we had to balance each other out. Yeah, there really wasn't any classroom management.

DISCUSSION

Findings from the study showed that teacher candidates at all levels found that interacting with students was a primary benefit of substitute teaching, paraprofessional work, and tutoring. This was reflected by the high number of relationship and classroom comments, which together totaled over 50% of the total comments given. As candidates gained more experience with building relationships and classroom management, they commented on their increased confidence, increased flexibility, and more rapid decision-making.

The preoccupation of teacher candidates with relationship and classroom management may be an indicator that teacher candidates need substantial experience in K–12 classrooms to learn these two dimensions of teaching. In fact, it may be that forming relationships and managing the classroom affect the performance of teacher candidates in their performance of every teaching skill specified by the InTASC standards. Therefore, these skills must be mastered before teacher candidates can move to more advanced levels of teaching.

The results also offer promise for addressing two challenging areas of learning in teacher preparation and classroom management. Through paid internships involving substitute teaching and paraprofessional work, teacher candidates can increase their interactions with K–12 students and deepen their understanding of classroom management principles. Further, by learning new strategies through extensive clinical work with individuals, small groups, and large groups of students, teacher candidates can enhance their ability to differentiate instruction.

The study also found differences among substitute teaching, paraprofessional work, and tutoring. For example, a long-term substitute teaching position affords different opportunities than substitute teaching that occurs in different classrooms with different students each day. The first affords more opportunity to learn about preparing lessons and teaching units over time. The second provides an opportunity to see a greater variation in how classrooms are organized and run. Depending on the type of position, paraprofessional work can encourage more or less autonomy. The teacher candidate who engaged in tutoring commented on the absence of classroom management from her experience. This may prove an advantage for a less experienced teacher candidate by allowing them to focus on instructional strategies rather than student behavior. It may not, however, be sufficient for a complete experience in clinical settings. Differences like the above suggest that close attention must be paid to the context of clinical placements to ensure teacher candidates have sufficient experience to develop the skills needed to master all aspects of teaching.

It is also important to note what the teacher candidates did not learn from substitute teaching and paraprofessional work. They spoke very little about assessment, an area that has challenged teacher preparation programs in the past. It does not appear any of these roles will provide sufficient preparation for assessment. In addition, day-by-day substitute teaching will probably not help teacher candidates plan for instruction. In that context, preparation was mentioned most often by teacher candidates commenting on the lesson plans they received from the regular teacher. In contrast, teacher candidates in a long-term substitute position talked about the challenges of preparing daily lessons. Thus, long term substitute teaching may offer a greater opportunity for learning how to prepare for teaching.

Finally, the preoccupation of teacher candidates may suggest first that mastering these two areas of teaching is vital to functioning effectively in the classroom, and second that college courses simply cannot substitute for engaging with K–12 students, probably because they cannot be learned outside of a K–12 classroom setting. Further, until these skills are mastered, the teacher candidate cannot move to higher levels of teaching. It is a viewpoint that is consistent with a theoretical model of learning to teach that purports our understanding of teaching is acquired through interactions that are gradually internalized mentally in the form of schemas.

IMPLICATIONS

The purpose of this work is not to gain employment for teacher candidates as substitute teachers, paraprofessionals, and tutors. Instead, the goal is to discover ways to utilize local school budgets to both provide paid internship experiences for teacher candidates and to simultaneously accomplish the work of the schools. The ultimate end is to create paid internships in which some of teacher candidate responsibilities include substitute teaching, paraprofessional work, and tutoring. To incorporate these roles into a viable teacher preparation clinical experience requires an understanding of what each role can and cannot do to facilitate teacher candidate learning. Learning that cannot be accomplished through the roles examined in this study, such as learning assessment, must be undertaken through a more traditional approach to clinical experiences or perhaps through a newer, more innovative approach.

As teacher educators consider new designs for clinical experiences, financial compensation for work performed in schools should be treated as one of the design principles. This study has taken a first step to using substitute teaching, paraprofessional work, and tutoring as vehicles for developing paid internships for teacher candidates. As we learn more about learning to teach in each of these experiences, we can become more sophisticated in our approach to designing clinical experiences that provide both a great learning experience and compensation for teacher candidates.

REFERENCES

Ashbaker, B. Y., & Morgan, J. (2013). *Paraprofessionals in the classroom: A survival guide* (2nd ed.). Pearson.

Borko, H., & Putnam, R. T. (1996). Learning to teach. In D. C. Berliner & R. C. Calfee (Eds.), *Handbook of educational psychology* (pp. 673–708). Macmillan.

Clinical Practice Commission. (2018). *A pivot toward clinical practice, its lexicon, and the renewal of educator preparation*. American Association of Colleges for Teacher Education.

Coron, J. P. (2017). *The substitute teacher's survival guide*. Hog Press.

DeMoss, K., Easton-Brooks, D., Hofman, A., Henning, J. E., & LeCelle-Perterson, M. (2017, March). *Sustainable funding for residency programs: Moving beyond grants for financial support* [Panel Presentation]. The American Association of Colleges for Teacher Education. Tampa, FL.

Dewey, J. (1963). *Experience and education*. Collier.

Fallon, B. (2017). *Investing in residencies, improving schools: How principals can fund better teaching and learning*. Bank Street College, Sustainable Funding Project. Human Sciences Press.

Fisher, P. J., Bates, A., & Gurvitz, D. J. (2014). *The complete guide to tutoring struggling readers—Mapping interventions to purpose and CCSS*. Teachers College Press.

Grossman, P., Hammerness, K., & McDonald, M. (2009). Redefining teacher: Re-imagining teacher education. *Teachers and Teaching: Theory and Practice*, *15*(2), 273–290.

Guha, R., Hyler, M. E., & Darling-Hammond, L. (2017, Spring). The teacher residency: A practical path to recruitment and retention. *American Educator, 41*(1), 31–34, 44.

Guha, R., Hyler, M. E., & Darling-Hammond, L. (2018). The power and potential of teacher residencies: An innovative model for preparing teachers. *Phi Delta Kappan 98*(8), 31–37.

Henning, J. E., Bragen, B. F., Mulvaney, T., & George, W. O., III. (2018). A sustainable teacher residency: Designing paid internships for teacher education. *School-University Partnerships*, *The Journal of the National Association for Professional Development Schools 11*(1). https://napds.org/member-only-resources/

Henning, J. E., Erb, D., Randles, H. S., Shoener, H., Fults, N., & Webb, K. (2016). Designing a curriculum for clinical experiences. *Issues in Teacher Education*, *25*(1), 23–38.

Henning, J. E., Gut, D. M., & Beam, P. C. (2019) *Building mentoring capacity in teacher education: A guide to clinically-based practice*. Routledge.

Kolb, D. A. (1984). *Experiential learning: Experience as the source of learning and development*. Prentice-Hall.

Korthagen, F. A. J. (2010). Situated learning theory and the pedagogy of teachereducation: Towards an integrated view of teacher behavior and teacher learning. *Teaching and Teacher Education, 26*, 98–106.

Korthagen, F. A. J., Kessels, J., Koster, B., Lagerwerf, B., & Wubbels, T. (2001). *Linking practice and theory: The pedagogy of realistic teacher education*. Routledge.

Langley, G. J., Moen, R. D., Nolan, K. M., Nolan, T. W. Norman C. L., & Provost, L. P. (2006). *The improvement guide: A practical approach to enhancing organizational performance* (2nd ed.). Jossey-Bass.

Lewin, K. (1946). Action research and minority problems. *Journal of Social Issues*, *2*(4), 34–46.

National Council for Accreditation of Teacher Education. (2010). *Transforming teacher education through clinical practice: A national strategy to prepare effective teachers* (Report of Blue Ribbon Panel on Clinical Preparation and Partnerships for Improved Student Learning).

Papay, J. F., West, M. R., Fullerton, J. B., & Kane, T. J. (2012). Does an urban residency increase student achievement? Early evidence from Boston. *Education Evaluation and Policy Analysis, 34*(4), 413–434. https://doi.org/10.3102/0162373712454328

Piaget, J. (1952). *The origins of intelligence in children.* International University Press.

Ronfeldt, M., & Reininger, M. (2012). More or better student teaching? *Teaching and Teacher Education, 28*(8), 1091–1106.

Sustainable Funding Project. (2016). *For the public good: Quality preparation for every teacher.* Bank Street College of Education.

TeachingWorks. (2012). *Great teachers aren't born. They're taught.* University of Michigan.

Vygotsky, L. S. (1986). *Thought and language.* MIT Press.

Washburn-Moses, L. (2017). A national descriptive survey of teacher residency programs. *School-University Partnerships, 10*(2), 33–41.

SECTION III

INNOVATIVE PARTNERSHIPS

CHAPTER 16

IMPLEMENTING THE PAIRED PLACEMENT MODEL

Foregrounding the Impact on Key Stakeholders

Marilyn E. Strutchens
Auburn University

Basil Conway IV
Columbus State University

Charmaine Mangram
University of Hawai'i at Mānoa

David Erickson
University of Montana-Missoula

Brea Ratliff
Auburn University

Preparing Quality Teachers:
Advances in Clinical Practice, pp. 357–380
Copyright © 2022 by Information Age Publishing
www.infoagepub.com

357

ABSTRACT

The authors describe the design and implementation of a paired placement model where teacher candidates complete intentionally-designed clinical practice experiences in pairs in classrooms during their clinical residency/ student teaching experience. Clinical educators are chosen by teacher educators and school partners based on the alignment of their teaching practices with the goals of the teacher education programs and their willingness to coach and mentor the teacher candidates.

For more than eight years a group of mathematics teacher educators, mathematicians, and mathematics teachers have been working together to effectively implement the paired placement clinical experience model (Strutchens et al., 2020). In the paired placement model, a pair of teacher candidates work daily with an experienced mathematics mentor teacher who is devoted to helping the teacher candidates address the craft of teaching, plan lessons jointly, and teach those same lessons while actively observing, reflecting, and revising (Leatham & Peterson, 2010). In a review of literature related to paired-placement clinical residencies, Mau (2013) reported that paired teacher candidates: (1) engaged in more frequent and varied communication; (2) increased their willingness to take pedagogical risks; (3) improved their levels of reflection; (4) found methods for collaboration and cooperation in the teaching action; (5) found ways to increase K–12 student learning; (6) had better classroom management; and (7) found strategies to handle tensions in perspective and performance (p. 54). Based on these findings, Mau recommended placing pairs of teacher candidates with one mentor teacher and implementing a model of learning to teach that encourages collaboration, pedagogical risk taking, increased reflection, and better classroom management.

This group focusing on the paired placement model is one of three sub-Research Action Clusters (sub-RACs) which make up the Clinical Experiences Research Action Cluster (CERAC) of the Mathematics Teacher Education Partnership, a network improvement community aimed at transforming secondary mathematics teacher education programs (Martin et al., 2020). The CERAC aims to design clinical experiences that help to prepare teacher candidates to implement the National Council of Teachers of Mathematics'[NCTM] eight mathematics teaching practices (NCTM, 2014). The eight mathematics teaching practices are: (1) Establish mathematics goals to focus learning; (2) Implement tasks that promote reasoning and problem solving; (3) Use and connect mathematical representations; (4) Facilitate meaningful mathematical discourse; (5) Pose purposeful questions; 6) Build procedural fluency from conceptual understanding; 7) Support productive struggle in learning mathematics; and 8) Elicit and use evidence of student thinking (NCTM, 2014, p. 10). Members of CERAC contend that these practices along with other equity-based strategies (Aguirre et al., 2013; Gutstein, 2006a & 2012; Ladson-Billings,1995; Paris, 2016) are central to teacher candidates learning to become effective student-centered teachers.

In order to implement the paired placement model in accordance with these goals, the paired placement sub-RAC has developed workshops for mentor teachers and teacher candidates, observation protocols for teacher candidates to use to focus on specific aspects of teaching and learning while they observe each other teach, syllabi to guide the interactions of the university supervisor, mentor teacher, and the pair of teacher candidates as they work together during the clinical residency, and other tools needed for effective implementation of the paired placement model. Over the years the paired placement sub-RAC has used Plan-Do-Study-Act (PDSA) cycles to improve the implementation of the model (Bryk et al., 2015). During the *Plan* phase the change is articulated and predictions about what we expect will happen are recorded. In the *Do* phase, the change is attempted, and the results of the change are recorded. Next in the *Study* phase, the results that occurred during the do phase are compared to the predictions made in the plan phase. Finally, during the *Act* phase decisions are made about what to do next (Bryk et al., 2015). The PDSA is a process for rapid cycles of learning from practice, coupled with three fundamental questions that drive improvement work: (1) What are we trying to accomplish? (2) How will we know that a change is an improvement? (3) What change can we make that will result in improvement? (Lewis, 2015).

Strategies that lead to successful implementation of the paired placement model based on the PDSA cycles conducted include:

1. Select pairs of teacher candidates that are compatible.
2. Select a mentor teacher whose practices are in alignment with program goals and who can serve as a coach for the pair.
3. Share possible pitfalls of the model and discuss how to avoid them.
4. Provide professional development about the model and co-planning and co-teaching strategies.
5. Check in early to see how the trio is working together.

Current members of the paired placement sub-RAC represent four university teams and their school partners. In this chapter, we share the impact that studying the implementation of the paired placement model through an equity lens has had on faculty members, university supervisors, mentor teachers, teacher candidates, and students.

AN EQUITY LENS:
TEACHER CANDIDATE AND STUDENT IMPACTS

It is important for mathematics teacher educators to use an equity lens to understand progress. Though there may be improvements for a general population, these improvements may be producing inequities in outcomes for certain subpopulations of the group. When educators use an equity lens to understand their practice, programs, classroom, relationships, and other elements, they examine systematic work that may be producing unequal outcomes.

Aguirre et al. (2013) defined five equitable teaching practices in mathematics education. These are practices that we would expect from teachers who make equity an important part of their professional practice. Teachers who do this (1) go deep with mathematics, focusing on content that matters, developing procedural fluency from conceptual understanding. While doing this, these teachers (2) leverage the multiple mathematical competencies that exist in their classroom highlighting students' mathematical thoughts and connecting these to shared goals. These teachers who purposefully select and leverage competencies use these attributes to (3) affirm their students' mathematical and personal identities by bringing voices often silenced to the forefront of discourse valuing their contributions to the classroom. When these voices are highlighted, these teachers (4) challenge spaces of marginality stifling the systems of oppression that have influenced the systems of education. Teachers who challenge spaces of marginality look deeply at the culturally relevant teaching and its tenants that develop students' critical consciousness and push them to identify, analyze, and solve real-world problems that result in societal injustices. These teachers thus (5) draw on multiple resources of knowledge that support students to affirm and appreciate their culture of origin while developing fluency in other cultures drawing on communities as assets to learning. In this section we show how the paired placement model impacts students who are in classrooms during paired placement clinical residencies.

Description of Data Sources

Universities that are part of the Paired-Placement sub-RAC used multiple sources of evidence to support the improvement of their clinical experiences and encourage critical reflection by teacher candidates. Teacher candidates were required to complete observations that related to specific principles such as assessment, equity, learning, management, tools, and technology. For each observation, teacher candidates used only one set of questions relating to these principles and recorded their observations in their journals. After the observation, teacher candidates debriefed with their mentor teacher and the person whom they observed. During debriefing, teacher candidates reflect on and discuss their recorded observations. Teacher candidates in the program also completed midterm and exit surveys and interviews either in focus groups or individually depending on university contexts. University supervisors observed preservice teachers and assessed their teaching using the Mathematics Classroom Observation Protocol for Practices (Gleason et al., 2017) to record qualitative data of preservice teaching episodes.

Analysis

Using the Aguirre et al. (2013) framework for equity-based teaching practices in mathematics education, the sub-RAC sought to understand more deeply the impact of the paired placement strategy on developing equitable practices of its teachers. Data sources previously described were read and analyzed by programs using these five equity-based practices and coded to highlight the impact of the model. These codes were then shared as a team to draw conclusions for the larger audience. The amount of data for each institution varied largely because of teacher candidates' enrollment and longevity of the model at each institution. Data shared across these five practices are actual quotes from participants of the paired placement model.

SYNTHESIS OF FINDINGS

Going Deep With Mathematics and Mathematics Teaching

Unfortunately, many students are systematically oppressed by classrooms that are a mile wide and an inch deep. However, teachers who go deep with mathematics emphasize learning for understanding over attending only to fluency with algorithms and facts (NCTM, 2014). In addition, teachers who go deep with mathematics understand how learning develops in a discourse-rich learning environment marked by conjecture, reasoning, and justification (Rubel, 2017). When reviewing data from the RAC, the team uncovered this expectation with both students and within the model itself.

Teacher candidates are similarly relegated by school structures that separate mathematics into certain units or domains. Many teachers, including preservice teachers, are forced to follow common lesson plans across a grade level or pacing guides from a district that ensure standards are covered before a standardized assessment. The structure of the placement however provided opportunities for members of the paired placement to go deep with mathematics and focus on content knowledge rather than testing and pacing guides.

The paired-placement model is extremely helpful in providing more opportunities to engage struggling learners. When members of the model were asked questions that focused on students' development of conceptual understanding or how procedural fluency was developed from conceptual understanding, many of the teacher candidates highlighted the effectiveness of the model. One teacher candidate stated the following:

> Having a co-teacher offers many benefits when you have good chemistry with them. It makes instruction flow smoother during activities since there are two expert bodies in the room that can move around and work with the students. Having a co-teacher also greatly benefits students who like individualized attention, as we are able to offer it more frequently.

A cooperating teacher described this as a "luxury of having three mathematics teachers in the room." Moreover, teacher candidates were able to lean on one another during lessons to ensure that each student had a focus on developing deeper mathematical understanding:

> Whenever my partner was teaching, I was able to walk around and help the struggling students in the class keep up with the classroom pace, and my partner was able to do the same when I was the lead teacher. We were able to work as a team to make sure all students were able to grow their learning throughout a lesson. The main students that were able to benefit from the paired placement model were the advanced and the struggling learners. We were able to focus on different learners and increase their understanding because we were able to have more one-on-one instruction than typically happens within a classroom.

In addition to developing deeper learning in secondary students, teacher candidates also thought more deeply about their lesson plans. Having a peer in the classroom throughout the semester challenged teacher candidates to improve practice and hold each other accountable:

> I think the biggest impact this has had on my teaching has been receiving feedback from my peer. It is beneficial to hear what made sense or where I could have done better from a co-intern. I know that the instructors have told us about effective practices but hearing how what I did either was successful or not from a peer helped me really question my methods.

This support provided more opportunities for preservice teachers to try out lesson ideas that they may have believed they could not have taught otherwise because of classroom management or lack of support. A preservice teacher shared this idea: "One of the benefits for the paired placement model was that there was less of a struggle with managing the classroom.

This allowed me to try different approaches that normally I would not have taken." The paired placement model was extremely valuable in providing opportunities for preservice teachers to go deep with mathematics in the classroom and go deep with their own mathematical teaching practices.

Leveraging Multiple Mathematical Competencies

Students and teacher candidates come with many valuable experiences and mathematical assets that should be leveraged in the classroom. Smith and Stein (2011) encouraged teacher candidates to purposefully use these assets in the classroom to connect to mathematical goals by monitoring, selecting, and sequencing students' contributions in a meaningful way. Teacher candidates in the paired placement have drawn on students' social experiences to highlight unjust practices of tracking (Conway et al., 2018) and mathematical competencies to build positive mathematical identity. Berry et al. (2020) drew from this work to relate it also to other teaching goals in a lesson such as the learning for social justice goals (Learning for Justice, 2016). The paired placement fostered this practice through increased collaboration during lesson planning, teaching, and critical reflection.

The paired placement model allowed teacher candidates to critically examine one another's practice. The teacher candidates often notice the differences in how students responded with one teacher as compared to another which caused them to question their practices. A teacher candidate responded in an interview:

> our students were struggling. Whenever my co-teaching partner would teach half the class responded well and whenever I taught the other half responded well. We would talk about what worked for us and what we thought did not work. We came to the conclusion that we were both only teaching half of the class.

Having a pair of teacher candidates go through the same experiences allows for them to support one another. Though this may be with differences in developing personal connections as above, it may also be with developing lesson plans or understanding content. Teacher candidates very often have time talking in the car as they carpool to a school in addition to their normal common planning times. In the following instance, this PST describes the interaction during internship that leveraged both of their mathematical competencies:

> My partner and I were constantly texting and talking about what would happen the next day and never just insisted that our one idea had to be taught a particular way. We would both listen to what the other had to say

and critique the idea without making the other feel inferior. We cared more about what was best for the students.

Affirming Mathematics Learners' Identities

Research in mathematics education has well documented the benefits of connecting mathematics to students, families, and communities, and to draw on these connections in their mathematics teaching (Turner et al., 2016). In addition, preservice teachers have been documented as drawing on these resources in their lesson planning and whose voices they highlight during their classes.

Though there are countless examples to describe the many ways this has happened in the paired placement, some teacher candidates in the model chose to make the affirmation of students' mathematical identities a focus (Conway et al., 2018). The teacher candidates purposefully planned for high school students to investigate issues of injustice that were taking place at a school in collaboration with their mentor teacher. During the class, students were asked to discuss the effects that school policy and tracking had on them socially and academically. The lesson focused on the statistical process of creating a statistical question, collecting data, analyzing data, and making inference using statistical tests. During the orchestration of the lesson, the triad of teachers purposefully allowed students to use different analysis techniques such as the chi-square test and the 2-sample t-test for analysis using that statistical analysis in the lesson to highlight multiple pathways to a solution. The teacher candidates purposefully selected students and their analysis in a way to sequence and connect the two analyzed results drawing on multiple competencies. During the lesson, Conway et al. (2018) described students affirming experiences they had of not being tracked during middle school. This teaching episode conducted during the paired placement model then became part of an effort to provide more opportunities for students at their school to enter into advanced coursework (Conway, 2021).

Challenging Spaces of Marginality

Aguirre et. al (2013) positioned the idea of challenging spaces of marginality with two different lenses. The first focused on who is being leveraged in the classroom by the teacher. Teachers who challenge these spaces look for opportunities to promote students who are traditionally marginalized into positive contributors academically, socially, and culturally to the classroom. The second focus places emphasis on the critical tenant of culturally relevant pedagogy, critical consciousness (Ladson-Billings, 1995). This idea resonates with the joint position papers by the National Council of

Supervisors of Mathematics and *TODOS: Mathematics for ALL* (2016), as well as the position paper of the Benjamin Banneker Association (2017), both of which argue that embracing social justice moves us beyond noticing issues and concerns about societal inequities and requires actions that confront oppression and/or marginalization. Teachers who challenge spaces of marginality incorporate opportunities to read and write the world with mathematics (Gutstein, 2006a).

Teacher candidates in the paired placement often used one another's strengths and weaknesses to think critically about their lessons and teaching.

> My co-teaching partner has a better relationship with some of the athletes in this class and thus they listened better. I learned that I left out the athletes sometimes in my questioning and in my teaching style. So, I was able to adapt my instruction, and I included more relevant tasks for athletes and kinesthetic learners so that they became more interested. I believe that this has increased the student-teacher rapport and grades for both of us have increased for the whole class, not just half of the class.

During the paired-placement, researchers have seen teacher candidates and their mentors use mathematics to explore, understand, and respond to social injustice. In one situation, a teacher candidate led a lesson that challenged students and the school system to re-evaluate the tracking system at the school (Conway et al., 2018). This lesson catalyzed student voices into a larger conversation on the lack of opportunity for students to enter advanced pipeline courses which in turn opened up more opportunities for students in lower grades (Conway, 2021). The paired model itself seemed to provide support for teacher candidates to take risks because they seemed to have allies during challenges. The mentor teacher in the classroom stated:

> I would like to think that I would have ventured out of my own comfort zone and completed such an activity [social justice lesson] in my class alone; however, having the paired placement definitely impacted this decision to pursue a particularly controversial issue.... There's no doubt however that the discussion influenced by the paired placement helped initiate conversations that led to this lesson!

Drawing on Multiple Resources of Knowledge

Mathematics teaching and learning is highly dependent on context, yet many teachers abstract mathematics away from students' own personal experiences and communities. Asset-based approaches are a deliberate positioning of students, parents, and their communities as positive and enabling resources for learning (Celedón-Pattichis et al., 2019). Teachers who draw on multiple resources of knowledge value students' language and culture, positioning them in the curriculum and letting their voices and experiences be a part of the classroom (Aguirre et al., 2013). Teacher candidates placed in the paired placement model seemed to both respect and highlight their partners assets as well as their students.

The paired placement model allowed for students to understand how their personal identities intersected with students during placement in ways that would not have been possible in traditional apprenticeship models. When these candidates noticed areas that they needed to improve, they used the curriculum as a way to connect with students. During interviews, preservice teachers often describe the model as an essential component to their success. They highlight the relationship with their peer that was developed through common planning, teaching debriefs, and venting while carpooling.

REFLECTIONS FROM PROGRAM COMPLETERS AFTER EXPERIENCING THE PAIRED PLACEMENT MODEL

Members of our team began implementing the paired placement model in the 2013–2014 academic year. We recently surveyed selected pairs from the past seven years to learn more about their experiences during the internship that helped candidates prepare for their professional careers. We developed an open-ended survey (see Appendix A) that looked to determine longitudinal effects of the placement that were experienced during the model such as confidence in overcoming challenges, persistence, self-reflection, leadership, collaboration, equity, and risk taking (Conway et al., 2017). We followed methods of Corbin and Strauss (2015) to code and analyze data. This section shares some themes that emerged as we surveyed five graduates (all pseudonyms) of our paired placement program seeking to learn "How does the paired placement model help candidates be prepared for their jobs?"

Cases of Paired Placement Interns Who Became Classroom Teachers

The first pair, Aria and Carlo, graduated in December 2013 after their paired placement internship with one of our sub-RAC team members who had taught high school mathematics for more than 30 years. Aria was immediately hired in the same district to fill a high school vacancy and has taught in the same school since, advancing to the co-chair of the mathematics department. Carlo took a high school mathematics teaching position for the next academic year out-of-state and after three years at that school, returned to teaching in-state at a larger high school for three years, and then became a high school principal in a different, smaller in-state district. The second pair, Shawn and Fiona, graduated in spring 2015 after their paired placement internship in seventh grade with a 25-plus year teacher of secondary mathematics. Each has taught five years in reservation high schools, most recently teaching advanced algebra or algebra readiness, and geometry. Fiona is a member of her school leadership team which focuses on improving the overall school climate. Hans, a member of the third pair, completed his paired placement internship in spring 2020 in Fiona's high school mathematics classroom teaching developmental algebra, advanced algebra, and geometry. He has completed his first half year in high school mathematics and coaching football.

When reviewing interviews in the three cases, three major themes emerged: communication, confidence, and life events. The following details impact of the paired placement model on teachers' reflecting over their past and their ability to communicate professionally, feel confident as a professional, and handle professional life and teaching.

Communication

The first major theme of all participants was communication. Carlo, now a high school principal, stated:

> Paired placement helped with my leadership responsibilities in the form of communication.... Clear communication and collaboration is a must across all facets of education. The internship was a great introductory level of what would develop into a foundational block for my success. It was not clearly noted at the time of the internship, but as I reflect on what was taken away from that experience, it was critical to who I am today. Being able to enjoy your job while working with others benefits the students unmeasurably.

Aria has become a leader in her school, working in collaboration with Carlo during their paired placement and recently serving as a cooperating teacher of other paired placement interns. She stated,

> As a professional educator, I have struggled with communication, people not wanting to work together, and not being open to new ideas. Thankfully the paired-placement model allowed me to explore other ways to communicate, share my ideas, try new things and to help others. While I still

face some of these difficulties, things are becoming easier, and I am able to support more staff.

Others mentioned the importance of failures during the internship, having the ability to see those in the partner, and being able to discuss them on a professional basis. Carlo shared his experiences learning to communicate the "good, the bad, and the ugly" stemmed from the failures and successes and learning how to work together, to "truly enjoy the working environment." Shawn shared that he is "more likely to seek out assistance/advice from another staff member since I was so used to having someone to bounce ideas off of." Fiona confirmed, "I was always communicating with and making mistakes in front of [my partner]; I felt very comfortable asking for help once I got a teaching job." As paired-placement teacher candidates move to their careers, the model seems to have strength in increasing communication ability to enhance collaboration and leadership in teachers' professional careers.

Confidence

Every respondent referred to the confidence they felt due to having constant communication. Hans did not use the term "confidence" as all the others did, but he expressed his feeling of being able to rely on his partner: "You had another person who knew exactly what you were talking about and that was watching and waiting to jump in if you got lost … we were on the same page and had constant communication." Fiona stated, "just having another person in the room with you gives you the confidence to try different things." Shawn, a relatively quiet individual, shared, "I felt more confident in making errors, knowing that I had another teacher there trying the same thing as me. If I was by myself, I think I would have been much more conservative in my approach." Aria also shared that she felt confident because of just having another teacher there: "During the paired placement, I felt like there were many times I was on my toes and adapting as needed … it was really exciting to see. I think this also allowed for me to try [risk taking] more often in my classroom."

Life Events

Several of the respondents addressed life events as challenges faced, a constant component of classrooms of learners, where each brings their busy life into the room, and not always with the same level of focus on learning mathematics. Carlo stated:

Having someone not follow through with what they were supposed to do because of life events. This is a very real thing that happens in education daily. It then makes the individual teacher think on their feet and to learn to be ready at a moment's notice.

Aria summarized her preparation which allowed for her moving beyond the pandemic:

Covid has been a difficult time for most teachers and learners. Due to different schedules and students' needs, I needed to adapt and support my learners. I completely flipped the way I taught, tried new things, and adapted as much as possible. I was nervous it wouldn't work, and it worked great. As I was going through the process, I shared and supported other teachers. I also supported three different district wide PLC teams. I took risks, found the right amount of flexibility and different instructional approaches to support learners' needs during this time. I also supported other teachers by providing strong communication, allowing for exchange of ideas, and continually supporting the idea that we are a team and can do this together.

Carlo and Aria's quotes allow us to recognize that the student teaching experience of teachers of mathematics includes preparing them for working with others.

Through PDSA work as a sub-RAC, the team asked, "How does the paired placement model help candidates be prepared for their jobs?" and we found the paired placement model candidates reported (a) having learned communication skills, (b) confidence as teachers, and (c) in general, a preparation for life events that naturally enter the classroom that all contribute to success in their future jobs.

MENTOR TEACHER IMPACTS

The Association of Mathematics Teacher Educators (2017) stated:

An effective mathematics teacher preparation program provides clinical experiences that are developed mutually with school partners, are scaffolded to build in complexity, include opportunities to work in diverse settings and with a range of learners, and are supervised by qualified mentors. (p. 37)

Furthermore, both experienced and novice teachers attest that clinical experiences (including student teaching) are powerful components of teacher preparation—more influential on long-term practices than preparation program coursework (Wilson et al., 2001). Even though the mentor teacher plays a critical role in what teacher candidates take away from the clinical residency experience, in the paired placement model mentor teachers benefit from the model much like the teacher candidates.

Data Collection

Mentor teachers participated in PDSA cycles, teacher candidate observation debriefings, and project focus groups. Data from these sources were examined, coded, and analyzed for emerging themes related to impacts from the implementation of the paired placement on mentor teachers.

Analysis Description

Four themes emerged from the data related to the impact of the paired placement model on mentor teachers: a professional learning community was formed between the teacher candidates and the mentor teacher, the mentor teachers could take risks that they might not normally take, they were able to use co-teaching and co-planning strategies to facilitate learning, and the mentor teachers saw themselves emerging as mathematics teacher educators. These themes have emerged consistently from implementation of the model.

Formation of Professional Learning Communities

The professional learning community (PLC) is a model in which educators work together to affect practices of schooling. School staff and others focus on learning rather than teaching, work collaboratively on matters related to learning, and hold themselves accountable for the kind of results that fuel continual improvement (DuFour, 2004).

One mentor teacher talked about how much he enjoyed having the teacher candidates there and just how much they helped him professionally. They helped him with organization and were willing to help do whatever tasks needed to be completed. The teacher also explained that it was not just him giving, he was really gaining a lot from the paired placement and appreciated what the teacher candidates brought to the situation.

In addition, one mentor teacher talked about how the three were able to determine that a student had problems seeing because each of them could take turns observing the student during class.

Another teacher said that she enjoyed how the paired placement provides a built-in professional learning community, which is difficult to have when you are an isolated teacher. She also mentioned how they respected the opinions of the other teachers although they were different as they worked toward a common goal. One mentor teacher in the model stated:

The paired placement model made me rethink through collaboration with my colleagues. Rather than me directing discussions on my own as a perceived expert in the field, I had a chance to listen and respond to interns' discussions and ideas as a practitioner. We worked together to think through ways to most effectively teach students. Our goals for students mathematically were held accountable by one another during discussion, lesson planning, and teaching. This has translated to my own practice. I believe I have sought my colleagues' advice and tried to encourage collaboration in my department more.

Risk Taking

Mentor teachers mentioned that the paired placement model enabled them to try lesson plans that required more preparation and student-to-student interactions than they might normally have attempted. The mentor teachers said that having the two teacher candidates in the classroom enabled them to bounce ideas off the candidates and to plan lessons where they could not easily predict what might happen with the students. As mentioned in the equity section, the trios taught social justice lessons and others that required them to facilitate courageous conversations. A mentor teacher in the paired placement model responded during an interview:

I would like to think that I would have ventured out of my own comfort zone and completed [a social justice activity] in my class alone; however, having the paired placement definitely impacted this decision to pursue a particularly controversial issue…. There's no doubt however that the discussion influenced by the paired placement helped initiate conversations that led to this lesson!

Use of Co-Planning and Co-Teaching Strategies

One of the other sub-RACs of the CERAC focuses on supporting collaborative pairs in using six co-teaching and co-planning strategies and developing resources that can help teachers enact co-teaching within a secondary mathematics context (Sears et al., 2020). Members of the paired placement sub-RAC have attended professional learning opportunities provided by the co-planning and co-teaching sub-RAC and have shared the strategies with their mentor teachers and teacher candidates. Consequently, the trios have used some of these strategies in their classrooms. In one paired placement setting, a seventh-grade class consisted of 30 students, a majority of which had special needs. The pair and their mentor teacher worked well together as a team. They used parallel teaching, which is when the class is divided with each teacher instructing half the students, addressing the same instructional topics, and using the same instructional strategies and materials; and the one teach—one other assists, in which one teacher has primary instructional responsibility while the other monitors behaviors or corrects assignments, often lending a voice to students or groups who hesitate to participate or add comments (Bacharach et al., 2010). They were very supportive of each other. They also used an inquiry-based curriculum which really helped the teacher candidates to grow in the use of the mathematics teaching practices and other equitable practices. By the end of the semester, the group of 30 students were performing well and could interact effectively together. The mentor teacher stated that she would not have been able to do alone what they did collectively for the students.

Emerging as Mathematics Teacher Educators

One mentor teacher stated that she felt more like a teacher educator when participating in the paired placement model. During the paired placement model, there is a greater focus on examining and improving teaching practices than during a traditional apprentice style internship model because of the collaboration and shared responsibilities. This leaves more time for the trio to focus on whether the students are learning instead of on managing and organizing the class. Furthermore, the observation protocols which the teacher candidates and the mentor teacher use to provide feedback to each other enable them to think deeply about teaching and learning.

Implications

The paired placement model benefits the mentor teacher and teacher candidates in multiple ways. If the mentor teacher and the teacher candidates work together well bidirectional benefits occur. Moreover, the teachers also have the potential to develop a more equitable classroom.

PROGRAM IMPACTS

Not only does the paired placement model result in increased learning for the secondary learners, teacher candidates, and their mentors, secondary mathematics teacher education faculty also benefit from learning to implement the model. One of the affordances of collaborating with other faculty who are studying the implementation of the paired placement model at their own institutions is that participating faculty formed a professional learning community or PLC (Stoll et al., 2006) focused on problem-solving, purposive change (Dill & Friendman, 1979), innovation[1] and programmatic level transformation. In this section, we share the voices of the members of our paired placement sub-RAC on the benefits of participating in a community of learners focused on implementing the paired placement model at their respective institutions. Members of the paired placement sub-RAC have met regularly since 2012, and monthly for the past three years.

Data Sources

Each faculty participant in the sub-RAC was surveyed to identify any changes in their teaching practice and any changes in their teacher education programs that were attributable to the faculty's participation in the sub-RAC. In addition to demographic questions, the survey consisted of four questions related to mathematics teacher educator practice. Five faculty responded to the survey which represents 100% of all faculty who are current members of the paired placement sub-RAC. Survey respondents had a range of experiences with teaching mathematics at the secondary level, teaching mathematics education seminars and field courses in higher education, and with their knowledge of the paired placement model. Respondents' experience teaching mathematics in secondary school ranged from 0 years to 12 years. Faculty have taught a range of mathematics education courses including elementary content and methods courses and secondary methods courses. All respondents have supervised secondary mathematics students in the field as a regular part of their work, and three of the five respondents are currently supporting secondary teacher candidates in the field. Only one respondent indicated that she/he had no knowledge or experience with the paired placement prior to joining the sub-RAC. Respondents had between two and nine years of experience participating in the paired placement sub-RAC (Strutchens et al., 2020).

Analysis Description

Survey responses were qualitatively coded and analyzed in relationship to the three themes: changes in field supervision practice, changes in secondary mathematics methods teaching practice, and program innovation. In addition to these a priori codes, two themes emerged from the analysis: design iteration and legitimacy. We have chosen direct quotes that help to illustrate each theme.

Changes in Field Supervision Practice

Unsurprisingly, faculty reported that their field supervision practice has changed, as a result of their participation in the sub-RAC. For example, Callie who had been an educator for 22 years shared:

> My participation in sub-RAC has really opened my eyes to alternate field placement models.... Prior to joining the paired placement model, I had never known of any other ways that students might engage in their student teaching field placement. The paired placement model provides the cognitive and affective support that many student teachers need given that they are often going into schools/departments that have a more traditional (direct) approach to teaching.

Madeline, who has been a mathematics teacher educator for 26 years, reported that working with the team "has pushed me to encourage teacher candidates to give critical feedback to each other." Moreover, even members of our sub-RAC who were not currently working in teacher education reported that there was value in collaborating with others to improve field practice. One such faculty shared, "[I] haven't had the opportunity yet but it has given me new ideas if I were to do field placement work again."

Changes in Secondary Methods Teaching Practice

Although the paired placement model sub-RAC meetings were not directly focused on changing teaching practice in relation to methods courses, faculty who are currently in teacher education reported that participating in the sub-RAC has changed instructional practice related to their secondary mathematics methods courses. For example, Ben who has been teaching for 18 years shared, "I have tried to use ideas from the placement model during my methods courses by placing candidates together before student teaching. This has allowed me to give students experiences that have related to a semester-long internship." Ben noted that the attention to equity and social justice in the PLC along with the attention to the teaching practices and mathematical practice standards in their work and data collection efforts has helped in creating clear and consistent goals in his program. Using instruments from the team for data collection has helped support the use of these practices and principles from research as a program.

Program Innovation

Participating faculty reported that being a member of the group has supported their capacity and ability to lead innovation at their respective universities. There were two primary ways that this was accomplished through our work together: the ability to iterate on the original paired placement design and by lending legitimacy to the work.

Design Iteration

Two respondents shared that being a part of the sub-RAC led to their ability to address the field placement needs of their programs in innovative ways by iterating on the original design of the paired placement model. For example, after having successfully implemented the paired placement model at his previous institution, one member of our sub-RAC reported that there were challenges with implementing the paired placement model at their new institution due to the organization of the programs. He stated,

> I moved from this university and went to a new university, similar in size, but separated candidates by postbaccalaureate, middle, and high school preparation. This has made it difficult to implement the paired placement model as it has been described and used previously because candidates were coming from different preparation areas. However, … I have also used ideas from the paired placement model in the creating and acceptance of a Noyce grant that places freshman and sophomore students in the secondary preparation program with juniors and seniors in the program. I have hoped that the "triad" of the interns, scholars, and mentors would reap many of the benefits that have been afforded through [t]he paired placement model.

Another respondent described being able to further iterate on the paired placement model after learning about Ben's success with a variation of the model.

> Given Ben's success with the "Triad model," this year I developed and proposed an iteration of the Paired Placement model to my department…. This model pairs one graduating teacher candidate during the student teaching semester with one incoming student together in one mentor teacher's classroom. In the proposed model, the graduating student would be responsible for contributing the researched based disciplinary practices (e.g., MTPs and equity practices), while the incoming student would be responsible for contributing their literacy and multicultural education knowledge to planning discussions. I developed this model in response to our department having very little time and support for

placing our incoming teacher candidates into the field for "observation" due to COVID-19 changing guidelines, but having full confidence that the classrooms of our current mentors along with our graduating teacher candidates would provide our incoming teacher candidates an excellent "observation" opportunity and would provide the student teacher and mentor one additional solid resource as they learn to navigate their new virtual classroom environment.

Legitimacy

Some participants reported that being a part of the sub-RACserved to legitimize their ideas as they pushed for purposive change within their departments and their universities, as Ben stated in the following:

> Joining the sub-RAC, I was able to advocate for switching the student teaching experience to a paired internship, just like our field experience courses had been since 1995 when we changed those at the secondary level for all future teachers.... The change was not just viewed as my idea, but a national organization, and that provided necessary support for the change.

Adopting Zelditch's (2001) definition, "something is legitimate if it is in accord with the norms, values, beliefs, practices, and procedures accepted by a group" (p. 33), we might understand membership in the paired placement model sub-RAC as providing one of the first steps in making the paired placement model legitimate to those beyond the mathematics education community. As articulated in Ben's quote below, by being able to cite and draw from evidence from a national network, participating faculty's voices and ideas are amplified.

> Now, I see the collaboration of individuals [as] the framework for true change. Moving and working together is really our strongest voice. Being able to rest on the work of my colleagues as I bring different ideas to my universities has made my impact of change in these environments much stronger. It's allowed me to provide evidence for trying something that may be different than what has always been done. (Ben, 18 years of experience)

Steps Forward

Faculty participating in the paired placement sub-RAC reported many benefits of their participation in the PLC, including changing their field supervision practice and supporting teacher education program innovation, broadly. Given these unexpected benefits, our team encourages faculty interested in implementing the paired placement model to seek out others who are either interested in or already implementing the model to form their own professional learning community. One such avenue is joining our sub-RAC, but there are other opportunities available through the Mathematics Teacher Education Partnership and the Association of Mathematics Teacher Educators.

CONCLUSION

Throughout the chapter we have shown that implementing the paired placement model can benefit all major stakeholders and create shared equitable classroom spaces. If the paired placement model is implemented well the teacher candidates develop into well-prepared teachers who implement effective and equity-based practices. Their mentor teachers report significant impact on their development both as teachers and as mentors. And the university supervisors experience growth in their understanding how much teacher candidates can grow given the right set of opportunities to learn. Furthermore, the paired placement model can be implemented across subject areas and grade levels. Collaboration, reflection, and equity and access are all affordances of the model for the teachers and their students when the model is implemented well.

REFERENCES

Aguirre, J. M., Mayfield-Ingram, K., & Martin, D. B. (2013). *The impact of identity in K–8 mathematics: Rethinking equity-based practices.* NCTM.

Association of Mathematics Teacher Educators. (2017). *Standards for preparing teachers of mathematics.* https://amte.net/standards

Bacharach, N., Heck, T. W., & Dahlberg, K. (2010). Changing the face of student teaching through coteaching. *Action in Teacher Education*, *32*(1), 3–14.

Benjamin Banneker Association. (2017). *Implementing a social justice curriculum: Practices to support the participation and success of African-American students in mathematics.* http://bbamath.org/index.php/2017/11/19/thebenjamin-banneker-social-justice-position-statement

Berry, R. Q., III, Conway IV, B. M., Lawler, B. R., & Staley, J. W. (2020). *High school mathematics lessons to explore, understand, and respond to social injustice.* Corwin Press.

Bryk, A. S., Gomez, L. M., Grunow, A., & LeMahieu, P. G. (2015). *Learning to improve: How America's schools can get better at getting better.* Harvard Education Press.

Celedón-Pattichis, S., Borden, L. L., Pape, S. J., Clements, D. H., Peters, S. A., Males, J. R., Chapman, O., & Leonard, J. (2018). Asset-based approaches to equitable mathematics education research and practice. *Journal for Research in Mathematics Education*, *49*(4), 373–389.

Conway, B., IV. (2021). An opportunity for the tracked. *School Science and Mathematics*, *121*(3), 175–186.

Conway, B., Erickson, D., Parish, C., Strutchens, S., & Whitfield, J. (2017, October*). An alternative approach to the traditional internship model* [Paper presentation]. The Georgia Association of Mathematics Teacher Educators. http:// digitalcommons.georgiasouthern.edu/gamte/

Conway, B., Strutchens, M., Martin, W. G., & Kenney, L. (2018). Using equitable pedagogy to increase students' participation in AP statistics. In D. White, A. Fernandes, & M. Civil (Eds.), *Access and equity: Promoting high quality mathematics in Grades 9–12.* (pp. 65–76). National Council of Teachers of Mathematics.

Corbin, J., & Strauss, A. (2015). *Basics of qualitative research: Techniques and procedures for developing grounded theory* (4th ed.). SAGE.

Dill, D. D., & Friedman, C. P. (1979). An analysis of frameworks for research on innovation and change in higher education. *Review of Educational Research*, *49*(3), 411–435.

Dufour, R. (2004). What is a "Professional Learning Community"? *Educational Leadership*, *61*(8), 6–11.

Gleason, J., Livers, S., & Zelkowski, J. (2017). Mathematics classroom observation protocol for practices (MCOP²): A validation study. *Investigations in Mathematics Learning*, *9*(3), 111–129.

Gutstein, E. (2006a). *Reading and writing the world with mathematics: Toward a pedagogy for social justice*. Taylor & Francis.

Gutstein, E. (2006b). Driving while Black or Brown: The mathematics of racial profiling. In D. Mewborn (Series Ed.), J. Masingila (Vol. Ed.), *Teachers engaged in research: Inquiry in mathematics classrooms, Grades 6–8* (Vol. 3, pp. 99–118). Information Age Publishing.

Gutstein, E. (2012). Reflections on teaching and learning mathematics for social justice in urban schools. In A. A. Wager & D. W. Stinson (Eds.), *Teaching mathematics for social justice: Conversations with educators* (pp. 63–78). National Council of Teachers of Mathematics.

Ladson-Billings, G. (1995). But that's just good teaching! The case for culturally relevant pedagogy. *Theory into Practice*, *34*(3), 159–165.

Learning for Justice. (2016). *Social justice standards: The teaching tolerance anti-bias framework*. https://www.learningforjustice.org/magazine/publications/social-justice-standards.

Leatham, K. R., & Peterson, B. E. (2010). Purposefully designing student teaching to focus on students' mathematical thinking. AMTE Monograph 7. In J. Luebeck & J. W. Lott (Eds.), *Mathematics teaching: Putting research into practice at all levels* (pp. 225–239). Association of Mathematics Teacher Educators.

Lewis, C. (2015). What is improvement science? Do we need it in education? *Educational Researcher*, *44*(1), 54–61.

Martin, W. G., Lawler, B. R., Lischka, A. E., & Smith, W. M. (Eds.), *The Mathematics Teacher Education Partnership: The power of a networked improvement community to transform secondary mathematics teacher preparation*. Information Age Publishing.

Mau, S. (2013). Letter from the editor: Better together? Considering paired-placements for student teaching. *School Science and Mathematics*, *113*(2), 53–55.

National Council of Teachers of Mathematics. (2014). *Principles to actions: Ensuring mathematical success for all.*

National Council of Supervisors of Mathematics & TODOS: Mathematics for ALL. (2016). *Mathematics education through the lens of social justice: Acknowledgment, actions, and accountability.* https://www.todos-math.org/socialjustice.

Paris, D. (2016). *On educating culturally sustaining teachers* [Teaching Works Unpublished manuscript, University of Michigan]. Ann Arbor, MI.

Rubel, L. (2017). Equity-directed instructional practices. *Journal of Urban Mathematics Education, 10*(2), 66–105.

Sears, R., Zelkowski, J., Edwards, B. P., & Castro-Minnehan, C. (2020). D*eveloping Infrastructure to Support Teacher Candidates during Emergency Remote Clinical Experiences.* Teaching and Learning Faculty Publications. 671. https://scholarcommons.usf.edu/tal_facpub/671

Smith, M., & Stein, M. K. (2011). *5 practices for orchestrating productive mathematics discussions.* National Council of Teachers of Mathematics.

Stoll, L., Bolam, R., McMahon, A., Wallace, M., & Thomas, S. (2006). Professional learning communities: A review of the literature. *Journal of Educational Change, 7*(4), 221–258.

Strutchens, M., Erickson, D., Sears, R., & Zelkowski, J. (2020). Clinical experiences for secondary mathematics teacher candidates. In W. G. Martin, B. R. Lawler, A. E. Lischka, & W. M. Smith (Eds.), *The mathematics teacher education partnership: The power of a networked improvement community to transform secondary mathematics teacher preparation* (pp. 179–198). Information Age Publishing.

Turner, E. E., Foote, M. Q., Stoehr, K. J., McDuffie, A. R., Aguirre, J. M., Bartell, T. G., & Drake, C. (2016). Learning to leverage children's multiple mathematical knowledge bases in mathematics instruction. *Journal of Urban Mathematics Education, 9*(1), 48–78.

Wilson, S. M., Floden, R. E., & Ferrini-Mundy, J. (2001). *Teacher preparation research: Current knowledge, gaps and recommendations.* A Research Report Prepared for the Department of Education and the Office for Educational Research and Improvement by the Center for the Study of Teaching and Policy in Collaboration with Michigan State University.

Zelditch, M., Jr. (2001). Theories of legitimacy. In J. T. Jost & B. Major (Eds.), *The psychology of legitimacy: Emerging perspectives on ideology, justice, and intergroup relations* (pp. 33–53). Cambridge University Press.

APPENDIX A

Interview Questions for Teachers who Experienced Paired Placement as Undergraduates

1. Could you briefly share with us your professional career as a mathematics educator, including how many years you have been teaching, where you have taught, and what you have taught?

2. What are attributes of the paired-placement model that contribute to successes as a professional educator?

3. How has the paired-placement model prepared you for any leadership responsibilities you have undertaken as a professional educator?

4. What are attributes of the paired-placement model that contribute to challenges you have faced as a professional educator?

5. How did the paired-placement internship prepare you to work and collaborate with other teachers to support student learning?

6. In what ways did the paired-placement internship enable you to effectively implement the eight mathematical teaching practices equitably?

7. How did the paired-placement internship prepare you to take risks and try new teaching approaches in your mathematics classroom?

8. Now that you have been teaching for years, what would you say are the components of the paired-placement internship that have positively impacted your current teaching practice?

9. Tell me about a time in your teaching career so far where you felt your experiences in the paired-placement internship impacted your actions?

NOTE

1. According to Dill and Friedman (1979), innovation is "the process of deliberately importing across organizational boundaries an identifiable package of technological information and putting this information to use in the activities the organization undertakes" (p. 414).

CHAPTER 17

A SIGNATURE PEDAGOGY

Empowerment Through Embedded Methods Courses

**Rachelle Curcio, Eliza Braden, Catherine Compton-Lilly,
Michele Myers, and Beth White**
University of South Carolina

ABSTRACT

There is widespread agreement that clinical practice should serve as a central design component for teacher preparation programs. In this chapter, we explore the many ways that the elementary education program at the University of South Carolina (UofSC) realizes the call of the 2018 AACTE Clinical Practice Commission Report. Specifically, we explore how the design of our program and its signature pedagogy—embedded methods courses and sustained attention to student diversity—empower teacher candidates to be active participants in the development of knowledge, skills, and dispositions for 21st century teaching. First, we share specifics about our elementary program and the professional development schools network it is situated within. Then, we delve into the design of the UofSC elementary embedded methods course model. Finally, we share findings from a collaborative interview-based study that explored recent alumni perceptions of the influence embedded

Preparing Quality Teachers:
Advances in Clinical Practice, pp. 381–396
Copyright © 2022 by Information Age Publishing
www.infoagepub.com

methods courses had on their teaching in schools, with specific emphasis their ability to serve children from a wide range of cultural and experiential backgrounds.

INTRODUCTION

In 2005, Shulman articulated the need for signature pedagogies related to the preparation of professionals—including educators. Signature pedagogies "are the forms of instruction that leap to mind when we first think about the preparation of members of particular professions" (p. 52). For the past 14 years, educators at the University of South Carolina (UofSC) have worked to create a set of educational experiences that exemplify high-quality elementary teacher education; the work is collaborative, intentional, and student-centered. It is no surprise that this model—deeply rooted in teacher education scholarship—simultaneously reflects the 2018 Report of the AACTE Clinical Practice Commission, *A Pivot Toward Clinical Practice, Its Lexicon, and the Renewal of Educator Preparation*. Specifically, this report calls for clinical practice to "serve as the central framework through which all teacher preparation programming is conceptualized and designed" (p. 14). Moreover, it has been posited that for teacher preparation to provide authentic interactive experiences in diverse learning environments, clinical practice is a "non-negotiable component of high-quality teacher preparation" (p. 14).

In this chapter, we explore the many ways that UofSC's elementary program realizes the call of the 2018 AACTE Report. Specifically, we explore how the elementary courses built around a signature pedagogy—embedded methods courses and sustained attention to student diversity—empower teacher candidates to be active participants in the development of knowledge, skills, and dispositions for 21st century teaching (AACTE, 2018).

Whereas our elementary program attends to multiple facets of AACTE's report (2018), our primary focus centers on how our clinical experiences embody the tenets of the "empowerment proclamation" (p. 31). In particular, an intentional "progression of embedded teaching and learning experiences" (p. 31) empower teacher candidates to better understand the cultural and contextual components of teaching through their involvement with children, rather than programs, from the onset of their preparation through graduation. In doing so, we empower teacher candidates to take active roles in embedded courses by fostering caring, culturally responsive relationships that enable them to be both lead learners and lead teachers.

We open with a review of literature that supports the development and continued refinement of our signature pedagogy—embedded methods courses and sustained attention to student diversity. We focus on literature directly connected to clinically-centered preparation and the need to cultivate care and a sense of critical consciousness within teacher candidates. We then describe our program and draw on data from an interview study to document how recent alumni view their preparation relative to their present work in the classroom. Finally, we conclude with some thoughts and implications for the field of teacher preparation at large.

A REVIEW OF LITERATURE

Darling-Hammond (2006) noted that the most powerful programs provide candidates extensive opportunities to observe and engage with expert models of practice throughout the duration of the program. As teacher preparation programs have been charged with placing clinical practice at its center (National Council for Accreditation of Teacher Education [NCATE], 2010), teacher education has embraced the cultivation of school-university partnerships that support clinical experiences throughout the entirety of a preparation program (AACTE, 2018; Darling-Hammond, 2006). Intentionally designed clinical experiences should regularly provide candidates opportunities to "reinforce, apply, and synthesize" (Darling-Hammond et al., 2005, p. 401) knowledge and pedagogy gained in coursework, while also obtaining an understanding of the logistical and relational demands of teaching (Feiman-Nemser, 2012). Essentially, purposeful participation in well-designed clinical experiences provides teacher candidates with guided practice in authentic classroom contexts.

Preparing teachers to meet the complexities of 21st century classrooms entail the development of the knowledge, skills, and dispositions needed to make informed decisions that contribute to the learning of all students (Bransford et al., 2005). However, preparation for the multitude of skills needed for classroom success cannot solely occur through university-based coursework. Teacher candidates' successful preparation requires consistent opportunities to enact content and pedagogical knowledge in authentic school-embedded settings (AACTE, 2018; NCATE, 2010). As the AACTE Clinical Practice Commission reported (2018), embedded experiences of this nature empower candidates to take active, not passive, roles as co-teachers, while authentically engaging them in the complexities of 21st century classrooms.

One pedagogical practice for centering clinical practice is the incorporation of embedded methods courses situated within school contexts. Methods courses situated at and within elementary schools and classrooms provide spaces to establish partnerships that enhance coherence and transform teacher preparation (Zeichner, 2010). These well-supervised, embedded experiences offer teacher candidates opportunities to "understand the problems of practice that currently face the profession" (AACTE, 2018, p. 8) in authentic settings under the guidance and support of university- and school-based teacher educators.

However, simply placing clinical practice at the center does not ensure an effective teacher preparation program; programs need to be well-designed and "sequenced to support candidates' developing knowledge and skill" (AACTE, 2018, p. 14). In particular, teacher educators should consider the role of care in developing critical consciousness in ways that empower candidates to be successful in complex and dynamic classroom structures. A review of the literature suggests that care is the foundation for relationships that makes all classroom experiences meaningful for both teachers and learners. It guides how educators instruct and manage students, organize the school day, and set policies for governance.

Care has many definitions. Thayer-Bacon (1997, 1998) offers a relational epistemological model in which caring relationships and student learning are connected. In this model, students are viewed holistically, and serious attention is given to their intellectual, emotional, social, and interactive needs. Other scholars demand culturally responsive care. For instance, Gay (2010) avers that culturally responsive care is an action driven, essential pillar when working with ethnically and linguistically diverse students. When describing care as action oriented, Gay asserts for, "a combination of concern, compassion, commitment, responsibility, and action ... manifested in the form of teacher attitudes, expectations, and behaviors about students' human value, intellectual capability, and performance responsibilities" (p. 48). In describing caring teachers, Ayers (2004) posits that caring teachers place students' interests and backgrounds at the center of all teaching and learning and draw on the students' individualized strengths when creating curriculum for and with them.

Connected to care is the need to cultivate teacher candidates' critical consciousness and agency. Teacher candidates need opportunities to examine institutions and structures that uphold racial oppression, and to challenge deficit orientations. According to Sharma and Lazar (2014), White monolingual teacher candidates' understandings of working with nondominant communities shifts when their coursework is grounded in pedagogies of discomfort. This work involves examining their own professional and personal values, beliefs, and assumptions and how these impact student learning. Additionally, candidates should be made aware on how to build upon the language and literacy resources of emergent bilingual students through course readings, field experiences, and videos. In particular, Landa and Stephens (2017) found that candidates can build cultural competence through engagements with children's literature. Whereas a lack of awareness can lead to apathy, when the fabric of coursework is steeped in developing critical cultural competence and embedded within authentic and diverse contexts, teacher candidates' attitudes, and dispositions shift.

THE ELEMENTARY EDUCATION PROGRAM AT UNIVERSITY OF SOUTH CAROLINA

As we hone in on the signature pedagogy that drives our elementary education program at UofSC, we review three essential programmatic features: (1) an active and supportive Professional Development School (PDS) network, (2) a strong team of educators deeply committed to teacher education, and (3) an established, yet evolving model of embedded methods courses.

An Active and Supportive Professional Development School Network

At UofSC the embedded elementary education coursework occurs within the structure of our PDS Network. The UofSC PDS Network was established in 1990 and is grounded in John Goodlad's (1994) scholarship related to educational renewal. Within the network, our 23 PDS school sites and newly established Professional Development School-District all maintain a commitment to cultivating spaces for "simultaneous and continuous renewal that benefits all stakeholders" (AACTE, 2018, p.18). According to the NCATE PDS Standards, we qualify as a leading PDS site; however, maintaining a PDS Network is an eternal process. New schools in our network are exploring what it means to be PDS sites and more established partnerships are building on past projects, nurturing emerging leaders, strengthening relationships, and encouraging novice educators to become active with PDS.

Across the PDS Network, university faculty are regularly called upon to observe novel instructional practices, provide professional development, facilitate study groups, gather data, model innovative teaching practices, and work with PK–12 students. From these reciprocal experiences, university faculty learn about challenges teachers face and mandates they endure. Additionally, faculty gain first-hand knowledge about novice teachers' challenges, thus enabling them to better craft coursework. Perhaps most importantly, our PDS partnerships provide candidates extensive opportunities to learn from authentic classroom experiences. In the elementary program, our embedded methods courses contribute to this learning.

A Commitment to Teacher Education

The work at UofSC is grounded in a long history of focused intentionality towards teacher education. We build our work on the shoulders of accomplished scholars (i.e., Field & Scoy, 2014; Hodges et al., 2017; Hodges & Mills, 2014) who have sustained the PDS network over time. For many years, UofSC did not have an undergraduate elementary education pathway. Since it was restablished in 2005, a set of embedded courses have become our signature pedagogy for teacher education.

In part, this signature pedagogy owes its existence to scholars who designed, implemented, and revised these practices. Whereas the methods courses in culturally sustaining pedagogy, math, science, and literacy all differ, they all hold central the tenets of kid-watching (Mills & O'Keefe, 2006) while authentically enacting theory into practice. In short, there is no single template for the embedded classes; but collaboration has allowed all members of the elementary team to learn from each other and our school-based colleagues to design and implement instruction that supports children's learning and reflects the demands of content areas. As Field and Van Scoy (2014) note, UofSC's on-site university courses enrich preservice teacher education classes through "demonstration lessons, small-group work, and guest lectures" (p. 438). These collaborations build efficacy and enthusiasm around practice.

Program innovations that made this work possible include regular meetings that address not just programmatic details, but also opportunities to talk about our work, align our courses so that they are manageable for our students, and collaboratively consider new possibilities. An essential element to our success has been the creation of clinical faculty roles; at UofSC clinical faculty are full members of the team who are recognized as expert teacher educators. They collaborate on research and publications while leading the team in issues related to teacher education.

Elementary Embedded Methods Course Model

Whereas we have crafted a unique model for embedded instruction, and while embedded experiences are the core of our signature pedagogy, they rest on a strong and enduring foundation of diversity and social justice. In fact, culturally sustaining pedagogy is the first fully-embedded course teacher candidates participate in—laying the groundwork for educating all students, particularly students of color and linguistically diverse students. The framework for the course requires our teacher candidates to critically exam themselves, their teaching, and society (Souto-Manning, 2013). In so doing, teacher candidates, explore their implicit and explicit biases, create curriculum to foreground ethnic groups who are often absent from textbooks, and have opportunities to read the world and take an active role in a cause that can benefit humanity. This embedded course provides teacher candidates with experiences to critically reflect and problematize challenges facing 21st century educators within authentic classroom settings alongside school- and university-based teacher educators.

After laying the foundation, our candidates participate in a sequence of embedded math, science, and literacy courses. The information that follows highlights how this model is enacted within our literacy courses (courses that all authors teach). First and foremost, each literacy course is situated at a local elementary school with instruction occurring dually in a "typical" college classroom setting (professor and teacher candidates) and within an elementary classroom. For one hour during each class, our candidates work with an elementary teacher and their students. Of note, we refer to the elementary children as *Small Teachers* because they provide our teacher candidates—whom we refer to as *Tall Teachers*—with valuable lessons about teaching, kidwatching, cultural competence, and building caring culturally responsive relationships. During this time in the elementary classroom, the course instructor and/or the classroom teacher demonstrates a mini-lesson with the children. Then, each *Tall Teacher* works with a *Small Teacher* for approximately thirty minutes, while collecting kidwatching data that will subsequently be used to plan curriculum for and with the child. During this instruction, the classroom teacher and course instructor provide in-action coaching to both *Small Teachers* and *Tall Teachers*.

After working with their *Small Teachers*, *Tall Teachers* reflect on their experiences, analyze student work, and discuss questions and experiences. Often, we collect writing samples, running reading records, videos, and other data for collaborative analysis. Since schools with diverse student populations are intentionally recruited as PDS schools, we know that our *Tall Teachers* will encounter *Small Teachers* who bring cultural, linguistic, and literacy differences.

Across the program, course instructors share a commitment to diversity (Zeichner, 2014; Zenkov & Pytash, 2018), and within our embedded literacy courses we challenge our candidates to consider linguistic and cultural differences that might affect how *Small Teachers* read and write their worlds. Specifically, we ask candidates to consider *Small Teachers'* negotiation of texts written in languages other than English, transnational literacy practices, use of native language to communicate in writing, different language structures that might affect reading, and language variations that might affect spelling.

At the end of each semester, candidates produce a case study in which they attend to their *Small Teachers'* literacy abilities and the funds of literacy knowledge they bring to schools (Moll, 1992). We attend to diversity not only when it appears on the syllabus, but also when *Tall Teachers* encounter it during their *Small Teacher* experiences. By participating in *Tall Teacher-Small Teacher* dyads, our students are exposed to a range of student diversity and are invited to reflect on the significance of that diversity as they collaborate with teacher educators (university- and school-based) who have a shared commitment to equity education.

METHODOLOGY

To learn more about the impact of our embedded methods courses on novice teachers, we designed a collaborative interview-based study. Our research questions were: (1) In what ways do alumni of the elementary education program believe that their experiences with the elementary education program and their embedded methods experiences inform their teaching in schools? and (2) In what ways do these experiences contribute to their ability to serve children from a wide range of cultural and experiential backgrounds?

Each of the five literacy instructors in the elementary program interviewed two former students to ascertain their perceptions about UofSC's elementary teacher preparation program; we recruited students who graduated from our programs within the last five years. This convenience sample of 10 alumni provides a lens into the experiences of students as they transition from teacher candidate to classroom teacher. As a research team, we crafted an interview protocol to explore the research questions we collectively raised about our program. Members of the research team met with alumni, and all interviews were audio recorded, transcribed in full, and uploaded to a shared online space.

To honor the perspectives and thoughts of our participants, we used grounded coding procedures (Saldaña, 2015; Strauss & Corbin, 1997). As we reread our interviews, we created grounded codes to represent segments of the transcripts. For each code, we created a name and a brief definition on a shared coding list. These codes were sorted relative to our research questions. During this process, we added codes, revised definitions, and then met to finalize the code list once all interviews had been individually coded. Once the code list was finalized, we each returned to our coded interviews and revised our coding in response to the changes made to the original code list; the finalized code list is presented in Appendix A.

After confirming the finalized code list, each author sorted their data by code. We then collaboratively read the data and discussed strong themes, surprises, apparently influential aspects of our program, and aspects of the program that were not discussed. In addition, we identified further questions and methodologies we might use to extend our work as we continue to reflect on and revise our signature pedagogy. Finally, we identified the salient themes that emerged from the data. These themes include: (1) course connections, (2) reflections on self and knowing, and (3) reservations and fear.

EMBEDDED METHODS COURSES: AN EMPOWERING PEDAGOGY

Below we present the themes collectively identified through our respective interviews. These interviews asked students to reflect back upon their experiences within the elementary program and to consider how these experiences connected to teaching and learning in their classrooms. In particular, we highlight the connections made between embedded teaching experiences to the ability to seek solutions, while striving to create equitable opportunities for all children to learn.

Course Connections: Insights and Influences

As alumni reflected on their elementary program experiences, they acknowledged professional impact from embedded courses and the professors and coaching teachers connected to these courses. Alumni highlighted *Small Teacher-Tall Teacher* dyads, feedback in the midst of teaching, and exposure to diverse classrooms in diverse schools. Additionally, whereas we primarily focused on literacy, alumni described the embedded courses' cumulative impact on gaining essential content and pedagogy across all content areas. The following notes the influence of consistent classroom immersion:

> It felt like we were actually able to live the experiences and grow. And I feel like we were able to grow before a lot of people figure out the things we figured out [our] junior and senior year during their first year of teaching. I think about just some of the things I see other people struggling with, I'm like, "I just ..." I felt so prepared with certain things because we were constantly in schools and working with teachers, not just watching them, working with them.

Alumni were empowered by embedded courses. Immersion in classrooms while learning theory and methodologies afforded these graduates opportunities to learn how to teach while actually teaching children. As candidates, they learned to teach by observing effective teachers who were carefully and intentionally selected for their aligned philosophical beliefs about teaching and learning.

In particular, alumni reflected on specific content knowledge and pedagogy gained from embedded experiences, and how they continue to draw on this knowledge to inform classroom instruction. From adapting kid-watching processes to referencing strategies for English-language learner students, alumni explicitly shared experiences and resources from their embedded courses. For example, several alumni noted their use of children's literature—a topic discussed in the literacy and culturally sustaining pedagogy courses. One alumnus reported "using children's literature as a responsive and reflective tool … to reach all of your readers and improve comprehension with intensive and extensive reading through specifically chosen children's books, you know the whole windows and mirrors thing." This alumnus, like others, realized that books are a platform to draw on students' strengths and center their lives in the classroom.

Other teachers noted the influence embedded experiences had on developing their knowledge about working with students from varying cultural and linguistic backgrounds. Alumni discussed getting to know students on multiple levels and the importance of coursework in grounding them "in intentionally planning instruction" and looking at what "students CAN do and building off of that." When reflecting on coursework, alumni often referenced the "multicultural education course" they engaged in and noted how this experience helped them to realize "that children come to school with that invisible backpack," and may have "a lot of things in their culture, that I am not aware of, because I didn't grow up in that culture." When asked how course participation assisted in learning about students' backgrounds one participant shared:

> The embedded courses helped me … I think it was because we were at so many different schools. It is not like we were at one school for all of the methods. And, we didn't just stick to one district, we didn't just stick to one school. In Columbia, there are so many different people, cultures, socio-economic status, everything. So, I think by going to the different schools and the one-on-one experiences with different students it gave you a little bit of everything. You had to learn the strategies to differentiate and it just provided a lot of differentiation for me as a learner.

These comments acknowledge the influence of embedded courses in preparing alumni to teach diverse student populations. All alumni described the importance of intentionality when creating spaces and curricula reflective of the children in their classrooms. Additionally, while they recognized that working with diverse student populations can be overwhelming, they referenced their ability to draw on coursework that grounded them in best practices and assisted them with feeling "more confident" about doing "what's right for my kids."

Reflections on Self and Knowing: A Sense of Empowerment

As alumni reflected on specific content and pedagogical insights gained from embedded courses, they also spoke about lessons learned and their continued application of this knowledge to act as culturally responsive advocates. In particular, several alumni discussed the ongoing need to rethink their own assumptions and push themselves to be open to new possibilities—a focus we intentionally reiterated. Our alumni had clear views on what teachers needed to know and recognized the need to appreciate and embrace diversity within their classrooms. Alumni consistently reflected on situations in which they applied coursework knowledge to advocate for a student, and as one graduate shared, "A kid might do something, that you might determine is being defiant, or maybe being a behavior issue, when sometimes it's linked to their culture."

Alumni presented an awareness of the diversity of their students and understood the importance of keeping an open mind. They described cultural, interactional, religious, and political differences as affecting what happens in classrooms. As an example, the following were shared:

Abby: In my classroom, the widest gap I experience is the different economic backgrounds from which students come. *Having grown up in the community* that I teach [in], this was the most surprising [thing] to me. There is also a lot of variety in the different family structures, including married parents, divorced parents, [and] students who live with grandparents.

Katie: *Growing up the way I did,* we were always taught when you talked with an adult you kept eye contact with that person. But I have taught different groups in the past, and they don't make eye contact because that's considered disrespect. So, I think just being a teacher, you have to understand and appreciate those cultures so that you can accommodate them in the classroom.

These comments reflect alumni's recognition that their students' experiences are different from their own. For example, Abby focused on children's economic backgrounds and family structures. She realized that even though she grew up in the same community where she now teaches, she continues to learn about the families and the children. These alumni shared an awareness of the limits of their own experiences and the need to remain open to alternative ways of being. However, they actively sought to identify assets and authentically connect to students. For example, Vivian described how her experiences as an emerging bilingual learner in schools informs her work with children, "So, they have the same struggles as I did.... They find it hilarious their teacher also struggled or is still struggling with it. So, we struggle with it together. I just try to have a connection."

Moreover, alumni described embedded courses as spaces where these important lessons were learned. Sandra shared the following when reflecting on her literacy courses:

> Here are twenty-five kids [you have to] get to know them all. So, starting with here's one or two or three and let me teach you how to build this relationship and let me teach you how to foster this [understanding]. To have that before you get plopped down into a school, where you are the teacher, where you are in charge of getting to know all of them. It was a good stepping stone.

The "stepping stone" provided by embedded courses provided alumni with confidence and a sense of empowerment. Alumni described a "sense of advocacy for the practices" learned within embedded courses and appreciated their "familiarity" with the resources they encountered in schools. This knowledge and familiarity led to confidence in their ability to make instructional decisions, connect to students' cultural backgrounds, and to learn and grow alongside their students. As Natasha shared:

> I am really conscious about it, because most of my kids don't look like me. I don't just want to put things in their head. I want to learn with them and grow with them. Think about what we don't know. Who'd voices did we not here? Can we amplify the stories to make them more powerful? My life experiences and my view is not reality for everybody. Allowing others to share their voice and lived experiences. That is something I got from my courses at UofSC.

Reservations and Fear

Whereas our alumni reported being empowered to make informed decisions on behalf of students, our interviews revealed reservations and fear when addressing equity and social justice. While aware of the importance of sociopolitical issues, Vivian shared her feelings as an English-Spanish speaking Hispanic teacher:

> Last year, it was my first year and there was this clear divide. My class was, I probably would say strongly opinionated. I wasn't really sure if this was because they felt this way or they were repeating from what their parents said. This year I feel like my class is strongly opinionated, but because they've been affected personally, they understood to a certain capacity, what's happening. I was scared last year to use my language and I didn't want to make anything worse.

As Vivian illustrated, alumni were aware of students' opinions about socio-political topics, but admitted that fear served as a barrier to engagement. They discussed their fear of repercussions from parents, "not doing it right," and how fear resulted in not discussing issues at all. Like teachers interviewed by Milner (2017), our teachers also feared how parents might consider engaging in political discussions and discussions around race, as Vivian explained:

> I mean it's not just the kids, cause those kids go back to their families and that's I guess a fear of mine as well. Cause I've had opinionated parents.

Elizabeth also discussed discomfort with discussing controversial topics. However, it was knowledge from coursework that made these discussions a bit easier. When asked about connections between coursework and supporting social justice, she responded:

> I think that's exactly what it [the program] did. It helped me understand how to have that social justice piece without being afraid to talk about it, because I think before I was like ... I'm scared that I'm going to offend somebody. I don't want to upset anybody.

As expressed by these teachers, fear often comes from not wanting to offend parents or students. However, alumni were encouraged by the support received from courses steeped in social justice.

Alumni interviewed for this study displayed agency by working through their fears to serve their students. As one teacher advocated, "Invite kid's culture into the classroom. Having that relationship first before we plan curriculum. So, we know who our kids are.... If we don't understand how their life is, then we're not able to connect with them."

DISCUSSION AND IMPLICATIONS

We recognize our program has room to grow and we appreciate our alumni's input. When asked, our teachers were honest. There were still things they wanted and needed. Alumni wanted additional insight on connecting literacy with issues of social justice and equity, more diverse text sets to reflect the students in their classrooms, and tools and strategies focused on differentiating instruction to better meet students' varying literacy needs. However, while alumni continue to struggle with the perennial problems of meeting multiple student needs and wanting more knowledge, our students reported that they were "learning over time" and "figuring that stuff out"—presenting themselves as capable problem solvers who remain committed to continual learning.

Additionally, we realize we cannot prepare teachers for every challenge they will face, and unfortunately, there will always be issues that teachers encounter in schools that we cannot predict. Because the range of problematic school policies and practices defies our imaginations as teacher educators, our response must be a focus on children and their abilities to learn and thrive.

This is the contribution of our signature pedagogy—embedded methods courses and sustained attention to student diversity. Through embedded courses, teacher preparation programs can provide well-supervised settings for teacher candidates to authentically "*think* like" and "*act* as a teacher" ([Emphasis original] Darling-Hammond, 2006, p. 305). Moreover, when coupled with a curriculum that emphasizes cultivating care and critical consciousness, candidates are situated to not only grapple with the realities of 21st century classrooms, but to create and advocate for equitable experiences for all learners. Additionally, the ability to learn with and from children—our *Small Teachers*—provides extensive opportunities to actively learn alongside school- and university-based teacher educators all while becoming empowered novice teachers.

REFERENCES

American Association of Colleges for Teacher Education (AACTE). (2018). *A pivot toward clinical practice, its lexicon, and the renewal of educator preparation* (A Report of the AACTE Clinical Practice Commission).

Ayers, W. (2004). *Teaching towards freedom: Moral commitments and ethical actions in the classroom.* Beacon Press

Bransford, J., Derry, S., Berliner, D., & Hammerness, K. (with Beckett, K. L.). (2005). Theories of learning and their roles in teaching. In L. Darling-Hammond & Bransford (Eds.), *Preparing teachers for a changing world: What teachers should learn and be able to do* (pp. 40–87). John Wiley & Sons.

Darling-Hammond, L. (2006). Constructing 21st century teacher education. *Journal of Teacher Education, 57*(3), 300–314.

Darling-Hammond, L., Hammerness, K., Grossman, P., Rust, F., & Shulman, L. (2005). The design of teacher education programs. In L. Darling-Hammond & J. Bransford (Eds.), *Preparing teachers for a changing world: What all teachers should learn to be able to do* (pp. 390–440). Jossey-Bass.

Field, B. E., & Scoy, I. J. V. (2014). The challenges never stop! Two decades of reaching for the best in clinical practice. *Peabody Journal of Education, 89*(4), 436–452.

Feiman-Nemser, S. (2012). *Teachers as learners.* Harvard Education Press.

Gay, G. (2010). *Culturally responsive teaching: Theory, research, and practice* (2nd ed.). Teacher College Press.

Goodlad, J. (1994). *Educational renewal: Better teachers, better schools.* Jossey-Bass.

Hodges, T. E., & Mills, H. (2014). Embedded field experiences as professional apprenticeships. In K. Karp (Ed.), *Annual perspectives in mathematics education* (pp. 249–260). National Council of Teachers of Mathematics.

Hodges, T. E., Mills, H., Blackwell, B., Scott, J., & Somerall, S. (2017). Learning to theorize from practice: The power of embedded field experiences. In D. Polly & C. Martin (Eds.), *Handbook of research on teacher education and professional development* (pp. 34–47). IGI Global.

Landa, M. S., & Stephens, G. (2017). Promoting cultural competence in preservice teacher education through children's literature. *Issues in Teacher Education, 26*(1), 53–71.

Mills, H., & O'Keefe, Y. (2006, Fall). From kid watching to responsive teaching: Coaching readers during independent reading. *South Carolina English Teacher,* 5–12.

Milner, R. (2017). Race, talk, opportunity gaps, and curriculum shifts in (teacher) education. *Literacy Research: Theory, Methods, and Practice, 66,* 73–94.

Moll, L. C., Amanti, C., Neff, D., & Gonzalez, N. (1992). Funds of knowledge for teaching: Using a qualitative approach to connect homes and classrooms. *Theory into Practice, 31*(1), 132–141.

National Council for Accreditation of Teacher Education. (2010). *Transforming teacher education through clinical practice: A national strategy to prepare effective educator* [Blue Ribbon Report].

Saldaña, J. (2015). *The coding manual for qualitative researchers*. SAGE.

Sharma, S., & Lazar, A. (2014). Pedagogies of discomfort: Shifting preservice teachers' deficit orientations toward language and literacy resources of emergent bilingual students. *Advances in Research on Teaching, 21,* 3–29.

Shulman, L. S. (2005). Signature pedagogies in the professions. *Daedalus, 134*(3), 52–59.

Strauss, A., & Corbin, J. M. (1997). *Grounded theory in practice*. SAGE.

Souto-Manning, M. (2013). *Multicultural teaching in the early childhood classroom: Approaches, strategies, and tools, preschool-2nd grade.* Teachers College Press.

Thayer-Bacon, B. (1997). The nurturing of a relational epistemology. *Educational Theory, 47,* 239–260.

Thayer-Bacon, B. (1998). Identification of caring professors in teacher education programs. *ENCOUNTER: Education for Meaning and Social Justice, 11,* 32–41.

Zeichner, K. (2010). Rethinking the connections between campus courses and field experiences in college- and university-based teacher education. *Journal of Teacher Education, 61*(1–2), 89–99.

Zenkov, K., & Pytash, K. E. (Eds.). (2018). Critical, project-based clinical experiences: Their origins and their elements. In *Clinical Experiences in Teacher Preparation* (pp. 1–17). Routledge.

APPENDIX A

Influence of Embedded Courses on Development of Cultural and Contextual Knowledge of Teaching	
Code	Definition
Course Insights	Reports about what was learned through the embedded courses
Constructs	Specific constructs/metaphors related to diversity or teaching that might be traced to coursework
Advice	What participants believe that teachers need to know or understand
Self	Examples of self-reflection revealing the limits or benefits of the teacher's personal perspective and experiences
Controversy	Discussions of dealing with controversial/political information in classrooms

Influence of Embedded Classes on Current Classroom Practice	
Code	Definition
Drawing On	Descriptions of drawing on the cultural/experiential knowledge of children
Children	Descriptions of how working directly with children informed their teaching
Instructor	Descriptions of how having a content area faculty instructor in the embedded classrooms and/or classroom teacher informed their teaching
Wish	Wishes, hopes, and needs related to teaching and children
Advocacy	Comments related to advocacy and confidence in alumni's emerging expertise
Theory/Practice Alignment	Actual reference to practices they employ in their classrooms that have strong theoretical support
Networks of Support	Techniques and strategies teachers use to communicate with key stakeholders or get to know them beyond the school walls
Negotiating Policies and Practices	Reports of navigating policies and practices that do not align with beliefs about teaching

CHAPTER 18

PARTNERSHIP BETWEEN SCHOOL AND UNIVERSITY LEADERS FOR TEACHER PREPARATION

Lauren J. Gibbs
University of North Florida and Tiger Academy (Jacksonville)

Matthew Ohlson
University of North Florida

Easter Brown
Resident Clinical Faculty, Clay County District Schools

Shelley Lester
Resident Clinical Faculty, Clay County District Schools

Justin Faulkner
Orange Park Junior High School

Stephanie Jackson
Grove Park Elementary School

Clayton Anderson
Orange Park High School

Preparing Quality Teachers:
Advances in Clinical Practice, pp. 397–411
Copyright © 2022 by Information Age Publishing
www.infoagepub.com

ABSTRACT

Stakeholders in a university/district professional development school (PDS) partnership report here on the first year of the partnership. Key achievements included professional development of teacher candidates and mentor teachers, and positive external relations in the form of conference presentations, community outreach and media coverage. Important contributors to the success of the partnership were a shared mission and vision, a clear organizational structure, dedication to regular communication, and the development of trust.

INTRODUCTION

During the 2018–2019 school year, the University of North Florida (UNF) College of Education and Human Services (COEHS) implemented a strategic plan to increase the number of hours teacher candidates (university students enrolled in a student teaching clinical experience in a K–12 school) spend in clinical settings. In addition, UNF increased the amount of supervision, coaching, and job-embedded professional development teacher candidates receive from both university supervisors and mentor teachers. In order to effectively supervise, coach, and facilitate the professional development of teacher candidates, mentor teachers and university supervisors must come to a common understanding of what development of teacher candidates looks like and how to approach the work. This article describes how UNF and the Clay County District Schools are working together to ensure quality professional development of teachers across the Clay County Professional Development School (PDS) network as well as innovative practices that provide teacher candidates with optimal clinical experiences.

District leaders, PDS principals, mentor teachers, boundary-spanning educators, UNF faculty, and teacher candidates meet multiple times a month as a Community of Practice (CoP) focused on strengthening the PDS partnership and providing UNF teacher candidates with the best possible clinical experience. The goal of the district/university CoP is to create an environment within the three PDSs (elementary, junior high, and high schools) that is focused on the simultaneous and continuous renewal of all the stakeholders in the partnership (American Association of Colleges for Teacher Education [AACTE], 2018). This article highlights the importance of the collaboration between the school district and university in forming and sustaining clinical partnerships.

REVIEW OF LITERATURE (CONCEPTUAL FRAMEWORK)

Examining the PDS partnership between Clay County District Schools and UNF requires an understanding of the empirical literature including the history of and best practices in PDSs, CoPs, principals as instructional leaders, and boundary-spanning teacher educators. The complex nature of the interactions among the PDS stakeholders lies at the heart of the "close coupling of theoretical and practical preparation" (National Council for Accreditation of Teacher Education [NCATE], 2010) needed for effective teacher candidate learning and practice.

History and Standards for PDSs

Teacher preparation and education in America has long been scrutinized. The *Nation at Risk* report (National Commission on Excellence in Education, 1983) put a spotlight on public education in the United States. While the report included concerns regarding teacher preparation, it did not provide recommendations for institutions of higher education on how to improve teacher education. In 1983 the No Child Left Behind Act (No Child Left Behind, 1983) placed an emphasis on teacher preparation but offered no recommendations regarding clinical experience. In 2001 the NCATE addressed the need for clinical practice recommendations when they released standards for PDSs (NCATE, 2001). Their report outlined developmental guidelines so PDSs could self-assess where they were in their work and establish next steps to advance their practice.

In 2005, the National Association for Professional Development Schools (NAPDS) was established, and in 2008 its Executive Council issued a list of Nine Essentials for a PDS, including "a comprehensive mission that is broader in its outreach and scope than the mission of any partner and that furthers the education profession and its responsibility to advance equity within schools and, by potential extension, the broader community" and "a school-university culture committed to the preparation of future educators that embraces their active engagement in the school community" (NAPDS, 2008, p. 2).

In 2010 an NCATE Blue Ribbon Panel released "Transforming Teacher Education through Clinical Practice: A National Strategy to Prepare Effective Teachers." The panel identified 10 principles to guide the development of clinically-based teacher preparation programs (NCATE, 2010). The 10th principle emphasizes that "Strategic partnerships are imperative for powerful clinical preparation" (p. 6). In 2016, the Council for the Accreditation of Educator Preparation (CAEP, n.d.) became the sole entity for the accreditation of educator preparation providers, replacing

NCATE. CAEP Standard 2, Clinical Partnerships and Practice stipulates (2.1) "partners co-construct mutually beneficial P–12 school and community arrangements"; (2.2) "partners co-select, prepare, evaluate, support, and retain high-quality clinical educators"; and (2.3) "the provider works with partners to design clinical experiences of sufficient depth, breadth, diversity, coherence, and duration to ensure that candidates demonstrate their developing effectiveness and positive impact on all students' learning and development" (http://caepnet.org/standards/standard-2).

In 2018 the American Association of Colleges for Teacher Education's Clinical Practice Commission (AACTE CPC) issued "A Pivot toward Clinical Practice, Its Lexicon, and the Renewal of Educator Preparation." The report laid out ten Proclamations that provided a "thorough conceptual framework and explanation of clinical practice with recommendations for implementation" (AACTE, 2018, p. 3). Proclamation 4, "The Partnership Proclamation," establishes that "clinical partnerships are the foundation of highly effective clinical practice" (p. 21).

Thus, NAPDS, CAEP, and AACTE CPC have all identified effective partnerships between postsecondary and P–12 institutions as essential elements of PDS work.

CoPs

CoP refers to a "group of people who share a concern, a set of problems, or a passion about a topic and who deepen their knowledge and expertise in this area by interacting on an ongoing basis" (Wenger et al., 2002, p. 4). CoPs emerged from the business sector and were formed as a means to increase expertise and build new knowledge (Wenger, 1998). Membership may include individuals who are community members and not necessarily a part of the organization. Learning within a CoP happens as a result of that community and its interactions (Kennedy, 2005). Wenger (1998) outlined three fundamental structures for a CoP: domain, community, and practice. CoPs are grounded in the collaborative sharing of knowledge in order to improve practice. As used herein, the term CoP is used to describe the collaborative work of the university, school, and district leadership.

Principals as Instructional Leaders

Although each member of the CoP plays an important role in the success of the PDS partnership, the three PDS principals are pivotal in its success. Principals are the instructional leaders of the school: "Effective instructional leadership is embedded in school culture; it is expected and routinely delivered" (Blase & Blase, 1999, p. 368). Instructional leaders focus their work on the teaching and learning that takes place at the school (Neumerski, 2012). A principal may also be referred to as the "head learner" of the school, because s/he is asked to create a learning organization in which everyone in the school is continually developing and learning through collaborative and reciprocal interactions (Yendol-Hoppey & Dana, 2010). This move towards the principal as an instructional leader or head learner is evidenced by the more recent implementation of new evaluation systems that expect principals to have a deep understanding of quality instruction (Jerald, 2012). School systems require incoming principals to demonstrate their ability to "accurately observe lessons and provide feedback to teachers or use data on teacher and student performance to plan and deliver high-quality professional development for teachers" (Jerald, 2012, p. 6). Principals are expected to take on the responsibility for the learning that takes place within their schools. This puts them in a unique position to maximize the learning that takes place and gives them the opportunity to develop and change the schools within which they work (Mullen & Hutinger, 2008).

Clement and Vandenberghe (2001) conducted an extensive case study of two elementary schools. The researchers spent five weeks in each school and interviewed 23 teachers and both principals. The purpose of the research was to determine "how school leaders can influence teachers' professional development positively through the creation of workplace conditions" (Clement & Vandenberghe, 2001, p. 45). The researchers found that it is crucial for principals to establish collegial relationships with their teachers in order for professional development and learning to occur. The researchers also stated that learning opportunities for teachers during the workday were scarce and learning opportunities that did exist were often not supported by appropriate learning spaces. These research findings highlight the importance of principals not only creating conditions (e.g., collegial relationships) conducive to professional development but also ensuring that the necessary content, structures, and processes for that professional development are in place.

Blase and Blase (1999) examined more than 800 "teachers' perspectives on principals' everyday instructional leadership characteristics and the impact of those characteristics on teachers" (p. 349). Teachers completed open-ended questionnaires to describe in detail the characteristics of principals that enhanced their classroom instruction. Blase and Blase found that effective instructional leadership consisted of two themes: promoting reflection by talking with teachers and promoting professional growth. Principals promote teacher reflection by making suggestions, giving feedback, modeling, and giving praise.

> Principals promote teacher professional growth by emphasizing the study
> of teaching and learning; supporting collaboration among educators;
> developing coaching relationships among educators; encouraging and
> supporting redesign programs; applying the principles of adult learning,
> growth, and development to staff development; and implementing action
> research to inform instructional decision making. (p. 363)

Blase and Blase's findings support the PDS CoP as a form of professional
development for principals and teachers. Specifically, the PDS CoP incorporates collaboration, feedback, studying teaching and learning, and
coaching relationships.

Boundary-Spanning Teacher Educators

Burns and Baker (2016) found through a meta-analysis that titles for and
definitions of boundary spanners were both unclear and highly variable.
The authors concluded that a wide variety of words and definitions were
used to describe the boundary-spanning role in PDSs. The individuals who
assumed these roles could be either university-based or school-based, and
there was little guidance about the qualifications required to assume these
roles. The tasks in which these boundary spanners engaged was varied as
well. They were teachers, intern supervisors, collaborators, and community
outreach partners.

Stevens (1995, as cited in Many et al., 2012) defined boundary spanners as individuals who commute, both literally and figuratively, between
public schools and university boundaries. Collay (1995) and Sandholtz
and Finan (1998) wrote that boundary spanners play an important role by
understanding and interpreting differing perspectives while maintaining
and often creating school-university partnerships. Miller and Silvernail
(2005) stated that a boundary spanner with experience in one arena is in a
unique position to develop connections between the research-driven theoretical world and the practical craft knowledge world. Many et al. (2012)
articulated three main themes as they relate to the work of the boundary spanner: understanding the other; deconstructing traditional power
relationships through support of and dialogue with stakeholders across
contexts; and drawing on prior knowledge to shape engagement with colleagues in their new spaces.

The boundary-spanning educators involved in the Clay County PDS
CoP are the Resident Clinical Faculty (RCF) who work daily to bridge the
university work to the work of the K–12 schools. They move the PDS work
forward by communicating daily with both university faculty and district/
school leadership. In the UNF/Clay model of PDS, the boundary-spanning
educators (RCF) are district teachers selected by UNF and the district who

are employed by the district but whose salary is paid jointly by UNF and Clay County District Schools. They work with teacher candidates, school and district administrators, and university faculty and staff. The basic principles articulated in the work of Many et al. (2012) and described in the previous paragraph are foundational to how we have conceptualized the role of the boundary-spanning educators in this partnership.

STRUCTURES FOR COLLABORATION

During the 2018–19 school year, the UNF and Clay County District Schools expanded and strengthened a partnership that was established over 30 years ago. In the past, the partnership often primarily focused on a select few University faculty supervising teacher candidates and presenting to the district staff ways to improve teaching and learning practices. The partnership now includes the district PDS director, the PDS director and faculty in residence from UNF, principals from the three PDSs, RCFs, mentor teachers, and teacher candidates. The mission of the CoP partnership is to design and implement a mutually beneficial learning and leadership partnership between UNF and the Clay County District Schools. Its visions are to (1) impact student achievement and grow the teaching field through real world application; (2) support students, teachers, and teacher candidates towards success; and (3) engage teachers in their own personal and professional development.

Enacting a memorandum of understanding (MOU) and co-constructing a mission and vision for the work were important first steps. The MOU defines the selection, funding, and roles of the RCFs. They serve as a communication bridge and resource for teacher candidates, mentor teachers, school and district administrators, and university faculty and staff. The MOU also specifies the professional development benefits that accrue to the RCFs. The RCFs supervise teacher candidates, teach on-site courses, and provide academic coaching and professional development to mentor teachers.

During regular meetings of the CoP, discussion includes updates on teacher candidates and mentors, as well as on the professional development and coursework of the PDS teachers. This wide-ranging discussion allows all of the PDS partners to support the educators in the PDS network. Time is allowed for the various CoP participants to bring dilemmas to the group that may or may not relate specifically to PDS work.

The establishment of the partnership enabled and required a shift in the traditional teacher preparation model, moving away from a mere supervision process to meet the minimum state requirements and towards a coaching model that fostered an exchange of ideas and best practices between university and district educators.

The voices of the principal partners are captured in the following vignettes, written by the three Clay County PDS principals. They provide context and an account of their experiences as members of the PDS team, as well as more details about the day-to-day operation of the PDSs.

Grove Park Elementary School

Grove Park Elementary is a K–6 school with 484 students. Minority students account for 71% of the student body, of which 42% are African American, 16% Hispanic, and 11% multiracial. Grove Park is a Title I school, with 100% of students economically disadvantaged.

As a PDS, Grove Park has become a clinical lab for future educators from UNF's COEHS. Teacher candidates are paired with skilled mentor teachers who have been selected based on input from the principal and the RCF. The co-teaching model of our PDS framework casts the mentor teacher and teacher candidate as vital facilitators of learning. Through this collaborative framework, the students of Grove Park are offered more targeted, individualized, small group instruction by both the mentor teacher and the teacher candidate.

Over the course of the clinical field experience, the roles of the mentor teacher and teacher candidate evolve. In the first few weeks, the mentor teacher leads in planning lessons and models delivering instruction while the teacher candidate actively supports the teacher in facilitating planned lessons and working with individual or small groups of students. No more than a month into the field experience, planning becomes collaborative, and all lessons are co- taught. The teacher candidate gains insight into the mentor teacher's craft by engaging in observation and debrief conversations targeted at understanding the most effective classroom management strategies; why the mentor teacher delivers lessons using a specific framework; what authentic engagement looks and sounds like; and how data is used to make instructional decisions. At Grove Park, this process is much like an instructional coaching cycle in which the mentor teacher guides the teacher candidate. As the field experience progresses toward the end of the semester, the teacher candidate leads the planning and development of lessons and supports the mentor teacher who works with individual or small groups of students. The teacher candidate serves an integral role during school-based CoP sessions and becomes more of the instructional coach during this phase.

Being a PDS is mutually beneficial for the university and the school. While the foundation of the partnership is to prepare future educators, it also serves as a venue for professional development for Grove Park teachers. Currently five Grove Park teachers, along with 25 other Clay County PDS teachers, are pursuing their master's degrees from UNF. The first course in the program is teacher action research (inquiry). The five Grove Park teachers are working as their own CoP as they reflect on and problematize their practice. Two of the five are mentor teachers for the UNF teacher candidates; the other three plan to mentor teacher candidates in the future. The graduate coursework is designed to support the development of the teachers as mentors and as educators.

The UNF/Grove Park PDS partnership has generated positive press for Grove Park Elementary and the surrounding community. Located in an historically underserved community, Grove Park Elementary has been hard to staff and is often negatively represented in the media. Since Grove Park has become a partner in the PDS network, Clay County teachers want to work here, and the school has received positive exposure in school district media, local newspapers, and at a national conference.

Orange Park Junior High School

Built in 1976, Orange Park Junior High School (OPJH) serves 775 students of rich diversity. Our minority student rate is 66%; 26% of the student body is African American, 17% Hispanic, and 10% multi-racial. Of our students, 72% are classified as economically disadvantaged and 100% receive free breakfast and lunch.

In our first year as a PDS, we have seen tremendous benefits. Teacher attendance has risen by 25% and student attendance is over 95% daily. Our teachers are growing in their instructional practice as they work to mold educators in training from UNF. Teacher candidates first observe their assigned mentor teacher, then work towards collaboration through instructional planning and co-teaching. By working with our RCF and administrative team, OPJH teachers are learning how to provide feedback to teacher candidates as they to elevate the work in the classroom in the service of students' academic growth.

We are currently working hard to transform our school culture. As we move towards a student-centered school community, we see increasing buy-in from teachers, staff, and stakeholders. We communicate regularly with parents through our community newsletter that highlights student success, teacher practice, and instructional initiatives. The newsletter is also used as a way to highlight the PDS work at the school. In February 2020 the principal and RCF from OPJH attended the NAPDS conference in Atlanta. During the three-day conference, they had opportunities to work collaboratively with other administrators and boundary-spanning educators engaged in PDS work around the country. This experience has helped the OPJH team plan for upcoming PDS work.

Orange Park High School

Orange Park High School (OPHS) is often judged by its dated facilities and the fact that it is the second oldest school in the district. To truly understand OPH, people have to come inside and talk to the faculty, parents, and students. These conversations give a different understanding of what it means to be a Raider.

At OPHS, we have the opportunity to meet the needs of 1600 students. One of our greatest attributes is our diversity. With a 52 (White)/48% (minority) split and one of the largest Hispanic populations (22%) in the county, it is truly the melting pot of the district. Sixty-one percent of our students receive free and reduced-price lunch. Because of our students' life circumstances, OPHS faculty focus not only on making a difference in the education of the students but also on how to break down the barriers students face outside of school that often hinder their achievement.

Currently 16 OPHS teachers are enrolled in graduate level coursework at UNF. They are working on collaborative inquiries focused on meeting the diverse needs of OPHS students. Because of the PDS partnership, OPHS teachers are afforded the opportunity to receive a free master's degree that will improve their practice and consequently have a positive impact on student achievement. The graduate coursework has also encouraged the teachers to mentor UNF teacher candidates. Those who were initially hesitant have gained confidence in their ability to serve as mentors for beginning teachers.

RESULTS

During a recent CoP meeting, the Clay PDS partners reflected on what makes the UNF/Clay PDS partnership successful. The group identified six key achievements of the PDS partnership in the first year:

- The number of UNF teacher candidates placed in the Clay County PDS has more than doubled.
- All of the PDSs in Clay County have seen an increase in teacher professional development participation.
- Twenty-nine teachers from the three PDS schools described here are taking graduate level courses that will lead to a teacher

leadership certificate and master's degree in a curriculum and instruction area.

- Two of the three principals and both RCFs attended the 2020 NAPDS conference; one of the principals and the RCFs presented on the work at their schools. The principals and faculty in residence are scheduled to share the collaborative work of the UNF/Clay CoP, as well as learn from other universities and districts engaged in PDS work, at a principal leadership conference (FASA) in summer 2020.
- The Clay County PDS network has received positive publicity in local and district media.

    o https://www.oneclay.net/site/default.aspx?PageType=3&DomainID=4&ModuleInstanceID=7291&ViewID=6446EE88-D30C-497E-9316-3F8874B3E108&RenderLoc=0&FlexDataID=24970&PageID=1

    o https://www.jacksonville.com/opinion/20181125/guest-column-unf-is-developing-next-generation-of-educators

- The first annual PDS celebration acknowledged the work of the teacher candidates and mentor teachers.

The vignettes from the principals echo the key milestones identified by the CoP. Although each of the six milestones is important, the vehicle for moving all of the work forward has been communication. The collaborative CoP meetings that take place monthly and at times twice monthly, along with regular email and phone communication, allow the principals and PDS teams to act as critical friends as we collaboratively design the unique work of the Clay County PDS network. Trust and dedication to the work are important elements of a thriving PDS partnership, and because of our dedication to regular meetings and open lines of communication between the CoP partners, we have built trust that enables us to troubleshoot obstacles and dilemmas as they arise and move forward in a way that is respectful to all partners.

The establishment of this partnership offered professional growth opportunities for the district staff. Meetings facilitated the building of genuine relationships and trust that allowed the clinical work to move forward in an intentional and meaningful way and evolved the group into a true CoP. The mentor teachers benefitted from the new Clinical Educator master's program at UNF. In addition, the RCFs received free tuition to pursue doctoral degrees at UNF. The group attended the 2019 NAPDS conference as a PDS team, presented at FASA and Student Success conferences, and co-authored this article. The Clay County Assistant Principals engaged in a yearlong UNF Instructional Leadership professional development program. Culturally responsive practices were specifically addressed in both leadership courses at UNF (taken by teachers and RCFs), which carried over to their work with teacher candidates. The partnership culminated with an Inquiry Showcase where participants spotlighted the processes and outcomes that emerged from what they learned because of this PDS partnership.

Other benefits to both UNF and the Clay County District Schools included a more authentic and practice-based teacher preparation program that was piloted in Clay County; more than doubling the number of UNF teacher candidates in the Clay County Schools; and increased hiring of UNF teacher candidates by Clay County after the completion of their internships. Clay County benefitted from community involvement and social justice work that was organized by the RCFs, including a "Walk of Understanding" in diverse neighborhoods within the greater community and cultural events at museums throughout Jacksonville.

DISCUSSION

Alignment With Standards

The UNF/Clay PDS partnership meets CAEP Standard 2 (Clinical Partnerships and Practice). It exemplifies Proclamation 4 (Partnership) outlined in the AACTE (2018) report through a dedicated CoP comprised of school and district leaders, RCFs, mentor teachers, university faculty, and teacher candidates.

The NAPDS (2008) Essentials have guided the work of the UNF and Clay County PDS partnership. Garin et al. (2018) constructed a crosswalk between the NAPDS Nine Essentials and the AACTE Proclamations, aligning the Partnership Proclamation (Proclamation 4) with most of the NAPDS Nine Essentials: 1 (comprehensive mission); 2 (school-university culture committed to the preparation of future educators); 4 (commitment to innovative and reflective practice); 6 (an articulation agreement); 7 (structure that allows all participants a forum); 8 (work by faculty across institutions); and 9 (shared resources and formal reward structures). The collaboration described herein incorporates all seven of these Essentials—thus, creating a truly mutually beneficial partnership.

Implications for Practice

The work of PDSs is complicated and nuanced; there is no right or wrong way to approach a PDS partnership. The people who make up the PDS network are truly the most important factor in determining the success of the partnership. It is important that each person's role within the PDS is collaboratively defined and consistently revisited.

Regular collaboration is essential in moving PDS work forward. That collaboration needs to include both university and district partners and must be built on a shared mission and vision, and on group norms that establish trust and promote collaboration. Other important elements of PDS partnerships include both participation of and buy-in by school and district leaders; having the right people in place; and continuous professional development that creates opportunities for all members of the PDS CoP.

CONCLUSION

Moving forward, the UNF/Clay PDS network will continue to meet monthly to support each other in the PDS work, set individual goals, and evaluate the current status of the partnership. Intentional data collection and systematic reflection are key next steps in the partnership. The members of the CoP will all receive copies of the texts that are being read by the PDS teachers who are taking graduate coursework so that the group can support and discuss the content with the PDS teachers.

Another goal of the CoP is to systematically involve the community in the PDS work. A Community Learning Exchange (Guajardo et al., 2016) is planned and will include university, district, school, and community members. One goal of the Community Learning Exchange is to have all community members collectively identify challenges and then develop solutions. The "Community" in a Community Learning Exchange goes beyond only those who live in a school neighborhood; it includes leaders, activists, educators, youth, and elders who work to better meet the needs of students while also supporting the development, growth, and happiness of all involved in equitable and just ways.

Although there are many areas in which the UNF/Clay PDS hopes to grow and improve, many accomplishments warrant recognition. Shared dedication to the PDS work on the part of both the university and district is imperative. When all partners are invested and dedicated, trust is built. This established trust can move the PDS work forward in a meaningful and systematic way.

REFERENCES

American Association of Colleges for Teacher Education. (2018). *A pivot toward clinical practice, its lexicon, and the renewal of teacher educator preparation: A report of the AACTE clinical practice commission*. https://secure.aacte.org/apps/rl/res_get. php?fid=3750&ref=rl

Blase, J. & Blase, J. (1999). Principals' instructional leadership and teacher development: Teachers' perspectives. *Educational Administration Quarterly, 35*(3), 349–378. https://doi.org/10.1177/0013161X99353003

Burns, R. W., & Baker, W. (2016). The boundary spanner in professional development schools: In search of common nomenclature. *School-University Partnerships, 9*(2), 28–39.

CAEP. (n.d.). *The CAEP standards.* http://caepnet.org/standards/introduction

Clement, M. & Vandenberghe, R. (2001). How school leaders can promote teachers' professional development. An account from the field. *School Leadership & Management, 21*(1), 43–57. https://doi.org/10.1080/13632430120033036

Collay, M. (1995) Creating a common ground: The facilitator's role in creating school-university partnerships. In H. G. Petrie (Ed.), *Professionalism, partnership, and power: Building professional development schools* (pp. 145–157). State University of New York Press.

Garin, E., Burns, R. W., & Polly, D. (2018). The intersection of the AACTE clinical practice report and the NAPDS nine essentials. *PDS Partners: Bridging Research to Practice, 13*(3), 5–7.

Guajardo, M.A., Guajardo, F., Janson, C., & Militello, M. (2016). *Reframing community partnerships in education: Uniting the power of the place and wisdom of people.* Routledge Taylor and Francis Group.

Jerald, C. (2012). *Leading for effective teaching: How school systems can support principal success.* Bill and Melinda Gates Foundation.

Kennedy, A. (2005). Models of continuing professional development: A framework for analysis. *Journal of In-service Education 31*(2), 235–250.

Many, J.E., Fisher, T. R., Ogletree, S., & Taylor, D. (2012, Fall). Crisscrossing the university and public-school contexts as professional development school boundary spanners. *Issues in Teacher Education, 21*(2),83–102.

Miller, L., & Silvernail, D. L. (2005). Wells Junior High School: Evolution of a professional development school. In L. Darling-Hammond (Ed.), *Professional development schools: Schools for developing a profession* (pp. 28–49). Teachers College Press.

Mullen, C. A., & Hutinger, J. L. (2008). The principal's role in fostering collaborative learning communities through faculty study group development. *Theory into Practice, 47*(4), 276–285. https://doi.org/10.1080/00405840802329136

National Association for Professional Development Schools. (2008). *The nine essentials of a professional development school.* https://napds.org/nine- essentials/

National Commission on Excellence in Education. (1983). *A nation at risk.* https://www2.ed.gov/pubs/NatAtRisk/appenda.html

National Council for Accreditation of Teacher Education. (2001). *Professional Development School Standards.* http://www.ncate.org/documents/pdsstandards.pdf

National Council for Accreditation of Teacher Education. (2010). *Transforming teacher education through clinical practice: A national strategy to prepare effective teachers. Report of the blue ribbon panel on clinical preparation and partnerships for improved student learning.* caepnet.org/~/media/Files/caep/accreditation-resources/blue-ribbon-panel.pdf [Document was not found on the web.]

No Child Left Behind. (2001). *United States Department of Education.* https://www2.ed.gov/policy/elsec/leg/esea02/index.html

Neumerski, C. M. (2012). Rethinking instructional leadership, a review: What do we know about principal, teacher, and coach instructional leadership, and where should we go from here. *Educational Administration Quarterly 49*(2), 310–347.

Sandholtz, J., & Finan, E. (1998). Blurring the boundaries to promote school/university partnerships. *Journal of Teacher Education, 49*(1), 13–25.

Wenger, E. (1998). *Learning, meaning and identity.* Cambridge University Press.

Wenger, E., McDermott, R., & Snyder, W. (2002). *Cultivating communities of practice.* Harvard Business School Press.

Yendol-Hoppey, D., & Dana, N. (2010). *Powerful professional development: Building expertise within the four walls of your school.* Corwin.

CHAPTER 19

PRACTICE-BASED INTEGRATED METHODS BLOCK

Reflecting on a Decade of Implementing an On-Site Cohort Model in a Teacher Preparation Program

Amy Good, Daniel M. Alston, Jean Vintinner, Ian Binns, Tracy Rock, and Michael Putman
UNC Charlotte

ABSTRACT

As part of our ongoing program development, UNC Charlotte restructured methods coursework and clinical experiences for undergraduate Elementary Education teacher candidates. University faculty worked with local elementary schools to create ongoing professional relationships meant to benefit all stakeholders, including teachers, elementary students, and our teacher candidates. This chapter describes how university faculty worked (a) collaboratively to create efficient, interdisciplinary instruction for methods clinical coursework, (b) with elementary schools to develop long-term clinical experience partnerships, (c) with elementary schools to create symbiotic, on-site

Preparing Quality Teachers:
Advances in Clinical Practice, pp. 413–428
Copyright © 2022 by Information Age Publishing
www.infoagepub.com
413

professional development opportunities, and (d) with practicing elementary teachers to create meaningful clinical experiences for teacher candidates.

"Adequate professional instruction of teachers is not exclusively theoretical, but involves a certain amount of practical work. The primary question as to the latter is the aim with which it shall be conducted" (Dewey, 1904).

Best practices for preparing educators has been debated for as long as there have been educators, as demonstrated by Dewey's (1904) quote. Nearly 12 years ago, teacher education programs were being called to action to transform the preparation of teachers through improved school-based clinical experiences. In November of 2010, the National Council for Accreditation of Teacher Education (NCATE) issued a Blue Ribbon Panel Report entitled, *Transforming teacher education through clinical practice: A national strategy to prepare effective teachers* (National Research Council, 2010). Changes were made and clinical partnerships with universities were formed. But there were so many different approaches and methods for clinical practice. Now, the AACTE, Clinical Practice Commission calls for a common definition for clinical practice, a common lexicon to support consistent discourse about clinical practice, and pathways through which to operationalize clinical practice (American Association of Colleges for Teacher Education, 2018).

The following chapter is a presentation of how one teacher education program created a more integrated and intense early clinical experience across the methods courses to provide a solid foundation of knowledge, skills, and attitudes necessary for continued growth and development of our teacher candidates. The elementary education program is part of a large, urban, southeastern United States university of over 25,000 students. In the second semester of the program, elementary education teacher candidates now take the majority of their core methods courses. Based on program evaluation data collected from graduates and school-based partners and employers, the yearlong internship is effective in providing sustained and meaningful clinical based experience; however, the data revealed that teacher candidate success could be enhanced with more systematic, coordinated, and intense *early* clinical experiences prior to the yearlong internship. Based on these program evaluation data, faculty desired to enhance our existing early clinical experiences, the opportunity provided by our state to "revision" our program, and the call to action from the field of teacher education, we began the work of transforming our early clinical experiences.

This chapter reviews our work with the program since 2010, where we restructured the early clinical experience of our teacher candidates as they take core methods courses in the second semester. We created an early clinical experience that was more intense, integrated, rigorous, and meaningful for teacher candidates and that required more engagement, monitoring, and collaboration among methods faculty and PK–6 schools. In this chapter, a synthesis of relevant literature is shared, a context for our program is discussed, narrative descriptions of two school partnerships are shared, and finally, the chapter concludes with implications.

CURRENT CONTEXT

As educational reform in the United States strives to move forward for current and future generations, it is important to pay attention to how the teachers who will shape and educate the minds of youth are prepared. The current educational climate, fueled by high-stakes testing and accountability, places precedence on the effectiveness of teachers and student achievement (Darling-Hammond, 2010). Innovative ways to prepare teachers are being developed to focus on the nation-wide teacher shortage (Pike & Carli, 2020). University-based teacher preparation programs produce 88% of teacher candidates (Snyder & Dillow, 2015) and are often scrutinized by researchers and other educational stakeholders. Stakeholders in education want to explore university-based teacher education programs to ascertain what features make them less or more effective at producing quality educators (Grossman et al., 2008; McDonald et al., 2013).

Given the careful examination of university-based teacher education programs, it is important to note the findings of researchers concerning the characteristics of these programs which assist in producing high quality teachers. One of the important characteristics is programs that have a clear vision of effective teaching and a solid grounding in effective pedagogical theories that are embedded throughout the program of study (Capraro et al., 2010). A second characteristic is making sure the educational curriculum is well built and structured (Darling-Hammond, 2000, 2006). A third important characteristic is making sure teacher candidates have the opportunity to engage in authentic field experiences for extended periods of time (Hammerness et al., 2005). A fourth characteristic is making sure there is alignment between what is learned in educational classes and what is experienced in field experiences. A fifth characteristic is making sure solid partnerships are formed between university faculty and K–12 school partners (Darling-Hammond, 2006, 2020). While these characteristics are positively impactful alone, the multiplicative impacts, when programs have several of these features, are even greater.

CHARACTERISTICS OF EFFECTIVE TEACHER EDUCATION PROGRAMS AND THE POWER OF INTEGRATION

It would seem logical, if the aforementioned characteristics are important, that they would be a part of all teacher preparation programs, but there are barriers to implementation (Knight et al., 2015). Despite the barriers that can prevent successful and sustaining change in teacher education programs, there are still charges to improve programs which prepare future teachers (AACTE, 2018; National Council for th Accreditation of Teacher Education [NCATE], 2010). Therefore, faculty of university-based teacher preparation programs are seeking to modify characteristics of their programs within the structural limitations they face.

Pedagogical Theory and Field Experience in Teacher Education Programs

Within university-based teacher preparation programs, foundational pedagogical theory is important in developing effective teachers (AACTE, 2018; Capraro et al., 2010). The authors of AACTE's Clinical Practice Commission recognize the importance of teaching educational theory and practice and included it as their second proclamation—The Pedagogy Proclamation (AACTE, 2018). Typically, candidates in teacher preparation programs receive adequate information about the theory of teaching (Lunenberg & Korthagen, 2009). Providing this knowledge assists teacher candidates in linking pedagogical theory with the content knowledge they are learning as they progress in their studies. Despite a solid foundation in pedagogical theory, teacher candidates often struggle to embrace these theories when they start teaching (Lunenberg & Korthagen, 2009). Lunenberg and Korthagen (2009) attribute this struggle to three factors: (1) Teacher candidates have prior knowledge and experiences about what teaching and learning looks, which can be a barrier to implementing new strategies they learn in their programs; (2) Pedagogical theories are not relevant to teacher candidates until they have experiences that connect to what they are learning; (3) There is limited utility of previous learned theory in complex, classroom situations when they need real-time assistance. Because of the phenomena of new teachers not engaging in the theory and practices they learned in their teacher preparation programs, researchers (e.g., Grossman et al., 2009) often criticize teacher preparation programs overly focused on the dissemination of pedagogical theory and content knowledge.

Field experience is another key characteristic in developing quality teachers and is the first proclamation—The Central Proclamation—in AACTE's Clinical Practice Commission (AACTE, 2018; Darling-Hammond,

2006). Field experiences are a way for candidates to put what they are learning into practice, as well as observe experienced teachers engage in instructional practices (Putman & Handler, 2016). NCATE (2008) defines field experiences as "school-based opportunities in which candidates may observe, assist, tutor, instruct, participate in service learning projects, or conduct applied research" (p. 38). Researchers (e.g., Ball & Forzani, 2009) encourage the intentional and consistent inclusion of field experiences—sometimes called clinical experiences—in teacher preparation programs because field experiences provide a low-stakes environment where candidates can engage in specific instructional strategies without paying attention to all classroom aspects. While field experiences and pedagogical theory are key features on their own, the purposeful combination of the two is influential in the growth of candidates' professional practice. Darling-Hammond (2006) spoke to the combination of theory and practice being the most impactful for producing high quality teachers. Proponents of practice-based teacher education also share the belief about the power of well-designed field experiences that link with pedagogical theory teacher candidates are learning (McDonald et al., 2013). Furthermore, researchers (e.g., Grossman & McDonald, 2008; Lampert & Graziani, 2009) advocate for extended and continuous field experiences throughout teacher preparation programs. These types of field experiences allow teacher candidates to have increased chances to implement instructional practices that align with the pedagogical theory they are learning in class.

Partnerships for Field Experiences

Without partnerships with K–12 schools, universities are limited in their ability to prepare teacher candidates. The authors of the Clinical Practice Commission include university and school partnerships as one of their 10 essential proclamations and tenets for highly effective clinical educator preparation. They call it "The Partnership Proclamation" (AACTE, 2018). Researchers note the significance of university and K–12 partners, as they provide teacher candidates with authentic spaces to practice what they are learning in their teacher preparation programs (Castle et al., 2006). When partnerships are formed between universities and K–12 schools it is important both share a desire for open communication and a vision for growth. Open communication increases the chance for professors and K–12 teachers and staff to be on a similar page regarding current teaching practices. This is critical as mismatched partnerships can lead to teacher candidates seeing instructional practices that contradict what they are learning in their university classes. This is problematic because often teacher candidates implement what they see in practice in schools rather than what they hear from professors in their classes (Moore, 2003; Putman, 2009).

This overlapping of domains is referred to as a "third space" which some scholars would describe as spaces which are "constructed through educational practices that provide and mediate rich learning opportunities within complex and often conflicting social contexts" (Martin et al., 2011, p. 300). Third spaces can be reconceptualized as places where all parties—in this instance university and school-based staff and educators—collaborate to develop experiences which lead to new and shared understandings (Martin et al., 2011; Zeichner, 2010). Teacher candidates exist within these third spaces created by university and school-based partnerships and can benefit from third spaces that are free from conflicting messages.

Having shared understandings for growth is important for universities and the schools they partner with as both parties can learn from the other and be influential in the preparation of teacher candidates. The authors of the Clinical Practice Commission refer to this idea of a third space which builds on and grows from university and school-based educators' shared understanding as "The Mutual Benefit Proclamation" (AACTE, 2018). It is important to note these synergistic third spaces between universities and schools take work. Boundary-spanning, when teacher educators teach their courses at the university and at PK–12 sites, is one of the important ingredients in developing partnerships that are grounded in shared understandings (Ikpeze et al., 2012).

INNOVATIVE APPROACHES TO CLINICAL PRACTICE

In 2008, our university was tasked with "revisioning" our undergraduate program for elementary education. A main goal of this effort was to increase the proficiency of our teacher candidates' in both pedagogical practice and content knowledge. The first step was to organize coursework in sequence, allowing courses to work as prerequisites developing schema, and eliminate the need for coursework to build background knowledge. This freed up some instructional time and allowed us to focus more on content and pedagogy. We integrated lesson planning into earlier coursework to allow methods classes to build on these skills in the context of specific subject matter. Our candidates have four semesters of education course work once they are admitted to the program, with the last two semesters devoted to final coursework and student teaching.

One benefit of this effort has been the ability to better anticipate course enrollments and offerings for both faculty and teacher candidates. Our department can anticipate the number of sections needed based on the number of candidates presently enrolled in the preceding coursework. Candidates can feel assured the courses they need will be offered as long as they follow the proper sequence.

During their second semester in the program, the Integrated Methods Block (IMB), our candidates take the majority of their content area methods coursework, including math for upper elementary grades, social studies, science, language arts with a focus on writing, and applied literacy methods. In an effort to provide knowledge of content and pedagogy efficiently, our faculty coordinates course topics and tries to model and implement interdisciplinary instruction whenever possible. There is a similar attitude towards clinical assignments; candidates create a portfolio of their work in classrooms and submit the entire assignment to all IMB faculty. This allowed us to eliminate redundant assignments, such as interviews of teachers and students, our teacher candidates had previously done for each course to create a context for clinical work and allowed time for more meaningful activities at school sites. We have compiled all the guidelines of this clinical work into a handbook that is shared with candidates, faculty, and partners at the clinical placement sites. In addition to presenting this information in our courses, we also have a collective, in-person orientation where our team of faculty review all expectations and begin the process of clinical placements.

Another issue we worked to overcome is the need for extended time in classrooms. Our teacher candidates needed more time to focus on lesson planning and implementation, building relationships with cooperating teachers and students, and getting the feel of the typical day of a teacher. Based on this need, teacher candidates are given two weeks off their IMB coursework and class meetings and are required to spend a minimum of 10 to 20 hours at their school placement site per IMB course. This results in teacher candidates spending, at a minimum, 40 to 60 hours out at their placements. By giving students two solid weeks in their assigned clinical classroom, they can spend entire school days at their placements and experience what it is like to arrive before the first bell and leave after kids are dismissed. This enables our teacher candidates to truly focus on the learning experiences they are obtaining in the schools instead of getting glimpses of a school day as occurs with the "get an hour here and an hour there" method. Further, our faculty coordinates with schools in our region to provide placements with schools and teachers who provide quality instruction. This increases the teacher candidates' learning as it allows candidates to experience classroom teaching that aligns with practices we discuss in coursework. Each IMB faculty member works as the liaison with the school so that we can meet with candidates, teachers, and administrators to answer questions, observe lessons, and develop a relationship with the school.

We are also able to gather information from schools about candidates' performance. For each lesson candidates teach, teachers offered feedback about their strengths and areas in which they could grow. In addition, teachers were asked a series of questions about candidates' dispositions towards students and teaching and their professional behavior. Each semester, we review this data to determine if any individuals need additional support before entering student teaching. Candidates who require support are asked to meet with faculty and develop a plan for growth and ask for any resources they need.

Over the course of a few semesters, we were pleased with the impact the intensive clinical had on our candidates. They left the experience with a better understanding of lesson planning, content knowledge, classroom management, and working in schools. Based on feedback from cooperating teachers, candidates, and our own experience, we realized that a greater amount of time in the classrooms could deepen this experience.

REFINING IDEAS INTO A NEW COHORT

In order to get candidates into classrooms earlier in the semester, we created a new model for clinical experiences requiring candidates to spend the same amount of time in classrooms but to spread this time over 10 weeks rather than the previously allotted two weeks. Starting the fourth or fifth week of school, candidates are now required to spend a minimum of five hours per week, all on one day, over the course of the semester. This allows more time between visits to reflect on classroom practices, develop lesson plans, gather resources, and build relationships with students and teachers.

In working with our IMB partner schools, we also noticed many amazing opportunities to work in concert with practices and initiatives at these sites. Schools providing STEM or STEAM programs offered opportunities for greater integration with science coursework. Schools providing intensive reading and writing development lent themselves to literacy coursework. We decided to consolidate our clinical placements to these schools and work closely with administration and teachers to align our instruction whenever possible. College faculty taught courses at these schools, and sometimes co-taught or modeled practices with classroom teachers to benefit both teacher candidates and elementary students. Candidates were able to see the practical application of course topics and interact with curriculum and materials in use at the school. Teacher candidates felt integrated into the school culture and all stakeholders worked as a team.

Long-Term Clinical Experience Partnership #1 (Panther STEM)

Panther STEM Elementary School is a Title 1 STEM magnet school that serves 470 students in kindergarten through fifth grade. Half of the students are from the surrounding neighborhood and the other half are from throughout the county. The enrollment by ethnicity is 36.6% White, 23.4% Hispanic, 22.1% African American, 12.1% Asian, 4.9% two or more ethnicities, and 0.9% American Indian. Our experience with this school started due to a relationship with the then STEM teacher, now STEM coach, Mrs. Jefferson. She worked with our candidates during their IMB semester prior to the development of our new cohort program. Our candidates always had high praise for the school. Many expressed interests in returning to the school for their student teaching experience and several hoped to eventually teach at the school after completing their programs. Panther STEM was a natural fit for our new cohort program.

As mentioned earlier, the cohort program incorporated a semester long clinical experience, methods courses meeting on-site, and close collaboration with our partners in the school. Our experiences with Panther STEM met all aspects of this program. Candidates were placed in this school for their clinical experience at the beginning of the semester and spent at least one day a week on-site. This was normal for all schools that participated in this cohort program. The main part that distinguished Panther STEM from other schools is the partnership we developed. The three times our methods courses met at Panther STEM were very different from our earlier experiences.

Our goal in working with Mrs. Jefferson was to make sure our on-site instruction was mutually beneficial. We did not want our methods instruction to just be what we normally did when at the university. In other words, our instruction had to be different. This included holding our classes in the STEM lab, observing classroom teachers, and meeting with the principal. All of this happened. What made this different from earlier experiences was how well our instruction integrated with what some of the teachers did at Panthers STEM. What follows is a brief description of what our candidates did during the three times our methods classes met at Panthers STEM.

Preparing for On-Site Class Visits. We believe it is important for teachers to be knowledgeable about the community that surrounds the school where they teach. Teachers should be sensitive to the (potential) differences that exist between themselves and the community and make efforts to learn more about the lives of their students outside of school. Such inquiry should be done with an open-mind and with an eye for the positive aspects of communities, rather than through a deficit-model (focusing solely on what the community lacks). A familiarity with the communities where students live can help teachers in several ways.

First, such knowledge can help teachers better identify, and become more sensitive to, the environments in which students spend the majority of their time—environments that may influence school learning. For example, learning that there are urban gardens developing throughout students' neighborhoods can help teachers realize how community members are both making use of land and meeting an economic need of the community. Or, learning that there is a scarcity of services—such as safe playgrounds—in a community; may cause teachers to be sensitive to students' need for outdoor play during the school day.

Second, a familiarity with the places and spaces students live can help teachers in planning big ideas, lessons, units, and homework assignments that, when relevant, reflect students' everyday worlds. For example, a government unit could include discussion of a local public issue of interest to students and their families. Third, teachers who know about the home communities of their students can begin to build meaningful home/school and community/school relationships. For example, local businesses and service-providers can become partners in school learning. In order to allow our candidates to experience the benefits of knowing the surrounding community of a school, we had them do a Community Mapping Assignment before they even stepped foot in the school. For this assignment, teacher candidates became visual sociologists, mapping out the social and historical geography of their placement school. This assignment had two purposes: (a) to raise levels of geographic consciousness about a school community; and (b) to report and analyze the social-cultural makeup of your school's community of students from various races, ethnicities, cultures, and backgrounds.

On-Site Class Visits. Once our candidates had an understanding of the community surrounding the school, we met at the school. Our first visit included an introduction to the school with a guided tour by Mrs. Jefferson. Candidates also met with the principal and some of our alumni who are now teachers at the school. Groups of candidates were sent to various classrooms to observe and learn about different reading instructional strategies. Additionally, during the time reserved for science methods instruction, Mrs. Jefferson and the course instructor set up six stations, each with a different instructional resource used with the elementary school students during their makerspace time. Our candidates were given tasks similar to the elementary students so they could learn how to use these different resources. We challenged them to learn how to use these resources and to reflect on how they could use them in their own instruction.

Our second meeting had some similarities to the first meeting in that our candidates visited various classrooms and met with the principal. For the science instruction, Mrs. Jefferson paired us with a fifth grade class during their technology class. The focus for this class was an introduction to coding. The technology instructor, Mrs. Adams, partnered up our candidates with the fifth grade students and had them work together in teams. It was one of the most beneficial experiences for our candidates.

As with the first two meetings, our third meeting visited various classrooms and met with the principal. This time, our candidates experienced a robotics lesson from Mrs. Adams. Although they were unable to work with fifth grade students during this experience, they did go through the same lesson and were given the same challenges that a fifth grade class experienced earlier in the week. This helped them to better understand what their future students may experience.

Long-Term Clinical Experience Partnership #2 (Knights Elementary)

Knights Elementary School is a public school that serves 811 students in grades PK, K–5 with a student-teacher ratio of 15 to 1. According to state test scores, 46% of students are at least proficient in math and 31% in reading. The enrollment by ethnicity is 4% White, 23% Hispanic, 64% African American, 6% Asian, 2% two or more ethnicities, and 1% American Indian.

Our experience with Knights Elementary School started because of a 12-year relationship with a principal, Mrs. Stone. She allowed us to have our own entrance to the school, parking next to the entrance, and our own room for our methods classes in the school. Mrs. Stone has always worked with our candidates and is currently one of our own doctoral candidates. All IMB faculty met with Mrs. Stone where we discussed the school calendar and how possible professional development would be a mutual part of this relationship. We planned to have teachers and professors deliver instruction together for both current teachers and teacher candidates.

On-Site Class Visits. The model for this clinical experience included our methods class meeting as normal and then classroom visits to see the theory, just discussed, in practice. For example, I introduced the concept of a morning meeting in order to set the classroom community in my social studies methods course. Then we walked down the halls to see the morning meeting in action in kindergarten and in Grade 2. We were fortunate to be able to do the same with writer's workshop.

One of the best features of the time at this school was the teacher candidates were able to see the whole day (bus drop off and pick up, transition times, recess, lockdown …) together, allowing for quality, real-time debrief and unpacking. These are things we can't do in a regular methods course. Our candidates were in pairs, and they were assigned to observe, plan, and practice teaching in the same classroom. The teachers who served as clinical educators also led professional seminars, along with Mrs. Stone. We had common reads with the clinical educators and plans for more common professional development.

Next Steps: Year-long Cohort Model

Because of the impact of the long-term clinical experience, we are now moving to place candidates with partner schools for an entire year. They will begin clinical work at these sites during their first semester in the elementary education program and continue at the site throughout their IMB semester. This long-term placement will allow for a deeper understanding of the school and eliminate any down time at the beginning of the IMB semester to arrange placements. To allow candidates diversity in their clinical experiences, these partner schools will be grouped by zones to allow candidates to gain some brief experiences at other schools in the zone while still maintaining their clinical placement. Adding this additional year-long placement, results in our candidates engaging in two year-long internships during their teacher preparation program and extends the intentionality and sustained clinical experiences that were possible in the final year of our teacher preparation program into the early clinical experiences as well.

IMPLICATIONS

Alignment With Clinical Experiences and High-Stakes Assessments

One of the challenges of teaching today is finding a way to prepare students for high-stakes assessments while providing meaningful and authentic instruction. In order to be granted licensure by the state, our candidates have to successfully complete an edTPA portfolio and pass two state licensure exams, one for literacy and one for math. Each of these assessments requires a great deal of preparation to become knowledgeable about the format and requirements of the evaluation tool itself rather than content. This knowledge is only loosely aligned with course topics, and it is difficult to sacrifice teaching content to explicitly support candidates' success on these tasks.

In creating an integrated approach to delivering content and clinical experiences, we have reclaimed a small bit of instructional time that can be used to help candidates translate coursework into tools to support their work on both edTPA and the exams. We have also worked to align some clinical assignments with edTPA expectations, such as planning a learning segment and recording lessons, to allow faculty to offer feedback on candidates' understanding of the portfolio requirements before completing this assessment independently in their final semester. By allowing candidates to work in classrooms, they are gaining a greater understanding of successful strategies and becoming a more effective practitioner.

Teacher Candidates Experiences With Best Practice

Elementary teacher candidates need to experience best practices in the classroom with all subjects. No longer can teacher education programs be a hierarchical structure with school systems, it needs to be democratic and inclusive (Zeichner, 2010). As mentioned, our faculty coordinates with school leaders in our region to provide placements with schools and teachers who provide quality instruction. This can be difficult because of the stereotypical disconnect between institutions of higher education and local schools. So far, our program allows candidates to experience teaching aligned with practices we discuss in coursework. Each IMB faculty member works as the liaison with the school so that we can meet with candidates, teachers, and administrators to answer questions, observe lessons, and develop a relationship with the school. As we continue this model, the partnership must be mutually beneficial, where the clinical instructors and school leaders agree on teaching methods and delivery. They will need to work together with the IMB university faculty. For example, this will only work when our faculty are seen in the schools delivering professional development and are respected as they are supporting classroom teachers, the school leaders and educators will value methods taught at the university and if there are differing opinions on reading, social studies, math, or science instruction, this can be discussed, and best practices can be agreed upon.

Future research is needed on the changing roles of all involved in teacher education and the preparation of teacher candidates, including supervisors, methods instructors, and adjuncts (Capello, 2020). If we are to prepare teacher candidates to be quality teachers, methods instructors can no longer be disconnected from the clinical classroom. No longer can teacher education programs be loosely connected to the schools, they will need to be "grown within" the schools where theory and practice can co-mingle (Gelfuso et al., 2015).

Integration of High-leverage Practices in Teacher Preparation Program

In addition to preparing our candidates for high-stakes assessments, there are other initiatives which impact what we teach in our classes. Specifically, the leadership in our college sees promise in developing faculty to teach high-leverage practices (HLPs) in our courses (Grossman et al., 2009). The focus on HLPs arises from an idea that teaching is complex and "unnatural" (Ball & Forzani, 2009) and developing as a teacher requires intricate work. Developing HLPs requires candidates watch, analyze, decompose, rehearse, and enact different core practices of teaching. By doing these processes, candidates are able to engage in approximations of practice which can lead to candidates having a firmer grasp on the intricacies of teaching (Grossman et al., 2009). Allowing candidates, the space to develop HLPs requires considerable time in programs to focus on the conceptual and practical aspects of complex teaching (McDonald et al., 2013). It also requires teacher candidates to have multiple opportunities to receive feedback on their approximations of practice. More research is needed on the integration of high-leverage practices in teacher preparation and frameworks have been provided we can incorporate (Burns et al., 2020).

By creating the long-term cohort model, we provided the time and opportunity for our candidates to rehearse and enact HLPs with multiple points for receiving feedback. Not only were candidates able to receive feedback from their cooperating teacher, but they were also able to receive feedback from university professors who were teaching and spending time at the long-term cohort sites. We feel there is still untapped potential, regarding the long-term cohort model and developing candidates' abilities to implement HLPs. We look forward to exploring more ways to make the long-term cohort model benefit ourselves, our candidates and the school leaders and teachers who partner with us.

REFERENCES

American Association of Colleges for Teacher Education. (2018). *A pivot toward clinical practice, its lexicon, and the renewal of educator preparation: A report of the AACTE Clinical Practice Commission.*

Ball, D. L., & Forzani, F. M. (2009). The work of teaching and the challenge of teacher education. *Journal of Teacher Education, 60,* 497–511.

Burns, R. W., Jacobs, J., & Yendol-Hoppey, D. (2020). A framework for naming the scope and nature of teacher candidate supervision in clinically-based teacher preparation: Tasks, high-leverage practices, and pedagogical routines of practice. *The Teacher Educator, 55*(2), 214–238.

Capello, S. (2020). Reexamining faculty roles in the supervision of pre-service teachers: Responding to the call for clinically-rich teacher education. *Journal of Educational Supervision, 3*(3), 18.

Capraro, M. M., Capraro, R. M., & Helfeldt, J. (2010). Do differing types of field experiences make a difference in teacher candidates' perceived level of competence? *Teacher Education Quarterly, 37*(1), 131–154.

Castle, S., Fox, R., & O'Hanlan Souder, K. (2006). Do professional development schools (PDSs) make a difference? A comparative study of PDS and non-PDS teacher candidates. *Journal of Teacher Education, 57,* 65–80. https://doi.org/10.1177/0022487105284211

Darling-Hammond, L. (2000). How teacher education matters. *Journal of Teacher Education, 51*(3), 166-173.

Darling-Hammond, L. (2006). Constructing 21st-century teacher education. *Journal of Teacher Education, 57*(3), 300–314.

Darling-Hammond, L. (2010). Teacher education and the American future. *Journal of Teacher Education, 61*(1-2), 35–47.

Darling-Hammond, L. (2020). Accountability in teacher education. *Action in Teacher Education, 42*(1), 60–71.

Dewey, J. (1904). The relation of theory to practice in education. In C. A. McMurry (Ed.), *The third yearbook of the National Society for the Scientific Study of Education* (pp. 9–30). The University of Chicago Press.

Gelfuso, A., Dennis, D. V., & Parker, A. (2015). Turning teacher education upside down: Enacting the inversion of teacher preparation through the symbiotic relationship of theory and practice. *Professional Educator, 39*(2), 2.

Grossman, P., Hammerness, K., & McDonald, M. (2009). Redefining teaching, re-imagining teacher education. *Teachers and Teaching: theory and practice, 15*(2), 273–289.

Hammerness, K., Darling-Hammond, L., Bransford, J., Berliner, D., Cochran-Smith, M., McDonald, M., & Zeichner, K. (2005). *How teachers learn and develop. Preparing teachers for a changing world: What teachers should learn and be able to do.* John Wiley & Sons.

Ikpeze, C. H., Broikou, K. A., Hildenbrand, S., & Gladstone-Brown, W. (2012). PDS collaboration as third space: An analysis of the quality of learning experiences in a PDS partnership. *Studying Teacher Education, 8*(3), 275–288.

Knight, S. L., Lloyd, G. M., Arbaugh, F., Gamson, D., McDonald, S. P., Nolan, J., & Whitney, A. E. (2015). Reconceptualizing teacher quality to inform pre-service and inservice professional development. *Journal of Teacher Education, 66*, 105–108.

Lampert, M., & Graziani, F. (2009). Instructional activities as a tool for teachers' and teacher educators' learning. *Elementary School Journal, 109*(5), 491–509. https://doi.org/10.1086/596998

Lunenberg, M., & Korthagen, F. (2009). Experience, theory, and practical wisdom in teaching and teacher education. *Teachers and Teaching: Theory and Practice, 15*(2), 225–240.

Martin, S. D., Snow, J. L., & Franklin Torrez, C. A. (2011). Navigating the terrain of third space: Tensions with/in relationships in school-university partnerships. *Journal of Teacher Education, 62*(3), 299–311.

McDonald, M., Kazemi, E., & Kavanagh, S. (2013). Core practices and pedagogies of teacher education: A call for a common language and collective activity. *Journal of Teacher Education, 64*(5), 378–386.

Moore, R. (2003). Reexamining the field experiences of preservice teachers. *Journal of Teacher Education, 54*, 31–42. https://doi.org/10.1177/0022487102238656

National Council for the Accreditation of Teacher Education. (2010). *Transforming teacher education through clinical practice: A national strategy to prepare effective teachers* (A report of the Blue Ribbon Panel on Clinical Preparation and Part-nership for Improved Student Learning).

Pike, L., & Carli, M. (2020). Leveraging best practice in teacher residency to enhance teacher preparation. *SRATE Journal, 29*(2), 2.

Putman, S. M. (2009). Grappling with classroom management: The orientations of preservice teachers and impact of student teaching. *The Teacher Educator, 44*, 232–247. https://doi.org/10.1080/08878730903180226

Putman, S. M., & Handler, L. K. (2016). Multi-semester community building in higher education: Examining the impact on teacher education candidates' development and teaching self-efficacy. In T. M. Petty, A. Good, & S. M. Putman (Eds.), *Handbook of research on professional development for quality teaching and learning* (pp. 346–369). IGI Global.

Snyder, T., & Dillow, S. (2015). *Digest of Education Statistics 2013* (NCES 2015-011). National Center for Education Statistics, Institute of Education Sciences, U.S. Department of Education. Washington, DC.

Zeichner, K. (2010). Rethinking the connections between campus courses and field experiences in college-and university-based teacher education. *Journal of Teacher Education*, *61*(1–2), 89–99.

CHAPTER 20

DEVELOPING A PRACTICUM MODEL THROUGH A DEMOCRATIC PROCESS

Faculty, Teachers, and Teacher Candidates Share Their Views and Experiences

**Carol Rees, Rupinder Deol Kaur, Beverly Ruberg,
Magdalena Maslowski, Brendon Bauhuis**
Thompson Rivers University

Grady Sjokvist, and Danielle Livingstone
Kamloops Thompson School District

ABSTRACT

This chapter developed from two points in the American Association of Colleges for Teacher Education [AACTE] (2018) report. The first point is that "local context matters when considering how to best operationalize clinical practice" (p. 4) and the second point is that there needs to be a "shared responsibility for teacher learning and development ... by university [and] school" (p. 35). The theoretical foundation of our work builds upon Zeichner

Preparing Quality Teachers:
Advances in Clinical Practice, pp. 429–458
Copyright © 2022 by Information Age Publishing
www.infoagepub.com

et al. (2015) who considered that if we are preparing teachers for a democratic society, we need to use a democratic process to get us there. We need to build our teacher education programs through a process that is itself democratic. We need the voices of teacher candidates, teacher mentors, university faculty and community members to be considered as having equitable value. This chapter shares the perspectives of teacher candidates, teacher mentors and university faculty who are involved in designing and piloting a co-teaching practicum model for a particular local context, a teacher education program for secondary teachers of science and mathematics. We share our process, our achievements, our difficulties, and our hopes for the future. The practicum experiences described overlapped the beginning of the COVID-19 pandemic and so we also share some experiences of co-teaching when practicum went online.

INTRODUCTION

Over the past decade we have seen a "turn" towards a more central role for practicum experiences (clinical practice) in initial teacher education (AACTE, 2018; Mattson et al., 2011). Evidence for the need for this shift, and a focus on what the practicum should include for the development of quality teachers, can be seen in studies from the United Kingdom (e.g., Burn & Mutton, 2015); Australia and Europe (Mattson et al., 2011); as well as the United States (Grossman et al., 2009; Zeichner, 2010) and Canada (Goodnough et al., 2009). In the United States, the recent report on clinical practice from the AACTE (2018) recommends a transformation of practicum experiences, and it suggests that this process of transformation should begin at the local level, "local context matters when considering how to best operationalize [practicum]" (p. 4). It also suggests that this process works best through discussions and studies that include voices from university, school and community, where there is "shared responsibility for teacher learning and development ... by university [and] school" (p. 35). This chapter takes up these two points to focus on one local context undergoing a three-year study for practicum transformation.

Our Local Context

In our local context, we have been using traditional aspects of practicum experiences, where a teacher candidate joins the classroom of a teacher mentor (cooperating teacher), first to observe and then to teach lessons independently. The teacher candidate receives feedback after their lessons and is assessed by their teacher mentor and a faculty mentor (a member of the university faculty who supports the teacher candidate with resources, and with planning, implementation, and reflection). This traditional model, described in detail by others (e.g., Patrick, 2013), can raise a multitude of problems. These problems include the isolation that the teacher candidate can feel, and the lack of collaboration that can exist between teacher mentor and teacher candidate (Rabin, 2020); a lack of respect that can occur for the knowledge that the teacher candidate brings (Zeichner, 2010); and ultimately, the existence of a hierarchy where the teacher candidate feels subordinate to the teacher mentor (Patrick, 2013). We know that issues like these exist in our program and that sometimes teacher candidates do not feel supported to implement new approaches to pedagogy that they have been learning about in their methods classes. This motivated us to look at new or alternative models for practicum that were developed, investigated, and implemented in other locations in the hopes of improving our situation (e.g., Darling-Hammond & Baratz-Snowden, 2007; Roth & Tobin, 2002; Goodnough et al., 2009). We were particularly interested in making teacher education more collaborative between teacher mentor and the teacher candidate (Rabin, 2020) and more democratic (Zeichner et al., 2015) and to help to bridge the gap between the university and schools (Zeichner, 2010).

We were drawn to the co-teaching model for practicum experiences because of the explicit focus on bringing the teacher mentor and the teacher candidate together on a more equitable footing and the value that is placed on the knowledge that both bring to the classroom (Murphy & Martin, 2015). We decided to explore the co-teaching model for our context.

In this chapter we first provide some of the background from the literature on co-teaching and the use of the co-teaching model for practicum. We then share our theoretical framework and our process for developing a co-teaching model for our local context. Next, we share our conceptual framework of five interconnected themes that was developed through our process of consulting the literature, speaking with experts and through our discussions as a local group of teacher candidates, teacher mentors (cooperating teachers) and faculty. Then we share the voices of the teacher candidates, teacher mentors, and faculty mentor who participated in a pilot or test-run of our co-teaching model. Finally, we discuss their experiences through the lens of our conceptual framework, sharing our achievements, our difficulties, and our hopes for the future for the next phase of our study.

BACKGROUND

In this section of the chapter, we share some of the relevant literature on co-teaching, co-teaching models and using co-teaching in teacher education.

Co-Teaching

The general term co-teaching refers to the practice of two or more teachers teaching together for the benefit of students. Co-teaching has been developed and used widely in the field of inclusive education to bring together special-needs teachers and classroom teachers in a variety of formats including the one-teach, one-assist format; station teaching; parallel teaching; and team teaching (Friend et al., 1993; Harbort et al., 2007; Pancsofar & Petroff, 2016). In parallel with the development of co-teaching in the field of inclusive education, co-teaching has been growing as a means to bring other forms of specialist knowledge into classrooms. Examples include English language learning (Im & Martin, 2015); social justice education (Sharma & Cobb, 2018), medical education (Daniel et al., 2018) and counselling education (Baltrinic et al., 2016).

Co-Teaching Models

The work on co-teaching in inclusive education gave rise to various models of ways that two teachers can actually work together in the classroom (Friend et al., 1993). In this section we describe these models. Rather than being mutually exclusive, these models can be brought together and modified to suit the particular context and needs of the students.

Friend et al. (1993) proposed that when general teachers and special educators are brought together, there are several instructional approaches to teaching that could be possible when there are two teachers working together in the classroom. These approaches or models described by Friend et al. are summarized in Table 20.1.

Using Co-Teaching in Teacher Education

Co-teaching can be a powerful method in teacher education. In this situation the teachers involved include one or more teacher candidates working alongside a teacher mentor in a practicum classroom. Early work on co-teaching in teacher education took place in the area of science education in western Canada (Roth, 1998; Roth et al., 1999) and the United States (e.g., Roth & Tobin, 2002; Roth et al., 2004, 2005). Through this work, a model of co-teaching was developed (e.g., Roth & Tobin, 2002; Tobin, 2006; Roth & Tobin, 2005) where co-teaching is coupled with cogenerative dialogue. Cogenerative dialogue involves meetings between teacher candidates, teacher mentors, faculty, and student representatives to plan and reflect with the intent to design and implement new curriculum.

Table 20.1

Instructional Approaches to Teaching

One teaching, one assisting	In this model, both teachers are present, but one takes the lead, and the other teacher generally observes the students and assists them as needed.
Station teaching	In this model of co-teaching, both teachers divide their content into two or more segments and deliver it to students at separate locations in the classroom. Eventually, students attend all the stations.
Parallel teaching	In parallel teaching, teachers jointly plan instructions, but each delivers to a diversified group consisting of half of the class.
Alternative teaching	In this type, one teacher works with a small group, for example students with special needs or a small group of students with a specific interest, while the other teacher instructs the larger group.
Team teaching	In team teaching, both teachers work as a team and share the instruction of students. They might take turns leading a discussion, one may speak while the other demonstrates, or takes notes for students.

Source: Modified from Friend et al. (1993, p. 10)

The co-teaching model for teacher education has expanded beyond the field of science education. Although not all programs refer to cogenerative dialogue, in all programs, the aim is for teacher candidate and teacher mentor to work together on all aspects of teaching; both are involved in co-planning, co-instruction and co-reflection.

Bacharach et al. (2010) explained that, for them, some of the chief differences between the traditional practicum model and the co-teaching practicum model are providing the teachers and faculty supervisors with guidance on working together through workshops and providing them with time to plan and reflect. Murphy (2016) identifies three elements of great importance in co-teaching for initial teacher education: co planning, co-practice, and co-reflection. In co-planning, teacher candidates and teacher mentors share expertise to plan learning opportunities for students; in co-practice, they share responsibilities for students' learning opportunities; and in co-reflection, they reflect on what went well for students' learning and what changes they need to make in their teaching.

Current research on co-teaching for teacher education includes studies that focus on elements to gain fluency in co-teaching (Thompson & Schademan, 2019); the role of care and collaboration (Rabin, 2020); and teacher efficacy within co-teaching (Hawkman et al., 2019); co-teachers' huddles during co-teaching (Soslau et al., 2018); and recent challenges of implementing co-teaching (Soslau et al., 2019).

THEORETICAL FRAMEWORK

The aim of our work is to develop a more democratic model for practicum as part of a wider transformative goal to support more democratic practices across teacher education generally (Zeichner et al., 2015). Quality teacher education requires a true partnership between university and school so that teachers new to the profession are well prepared for the realities that they will face. We aim to recognize the voices of teacher candidates, teacher mentors and faculty in our process to reduce the hierarchy that can exist.

We share the view of Zeichner et al. (2015) that we need to recognize the particular knowledges and perceptions that teacher candidates, teacher mentors, and faculty bring to the communal activity of developing our practicum model. Within our process we need to equally value the professional expertise of each contributor. To create teachers for democratic education we need to use a democratic process to get us there. In the words of Zeichner et al (2015) "the preparation of teachers for a democratic society should be based on an epistemology that in itself is democratic" (p. 124).

Our Process

Our three-year project follows a process that brings together the voices of teacher candidates, teachers, and faculty each year to explore and develop a practicum model that is right for our context. Our process each year involves a cycle of workshop and discussion; model design and refinement; implementation and pilot project; reflection and recommendations for the next cycle (Figure 20.1).

The next section of the chapter details the steps in our process through our first year of this three-year study.

Workshop and Discussion (August 2019)

We invited Colette Murphy from Trinity College Dublin, and her collaborator Jim Beggs, as visiting scholars to lead a two-day workshop for our participants in August 2019. We chose Colette and Jim because of their extensive experience with co-teaching. Our participants at this stage of our study included eight teacher candidates, four teacher mentors, and four faculty members. We arranged the workshop so that Colette first gave our participants a knowledge base from the literature on co-teaching for

Figure 20.1

Steps in the Process Used to Develop and Test Our Model

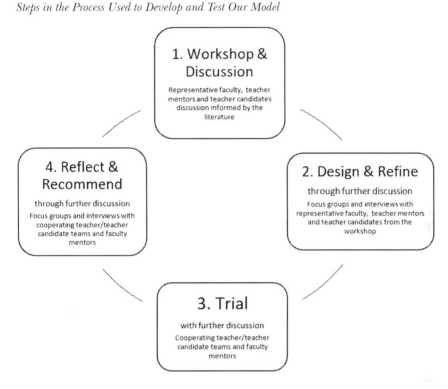

teacher education and then we divided participants into interprofessional groups (two teacher candidates with one teacher mentor and one faculty member) to discuss the importance for them of particular elements of co-teaching models gleaned from the literature. Colette brought us two activities that were ideal for our aims and have been described elsewhere (Rees et al., 2020). Groups presented results from their discussion and we video recorded the presentations.

Design and Refine Our Model (September–December 2019)

Following thematic analysis of materials from the activities and discussions at the workshop, we created our conceptual framework of five interconnected themes. Our conceptual framework is represented in Figure 20.2 (modified from Rees et al., 2020).

Through a teacher candidate focus group and teacher interviews we brought these themes to our workshop participants for further discussion.

Figure 20.2

Our Conceptual Framework

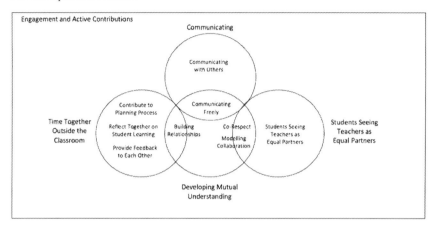

These themes were "Time together outside the classroom," "Developing mutual understanding," "Making equity visible," "Engagement and active contributions" and "Communicating." From this work we designed and refined our conceptual framework and our co-teaching model and drew up a plan for our pilot for an eight-week practicum that would be taking place from late February to late April. Details and outcomes of the Workshop and Discussion and the Design and Refine phases are presented elsewhere (Rees et al., 2020). This chapter focuses on the pilot and Reflect and Recommend steps in our process. The practicum weeks and meetings are laid out schematically in Figure 20.3.

Trial—Examining our Model in Action

Overview (this section is written by our FM)

As the Faculty Mentor Assigned from the School of Education for the teacher candidates (B&M), it was indeed a wonderful opportunity for me to be involved in the co-teaching research project. Our first two sessions were meetings of all the participants for a half day each (Figure 20.3).

The first meeting with the researchers, teacher candidates, teacher mentors, and faculty mentor was spent getting to know everyone and to review the philosophy of co-teaching. The Teams M&D and B&G were given time to discuss the practicum and what topics might be covered. I

Figure 20.3

Our Practicum: This Diagram Shows the Weeks of Practicum, and the Timing of Planning and Reflection Meetings and of the Faculty Mentor Observations

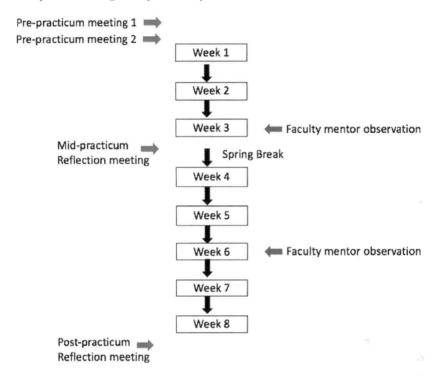

was able to listen in to their conversations and answer any questions they might have about the practicum. I noticed an immediate professional respect between all parties. Everyone was listening attentively to each other and contributing to the discussion. It was so beneficial for them to have this precious time to begin their planning. Instead of the traditional teacher mentor role, where an individual who is experienced and shares this knowledge, I saw a different dynamic taking place. The mentors concentrated on the experience of the teacher candidates in their recent schooling and experience in the work world. As they discussed topics, they ran ideas back and forth on how to make lessons authentic and engaging for their learners.

The second meeting was primarily a planning session between the teacher candidates and their teacher mentors. One topic put forward for them to discuss was the importance of students seeing them as equals. It would be unique for the students to have a teacher candidate that was in a different role than the traditional one. Clear communication between the teacher mentor and teacher candidate was crucial. This would include classroom procedures. They took time to discuss these items and then started a more structured planning session. One group (M&D) constructed a blueprint looking at the curriculum and the topics they would cover while the other designed a graphic image in multiple colours depicting the lessons, activities, and possible co-teaching methods. As the faculty mentor, I stood back giving them lots of time together, then meeting with each group to answer questions and learning from them. This is unique for a faculty mentor. First, getting to know the teacher mentors and teacher candidates in more depth before a practicum, strengthens the connection and relationship between all three parties. Hearing ideas for lessons is exciting and something to look forward to!

Just as the practicum was to begin, there was a glitch. One teacher candidate through no fault of his/her own, had to move to another school. Luckily, an elementary teacher was keen to join into the co-teaching pair role to upgrade her knowledge of secondary school teaching. Team B&G became team C&G. In Week 2 of the practicum, I, as the Faculty Mentor, got to observe Team C&G. It was a different role than usual. I was there to see co-teaching in action. I quickly picked up on the mutual respect each had for the other. As they used different co-teaching methods there was a smooth transition between the pair. It actually seemed like a well-orchestrated piece! Obviously there had been lots of planning previously but there was also a natural ebb and flow between them. They were both very enthusiastic and focused on the lesson and their learners. Having time after the lesson to discuss and reflect on the lesson was beneficial for all.

Team M&D started their course in the third week of the practicum (week of March 9, 2020). I was scheduled to observe them in Week Four (after the spring break). Unfortunately, COVID 19 closed the school and abruptly ended face-to-face classes. M did continue to co-teach with D for another 10 days using a virtual platform. It was a different experience but those first planning meetings and time to get to know each other and the curriculum were very beneficial. They were both immersed in the planning, developing online resources, and assessing their students. Students saw them both as their teacher and responded well. As the faculty mentor, I was still in communication with them and admired the mutual respect and time they put into developing meaningful learning activities for their students.

Team C&G moved into online co-teaching and plan on continuing to the end of the semester (June 2020) below C shares an overview of their face-to-face and online teaching.

C & G's Practicum Experience—the First Three Weeks (this section is written by C)

For the first week of classes I observed and helped in one of the two physics 11 classes that G taught. We had decided we would do a project on electric cars over the next two weeks, so I gathered the materials needed and built a prototype. We had two meetings to look at the materials and the prototype, and to plan the details of the project together. Our planning sessions were grabbed after school and in G's prep period (when G had lots of other prep he needed to do) and were short compared to the rich planning opportunities B&G had in the January meetings.

The area of curriculum we were working on was Newton's second law. The plan was to build model cars that could be battery or solar powered, then support students to design their own experiments to test the impact of a variable on the acceleration of their car, and finally make modifications to create their own innovative machine 2.0 that worked even better than the original version. We invited engineers from the university to visit twice—first to help the students get started on their inventions and then to attend the presentations at the end of the unit and provide feedback for students. We planned that our teachers' assessment would take place on these group presentations of learning and individual lab reports that the students would submit. I also developed detailed unit and lesson plans required by the teacher education program and shared these with G and with our faculty mentor (B).

We had little time to fine-tune their co-teaching plans on a daily or weekly basis. The days were completely filled with involvement with students. All we could fit in were brief check-ins before or following class about things we needed to change to the lesson plan for the following day. In the January planning sessions, G&B had decided that the fundamental thing was to build off of each other's strengths. G's strengths included his wealth of experience with teaching physics, his use of student-led projects, his use of education technology such as graphing tools and his ability to engage the students using popular media and real-world references. My strength came from my past experience developing hands-on engineering type projects for middle school students and my knowledge of supporting student-led inquiry. We shared an interest in using popular media and real-world relevance to engage students, so we had fun collecting and sharing these connections.

As co-teachers, we decided that it would be good if I introduced the unit so that the class would see me as a teacher (rather than student-teacher) and know that it was me who had taken a lead in developing this particular project. Linking to the physics problems was an essential part of the class and we decided that G would take the lead on these components.

On March 11, B, the faculty mentor visited the class for her first observation, she noted that we switched smoothly back and forth with who was leading the class at any given time and that at all times both of us were involved in the class. The teacher who was not leading stepped in and assisted, for example managing the technology or distributing the resources. During hands-on group work, which was the majority of the time, both of us circulated, interacting with the students in their small groups.

At the presentations at the end of the two-week project, we were both really impressed with the work of the students, as were the engineers, and the principal and vice principal who attended the presentations. The students had done a great job, as well as creating their innovative car machine 2.0, students had conducted experiments to measure the impact of a change in their original car on the acceleration. They had made videos of their cars movement and used video physics software to determine acceleration with as many as five different treatment values and produced final graphs of acceleration versus treatment level to show the impact of their variable on the acceleration of their car.

After these first three weeks of the practicum was the week of spring break (March 16–20, 2020). We had planned that following the break they would start a new Rube Goldberg project with this Physics 11 class (11A) and use this to support the students' learning about different forms of energy, calculations of energy, work and power, energy conversions, efficiency of energy conversion. As well, we had planned for the other Physics 11 class (11B), to have a chance to do the electric car project. Over the spring break the decision was made not to reopen the schools, the COVID-19 pandemic had reached BC, Canada. It took time and perseverance to arrange for a continuation of classes online and a continuation of the practicum experience for our participants, but, by April 21, 2020, we were up and running again.

C & G's Practicum Experience Online (April–June)

We had put together and distributed the materials for the car project for the Physics 11 B class as individual kits (all cleaned and sterilized). We introduced this project to them (Physics 11 B) through google classroom. For the class who had just finished the car project as face-to-face (Physics 11 A), we introduced the Rube Goldberg project. Then in Zoom classes, with us co-teaching, twice each week we supported students to complete their projects at home.

At the time of writing this chapter, we are continuing to co-teach online. Of course, teaching and learning online during the COVID-19 pandemic is very difficult. The students and teachers are experiencing anxiety and concern about the future and the need to care for everyone's well-being takes precedence to all else. Some of the difficulties that directly impacted our plans included the loss of group work for the students and difficulties with encouraging students to talk in video sessions. However, doing the projects at home seems to have been a positive learning experience for many students, and they seemed enthusiastic to share their creations and their findings. Unfortunately, there are students who could not maintain contact with us online and we hope to catch up with those students when face-to-face classes resume. Regardless of the difficulties, we believe that the students who participated learned lots and that there were some aspects of co-teaching that were enhanced through the online process.

One source of learning came from experimenting with teaching materials to engage the students online. We each engaged extensively in this process, and we shared our new developing skills in education technology at our weekly meetings (we created videos, google forms and pear deck slides). As co-teachers, online classes allowed us more time for daily and weekly check-ins. In the Zoom classes we developed a kind of light-hearted rapport not unlike a pair of sports commentators. We interjected frequently to comment on each other's "lesson" supporting each other and offering alternative ways of explaining a concept or alternative examples to illustrate it. We each built on our own strengths and learned from each other. There is no doubt that the learning experience was a two-way street, just as I learned to be a secondary school teacher, G gained much professional development experience through co-teaching as well.

In the next section M, who was the teacher candidate in M&D's group, shares her views of their co-teaching experience.

M&D's Practicum Experience—The First Three Weeks (this section was written by M)

D's class that I joined for practicum was Grade 11 Workplace Math. For my practicum, I was also joining the class of another teacher for Grade 11 and Grade 12 Chemistry. Chemistry was my subject area, and I was joining D's class for the experience of co-teaching with D teaching math. I also wanted the experience of teaching a class where more students experienced difficulty with the subject area.

D used lots of project-based learning and the subject matter was very practical for the most part. However, there was one area of curriculum that we were covering that was totally new for me. The big idea was "3D objects are often represented and described in 2D space." This is an important curricular area for many workplaces. Students develop their knowledge of how to represent 3 D objects in two dimensions and are therefore focusing on angles, views, and scale diagrams. We decided together to plan a unit on this big idea. We began our planning conversations in January. Since the area of curriculum was totally new to me, we decided to develop our unit based upon D's prior work.

I created my unit and lessons and shared with D and with our faculty mentor (B). I only got to teach one week of this unit before the spring break. We had decided that the best means of beginning would be for me to take the lead in the class and D to assist, since this would maximize the opportunity for the students to see me as an equal partner teacher in the classroom.

M&D's Practicum Experience Online (this section is written by M)

As explained previously, during the spring break the decision was made not to resume classes following spring break. I resumed teaching with D on the week of April 14, 2020. Our school district supported teachers to make the decision about the form of online teaching that would work best for their class. D knew that many of her students would not have ready access to online video classes. D decided on asynchronous teaching where she prepared videos and documents for her class to support them in their projects. Joining D for online teaching gave me the opportunity to create videos for the class, source background information, create lessons and work on assessment. I expanded my teaching with D to include D's Earth science class. Planning worked really well online. We had video meetings twice weekly and checked in most days via e-mail.

In the next section of the chapter, following the fourth step in our process (Figure 20.1), we share reflections and recommendations from our work putting our model into action. These reflections were made when we got together as a whole group. This larger group, including the two co-teaching teams (G&C; M&D) their faculty mentor (B) and the two researchers (C&R) got together for reflection meetings twice so far (April 3 and May 1, 2020).

Reflect and Recommend (April 3 and May 1, 2020)

Our mid-practicum reflection meeting (April 3) gave us a chance to check in on how our co-teaching model was going after the first three weeks of face-to-face classes. We reflected by going through each of our five themes from our conceptual model (Figure 20.2). Each teacher candidate/

teacher mentor team first made reflection notes on how co-teaching went in relation to each theme. Each pair shared their reflections at the meeting, and we discussed. For our final post-practicum meeting (May 1), each teacher candidate, teacher mentor and faculty mentor reflected on the whole experience with co-teaching, including teaching face-to-face and teaching online. We have been taking our findings from these two meetings and from all participants and synthesized them into four representative voices: the teacher candidate, the teacher mentor, the faculty mentor, and the researcher. In the next section we share these voices with respect to the five themes of our conceptual framework. In each section the researcher speaks last and when she speaks, she reflects on the comments of the other three voices, and she relates this to the literature.

Examining Our Points of View Through the Lens of Our Conceptual Framework

The next sections come from our reflections as described above. They are presented as direct quotes in turn from the teacher candidate, teacher mentor, faculty mentor and researcher. Each section concerns one of the five aspects of our conceptual framework shown in Figure 20.2: *Time Together Outside the Classroom, Developing Mutual Understanding, Seeing Co-Teachers as Equal Partners, Engagement and Active Contribution From Teachers and Students, Communication.*

Time Together Outside the Classroom. In this section we share, as direct quotes, the perspectives of teacher candidate, teacher mentor, faculty mentor, and researcher in turn, on the importance of *Time Together Outside the Classroom* in co-teaching. This is the first aspect of our conceptual framework (Figure 20.2).

> *Teacher Candidate:* Starting the planning together pre-practicum (in January), like we did, was great. I was able to start developing my relationship with my TM who knew already what the class would be doing and had taught this class and this material before. My TM had already established relationships with some of the students in their prior classes together. When we started co-planning and discussed trying new strategies, my TM, as an experienced teacher, was able to say, "well this is what might work well in this class and this might not." So, I think that the advanced planning is very important. Having that time was very precious and it was a blessing, and I would hope that in future practica all of our TCs have a way that they could all get more planning time.

If you cannot get the planning time as release time for the TMs (meaning a teacher on call is hired to replace the TM so that they can meet during school-time), as we did in the co-teaching project, another way is for the TCs to volunteer in their TMs' classes. Then the TCs have an opportunity to check-in with their TMs. The pre-practicum planning was just invaluable so that we were ready to hit the ground running come Day 1.

Once we started practicum, it was really difficult to find day-to-day planning and reflection time—every moment was busy with students. I didn't want to take time away from students. For daily check-ins we snatched some quick meetings where we could. In these rushed meetings we focused on major needs, such as a change of plan for the following day. For us, a weekly meeting after school was best. It is essential that co-teachers coplan to make co-teaching successful. In addition, co-evaluation is important because without reflecting on the lesson together, improvements cannot be made, or students' best interest achieved.

Another thing about time was just the time it takes to get comfortable with each other. I was not always sure when was the right time to jump in with a question for my TM. I tended to hover to wait for the right moment. I recognized that I needed to know what was going on in the student-teacher consults so that I was in sync with the needs and knew when it might be okay to jump in. I could see this was coming, but it really takes time. Also, I needed to learn to be clear and concise—so as not to waste time when I did jump in. Teaching online did give us more time for those daily and weekly meetings.

Teacher Mentor: Although the other themes are important, without time outside of the classroom there would be no opportunity to make the other themes fall into place. The planning time in January was great. Each of us (me and my TC) had our own specialty. TCs have a fresh look at things. We were sharing ideas; the whole was greater than the sum of the parts. We were able to design our plans and play on each other's strengths. I agree the day-to-day at school is very busy. I could see that as time went on it was getting easier to find those quick moments to talk between classes and even within classes when the students were working. When we were teaching online, we had time for two weekly meetings each week and we were checking in with each other every day by e-mail.

Faculty Mentor: The pre-practicum meetings gave teacher candidates and teacher mentors precious time, and it was great for me to be able to step back and listen in on these conversations. The whole second meeting was a planning session and normally in our practicum the TC and TM don't have that time. I know that it's busy at school and TCs and TMs found it difficult to fit in meetings especially when the TC is with two different TMs. One of the benefits of the online co-teaching was that there was more time for the TC and TM to talk.

Researcher: All agreed that the pre-practicum planning meetings were very successful and that there were problems with getting time in the day-to-day busyness of school for the daily and weekly meeting that we had planned.

In several of the studies in the literature the importance of setting aside time together outside the classroom is also emphasized; for co-planning, feedback and for reflection (e.g., Guise et al., 2017; Murphy & Beggs, 2005; Roth & Tobin, 2002; Soslau et al., 2019). Setting up specific meeting times is also recommended. For example, Bacharach et al (2010 recommended that "In the co-teaching practicum model "[Teacher candidates and teacher mentors] … identify a specific planning time where the primary focus includes the details of how, when, and which co-teaching strategies to use for upcoming lessons" (p. 8).

Although this daily check-in time and weekly planning time is very important, one potential advantage to the co-teaching model is that teachers can speak up and make alterations right there and then during the class. As TM/TC teams get more comfortable with each other, we hope this could develop. Another interesting observation from our study is that once the co-teaching teams were teaching together online, they found they had more time for daily and weekly check-ins. It may be that we can exploit this in our planning for the future and help TC TM teams find ways that work for them to use online means for their check-in.

In the next section we turn to the second aspect of our conceptual framework Figure 20.2), developing mutual understanding. Once again, we share the perspective of each role, teacher candidate, teacher mentor, faculty mentor, and researcher. These are written as direct quotes from each role in turn. The researcher reflects back on the reflections of the other three.

Developing Mutual Understanding. In this section we share, as direct quotes, the perspectives of teacher candidate, teacher mentor, faculty mentor, and researcher in turn, on the importance of *Developing Mutual Understanding* in co-teaching. This is the second aspect of our conceptual framework (Figure 20.2).

Teacher Candidate: For me, building relationships was key because this led to mutual understanding. A fundamental requirement for developing mutual understanding is respect and I felt that respect between me and my TM was established, and I was given a voice through all of the co-planning.

I came to understand that for teachers, the focus is the students all the time. But I didn't get that right away, once I got that, it helped. At first, I was thinking about the project, the lessons, mostly (more than the students) and wanted to be checking in with my TM about our planning, but I didn't want to interrupt when the students were asking questions before and after class.

As we went on, we got to understand each other, and we did coteach more naturally. I think that so long as the TM is not actively trying to remove themselves in a purposeful way (because they might be worried about stepping on the TCs toes) co-teaching could be quite natural once both teachers are engaged. In the traditional model, I can see that the TM would not want to jump in as they would worry that was not the correct thing to do because they should give over the class to the TC.

I'm not sure why, but when we were teaching online together it became much easier to jump in and add to each other's teaching. This may have happened anyway in face-to-face if we had of had more time to become comfortable with each other. It is hard to know if the increased "jumping in" was because we were teaching together longer or because we were online.

Teacher Mentor: As things went on, we became more comfortable. Initially we each might be wanting to join in and add to the lesson but felt maybe it is not our place. As we went further, we would step in and say something like "okay, let me add something to that." It would be good to facilitate that happening sooner as it was really effective. I think that the TC and TM need to feel sure of each other, to have that mutual understanding, for this to happen.

Faculty Mentor: Developing trust is so important and this comes from mutual understanding, really seeing where the other person is coming from. Sometimes it's hard for TMs to remember what it's like to be a TC who is in front of the class for the first time. It's so important to reserve judgement, there is this point, usually about four weeks into the practicum, when the teacher candidate has the confidence, when they're comfortable, it's a magical moment.

Researcher: Everyone agreed that TCs and TMs need to reach mutual understanding so that they have trust in each other. Our theme of 'Developing mutual understanding' was indicated in other studies in the literature, albeit by a different name. In Thompson and Schademan's (2019) study, they called this "Negotiating Difference" (Thompson & Schademan, 2019, p. 4). Like our concept of *Developing Mutual Understanding, Negotiating Difference* depends on co-respect. Thompson and Schademan (2019) found that "the successful negotiation of difference was only possible when pairs were willing to engage tensions directly and work through them" (p. 4). We know that our TM/TC pairs would find it very difficult to engage tensions directly. This might be a cultural thing, here in Canada we are very careful not to upset each other in our professional interactions.

This raises questions for us, for example "How do we aid mutual understanding when the TCs and TMs have unequal roles? Even if the TM is not formally assessing the TC, the TC might worry that the TM can impact the TCs hiring into the school district, how can we deal with this inequity? Also, it might be difficult for the TM to remember their first class in front of students, how can we encourage the TM to reserve judgement and trust that the TC will get there in time? When TCs begin they can be in very different places they can have different backgrounds and therefore different journeys to travel.

In the next section we turn to the third aspect of our conceptual framework (Figure 20.2), co-teachers as equal partners. Once again, we share the perspective of each role: teacher candidate, teacher mentor, faculty mentor, and researcher. These are written as direct quotes from each role in turn. The researcher reflects back on the reflections of the other three.

Seeing Co-Teachers as Equal Partners. In this section we share, as direct quotes, the perspectives of teacher candidate, teacher mentor, faculty mentor, and researcher in turn, on the importance of *Co-teachers as Equal Partners* in co-teaching. This is the third aspect of our conceptual framework (Figure 20.2).

Teacher Candidate: My TM suggested we first use the model one-teach, one-assist, with me as the lead-teacher and my TM assisting me for the first 4 days. The 5th day, I was the assist to help to show us as equal partners. Also, my TM introduced me as a co-teacher and demonstrated this to students by saying that students can go to either of us for questions (such as asking permission to leave the class). I did feel though, that the students saw my TM as the teacher because she already had developed relationships with the students and taught the class from the start of the semester.

Of course, it took time to develop a position in the classroom where I was seen as a teacher like my teacher mentor. However, being proud of the activities I brought to the classroom helped me to feel strong. I was very happy about the car project that I was bringing to the students. I felt I was bringing something that they would find engaging and that was useful for their learning. Another thing that really helped me was starting the class some days, as then the students saw me as the *lead* teacher and my TM was assisting me. I knew that I needed to act as if I was surer of myself.

Once we moved to online teaching, I found my feet. I'm not sure if this was a time thing and was just because I was more comfortable with my TM and the students, or some other reason.

I am not sure where this point would be more applicable, but I think it would have been helpful to discuss with my TM some of the classroom management strategies and what works. I am still learning classroom management and that is why I think this would be helpful, although my TM and I discussed classroom management after the lesson which I certainly learnt from, and we enacted the following day.

Teacher Mentor: As mentioned by M, I suggested to her that she take a lead role early on in practicum to help the students see us both as teachers in the classroom. This is something we talked about with our FM. Also, hen we were talking with our FM, I know that we talked about how perhaps I might be able to share strategies for classroom management with M. It sounds like such a simple idea in theory that us TMs can just bestow all this classroom management knowledge onto the TC and then when they go, they are ready to go. But it needs to be *try it, observe, and comment,* right? I mean I can't possibly predict how my students are going to react to a different person. I can barely even summarize my own strategies because I just do them. Someone can say, "I noticed you did this" and I'm like "Oh, did I? "I didn't notice." So, it sounds great in theory that TMs can bestow the knowledge but until the TC is actually in there, it's just theoretical, right?

It does take TCs time to gain confidence though, and the students pick up on that. If the students see a confident teacher in front of them, they'll respond to that but if they see a TC showing insecurity, showing a lack of confidence, showing the fear, then they can eat a TC for breakfast. It's like that idea of being like a duck, where all anyone sees is you calmly gliding on the water, and they don't see the feet swimming like crazy underneath.

Faculty Mentor: Establishing the relationship where the teachers are seen as more equal by the students is hard. Especially when the relationship between the teacher mentor and the students is already established. Of course, having TCs start right at the beginning of the semester would be great but if that cannot happen the TC needs to visit the class—maybe do an icebreaker with the class, introduce themselves, get to know the students a little before their teaching begins. TC leading the lessons from the beginning is so important. M had to be seen as the person leading the lessons so that students would perceive her as the teacher. In G and C's class, G was away one day and a teacher, teaching on call, was in. So that day, C effectively led the class.

Researcher: We can see that this *Seeing Teachers as Equal Partners* is very difficult to establish. We hoped that TCs and TMs would establish a rapport so that they both felt comfortable for TMs to jump in during the TCs lesson, to model, especially in situations where things were going a little sideways for the TC. However, our participants' conversation shows that they did not agree. Everyone agreed that the TC needed to show their ability to be a confident teacher, on their own, first. People felt that, really, there was not much that the TM could do 'in the moment' to help them. With time, we do hope that this kind of supportive interaction could develop and could assist the TC right in the moment and help the TC learn some of these needed skills. In our view, this is one of the great values of co-teaching as opposed to the traditional "sink or swim" or "pilot by fire" model.

In the literature the importance of seeing teachers as equal partners was also discussed. For example, Thompson and Schademan (2019) talked about the TC and TM 'sharing authority.' They suggested that it is when the TC feels they truly belong in the classroom and at the school that sharing authority can happen. We wondered how it might be possible to support the TC even more so that sense of real belonging develops.

In the next section we turn to the fourth aspect of our conceptual framework (Figure 20.2), *Engagement and Active Contribution of Teachers and Students*. Once again, we share the perspective of each role: teacher candidate, teacher mentor, faculty mentor, and researcher. These are written as direct quotes from each role in turn. The researcher reflects back on the reflections of the other three.

Engagement and Active Contribution of Teachers and Students. In this section we share, as direct quotes, the perspectives of teacher candidate, teacher mentor, faculty mentor, and researcher in turn, on the importance of *Engagement and Active Contribution of Teachers and Students* in co-teaching. This is the fourth aspect of our conceptual framework (Figure 20.2).

Teacher Candidate: Co-teacher engagement was great - we were both engaged all the time. This was really helpful because my TM noticed what I needed without me asking and stepped in to do that thing, such as help me with the technology or giving the students their bags of materials.

For the car project student engagement was really good for the car building but sometimes students didn't complete some tasks such as doing all the graphs they should have—in other words—they were all engaged—but were they engaged in the right things?

Co-teacher engagement was great but at times student engagement was not. When I was introducing activities for example, I know that some of the students were not engaged but I found it difficult to notice and react immediately, in the moment, because I so focussed on what I was doing.

When we went to online teaching, student engagement was extremely difficult to read. The students often did not turn on their mics or their video. We tried a bunch of ways to find out how they were receiving our output, such as direct questions to them, google forms where they completed tasks and submitted findings that we could see immediately. We tried pear deck which is an interactive method using questions for the students to respond to, built right into the presentation. At the point of the question, the teacher simply waits for the students to respond by typing in an answer and the teacher can see the responses immediately. Of course, we did try engaging the students in discussion by asking them a question, but we often got no takers when we did this in the moment. When you gave them notice, such as when we invited in our engineer guest, they were great. They turned on the video camera and the microphone and shared. This is still a work in progress for us.

Teacher Mentor: We were both engaged and actively contributed during lesson co-planning and for preparation of resources. In the classroom too, we were both as engaged with the class. I think we developed a new co-teaching model; instead of "one teach, one assist," I think we were doing "one teach, one facilitate" because we were noticing what was needed and doing that.

There is a tricky issue of when to step in to help when you don't know the TC that well. You ask yourself; do they want help? Also, would you undermine them if you stepped in?

As far as engaging students online this is certainly an issue that we're working on. We also tried a fun question that we asked students to respond to in the chat feature. We thought that students might interact about those questions. Such as, "Which Marvel character is your favorite?" One day we did a star-wars quiz. Both of these were quite successful, and we had lots of comments in the chat.

Faculty Mentor: One area that could perhaps fit into "Engagement of teachers and students" would be developing a relationship between the students and the teacher candidate before entering into a full co-teaching style. The students already know their teacher and having a new "teacher" in the class and accepting this person takes some time. Perhaps there could be some activities around "Getting to Know You" where both the TC and TM present together and separate. Small group rotations for discussion with students and the TC could happen while the TM continues on with work assignments with the rest of the class. My suggestion would be that the co-teaching class begin in the first week of the practicum. Rather than the TC observing in that class they start co-teaching in there right away.

Researcher: It was great to see the co-teachers so engaged and invested. Of course, we understand the comments about student engagement. It takes time for the students to get to know the TC and engagement of students can be difficult for TCs to achieve. For TCs and TMs, teaching online with no interaction can be disheartening. Finding ways to incorporate student interaction online is fundamental for next steps.

The importance of both teachers remaining engaged at all times was also mentioned in the literature. Bacharach et al (2010) explained the importance of active, engaged participation by both co-teachers, "in co-teaching both teachers work together to remain actively involved" (p. 7). Although the importance of students' engagement is fundamental for student learning, in the co-teaching students' voice is not often mentioned. We did note that in cogenerative dialogue in Roth and Tobin's (Tobin, 2006) work they included students in these discussion, reflection, and planning meetings.

Including students' voice in this way did increase students' engagement in their own and their co-teachers' learning.

In the next section we turn to the fifth and final aspect of our conceptual framework (Figure 20.2), *Communication*. Once again, we share the perspective of each role; teacher candidate, teacher mentor, faculty mentor and researcher. These are written as direct quotes from each role in turn. The researcher reflects back on the reflections of the other three.

Communication. In this section we share, as direct quotes, the perspectives of teacher candidate, teacher mentor, faculty mentor, and researcher in turn, on the importance of *Communication in Co-teaching*. This is the fifth and final aspect of our conceptual framework (Figure 20.2).

Teacher Candidate: As mentioned earlier, in the first three weeks I realized how busy school was. The students needed to come first, and I didn't want to take away from that. I wasn't sure when it was okay to communicate about the project, I felt I needed a signal, or maybe an appointment time. E-mail was a good way from me to get my thoughts in order and send but I felt I needed to work on being concise, so I was not sending long burdensome e-mails.

I think this point is similar to "time together outside the classroom" in that it is hard to find a time to meet during the school day to actually communicate, exchange ideas, and co-evaluate lessons. Communication is critical, it is integral for building any relationship, resolving conflicts, co-planning, and co-evaluating.

Teacher Mentor: Communication is so important—the 5-minute class change doesn't give us time. Daily communication was especially important when we moved online. We did a zoom meeting every two days—we were communicating over e-mail everyday and keeping that connection going was really important and may be a sub-topic under that is developing a relationship between TC and students.

Faculty Mentor: After the FM observes a lesson, debriefing with the Faculty Mentor, Teacher Mentor, and Teacher Candidate together are very rich. The FM takes the role of "guide on the side," or "learning partner" looking at co-teaching.

Researcher: Our teams found day-to-day communication very difficult at school and interestingly they found communication easier during online teaching. This issue was also talked about in the literature. For example, in Gallo-Fox and Scantlebury's (2016) study, co-teaching participants also talked about difficulties with keeping up with communication on an ongoing day-to-day basis. They noted that "communication about each lesson proved to be more challenging" (p. 334). One potential solution to the difficulties with communication in school might be to use an appropriate online medium.

CONCLUSIONS AND IMPLICATIONS

In this chapter we have shared our democratic process of engaging all voices in the first year of designing, piloting, and reflecting on a co-teaching practicum model for our particular context. Our experiences have led us to conclusions that have implications for the next second of our study. In this final section of the chapter, we share these conclusions regarding each of the five concepts in our conceptual framework: *Time Together Outside the Classroom*; *Developing Mutual Understanding; Seeing Teachers as Equal Partners; Engagement and Active Contributions; Communication.*

Time Together Outside the Classroom

Although the set planning meetings and reflection meetings that we arranged worked well, there was little time for planning and reflection on a day-to-day basis. Fitting in even a weekly meeting during face-to-face practicum was difficult for one of our teams. Although of course we would not wish online practicum on our teacher candidate or teachers and students, online practicum did provide more opportunities for planning and reflection on a day-to-day and weekly basis. This leads to a question for discussion by our group to discuss at the workshop in the second round of our process. This question is "Could TC and TM teams use online means to communicate daily, and weekly?"

Developing Mutual Understanding

Although our TC/TM pairs were trying hard to work together well, we wondered how to help them to develop their mutual understanding and trust even more, or even more quickly? The TC needs to trust that the TM will support them when they are teaching. We know that in the "sink or swim" model of the traditional practicum, the idea was to put the TC in the teaching situation and see if they had the "right stuff" for teaching. This old model is built upon the idea that teaching is an innate ability, rather

than a set of skills to be learned. We cannot expect TCs to know already
how to manage a class. At the same time, TMs have developed their teaching abilities through a "trial and error" mode and so it is difficult for them
to be able to tell the TC what to do if students are acting inappropriately.
Teachers notice and react but are not necessarily self-aware of the things
that they are doing that are working well. In other words, they know when
it is working but they may not be able to tell the TC how to do it. As TC/TM
teams gain mutual understanding and see this situation from each other's
perspective, further support is possible and teams can find concrete ways
to support the TC even more, in their early attempts at teaching. We are
thinking about incorporating discussion of this topic into our workshop
on the second round of the study. The question to address is "What are
some concrete ways that TC/TM teams could support the TC in their early
attempts at teaching?"

Seeing Teachers as Equal Partners

Our TMs make a real effort to welcome the TCs and introduce them as
co-teachers, but it still took time for them to be accepted as such. Although
we do understand that this takes time, we do have further ideas that might
help. For example, C&G, during co-teaching online made collaboration
visible to the students in a purposeful way, which was definitely helpful.
Comments to the class like "When we [co-teachers] were talking yesterday
about that activity, we thought that we should do that with you." The use
of the pronoun 'we' and the reporting of consultation together really make
explicit to the students that the teachers are working together as equals.
The teacher candidate C noticed that following these kinds of comments
from G, the students did come to her more often with a question, rather
than always going to G. This implies that a discussion question we would
bring to our future workshop is *What are the ways that TC/TM teams could
make their collaboration more visible for students?*

Engagement and Active Contributions

Although both teachers in our TC/TM pairs were actively engaged as
teachers, we did see that students were not always engaged by TCs lessons
and TM were not sure how to help that situation. This implies further questions for us that we will bring to our workshop for discussion in the second
round of the study. Our questions are: *How can the teachers work together to
engage the students even if the TC is not able to do this alone? What can TMs do
to help without undermining the TC?*

Communication

The big lesson we learned was that communication became easier during online co-teaching, which seems opposite to what we might have expected. Communication was easier because it became possible to find time daily to write an e-mail or chat before and after a Zoom session. This implies that one of the questions to bring back to our team is: *How could we make use of what we have learned through online co-teaching to make communication easier when we are doing face-to-face teaching?*

Limitations and Future Work

Our pilot project with our co-teaching model was very small, involving only two co-teaching teams. We began with just two teams because we want to look in depth as what works and how any issues that arise can be improved. In the second round of our study, we plan to expand to four teams, as soon as we can resume (following the COVID-19 pandemic). We had a teacher candidate drop out of the study (through no fault of his own he had to move to a different school). Recruiting further TCs and TMs willing to jump in would allow us to more seamlessly deal with such an issue in future. The COVID-19 pandemic created a situation where we had to move our study online. Although this created problems in that we could no longer observe the teachers co-teaching face-to-face, it allowed us to investigate a novel area. To the best of our knowledge there are no studies at present looking at co-teaching online. Future work will definitely involve further exploration of this area.

Implications of our pilot project are the questions generated in relation to each theme in our conceptual framework. These are questions that we plan to bring to our workshop participants for discussion in the second round of our study.

Significance

This chapter is linked to two of the recommendations of the AACTE (2018) report: *Developing in a Local Context* and *Sharing the Voices of Multiple Stakeholders*. In the chapter we have shared the process that we are using to democratically develop a co-teaching practicum model that works on our local context. We hope that other programs in other contexts might find this useful.

The impact of the COVID-19 pandemic and the movement of teaching and learning online, offered an unforeseen issue for us to study, namely, co-teaching online. This study offers a view into the experiences of teacher candidates and teacher mentors working online together to support students learning in this unique situation.

REFERENCES

AACTE [American Association of Colleges for Teacher Education] (2018). *A pivot towards clinical practice, its lexicon, and the renewal of educator preparation* (A report of the AACTE clinical practice commission). http://www.nysed.gov/common/nysed/files/cpc-aactecpcreport.pdf

Bacharach, N., Heck, T. W., & Dahlberg, K. (2010). Changing the face of student teaching through co-teaching. *Action in Teacher Education*, *32*(1), 3–14.

Baltrinic, E. R., Jencius, M., & McGlothlin, J. (2016). co-teaching in counselor education: Preparing doctoral students for future teaching. *Counselor Education and Supervision*, *55*(1), 31–45.

Burn, K., & Mutton, T. (2015). Review of 'research-informed clinical practice' in initial teacher education. *Oxford Review of Education*, *41*(2), 217–233.

Daniel, M. M., Ross, P., Stalmeijer, R. E., & de Grave, W. (2018). Teacher perspectives of interdisciplinary co-teaching relationships in a clinical skills course: A relational coordination theory analysis. *Teaching and Learning in Medicine*, *30*(2), 141–151.

Darling-Hammond, L., & Baratz-Snowden, J. (2007). A good teacher in every classroom: Preparing the highly qualified teachers our children deserve. *Educational Horizons*, *85*(2), 111–132.

Friend, M., Reising, M., & Cook, L. (1993). Co-teaching: An overview of the past, a glimpse at the present, and considerations for the future. *Preventing School Failure: Alternative Education for Children and Youth*, *37*(4), 6–10.

Gallo-Fox, J., & Scantlebury, K. (2015). "It isn't necessarily sunshine and daisies every time": Coplanning opportunities and challenges when student teaching. *Asia-Pacific Journal of Teacher Education*, *43*(4), 324–337.

Gallo-Fox, J., & Scantlebury, K. (2016). co-teaching as professional development for teacher mentors. *Teaching and Teacher Education*, *60*, 191–202.

Goodnough, K., Osmond, P., Dibbon, D., Glassman, M., & Stevens, K. (2009). Exploring a triad model of student teaching: Pre-service teacher and cooperating teacher perceptions. *Teaching and Teacher Education*, *25*(2), 285–296.

Grossman, P., Hammerness, K. M., & McDonald, M. (2009). Redefining teaching, re-imagining teacher education. *Teachers and Teaching*, *15*(2), 273–289.

Guise, M., Habib, M., Thiessen, K., & Robbins, A. (2017). Continuum of co-teaching implementation: Moving from traditional student teaching to co-teaching. *Teaching and Teacher Education*, *66*, 370–382.

Harbort, G., Gunter, P. L., Hull, K., Brown, Q., Venn, M. L., Wiley, L. P., & Wiley, E. W. (2007). Behaviors of teachers in co-taught classes in a secondary school. *Teacher Education and Special Education*, *30*(1), 13–23.

Hawkman, A. M., Chval, K. B., & Kingsley, L. H. (2019). 'I feel like I can do it now': preservice teacher efficacy in a co-teaching community of practice. *Teaching Education*, *30*(1), 86–104.

Im, S., & Martin, S. N. (2015). Using cogenerative dialogues to improve co-teaching for language learner (LL) students in an inclusion science classroom. *Asia-Pacific Journal of Teacher Education*, *43*(4), 355–369.

Mattson, M., Eilertson, T. & Rorrison, D. (2011). *A practicum turn in teacher education*. Sense.

Murphy, C. (2016). *Coteaching in teacher education: Innovative pedagogy for excellence*. Critical Publishing.

Murphy, C., & Beggs, J. (2005). Coteaching as an approach to enhance science learning and teaching in primary schools. In: W.-M. Roth &; K. Tobin (Eds.), *Teaching together, learning together* (pp. 207–223). Peter Lang.

Murphy, C., & Martin, S. N. (Eds.). (2015). Coteaching in teacher education: Research and practice. [Special Issue] *Asia-Pacific Journal of Teacher Education*, *43*(4).

Pancsofar, N., & Petroff, J. G. (2016). Teachers' experiences with co-teaching as a model for inclusive education. *International Journal of Inclusive Education*, *20*(10), 1043–1053.

Patrick, R. (2013). "Don't rock the boat": Conflicting mentor and pre-service teacher narratives of professional experience. *The Australian Educational Researcher*, *40*(2), 207–226.

Rabin, C. (2020). Co-Teaching: Collaborative and caring teacher preparation. *Journal of Teacher Education*, *7*(1), 135–147.

Rees, C. A., Murphy, C., & Kaur, R. D. (2020). Inquire together: Teacher candidates, teachers and faculty share ideas regarding a coteaching model. Manuscript submitted for publication.

Roth, W. M. (1998). Science teaching as knowledgeability: A case study of knowing and learning during co-teaching. *Science Education*, *82*(3), 357–377.

Roth, W. M., Masciotra, D., & Boyd, N. (1999). Becoming-in-the-classroom: A case study of teacher development through co-teaching. *Teaching and Teacher Education*, *15*(7), 771–784.

Roth, W.-M., & Tobin, K. (2002). *At the elbow of another: Learning to teach by co-teaching*. Peter Lang.

Roth, W. M., & Tobin, K. G. (2005). *Teaching together, learning together*. Peter Lang.

Roth, W. M., Tobin, K., Carambo, C., & Dalland, C. (2004). Coteaching: Creating resources for learning and learning to teach chemistry in urban high schools. *Journal of Research in Science Teaching*, *41*(9), 882–904.

Roth, W. M., Tobin, K., Carambo, C., & Dalland, C. (2005). Coordination in coteaching: Producing alignment in real time. *Science Education*, *89*(4), 675–702.

Sharma, M., & Cobb, C. (2018). Exploring co-teaching with a social justice perspective: A conceptual study. *Journal on Excellence in College Teaching*, *29*(1), 153–176.

Soslau, E., Kotch-Jester, S., Scantlebury, K., & Gleason, S. (2018). Coteachers' huddles: Developing adaptive teaching expertise during student teaching. *Teaching and Teacher Education*, *73*(1), 99–108.

Soslau, E., Gallo-Fox, J., & Scantlebury, K. (2019). The promises and realities of implementing a coteaching model of student teaching. *Journal of Teacher Education*, *70*(3), 265–279.

Thompson, M., & Schademan, A. (2019). Gaining fluency: Five practices that mediate effective co-teaching between pre-service and mentor teachers. *Teaching and Teacher Education*, *86*, 102903.

Tobin, K. (2006). Learning to teach through coteaching and cogenerative dialogue. *Teaching Education*, *17*(2), 133 142.

Tobin, K., & Roth, W. M. (2005). Implementing coteaching and cogenerative dialoguing in urban science education. *School Science and Mathematics*, *105*(6), 313–322.

Zeichner, K. (2010). Rethinking the connections between campus courses and field experiences in college- and university-based teacher education. *Journal of Teacher Education, 61*, 89–99.

Zeichner, K., Payne, K. A., & Brayko, K. (2015). Democratizing teacher education. *Journal of Teacher Education*, *66*(2), 122–135.

CHAPTER 21

REDESIGNING TEACHER PREPARATION

A Community-Embedded Approach

Rebecca Hines
University of Central Florida

Eileen M. Glavey
Western Carolina University

Whitney Hanley
Gwinnett County Public Schools, GA

Annette Romualdo
University of Minnesota, Duluth

ABSTRACT

In 2017, the Exceptional Education Department at the University of Central Florida (UCF) relaunched the Bachelor of Science in Exceptional Education teacher preparation program after a 6-year hiatus. The relaunch included a redesign of the program from a traditional model to one that is community-embedded, providing ongoing field-based experiences aligned with academic coursework. This chapter describes the community-embedded, experiential learning process used in this program and a discussion of program effective-

Preparing Quality Teachers:
Advances in Clinical Practice, pp. 459–477
Copyright © 2022 by Information Age Publishing
www.infoagepub.com

ness. Key components of the model in use at UCF, along with initial program outcomes and student feedback are reported.

INTRODUCTION

Underprepared for the challenges of today's classrooms, approximately 44% of new teachers leave the profession within five years (Ingersoll et al., 2018). Coupled with a 23% decline in teacher-preparation program enrollment between 2007–2008 and 2015–2016 academic years, teacher education is in crisis (American Association of Colleges for Teacher Education [AACTE], 2018a). Colleges of education are responding to the problem of early-career attrition among teachers by changing teacher education programs to improve graduates' readiness, confidence, and enjoyment of teaching.

The 2010 National Council for Accreditation of Teacher Education (NCATE) Blue Ribbon Panel report, *Transforming Teacher Education Through Clinical Practice: A National Strategy to Prepare Effective Teachers*, and the 2018 follow-up report by the American Association of Colleges and Teacher Education (AACTE), *A Pivot Toward Clinical Practice, Its Lexicon, and the Renewal of Educator Preparation*, advocate for a departure from traditional teacher preparation program models that loosely link school-based experiences to academic coursework (NCATE, 2010; AACTE, 2018a). Both NCATE and AACTE support educating effective teachers moves well beyond the university and into the community where teacher candidates are engaged more closely in schools. As such, NCATE (2010) calls for "dynamic integration of clinical preparation through every facet of teacher education, in course work, laboratory-based experiences, and in school-embedded practice" (p. 5).

New and experienced teachers cite clinical practice as the most highly influential element of their teacher preparation (Darling-Hammond, 2006; Moulding et al., 2014; Ronfeldt, 2012), yet most traditional programs lack ongoing, coherent integration of courses with highly supervised field work in schools and often leave the bulk of clinical practice as a culminating experience that occurs post-coursework (AACTE, 2018a; Darling-Hammond, 2010). The AACTE 2013 Professional Education Data System (PEDS) report *The Changing Teacher Preparation Profession* maintains teacher preparation programs which focus more on classroom experiences and authentic teaching practices are more likely to graduate teacher candidates who remain in the field versus those trained in programs with less emphasis in clinical experience.

Background

The PEDS report shows virtually all teacher preparation programs require supervised student teaching or internship, but the duration varies.

The average bachelor level clinical requirement ranges from 500–562 total clock hours (mean = 14.5 weeks). The average participation in early field experiences ranges from 114–189 clock hours. At the university that this chapter focuses on the existing teacher preparation programs require two internships for teacher candidates during their final year. The first internship places students in school-based classrooms part-time, two days per week, while completing corequisite courses. They have the opportunity to observe teaching, to work with small groups of students, and to complete independent study projects in order to engage in experiential learning. As with most traditional internships, collaborating teachers and university coordinators observe the intern working with students and provide essential feedback about their performance.

The culminating teacher preparation course is nine credit hours and equivalent to a full-time teaching position; the semester-long student teaching position in a school provides a structured, supervised process in which interns work with collaborating teachers to develop their teaching skills. Interns practice to develop knowledge, skills, and dispositions of the teaching profession as measured by the Florida Educator Accomplished Practices (FEAPs) and are provided feedback from collaborating teachers and university coordinators.

The frequency of formal observations and feedback varies from Internship 1 to Internship 2. During Internship 1, supervising teachers complete three observations and clinical coordinators complete two observations. During Internship 2, supervising teachers complete five formal observations and clinical coordinators complete three. In addition, during both Internship 1 and Internship 2 the supervising teacher and clinical coordinator meet with the preservice teacher for midpoint and final evaluations to discuss areas of strength and areas for improvement which includes the student's self-assessment of their teaching and learning experience.

Moving to a Community-Embedded Approach

With the belief teacher candidates must be better prepared to respond to the wide range of student needs in contemporary schools, the undergraduate special education program at a large university responded to the call for increased school-embedded coursework with a redesign and relaunch of its undergraduate special education program in 2017. Prior to 2017, the undergraduate special education program was dormant for six years and allowed no new students. The program enrollment was zero by the 2016 school year and students interested in special education were offered only a minor in the subject and dual certification. Faced with a decision of whether to dissolve the program completely, program faculty voted to reinstate with a full redesign. Site-based course delivery and clinical practice were critical elements added to the new program, which is now described as "community-embedded" in the university course catalog, to ensure students understand its immersive, nontraditional nature.

Drawing from the recommendations of the 2010 report, details of the program specifically include:

1. An emphasis on improving outcomes for local students, with experiences developed in collaboration with K–12 partners and tailored to meet specific problems of practice while tied to specific university course objectives
2. A shift from faculty-directed to student-directed scheduling of experiences using a commercial scheduling software, so students customize their own experiences
3. Teaching residencies that allow students to work as paid paraprofessionals in partnering districts during their senior year, while receiving real-time and remote audio coaching from university mentors related to course objectives.
4. A cohort model that includes doctoral students as site-based advisors in schools

The program specifically addresses the 10 design principles identified by the Blue-Ribbon Panel as described in Table 21.1.

Table 21.1

Program Design Principles and Practices

Design Principle	Operationalized in Special Education Redesign
Focus on PK-12 student learning	Experience in high-achieving school with mentor teachers; Reading clubs; Reading case studies
Dynamic integration of clinical preparation throughout every facet of teacher education	Break room; Content lessons at TLA; Reading clubs; Tech clubs; Residencies and internships
Continuous evaluation of a teacher candidate's progress and of the elements of a preparation program	Performance lab; degree audits; certification tests
Preparation of teachers who are simultaneously content experts and innovators, collaborators, and problem solvers	Break room; Content lessons at TLA; Reading clubs; Tech clubs
Candidate engagement in interactive professional learning communities	Cohort model; formal and informal meetings on-site as regular part of residencies

(Table continued on next page)

Table 21.1 (Continued)

Program Design Principles and Practices

Design Principle	Operationalized in Special Education Redesign
Rigorous selection of clinical educators and coaches from both higher education and the PK–12 sector	Supervision provided by only faculty and qualified doc students; clinical educators hand selected by program rather than school system
Designation of specific sites funded to support embedded clinical preparation	Partner schools with UCP; newly entered agreement between CCIE and UCP; new building
Integration of technology to foster high-impact preparation	Online modules from IRIS, Transition Co-alition, Florida's CPalms;
	Technology clubs on-site at Bailes
Creation of powerful research and development agendas and systematic gathering and use of data to support continuous improvement in teacher preparation	Qualtrics surveys each year, focus groups, follow-up with graduates
Establishment of strategic partnerships for powerful clinical preparation	UCP of Central Florida
	CARD Center

In order to begin the process of relaunching the special education program with the enhanced field experience model, three overarching program goals were identified: Creating self-directed preservice teachers who understand the challenges and are committed to teaching; Meeting program and State goals and objectives for preservice teachers; Serving local schools and community while building a sustainable teaching workforce. Specific experiences were aligned with each semester of the program, and more than 50% of the courses were moved to site-based locations for face-to-face meetings (see Table 21.2).

SHORT-TERM IMPACT

Strong Methods for Training and Monitoring of Teacher Candidates

Cohort Model and Mentoring

The community-embedded program used the cohort model, which encourages a collaborative experience while completing the program as

Table 21.2

Logic Model for Redesigned, Community-Embedded Program

Resources	Activities	Outputs	Short-Term Outcomes(18 months)	Long-Term Outcomes (2–5 years)
• College/Program • Special Education faculty and doctoral student mentors • Well-established university education program • Partner School District • Cadre of master teachers in schools • University administrative support • Undergraduate Special Education majors	• Train selected cadre of master teachers • Redesign coursework as field-embedded • Develop personalized, flexible scheduling system • Establish "Teacher in Residence" (TIR) internship model	• Cadre of master teachers who are certified clinical education supervisors • Campus-district hiring pipeline established • New field-embedded coursework	• Strong methods for training and monitoring of Special Education teacher candidates • Increased coordination between college and community • Pipeline of well-prepared teachers for partner district	• Firmly institutionalized district/campus partnership • Well-established residency program in Special Education • Strong set of field-embedded courses • Institutionalized monitoring system of program components
• Teacher candidates • Undergraduate Special Education majors	• Enroll cohort of candidates in program • Cohort take newly designed coursework • Teacher candidates hired as paraprofessionals and complete TIR internship	• Cohort of highly skilled Special Education teachers graduating • Resident learning community established	• Highly skilled graduates with positions in partner district schools	• Multiple cohorts of novice teachers successfully demonstrating evidence based practices • Increased student achievement

well as provides support, feedback, and encouragement from colleagues. Research shows the use of such models increases the likelihood of program completion (Jay & Miller, 2016). Students received mentorship from current doctoral students in the special education program. Mentoring involved both monthly group meetings and individualized guidance available weekly throughout the program. Field-based experiences, beginning in semester one, provided opportunities for observation of, and immersion in, the practice of teaching as supported by research (Cummins & Asempapa, 2013). Learning communities are formed in content courses; virtual and face to face meetings serve as opportunities for students to engage in the sharing of ideas, enhance understanding of content through faculty led group discussions and check in on progress and possible questions or concerns with on-site course work and assignments throughout each semester.

During the teaching residencies and throughout the entire teacher preparation experience, students had direct contact to the program coordinator and doctoral mentors through text, phone calls, and e-mail seven days per week. Students regularly texted or called with questions ranging from advising questions, requests for teaching feedback and classroom observations, and course assignment clarification. Access to the program coordinator and mentors was unlimited as an intentional part of offering a "customer service" model for gaining and retaining students. Three key elements of business-based customer service were considered as the program was developed:

- Making it easy for students to talk to advising team
- Making processes within the college easy to understand and readily accessible
- "On demand" support and student-centered scheduling (adapted from Lake, 2018).

To ensure students have a personalized experience to set the stage for the program, an interview was required for prospective students before starting the program. The goal of the interview was to let students know the program is nontraditional and that the expectation is that students will be ready to go "above and beyond" in improving the lives of children. The program coordinator and two doctoral assistants, the advising team, provided their cell phone number and performed the interview and an orientation "on demand" to prospective students so that each one had a personal experience to begin the program. All members of the team were informed of the customer service approach and the commitment to finding solutions to whatever issues they faced.

Through the personal interviews, students stated that many of the problems they faced in the initial phase of starting the program had to do with college requirements. The program coordinator conducted a program review to determine which requirements came from the state, university, or college.

Customized Learning and School Partnerships

To meet scheduling needs of students consistent with increased field work, most courses in the program were delivered as mixed mode, with both face-to-face and online components. Coursework used the principles of Universal Design for Learning (UDL) including multiple forms of representation, action, and expression, and means of engagement (Rose & Meyer, 2002). The use of flexible digital media provided multiple alternatives and opportunities to customize teaching and learning. In online and hybrid courses instructor-to-student and student-to-student interactions were facilitated with individual and group video conferencing via Adobe Connect, Zoom, as well as synchronous and asynchronous chats.

Competencies embedded in this specialized program of study were derived from a combination of current national and state adopted standards including the Council for Exceptional Children's (CEC) *Initial and Advanced Professional Content Standards and Knowledge and Skill Sets*, CEC's *Initial Special Education Teachers of Individuals with Exceptional Learning Needs with Developmental Disabilities and/or Autism*; Florida Department of Education's *Florida Educator Accomplished Practices*, *Florida Professional Education Competencies*, *Exceptional Student Education Subject Area Competencies*, and *English for Speakers of Other Languages*.

Partnerships with the Toni Jennings Exceptional Education Institute's (TJEEI), the UCF Center for Autism and Related Disabilities (CARD), Lighthouse of Central Florida, the Down Syndrome Association of Central Florida, United Cerebral Palsy of Central Florida, and local school districts were used to develop field experiences and content modules that meet the needs of scholars, schools, and the community.

Early field placements largely take place in a highly successful public charter school near campus. The school, one of six run by UCP of Central Florida, focuses on inclusion with integrated classrooms serving 50% students without disabilities and 50% students with disabilities including autism spectrum disorders, physical disabilities, intellectual disabilities, learning disabilities, emotional/behavioral disorders, and other health impairment. In spite of an extremely wide range of learners in every classroom, the school received recognition from the governor for the 2016–2017 school year for being in the top 10 out of more than 3,000 Florida schools in the area of raising student achievement in reading.

Increased Coordination Between College and Community

Field Experiences and Personalized Flexible Scheduling

A reality for higher education faculty and those facilitating clinical experiences is scheduling and planning community and school-embedded experiences can be labor intensive and difficult to manage. Turning to technology for student-centered planning, scheduling, and management was key in managing community experiences. To connect students with field-based activities, each semester a schedule of opportunities submitted by local partnering schools and agencies is created. An education subscription to *SCHED*, a commercial web-based event management software, was purchased to add a layer of ease to faculty as well as students. The program includes tools for scheduling, check-in, push notifications, and other related features. Using SCHED, students selected their own experience each semester by pulling up the semester calendar such as the sample in Figure 21.1.

Students planned around their own coursework, work schedules, personal commitments, and so forth, as they fulfilled course requirements and met the needs of community partners. Sample projects included leading after-school technology clubs as a part of a mixed-mode technology course, and leading school-based reading clinics as a part of a reading course taught on-site at a partnering school.

Responsive Community-Embedded Service

Each semester students engaged in one or more field experiences tied to coursework and designed to meet the needs of a school or classroom in the area. Course sequence was adjusted so that topics were clustered for maximum learning. The first semester included a focus on behavior management, a consistent problem area for new teachers. According to Akalin and Sucuoglu (2015), new teachers often lack the proper training and expertise in classroom management. Understanding that behavior management and the inability to effectively implement highly effective behavior management techniques is often cited as one of the biggest issues among new teachers and the cause for many to leave the profession (Briere, et al., 2015), the program planners intentionally focused on clustering

Figure 21.1

Sample Schedule for Student-Centered Planning of Field Activities

coursework in this area early in the preparation sequence. The coursework was tied to a specific program-wide school-based project to reinforce the principles of behavior change while contributing to the community.

For the first semester, the behavior project was designed in response to a request from a local high need elementary school. The school, struggling to reduce the number of suspensions, asked for support from the university. With support from doctoral students, the program coordinator designed a "Break Room" to support the school in its PBIS efforts while allowing a place for undergraduates to spend time learning and practicing self-regulation and other management strategies in real-world setting. The break room intervention was designed based on literature showing that "class pass" style interventions that include positive reinforcement can encourage academically engaged behavior and socially acceptable requests for breaks in the classroom (Boyd & Anderson, 2013; Collins et al., 2016; Stormont et al., 2016). The faculty member coordinating the break room, who is a former teacher of students with emotional/behavioral disorders, designed a management routine as a protocol to be used each time students were sent to the break room (Figure 21.2). Doctoral students supervised the break room and modeled the use of the protocol, and undergraduate students were taught to use the system. Students signed up for "shifts" in the break room each week based on their own availability and documented each visit.

Figure 21.2

Break Room Protocol

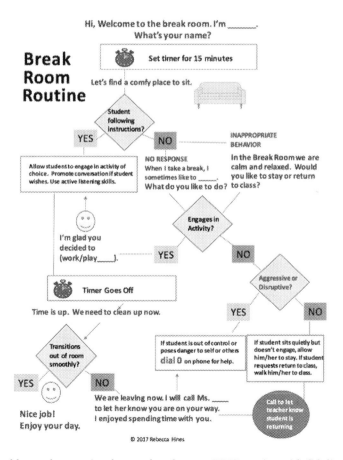

Note. Used by students to implement break room PBIS routine with fidelity.

The Break Room was a drop-in system in which teachers could send students for a 15-minute break during the school day at initial signs of problematic behaviors. The university faculty member who designed and led the break room initiative presented an overview of the break room to faculty at a staff meeting and provided pre-made passes for teachers to use to send students. Teachers were aware that students were welcomed to visit the break room as a "cool down" opportunity or as a reinforcement at the teacher discretion, and that the break would be specifically 15-minutes and that students would be returning immediately afterward. University teacher candidates were involved in all phases of developing the Break Room including picking out furniture and materials, designing the layout, and decorating. Teacher candidates were trained in Break Room procedures by university faculty on site at the school prior to the first day, and a video model was produced for students to watch in class. As part of the Break Room procedures, teacher candidates completed a brief intake survey and wrote summative anecdotal information as students left the room as shown in Table 21.3.

Table 21.3

Break Room Anecdotal Record Sample

"Student came in very upset. She had been sitting in the front office for a few minutes after hitting another girl. We discussed ways she can handle the situation better next time. I suggested her to count to 10 to cool down. After a few minutes, she felt a lot better and played with sensory toys. On the walk back to class, she told me she would apologize."
"Student came in for reward. When talking on the way back to class, we discussed why she came in and what she did that gave her the reward. She stated that she listened to her teacher and payed attention to her teacher and got the reward. She said, "if I listen more to (teacher's name), then I can come back right?" I think this was an effective reward for her."
"Student came in due to being bullied. She was sad and upset because someone said she was fat. We discussed how everyone is different, unique, and special in a way. We talked until she calmed down. I let her talk and vent out her emotions mostly. She said they were mean and she felt embarrassed. She was crying when she came in. After talking and relaxing in the cozy corner with a stress toy, she stopped crying and went back to class with a smile."
"The student walked in very agitated and crying. He was very bothered and frustrated over the incident in the classroom. He chose to lay on the floor and play with the textured tiles and payed with squishy toys. After 15 minutes, he walked out happy and energized. There was a drastic and positive behavior change. These 15 minutes truly helped the student finish his day a lot better."
"The student walked in bothered and walked out in a better mood. On the walk back, he said he liked being here and he would behave better and listen to his teacher."

Of the 252 documented visits to the break room, university students rated their own performance as effective or very effective 98% of the time. They also reported that students entered the break room "calm" 45% of the time, and left "calm" 88% of the time. Because the break room was drop-in only, university students often had "down time" in which they worked on other assignments and online course modules. The experience was specifically aligned with an online classroom management course.

During the second semester teacher candidates worked together to teach a unit on Romeo and Juliet to a high school class of young adults with intellectual disabilities as a part of a Teaching Adolescents and Adults with Disabilities course. The professor modeled for teacher candidates by teaching the first lesson to the classroom of high school students. Students then worked in pairs to build on the unit over the course of the semester concluding with a production of the play. All planning and coordinating of the lessons took place online or in ad hoc group meetings planned by students. During this semester, students also led technology and reading clubs tied to other courses. The third and fourth semesters of the program included traditional coursework and teaching residencies.

Pipeline of Well-Prepared Teachers for Partner School District

Teachers in Residence

After completing year one in various community settings and activities, teacher candidates had the option of completing a full-year teaching residency as "Teachers in Residence" as their culminating internship experience. The Teachers in Residence model used key elements of residencies as identified by Guha et al. (2016), including: strong district/university partnerships; coursework about teaching and learning tightly integrated with clinical practice; full-year residency teaching alongside an expert mentor teacher; high-ability, diverse candidates recruited to meet specific district hiring needs; and cohorts of residents placed in "teaching schools" that demonstrate effective pedagogies/practices with diverse learners and are committed to help novices learn to teach.

To participate in the Teachers in Residence experience, students were made aware of teaching assistant or paraprofessional openings in inclusive classrooms in partnering schools. Students interviewed for the positions as they would any other job for which they are applying, and school administrators hired based on their own criteria. There were multiple opportunities available, so while not all students were hired in their preferred location, all

472   R. HINES ET AL.

students seeking the full year residency found employment and completed the internships.

Students worked for the full school year as teaching assistants in the classroom using the same job description the partnering schools use in hiring other teaching assistants/paraprofessionals. Students were simultaneously enrolled in university internship hours and completed clinical experience assignments consistent with other education majors at the university. Under the university's existing internship requirements, students received formal feedback a minimum of four times per semester from their UCF Clinical Internship Coordinator depending on the level of internship. In addition, faculty and doctoral mentors provided informal feedback during weekly school visits and as requested by teacher candidates. Teachers on-site who had received the clinical supervision training also served as mentors and conducted a minimum of three formal observations and twp formal evaluation meetings throughout the year depending on the level of internship.

PRELIMINARY REVIEW OF PROGRAM EFFECTIVENESS

By the second year of the program the number of participants in the special education undergraduate program grew from 12 students in year one to 72 students in year two. As a program review, data on effectiveness of the program in preparing effective special education teachers was collected by means of teacher candidate surveys and interviews, focus groups, and internship observations to determine the extent to which the program operated as intended. Data collected during all phases of the project (ongoing, monthly, each semester, and annually) was used for formative evaluation at the end of the first year of the program to determine needed changes in course design and delivery. Data was also used to refine logistical procedures, catalog description, course delivery, and program options. Data from the original 2017–2018 cohort of 11 students is shared in this section.

In an end-of-experience survey, 100% of preservice teachers reported that experience in schools was the greatest contributor to their learning (see Figure 21.4). In response to the question, *In what area do you feel most prepared?* the most frequent responses were collaborating with others and making modifications and accommodations. The areas receiving the fewest responses were lesson planning and teaching math.

Survey results were sorted by year in the program to gain and understanding of student growth in the program. By their third and fourth semesters, 100% of students in the community-embedded program self-reported proficiency in aligning instruction with state-adopted standards and in adapting the learning environment to accommodate the needs of a diverse student population (see Figure 21.3). Students reported over

65% growth in their proficiency between their first and second year in the program in the area of managing individual and classroom behaviors (see Figure 21.3). Students attributed their growth in confidence to the program emphasis on proactive behavior management plans, as demonstrated by embedding the *Break Room Protocol* in two partner schools, and the Teachers in Residence experience.

Figure 21.3

Preservice Teacher Self-Reported Greatest Contributors to Learning

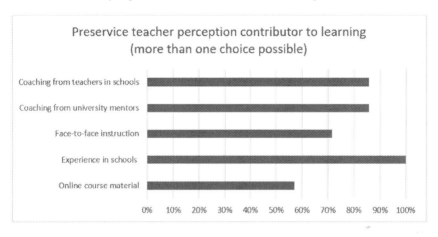

Looking more deeply at students' ratings of their proficiency in accomplished practices, students felt confident supporting, encouraging, and providing immediate and specific feedback to students; concurrently, they felt able to effectively design assessments to adapt instruction based on student need—thereby increasing student achievement. Finally, a defining characteristic of current preservice teachers and recent graduates is their ability to deliver engaging and challenging lessons in a manner to maximize student understanding—with 50% growth in self-perceived ability over the course of their experience (see Figure 21.4).

DISCUSSION

The goals of the undergraduate program redesign presented in this chapter were to create self-directed teacher candidates who are committed to teaching and understand its challenges, who can meet program and state goals and objectives for teacher candidates, and who become a part of a sustainable teaching workforce. Using a cohort model, increased classroom-based

Figure 21.4

Preservice Teacher Confidence in Their Knowledge and Skills With FEAPs

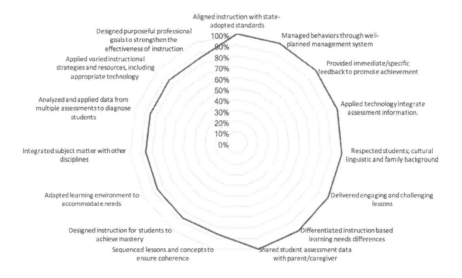

3rd and 4th Semester Teacher in Residence
Confidence in Accomplished Practices

experiences, a customer-service style communication system, and teaching residencies the program met its initial goals.

In the first two years of the program, the number of students jumped from 11 in fall 2017 to 72 by spring 2019. Based on information collected in an initial program review after the first two years of existence, students in the program felt well prepared in all of the State's accomplished practices. By December 2019 there were 20 program graduates, 18 of whom are currently teaching. Of those, 16 completed the Teachers in Residence experience, and 14 have remained in the district in which they completed the teaching residency.

At a time when teacher recruitment and retention is a critical need in the field of education and the state of Florida has been plagued with a critical shortage of special education teachers for decades, the preliminary outcomes of the community-embedded approach to teacher preparation are promising. Teacher candidates engaged in field-embedded training designed with flexibility, modeling of evidence-based practices, and support, appear well positioned to meet the immediate and long-term needs of schools in their community. In one of the toughest fields for recruiting, community-embedded teacher preparation may afford the opportunity to build a sustainable workforce of teachers who feel experienced and confident. This approach calls for university faculty of educator preparation programs to make a commitment to move away from a traditional mindset of campus-based instruction followed by school-based experiences and to build flexibility into scheduling, communications, and coursework as they prepare educators for today's classrooms.

IMPLICATIONS FOR RESEARCH AND PRACTICE

The NEA formally recommended that traditional teacher preparation for undergraduates incorporate resident teacher program principles that move beyond the traditional internship and include a full one-year residency to prepare fully "profession-ready" teachers. On a practical level, however, planning and managing more clinical placements and residencies may be more costly to traditional programs with limited resources for supervision and coordination. A key to making this change is moving away from a prescriptive university-need-based program to a focus on building key partnerships and working closely with area schools who are eager for additional support. The call for "authentic partnerships" by the NEA includes partners who co-construct and co-own all aspects of the experience, including staffing, funding, accountability, and program improvement (Coffman & Patterson, 2013). Allowing clinical experiences and residencies to become an integral part of a school or school system and allowing K–12 teachers and administrators to help shape the partnership based on school needs can allow school faculty and staff to find the best fit for candidates. Placing students in cohorts or clusters greatly reduces the travel and supervision needs for university faculty and staff.

In 2014 the U.S. Department of Education (Silva et al., 2014) reported that novice residency program teachers felt more prepared in seven of eight teaching activities than nonresidency novice teachers, with key areas such as classroom management and adapting classroom materials showing a 17% difference in perceived proficiency. These key areas were also reported as perceived strengths by participants in the community-embedded program described in this chapter.

As the profession continues to struggle with the high cost of teacher turnover, residencies may offer a solution and should continue to be examined. A National Center for Teaching Residencies study (2016) across 14 cities in the United States found that for those completing residencies the three-year attrition rate for teachers was 16% compared to the national average of 33%. Further research into the specific experiences of teacher candidates is recommended to help define and understand these trends. In addition, research on the effectiveness of graduates of residency programs, including whether they are more successful in reducing referrals and suspensions, would move the discussion of the need for residencies forward and tie more directly to its impact on classrooms and students.

Lastly, ease of communication was a fundamental factor contributing to the success of the newly designed teacher preparation program. Communication between university faculty and school partners, as well as communication with students enrolled in the program was ongoing and steady. Anecdotally, the researchers note students used texting far more than any other means of communication. Additionally, texting with principals and teachers at partner school sites became a primary means of communication about job openings, recommendations, meetings, and "check-ins" on teacher candidates. The ability to maintain a responsive customer service approach with both students and partner school sites via text messages cannot be underscored. Future research should focus on how this personalized approach impacts teacher recruitment and retention.

REFERENCES

Akalin, S. & Sucuoglu, B. (2015). Effects of classroom management intervention based on teacher training and performance feedback on outcomes of teacher-student dyads in inclusive classrooms. *Educational Sciences: Theory & Practice, 15*(2), 739–758.

American Association of Colleges for Teacher Education. (2018a). *A pivot toward clinical practice, its lexicon, and the renewal of educator preparation: A report of the AACTE clinical practice commission.when* https://aacte.org/resources/clinical-practice-commission

Boyd, R. J., & Anderson, C. M. (2013). Breaks are better: A tier II social behavior intervention. *Journal of Behavioral Education, 22*(4), 348–365.

Briere, D. E., Simonsen, B., Sugai, G., & Myers, D. (2015). Increasing new teachers' specific praise using a within-school consultation intervention. *Journal of Positive Behavior Interventions, 17*(1), 50–60. https://doi.org/10.1177/1098300713497098

Collins, T. A., Cook, C. R., Dart, E. H., Socie, D. G., Renshaw, T. L., & Long, A. C. (2016). Improving classroom engagement among high school students with disruptive behavior: Evaluation of the class pass intervention. *Psychology in the Schools, 53*(2), 204–219.

Cummins, L., & Asempapa, B. (2013). Fostering teacher candidate dispositions in teacher education programs. *Journal of the Scholarship of Teaching and Learning, 13*(3), 99–119.

Coffman, A. N., & Patterson, R. (2013). *Teacher residencies: Redefining preparation through partnerships.* National Education Association.

Darling-Hammond, L. (2006). Constructing 21st-century teacher education. *Journal of Teacher Education, 57*(3), 300–314.

Darling-Hammond, L. (2010). Teacher education and the American future. *Journal of Teacher Education*, *61*(1-2), 35–47.

Guha, R., Hyler, M. E., & Darling-Hammond, L. (2016). *The teacher residency: An innovative model for preparing teachers*. https://learningpolicyinstitute.org/sites/default/files/product-files/Teacher_Residency_Innovative_Model_Preparing_Teachers_REPORT.pdf

Ingersoll, R., Merrill, E., Stuckey, D., & Collins, G. (2018). *Seven trends: The transformation of the teaching force—updated October 2018*. CPRE Research Reports. https://repository.upenn.edu/cpre_researchreports/108

Jay, J., & Miller, H. (2016). Immersing teacher candidates in experiential learning: Cohorts, learning communities, and mentoring. *Global Education Review*, *3*(4), 169–175.

Lake, L. (2018). *Top 5 customer service best practices*. https://www.thebalancesmb.com/best-practices-for-excelling-at-customer-service-2295990

Moulding, L., Stewart, P., & Dunmeyer, M. (2014). Pre-service teachers' sense of efficacy: Relationship to academic ability, student teaching placement characteristics, and mentor support. *Teaching and Teacher Education*, *41*, 60–66.

National Council for Accreditation of Teacher Education Blue Ribbon Panel on Clinical Preparation and Partnerships for Improved Student Learning. (2010). *Transforming teacher education through clinical practice: A national strategy to prepare effective teachers*. http://www.ncate.org/LinkClick.aspx?fileticket=zzeiB1OoqPk%3D

National Center for Teacher Residencies. (2016). *NCTR network partner report 2015–16*.

Ronfeldt, M. (2012). Where should student teachers learn to teach? Effects of field placement school characteristics on teacher retention and effectiveness. *Educational Evaluation and Policy Analysis*, *34*(1), 3–26.

Rose, D. H., & Meyer, A. (2002). *Teaching every student in the digital age: Universal Design for Learning*. Elsevier.

Silva, T., McKie, A., Knechtel, V., Gleason, P., & Makowsky, L. (2014). *Teaching residency programs: A multisite look at a new model to prepare teachers for high-need schools*. National Center for Education Evaluation and Regional Assistance, Institute for Education Sciences.

Stormont, M. A., Rodriguez, B. J., & Reinke, W. M. (2016). Teaching students with behavior problems to take a break. *Intervention in School and Clinic*, *51*(5), 301–306.

CHAPTER 22

RELATIONSHIPS IN CLINICAL PRACTICE EXPERIENCES

An Examination of Student Teaching Triads in a Science Education Program

Lesley J. Shapiro
Classical High School

Rudolf V. Kraus II
Rhode Island College

ABSTRACT

Clinical practice, like most aspects of teacher education, is built on partnerships and relationships between faculty, teacher educators, clinical educators, and other participants. Through a series of interviews, this study examines the role of relationships in an exemplary clinical practice environment. Data show that teacher candidates thrive most when they feel supported and when relationships are sources of mutual benefit.

Preparing Quality Teachers:
Advances in Clinical Practice, pp. 479–496
Copyright © 2022 by Information Age Publishing
www.infoagepub.com

479

INTRODUCTION

Within the context of teacher education, the emphasis on clinical experiences has increased in recent years (American Association of Colleges for Teacher Education [AACTE], 2018; Council for the Accreditation of Educator Preparation [CAEP], 2018; National Council for Accreditation of Teacher Education [NCATE], 2010) across all educational domains. These clinical practice experiences, particularly student teaching, present profound opportunities for growth and development for teacher candidates including in our field of science education. At the same time, this increased focus on clinical experience creates an opportunity for teacher educators to return to K–12 schools and engage with practicing teachers in a manner that fosters deeper professional relationships and presents opportunities to bridge the gap between research and practice.

Critical to any clinical experience process is the selection of a strong mentor teacher as this person will spend far more one-on-one time with the teacher candidate than the university faculty member. However, there is little in the literature about the criteria for selecting a strong mentor teacher, nor is there much to define what makes a relationship strong (Steadman & Brown, 2011). We set out to examine the past practice of our own secondary science education program, because we are fortunate enough to have several long-term relationships which are working very well for the university faculty member, the mentor teacher, and the teacher candidate. This examination was guided by the following question: What are the features of a strong triad relationship that lead to success?

In this chapter we explore the findings from an exemplary case study on the relationships that are established and developed within the context of our own student teaching triads. We share the lessons that we have learned and discuss how this self-reflection has sharpened the clinical placement experience in our secondary science education program.

LITERATURE REVIEW

While clinical practice has become a priority in teacher education, this is a relatively under-researched area of study. Of the roughly 2,000 pages that make up the first and second *Handbook on Teacher Education*, only seven pages are devoted to the members of the student teaching triad; including the college supervisor, the mentor teacher, and the teacher candidate (Steadman & Brown, 2011). Because much of the activity of the triad is context-based and collectively focused on individual classrooms, the collective autobiography approach to practitioner research is an appropriate methodology (Dewey, 1910; Gordon, 2016).

Our definition of triad includes the college supervisor, the mentor teacher, and the teacher candidate (Steadman & Brown, 2011). Within this definition it is assumed that the college supervisor is a teacher education faculty member. This differs from the more common model where the college supervisor is not a teacher education faculty member (Rozelle & Wilson, 2012) and instead is a graduate student with teaching experience, a retired teacher, or a retired principal hired by the college for the purposes of observing teacher candidates in the field (Koerner et al., 2002; Slick, 1997). This differs from the role of the college supervisor described by Koster et al. (1998) and Nguyen (2009) who describe this role as a liaison between teacher education faculty and mentor teachers. A diagram contrasting these two paradigms is shown in Figure 22.1.

Figure 22.1

Paradigms of Clinical Practice

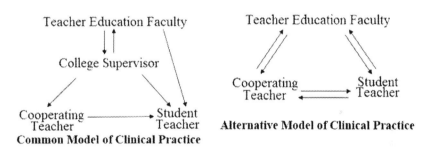

Other models of the hierarchy of relationships and roles within the student teaching experience have been proposed. Veal and Rikard (1998) suggest that there are two relationship triads, an institutional triad, and a functional triad, extant in the context of student teaching. The institutional triad focuses on the context of teacher preparation and includes the college supervisor, mentor teacher, and teacher candidate. The functional triad includes the mentor teacher, teacher candidate, and the K–12 students. Another model, proposed by Talvitie and colleagues (2000) envision the relationships within student teaching as a quadrilateral which includes the college supervisor, mentor teacher, teacher candidate, and also includes the teacher candidate's peers. While we recognize that other models of relationships exist, our examination focused only on the relationships of the members of the institutional triad, and we are defining the triad as the entirety of our case study. Other models such as the ones proposed by

Veal and Rikard (1998) and Talvitie and colleagues (2000) are outside the boundaries of our case.

The research published in this area demonstrates that supervising teacher candidates is complex. There is an inherent contradiction in the dual roles of the people involved in the supervision and assessment of teacher candidates (Acheson & Gaul, 2003; Feiman-Nemser, 1996; Slick, 1997). The college supervisor, who may or may not be a teacher education faculty member, needs to both support and evaluate the teacher candidate. The tension inherent in this role leads college supervisors and teacher education faculty members to focus on specific skill sets in teaching practice (Zeichner, 2005).

As defined by Nguyen (2009), mentor teachers oversee their mentee's daily activities, assist them in solving classroom situations, and evaluate their performance. Mentor teachers tend to exert influence in different areas from their college-level colleagues, including the development of the teacher candidate's educational philosophy (Boschee et al., 1979) and their self-concept as a teacher (Rozelle & Wison, 2012). Despite this important role, mentor teachers are often untrained and are either unpaid or underpaid for their work (Young & MacPhail, 2015; Zeichner, 2005). Zeichner (2005) states that in the United States most teachers are asked to mentor without any formal preparation or ongoing support (Hoffman et al., 2015). In selecting mentor teachers, attention needs to be paid to the quality of the teacher's instructional practice (Rozelle & Wilson, 2012; Zeichner, 2002) as well as their ability to explain their own practices to others.

The learning that occurs during student teaching occurs in two separate contexts, the K–12 classroom and the college classroom (Cuenca, 2011). Shifting between these two contexts forces the teacher candidate to repeatedly shift their identity, from teacher to student, according to the environment (Veal & Rikard, 1998). Additional stresses have been noted for teacher candidates from different cultural backgrounds and also for those who struggle financially (Nguyen, 2009; Slick, 1997).

EXISTING PROGRAM AND CONTEXT

As the largest teacher education program in a small New England state, we have several advantages with regard to the placement of teacher candidates for their clinical experiences. The first is the relative ease of conducting observations, which can be done in person due to the small size of our state. The second advantage is that in our institution's secondary teacher education programs the students have developed a relationship with the college faculty member through the advising process long before they reach student teaching. It is also common for education majors to have had their college supervisor as a faculty member in a previous course. The third advantage is that faculty members conduct the observations of their teacher candidates during student teaching and other clinical practice experiences which results in a tighter alignment between these experiences and class-room-based instruction. Student teachers are observed a minimum of three times by the college supervisor prior to full-time student teaching. The final advantage is that our program allows for the placement of teacher candidates by teacher education faculty members. Thus, faculty members are able to recruit mentor teachers who serve as clinical educators and who exhibit the dispositions and reform-based pedagogical practices that our program values in secondary science teachers that they have seen in the classroom, encountered in other professional environments, from the college's graduate education programs, or referred from highly successful cooperating teachers.

Throughout our program there is a strong emphasis on clinical experi-ences and clinical practice. Teacher candidates in their early education coursework conduct observations, interview teachers, and serve as school-based tutors. In all, our teacher candidates complete over 100 hours of clinical practice prior to student teaching. In their final year of teacher education, teacher candidates complete both a 60-hour practicum in the fall semester and a 14-week full-time student teaching placement in the spring semester. At the time of publication, plans to dramatically increase the amount of clinical practice in our program are underway and will go into effect with the class of 2023.

We feel that we have been highly successful in preparing future science teachers. Over 90% of the graduates of our secondary science education program since 2012 remain classroom teachers, greatly exceeding the national retention rate. Since 2014, program graduates and mentor teach-ers from our stronger triads have presented at state and national level practitioner science education conferences and have taken leadership roles in district-wide curricular reform.

METHODOLOGY

In this chapter we draw on the framework of an exemplar case study (Yin, 2014) to provide more data related to the case of triads of two mentor teachers who worked with teacher candidates between 2013–2017. These mentor teachers were purposefully selected (Patton, 2014) show a high level of success and did not demonstrate any barriers historically identified in the literature (Applegate & Lasley, 1982; Hoffman et al., 2015; Richard-son-Koehler, 1988). Based on our bias and involvement in the project we also draw on the paradigm of collective autobiography (Gordon, 2016) to capture our positionality within the context or our work. The goal of this is to use data to tell our story, draw conclusions, and interpret about how this work may influence future clinical practice endeavors.

Defining a Triad

Our definition of a triad originates with Barrows (1979) as a three-person relationship including the college supervisor, Rudolf Kraus, the mentor teacher, sometimes Lesley Shapiro, and the teacher candidate. All individuals have the opportunity to teach and learn from each other. Our view of the relationship between the members of the student teaching triad is one where all three individuals serve to both inform and support the others as seen in Figure 22.2. This bridge between theory and practice serves to educate all members of the triad as they engage with one another through continuous dialogue surrounding the development of teaching practice. The learning that occurs within the context of these relationships is used to inform and structure continuous program improvement.

Figure 22.2

Triad Relationships and Information Flow

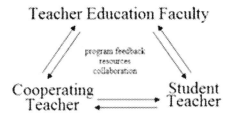

Data Collection and Analysis

Data were gathered through a series of semistructured interviews which focused on the triad member's experiences within the triad and their relationships with the other members of the triad. All interviews lasted between 30 and 45 minutes and each was audio-recorded and transcribed. Initial coding was done using a constant-comparative method (Lincoln & Guba, 1985) and conducted independently by each author. Once the initial codes were completed, the authors met to confer until agreement was reached. In this way, we constructed a collective autobiography built from the voices of all triad participants.

This collaborative examination of our shared experience within the triad relationship led to findings which we would not have come across without these efforts. As a result of the findings below, we are working to improve and expand our clinical placement process.

FINDINGS

Data analysis yielded five themes common to highly successful triad relationships. The themes that emerged are the importance of the teacher candidates feeling supported, the perspective that the triad relationships allow for members to act as resources for each other, the system's transmission of values as well as knowledge, the persistence of strong relationships, and the importance of carefully matching teacher candidates with mentor teachers. Figure 22.3 presents an overview of the findings, and the following subsections will discuss each of the findings in detail.

Figure 22.3

Overview of Findings

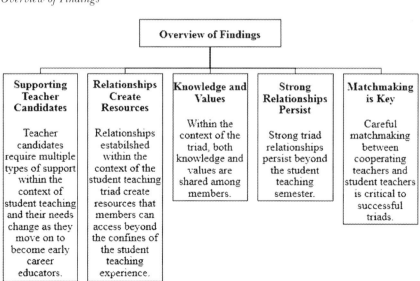

Supporting Teacher Candidates

During clinical placement, support in science teaching "focuses on pedagogy and classroom management with the goal of developing teaching skills and fostering the teacher candidate's self-efficacy." One teacher candidate, Susan, said

> It's really easy to just think that it's mentor teacher and teacher candidate and there's no connection of the mentor teacher to the professor. But in my case, that connection was strong, and therefore it benefited me in terms of my growth because they were having conversations about what was going on day-to-day in the classroom and what resources I needed, from not only the mentor teacher but from the professor to help me gain the skills I needed to be a successful classroom teacher.

Our data show that teacher candidates need to feel supported by both their mentor teacher and teacher education faculty member in a broad range of contexts. In our program, day-to-day support is provided by the mentor teacher and is bolstered through weekly interactions with the teacher education faculty member during the student teaching seminar. Frequent communication between the teacher education faculty member and the mentor teachers is used to structure seminar sessions based on the needs of the teacher candidates in that year's cohort.

Support during clinical practice, particularly between mentor teachers and teacher candidates, can also be more personal in nature (Maria-Monica & Alina, 2014). For traditional college students, the clinical practice experience coincides with their transition from college student to early-career teacher. For nontraditional college students, spending a semester in clinical practice can create personal and financial hardships. Winston, a mentor teacher explained this as:

> For people who are not traditional students, who may be working full-time trying to get into teaching as a new career, it's very difficult for them. It's almost set up for them to fail. They have to commit to student teaching. They have to commit to a full-time, unpaid student teaching position. And if they have a family, if they try to support themselves or their family, it's really, really difficult. So, a lot of things give because of that.

In either case, both mentor teachers and teacher education faculty members must be able to provide support to the teacher candidate as they encounter difficulties. Further, long-term relationships between mentor teachers and programs of teacher education allow for mentor teachers to be familiar with the wide range of supports offered by the university, including social and financial support as well as healthcare.

As teacher candidates transition out of their clinical practice placement, their needs for support change, but often do not diminish. Having the ability to reach out to the teacher education faculty member or mentor teacher for support can be very helpful. During the preemployment period, teacher candidates can require support as they move through the job application process. This type of support can include letters of reference or recommendations from the teacher education faculty member and mentor teacher, answers to questions about the interview process, and ultimately feedback on decisions about job offers. Heidi, a teacher candidate, pointed out that her mentor teacher was:

> A really good ally in my personal life. I wasn't in a great spot so Ms. Shapiro was a good ally to kind of encourage me to break out of where I was at and take on a new opportunity.

The shift from teacher candidate to beginning teacher represents a significant change both in the individual's self-concept and their professional responsibilities. As such, they may require ongoing support in their first few years of practice. This need for support can be magnified in instances where the school or school district lacks a robust mentoring and induction program. The ability to reach back to the other members of the triad creates an important lifeline for beginning teachers to express fears, ask questions, and receive feedback. Lexi, a teacher candidate, shared:

> A lot of the times mentor teachers and professors leave that relationship when you graduate, and when you're done in May. But having both of you continue to be like, "Hey, what's going on? Do you need help? How can we support you, not just now that you're done student teaching, now that you're an actual teacher, how can we still support you in that?" Which makes me more effective, because I have other people that aren't just in my department that are supporting me, because my department is not supportive.

This was also echoed by one mentor teacher who said:

> I believe that the student teaching relationship doesn't end when they leave me in May. I occasionally jokingly call it lifetime tech support, and so they call me. Since the beginning of this year, I fielded questions from four of my five previous teacher candidates, even though some of them have been in the classroom for three years.

Relationships Serve as Resources

In a healthy triad, relationships are multidirectional and result in a situation where all members act as resources for each other. While college faculty are expected to have subject matter expertise, it is the mentor teacher who knows the students and the school best. As such, mentor teachers can serve as an invaluable resource for personalizing the experience of the teacher candidate. These teachers can be valuable to the college program in many other ways, including serving on advisory panels, participating in mock interviews to prepare teacher candidates for the job search, opening their classroom doors for observations, and connecting college faculty with other colleagues in their school or discipline. Additionally, both the mentor teacher and the teacher candidate are in a position to provide feedback on the effectiveness of the college's teacher education program. Susan, a teacher candidate, explained:

> I think that Lesley has been very reflective on what she's done with me as her student teacher and has taken that reflectiveness and applied it to her future student teachers, who I actually am in contact with as well, and share advice and talk to a lot about working with my mentor teacher and how to make the relationship work, and the benefits of the relationship that you will have with the mentor teacher. So, I think that with her reflecting on my practice and giving her my direct feedback on working with her through student teaching, she's been able to also use that to better herself as a mentor teacher.

Through their participation in the triad relationship, mentor teachers access a different series of resources. These resources focus on access to the expertise of the college faculty member in areas unrelated to the preparation of the teacher candidate. This can open up additional opportunities for professional development and graduate-level education. The college faculty member, by being part of multiple triad relationships, is also in a position to facilitate teachers learning from each other. One mentor teacher pointed out:

> It's nice because when Dr. Kraus comes in for observations, I get to talk to him, and it's always interesting because he visits most of the schools in the state. So, he has firsthand knowledge of what other teachers are doing in the state, and it's nice to tap into that experience and tap into those observations that he has. For example, I had some questions about standards-based grading and standards-based reporting, and he was able to tell me, "Well, yeah, at [District A] they do this, and in [District B] they do this, and there's a teacher in [District C] who's using this program," and that would be impossible to get from anyone else. So, in that sense, it's nice having that resource. In fact, a couple times I e-mailed him with questions about standards-based grading, and he was able to provide some resources right off the top of his head. So, in that sense, it's just having a good resource.

Knowledge and Values

Clinical preparation is not strictly about instructional methods and classroom management. The process of being a teacher candidate communicates much more. Questions like "What should we be spending our limited time on?" and "What is the job of a teacher, really?" come to be answered by observing and listening to the mentor teacher. Our data show that mentor teachers and teacher candidates usually share views of what successful teaching looks like (Rozelle & Wilson, 2012). They share beliefs about the role of the teacher, the role of the school, and other beliefs and values.

In the community of science teacher educators, one of our goals is to ensure that the teacher candidates we graduate remain members of the professional communities of science teachers. Our findings indicate that teacher candidates often come to adopt their mentor teacher's views on what it means to participate in the community of educators. Another teacher candidate, Lexi, pointed out:

> I would not have the professional goals, I guess. If I was with a mentor teacher and a professor that didn't also do other things outside. Like if their main goal was just teaching in a classroom, being a professor, and that's all they did, I wouldn't have the exposure to doing something like … well the Rhode Island Science Teachers Association conference is easy, but NSTA, because I wouldn't have known about it. I didn't know about it at all until you guys kind of brought that up, and kind of pushed me not so gently towards that. So, I wouldn't have had that opportunity, I guess.

In turn, mentor teachers who are not involved in their respective professional communities can have their interest ignited by their relationship with the teacher education faculty member. Rachel, a mentor teacher, said, "I don't know that I would have started presenting at conferences had Dr. Kraus not pushed me to do that for the first time."

Strong Relationships Persist

The relationship between the members of the triad does not end at the expiration of the clinical placement term at the end of the student teaching semester. In our small state, where most graduates remain after earning their degree, they remain part of the community. As such, the new beginning teachers feel comfortable contacting members of the triad for advice or feedback. As they progress further in their career, these relationships provide opportunities for collaboration. Susan points out:

Lesley and I have had a very long-term relationship outside of student teaching. She has been my sounding board; she has been kind of my cheer-leader even after student teaching has ended. We have in-depth conversa-tions about what's going on that did not occur in student teaching only because I didn't have my own personal experience being the main teacher in the classroom. So, our conversations have gotten more in-depth, more specific to what goes on in a classroom and how to best present material to students. We have also both presented many times together at different state and national conferences.

Strong relationships between mentor teachers and the teacher educa-tion faculty members are equally fruitful. Mentor teachers and the teacher education faculty members find themselves working together in other contexts, including graduate education, the state's Science Olympiad, or administration of the state's science teacher association.

Matchmaking Is Key

Careful matching of mentor teachers and teacher candidates is impor-tant and pays off tremendously when done well. Knowledge of both the mentor teacher and teacher candidate as people allows placements to be made not just on the basis of certification and availability but also on tem-perament, strengths, interests, and goals. One teacher education faculty member stated:

It really helps me pair up individual student teachers with mentor teach-ers, because I know what our students need. And then I know what the strengths are out in the field, and I can make matches, which will benefit both of them, as opposed to just "I found you a room. Good enough. See you in May."

This was echoed by Rachel, a mentor teacher, who said:

I think that initial discussions about needs are important. Having worked with Dr. Kraus multiple times, the discussion when I get a student teacher isn't, "Okay, here you go. Here are the forms." It's, "all right, this is what I assessed as what I think this person needs through practicum. These are the strengths and weaknesses." That's allowed me to give the student teach-er more targeted feedback. It also lets me talk to the student teacher in a different way and say, "Okay, how can I help you? What are your needs?"

Veteran mentor teachers know the college's program, and this means that they are familiar with the expectations and associated paperwork. When less time can be spent on introductions, more time can be spent on the teacher candidate. Our secondary criteria for mentor teacher selection include a willingness to cede control over their classroom, ability to prioritize feedback without overwhelming the teacher candidate, and investment in the process of developing beginning teachers.

Summary of Findings

Relationships within the student teaching triad are multidimensional, complex, and extend beyond the term of the student teaching experience. Within student teaching and beyond, teacher candidates are supported by both their mentor teacher and the teacher education faculty member. Continued persistence of these relationships creates a network of accessible resources for all members. Pedagogical knowledge and pedagogical content knowledge are only part of what is transmitted within the context of the triad relationship; values, such as what it means to be a teacher and what it means to be an engaged member of the professional community, are modeled and supported. Outside of the creation of resources, highly successful triad relationships persist long after graduation. Maximizing the potential of a student teaching triad requires careful matching of mentor teachers and teacher candidates.

DISCUSSION AND FUTURE DIRECTIONS

Discussion of Findings

Sustained relationships between the mentor teacher and the teacher education faculty member allow for the creation of a shared vision where both individuals are familiar with the context of the other. In addition to a shared understanding of the processes and procedures of both institutions, a strong relationship also allows for the growth of trust, which is essential to both parties (Koerner, 1992; Rikard & Veal, 1996). A sustained relationship between the mentor teacher and university-based teacher educator is also important because learning to mentor teacher candidates takes years and not months (AACTE, 2018; Aspfors & Fransson, 2015). Teacher education programs benefit by going back to strong mentor teachers year after year.

A teacher candidate should be delivered from a university campus to a K–12 classroom with a discussion of that individual's strengths and weaknesses. In a similar way, the strengths and weaknesses of the mentor teacher should factor into decisions about whom they will be assigned. Further, the observations of the mentor teachers should feed into the structure of the student teaching experience and the topics for the student teaching seminar course. Additionally, feedback from all members of the triad should be used to inform future clinical practice experiences at all stages. This is not commonly the process that exists in teacher candidate placement (Wang & Odell, 2002; Ulvik & Sunde, 2013).

While clinical practice experiences are defined within a set time period, we observe and experience that these mutually beneficial relationships sustain themselves after the 14 weeks of student teaching have come to a close. When strong relationships exist, teacher candidates continue to draw upon the other members of the triad for support, which offers them access to continued mentoring during the induction years and sometimes beyond.

Mentor teachers are not only a resource for their teacher candidates, they also act as a resource for the teacher education faculty member. In fact, the impetus for this study came from author two's observation that our program's outcomes exceed the national averages in terms of persistence in the field. We felt that we were doing something right and decided to try and document exactly what that was through collective autobiography. In so doing, we have clarified for ourselves the usefulness of the AACTE (2018) recommendations.

This interdependence among triad members falls under the collaborative inquiry model suggested by Wang and Odell (2002). Deeper collaboration of this type can take the form of testing materials or serving as a site for research and observation. Further, these relationships can be expanded so that mentor teachers from different contexts can be introduced to provide each other support.

From the perspective of a mentor teacher, it is important that the college supervisor is the same individual as the teacher education faculty member. This creates a coherence of view that is helpful for providing focus to a process that can seem amorphous. Continued work with the same teacher education faculty member not only benefits the teacher candidates with clarification of process and shared vision, but also pushes the mentor teacher into expanded roles through their continuous interactions with the teacher education faculty member (Applegate & Lasley, 1982). One mentor teacher, author two, credits her relationship with the teacher education faculty member for encouraging her to present her work locally and nationally as well as her pursuit of a doctorate in education.

As a teacher education faculty member, Rudolf Kraus finds that returning to a location is useful because of the familiarity with the policies, personnel, and students of a district. This avoids the problems cited in Applegate and Lasley (1982). Curricular and technological resources are also known, and this information can be shared with the teacher candidate in advance. Knowledge of individual mentor teachers allows placements to be made on the basis of temperament and teaching philosophy instead of merely certification and geography (Hoffman et al., 2015). This prevents the teacher candidates from being used as an emergency supplement to the workforce at the expense of their own development as teachers.

In science education, there is an extensive push on the part of CAEP and the National Science Teachers Association for teacher candidates' involvement in the professional community. Our limited data show that this type of engagement can be fostered when mentor teachers are themselves actively engaged in their professional communities. This can result in the sharing of values and practices (Rozelle & Wilson, 2012), including conference presentations and active participation in the professional community of educators.

Future Directions

The work of a mentor teacher is really the work of a clinical education faculty member. A strong mentor teacher serves as a model of best practice, observes, and provides feedback to the teacher candidate, engages in clinical coaching, and helps them grow into their new profession (Maria-Monica & Alina, 2014). While onerous, the care and diligence that goes into hiring a new university colleague should be brought to bear on the selection of mentor teachers as well.

In establishing a relationship with a mentor teacher, university-based teacher educators are building clinical partnerships. Instead of simply relabeling existing one-way practices as "partnerships," work needs to be done to help all members work toward their shared goal of creating the best possible teachers. This requires an openness to listening and addressing any shortcomings in one's own practice. We find that this aligns with Tenet 2 of AACTE's The Partnership Proclamation.

Tenet 1 of The Central Proclamation necessitates that great care needs to be taken when matching teacher candidates with mentor teachers (Hoffman et al., 2015; AACTE, 2018). If this matching is done solely on the basis of "Who has room for a teacher candidate?" then results will remain lackluster. If the teacher education faculty member can invest their time into speaking with classroom teachers and finding out what their values and practices are, then the process of assigning teacher candidates can become deliberate and much more fruitful.

One way to foster these kinds of relationships is to encourage university administration to value this kind of time-intensive work. Currently, this is a barrier in our context that requires the university-based teacher educator to work well outside the established contract for other faculty; teacher educators are also partly administrators. Work needs to be done to make this critical task more sustainable. Building relationships with practicing teachers needs to be viewed as a valuable part of the work of preparing teacher candidates. This is not a new phenomenon, Johnston et al. (1996) points out that "while school/university partnerships are being developed as part of educational reform nationwide, universities and colleges do not often reward the supervisor [the teacher education faculty member] who spends time in the field talking to teachers" (p. 177).

CONCLUSION

Honoring the contributions of all the members of the student teaching triad is an essential part of moving these relationships forward and improving program results. As AACTE attests, clinical practice is moving from being the final capstone of teachers' education to a cornerstone upon which to build teacher education programs. This change means that the importance of school-based teacher educators increases and the establishes the need for boundary-spanning teacher educators.

In the end, it all comes down to relationships. Johnston and colleagues (1996, p. 175) stated:

> The closeness, due perhaps to the size of our community and Colgate, or more likely to the connection we have to Kay [university teacher education faculty member] and the education program allows us to have a more intimate relationship with the student teachers. We have been invited to their seminars and to hear their guest speakers. They attend our school functions and professional meetings in addition we see them in the local stores, restaurants, and sporting events. All of these reasons help to create an atmosphere that makes learning together more natural.

Relationships in the student teaching triad exist among all members and have the ability to develop or disappear based on the engagement of the individuals. Our results mirror the assertions of Chaliès et al. (2010) and show important and lasting benefits to having the collegiate teaching faculty be the same people who conduct classroom observations. Having a three-person dynamic accelerates the feedback cycle and allows teacher candidates therefore to make more progress in the same amount of time. These tighter relationships are, the more likely they are to sustain themselves after graduation.

As we look forward, several teacher candidates from the triads in this study are now eligible to host their own teacher candidate. We are excited to see how individuals with previously established relationships work within their own triads.

REFERENCES

Acheson, K. A., & Gall, M. D. (2003). *Techniques in the clinical supervision of teachers. Preservice and inservice applications.* Longman.

American Association of Colleges for Teacher Education. (2018). *A pivot toward clinical practice, its lexicon, and the renewal of education preparation: A report of the AACTE Clinical Practice Commission.*

Applegate, J. H., & Lasley, T. J. (1982). Mentor teachers' problems with preservice field experience students. *Journal of Teacher Education, 33*(2), 15–18.

Aspfors, J, & Fransson, G. (2015). Research on mentor education for mentors of newly qualified teachers: A qualitative meta-synthesis. *Teaching and Teacher Education, 48*(C), 75–86.

Barrows, L. (1979). *Power relationships in the student teaching triad* [Paper presentation]. The annual meeting of the American Educational Research Association, San Francisco, CA. (ERIC Document Reproduction Service No. ED 173 335).

Boschee, F., Prescott, D. R., & Hein, D. D. (1978). Do mentor teachers influence the educational philosophy of student teachers? *Journal of Teacher Education, 29*(2), 57–61.

Chaliès, S., Bruno-Méard, F., Méard, J., & Bertone, S. (2010). Training preservice teachers rapidly: the need to articulate the training given by university supervisors and mentor teachers. *Teaching and Teacher Education, 26*(4), 767–774.

Council for the Accreditation of Educator Preparation [CAEP]. (2018). Retrieved on June 26, 2018, http://caepnet.org/standards/standard-2

Cuenca, A. (2011). The role of legitimacy in student teaching: Learning to "feel" like a teacher. *Teacher Education Quarterly, 38*(2), 117–130.

Dewey, J. (1910). *How we think.* D. C. Heath & Co.

Feiman-Nemser, S. (1996). *Teacher mentoring: A critical review.* ERIC Clearinghouse on Teaching and Teacher Education. (ERIC Document Reproduction Service No. ED39760)

Gordon, S. (2016). Expanding our horizons: Alternative approaches to practitioner research. *Journal of Practitioner Research, 1*(1), 1–18.

Hoffman, J. V., Wetzel, M. M., Maloch, B., Greeter, E., Taylor, L., Dejulio, S. R., & Vlach, S K. (2015). What can we learn from studying the coaching interactions between mentor teachers and preservice teachers? A literature review. *Teaching and Teacher Education, 52*(C), 99–112.

Johnston, D. K., Duvernoy, R., McGill, P., & Will, J. F. (1996). Educating teachers together: Teachers as learners, talkers, and collaborators. *Theory into Practice, 35*(3), 173–178.

Koerner, M. (1992). The mentor teacher: An ambivalent participant in student teaching. *Journal of Teacher Education, 43*(1), 46–56.

Koerner, M., Rust, F. O. C., & Baumgartner, F. (2002). Exploring roles in student teaching placements. *Teacher Education Quarterly, 29*(2), 35–58.

Koster, B., Korthagen, F. A. J., & Wubbels, T. (1998). Is there anything left for us? Functions of mentor teachers and teacher educators. *European Journal of Teacher Education, 21*(1), 75–89.

Lincoln, Y., & Guba, E. (1985). *Naturalistic inquiry.* SAGE.

Maria-Monica, P., & Alina, M. (2014). Students-teacher perspectives on the qualities of mentor-teachers. *Procedia—Social and Behavioral Sciences, 116*, 3559–3563.

National Council for Accreditation of Teacher Education [NCATE]. (2010). *Transforming teacher education through clinical practice: A national strategy to prepare effective teachers.*

Nguyen, H. T. (2009). An inquiry-based practicum model: What knowledge, practices, and relationships typify empowering teaching and learning experiences for student teachers, mentor teachers and college supervisors? *Teaching and Teacher Education, 25*(5), 655–662.

Patton, M. Q. (2014). *Qualitative research & evaluation methods: Integrating theory and practice.* SAGE.

Richardson-Koehler, V. (1988). Barriers to the Effective supervision of student teaching: A field study. *Journal of Teacher Education, 39*(2), 28–34.

Rikard, G. L., & Veal, M. L. (1996). Mentor teachers: Insight into their preparation, beliefs, and practices. *Journal of Teaching in Physical Education, 15*(3), 279–96.

Rozelle, J. J., & Wilson, S. M. (2012). Opening the black box of field experiences: How mentor teachers' beliefs and practices shape student teachers' beliefs and practices. *Teaching and Teacher Education, 28*(8), 1196–1205.

Slick, S. K. (1997). Assessing versus assisting: The supervisor's roles in the complex dynamics of the student teaching triad. *Teaching and Teacher education, 13*(7), 713–726.

Steadman, S., & Brown, S. (2011). Defining the job of university supervisor: A department-wide study of university supervisor's practices. *Issues in Teacher Education, 20*(1), 51–68.

Talvitie, U., Peltokallio, L., & Mannisto, P. (2000). Student teachers' views about their relationships with university supervisors, mentor teachers and peer student teachers. *Scandinavian Journal of Educational Research, 44*(1), 79–88.

Ulvik, M., & Sunde, E. (2013). The impact of mentor education: Does mentor education matter? *Professional Development in Education, 39*(5), 754–770.

Veal, M. L., & Rikard, L. (1998). Mentor teachers' perspectives on the student teaching triad. *Journal of Teacher Education, 49*(2), 108–119.

Wang, J. & Odell, S. (2002). Mentored learning to teach according to standards-based reform: A critical review. *Review of Educational Research, 72*(3), 481–546.

Yin, R. K. (2014). *Case study research: Design and methods.* SAGE.

Young, A. M., & MacPhail, A. (2015). 'Standing on the periphery' Mentor teachers' perceptions and responses to the role of supervision. *European Physical Education Review, 21*(2), 222–237.

Zeichner, K. (2002). Beyond traditional structures of student teaching. *Teacher Education Quarterly, 29*(2), 59–64.

Zeichner, K. (2005). Becoming a teacher educator: A personal perspective. *Teaching and teacher education, 21*(2), 117–124.

SECTION IV

OTHER INNOVATIVE IDEAS AND APPROACHES

CHAPTER 23

INNOVATION AT ITS BEST

The Integration of Self-Reflection During the Student Teaching Experience

Paula E. Egelson
Southern Regional Educational Boar

Jacob Hardesty
Rockford University

ABSTRACT

Innovative ideas and practices are rarely entirely new. Innovative ideas are those that have existed for some time but have not been widely adopted or adapted in a particular way. For instance, scholars are increasingly recognizing self-reflection in its value for teacher education. This chapter discusses research for innovative clinical practice, research on the benefits and impact of teacher self-reflection and the results of a student teacher self-reflection study. As this case study demonstrates, preservice teacher reflection is about more than only reflection. Instead, Will Hernandez's reflections demonstrate how influential that practice can be to shape the pedagogical and social practices of preservice teachers.

Preparing Quality Teachers:
Advances in Clinical Practice, pp. 499–515
Copyright © 2022 by Information Age Publishing
www.infoagepub.com
499

INTRODUCTION

The semester that preservice teachers spend student teaching can be one of the most rewarding as well as one of the most challenging of their nascent teaching careers. Student teachers often report feeling a range of emotions as they progress through the semester. Guilt, exasperation, emotional exhaustion and gratitude often make up the emotional component of the student teachers experience. Student teaching is also an opportunity for early career educators to synthesize their coursework into a pedagogical whole. Instead of thinking of classroom management, lesson planning, and exceptional student accommodations as separate topics as in their coursework, the aim of student teaching is to think more about how these topics together provide the pedagogical tools for an early career educator. This study tracks how one student teacher, Will Hernandez [a pseudonym], thought through the challenges and opportunities of his student teaching semester. Using guided monthly reflections, authors analyzed how Will's thinking about his pedagogical effectiveness changed over the course of the semester. Results indicate having student teachers engage in some regular reflections helps them make sense of an often chaotic semester, helping them more accurately identify pedagogical strengths and areas for professional growth.

SUPPORTING INNOVATIVE CLINICAL PRACTICE RESEARCH

Koerner et al. (2002) describe the relationships among the student teacher, supervising teacher, and cooperating teacher, as comprising the "triad" of student teacher clinical practice (p. 38). As they convincingly argue, an effective student teaching experience requires clear roles and expectations among all three. While they acknowledge some surprise as the level of "clear demarcation of roles," they also point out not all roles are the same, since the student teachers have to "walk a delicate line" simultaneously as students and teachers (pp. 39, 55). Zeichner (2002) is more cautious about whether such a demarcation is beneficial: perhaps beneficial; perhaps it is unnecessary. Writing in the same *Teacher Education Quarterly* issue, he criticizes colleges and universities for seeing student teaching as a "low status activity," one that has changed little over time, largely because of schools' lack of interest in it (p. 60). Part of his solution involves "good human relations," including ensuring each triad member has a similar pedagogical philosophy (p. 61). In contrast, members of the National Council for Accreditation of Teacher Education's [NCATE] (2010) Blue Ribbon Panel on Clinical Preparations and Partnership for Improved Student Learning looked less at the human relations involved to improve teacher education and more at the teacher education programs themselves. While they acknowledged the need for "supportive partnerships between" universities and K–12 schools, they argued that must go together with other recommendations, including "More Rigorous Accountability" and "Revamping Curriculum."

Following that 2010 NCATE report, a variety of ideas and solutions were proposed to improve the student teaching experience for all involved. In a review of those efforts, the American Association of Colleges for Teacher Education [AACTE] vice president Rodrick Lucero concluded, "Many of these efforts have resulted in thriving, mutually beneficial partnerships between preparation programs and local schools that serve as laboratories of practice and innovation—but others have not" (AACTE, 2018). In response, the AACTE convened its own commission of forty educators, the majority working as educators in K–12 schools or in teacher education programs at colleges and universities. The group reviewed the variety of recommendations that followed the NCATE report's publication to identify those with the most promise and those deemed less effective. The resulting AACTE report, *A Pivot toward Clinical Practice, Its Lexicon, and the Renewal of Educator Preparation* (AACTE, 2018) offered 10 proclamations, that is, practices in student teaching that would be adaptable in the variety of AACTE member institutions, from liberal arts colleges to state universities alike. While some of the proclamations focus on school-university partnership, the majority emphasize the pedagogical development of preservice teachers.

Other scholarship into student teaching has placed a greater emphasis on the importance of school-university partnerships. Joyce Epstein and colleagues' (2009) oft-referenced text, *School, Family, and Community Partnerships: Your Handbook for Action*, is a comprehensive look at elementary and high schools partnering with other institutions, including colleges and universities. The authors cover a variety of "lessons learned in research and fieldwork" on issues related to partnerships (p. 3). These lessons range from educating district and state leaders about the value of partnerships between colleges and various civic organizations to strategies for involving college parents in their child's civic education. Indeed, much of Epstein's scholarship highlights the multitude of actors involved in school partnership. For instance, a 2010 article with Frances Van Voorhis argues that "students learn more when parents, educators, and others in the community recognize their shared goals and responsibilities" (p. 1). Epstein and Van Voorhis extended that reasoning to call for school counselors to spend 20% of their time strengthening school partnerships. Likewise, a 2016 study with Sheldon (2016) looked at data from 347 schools in 21 districts to identify factors influencing family engagement. Like the aforementioned study, this study clarified shared purpose among parents and school personnel, leading to multiple benefits, including more widespread parent engagement and greater school attendance (p. 215). Similarly, Bryan and Holcomb-McCoy (2007) looked at levels of, and reasons for, school counselor involvement in school-family-community partnerships. Using data drawn from 235 participants, they found school counselors felt they were only "somewhat involved" in most areas of partnership, though indicate a "positive attitude" about those involvements (pp. 448, 450).

THE VALUE OF PRESERVICE TEACHER SELF-REFLECTION DURING STUDENT TEACHING

Historically, scholars have emphasized the importance of reflection in teacher education. The late 1980s and 1990s saw a great deal of writing on the role of reflection in student teaching. Much of this research foregrounded structural issues, particularly how well teacher education programs help preservice teachers develop reflective habits. Zeichner and Liston (1987) argued for a program that is more "inquiry oriented" to ultimately help preservice teachers "develop the desire and ability to assume greater roles in determining the direction of the classroom" (p. 25). They looked at the teacher education program at the University of Wisconsin, seeking to evaluate how effective program-wide changes were in developing more reflective preservice teachers. And while they concede certain problems did arise in moving from planning to implementation, they remained optimistic such a heuristic could serve as an effective model for greater reflection in the future. Colton and Sparks-Langer (1993) similarly outlined a teacher education program designed to produce the "teacher as a 'reflective decision maker'" (p. 45). The four-part framework they developed was not designed to be connected to any single institution, but instead to create an environment in which the preservice teacher's feelings take on a larger pedagogical role. Like Zeichner and Liston, Colton and Sparks-Langer wrote convincingly about the need for reflective preservice teaching, noting "Technical [teaching] proficiency is not enough; morals and democratic principles must also guide reflective teachers' actions" (p. 45). Indeed, such passionate calls for greater preservice teacher reflection are common. In a *Teacher Education Quarterly* study, LaBoskey (1993) also concluded "We owe it to all students to endeavor to provide them with teachers who are thoughtful, passionate, and principled educational decision-makers" (p. 12).

Other scholars working in the late 1980s and early 1990s looked to how to analyze the effectiveness of student teacher pedagogy reflection. Marshall (1990) suggested working with student teachers to develop metaphorical thinking skills. She contrasted two metaphors—classroom-as-work-place and classroom-as-learning-place - to help student teachers think through how they would behave in different environments. The former led to student teachers acting more as managers, chiding students for being off topic, while the latter led the student teachers to act more as educational guides. McLaughlin (1991) sought to understand how well individual student teachers were doing using reflective tools. Using journals, pre- and post-student teaching interviews, and other written self-evaluations, he worked to develop an "interactive self-evaluation" student teachers could use going forward (p. 141). Ultimately, scholars writing on the topic currently sought to establish the scholarly foundation to include reflection as a necessary part of student teaching

More recent research has explored how reflection is impacted by the subject areas the preservice educators teach, finding that students reflect differently if they are teaching math or music. Baumgartner and Councill (2019) focused specifically on how student teachers in music education thought through some of the challenges and opportunities they experienced. Drawing on data from student teachers at three Midwestern universities, they found that student teachers viewed their weekly seminar courses as a "safe space" to discuss a variety of issues. Some topics discussed were effective verbal self-reflection techniques following rehearsals, though others were more general, including future employment opportunities. Stegman (2007) also looked at the reflective practices of student teachers in music classrooms, though her attention was focused to reflective dialogues between those preservice teachers and their cooperating and supervising teachers. She found those discussions typically avoided "critical" issues on topics such as funding inequality, instead emphasizing technical, clinical, and personal issues. Research on preservice teachers working with English language learning (ELL) students also points to how such practices can be subject-area specific. Köksal and Genc (2019) used reflective journals and semi-structured questionnaires to understand the development of preservice teachers' reflective skills. They found that specific concerns about ELL pedagogy was one of three areas student teachers reflected on the most, along with developing professional identity and developing positive feelings. Likewise, Lucas and Villegas (2013) view reflection as a "time-honored approach to exploring one's beliefs and values" (p. 104). They extoll the benefits of a more structured preservice teacher program, arguing a set of "central tasks" can help future full time teachers address the unique pedagogical needs of ELL students.

Other contemporary education scholars have looked at how technology can impact student teachers' ability to reflect on their teaching. Wegner et al. (2014) note that technology, when used correctly, can positively add greater structure to how students reflect. Looking specifically at student teachers in German biology classes, they had students use a "Reflection-

Wiki," a website that permits collaborative editing of its content, to analyze their teaching. The Wiki is structured to help students look at six areas of pedagogy, such as classroom management and body language, to improve their pedagogy. Snyder (2011) has similarly applauded how technology can be an asset to student teachers. He discusses that simply asking student teachers to video record themselves can help them improve, for instance, the amount of over explaining or "teacher talk" (p. 58). Snyder perceptively concludes "Video reflection provides insight into the teacher psyche because reflective comments reveal where the teacher's attention is being placed" (p. 60). And, as Beyerbach et al. (2001) remind us, how student teachers use technology is not a fixed entity itself. They correctly point out that for preservice and in-service teachers alike, the more educators incorporate technology, and in different ways, the more comfortable they become with it.

Like the previously discussed studies that emerged in the 1990s, scholars continue to look at how effective programs are in instilling reflective values among student teachers, though over a longer period. These longitudinal studies have sought to track how various teacher education programs have impacted student reflection over more than the typical student teaching semester. Miksza and Berg (2013) looked at eight teachers' perceptions of what they were focused on, drawing on Fuller and Brown's teacher-concern model. They found that participants expressed decreased concern for "self-survival" and greater concern for "making an impact" as time progressed (p. 56). More recently, Doppen and Shahri (2019) examined data over a 10 year period of preservice teachers who did their student teaching in a country other than the United States. Seeking to partially unpack Crevecoeur's deceptively complex question "What is an American?" they found that student teachers identified how their individual lives contributed to a "national identity constructed on ... collective values"—a finding they note spanned Democratic and Republican administrations alike (p. 87).

STUDENT TEACHER SELF-REFLECTION

As we begin to investigate the innovative practice of student teacher self-reflection, it is critical to understand what reflection is. Teacher self-reflection is the process in which teachers think about a specific practice, examine how something (like a lesson plan, an assessment, written communication with parents) they developed, communicated, presented and/or administered, and analyzes how it might be improved or changed for the better (TeacherHub, 2020). Another definition for self-reflection is continuous learning (Costa & Kalleck, 2008). A key rationale for reflective practice is that an experience by itself does not necessarily lead to learning; a deliberate reflection on the experience is paramount.

Early in the 20th century John Dewey wrote about reflective practice with his exploration of experience, interaction, and reflection (Dewey, 1907). Terry Borton's 1970 book *Reach, Touch, and Teach* popularized a simple learning cycle comprised of three questions: What? So what? Now what? David Kolb (1975) drew on the work of Dewey (1907) and Piaget (1926) to develop a reflective model that emphasized experiential learning, transforming information into knowledge after the learning experience has occurred. Chris Argyris and Donald Schon created the idea of single-loop and double-loop learning in 1978. Single-loop learning stays with current strategies even though an error has occurred. Double-loop learning involves modification of objectives, strategies or policies after an error has taken place. Don Schon (1983) talks about two types of reflective practice. The first, reflection-on-action, is reflection on an experience that has already taken place. The second is reflection-in-action, reflecting on actions as they are occurring. Schon's book *The Reflective Practitioner* is a landmark publication of how professionals meet the challenges of their work in part through reflection.

Stephen Brookfield (1998) said that reflective practitioners continually examine their assumptions by viewing their practice via four connected lenses: (1) Our autobiography as a learner. (2) Seeing ourselves through our learners' eyes. (3) Our collective experiences and (4) Theoretical literature.

AN EXAMINATION OF
SELF-REFLECTION DURING STUDENT TEACHING

This study on self-reflection during student teaching, we asked student teachers at a Midwestern college to volunteer to self-reflect during their semester-long student teacher experience. Eight student teachers across a variety of teaching areas and grade configurations agreed to participate. They took part in a student teacher self-reflection training that included the theory and impact of teacher self-reflection and were then instructed on how to complete a student teacher self-reflection each month during student teaching. On the self-reflection form they filled in their name, the school they were assigned to for student teaching, grade level, content area, the date, and selected a self-reflection topic: (1) instructional planning, (2) instruction, (3) assessment, (4) parent communication, or (5) classroom management. The student teacher then responded to the following statements or questions that were adapted from Graham Gibbs (1988):

1. Describe what happened.
2. What were your reactions and feelings?
3. What was good or bad about the experience?
4. What sense can you make of this situation? What was going on?

5. What can be concluded from this experience and analysis you have conducted?
6. What actions are you doing differently in this type of situation next time?

Students then emailed their monthly reflections to the principal investigators. For the purposes of this chapter, it was decided to use the self-reflections of one student teacher, Will Hernandez.

We used researcher Terry Borton's (1970) learning cycle of *What? So what? Now what?* to help explain the student teacher self-reflections. Student teachers' reflections were then coded by the emergent themes: (1) assessment, (2) classroom management, (3) interaction with parents, (4) planning and instruction, (5) role of cooperating teacher, (6) student academic success, (7) student reactions to student teacher, and (8) student academic success. Next, the coded reflections were examined for impact and effectiveness in developing a comprehensive story about the impact of student teacher self-reflection. Based on this, the number of reflections was narrowed. The selected reflections were then integrated into a composite of a student teacher learning the practice of teaching.

WILL HERNANDEZ'S STUDENT TEACHER SELF-REFLECTIONS

Will Hernandez's self-reflections were chosen for this chapter because of their comprehensiveness and expressiveness in portraying the full teaching experience using self-reflection. Will is a student teacher in eighth grade social studies at a middle school on the outskirts of a large midwestern city. He is a strong student academically and expresses himself well in his self-reflections. Will is a traditional college student, is 21-years old and has completed three years of undergraduate work. Hernandez connects with his students and seems to understand them. He does experience stress during student teaching. There is conflict with his supervising teacher and there are some classroom management issues that are serious. We follow Will throughout his five-month study teaching experience via his self-reflective writings. Will chooses a different area of the teaching experience to self-reflect on each month.

Month 1, September—Will Hernandez—Focus: Instructional Planning

Instructional planning is the process where an educator examines appropriate curricula, instructional strategies, resources, and data during the planning process to address the various needs of their students (Georgia Department of Education, 2020). Will tackles instructional planning early in his student teaching experience. He does not have a lot of support from his supervising teacher and feels like he is on his own. It is difficult work, but it brings him great benefits. The *What?* for this month is Will's experiences in beginning instructional planning, how he approaches and how he struggles. Will relates that, over time, he got better at instructional planning because of his practice in doing it. He reports to feeling stressed because he must take on instructional planning with so little support but reports that he can now make student accommodations and learns more about his content area because of doing the planning. The *So what?* is Will's increasing confidence and skill in doing instructional planning. Will also learns more about lesson plan structures and discovers a variety of instructional strategies. He writes:

> Overall, instructional planning was a good experience. While I felt overwhelmed and stressed at times, I was successfully able to create my own lessons and got much better at doing so as time went on. I gained more knowledge of my content area and learned a lot about instructional planning (such as different lesson plan structures and different instructional strategies) in crafting my own lessons versus using my cooperating teacher's resources or those of other teachers' online. In creating everything from scratch, I also was able to make more accommodations for my students, shifting my lessons to help them improve their weaknesses or focusing on their interests. (Hernandez, 2019)

Will is intent on planning instruction that is interactive and motivational for his students. He makes accommodations for his students with special needs. He states:

> Instructional planning is extremely time consuming and research intensive; however, it is essential for the success of the classroom. If you can craft really interactive lessons, geared towards the interests of your students, the classroom will function efficiently. My students have readily enjoyed my instruction but have also rapidly improved their test scores (average post-test scores in all of my classes is a 90% versus a 25% on pre-tests). Instructional planning is key in the success of your students but also the success of myself in teaching. (Hernandez, 2019)

The *Now what?* of this reflective work is Will's continuing growth and the application of instructional planning. Will is pleased his students enjoy his instruction and have improved their posttest scores. He views good instructional planning as a key to classroom success.

Month 2, October—Will Hernandez —Focus: Classroom Management

Will encounters some serious roadblocks with classroom management. Two students continually disrupted his class at the beginning of his student teaching experience and were disrespectful to Will. The *What?* for this month is Will's struggle with classroom management, especially with two students. Will's supervising teacher tells him that he needs to write the two students up. Will relates:

> The bad part of this experience was the feelings associated with writing up students as well as being openly disrespected in class. A great thing happened out of writing the referral, however, as I had a meeting with the two students the following week (set up by the assistant principal). In talking with the students, they apologized for their behavior and gave reason for their disrespect (have a home-life which encourages disrespect of authority). In understanding the students better, and in turn they understood where I was coming from, we came up with a behavior management plan. Going forward, the two students have been excellent and have readily participated in class. This resolution only resulted because of writing the referral, in my opinion. (Hernandez, 2019)

Fortunately, the school where Will was working took the students' bad behavior seriously and worked out a behavior plan for the students. The students also apologized to Will. Will saw a huge positive change in the students' behavior after the talk with the assistant principal and the behavior plan was put in place. The *So what?* for this passage is that Will faced a serious discipline issue in his classroom and was able to resolve it with the help of the school administration.

Will came to realize the critical importance of a viable classroom management plan and that sometimes drastic measures had to be taken to ensure classroom tranquility and learning. He says:

> Behavior management is a key in a healthy learning environment. While most behavioral disruptions can be fixed with simple re-direction; some students will need more serious consequences such as a referral. Referrals can lead to a greater conversation with the student about their behavior, where true learning and even healing can occur. (Hernandez, 2019)

Will went through the steps of effective classroom management and experienced the talking, communication, and healing that are a part of it. The *Now what?* is that Will has foundational experience with classroom management that he can now apply to classroom situations in the future.

Month 3, November—Will Hernandez—Focus: Instruction

Will did a simulation of a component of the French Revolution with his students in November. The *What?* for this month is Will's move from instructional planning to actual instruction and the results of that instruction. He plans his instruction thoroughly and it is time consuming, but the planning and actual instruction are worth the positive student outcomes. Writes Will:

> Overall, this was a very good experience! My students interacted with not only the content, but also with their own peers far more than they ever had in the past. To this day, my students are able to describe the French Revolution in depth and definitely have a personal experience to justify their beliefs. From a teaching standpoint, the simulation required a lot of preparation but had students engaged for the entirety of the lesson. (Hernandez, 2019)

Will is pleased with the depth of knowledge his students have gleaned from the simulation, their enjoyment with the instructional approaches, and their communication with each other. He is also feels justified that his students can support their thoroughly communicate their knowledge of the French Revolution. The *So what?* of this passage is the deep student learning that takes place because of this simulation. He mentions the various instruction techniques (like project-based learning and interactive lessons) he employed positively, and that the overall simulation as an instructional tool was a success. Reflects Will:

> My conclusion from the French Revolution simulation is that students not only enjoy project-based learning opportunities and interactive lessons, but their comprehension of the material greatly improves. Following the simulation, my students took an exam in which they had to answer a short answer question on the French Revolution. Every student was able to answer the question and receive at least half-credit, potentially forgetting to answer the question in its entirety (there were multiple parts to the question). (Hernandez, 2019)

In his self-reflections, Will often uses student assessment results to demonstrate and support student growth. He adds that simulations aid in the deep student comprehension of the material. The *Now what?* of this passage is Will's realization that simulations if implemented properly can be used in the future as an effective instructional strategy.

Month 4, December—Will Hernandez—Focus: Parent Communication

Will is fortunate that he is able to have formalized parent-teacher interactions during his student teaching experience. However, his cooperating teacher does limit his interactions with parents. The *What?* of this month is how much Will enjoys communicating with his students' parents and feels he has made a difference, however limited his time with parents was. Relates Will:

> Parent-teacher conferences were overall a good experience. Not only were parents receptive to the feedback I offered but spoke with their student about things to improve which I could see in class going forward (a change in certain students' behavior). The bad part of parent-teacher conferences was in relation to my co-op. While I had grown to know these students, my co-op was determined to limit my voice because I was not their true instructor. Multiple times I was told not to speak or intervene, which was frustrating since I had a lot of information to offer. Either way, I feel that I made a difference and loved interacting with the parents. (Hernandez, 2019)

Will developed a connection with his students and knows their academic strengths and weaknesses. He thinks he was not able to fully contribute during the parent-teacher conferences due his cooperating teacher cutting him off. The *So what?* of this passage understanding that even if a professional experience is not perfect it can still be valuable and positive.

Will discovers the parents with whom he needs to talk to the most, due to poor student academic standings or discipline problems, are not the ones who show up for the conferences. The parents of the students who are doing well are the ones who attend. He laments:

> As is common, the parents that I did interact with were not the ones I needed to interact with. Almost all of the parents that showed up had students that were currently receiving A's or B's and whose behavior was not a problem. The students that were not performing well academically and who poised behavior problems on a daily/weekly basis, their parents/guardians never arrived. It seems that parent-teacher conferences are useful in establishing a rapport with parents and for helping to change behavior, yet it is not effective in reaching the students that needs it due to minimal parental involvement. (Hernandez, 2019)

Will does see the teacher-parent conferences as a vehicle for building rapport with the parents and to help change student behavior for the better. The *Now what?* will have Will building on his positive initial experiences with parents when he starts teaching.

Month 5, January—Will Hernandez—Focus: Assessment

There are several types of student assessment. There is assessment of learning (summative assessment), assessment for learning (formative assessment) and a combination of formative and summative assessment. Will focuses on the creation of assessments for this month. The *What?* of this passage is Will's ability to create effective assessments. He says:

> Overall, assessment development was a good experience. I learned how to make a rigorous examination that is also attainable for students to ace. Assessment development is a skill that I use on a constant basis now that I am teaching my own classes. Without learning how to do so in student-teaching, first-year teaching would be much more difficult. (Hernandez, 2020)

Will is focused on creating both challenging and "the ability to get an A" type of assessments for students. Rigor and success in creating assessments is a tall order and Will achieves it. This is the *So what?* for this month. Hernandez will use his assessment creation skills constantly as a teacher.

Based on his experience, Will prefers assessments he creates rather than ones that are developed by the district or textbook companies. The pre-made assessments have tendency to be confusing and not on target for students. With assessments he crafted the pre- and posttest student score differences are greater and they build student confidence. Will says:

> Students do much better on self-crafted examinations versus those from the text-book company. My students, on average, would improve at least 50% on pre/posttests that I would administer based upon what I actually taught and crafted to student abilities) versus only 10-20% on textbook quizzes and district assessments. Most of the time, pre-made assessments were confusing for students. My self-crafted examinations, however, students felt confident in answering questions because they remembered specific lectures or activities that I had done in relation to those words/concepts. Assessment development, while time consuming, is necessary in order to ensure the success and confidence of your students in taking examinations. (Hernandez, 2020)

Will writes repeatedly how assessment development and instructional planning are time-consuming but are worth the effort due to student success in mastering the content. The *Now what?* is the understanding that positive student outcomes are partly the result of good instruction and assessment design and execution.

Self-Reflection Student Teaching Summary, January—
Will Hernandez

As Will sums up his student teaching experience, he realizes that he, for a variety of reasons, had to self-reflect about his teaching from Day 1. He mentions how critically important self-reflection is to his improvement as a teacher. Will states:

> Self-reflection is an essential part of teaching. From day one, my cooperating teacher forced me to self-reflect with his constant critique. Yet, I felt it was necessary to self-reflect so I could make changes for the unit, the week, the day, or even the next class period the same day. Writing my self-reflections down helped me better work through my thoughts and identify what actually occurred and what I needed to change for the future. (Hernandez, 2020)

Although student teaching is for a fairly short period of time, Will notes the changes in himself, how he approaches his new-found profession, and that his self-reflections have changed. He realizes that his lessons do not have to be perfect, that he needs to be less self-critical of himself, and that he will not reach every student. He notes that writing his reflections is critical to his professional growth. He comments:

> Yes, my self-reflections did change over time. At first, I was very hypercritical of everything I did (mainly due to the frequency of the cooperating teacher's critiques). I wanted to teach a perfect lesson so I would not be critiqued but then also to maximize my student interest. As time went on, I realized that there is no such thing as a perfect lesson. No matter what I would do/change, my cooperating teacher would have something negative to say. Also, each lesson will not reach every student. In learning this, I became less critical of myself and my instruction, and focused just on what to change for the future, allowing myself to make mistakes. (Hernandez, 2020)

Finally, Will realizes that he does self-reflection well and frequently. It is a part of his professional life and is grounded in research and theory. He is open to changing what he does in the classroom to improve his assessment techniques, classroom management, instruction, and parent communication. Will summarizes:

> would give myself a proficient or exceeds in terms of self-reflecting. Almost everything that I do, I think about before, during, and after the fact in relation to my teaching. My methods are ground in research and theory, and if something does not go well, I am willing to change it for the future. I think very much about what I can do, specifically, to improve the instruction to my students. (Hernandez, 2020)

Will Hernandez's story speaks to the usefulness and agency of reflecting on student teaching. As Will makes clear, reflection is not meant as an end unto itself. Instead, preservice teachers use reflection as a tool to improve not just their pedagogy, but also the various factors that go into student teaching, including lesson planning and interpersonal communication. If done well, such reflection is not a singular event or even one done occasionally when a situation may warrant. Instead, student teachers are learning to incorporate reflection as an ongoing part of their future in-service work as well. Ultimately, that teacher self-reflection is an innovative practice that can benefit all student teaching programs. It improves overall teacher practice and supports continuous improvement in assessment, classroom management, instruction, and parent communication.

The major takeaways of this chapter are many. If done properly, student teacher self-reflection makes a strong and positive impact on the student teaching experience. It can assist in solving classroom challenges and reinforces practices that are going well. It builds confidence in students teachers. The practice of self-reflection in teachers also demonstrates the importance of planning ... planning instruction, planning content, planning assessment. Good planning leads to good execution and good outcomes for students.

For those wanting to implement a student teacher self-reflection component, one of the best ways to start is to begin is with a pilot project of a few student teacher volunteers. Use the reflection format that is found in this chapter and train participating student teachers on self-reflection theory and practice. Ask that student teachers provide reflections to you on a regular basis and comment on what they have offered. At the conclusion of the student teaching experience, run a focus group with these individuals to determine what has worked well with the reflection process and what hasn't. Make needed changes to the self-reflection process. Expand the project to include all student teachers in the next cycle. Initiating student self-reflection into the student teaching experience will be well worth the time expended!

REFERENCES

American Association of Colleges for Teacher Education. (2008). *AACTE Commission Issues Proclamations for Effective Clinical Educator Preparation* (News release). January 17, 2018, https://aacte.org/2018/01/aacte-commission-issues-proclamations-for-effective-clinical-educator-preparation/.

Argyris, C., & Schon. D. (1974). *Theory in practice: Increasing professional effectiveness.* Wiley.

Baumgartner, C., & Councill, K. (2019, October). Music student teachers' perceptions of their seminar experience: An exploratory study. *Journal of Music Teacher Education, 29*(1), 11–25.

Beyerbach, B., Walsh, C., & Vannatta, R. (2001, January). From teaching technology to using technology to enhance student learning: Preservice teachers' changing perceptions of technology infusion. *Journal of Technology and Teacher Education. 9*(1), 105–127.

Borton, T. (1970). *Reach, touch, and teach.* McGraw-Hill.

Bryan, J., & Holcomb-McCoy, C. (2007). An examination of school counselor involvement in school-family-community partnerships. *Professional School Counseling. 10*(5), 441–454.

Brookfield, S. (1988, Fall). Theoretical foundations. *Journal of Continuing Education in the Health Professions. 18*(4), 197–205.

Colton, A., & Sparks-Langer, G. (1993). A conceptual framework to guide the development of teacher reflection and decision making. *Journal of Teacher Education, 44*(1), 45–54.

Costa, A., & Kallick, B. (2008). *Learning and leading with habits of mind.* ASCD.

Dewey, J. (1907). *School and society.* University of Chicago Press.

Doppen, F., & Bahman S. (2019). Overseas student teachers' reflections on American national identity: A longitudinal study. *Journal of International Social Studies, (9)*1, 72–92.

Epstein, J., & Associates. (2009). *School, family, and community partnerships: Your handbook for action* (3rd ed.). SAGE.

Epstein, J., L., & Sheldon, S., B. (2016). Necessary but not sufficient: The role of policy for advancing programs of school, family, and community partnerships. *RSF: The Russell Sage Foundation Journal of the Social Sciences, 2*(5), 202–219. https://doi.org/10.7758/rsf.2016.2.5.10

Epstein, J. L., & Van Voorhis, F. L. (2010). School counselors' roles in developing partnerships with families and communities for student success. *Professional School Counseling, 14*(1), 1–14.

Georgia Department of Education. (2020). Instructional planning. Retrieved May 30, 2020, from https://www.gadoe.org

Gibbs, G. (1988). *Learning by doing.* Oxford Polytechnic.

Kolb, D. (1975). *Experiential learning.* Wiley-Blackwell.

Köksal, D., & Gülten, G. (2019, January). Learning while teaching: Student teachers› reflections on their teaching practicum. *Journal of Language and Linguistic Studies, 15*(3), 895–913.

Koerner, M., Rust, F., & Baumgartner, F. (2002). Exploring roles in student teaching placements. *Teacher Education Quarterly, 29*(2), 35–58.

LaBoskey, V. (1993). Why reflection in teacher education? *Teacher Education Quarterly, 20*(1), 9–12.

Lucas, T., & Villegas, A. (2013). Preparing linguistically responsive teachers: Laying the foundation in preservice teacher education. *Theory into Practice, 52*(2), 98–109.

Marshall, H. (1990). Metaphor as an instructional tool in encouraging student teacher reflection. *Theory into Practice, 29*(2), 128–132.

McLaughlin, H. (1991). The reflection on the blackboard: student teacher self-evaluation. *International Journal of Qualitative Studies in Education, 4*(2), 141–59.

Miksza, P., & Berg, M. (2013). A longitudinal study of preservice music teacher development: Application and advancement of the fuller and brown teacher-concerns model. *Journal of Research in Music Education, 61*(1), 44–62.

National Council for Accreditation of Teacher Education [NCATE]. (2010). Transforming teacher education through clinical practice: A national strategy to prepare effective teachers. http://www.highered.nysed.gov/pdf/NCATECR.pdf

Piaget, J. (1926). *The language and thought of a child.* Routledge & Kegan Paul.

Schon, D. (1983). *The reflective practitioner: How professionals think in action.* Basic Books.

Stegman, S. (2007). An exploration of reflective dialogue between student teachers in music and their cooperating teachers. *Journal of Research in Music Education, 55*(1), 65.

Snyder, D. (2011). Preparing for teaching through reflection. *Music Educators Journal, 97*(3), 56–60.

TeacherHub. (2020). *Teacher self-reflection.* Retrieved May 30, 2020, from TeacherHub.com

Wegner, C., Remmert, K., & Strehlke, F. (2014). Professionalizing the self-reflection of student teachers by using a Wiki. *Educational Technology, 54*(4), 38–42.

Zeichner, K. (2002). Beyond traditional structures of student teaching. *Teacher Education Quarterly, 29*(2), 59–64.

Zeichner, K., & Liston, D. (1987). Teaching student teachers to reflect. *Harvard Educational Review, 57*(1), 23–49.

CHAPTER 24

COLLABORATING TEACHERS AND PRESERVICE TEACHERS ATTENTION TO THE ELEMENTS OF THE APPRENTICESHIP MODEL FOR LEARNING DURING CLINICAL EXPERIENCES

Ruthmae Sears
University of South Florida

Patricia Brosnan
Ohio State University

Cynthia Castro-Minnehan
University of South Florida

Pier Junor Clarke
Georgia State University

Jamalee Stone
Black Hill State University

Preparing Quality Teachers:
Advances in Clinical Practice, pp. 517–541
Copyright © 2022 by Information Age Publishing
www.infoagepub.com

ABSTRACT

This chapter describes how preservice teachers and collaborating teachers attended to elements of the apprenticeship model for learning during clinical experiences. The elements of the model are: students' thinking, co-planning and co-teaching, diverse students in classroom settings, and Cognitive Coaching^SM. The elements intersect to promote students' learning. Data were garnered via two focus groups, one for 21 preservice teachers and the other for 24 collaborating teachers. Subsequently, the data were analyzed using a thematic analysis with the apprenticeship model for learning being used as a theoretical lens. The results suggest that the use of the model fostered productive and purposeful collaboration and facilitated synchronized efforts to promote students' learning. The results of the study have implications on programmatic efforts to enhance the nature of clinical experiences in teacher preparation programs.

INTRODUCTION

Clinical experiences are considered a core component of teacher preparation programs (American Association of Colleges of Teacher Education [AACTE], 2018; Cuenca, 2012; Darling-Hammond, 2014). In fact, the National Council for Accreditation of Teacher Education [NCATE] Blue Ribbon Report (2010) advocated that teacher preparation programs should employ a clinically-rich based approach to facilitate opportunities for preservice teachers to learn by doing, thereby developing both their academic and practitioner knowledge. The report also advocated for opportunities for preservice teachers to collect and reflect on data relative to whether their students learned. The apprenticeship model for learning could be used during clinical experiences to facilitate learning opportunities for preservice teachers and their students (Brosnan et al., 2014, National Council of Teachers of Mathematics [NCTM], 2014b). This model suggests that what ultimately is learned during clinical experiences is the result of the interplay between student thinking, co-planning and co-teaching, Cognitive Coaching^SM, and consideration to the diverse settings; and that student learning should be at the intersection of all the elements. Hence, in this chapter, we will describe how collaborative pairs (collaborating teachers and preservice teachers) used the apprenticeship model for learning during their clinical experiences to facilitate student learning in diverse settings. Thus, our research answers the following question: (1) To what extent do collaborating teachers and preservice teachers attend to elements of the apprenticeship model for learning during clinical experiences?

THE APPRENTICESHIP MODEL FOR LEARNING

The roles teachers play is vast; nevertheless, their ultimate goal is to support student learning (Brosnan et al., 2014; NCTM, 2014a). Considering that clinical experiences provide preservice teachers an opportunity to bridge research to practice, and to reflect on means to promote learning, the nature of the interaction between the preservice teachers and their collaborating teachers can have implications on what preservice teachers' actually learn. Therefore, the apprenticeship model for learning can be utilized by the collaborative pair to support students' learning (Brosnan et al., 2014; NCTM, 2014b). The elements of the apprenticeship model for learning seek to: reflect on means to integrate students' thinking into the classroom discourse; foster collaboration via co-planning and co-teaching; embrace the diversity of the students within the classroom settings; and facilitate structured conversations through Cognitive Coaching^{SM}. This model is illustrated in Figure 24.1.

During clinical experiences, we perceive that the apprenticeship model for learning can support the collaborative pair to focus on students' learning during planning, enactment, and assessment of instruction. When co-planning, the collaborative pair can reflect on what students need to learn, what will constitute evidence of learning, and the nature of the tasks with which students engage that will support their learning. For the enacted lessons, the collaborative pair may use various co-teaching strategies to facilitate learning and assess students' depth of understanding

Figure 24.1

Apprenticeship Model for Learning

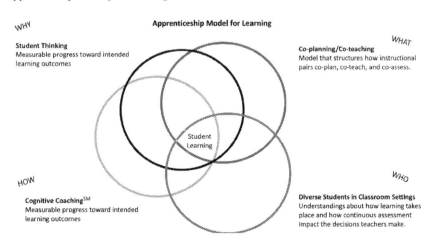

(Sears et al., 2017; Sears et al., 2019; Grady et al., 2020). Hence, they will need to notice and utilize students' thinking, actively seek to embrace the diversity in the classroom, and integrate effective teaching strategies that can foster equitable learning opportunities. After the lesson, the collaborative pair can utilize Cognitive Coaching[SM] to reflect on the effectiveness of their instructional practices and means to further support students' learning. The collaborative pair may also engage in planning for future lessons. Therefore, during clinical experiences the apprenticeship model for learning can be used to support learning via a cyclic process (Brosnan et al., 2014). This cyclic process is illustrated in Figure 24.2. In the subsections below, we discuss each element of the apprenticeship model for learning.

Student Thinking

Student thinking within a classroom can be observed based on how they make inferences, and articulate ideas (Leatham et al., 2015). Thus, during clinical experiences the collaborative pair should notice observable characteristics (Leatham et al., 2015). Franke and Kazemi (2001) noted, "Constructing models of children's thinking entails focusing on organized,

Figure 24.2

Focus on Learning During Field Experiences

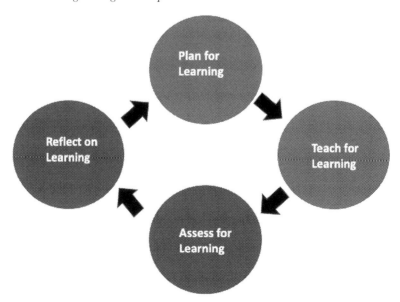

principled knowledge about problems within the various content domains, along with the range of strategies children often use to solve the problems" (p. 103). Thus, the collaborative pair should attend to students' thinking, interpret what students are conveying from a content perspective, and determine a suitable response that can move the learning forward (Stockero et al., 2015). The collaborative pair may also plan to employ decentering actions, to reflect on how students are thinking when they interact with them (Teuscher et al., 2016).

Furthermore, to capitalize on students' thinking within a classroom, Stein et al. (2015) recommended teachers orchestrate discourse in which they anticipate, monitor, select, sequence, and make connections amongst students' responses. Thus, the collaborative pair should consider the cognitive demand of the tasks during the enacted lessons and means to maintain the cognitive rigor of tasks posed (Boston & Smith, 2011). Burns and Badiali (2018) discussed pedagogical skills (inclusive of ignoring, noticing, pointing, intervening, processing, and unpacking), and means to sequence them, to help preservice teachers facilitate learning within the classroom setting.

Additionally, teachers can utilize students' misconceptions to explicate incorrect schematic connections that students made in their thinking (Ojose, 2015). Teachers can use the insights garnered about students' misconceptions to support students' engagement in learning the content being taught, and address more rigorous cognitive processes (Roh & Lee, 2017; Schoenfeld, 2015; Thames & Ball, 2013).

Co-Planning and Co-Teaching

During co-teaching, the collaborative pair is in the same classroom and have shared responsibility for instruction (Baeten & Simons, 2014; Friend & Cook, 2007). The roles of the teachers are negotiated, and they work collaboratively to maximize student-learning opportunities (Friend & Cook, 2007; Sears et al., 2017; Sears et al., 2018; Grady et al., 2020). Guise et al. (2017) found that collaborative pairs fell "on a continuum" of co-teaching traits ranging from highly traditional to highly collaborative.

Various strategies for co-teaching may include: one teach, one observe; one teach, one assist; parallel teaching; alternative teaching; team teaching; and station teaching (Sears et al., 2018). Researchers noted that station teaching, team teaching, and parallel teaching strategies increased equitable learning opportunities, even though they were not frequently used during clinical experiences (Mangram et al., 2020; Sears et al., 2017; Sears et al., 2019, Grady et al., 2020). The researchers also noted that the collaborative pairs more frequently utilized the one teach, one observe strategy, which mirrored a traditional mode of instruction (Mangram et al., 2020; Sears et al., 2018; Sears et al., 2017). Guise et al. (2017) noted that when one teach, one observe is used, with the preservice teacher as the observer, there is a power differential, with the collaborating teacher assuming the expert role.

Co-teaching cannot occur in isolation. Thus, co-planning is needed if co-teaching is to be achieved (Dieker, 2001; Howard & Potts, 2009; Magiera et al., 2005; Murawski & Lochner, 2011). Cayton et al. (2016) identified six co-planning strategies, namely: one plans, one assists; partner planning; one reflects, one plans; one plans, one reacts; parallel planning; and team planning. Co-planning may occur in a variety of forms: face-to-face planning, electronic daily planning, or on-the-spot planning (Friend & Cook, 2007).

Cognitive Coaching^{SM}

Cognitive Coaching^{SM} uses conversations to plan, reflect and problem solve (Ellison & Hayes, 2008; Knight, 2008); thereby promoting self-directed learning, efficacy, interdependence, consciousness, and craftsmanship via a nonjudgmental process (Bengo, 2016; Costa & Garmston, 2015; Ellison & Hayes, 2008; Knight, 2008). The use of Cognitive Coaching^{SM} can also strengthen preservice teachers' self-efficacy by facilitating reflection on means to overcome challenges faced within the classroom setting (Wooten-Burnett, 2016). Hence, in facilitating Cognitive Coaching^{SM}, the facilitator becomes a good listener and asks purposeful questions to increase opportunities for individuals to self-reflect and grow professionally. A synthesis of research found that when Cognitive Coaching^{SM} is employed, there is an increase in: students' performance, teachers' reflectiveness, collaboration, professional assistance offered to teachers, and job satisfaction (Edwards, 2016).

Edwards (2016) provided recommendations for implementing Cognitive Coaching^{SM}. Some of the recommendations were as follows: provide appropriate training to support the implementation of Cognitive Coaching^{SM}, establish norms for collaboration, make a distinction between evaluation and coaching, highlight the significance of reflecting, and allocate time for Cognitive Coaching^{SM}. Thus, if Cognitive Coaching^{SM} is to be utilized during clinical experiences, teacher preparation programs ought to provide training.

Diverse Students in Classroom Settings

Schools are becoming increasingly diverse (Bryant et al., 2017). Diversity within the classroom setting is multifaceted and socially constructed

(Knights & Omanovic, 2015; Males et al., 2020). Common characteristics used to describe student diversity may include: gender, race/ethnicity, socioeconomic status (SES), age, disability, and sexual orientation/gender identity (Rowe & Trickett, 2018). Thus, teacher preparation programs, ought to consider means to support preservice teachers to be effective in diverse spaces (Darling-Hammond, 2000; Koehler & Mishra, 2009).

During clinical experiences, attending to student learning involves recognizing the increasingly diverse and heterogeneous nature of classrooms (Tomlinson, 2017). This heterogeneity calls for the collaborative pair to address academic, socio-emotional, and cultural needs of the diverse student population (AMTE, 2017; AACTE, 2018; NCATE, 2010). Particularly, the collaborative pair should be proactive in identifying the role that culture plays, negating stereotypes, and taking actions that move toward inclusion of all students (Darling-Hammond, 2010, 2012, 2014). In order to do so, the collaborative pair should honor students' history, language, and students' cultural ways of learning unique to their backgrounds (Gutiérrez & Rogoff, 2003; Moschkovich, 2013). Thus, being cognizant of the contextual norms and students' experiences can assist in planning lessons that are culturally relevant (Irvine, 2010; Leonard, 2018; Banks, 2015; NCTM, 2014b). Additionally, the collaborative pair can seek to make connections with families and engage in community outreach efforts (King & Butler, 2015). Therefore, during clinical experiences, students' diversity should be valued (Seah & Andersson, 2015). Moreover, the collaborative pair is encouraged to differentiate instruction to cater to the diverse needs of students (Suprayogi et al., 2017). Differentiated instruction emphasizes that a single teaching style would not meet the needs of each student; since students are diverse and may learn differently. Thus, the collaborative pair can plan to differentiate content, vary the learning activities, and utilize various forms of assessments to better meet the needs of all students (Suprayogi et al., 2017; Tomlinson, 2017).

Summary of the Apprenticeship Model for Learning

The apprenticeship model for learning provides a lens to examine the nature of clinical experiences and interactions between collaborative pairs, while keeping students' learning as the focus of the interaction. The model skillfully captures the nature of planning, enactment, context, Cognitive Coaching[SM] support, and means to attend to students' thinking.

METHODS

We used qualitative research approaches to examine how collaborative pairs attended to elements of the apprenticeship model for learning during clinical experiences. The data were garnered from focus group interviews. In the subsequent paragraphs, we describe the participants, data collection process, and systematic approach used to analyze the data.

Participants

The focus group participants consisted of 24 collaborating teachers and 21 preservice teachers. The collaborating teachers were in secondary mathematics, science, and foreign language. Most of the collaborating teachers had at least three years of experience providing instructional support during clinical experiences.

The preservice teachers were in their fifth year of their teacher preparation program. At the end of the teacher preparation program, the preservice teachers received a master's degree and a secondary teaching license in their specialty area. For their teacher certification program, the preservice teachers completed a year-long placement with the same collaborating teachers. During the first semester, the preservice teachers were expected to engage in half-day instructional activities; and during the second semester, they had to engage in full-day instructional activities as a final internship requirement. Additionally, participating preservice teachers enrolled in an Urban Teaching Seminar. During the seminar, they discussed their own beliefs and assumptions relative to teaching and learning. They also discussed all the elements of the apprenticeship model for learning. The collaborating teachers were exposed to similar content and objectives that were addressed in the Urban Teaching Seminar via a professional development training that was organized by the university.

Diverse School Context

The collaborating teachers worked in diverse school settings, which met the federal guidelines for high-need schools. According to the 2013–2014 school district data, for which the collaborating teachers worked, there were 53,327 students enrolled in schools within this district. Of the total number of students in the schools, 73% were Students of Color, 79% were students who were socioeconomically disadvantaged, and 12% were students with limited English proficiency. In addition, the student mobility rate was 17% (Columbus City Schools, 2014).

Data Collection

We used data from two focus group interviews, one with 24 collaborating teachers and the other with 21 preservice teachers. The fishbowl focus group method was used to collect data on certain topics from a large group of people to gain multiple perspectives and experiences that otherwise would be unavailable (Carey, 1994; Lewis & Winkelman, 2017; Walsh & Sattes, 2015). A summary of the process we used follows.

Focus Group Interviews

The participants provided insights into the extent they attended to the apprenticeship model for learning. Two project leaders preplanned the open-ended questions for the focus group interviews. Sample questions posed were: How has your experience with [university program initiative] influenced your thinking about teaching and learning? How has your experience with your preservice teacher/collaborating teacher impacted your planning? How has your experience with your preservice teacher/ collaborating teacher impacted your teaching? How has your experience with [university program initiative] influenced your capacity to support the thinking of others? In what ways did this work impact student learning? What benefits did the Urban Teaching Seminar provide? What other comments do you have?

Participants were allocated five minutes to answer each question. Using a fishbowl format (Walsh & Sattes, 2015), half of the teachers sat in an inner circle, and the other half in an outer circle. For the first half of the interview, teachers in the inner circle responded verbally, while teachers in the outer circle took notes, and reflected on trends and thoughts about the conversation. Subsequently, participants switched places with the inner/ outer circle participants and shared their responses. The duration of each focus group interview was 60 minutes. The focus group interviews were audio and video recorded. Not all participants responded to all questions. The video data was subsequently transcribed.

Data Analysis

The data were analyzed qualitatively (Clarke & Braun, 2014). We engaged in a thematic analysis informed by the "experiential" and "critical" orientations (Terry et al., 2014). According to Terry et al. (2017), "Experiential orientations focus on what participants think, feel, and do, and are underpinned by the theoretical assumption that language reflects reality…. Critical orientations seek to interrogate dominant patterns of meaning and theoretically understand language as creating, rather than reflecting reality" (p. 25).

Hence, from an experiential lens, we considered how the collaborative pairs felt, and used their language to mirror reality. We also adhered to a critical orientation because their language provided insights into the power dynamics in shared spaces and influenced how decisions were ultimately made. Moreover, we adhered to Terry et al. (2017) six stages of thematic analysis, namely: *familiarizing with the data*, *generating codes, constructing themes*, *reviewing potential themes, defining, and naming themes,* and *producing the report*. Hence, we reviewed the transcripts of the focus groups to become familiar with the data. We also considered the constructs of the university's program and expectations that may have influenced the actions of the collaborative pair.

Afterwards, two of the researchers coded the data in NVivo Software. We utilized a deductive approach, by analyzing the data through the theoretical frame of the apprenticeship model for learning. Open coding was also used to identify segments that could be relevant to answer our research question. For instance, we noticed in considering students' thinking, the collaborative pairs would utilize language that questioned the evidence of students' learning to explicate it. Thus, phrases relative to "evidence of learning" were coded as attending to the element of student thinking in the model.

Next, we constructed themes from the data. Although the elements from the model were the dominant themes, we considered ideas that were being amplified within the codes. For instance, we considered how the collaborative pairs focused on de-centering when addressing student thinking.

Subsequently, four researchers reviewed the themes and determined the extent it captured the data and adequately answered the research questions. The researchers generated frequencies of coding, to explore similarities and differences among the responses provided by the collaborating teachers and preservice teachers. There was a consensus, that our conceptions of the elements, as articulated within the literature review, provided a concise description to define and name our themes. Finally, the group engaged in online writing sessions to collectively develop the narrative.

RESULTS

The results of the study indicated that the collaborative pairs attended to the elements of the apprenticeship model for learning, and it helped to focus on students' learning. Both the collaborating teachers and the preservice teachers suggested that the focus on student learning created opportunities for them to reflect not just on what they were doing, but also on what they ultimately hoped for students to achieve. Despite their similar viewpoints about the value of using the model during clinical experiences, there were differences in elements that they focused on more readily. For instance, we noticed that collaborating teachers provided greater insights on the co-planning and co-teaching strategies, and the preservice teachers were more likely to focus on their beliefs about diverse settings. Table 24.1 is a summary of the frequency of codes based on the elements of the model. Although the length of the text varied among the various codes, Table 24.1 highlights the differences between the dominant codes for the collaborating teachers and preservice teachers.

Table 24.1

Frequency of Codes for Elements of the Apprenticeship Model for Learning From the Focus Groups Data Set

Codes	Collaborating Teachers	Preservice Teachers
Student Thinking	11	10
Co-planning and Co-teaching	26	12
Cognitive Coaching[SM]	10	7
Diverse environment	14	28

In the subsequent paragraphs, we describe how the collaborating teachers and preservice teachers attended to each element of the model.

Student Thinking

The collaborative pairs sought to explicate students' thinking by focusing on evidence of learning. Thus, they shared what they noticed about students' responses, which also provided insights into what students learned (Burns & Badiali, 2018; Stein et al., 2015). For example, a collaborating teacher noted,

> When I had student teachers in the past, it was always learning for the teacher and the intern, but not necessarily on student learning. So, this is a huge paradigm shift for me ... I really got into looking for student learning, looking for evidence of student learning, and everything we do with our kids. (Collaborating Teacher 6)

Thus, the teachers began to question, what is it that they want the students to learn and how will they actually know that the students learned it. For example, another collaborating teacher noted,

> I ... focus on really what do I want the students to learn and really analyz-ing it that day, you know how did we do ... did they get it? How do I know they got it? And just really chunking more, like day-to-day, and looking deeper at student learning than I probably did before. So, I know I had an outcome that I had to teach and come up with a lesson to do it, but the focus of where are they at right now. Where did it take them? (Collaborat-ing Teacher 1)

The collaborating teacher's remarks highlighted that their focus changed from reflecting solely on their own understanding, to determining the extent students learned. The collaborating teacher in the last quotation perceived that the instructional strategy of chunking enhanced the depth of students' thinking of the subject matter being taught.

The collaborating teachers also engaged in decentering actions, and considered how their interactions with the students, impacted students' thinking (Teuscher et al., 2016). Hence, as the collaborating teachers expli-cated students' thinking, they were also reflecting and questioning their own actions and the extent it cultivated learning. For instance, a teacher noted, "I feel like my students might have suffered previously ... we are working together to make sure our students get quality instruction. I feel so much more comfortable with my students' learning" (Collaborating Teacher 15). Therefore, by reflecting on what is the evidence of students' learning, and decentering the teachers' actions, provided the collaborating pairs an opportunity to unpack the nature of students' thinking.

Likewise, the preservice teachers also sought to notice students' behaviors and comments to explicate students' thinking. For instance, a preservice teacher said,

> I was observing every single move and the first impression from the students ... I was trying to see a reaction to see if the student like those things ... I was trying to observe if students were actually using their phone to do homework or something else ... I observe a lot ... so when I was ready to teach I already knew what the students were expecting. (Preservice Teacher 1)

Hence, the preservice teacher suggested they were noticing to orchestrate the discourse within the classroom setting. Another preservice teacher sug-gested the need to question to explicate students' thinking and facilitate learning. The preservice teacher noted,

I break things down into fundamental parts so there's like every problem has, what is the question asking, what is the problem telling you, how can you visualize, conceptualize and describe it in math terms and how are you going to solve it? .... And those fundamental skills can be across ... problem solving as a whole. (Preservice Teacher 2)

Thus, in attending to students' thinking, preservice teachers considered means to question students effectively, such that students can convey their thought process, verbally, visually, and via other forms of representations. The preservice teachers also suggested that effective questioning can be used to develop students' problem-solving skills.

Moreover, the preservice teachers, also engaged in decentering, when considering students' thinking. One preservice teacher indicated that due to their dominant personality the students might have mirrored their action. The preservice teacher said, "You can demonstrate how you are an alpha in the classroom, the students will follow you no matter what" (Preservice Teacher 6). Thus, in attempting to explicate student thinking, the preservice teacher was mindful that their personalities can potentially impact the extent students share their thinking and participate in the classroom discussions.

The collaborating teachers' feedback helped preservice teachers decenter and consider how they impact students' thinking. For instance, a preservice teacher noted, she's able to,

see through the student's eyes what I am not able to see. That helped me to adjust many ... lessons and ... also the way I present some of the information ... [and] the way I communicate information to the students. (Preservice Teacher 11)

Thus, having collaborating teachers in the classroom helped the preservice teachers to reflect on how their actions can contribute to what was learned.

Co-Planning and Co-Teaching

Findings from the data revealed that the collaborative pairs implemented co-planning and co-teaching strategies. In the subsection below, we describe how they attended to co planning and co-teaching.

Co-Planning Strategies

The collaborative pairs engaged in co-planning. The planning sessions were sometimes planned, or impromptu. The goal of the planning was to reflect on means to plan, teach, and assess to promote learning. For instance, a collaborating teacher noted,

> I think our conversations center more around, you know, … focus more on interventions, how do we extend this child, and then how do we help this child … our … planning is evolving…. That is why we want to parallel teach. (Collaborating Teacher 1)

Similarly, another collaborating teacher noted,

> I have a clearer context to discuss the planning piece of things, a clearer focus on the evidence of the student learning it always there …, but, now it is there out in the open as the centerpiece. So, I feel like the discussions are deeper, more focused, then again, there is context, there is common vocabulary. (Collaborating Teacher 2)

Thus, the collaborating teachers noted that they became intentional in utilizing co-planning to promote students' learning.

The collaborating teachers also acknowledged that they employed one plans and one reacts co-planning strategy (Cayton et al., 2016). For example, a collaborating teacher noted,

> I would be planning the lessons and sharing what we would like to do with them, and then they would take over planning the lessons, and I would kind of review it and offer suggestions, things like that. So, it's a very different process in planning now, … together sharing ideas. (Collaborating Teacher 13)

Thus, the collaborating teachers sought to model planning, as well as provide opportunities for preservice teachers to create their own plans.

The preservice teachers acknowledged that they planned with their collaborating teachers. Their responses focused on what was being planned, rather than on the type of co-planning utilized. For example, a preservice teacher noted, "I am involved in IEP [Individualized Educational Plan] meetings and conferences, I speak my own piece whenever I feel necessary, and they listen to what I have to say too" (Preservice Teacher 3). Thus, in this example, the preservice teacher is engaged in planning meetings focused on supporting the diverse needs of students. Another preservice teacher indicated,

> Our planning mainly consists of us doing … problems on the board and then saying, which way is the most clear—how [do] we present this to the students and … what problem types are we going to go to next, how are we going to step up one notch so that they can do it and are still challenged. (Preservice Teacher 6)

Thus, the preservice teacher's quote suggested that they planned to maintain content rigor, and considered the clarity of the content conveyed.

Co-Teaching Strategies

The collaborating teachers sought to utilize a variety of the co-teaching strategies. For instance, one teacher noted, "I am excited about the possibilities of using the different co-teaching styles" (Collaborating Teacher 1). The collaborating teachers acknowledged that they desired to use various strategies, such as parallel teaching, and team teaching. For instance, a collaborating teacher noted, "We really want to try parallel teaching" (Collaborating Teacher 1), and another indicated "the two of us teach in teams for the most of it" (Collaborating Teacher 3). Moreover, the collaborating teachers considered means to support preservice teachers' growth and independence via co-teaching. For example, in working with preservice teachers, the collaborating teachers may initially utilize one teach, one observes or one teach, one assist, in which they facilitate most of the instruction, and then transition to team teaching. Once the collaborating teachers perceived that the preservice teachers are able to facilitate instruction independently, they subsequently utilized the one teach, one observe strategy, in which the preservice teachers served as the primary facilitator of instruction. For instance, a collaborating teacher noted,

> I will teach the first period, then second period we will start working together team teaching. Then by the second and third period we are on a roll, and by the fourth period, they kind of take over themselves. (Collaborating Teacher 4)

Thus, the collaborating teacher sought to use co-teaching to support preservice teachers' instructional independence over time.

Similar to the collaborating teachers, the preservice teachers confirmed that they utilized various co-teaching strategies and were excited to implement them. For instance, a preservice teacher indicated,

> She comes into the class with a whole bunch of methods of CPCT [co planning and co-teaching], of how she can integrate both of us equally in the classroom, in order to maximize or try basically a whole bunch of new things whenever possible. So just to have that experience and try those different forms of teaching like small group, … co-teaching, team teaching, all those different methods, has been absolutely fantastic in my opinion. (Preservice teacher 14)

Thus, the quote suggested that the preservice teacher perceived that their collaborating teacher was enthused about implementing co-teaching strategies and wanted to integrate them equally as a teacher in the classroom setting.

Cognitive Coaching^SM

During clinical experiences, Cognitive Coaching^SM was used to clarify and support learning outcomes. Collaborating teachers perceived that Cognitive Coaching^SM improved the communication channels between them and their preservice teachers. For instance, one collaborating teacher noted,

> I think that Cognitive Coaching^SM has helped support us, you know ... the more I got into it I was like, oh this makes sense, ... I've learned that I need to keep my mouth shut, and I need to ask certain questions and let them do the thinking and processing and come up with their ideas. So I mean how cool is that...? (Collaborating teacher 5)

As a result of utilizing Cognitive Coaching^SM, the collaborating teachers began to pose questions more frequently to the preservice teachers during the planning and post lessons discussions. For instance, the collaborating teachers asked questions such as "Where do you see that going? How do you plan to notice that the students are learning?" (Collaborating Teacher 3). Thus, the collaborating teachers posed questions to help preservice teachers reflect on suitable instructional approaches rather than simply tell the preservice teachers what to do.

Furthermore, Cognitive Coaching^SM helped collaborating teachers learn how to listen. According to a collaborating teacher, "Cognitive Coaching^SM plays a big role ... in just learning how to listen better. All the collaborative components help us to fine tune our own skills" (Collaborating Teacher 8). Thus, the use of Cognitive Coaching^SM provided collaborative teachers an opportunity to listen, and increased opportunities for preservice teachers to participate in conversations about the nature of instructional strategies.

Furthermore, the collaborating teachers perceived that Cognitive Coaching^SM fostered all parties to be responsible for instruction, and developed rapport. For instance, one collaborating teacher noted,

> My thinking about it [clinical experiences] has changed ... It's dual ownership, just not the know-it-all, you're not the expert ... you have to empower the intern... and work together, work on an even level from the beginning ... I think what the most important part is letting your guard down, allowing yourself to not be successful in front of the intern, being able to reflect

back with your intern on that…. You're building a professional rapport with these interns. (Collaborative Teacher 9)

Thus, the collaborative teachers perceived that Cognitive Coaching^SM provided them an opportunity to discuss their personal limitations without fear of judgment, and helped to empower the preservice teachers.

The preservice teachers acknowledged that Cognitive Coaching^SM increased opportunities to reflect upon and improve lessons. For instance, a preservice teacher noted, "Cognitive Coaching^SM, second period, we sit down, and she goes how do you think that could have worked better? or how do you think it went? … she's like don't get frustrated let's just think about it" (Preservice Teacher 4). Thus, the preservice teachers perceived that Cognitive Coaching^SM provided a solace to address obstacles that might have arisen in the lesson. Moreover, the preservice teachers acknowledged that Cognitive Coaching^SM facilitated self-reflection. For example, a preservice teacher indicated,

> [Cognitive Coaching^SM] has made me realize almost the power of reflection, and self-reflection, in your teaching practices, and your lessons … what you could have done better, what you did well, what could you tweak, … I never really understood how important that was until I had the experience … I've learned a lot. (Preservice Teacher 5)

Thus, the use of Cognitive Coaching^SM during clinical experiences empowered the preservice teachers to consider means of how to enhance their instructional craft. On the other hand, Cognitive Coaching^SM assisted the collaborating teachers to develop skills, which empowered the preservice teachers.

Diverse Students in Classroom Settings

The collaborative teachers embraced the diversity of their students and reflected on means to integrate students' culture and language into the lessons. For instance, a collaborating teacher noted,

> I really try to think about, we call that comprehensive input: how much language I use to expose, to give to students. So, I was very cautious of trying to use native language, the common language, like Chinese, to explain tasks, to, uh, you know, explain procedures. But before I had an intern, you know, I was focusing on if I get my lesson done, English was easier. So, now I'm like, even though it takes some time, I try to use so much more Chinese. And I realized, the students can really follow and get it. You know, it takes some time, but he gets it. And it's getting easier. (Collaborating Teacher 15)

Thus, the collaborating teacher considered means to support students' native language in lessons, and noticed that it facilitated learning. The collaborating teachers also identified strategies that can support students learning, such as technology. For instance, a collaborating teacher noted,

> I have a very high ESL population at my school so it's one of the strategies, is visual! So, having the SMART Board, to be able to just take a picture of anything of the internet, it helps tremendously. (Collaborating Teacher 5)

Thus, the collaborative teachers were appreciative of the technological resources the university provided because it increased students' access to various content. For example, a collaborating teacher noted,

> it provided access to some of these newer technologies like SMART Boards, like clickers. The people would not have had access … otherwise, and are able to now use as part of instruction and learning, and are making much richer classroom experiences for their kids because they've had access to it. (Collaborating Teacher 3)

In addition, to utilizing technology, the collaborative teachers believed that co-teaching can help to differentiate instruction and meet the needs of the diverse student population. For instance, a collaborating teacher noted,

> I have a significant amount of students that are special education. Or it's just, learning language is hard, and I found that we are able to plan ahead, and even divide in different ways or do different things where students are getting more individualized instruction. And I definitely feel that they're doing better than students that could get lost in a crowd of thirty and it's not even close to happening just with us around helping. (Collaborating Teacher 18)

Another, collaborating teacher echoed these sentiments and considered how they could use co-teaching to cater to their diverse population. The collaborating teacher noted,

> there are a whole different variety, or levels of what we are looking at, and how we will address the different ways that students learn. Um having an activity where they are up moving around, versus having something that they are manipulating with their hands, um to going back to the pencil and paper, and using technology. There's … so many different strategies out there. (Collaborating Teacher 7)

Thus, the collaborating teachers, perceived the use of co-teaching can increase the use of individualized approaches, and differentiated instruction to better meet the needs of students.

In discussing the diverse settings, preservice teachers reflected on how to facilitate equitable opportunities, and culturally responsive pedagogies. The preservice teachers acknowledged that differences exist between studying issues relative to equitable opportunities and enacting them during their instruction. Additionally, the preservice teachers engaged in self-reflection when they considered their beliefs about students' ability to learn. For example, a preservice teacher said,

> It is one thing to study social justice critical pedagogy in the classroom and then go see it worked out, and so I think that's probably the experience, having a mentor teacher in the field is the most I've gotten out of it because it links your theory with knowledge and practices, and it makes it come alive.... I think that has been the biggest thing for me. I feel like for me it has erased stereotypes for me—not stereotypes—but assumptions. You have kids in your classroom who you are thinking, does this kid not want to work, or is this kid having trouble understanding? And your mentor teacher can really help you understand—well think about this, think about this.. . . And you do realize it's OK to say some kids are just not working hard enough. This kid actually has a learning disability; this kid needs extra support.... That is really nice—it helps you realize what each kid needs. (Preservice Teacher 7)

The preservice teacher also noted,

> It is one thing to talk about it in the classroom and read case studies. These kids are not case studies. Everyone is different, everyone is going through a different thing. That has been the biggest thing that has impacted me—get to know kids in your setting and not just take this idea and I know what this is.... Just getting feedback from your mentor teacher totally changes the game. (Preservice Teacher 7)

Therefore, allowing preservice teachers to complete their clinical experiences in diverse settings broadened their perspectives of inequities that may exist, and created opportunities to reflect on means to embrace diversity.

Building relationships with students was perceived as central to the success of the preservice teachers working in a diverse environment. The preservice teachers frequently suggested that knowing the students you will teach and exhibiting good classroom management skills is necessary in a diverse setting. For example, a preservice teacher noted,

> One thing I've been thinking about a lot, these classes have kind of pointed out to me that in urban education managing a classroom is just, as if not, more important than teaching the content, because if you cannot successfully manage the classroom they are not going to pick up any of the con-

tent anyway. And a lot of managing the classroom in an urban setting has to do with creating and developing relationships with students. And that is something I did not think a whole lot about before. (Preservice Teacher 13)

Hence, working in a diverse context highlighted the importance of building relationships with the students.

SUMMARY OF RESULTS

Therefore, attending to each element of the apprenticeship model for learning, facilitated opportunities for the collaborative pairs to focus on students' learning during clinical experiences. In attending to students' thinking, the collaborative pairs sought to document evidence of learning. Co-planning and co-teaching provided opportunities for the collaborative pairs to carefully plan and enact lessons that engaged students and increased learning opportunities. Cognitive Coaching^{SM} provided the collaborative pairs an outlet to reflect and listen to each other. Moreover, in working in diverse settings, the collaborative pairs sought to implement strategies that are culturally relevant. The preservice teachers also became more aware of their beliefs that were potentially productive or unproductive (NCTM, 2014b; Philipp, 2007).

DISCUSSION

During clinical experiences, having collaborative pairs attend to the various elements of the apprenticeship model for learning promoted students' learning, and encouraged productive and purposeful collaboration. Thus, utilizing the model helped in developing preservice teachers' ability to facilitate instruction, reflect on obstacles, and consider appropriate strategies to address them.

The results also provided clarity on the interplay of actions that occur during clinical experiences, based on the intersection of elements in the apprenticeship model for learning. For instance, Cognitive Coaching^{SM} can be used to help preservice teachers plan more carefully, and consider means to explicate students' thinking and promote learning. It can also facilitate opportunities for the preservice teachers to reflect on the extent they addressed the diverse needs of students. Thus, gaining insights into the intersection of elements of the apprenticeship model for learning can be valuable in amplifying actions that may need to be attended to promote students' learning. Hence, researchers, may seek to examine each element or the intersection of multiple elements of the apprenticeship model for learning with greater depth in the future. Moreover, the results suggested that having clinical experiences in diverse settings can increase the likelihood the collaborative pairs considered means to promote diversity and support equitable opportunities within their instructional practices. For instance, the preservice teachers acknowledged that they became more aware of their beliefs about diverse learning environments. Thus, being aware of their productive and unproductive beliefs helped them consider means to provide access and attend to equity within the classroom settings (NCTM, 2014b).

Furthermore, this study can serve as a catalyst for research seeking to support student learning during clinical experiences. Hence, future studies can examine how the model is enacted in various discipline-specific clinical experiences, and at various grade levels. Researchers may also consider examining how the model may be applied in different school settings (e.g., urban, suburban and rural), and considering potential similarities and differences in the nature of the experiences. Additionally, consideration may be given as to how the apprenticeship model for learning can be used to support clinical experiences that may occur in an online setting. Studies of this nature can be valuable considering the increased demand for remote instruction, as a result of the paradigm shift to facilitate continuous learning opportunities during the era of the coronavirus disease 2019 (COVID 19).

CONCLUSION

In closing, the apprenticeship model for learning can be used during clinical experiences to support students' learning. The elements of the model provided opportunities for collaborative pairs to place a greater focus on learning and meet the needs of diverse student populations. The results of the study indicated that differences exist in what collaborating teachers and preservice teachers may focus on when utilizing the model. Particularly, the collaborating teachers were more likely to focus on co-planning and co teaching, while the preservice teachers were more reflective on diverse students in classroom settings. Therefore, teacher preparation programs, can use the results from this study to inform their efforts to support collaborative pairs during clinical experiences, particularly in diverse settings.

REFERENCES

Association of Mathematics Teacher Educators, A. (2017). *Standards for Preparing Teachers of Mathematics.*

American Association of Colleges of Teacher Education Clinical Practice Commission. (2018). *A pivot toward clinical practice, its lexicon, and the renewal of educator preparation: A report of the AACTE Clinical Practice Commission.*

Baeten, M., & Simons, M. (2014). Student teachers' team teaching: Models, effects, and conditions for implementation. *Teaching and Teacher Education, 41*, 92–110.

Banks, J. A. (2015). *Cultural diversity and education: Foundations, curriculum, and teaching*. Routledge.

Bengo, P. (2016). Secondary mathematics coaching: The components of effective mathematics coaching and implications. *Teaching and Teacher Education, 60*, 88–96.

Boston, M. D., & Smith, M. S. (2011). A 'task-centric approach' to professional development: Enhancing and sustaining mathematics teachers' ability to implement cognitively challenging mathematical tasks. *ZDM, 43*(6–7), 965–977.

Brosnan, P., Jaede, M., Brownstein, E., & Stroot, S. A. (2014, April). *Co-planning and co-teaching in an urban context*. Annual Meeting of the American Educational Research Association, Philadelphia, PA.

Bryant, A., Triplett, C., Watson, N., & Lewis, P. (2017). The browning of American public schools: Evidence of increasing racial diversity and the implications for policy, practice, and student outcomes. *The Urban Review, 49*(2), 263–278.

Burns, R. W., & Badiali, B. J. (2018). Clinical pedagogy and pathways of clinical pedagogical practice: A conceptual framework for teaching about teaching in clinical experiences. *Action in Teacher Education, 40*(4), 428–446.

Carey, M. (1994). The group effect in focus groups: Planning, implementing and interpreting focus group research. In J. Morse (Ed.), *Critical issues in qualitative research methods* (pp. 225–251). SAGE.

Cayton, C., Grady, M., Preston, R., & Sinicrope, R. (2016). Co-Planning strategies to support intern development. In *Proceedings of the fifth annual Mathematics Teacher Education Partnership conference*, pp. 150–155.

Clarke, V., & Braun, V. (2014). Thematic analysis. In T. Teo (Ed.), *Encyclopedia of critical psychology* (pp. 1947–1952). Springer.

Columbus City Schools. (2014). *Our spirit of success: Columbus City Schools 2013–2014*. Retrieved June 15, 2016, from http://www.columbus.k12.oh.us/progressreport/page4.html

Costa, A. L., & Garmston, R. J. (2015). *Cognitive Coaching^{SM}: Developing self-directed leaders and learners*. Rowman & Littlefield.

Cuenca, A. (2012). *Supervising student teachers: Issues, perspectives and future directions*. Sense.

Darling-Hammond, L. (2000). How teacher education matters. *Journal of Teacher Education, 51*(3), 166–173.

Darling-Hammond, L. (2010). Recruiting and retaining teachers: Turning around the race to the bottom in high-need schools. *Journal of Curriculum and Instruction, 4*(1), 16–32.

Darling-Hammond, L. (2012). *Powerful teacher education: Lessons from exemplary programs*. John Wiley & Sons.

Darling-Hammond, L. (2014). Strengthening clinical preparation: The holy grail of teacher education. *Peabody Journal of Education, 89*(4), 547–561.

Dieker, L. A. (2001). What are the characteristics of "effective" middle and high school co taught teams for students with disabilities? *Preventing School Failure: Alternative Education for Children and Youth*, *46*(1), 14–23.

Edwards, J. L. (2016). *Cognitive Coaching^SM: A synthesis of the research* (12th ed.). Center for Cognitive Coaching^SM.

Ellison, J., & Hayes, C. (2008). Cognitive Coaching^SM. In J. Knight (Ed.), *Coaching: Approaches and perspectives*. Corwin Press.

Franke, M. L., & Kazemi, E. (2001). Learning to teach mathematics: Focus on student thinking. *Theory into practice*, *40*(2), 102–109.

Friend, M., & Cook, L. (2007). Co-teaching. *Interactions: collaboration skills for professionals* (5th ed.). Pearson.

Grady, M., Sears, R., Stone, J., & Biagetti, S. (2020). Using co-planning and co-teaching strategies to transform secondary mathematics clinical experiences. In W. G. Martin, B. R. Lawler, A. E. Lischka, & W. M. Smith (Eds.), *The mathematics teacher education partnership: The power of a networked improvement community to transform secondary mathematics teacher preparation* (p. 235). Information Age Publishing.

Guise, M., Habib, M., Thiessen, K., & Robbins, A. (2017). Continuum of co-teaching implementation: Moving from traditional student teaching to co-teaching. *Teaching and Teacher Education*, *66*, 370–382.

Gutiérrez, K. D., & Rogoff, B. (2003). Cultural ways of learning: Individual traits or repertoires of practice. *Educational Researcher*, *32*(5), 19–25.

Howard, L., & Potts, E. A. (2009). Using co-planning time: Strategies for a successful co teaching marriage. *Teaching Exceptional Children Plus*, *5*(4), 2–11.

Irvine, J. J. (2010). Culturally relevant pedagogy. *Education Digest: Essential Readings Condensed for Quick Review*, *75*(8), 57–61.

King, E., & Butler, B. R. (2015). Who cares about diversity? A preliminary investigation of diversity exposure in teacher preparation programs. *Multicultural Perspectives*, *17*(1), 46–52.

Knight, J. (Ed.) (2008). *Coaching: Approaches and perspectives*. Corwin Press.

Knights, D., & Omanovic, V. (2015). Rethinking diversity in organizations and society. In R. Bendl, I. Bleijenbergh, E. Hentthonen, & A. J. Mills (Eds.), *The Oxford handbook of diversity in organizations* (pp. 83–108). Oxford University Press.

Koehler, M. J., & Mishra, P. (2009). What is technological pedagogical content knowledge? *Contemporary Issues in Technology and Teacher Education*, *9*(1), 60–70.

Leatham, K. R., Peterson, B. E., Stockero, S. L., & Van Zoest, L. R. (2015). Conceptualizing mathematically significant pedagogical opportunities to build on student thinking. *Journal for Research in Mathematics Education*, *46*(1), 88–124.

Leonard, J. (2018). *Culturally specific pedagogy in the mathematics classroom: Strategies for teachers and students*. Routledge

Lewis, R. E., & Winkelman, P. (2017). *Lifescaping practices in school communities: Implementing action research and appreciative inquiry*. Routledge.

Magiera, K., Smith, C., Zigmond, N., & Gebauer, K. (2005). Benefits of co-teaching in secondary mathematics classes. *Teaching Exceptional Children*, *37*(3), 20–24.

Moschkovich, J. (2013). Principles and guidelines for equitable mathematics teaching practices and materials for English language learners. *Journal of Urban Mathematics Education, 6*(1), 45–57.

Males, L. M., Sears, R., & Lawler, B. R. (2020). Equity and justice in the preparation of secondary mathematics teachers. In W. G. Martin, B. R. Lawler, A. E. Lischka, & W. M. Smith (Eds.), *The mathematics teacher education partnership: The power of a networked improvement community to transform secondary mathematics teacher preparation* (p. 57). Information Age Publishing.

Mangram, C., Clarke, P. A. J., Waller, P., Ellis, R. L., & Castro-Minnehan, C. (2020). Focus on improving clinical experiences in secondary mathematics teacher preparation. In W. G. Martin, B. R. Lawler, A. E. Lischka, & W. M. Smith (Eds.), *The mathematics teacher education partnership: The power of a networked improvement community to transform secondary mathematics teacher preparation* (p. 281). Information Age Publishing.

Murawski, W. W., & Lochner, W. W. (2011). Observing co-teaching: What to ask for, look or, and listen for. *Intervention in School and Clinic, 46*(3), 174–183.

National Council for Accreditation of Teacher Education. (2010, November). *Transforming teacher education through clinical practice: A national strategy to prepare effective teachers*. Report of the Blue Ribbon Panel on Clinical Preparation and Partnerships for Improved Student Learning. Eric Clearinghouse.

National Council of Teachers of Mathematics. (2014a). *Principles to action: Ensuring mathematical success for all.*

National Council of Teachers of Mathematics. (2014b). *Access and Equity Position Statement.* https://www.nctm.org/uploadedFiles/Standards_and_Positions/ Position_Statements/ Access_and_Equity.pdf

Ojose, B. (2015). *Common misconceptions in mathematics: Strategies to correct them.* University Press of America

Philipp, R. A. (2007). Mathematics teachers' beliefs and affect. In F. K. Lester Jr. (Ed.), *Second handbook of research on mathematics teaching and learning* (pp. 257–315). Information Age Publishing.

Roh, K. H., & Lee, Y. H. (2017). Designing tasks of introductory real analysis to bridge a gap between students' intuition and mathematical rigor: The case of the convergence of a sequence. *International Journal of Research in Undergraduate Mathematics Education, 3*(1), 34–68.

Rowe, H. L., & Trickett, E. J. (2018). Student diversity representation and reporting in universal school-based social and emotional learning programs: Implications for generalizability. *Educational Psychology Review, 30*(2), 559–583.

Schoenfeld, A. H. (2015). Summative and formative assessments in mathematics supporting the goals of the common core standards. *Theory Into Practice, 54*(3), 183–194.

Seah, W. T., & Andersson, A. (2015). Valuing diversity in mathematics pedagogy through the volitional nature and alignment of values. In A. Bishop, H. Tan, T. N. Barkatsas (Eds.), *Diversity in Mathematics Education* (pp. 167–183). Springer.

Sears, R., Brosnan, P., Gainsburg, J., Stone, J., Spencer, C., Riggs, L., Biagetti, S., Cayton, C., Grady, M., Clarke, J. P., & Andreasan, J. (2017). Using improvement science to transform internship experiences through co-teaching strategies. In L. West (Ed.), *Reflective and collaborative processes to improve mathematics teaching*. National Council of Teachers of Mathematics.

Sears, R., Grady, M., Cayton, C., Brosnan, P., Ahmad, S., & Castro-Minnehan, C. (2018). *Implications of a co-planning and co-teaching professional development training for pre-service teachers and collaborating teachers*. https://digitalcommons.usf.edu/tal_facpub/234/

Sears, R., Kersaint, G., Burgos, F., & Wooten, R. (2019). Collaborative effort to develop middle school preservice teachers' mathematical knowledge. *PRIMUS, 29*(9), 965–981.

Stein, M. K., Engle, R. A., Smith, M. S., & Hughes, E. K. (2015). Orchestrating productive mathematical discussion: Helping teachers learn to better incorporate student thinking. In L. B. Resnick, C. S. C. Asterhan, & S. N. Clarke (Eds.), *Socializing intelligence through academic talk and dialogue* (pp. 357–388). American Educational Research Association.

Stockero, S. L., Rupnow, R. L., & Pascoe, A. E. (2015). *Noticing student mathematical thinking in the complexity of classroom instruction*. North American Chapter of the International Group for the Psychology of Mathematics Education [Paper presentation]. The Annual Meeting of the North American Chapter of the International Group for the Psychology of Mathematics.

Suprayogi, M. N., Valcke, M., & Godwin, R. (2017). Teachers and their implementation of differentiated instruction in the classroom. *Teaching and Teacher Education, 67*, 291–301.

Terry, G., Hayfield, N., Clarke, V., & Braun, V. (2017). Thematic analysis. In C. Willing & W. Stainton-Rogers (Eds.), *The SAGE handbook of qualitative research in psychology* (pp. 17–37). SAGE.

Teuscher, D., Moore, K. C., & Carlson, M. P. (2016). Decentering: A construct to analyze and explain teacher actions as they relate to student thinking. *Journal of Mathematics Teacher Education, 19*(5), 433–456.

Thames, M. H. & Ball, D. L. (2013). Making progress in US mathematics education: Lessons learned—past, present, and future. In K. R. Leatham (Ed.), *Vital directions for mathematics education research* (pp. 15–44). Springer.

Tomlinson, C. A. (2017). *How to differentiate instruction in academically diverse classrooms*. ASCD.

Walsh, J. A., & Sattes, B. D. (2015). *Questioning for classroom discussion: Purposeful speaking, engaged listening, deep thinking*. ASCD.

Wooten-Burnett, S. C. (2016). "Cognitive Coaching[SM]: The impact on teacher candidates' teacher efficacy." *Research Quarterly for Exercise and Sport, 87*(S2), A1.

.

CHAPTER 25

HYBRID METHODS COURSE MODEL FOR TEACHER EDUCATION CANDIDATES

Implementation Evidence From the Field

Austin Kureethara Manuel, Christina Janise McIntyre, Emily K. Reeves, and Daphney L. Curry
Midwestern State University

ABSTRACT

While the hybrid education trend is growing, teacher preparation is in a unique situation because of the opportunity to blend both online learning and internship obligations using a hybrid model for teacher preparation. This study specifically explores the benefits of a hybrid model to teach preservice methods courses the two semesters before clinical teaching. After exploring the underlying dimensions that determine the tenets of the two assessments—one assessed by the mentor teachers at professional development schools, and another assessed by professors of the teacher candidates—a comparison of hybrid and non-hybrid methods on these tenets were conducted using data from 78 teacher candidates. In the ever-changing landscape of higher education, this study demonstrates that the hybrid model is just as successful and, in some situations, even more beneficial than the traditional face-to-face format.

Preparing Quality Teachers:
Advances in Clinical Practice, pp. 543–559
Copyright © 2022 by Information Age Publishing
www.infoagepub.com
543

INTRODUCTION

Online coursework has had a relatively long history in higher education, demonstrating usefulness for nontraditional and traditional students alike (Dolan, 2009). Due to its asynchronous nature, apart from granting traditional students greater flexibility when scheduling academic coursework, online coursework has allowed nontraditional students to complete undergraduate degrees and seek graduate credentials simultaneously. With its steadily increasing popularity, a focus on quality instruction has helped ensure the caliber of content delivered online remains high. The face-to-face components of hybrid courses can be synchronously delivered through virtual meeting software or asynchronously through recorded videos, thus, allowing flexibility for both students and professors (Hass & Joseph, 2018; Lei & Lei 2019; Tuckman, 2002). The hybrid courses featuring internship components that require both instruction and clinical experiences can benefit from this format and is ideal for teacher education during the clinical phase (Hurlbut, 2018). Further, the model has shown a high level of promise for allowing students to receive quality content instruction while allotting them more time working with in-service teachers in the field.

Even when conducted in classrooms at professional development schools (PDS), feedback from the secondary methods courses demonstrated clear frustration with the traditional course model. The teacher candidates consistently reported that the traditional course model, which divides teacher candidates' time between their course work in face-to-face class and the field activities, had not helped to improve their opportunities to demonstrate their teaching skills at PDS. After considering the benefits that feature internships and clinical placements, a hybrid secondary methods course model was designed and delivered with dramatically different results and feedback from all data collection points, including teacher candidates and PDS mentor teachers.

One enduring common complaint among teachers and students, however, has been the lack of connection and engagement among students and instructors (Bolliger et al., 2019; Dolan, 2009; Sanga, 2018). Even this area of concern is being addressed by advancements in technology such as high-speed internet, quality digital video formats, social media discussion platforms, and widely available file-sharing programs. These have increased the engagement capabilities of online coursework, making online courses more effective and more satisfying for those seeking a more interactive experience (Bolliger et al., 2019; Brunken, 2019). With this online shift and a movement toward a more flexible educational experience, hybrid courses have been developed that possess both online and face-to-face components.

The Hybrid Model

According to the Education Department's National Center for Education Statistics, while enrollment across the country in higher education has declined as a whole, enrollment in online courses has increased (Ginder et al., 2018). For many students, online courses are more feasible because they allow flexibility for interns to gain experience, work, and outside responsibilities (Ortagus & Tanner, 2019). While this trend is growing, teacher preparation is in a unique situation because of the opportunity to blend both online learning and internship obligations using a hybrid model for teacher preparation. Particularly during the two semesters leading up to clinical teaching or a full-year internship, teacher candidates enrolled in a hybrid teacher preparation program can fulfill the content expectations online while spending their traditional face-to-face class time in a K–12 classroom gaining experience. Using several of the National Association for Professional Development Schools (NAPDS, 2008) Nine Essentials as an anchor in our PDS, we carefully developed a hybrid secondary methods course that balanced online content with a much higher number of hours of actual co-teaching time in the K–12 setting.

A school-university culture committed to the preparation of future educators that embraces their active engagement in the school community (NAPDS Essential 2) played a critical role in this model. Traditionally, teacher candidates spent about half of their semester in the field and the other half in classrooms with professors working on content. Using NAPDS Essential 2, the school-university partnership met and agreed that 100% of the semester would be more beneficial in terms of having teacher candidates in the K–12 classroom working with students. This included tutoring, being involved in school-community events, and traditional K–12 classroom work. The outcome resulted in students going from about 45 hours of experience during the semester to over 90 hours of experience and the feedback from teacher candidates was very positive.

Ongoing and reciprocal professional development for all participants guided by need (NAPDS Essential 3) was a driving force for the online content development. Not only did teacher candidates need online content support, but mentor teachers also needed professional development for co-teaching support. For teacher candidates, content was delivered using the online learning platform used by the university for traditional online courses. This allowed for students to track their progress using the grade book which helped ease their natural worries about grades and focus on their actual development as a teacher. The main features of the online learning platform used were discussion boards, quizzes, reading assignments, and written assignment submission. Teacher candidates appreciated the discussion board feature as one teacher candidates reported on her course reflection form, "I loved the discussion boards because we were in the field with our classes but also got to discuss what we were doing with our peers." For mentor teachers, we created a website that included training videos, forms, guidelines, and additional supports.

Professors actively worked with both teacher candidates and mentor teachers by providing support, guidance, and resources. Further, professors conducted Saturday workshops to support teacher candidates. Professors made themselves a valuable and accessible resource. This dynamic exemplifies NAPDS Essential 7 by creating a structure that allows all participants a forum for ongoing governance, reflection, and collaboration and NAPDS Essential 4, shared commitment to innovative and reflective practice by all participants.

Hybrid Model Components

The following are featured in the current hybrid model discussed in this chapter. Literature circles delivered in blog format increased student collaboration and connectedness as well as modeled best practice pedagogy. A video feedback platform, such as GoReact (Speakworks, 2018) allowed students to record their teaching and receive time stamped comments and feedback from supervisors and peers. Self-paced software, such as Certify Teacher, are provided to teacher candidates to practice the certification exams. The interactive study methods and practice quizzes were helpful to prepare the teacher candidates to prepare for their upcoming certification exams. Pre- and post-synchronous teaching conferences with instructors could have been held in person but were mostly conducted using virtual meeting software such as Zoom which allowed for location flexibility (Zoom Video Communications, 2020). For immediate communication, a communication app, Remind 101, was used to broadcast important announcements to the whole class or communicate with each student (Remind, 2020). As an alternative to meetings and lengthy e-mails, faculty shared a google site with mentor teachers which included all pertinent information related with the course work. This also contained co-teaching training where new mentors could engage in learning about the co-teaching process and experienced mentors could review information as needed. Students also used digital time logs to document hours in their clinical setting, which allowed mentor teachers and professors to track and verify individual students' time in the field.

METHOD

Based on our creation of the hybrid teacher education program we wanted to determine the efficacy of the hybrid model of instruction for the methods courses. Data from mentor surveys and unit plan assessment were collected and analyzed for a group of 78 teacher candidates. Specifically, we examined the research questions: Will there be statistically significant differences between the non-hybrid and the hybrid groups for data sets (1) mentor surveys and (2) unit plan results, for different underlying dimensions of each set of data? For the former research question, data from the mentor survey, which provided information on how well the teacher candidates internalized the content, was used. For the latter research question, data from the unit plan assessment, in which teacher candidates' ability to plan their lessons was used. Notably, the data from the mentor survey would provide information regarding teacher candidates' level of internalization of content and the application thereof, as observed by the mentor teacher, illustrated by positive impacts on K–12 students. Further, the results from the unit plan assessment would demonstrate the teacher candidates' ability to apply what they learned in the course content. Additionally, the unit plan assessment has undergone validity and reliability tests, specifically inter-rater reliability measures, which strengthen the quality of the data. Two data sources were examined for the students who received at least one methods instruction in the hybrid format and compared with the same data from students who had received methods instruction in the traditional format, in previous semesters. The traditional format consisted of a variation of three weeks in the classroom before being placed in the field to shadow a mentor teacher. After the placement, students would be in the field one day a week and would attend class the other day. However, using the hybrid model, students were placed in the field for the entire semester after their first week of the semester. The placement was possible because the course work was provided online in the hybrid model. The teacher candidates in the hybrid model, thus, had more clinical hours compared to teacher candidates who were not placed in hybrid model course. The required pre- and post-teaching conferences were provided using virtual meeting platforms.

Dimensions Defining Mentor Survey Results and Model Comparison

Initially, mentor teacher survey data from the academic years that ended in 2018 and 2019 was collected. The survey collected the mentor teachers' observation of the teacher candidates' performance under their supervision. The mentor teachers observed their teacher candidates' involvement in the educational activities in the school setting and determined the level of benefits to the students in the classroom. The level of acquired benefit for the classroom was calibrated on a 4-point scale, namely no benefit at all (0), little benefit (1), some benefit (2), and significant benefit (3). If the teacher candidates did not participate in the activity, the mentor teacher would mark it as *not applicable* (NA). We denoted it with a 4 in our analysis. It is to be noted that the item classroom observation was mandatory for all teacher candidates and NA was not allotted for any of them in this category. The other categories that the mentor teachers observed were individual student observations, where the teacher candidates were involved in engaging the K–12 students in the classroom; teacher assistant, where the teacher candidates would assist the mentor teachers in educational activities in the school setting; lab assistant, where the teacher candidates would assist the mentor teachers in educational scientific activities in the school lab setting; Tutoring, where the teacher candidates would provide additional, special, remedial, or accelerated instruction involving a single student or very small group; whole group instruction, where the teacher candidates would instruct or provide support to the mentor teacher to instruct the whole class; small group instruction, where the teacher candidates would instruct or provide support to the mentor teacher to instruct students working in small groups; and field-based projects, where the teacher candidates would support the K–12 students outside the typical classroom setting under the supervision of their mentor teachers.

Descriptive Data and Inferences

Tables 25.1–25.8 are based on descriptive data analyses and explain how each benefit varied between two groups of teacher candidates across two years. Further, the tables indicate how the benefits of each category varied when the method of instruction changed from non-hybrid to hybrid status. The percentage of benefit was used for each category for all the tables.

Table 25.1

Variation of Classroom Observation Benefit Across Two Years

Year	Type	No Benefit to Class(0)	Little Benefit to Class(1)	Some Benefit to Class(2)	Significant Benefit to Class(3)
2018	Not Hybrid	2.94%	5.88%	35.29%	55.88%
2018	Not Hybrid Previously	0.00%	10.53%	26.32%	63.16%
2019	Not Hybrid	5.56%	5.56%	50.00%	38.89%
2019	Hybrid	0.00%	0.00%	42.86%	57.14%

Table 25.2

Variation of Individual Student Observation Benefit Across Two Years

Year	Type	Little Benefit to Class(1)	Some Benefit to Class(2)	Significant Benefit to Class(3)	NA
2018	Not Hybrid	2.94%	23.53%	50.00%	23.53%
2018	Not Hybrid Previously	10.53%	15.79%	68.42%	5.26%
2019	Not Hybrid	5.56%	44.44%	44.44%	5.56%
2019	Hybrid	0.00%	28.57%	71.43%	0.00%

Table 25.3

Variation of Teacher Assistant Benefit Across Two Years

Year	Type	Little Benefit to Class(1)	Some Benefit to Class(2)	Significant Benefit to Class(3)	NA
2018	Not Hybrid	0.00%	11.76%	82.35%	5.88%
2018	Not Hybrid Previously	5.26%	10.53%	68.42%	15.79%
2019	Not Hybrid	0.00%	16.67%	77.78%	5.56%
2019	Hybrid	0.00%	0.00%	100.00%	0.00%

Table 25.4

Variation of Lab Assistant Benefit Across Two Years

Year	Type	Some Benefit to Class(2)	Significant Benefit to Class(3)	NA
2018	Not Hybrid	5.88%	23.53%	70.59%
2018	Not Hybrid Previously	10.53%	26.32%	63.16%
2019	Not Hybrid	0.00%	5.56%	94.44%
2019	Hybrid	0.00%	42.86%	57.14%

Table 25.5

Variation of Tutoring Benefit Across Two Years

Year	Type	Some Benefit to Class(2)	Significant Benefit to Class(3)	NA
2018	Not Hybrid	0.00%	47.06%	52.94%
2018	Not Hybrid Previously	10.53%	26.32%	63.16%
2019	Not Hybrid	5.56%	33.33%	61.11%
2019	Hybrid	0.00%	42.86%	57.14%

Table 25.6

Variation of Group Instruction Benefit Across Two Years

Year	Type	Little Benefit to Class(1)	Some Benefit to Class(2)	Significant Benefit to Class(3)	NA
2018	Not Hybrid	2.94%	29.41%	64.71%	2.94%
2018	Not Hybrid Previously	5.26%	26.32%	68.42%	0.00%
2019	Not Hybrid	0.00%	27.78%	72.22%	0.00%
2019	Hybrid	0.00%	28.57%	71.43%	0.00%

Table 25.7

Variation of Small Group Instruction Benefit Across Two Years

Year	Type	Little Benefit to Class(1)	Some Benefit to Class(2)	Significant Benefit to Class(3)	NA
2018	Not Hybrid	2.94%	14.71%	79.41%	2.94%
2018	Not Hybrid Previously	0.00%	15.79%	57.89%	26.32%
2019	Not Hybrid	0.00%	27.78%	61.11%	11.11%
2019	Hybrid	0.00%	28.57%	71.43%	0.00%

Table 25.8

Variation of Field-Based Projects Benefit Across Two Years

Year	Type	Little Benefit to Class(1)	Some Benefit to Class(2)	Significant Benefit to Class(3)	NA
2018	Not Hybrid	2.94%	2.94%	32.35%	61.76%
2018	Not Hybrid Previously	0.00%	10.53%	36.84%	52.63%
2019	Not Hybrid	0.00%	0.00%	38.89%	61.11%
2019	Hybrid	0.00%	14.29%	85.71%	0.00%

Examining Benefits of Hybrid Model

Data from 78 teacher candidates were reported by their mentor teachers. First, it was examined whether any variables could be eliminated by running a factor analysis among the benefit variables. The Bartlett's Test of Sphericity and Kaiser-Meyer-Olkin (KMO) was conducted. The measure of sampling adequacy for all the benefit variables found that even though the Bartlett's revealed that the factor analysis is highly significant, $\chi^2 (28) = 80.58$, $p < .001$, the KMO values for Lab Assistant Benefit (.44) and Small Group Instruction Benefit (.36) were below .55. Therefore, the two variables were removed from the factor analysis. On rechecking the adequacy of the factor analyses with the rest of the variables were established (Bartlett's test, $\chi^2(15) = 58.50$, $p < .001$ and KMO values for all variables were greater than .5 (Classroom Observation Benefit (0.69), Individual Student Observation Benefit (0.71), Teacher Assistant Benefit (0.64), Tutoring Benefit (0.67), Whole Group Instruction Benefit (0.67) and Field Project Benefit (0.62)). Further, the overall Measure of Sampling Adequacy was .67. Again, the determinant of the correlational matrix (*det* = .45) was greater than the required value for the determinant, 0.00001(Field et al., 2012). Subsequently, running a factor analysis was appropriate for this adjusted benefit data.

An initial factor analysis was run to obtain the eigenvalues for each variable. After running the factor analysis based on eigenvalues there were two eigenvalues greater than 1. This finding was confirmed by the corresponding scree-plot, which is given in Figure 25.1. Thus, all the benefit variables except the Lab Assistant and the Small Group Instruction Benefit were significant. The oblimin rotation was used to maximize the loading of each variable on the three named factors as shown in Table 25.9.

Figure 25.1

Scree Plot to Determine Factors

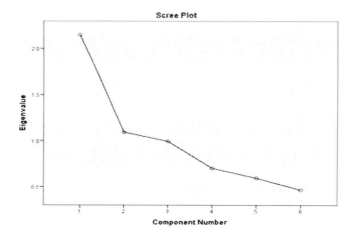

Table 25.9

Factor Analysis Loadings

Factors	Classroom Activities Benefit	Outside Classroom Activities Benefit
Individual Student Observation Benefit	0.76	
Whole Group Instruction Benefit	0.69	
Teaching Assistant Benefit	0.68	
Classroom Observation Benefit	0.63	
Tutoring Benefit		0.78
Field Project Benefit		0.62

The first cluster of benefit variables was named *Classroom Activities Benefit*, which included Individual Student Observation Benefit, Whole Group Instruction Benefit, Teaching Assistant Benefit, and Classroom Observation Benefit. A second cluster, which included Tutoring Benefit and Field Project Benefit was named *Outside Classroom Activities Benefit*. Thus, the eight variables were successfully reduced to four factors, namely *Classroom Activities Benefit, Outside Classroom Activities Benefit, Lab Assistant Benefit*, and *Small Group Instruction Benefit*.

Comparisons Between the Hybrid and Non-Hybrid Models

Two groups of students were identified, the hybrid group that included students who had the hybrid class experience and the non-hybrid group that included students who did not have hybrid class experience. A parametric analysis was not appropriate because the sampling distribution was not normally distributed (Field et al., 2012). Instead, a non-parametric test, the Wilcoxon rank-sum test, was utilized.

In the first model, students were grouped according to the class delivery format. Those who experienced non-hybrid model ($N = 71$) and those students who experienced hybrid model ($N = 7$) were grouped separately to compare how the benefits of each factor affected them. Classroom Activity Benefit for non-hybrid group ($Mdn = 12$) did not differ significantly from the hybrid group ($Mdn = 12$), $W = 241$, $p = .887$, $r = -.02$. Lab Assistant Benefit for non-hybrid group ($Mdn = 4$) also did not differ significantly from the hybrid group ($Mdn = 4$), $W = 286$, $p = .397$, $r = -.1$. Small Group Instruction for the two groups, non-hybrid ($Mdn = 3$) and hybrid ($Mdn = 3$) did not differ significantly ($W = 289.5$, $p = .378$, $r = -.1$). For Outside Classroom Activity Benefit, there was a difference in the median measure for non-hybrid group ($Mdn = 7$) and hybrid group ($Mdn = 6$). However, the slight increase in median for the non-hybrid group was not statistically significant ($W = 354.5$, $p = .0504$, $r = -.22$).

In the next model, an examination of whether there were any differences between the values of the different factors for the courses that changed from non-hybrid to hybrid status was conducted. Results from Wilcoxon rank-sum test indicated that none of the factors were significantly different between the hybrid and non-hybrid methods for Classroom Activity Benefit ($W = 68.5$, $p = .895$, $r = -0.03$), Outside Classroom Activity Benefit ($W = 86.5$, $p = 0.219$, $r = -.24$), Lab Assistant Benefit ($W = 67.5$, $p = 0.946$, $r = -.01$), or Small Group Instruction Benefit ($W = 87.5$, $p = 0.162$, $r = -0.27$). Each factor had identical median values for hybrid and non-hybrid methods (Classroom Activity Benefit ($Mdn = 12$), Outside Classroom Activity Benefit ($Mdn = 7$), Lab Assistant Benefit ($Mdn = 4$), or Small Group Instruction Benefit ($Mdn = 3$).

Dimensions Defining Unit Plan Results and Model Comparison

Unit plan data is collected using a standardized rubric that quantifies teacher candidates' ability to effectively plan instruction in a unit format. The rubric is on a four-point scale as follows: 3-Exemplary, 2-competent, 1-Needs Improvement, and 0-Unsatisfactory. Out of the nine areas assessed using this 4-point scale, the first one is *Students and Instructionally Significant Environmental Factors* which assesses teacher candidates' ability to plan quality instruction for a specific set of students based on their given contextual factors. Area two is *Instructional Decision Making* which assesses teacher candidates' ability to plan for specific student's special needs including considerations of diversity and background. Area three is *Collaboration* which assesses teacher candidates' understanding of the importance of collaboration to meet the learning objectives of their students. Area four is *Planning Process and Content* which assesses teacher candidates' ability to align the content standards, higher order thinking skills and students' needs when planning instruction. Area five, *Technology Integration*, assesses teacher candidates' ability to plan instruction that integrates digital tools and resources that support instruction. Area six is *Assessment* which assesses teacher candidates' ability to construct and utilize multiple valid and reliable formative and summative assessments that are clearly and explicitly aligned with student factors and unit outcomes. Area seven, *Assessment Technology*, measures teacher candidates' ability to construct and utilize formative and summative assessments that are aligned with technology standards and provide a path to use resulting data to inform student learning. Area eight is *Instructional Delivery and Alignment of Lessons* which assesses teacher candidates' ability to logically organize and align instructional activities and objective with unit outcomes, while promoting active student engagement with higher order thinking and varying strategies. Area nine, *Communication*, assesses teacher candidates' ability to communicate their lessons clearly and concisely in an organized and logical manner.

The Unit Plan data was analyzed by organizing the teacher candidates into three groups: the teacher candidates who were in classes that had not yet started to use the hybrid methods format (*Regular*, $n = 50$), teacher candidates who were currently in class the hybrid methods but before the instructors using the method (*NoHybrid*, $n = 4$) and the teacher candidates who were in the classes that use hybrid methods and had previously experienced the hybrid model (*Hybrid*, $n = 11$). The details of the data analyses are as follows.

The sample size for *NoHybrid* section was too small to consider when following a normal distribution. There was not enough variance among the Rubric Score values of the students in the group *Hybrid* to consider it following a normal distribution. Consequently, Kruskal-Wallis nonparametric comparison of median was used to make conclusions.

Comparisons Among the Three Situations

The Kruskal-Wallis test indicated that the differences in the median Rubric Scores were statistically significant (*Regular* (*Mdn* = 34), *NoHybrid*

(Mdn = 27), and *Hybrid* (Mdn = 27), $H(2)$ = 25.78, p <.001). In the following post hoc pair-wise comparisons, using Mann-Whitney U Tests, the average median Rubric Score was greater for *Regular* (Mdn = 34) than for *Hybrid* (Mdn = 27, U = 28.9, p < .001) and for *NoHybrid* (Mdn = 27, U = 24.53, p = .034). There was no difference in the median Rubric Scores between *Hybrid* and *NoHybrid* (Mdn = 27). However, it is important to note that there were not enough cases of *NoHybrid* and *Hybrid* situations.

A factor analysis was conducted to find the variables in the unit plan assessment that tied together. The KMO values of all the variables (>.5) and the overall KMO value (.77), together with the results from the Bartlett's test ((36) = 327.63, p <.001) confirmed the appropriateness of factor analysis. The two factors that the variables were loaded on to were named Active Instruction and Planning as detailed below in Table 25.10.

Table 25.10

Factor Analysis Loadings of Unit Plan Assessment[a]

	Active Instruction	Planning
Communication	.83	
Technology Integration	.80	
Collaboration	.77	
Assessment Technology	.77	
Instructional Delivery/Alignment of Lessons to Unit	.72	
Students and instructional significant environmental factors	.57	
Assessment		.87
Planning Process and Content		.64
Instructional decision making		.42

Extraction Method: Principal Component Analysis. Rotation Method: Oblimin with Kaiser Normalization. [a]Rotation converged in 14 iterations.

Comparisons Using Factors

Correspondingly, it was investigated whether there were statistically significant differences among the three situations of the hybrid methodology. The *Hybrid* group had no variance for both the factors, Active Instruction and Planning. Even though there were variances for other two groups, *NoHybrid* and *Regular*, both of them did not follow a normal distribution. A Kruskal-Wallis test revealed that the differences in median for the three groups were statistically significant with both factors, namely Active Instruction ($H(2) = 31.1$, $p < .001$) and Planning ($H(2) = 11.85$, $p = .003$).

Pairwise comparisons for Active Instruction using Mann-Whitney tests revealed that there were statistically significant differences in the median between *Hybrid* group (*Mdn* = 18) and *Regular* group (*Mdn* = 24)(U=28.86, $p < .001$) and between *NoHybrid* group (*Mdn* = 17) and *Regular* group (*Mdn* = 24)($U = 32.11$, $p = .002$). The difference in medians of *NoHybrid* (*Mdn* = 17) and *Hybrid* (*Mdn* = 18) groups was not significant ($U = 3.25$, $p = .759$).

Pairwise comparisons for Planning using Mann-Whitney tests revealed that there were no statistically significant differences in the median between the medians of *NoHybrid* (*Mdn* = 10) and *Hybrid* (*Mdn* = 9) ($U = 14.125$, $p = .564$) and between *NoHybrid* group (*Mdn* = 10) and *Regular* group (*Mdn* = 11)($U = 6.85$, $p = .47$). The difference in the *Hybrid* group (*Mdn* = 9) and *Regular* group (*Mdn* = 11)($U = 20.97$, $p = .002$) was statistically significant.

Summary of Findings

Obviously, the factor analyses on the variables from the Teacher Survey helped create a better picture of the students' activities based on the mentor teacher surveys and unit plan assessments. The four factors, namely, benefits from classroom activities, outside classroom activities, small group instruction, and lab assistant activities made an effective model to further analyze the characteristics of the available data. There were no statistically significant differences among the benefits acquired by the students who attended both types of classes—the hybrid and the non-hybrid.

Further, the lack of variances in the individual criteria and the small sample size of the data did not allow any parametric analyses. The various Kruskall-Wallis tests suggested that there were significant differences between using hybrid methods and non-hybrid methods. However, these results did not demonstrate a big advantage of the hybrid methods. The factorial analysis to reduce variables and to find converging factors resulted in two factors, namely, active instruction and planning. The Kruskall-Wallis tests and the follow up post hoc tests—Mann Whitney U tests—did not suggest any favorable statistically significant difference in using hybrid methods over using non-hybrid methods.

The results from the data analyses may not accurately represent the benefits of the hybrid model completely and may be different from the individual responses of the teacher candidates' mentor teachers. The disparity may be attributed to a smaller number of students who experienced the hybrid model ($N = 7$) when compared with those who experienced the non-hybrid model ($N = 71$). Further data collection, as we proceed with our hybrid model, in the coming academic years, might reveal the differences in the hybrid methodology and non-hybrid methodology more effectively.

DISCUSSION

Although the data and subsequent analysis did not show a statistically significant difference between the face-to-face and hybrid course models, there were still findings worthy of discussion and consideration for future work. Online delivery has often garnered criticisms on the part of both students and instructors because of its challenges to provide a cohesive and engaging environment due to the lack of interactions among the parties involved. The fact that the data showed little statistical difference in delivery method perhaps is important and of note as the data showed the hybrid format either met, or in some cases exceeded, the benefits of the traditional face-to-face delivery method. In the ever-changing landscape of higher education this study demonstrates that the hybrid model is just as successful and, in some arenas, even more beneficial than the traditional face-to-face format. As online delivery and varied online degree options become more prevalent and demands on traditional and non-traditional students increase, flexibility on the part of universities and education preparation providers will be the only way to stay relevant (Ortagus & Tanner, 2019). Even the recent outbreak of COVID-19 has shown that online course delivery options are beneficial when trying to accommodate the challenging situations that we have today that perhaps been not an issue a decade ago. Also, hybrid delivery is more flexible and accommodating for today's learners and their unique situations, and this small study demonstrates that teacher students' learning during their methods field placement does not suffer through online course delivery.

Even though performance assessment data seemed consistent among compared groups, perhaps the most compelling reason to weigh the hybrid model's feasibility is the opinions of the mentor teachers and the teacher candidates. Mentor teachers were positive and displayed great enthusiasm in the field, particularly when referring to the traditional model. One mentor had a difficult time the year prior because of the time split and the confusion it caused with the bell schedule. After a semester with the hybrid model, she very enthusiastically stated, "This has been awesome! My preservice teacher is here more than required and we are truly practicing the co-teaching model. This semester has been good for me also." Her point really highlights the mutually beneficial component of PDS and the hybrid's advantage of allowing for teacher candidates to have more time in the field.

Teacher candidates appreciated the flexibility of the format and the availability of additional time to work with students in the K–12 classrooms. Teacher candidates felt they were able to establish better relationships with the K–12 students because their increased rapport with them. They also indicated that they were able to establish a better connection with their mentor teachers and to be involved in a true expert-novice internship experience. Another teacher candidate stated, "having the time to practice with the different co-teaching models helped me feel more involved, and I never felt like I was just there to observe."

Other points teacher candidates appreciated about the model aside from extra time in the field and more time teaching included the state test preparation options, optional Saturday workshops, and increased communication using online platforms, including Remind 101 and Zoom (Remind, 2020; Zoom Video Communications, 2020). Teacher candidates felt there was increased time devoted to coursework focusing on content pedagogy. Additionally, lessons observed by university supervisors seem more student-centered and responsive and less scripted and mechanical, indicating, perhaps, the benefits of teacher candidates' strengthened relationships with students. As we gather additional data including performance data on clinical teaching experiences and certification data, we will be able to create a clearer picture of the hybrid model's capabilities. Furthermore, the model will continue to evolve as we gather data on the changes we have made, and we will continue to make efforts to maximize our mutually beneficial relationship with our PDS partners.

REFERENCES

Bolliger, D. U., Shepherd, C. E., & Bryant, H. V. (2019). Faculty members' perceptions of online program community and their efforts to sustain it. *British Journal of Educational Technology, 50*(6), 3283–3299. https://doiorg.databases.msutexas.edu/10.1111/bjet.12734

Brunken, J. (2019). Harness interactivity for e-learning. TD: *Talent Development, 73*(5), 77LT–80LT.

Dolan, K. (2009). Student performance and satisfaction: Online vs. face to face. *Teaching Professor, 23*(4), 5–4.

Field, A., Miles, J., & Field, Z. (2012). *Discovering statistics using R* (1st ed.). SAGE.

Ginder, S. A., Kelly-Reid, J. E., & Mann, F. B. (2018). *Enrollment and employees in postsecondary institutions, Fall 2017; and financial statistics and academic libraries, fiscal year 2017: First look (provisional data) (NCES 2019- 021REV)*. U.S. Department of Education. Washington, DC: National Center for Education Statistics. Retrieved from https://nces.ed.gov/pubs2019/2019021REV.pdf

Hass, A., & Joseph, M. (2018). Investigating different options in course delivery— traditional vs online: is there another option? *International Journal of Information & Learning Technology, 35*(4), 230–239. https://doi.org/databases. msutexas.edu/10.1108/IJILT-09-2017-0096

Hurlbut, A. R. (2018). Online vs. traditional learning in teacher education: a comparison of student progress. *American Journal of Distance Education, 32*(4), 248–266. https://doi.org/databases.msutexas.edu/10.1080/08923647.2018. 1509265

Lei, S. A., & Lei, S. Y. (2019). Evaluating benefits and drawbacks of hybrid courses: Perspectives of college instructors. *Education, 140*(1), 1–8.

National Association for Professional Development Schools. (2008). *What it means to be a professional development school.* https://napds.org/nine-essentials/

Ortagus, J. C., & Tanner, M. J. (2019). Going to college without going to campus: A case study of online student recruitment. *Innovative Higher Education, 44*(1), 53–67. https://doi.org/databases.msutexas.edu/10.1007/s10755-018-9448-9

Remind. (2020). https://www.remind.com/

Sanga, M. W. (2018). Getting to master online teaching: Insights from purposefully organized course development training. *Quarterly Review of Distance Education, 19*(2), 15–25.

Speakworks. (2018). *GoReact.* https://get.goreact.com/

Tuckman, B. W. (2002). Evaluating ADAPT: A hybrid instructional model combining web-based and classroom components. *Computers & Education, 39*(3), 261. https://doi.org/msutexas.edu/10.1016/S0360-1315(02)00045-3

Zoom Video Communications. (2020). *Video conferencing, web conferencing, webinars, screen sharing.* https://zoom.us/

CHAPTER 26

INNOVATION IN CLINICAL PRACTICE

Content Cohorts, Partnerships, and Micro-Credentialing

Tina Wagle, Michelle R. Eades-Baird, and Donna Mahar
SUNY Empire State College

ABSTRACT

Clinical work has become a focal point in teacher preparation in the last several years. Discussions have concentrated on length and location of placement, work with local K–12 partners, and meaningful praxis. Teacher preparation, including clinical work, needs to be improved continuously through reflection and new ideas based on best practice and feedback from key stakeholders. This chapter focuses on a revision to the clinical model in a state-wide teacher preparation program to include the placement of students by content cohorts in clinical courses, enhanced work with K–12 partners as well as the introduction of micro-credentialing to identify important pedagogical skills mastered in the program.

Preparing Quality Teachers:
Advances in Clinical Practice, pp. 561–577
Copyright © 2022 by Information Age Publishing
www.infoagepub.com
561

The clinical component of educator preparation has become a focal point of discussion regarding best practices since the turn of the century. Major organizations and scholars (American Academy of Colleges for Teacher Education [AACTE], 2018; Association for Advancing the Quality in Educator Preparation [AAQEP], 2020; Darling-Hammond, 2014; National Board for Professional Teaching Standards [NBPTS], 2007; National Council for Accreditation of Teacher Education [NCATE], 2010; National Research Council [NRC], 2010) have published their thoughts about best practices in clinical educator preparation. Common themes have emerged, including the length of clinical practice, mutually beneficial partnerships between P–12 and higher education institutions, and a seamless integration of theory and practice.

Attributes of High-Quality Teacher Preparation Programs

Recently in 2018, the American Association of Colleges for Teacher Education (AACTE) published its report on clinical practice in teacher preparation. This document includes 10 proclamations all supporting the central tenant that clinical practice is central to high quality educator preparation. The remaining proclamations include important programmatic necessities including skills, sound pedagogy, partnerships that are mutually beneficial, infrastructure, empowerment, and expertise. (AACTE, 2018). In 2010, The National Research Council identified the three critical aspects of teacher preparation that create positive outcomes for students: (1) candidate content knowledge; (2) quality of teacher candidates; and (3) field (or clinical) experience. This report contributed to the development of the Council for the Accreditation of Educator Preparation (CAEP) (2011) standards particularly Standard 2, which explicitly addresses clinical partnerships and practice. Standard 2.3 states that clinical experiences should be "of sufficient depth, breadth, diversity, coherence, and duration to ensure that candidates demonstrate their developing effectiveness and positive impact on all students' learning and development" (http://caepnet.org/standards/standard-2). Similarly, the Association for Advancing Quality in Educator Preparation (AAQEP) standards point to the need for the development and implementation of "quality clinical experiences." Standard 3b goes on to suggest these experiences should be in the "context of documented and effective partnerships with P-12 schools and districts" (https://aaqep.org/wp-content/uploads/2020/01/2020-Guide-to-AAQEP-Accreditation.pdf, p. 7). Additionally, Darling-Hammond (2006) describes the need for continuous improvement of teacher preparation and argues that quality programs should include an inextricable link between coursework clinical work, and supervision of that clinical work, as well as strong partnerships with schools that have demonstrated success in teaching diverse learners.

As noted above, educators and other practitioners have expressed their beliefs about the essential components in teacher preparation related to clinical practice. At the State University of New York Empire State College (SUNY ESC), this ideology is shared, but we also believe in innovation, continual reflection, and progression on how to improve the program. These reasons have urged us to pursue some clinical changes related to competency-based education and micro-credentialing.

Competency-Based Education (CBE)

CBE has gained more visibility over the last decade when student tuition debt became an important news story. With the incredible rise of student debt, the government and various educational institutions discussed means of moving from this financial hardship for young adults, proving to be a drawback for the economy. CBE has potential to make higher education more affordable. "CBE focuses on what students know as demonstrated by mastery of competencies and differs significantly from the traditional, course-sequenced, credit-based college degree program" (Ordonez, 2014, p. 47). Institutions offering CBE programs vary in their approach, but the central key principles include: (1) students completing assessments at a variable pace while receiving appropriate support; (2) the competencies align with industry standards; (3) the learning resources are readily available and reusable; and (4) there is explicit mapping of competencies to courses learning outcomes and assessments (Johnstone & Soares, 2014; Ordonez, 2014). Such institutions are often nontraditional and student-centered; ESC is a long standing, nontraditional institution that frequently utilizes competency-based education based on its adult student population and student-centered approach to learning.

Related to CBE, SUNY ESC has a long history of offering student credit for experiential learning, or Prior Learning Assessment (PLA). PLA is the evaluation of "college-relevant learning that [students] acquired through work experiences, employer training programs, volunteer work, self-study, or military training and experiences" (Klein-Collins & Hudson, 2018). Klein-Collins and Hudson (2017) found that adult students who utilized PLA were two and a half more times likely to have a postsecondary degree than students who did not have PLA credits. Hence, there is evidence that offering a student-centered, innovative approach to earning credits aids in student degree completion. While the teacher education programs at Empire State College do not currently offer prior learning assessment, this paper will discuss the idea of asking students to perform tasks and assessments to earn micro-credentials, a form of CBE to represent their knowledge gained in their clinical experiences.

Micro-credentials (here, in the form of digital badges) "are designed to make visible and validate learning in both formal and informal settings, and hold the potential to help transform where and how learning is valued" (French & Barry, 2017, p. 38). According to the Center for Collaborative Education, micro-credentials are aligned to performance assessments—from basic to advanced, and help build learning communities (French & Barry, 2017). Specifically, for teacher related micro-credentials, French and Barry state that they are "suited for anytime/anywhere learning and allow teachers to show what they can do, not only what they know" (French & Barry, 2017, p. 38). Digital badges represent the verification of skills that are not obvious on a traditional transcript (LaMagna, 2017). Therefore, a badge could verify that not only has a student mastered a particular skill like lesson planning when s/he earns the badge for that skill, but also, it will be apparent to an outside agency what lesson plan proficiency actually entails (Braxton et al., 2019). CBE "reorients the educational process toward demonstrated mastery and the application of knowledge and skills in the real world" (Johnstone & Soares, 2014, p. 12). This application is the rationale of placing innovative micro-credentialing into teacher education clinical courses, where students are in both theoretical courses and teaching in the classroom.

ESC's Master of Arts in Teaching (MAT) Program

Both the faculty and the administration of ESC embody the belief that early clinical experiences in high-needs school contexts, extensive mentoring and continuous supervision, individualized instruction by adult and urban education specialists, cohort-based instructional models, an integrated curriculum that supports systematic reflection, intensive collaboration with local school districts, financial support, and authentic assessment of outcomes are the components that make the difference in recruiting, training and retaining high quality candidates (Burbank & Kauchak, 2003). Catering to adult career changers, the ESC MAT program is an alternative, graduate-level teacher preparation program based on a clinical model that enables a prospective teacher to earn a secondary (Grades 5–12) New York State (NYS) Initial Teaching Certification License in a content area (English, Languages Other Than English (LOTE), mathematics, science, or social studies) while working as full-time teachers in predominantly high-needs schools across New York State. The MAT program has two phases: the foundational and clinical phases.

Foundational phase. The two- (Transitional B Intensified Mentored Teaching [Trans B IMT]) or three-year (Transitional B Mentored Teaching [Trans B MT) Tracks in the MAT program begin with a year of part-time coursework that includes courses in educational foundations, methods, culturally responsive pedagogy, and differentiation. During this phase, students are also required to complete the NYS required field observations associated with preservice teaching, required New York State workshops and successfully complete two NYS Teacher licensing examinations. During this foundational coursework, students are exposed to educational theory and practice, which informs their full-time classroom teaching in the clinical phase during years two and three of the program.

Clinical phase. The MAT program utilizes the New York State Transitional B Teaching license, which enables teacher candidates to begin teaching full-time as teachers of record during the second year of the program. During the clinical phase, the teacher candidate is continuously mentored by faculty and field supervisors in the classroom while they complete program coursework. This coursework aligns with the daily tasks and challenges of their classroom practice including lesson and unit planning, classroom management, literacy, and assessment as well as the four seminars where students come together with their faculty mentor to discuss critical themes related to their clinical component of their degree.

During their time in the program, each teacher candidate is observed five to seven times a semester by faculty and are provided with detailed feedback using a validated Classroom Observation Rubric (COR) which is an adapted version of the Danielson (2011) rubric. After the classroom observation, the faculty member or field supervisor holds a debriefing session with the student. Thus, ESC faculty are active members of this intense support and ongoing induction process. To ensure that each new teacher has continuous, day-to-day support in their school building, s/he is assigned an experienced, school-based mentor who is employed as a teacher by the school or school district in the same content area as the teacher candidate. This mentor agrees to serve in this supportive capacity until the teacher candidate finishes the MAT program. At the successful completion of the MAT program, the teacher candidate is recommended for a NYS Initial Teaching License.

Praxis development. Darling-Hammond (2006) describes one of the most challenging aspects of teacher preparation as the successful integration of theory into practice. Empire State College's program allows for the balance to which Darling-Hammond describes as "elusive" by requiring teacher candidates to engage in course work at the same time they are teaching in order to actively reflect upon theoretical application in their own classroom context. In particular, the clinical seminars support this type of learning and continued development by using a professional learning community (PLC) (Hord, 1997) model to encourage collaboration and support among clinical students. In addition, it provides opportunities to support teacher candidates and teachers of record through ongoing mentoring and instructional assistance and collaboration as they continue their coursework. This period of clinical work also supports the recommendations from the *NCATE Blue Ribbon Panel Report, 10 Design Principles for Clinically Based Practice*. Principle #2 states: "Clinical preparation is integrated throughout every facet of teacher education in a dynamic way" (NCATE Blue Ribbon Panel Report, 2010, p. 5). In the Empire State College program, content and pedagogy are woven around clinical practice as demonstrated by the 50 classroom observation hours in the first year; these clinical observations are brought into assignments across the foundational phase courses. This deliberate connection of early clinical experiences to pedagogy lays the foundation required for developing teaching praxis and the habits of mind necessary for reflective practice in preservice teacher candidates. Clinical progress goes beyond site-based visits by field supervisors; faculty review assignments connected to work done in the field, making clinical work a recursive process within the program. The clinical seminars support this type of learning and continued development while also providing opportunities to support teacher candidates and teachers of record through ongoing mentoring, instructional assistance, and student collaboration as they continue their coursework.

ESC teacher candidates enroll in a Capstone course during the last semester of the program, which is a culmination of the theoretical knowledge and clinical work they have mastered in the program (Loe & Rezak, 2006). The final project students write includes four components: their professional identity as a teacher, advanced knowledge of content area materials and standards, praxis, and assessment. Through this paper, students must demonstrate mastery on the following criteria: Articulates an understanding of her/his professional identity as a teacher; Demonstrates advanced level learning in the content area; Demonstrates integration of educational theory as it applies to teaching in the content area; Demonstrates the ability to use a variety of appropriate assessments to inform practice; Demonstrates appropriate uses of technologies for teaching and learning; and Demonstrates graduate-level writing quality. Students also must be observed twice using the 4-point classroom observation rubric and cannot receive a score below a two on any of the indicators.

Residency clinical track. To address the previously cited statement from Darling-Hammond with regards to extensive clinical placements, ESC's MAT program introduced a new clinically rich residency track in 2011. This track stems from teacher preparation best practices for residency models including the Boston teacher residency and the Academy for Urban School Leadership in Chicago with regards to their extended time in the classroom under the tutelage of a veteran teacher (Berry et al., 2009). The inclusion of residencies in the design of the program was informed by the National Board for Professional Teaching Standards, as one of the authors and developer of this program is a National Board Certified K–12 teacher. These standards include: Teachers are committed to students and their learning; Teachers know the subjects they teach and how to teach those subjects to students; Teachers are responsible for managing and monitoring student learning; Teachers think systematically about their practice and learn from experience; and Teachers are members of learning communities (NBPTS, 2007). This framework also serves as a partial basis for the micro-credentialing being proposed and discussed in this chapter.

Students in ESC's MAT residency model begin in the school with their clinical educator from the beginning of the school year and remain until the beginning of May. Clinical educators utilize the gradual release of responsibility (GRD) (Pearson & Gallagher, 1983) instructional framework over the course of the year emphasizing co-teaching, culminating in an eight-week immersion period in which the resident assumes responsibility for all classes. This model allows for students to gain a full year of teaching experience, which is invaluable in anticipating planning, addressing classroom management, and garnering a sense of what an entire year of teaching entails. Like the Transitional B track, each semester, the resident is observed by college faculty five times a semester. The clinical educator is also asked to complete one of the resident's observations. In preparation for teach visit, the student fills out a pre-observation form (Danielson, 2011) and submits a lesson plan. After the lesson has occurred, the student then fills out the post-observation form to ensure reflective practice (Loughran, 2002).

Partnerships. In the introduction, the importance of partnerships in clinical work was highlighted. SUNY ESC is in a unique position to serve several areas of New York State, as there are 34 different satellite locations of the college. As a result, the outreach to developing partnerships across the state is vast and diverse. The faculty and staff have worked hard to focus on the needs of every district with which the college partners. ESC has a Teacher Education Advisory Board that encompasses SUNY ESC faculty and staff, current students and program alumni and key partner stakeholders including state-wide school and district leaders, and representatives from the New York State United Teachers (NYSUT) and the Board of Cooperative Educational Services (BOCES). These stakeholders are vital to relaying the local community and school needs back to SUNY ESC, so that continuous programmatic improvements can be made. Faculty, current students, and alumni are joined by school-based mentor teachers, school district leaders, representatives from the New York State United Teachers Educational Learning Trust (NYSUT ELT)to address the needs of all K–12 students, with emphasis on high needs schools. Advisory Board members play a key role in program development. The proposed changes to clinical preparation are in part based on needs in the K–12 classroom identified by board members. Our partnership with the NYSUT ELT allowed us to create and sponsor four graduate courses that guide classroom teachers through the National Board certification process.

When students arrive at the clinical portion of the program, SUNY ESC staff meets with every school in which a student is placed. In the Transitional B track, school-based mentors are selected, and they sign an agreement to help develop the teacher candidates as they adjust to the role of head classroom teacher. In the residency track, the coordinator of clinical placements meets with a building leader, the student, and the clinical educator to ensure everyone understands the expectations of the program and that there are benefits for both the school and the ESC student that make this partnership positive for all involved.

An example of how SUNY ESC simultaneously meets the needs of the local schools, and its own students is a unique pathway within the Residency track. Students who enter the MAT program who also serve as teaching assistants (TA) in their schools can maintain their TA position while working towards completion of the degree and certification requirements. They work with a clinical educator while maintaining their TA responsibilities and take an eight-week leave of absence in the spring term to fulfill the required immersion period. This grew out of research faculty conducted as part of a "grow your own" initiative (Madda & Schultz, 2009; Skinner et al., 2011), as there is a need to establish connections between communities and schools. This pathway allows TAs who are familiar with the school and students to become head classroom teachers, again making the partnership between ESC and the school mutually beneficial.

A couple of other partnerships that the residency track is involved with to support a reciprocal arrangement include two relatively new initiatives. The first is an additional option to the residency track that enables students to be in their residency placements three days a week and work as substitute teachers in the building two days a week. It also helps the school find a certified-ready substitute who is familiar with the school, policies, and students. Thus, this pathway is beneficial for both entities. The second is a newly signed partnership between SUNY ESC and the National Education Association (NEA) Classroom Academy. In this model, residency students may opt for a two-year placement instead of one. However, the students also receive a stipend for those two years, making this opportunity helpful financially. It also speaks to the importance of a long-term clinical placement. SUNY ESC is looking to place its first student in this pathway this coming year, so data will be collected on the success of this experience.

Another example is with the National Board of Professional Teaching Standards. This partnership with the National Board of Professional Teaching Standards (NBPTS) is a corner stone of the residency program and benefits both Residency and Transitional B students by providing access to the ATLAS (Accomplished Teaching, Learning, and Schools) video library. Empire State College science and literacy professors became part of the ATLAS science initiative for teacher preparation programs in 2016. Working with teacher preparation programs throughout the United States allowed the faculty to develop best practices in using the videos. ESC has access to the entire K–12, cross-discipline library of over 1,300 videos and case studies of NBPTS teachers providing visual and written representations of what standards-based teaching looks like because of a collaboration our National Board certified faculty member has with NBPTS. When designing the badges for the new approach to clinical preparation, the ATLAS videos play a critical role. Content area faculty will select videos to meet the standard being addressed by the badge. Knowing that the videos have been mapped to NBPTS, TASC standards provides assurance that the videos focusing on the same skill across content areas provide all students in the program with the information needed to master the badge learning outcomes. The NBPTS ATLAS science collaborative used the MAT capstone course to highlight how the videos can be used throughout clinical preparation (Arias et al., 2020; Forsythe et al., 2021). The MAT faculty involved in the science collaborative shared how students reviewed ATLAS videos as part of the capstone, not from the eyes of a novice, but from the perspective of a practitioner. Students move from a novice stage of video analysis where the instructor models and guides the analysis to the capstone experience that requires traits evidenced-based analysis and connections to broader educational issues. The proposed clinical changes to our MAT program will position graduate students to segue into this NBPTS pathway thus creating a pipeline from certification to continual renewal and reflection of classroom practice.

Assessment of clinical practice. The ESC MAT program employs a multi-faceted approach to evaluating the quality of their teacher preparation program. Teacher candidates' clinical performance evaluated by MAT faculty, field supervisors, and clinical educators for spring residents) using a Classroom Observation Rubric (COR) which is based on Danielson's (2011) rubric. Using Rasch (1960) analysis, the original rubric was adapted, validated, and honed to best evaluate and support novice teachers' practice in the classroom. During the Fall semester of clinical work, a fundamental version of the COR, the Residency Fall Observation Rubric (RFOF), is used to evaluate residency students' teaching. Annually, the COR is normed to ensure its consistent use and undergoes psychometric analysis to measure validity and reliability. During the annual Rasch analysis, differential item functioning (DIF) provides insight into performance of students within specific clinical pathways and content areas; this informs areas of strengths and weaknesses that can be addressed in program coursework. In addition to using the COR, mentor teachers complete a questionnaire twice a year on the Trans B student that they mentor which provides both classroom performance and disposition-related feedback; the clinical educator provides similar feedback and conducts one Spring observation for their Resident. Teacher candidates provide feedback on clinical educators and field supervisors.

Proposed New Clinical Structure

Teacher effectiveness and student achievement is contingent upon instructional practices in the subject area (NCATE, 2010). One goal of revising SUNY ESC's existing clinical course structure is to better align teacher candidates with faculty experts in the same content area, thereby shifting from a focus on developing praxis (transferring pedagogical theory into teaching practice) to that of developing highly specialized pedagogical content knowledge (PCK) (Shulman, 1986, 1987). PCK has been described as a special amalgam of teachers' content knowledge in their discipline and knowledge of general pedagogy while considering the curriculum, assessment, educational outcomes, and teaching context (Morine-Dershimer & Kent, 1999); it is "grounded in a focus on student learning [in a particular content area] and thus responsive to diversity, multiculturalism, and equity" (Hayden & Eades-Baird, 2017, p. 37).

Reorganization of clinical students. SUNY Empire State College's clinical education courses have long addressed praxis by utilizing traditional resources: textbooks, articles, synchronous webinars, and videos. During the clinical phase of the program, faculty, and field supervisors mentor teacher candidates on praxis. Prior to this newly proposed restructuring, teacher candidates enrolled in clinical courses that aligned to their clinical track (Transitional B or Residency), putting them into a course with peers on the same clinical track but in mixed content areas. Each clinical course was previously taught by a faculty member who may or may not be an expert in the same teaching discipline as the teacher candidates in the course. The increased support of our teacher candidates improves alignment with experts in their field of study. The main goal of rethinking and restructuring our clinical course structure is to align faculty's content-specific pedagogical content knowledge with the teacher candidates' disciplines in order to better support them in the field during the critical new teacher induction period and to better prepare them for their subject-specific edTPA portfolio submissions. The edTPA is a content-based, performance-based assessment borne out of the Stanford Center for Assessment, Learning, and Equity (SCALE). The edTPA is also in alignment with the National Board for Professional Teaching Standards (https://www.nbpts.org/wp-content/uploads/ATLAS-One-Pager.pdf). New York State has adopted this assessment as a high-stakes assessment requiring that preservice teachers need to pass this test in order to attain their initial teaching license.

The new clinical model involves the creation of another learning management system (LMS) shell directly related to the ongoing revision of our clinical course work. All clinical students will be placed in the same content (science, Spanish, English language arts, mathematics, social studies) online LMS shell with breakout groups according to students' program pathway. In this shell, they will receive theoretical content and engaging discussions about teaching. Faculty will offer a range of topics such as assessment, differentiation of instruction, technology integration, and so forth. Webinars (one created for each badge) will also address issues that may emerge in real time, such as school safety or statewide curriculum changes. For the webinars, experts in the field, as well as our full-time faculty, will offer current research-based knowledge on given topics to help prepare our pre- and in-service teachers.

Digital badging. The proposed innovative clinical course redesign will utilize digital badging (of micro-credentials) to ensure greater connections between theoretical and content knowledge, and observable classroom practice. As students demonstrate mastery of a particular skill or topic (such as differentiation or technology integration) in their pre-service classrooms, they will earn a badge for that particular skill. The badges themselves will be housed in a Virtual Teaching Laboratory (i.e., a Moodle shell developed by a SUNY Empire State Instructional Designer). Empire State College recently acquired a license to Credly, which is a digital platform that houses digital badges and makes them portable. Credly is recognized nationally and internationally, making the awarding of these badges important and recognizable.

During their clinical work, students will be observed by MAT clinical faculty, adjunct field supervisors, and K–12 teachers in public school systems. Using feedback from those observers, as well as their own observations, the clinical course faculty will award the badges as they are earned. While this new structure is not in full alignment with competency-based education since there is additional coursework involved, the badges do bring in elements of CBE with regards to completing a task in order to demonstrate proficiency in a skill. Part of this demonstration will be based on their classroom observation reports, showing real-life application of knowledge gained. In an article titled "Teachers, Micro-Credential, and the Performance Assessment Movement," the authors state that "micro-credentials are viewed as a valuable means for teachers to improve their practice" (French & Barry, 2017, p. 41). The hope is that students will find this practice valuable and helpful in improving their practice. Housing the digital badges in a virtual space open to all faculty and students provides students with an "interactive professional community" and "technology applications that foster high impact preparation" (NCATE Blue Ribbon Panel on Clinical Preparation, 2010, pp. 5–6). This community also supports the aforementioned desired outcomes of The Center for Collaborative Education's micro-credentialing.

This course restructuring builds on the work accomplished through a 2018–2019 TeachNY grant titled "Digital Badges, Micro-Credentials, and Cross-Level Collaboration in a Virtual Teaching Laboratory." Through that grant, SUNY ESC has created a Learning Management System (LMS) laboratory, which:

> is a virtual laboratory for pre-service teachers and in-service teachers where high-quality professional development can be implemented with the result being micro-credentials that document what the teachers, regardless of their years in the profession, know and are able to do. Again, the micro-credentials are based on the National Board of Professional Teaching Standard's 5 Core Propositions, standards cited in the TeachNY Advisory Council's Report of Findings and Recommendations. (TeachNY Advisory Council, 2016).

The use of Credly will make the laboratory be available to in-service teachers as well.

Partners. ESC has approached the following organizations as initial partners in the development of badging content: Onondaga-Cortland-Madison BOCES; Buffalo Public Schools' Math, Science and Technology Preparatory School, and Syracuse City School District. The college will consider additional high-need partnerships as they become available. These K–12 partners will allow school district mentoring to become aligned with our clinical courses through access to the badging system and the virtual learning space where the badges reside. Although all members of the teacher preparation faculty are certified teachers with K–12 classroom teaching experience, being away from the K–12 classroom can lessen the connections between what working theory, and how it actually plays out in practice. This supports the recommendations from accrediting bodies and agencies related to mutually beneficial partnerships being critical not only to prepare skilled and competent teachers, but to facilitate a smooth transition and induction to full time teaching.

With the proposed badging system, students must demonstrate mastery on a certain topic (such as differentiation or technology integration) to earn that merit. The badges, since they are standardized, become a valid measure of student skill mastery, thus overcoming the disconnections between course assignments and classroom observations. The badges are standardized across programs by looking at communalities across content-area edTPA rubrics. For example, all content areas require teachers to be proficient in using both academic and content specific vocabulary to increase the depth and breadth of content knowledge beyond isolated lessons. In addition, there is expected to be greater connection among students, faculty, field supervisors, MAT faculty, and K–12 classroom teachers.

Evaluation of proposed model. All innovative practices need to be assessed to evaluate their effectiveness. Focus groups will be conducted by MAT faculty with K–12 teachers, school administrators, and community partners; information sought from them will include identification of essential and desired skills needed by education graduates, interest level in having access to the virtual teaching lab (the LMS) in order to see student progress, and potential future interest in directly working with the badging system if it counts toward professional development. Clinical faculty will meet regularly to discuss the new model and how it can continue to be revised based on their teaching the course and student learning.

The sequential badging system will serve as a source of evaluation by determining if the teacher candidates meet the criteria to earn content and pedagogically related badges will become an assessment of student mastery. Every semester, students are given a Student Assessment of Learning Experience (SALE). Aggregated results from each clinical course will demonstrate whether students rate the courses highly and where there is room for improvement. Students will be surveyed regularly on the badging system and how it relates to clinical supervision. The first two semesters' feedback from students who are transitioning from the old system to the new system will also be utilized in the improvement loop. Seeking feedback from the P–12 partner schools as well as the critic teachers, in the case of the residents, will also be incorporated. These data points will demonstrate the success of the restructuring and how it can be improved continuously. This new clinical model is fluid- just as the teaching profession must be. This cannot be a one and done revision—rather through continual dialogue among all stakeholders. Given the modality of the online clinical component and virtual laboratory, it is anticipated that the badging system can be accessed and utilized by other SUNY teacher preparation programs, strengthening the K–20 pipeline.

CONCLUSION

Teacher preparation is a fluid field, perhaps now more than ever as schools and colleges are adapting to online and hybrid learning due to the COVID-

19 pandemic. The faculty in Empire State College's MAT program believe our current model has proven to be robust and innovative while adhering to best practices in teacher preparation as outlined by AACTE and verified by AAQEP accreditation. K–12 partners, as well as other teacher preparation programs within our large university system looked to use for guidance, as K–12 instruction and teacher preparation moved into uncharted territory in March 2020. As we shared our current model with partners and colleagues, we were able to solicit feedback on the revisions discussed in this chapter. Although unusual in pre-pandemic academia, this broad feedback provided opportunities to collaborate across institutions that we recommend continuing in a post-pandemic world.

In anticipation of the change to a content-based clinical model, graduate students are submitting videos of their classroom instruction to the faculty member teaching their content methods class. Although during the transition students remain grouped across content areas in the clinical course, working closely with the content area faculty member allows connections to be made to specific content area texts, pedagogy, and edTPA expectations. Feedback from students, content course instructors, and K–12 partners indicate that this praxis-based approach to clinical instruction leads to a rich learning experience for all stakeholders, including the college faculty. Praxis as described in the most detailed text is no substitute for the college content faculty to see how strategies unfold in an actual classroom.

It is important for students to observe and unpack standards-based teaching prior to implementing it. The National Board for Professional Teaching Standards ATLAS video library affords us the opportunity to select videos focused on specific standards that cut across content areas. Implementing academic vocabulary may introduce words and terms in different ways across content areas, but the importance of providing ongoing, consistent instruction using academic vocabulary is a key tenant regardless of the content being taught. Mapping standards across the content areas is a first step to achieving this consistency in achieving program outcomes. Micro-credentials provide a way for students, faculty, and mentors at K–12 placements to know what to expect from individual graduate students as well as what areas must be targeted.

The 20th century remained tethered to the agrarian model of K–12 education that was best suited to the century before it. The need to accept hybrid and distance learning on a national level provided the impetus to reconceptualize what it means to be both a teacher and student. Our new content-based, clinical model using micro-credentials provides a path forward for our students, faculty, K–12 partners, and colleagues to build on as we reconceptualize our world.

REFERENCES

American Association of Colleges of Teacher Education. (2018). *A pivot toward clinical practice, its lexicon, and the renewal of educator preparation: A report of the AACTE Clinical Practice Commission*. Washington, DC.

Arias, A., Criswell, B., Ellis, J., Escaladea, L., Forsythe, M., Johnson, H., Palmieri, A., Parker, M., & Ricco, J. (2020). The framework for analyzing video in science teacher education: Examples of its broad applicability. *Innovations in Science Teacher Education*.

Association for Advancing the Quality in Educator Preparation Guide to AAQEP Accreditation. (2020). https://aaqep.org/wp-content/uploads/2020/01/2020-Guide-to-AAQEP-Accreditation.pdf.

Berry, B., Montgomery, D., Curtis, R., Hernandez, M., Wurtzel, J., & Snyder, J. D. (2008, Summer). Urban teacher residencies: A new way to recruit, prepare, develop, and retain effective teachers on high-needs districts. *Voices in Urban Education*, 13–24.

Braxton, S. Bohrer, J., Jacobson, T., Moore, Leuba, M., Proctor, C., & Reed, A. (2019). *7 things you need to know about digital badges*. Educause Learning Initiative.

NCATE Blue Ribbon Panel on Clinical Preparation and Partnerships. (2010). *Transforming teacher education through clinical practice: A national strategy to prepare teachers*. NCATE.

Danielson, C. (2011). *Enhancing professional practice: A framework for teaching*. ASCD.

Darling-Hammond, L. (2006). Constructing 21st-century teacher education. *Journal of teacher education*, *57*(3), 300–314.

Darling-Hammond, L. (2014). Strengthening clinical preparation: The Holy Grail of teacher education. *Peabody Journal of Education, 89*(4), 547–561.

Forsythe, M. E., Criswell, B. A., Arias, A. M., Ellis, J. A., Escalada, L., Johnson, H. J., Palmeri, A. B., Riccio, J., & Parker, M. E. (2021). The Framework for Analyzing Video in Science Teacher Education (FAVSTE). *Journal of Science Teacher Education*, http://doi.org/10.1080/1046560X.2021.1970698

French, D., & Berry, B. (2017). Teachers, Micro-Credentials, and the Performance Assessment Movement. *Voices in Urban Education*, *46*, 37–43. https://search-ebscohost-com.library.esc.edu/login.aspx?direct=true&db=eric&AN=EJ1148462&site=ehost-live

Hayden, H. E., & Eades-Baird, M. (2017). Not a stale metaphor: The continued relevance of pedagogical content knowledge for science research and education. *Pedagogies: An International Journal*, *13*(1), 36–55.

Hord S. M. (1997). *Professional learning communities: Communities of continuous inquiry and improvement*. Southwest Educational Development Laboratory, Austin, Texas

Johnstone, S. M., & Soares, L. (2014). Principles for developing competency-based education programs. *Change: The Magazine of Higher Learning, 46*(2), 12–19.

Klein-Collins, R., Hudson, S., National Student Clearinghouse, & Council for Adult and Experiential Learning (CAEL). (2017). *What Happens When Learning "Counts"? Measuring the benefits of prior learning assessment for the adult learner—A CAEL self-study of the academic outcomes of learning counts students.* Council for Adult and Experiential Learning.

Klein-Collins, R., Hudson, S., & Council for Adult and Experiential Learning. (2018). *Do methods matter? PLA, portfolio assessment, and the road to completion and persistence. A Study of Prior Learning Assessment and Adult Students' Academic Outcomes at Four Learning Counts Partner Colleges.* Council for Adult and Experiential Learning.

LaMagna, M. (2017). Placing digital badges and micro-credentials in context. *Journal of Electronic Resources Librarianship, 29*(4), 206–210.

Loe, M., & Rezak, H. (2006). Creating and implementing a capstone course for future secondary mathematics teachers. In K. Lynch-Davis & R. L. Rider (Eds.), *The work of mathematics teacher educators: Continuing the conversation Monograph Series, 3,* pp. 45–62). AMTE.

Loughran, J. J. (2002). Effective reflective practice: In search of meaning in learning about teaching. *Journal of Teacher Education, 53*(1). 33–43.

Madda, C. & Schultz, B. (2009). (Re)Constructing ideals of multicultural education through grow your own teachers. *Multicultural Perspectives, 11,* 204–207.

Morine-Dershimer, G., & Kent, T. (1999). The complex nature and sources of teachers' pedagogical knowledge. In J. Gess-Newsome & N. G Lederman (Eds.), *Pedagogical content knowledge: The construct and its implications for science education,* (pp. 21–50). Kluwer.

National Board for Professional Teaching Standards. (2007). *What teachers should know and be able to do.*

National Council for Accreditation of Teacher Education. (2010). *Transforming teacher education through clinical practice: A national strategy to prepare effective teachers.* http://www.ncate.org/LinkClick.aspx?fileticket=qhvOTxP2Gm0%3D&tabid=715

National Research Council. (2010). *Preparing teachers: Building evidence for sound policy.* Committee on the Study of Teacher Preparation Programs in the United States, Center for Education. Division of Behavioral and Social Sciences and Education. Washington, DC: The National Academies Press.

Ordonez, B. (2014). Competency-based education: Changing the traditional college degree power, policy, and practice. *New Horizons in Adult Education & Human Resource Development, 26,* 47–53. https://doi.org/10.1002/nha3.20085

Pearson, P. D., & Gallagher, M. C. (1983). The instruction of reading comprehension, *Contemporary Educational Psychology, 8,* 317–344.

Rasch, G. (1960). *Probabilistic models for some intelligence and attainment tests.* Danmarks Paedagogiske Institut.

Shulman, L. S. (1986). Those who understand: Knowledge growth in teaching. *Educational Researcher, 15*(2), 4–14.

Shulman. L. S., (1987). Shulman, L. S. (1987). Knowledge and teaching: Foundations of the new reform. *Harvard Educational Review, 57,* 1–22

Skinner, E. A., Garreton, M. T., & Schultz, B. D. (2011). *Grow your own teachers: Grassroots change for teacher education. teaching for social Justice.* Teachers College Press.

CHAPTER 27

LINKING THE FIELD-BASED MENTOR TEACHER TO UNIVERSITY COURSEWORK

Methods Course Modules for Completing the Triad of Learning for Mathematics Teacher Candidates

Jeremy Zelkowski
The University of Alabama

Jan Yow
University of South Carolina

Patrice Waller
California State University, Fullerton

Belinda P. Edwards
Kennesaw State University

Holly G. Anthony
Tennessee Tech University

Tye Campbell ^
Crandall University

Anna Keefe
The University of Alabama

Carey Wilson
Tennessee Tech University

Preparing Quality Teachers:
Advances in Clinical Practice, pp. 579–607
Copyright © 2022 by Information Age Publishing
www.infoagepub.com
      579

ABSTRACT

This chapter presents work across the Mathematics Teacher Education Partnership's Clinical Experiences Research Action Cluster subgroup focused on integrating modules into methods courses that link university coursework to field-placement in secondary (middle, high) mathematics classrolems. Four modules are described that link the triad (i.e., university faculty, teacher candidate, mentor teacher) of clinical preparation. The four modules focus on the Standards for Mathematical Practice, Lesson Planning, Quality Feedback for Learning, and Task Development. Each module has multiple methods for how to implement and/or using data to inform program assessment of teacher candidates and the impact of the modules in the field-placement classroom. Mentor teachers are asked to engage enough to provide program faculty enough information about the learning experience of the module for teacher candidates and mentor teachers. Descriptive results are presented from the implementation of each module as well as their development.

INTRODUCTION

Over the course of the last two decades, there has been increasing pressure to make teacher clinical preparation to be the foundation and driving force of program design (American Association of Colleges for Teacher Education [AACTE], 2018), Darling-Hammond, 2006, 2012, 2014). In 2010, the National Council for the Accreditation of Teacher Education (NCATE) stated,

> The education of teachers in the United States needs to be turned upside down. Teacher education must shift away from emphasizing academic preparation and course work loosely linked to school-based experiences to programs fully grounded in clinical practice and interwoven with academic content and professional courses. (NCATE, 2010, p. ii)

More specific to mathematics teacher education, the Mathematics Teacher Education Partnership (MTEP) collaboratively developed guiding principles that shape program transformations to produce well-prepared new teachers of mathematics, as opposed to being just-barely qualified (MTEP, 2014). The guiding principles promote advancing clinical experiences through embedded, early, sequential, intensive, and well-supervised classroom field work that aligns with program goals decided upon by the preparation institution, the cooperating mentor teacher, and program faculty. To move program transformations forward, our Network Improvement Community or NIC (Bryk et al., 2010; Martin & Gobstein, 2015; Strutchens et al., 2020) established a Clinical Experiences Research Action Cluster to study the impact of lessons, activities, and the integration of the mentor teacher as a critical point of alignment to improve mathematics teacher readiness entering the profession.

The Clinical Experience Research Action Cluster (CERAC) has three central sub-groups engaged in the study of clinical experience models for producing well-prepared first-year mathematics teachers. The three subgroup focus areas include (a) paired teacher candidates in internships or student teaching, (b) co-planning and co-teaching internships, and (c) clinical field experiences in teaching or methods courses. The focus of the author team's work has been on the third subgroup with a central alignment to our guiding principles which states that clinical practice for teacher candidates is critical and must involve mentor teachers having shared values and visions with program faculty on the teaching and learning of mathematics.

This chapter reports on the work of four different clinical experience modules (collection of sequenced activities) that purposefully and strategically integrate the mentor cooperating teacher into teacher preparation programs by connecting university coursework in the field experiences of teacher candidates. Effectively, our work introduces new ideas and constructs for teacher candidates in university settings (e.g., classes, assignments, activities), builds early knowledge and skills around core topics, and capstones the module experiences by engaging teacher candidates and mentor teachers collaboratively to complete a task as part of the preparation of new mathematics teachers.

RELEVANT LITERATURE

The AACTE provided essential tenets with respect to highly effective clinical educator preparation. Those tenets include language centered on (a) partnerships, (b) infrastructure, (c) development, (d) empowerment, and (e) mutual benefit. The AACTE (2018) states, "A strong research base supports the benefits of clinical partnerships for both schools and teacher preparation programs, resulting in benefits for the improved preparation of teacher candidates and success of PK–12 students" (p. 14). There is little question as to whether strong clinical practice should be a primary focus of [mathematics] teacher preparation. Rather, the larger questions relate to programmatic requirements, structural designs, and the expertise of educators involved in the preparation of teacher candidates.

For two decades, the programmatic requirements for the preparation of secondary mathematics teachers has normally included a major in mathematics (Association of Mathematics Teacher Educators [AMTE], 2017; Conference Board for Mathematical Sciences, 2001, 2012) as a result of the No Child Left Behind Act signed in 2002. In addition to completing a major in mathematics, state and local jurisdictions generally further require a minimum number of professional study courses (e.g., teaching methods, learning theories, educational foundations) and clinical field hours in secondary mathematics classrooms. For example, the *AMTE Standards for Preparing Teachers of Mathematics* at the high school level states that teacher candidates should complete three mathematics teaching methods courses, but virtually no state or province (i.e., jurisdiction) requires such an experience (AMTE, 2017). With respect to clinical experiences, some jurisdictions require a minimum number of field hours prior to a student teaching internship, while others may only require a total number of hours at the conclusion of the program. With less consistency between jurisdictions (e.g., state or provincial departments of education), clinical experience requirements have greater variability than just about any other factor of mathematics teacher preparation.

While program requirements vary, program designs play a large role in the developmental progressions of teacher candidates (AACTE, 2018; Zelkowski et al., in press; Zelkowski et al., under review). What is clear from the literature is the need for sequenced clinical experiences with purposeful objectives during each field experience (AMTE, 2017; Darling-Hammond, 2014; MTEP, 2014). The National Council of Teachers of Mathematics (NCTM) Specialized Professional Association standards has consistently stated that planned and sequenced clinical field experiences in diverse settings prior to full-time student teaching is a requirement to be a nationally recognized program (Council for the Accreditation of Education Preparation, 2012, 2020). While there are contracting views on clinical experiences (e.g., hours, semesters), the overlap of recommendations suggests multiple semesters of field experiences before full time student teaching internships mentored by highly skilled mentor teachers; Further, the implementation of program design and sequencing of field experiences is critical to the development of mathematics teacher candidates' overall readiness for first-year teaching (Ball et al., 2009; Forzani, 2014; Zeichner, 2010).

Expertise of Educators and Design-Bbased Research

While the expertise and experience of university faculty play a critical role in the development of knowledge and skills of mathematics teacher candidates, the mentor teacher plays an equally critical role in the preparation of new teachers (MTEP, 2014; Slick, 1998a, 1998b). In more recent calls, there has been a larger emphasis on the professional development of the mentor teacher in supervising teacher candidates (Gareis & Grant, 2015; Hoffman et al., 2015). Tatto (1998) and Darling-Hammond (2006) suggest that program faculty that have strong relationships and shared values with mentor teachers ultimately produce early career teachers with those same shared visions of teaching. More specifically, strong evaluation of program modeling in relation to candidate outcomes, including the effects of mentor teachers, is suggested as an important factor in evaluating mathematics teacher preparation programs (Tatto, 2018). Without such professional development for mentor teachers and shared values across the triad, teacher candidates may experience negative outcomes or lack of professional growth (Izadinia, 2015, 2016). The triad of the methods professor, the mentor teacher, and the teacher candidate must have shared visions of teaching and learning mathematics to effectively progress teacher candidates to internship readiness (Lawley et al., 2014; Strutchens et al., 2020; Zelkowski et al., 2020).

The Plan, Do, Study, Act (PDSA) Cycle of Knowledge Generation is a well-tested model for generating data, testing, and answering questions, and refining educational aspects to produce higher quality outcomes than those absent of PDSA cycles (Deming, 1950, 1993; Sears et al., 2019; Shakman et al., 2020). The PDSA cycle implementation in our work is centered on learning about primary and secondary clinical experience drivers (discussed in upcoming section) and making appropriate changes that improves the symbiotic and bidirectional learning between teacher candidate and mentor teacher. A catalyst for the adoption of design-based implementation research emphasizes the local context and collaboration between researchers and practitioners (Tichnor-Wagner et al., 2017). Design-based research methods in the context of clinical experiences for teacher candidates lends a reliable framework for the advancement of clinical practices in the sense of more recent calls to action and transformation.

Context and Background of Advanced Clinical Practices

The advancement of clinical practice improvement models has included the development and testing of many university settings and field-based clinical experience models since 2012 (Zelkowski et al., 2020; Yow et al., 2018). Our design-based implementation research emphasizes extensive planning across our CERAC NIC for field-based methods courses. Our national collaborative work is centered on the primary and secondary drivers of the CERAC (see Figure 27.1). Our primary drivers for this work are: (a) the interdependency of methods courses and early field experiences, (b) the transparent and coherent system of mentor teacher selection and support, and (c) a focus on equity and access to quality clinical experiences. Our secondary drivers include an increased attention to: (a) the mathematical practices of students and teachers, (b) a deliberate focus on connecting coursework and field experiences, and (c) developing infrastructure for improving clinical experiences for teacher candidates.

Figure 27.1

Drivers of the CERAC

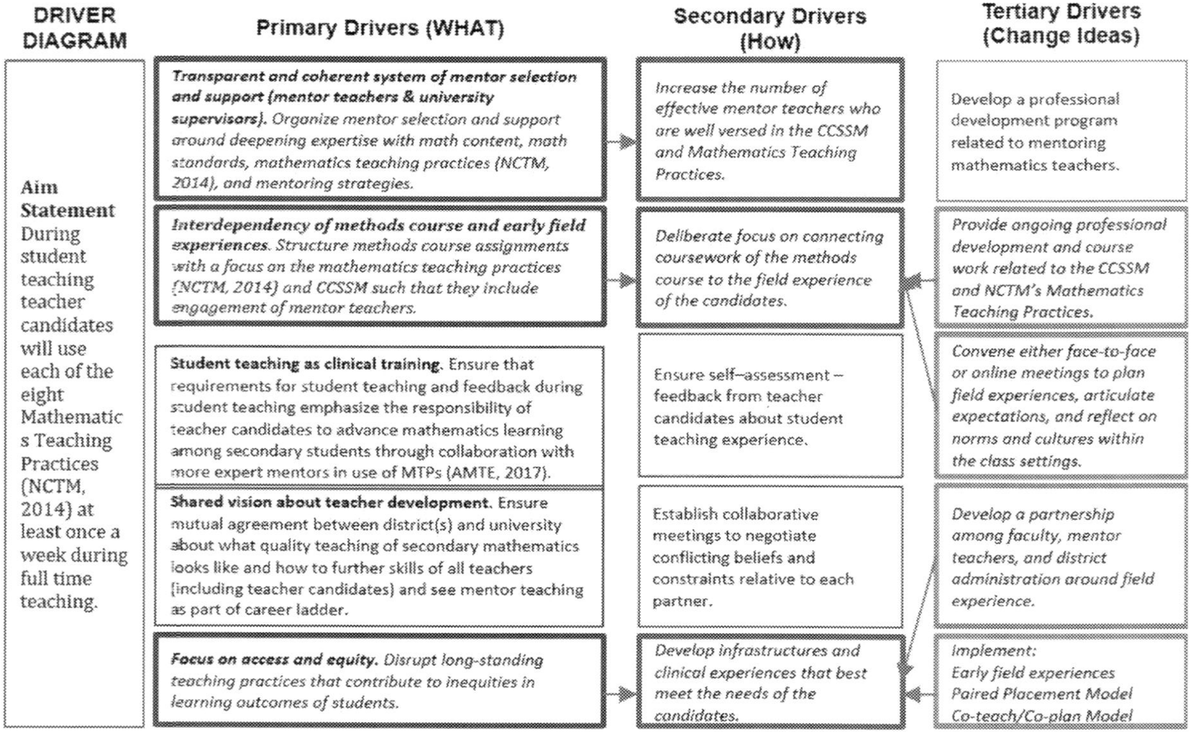

DRIVER DIAGRAM

Primary Drivers (WHAT)

Secondary Drivers (How)

Tertiary Drivers (Change Ideas)

Aim Statement
During student teaching teacher candidates will use each of the eight Mathematics Teaching Practices (NCTM, 2014) at least once a week during full time teaching.

Transparent and coherent system of mentor selection and support (mentor teachers & university supervisors). Organize mentor selection and support around deepening expertise with math content, math standards, mathematics teaching practices (NCTM, 2014), and mentoring strategies.

Interdependency of methods course and early field experiences. Structure mathematics course assignments with a focus on the mathematics teaching practices (NCTM, 2014) and CCSSM such that they include engagement of mentor teachers.

Student teaching as clinical training. Ensure that requirements for student teaching and feedback during student teaching emphasize the responsibility of teacher candidates to advance mathematics learning among secondary students through collaboration with more expert mentors in use of MTPs (AMTE, 2017).

Shared vision about teacher development. Ensure mutual agreement between district(s) and university about what quality teaching of secondary mathematics looks like and how to further skills of all teachers (including teacher candidates) and see mentor teaching as part of career ladder.

Focus on access and equity. Disrupt long-standing teaching practices that contribute to inequities in learning outcomes of students.

Increase the number of effective mentor teachers who are well versed in the CCSSM and Mathematics Teaching Practices.

Deliberate focus on connecting coursework of the methods course to the field experience of the candidates.

Ensure self-assessment – feedback from teacher candidates about student teaching experience.

Establish collaborative meetings to negotiate conflicting beliefs and constraints relative to each partner.

Develop infrastructures and clinical experiences that best meet the needs of the candidates.

Develop a professional development program related to mentoring mathematics teachers.

Provide ongoing professional development and course work related to the CCSSM and NCTM's Mathematics Teaching Practices.

Convene either face-to-face or online meetings to plan field experiences, articulate expectations, and reflect on norms and cultures within the class settings.

Develop a partnership among faculty, mentor teachers, and district administration around field experience.

Implement: Early field experiences Paired Placement Model Co-teach/Co-plan Model

The four modules developed in PDSA cycles focus on the following topics:

1. The Standards for Mathematical Practice (SMP) from the Common Core which were predicated on the NCTM Process Standards (National Governors Association Center for Best Practices & Council of Chief State School Officers [NGACBP & CCSSO], 2010).
2. Lesson Planning (LP) in connection to the eight efleective Mathematics Teaching Practices (NCTM, 2014).
3. Feedback as an effective learning tool (Hattie & Temperley, 2007; Wiggins, 2012)
4. Mathematical Task Writing (TW) (Anderson & Signe, 2011; Slavit & Nelson, 2009; Stein et al., 2008).

We share select results from the implementation of these modules across our CERAC NIC for methods courses after brief descriptions of the modules themselves. For more information and information to access the modules materials, please consult our website: https://cerac-methods.ua.edu/

STANDARDS FOR MATHEMATICAL PRACTICE MODULE

The Standards for Mathematical Practices (SMP) Module consists of three activities focused on helping teacher candidates and mentor teachers think more deeply about the Standards for Mathematical Practices (SMPs) within the Common Core State Standards for Mathematics (NGACBP & CCSSO, 2010). It consists of three activities designed to be completed while teacher candidates are in a clinical placement, with the final activity to be completed alongside the teacher candidate's mentor teacher.

Activity 1 begins by asking the teacher candidates to answer the following prompt, based on their own experiences as a secondary mathematics student and their observations of secondary students in their clinical placements: *Write down as much as you can to describe the habits of doing math the typical student has by 10th grade.* Teachers candidates tend to list less-than-positive responses such as: *random guess-and-check* and *trusting the calculator even when the answer does not make sense.* Then, teacher candidates are divided into smaller groups to learn more about the SMPs. The suggested text to use is Koestler et al.'s (2013) *Connecting the NCTM Process Standards and the CCSSM Practices.* Though this text offers an excellent crosswalk between the NCTM Process Standards (NCTM, 2000) and the SMPs, instructors could choose an alternative, more widely available resource for teacher candidates to investigate the SMPs more deeply. Once the teacher candidates learn more about the SMPs and share those learnings with classmates, we return to the initial brainstormed list of a 10th grader's typical habits of doing mathematics and talk through how that list compares to what we now know about the desired eight SMPs and how we as teachers can help scaffold learning experiences that helps students move closer to the eight SMPs.

Activity 2 centers on teacher candidates participating in a 10th grade inquiry geometry lesson as students with the methods course instructor as the classroom teacher. After completing the lesson, teacher candidates engage in discussing how the SMPs were addressed during the teaching and learning of that lesson. The lesson used in the SMP Module is found at insidemathematics.org and focused on the properties of quadrilaterals (Inside Mathematics, 2017). We chose this website because it houses publicly available, high-quality inquiry mathematics videos alongside other valuable supplemental material such as teacher notes. However, similar to the above comment on the Koestler et al. (2013) text, any publicly available, high-quality inquiry mathematics videos could be used in the SMP Module. Since mentor teachers will also need to access the videos, it is key that they be publicly available—or at least available to the teacher candidate's mentor teachers. Once teacher candidates participate as secondary students would in the activity, we discuss how the instructor facilitated the lesson to encourage the SMPs and how the facilitation could have been improved to encourage an even deeper evolution of the SMPs among secondary students. Teacher candidates engage with two observational instruments (Elementary Mathematics Specialists & Teacher Leader Project, 2012; Maletta et al., 2011) to help them further investigate SMPs evoked during the teaching and learning or the quadrilaterals lesson in part, in preparation for the final mentor teacher activity of the module.

Activities 1 and 2 prepare teacher candidates for the final culminating experience in Activity 3 which involves a joint investigation between the teacher candidate and mentor teacher of a video segment from the lesson on properties of quadrilaterals. Together, the teacher candidate and mentor teacher view a 10-minute video clip of this lesson that the teacher candidate has already completed as a student, discussed among fellow teacher candidates, and reflected on individually in Activity 2. Now, the teacher candidate has a chance to watch a portion of the video again alongside the mentor teacher in order to facilitate a conversation focused on the SMPs witnessed within the video. The pair is asked to use the Student Column of the Looks Fors rubric (Elementary Mathematics Specialists & Teacher Leader Project, 2012) to help them address the following prompts:

1. What were the students doing? What content were they discussing? How would you describe their level of engagement?

2. Using the "Students" column of the Mathematical Practices Look-Fors, read through the indicators for each of the SMPs and discuss whether these characterize any of the interactions from the video. Provide specific evidence from the video to support your claims. (Note: some SMPs may not be demonstrated in this video clip).

3. What can you take-away from this clip that could impact your own instruction?

Teacher candidates then complete a detailed narrative describing and reflecting on their conversation with the mentor teachers. The goal of Activity 3 is to help both the teacher candidate and mentor teacher gain an even deeper understanding of the SMPs and offer an example of a lesson where the SMPs may be enacted in an inquiry lesson.

Data and Description of Impact: Teacher candidates and mentor teachers both take a pre- and post-survey to gauge their knowledge and understanding of the SMPs before and after the Module. Teacher candidates also complete an exit slip after each activity to also offer insight into their thinking as they progress through the Module. Previous findings from an analysis of the mentor teacher data demonstrated some growth among the mentor teachers in particular areas (Yow et al., 2018). For example, mentor teacher responses on the post-survey items, as compared to their responses on the same pre-survey items, suggested an increased understanding of the SMPs highlighted in Module 1, such as SMP 4 (model with mathematics) and SMP 5 (Use appropriate tools strategically) (NGACBP & CCSSO, 2010). Survey results also suggested that MTs improved their implementation of some of the core SMPs and were more purposeful in facilitating student learning in their classrooms, such as called for in SMP 3 asking students to "critique the reasoning of others" (NGACBP & CCSSO, 2010).

In our previous study (Yow et al., 2018), we also found evidence that collegial conversations were another benefit of the joint endeavor in Activity 3 between the teacher candidate and mentor teacher. For example, whereas normally a teacher candidate-mentor teacher lesson discussion would focus on either a lesson the mentor teacher taught or a lesson the teacher candidate taught, watching a video of another teacher teaching created a "safe" space to discuss the lesson together. The pair was reflecting on someone else's lesson rather than their own. Activity 3 gave them the opportunity to speak as colleagues rather than mentor and mentee. Additionally, Activity 3 gave them the opportunity to sit down together—if only briefly—to talk about teaching in a structured way. Oftentimes in the reality of schooling and internships, the business of students coming in and out of classes results in limited time for teacher candidates and mentor teachers to have meaningful conversations about teaching, but this assignment offers that opportunity (Yow et al., 2018).

Data reviewed since our previous study offered additional insights into the teacher candidate-mentor teacher experience with Activity 3. Exit slip data spoke to a varied experience across the teacher candidates as well as the teacher candidate-mentor teacher pairings. For example, when asked how the conversation with their MT about the video compared with our class conversation about the video, one teacher candidate wrote, "The discussion with my mentor teacher was less in depth. During class we were able to really pick the video apart and see when and where students were engaging with the SMPs. With my mentor teachers, our conversations were normally brief and simply an overview of things we saw or didn't see." In contrast, another teacher candidate wrote, "While in class, we simply discussed all of the SMPs that this video addressed and why. Thus, it seemed more like a checklist in class with more analysis with my coaching teacher."

One additional point highlighted in the data was the question of the most effective way to engage the teacher candidate and subsequently the mentor teacher in the discussion around the video clip. Our previous findings indicated that although it was beneficial to have the teacher candidates engaged in one lesson (the properties of quadrilaterals) over multiple Activities (2 and 3), they sometimes felt fatigued from watching the same lesson multiple times. Although they could also see the value of viewing the same video clip multiple times with at least two different mentor teachers, it also felt as if they reached a point of saturation and wondered if viewing different video clips may be more helpful (Yow et al., 2018). Subsequent data also highlighted the additional challenge of the time spent with the mentor teachers viewing and discussing the video clip. Much time and deliberation occurred among the original Module 1 design team about how best to engage mentor teachers without placing too much of an additional burden on their time. Some teacher candidates noted that it was difficult to even find the time to complete the assignment with their mentor teachers given the often-hectic atmosphere of secondary schools, while others noted that even more time to set-up and explain the video lesson to their mentor teachers was helpful:

> Before I showed my mentor teacher the video clip, I showed her the copy of the task the students were completing that I had. I also gave her some background information on what the teacher asked students to keep track of to turn in to her. I felt like all of these things were important for her to know so that she could follow the video more easily.... After we watched the video clip we were both very glad I gave her the background information beforehand. Without it I think the video would have been very difficult to follow.

Further iterations of Activity 3 along with more data collection are war-ranted to find more effective ways to engage the mentor teacher during this time. Data demonstrated that the activity was beneficial to both the teacher candidate and mentor teacher in terms of increased understanding of the SMPs and teacher candidates overwhelmingly noted the benefits of the engagement, but finding the most efficient and effective way to maximize this time spent with the mentor teacher is critical.

LESSON PLANNING MODULE

The Lesson Planning (LP) Module is designed to discover teacher candi-dates' preconceived beliefs about lesson planning and move them towards a greater understanding of the components of high-quality lesson plans embedded in the Mathematics Teaching Practices designed to engage stu-dents in the Standards for Mathematical Practice. The LP Module consists of 3 activities—the first activity focuses on the teacher candidates current understanding (or beliefs) of mathematics lesson planning and highlights already established ideas regarding mathematics teaching and learning practices. Activity 2 gives teacher candidates the opportunity to evalu-ate and revise their already planned lessons after having received some instruction on lesson planning between Activities 1 and 2. Activity 3 allows teacher candidates to put their lessons into practice with support from the mentor teacher.

The LP Module is predicated on the Mathematical Classroom Observa-tion Protocol for Practices (MCOP^2) (Gleason et al., 2017) focusing on the developmental trajectory of teacher candidates to become ambitious lesson planners for their early instructional decisions. The LP Module is designed to be implemented in a mathematics methods course which is centered on developing the ideas of equitable instructional practices in lesson planning that promote mathematics learning through making explicit connections to the NCTM Mathematics Teaching Practices (NCTM, 2014) and the Standards for Mathematical Practice (NGACBP & CCSSO, 2010).

Activity 1—Baseline Beliefs about Lesson Planning

Activity 1 begins with the assumption that this is the teacher candidate's first attempt at writing a lesson plan, prior to any specific mathematics lesson planning instruction. Teacher candidates are asked to examine a potential quiz on slope for which the instructor provides context (i.e., grade level, standards, etc.) and write a lesson plan in 45 minutes using any resources available. The purpose of this first lesson plan draft is to provide an opportunity for methods faculty to understand teacher candidates' beliefs and knowledge about lesson planning and quality (or not) teaching practices as they are beginning their first methods course (Zelkowski et al., 2020). Teacher candidates will likely create a lesson plan that is brief and focused on procedures with rote practice examples.

After writing the lesson plan, teacher candidates complete the Pre-MCOP² Lesson Plan Evaluation which allows them to self-evaluate their plans using the MCOP² Lesson Planning Rubric. The MCOP² Lesson Planning Rubric encourages teacher candidates to reflect on their lesson plan using at most a three-point rubric that assesses whether or not the lesson plan provides evidence that certain criteria (problem solving, multiple representation) are present within the plan. After completing this one assessment, teacher candidates will then submit their lesson plans to be assessed using the same lesson planning rubric by the instructor.

Prior to Activity 2, teacher candidates should be exposed to the normal instruction related to learning how to write secondary mathematics lesson plans that they would typically undergo within the program. We suggest discussing the difference between procedural and conceptual questions and the difference between problem solving and skill building. We also encourage instructors to have TCs to evaluate a student's ability to respond to the assessment questions after their lesson.

Activity 2—Evaluating and Revising Lesson Plans

The purpose of Activity 2 is for teacher candidates to have an opportunity to work with a teacher candidate peer/partner to reflect on MCOP² Lesson Planning Rubric scores from Activity 1 and consider ways in which they might improve the lesson plan as it relates to MCOP² Lesson Planning Rubric scores. Keeping in mind that the Lesson Planning rubric is centered on the Mathematics Teaching Practices (NCTM, 2014) and the Standards for Mathematical Practices (SMPs). It is vital that teacher candidates engage with lesson planning with these tools in mind. This peer-to-peer interaction allows for rich discourse and revisions that refocus the lesson in a student-centered manner. teacher candidates then have the opportunity to revise and resubmit their lesson plans.

Activity 3—Engaging the Mentor Teacher in the Clinical Experience

The purpose of Activity 3 is to engage the cooperating mentor teacher with the teacher candidates in the lesson planning and self-assessment process. Activity 3 requires that teacher candidates plan, implement, and reflect on a lesson or quality task in a mathematics classroom. During the clinical experience the teacher candidates and the mentor teacher work collaboratively to plan a lesson using the MCOP^2 Lesson Planning Rubric to ensure that the lesson is student centered and engaging. After planning the lesson, the teacher candidate implements the lesson while the mentor teacher observes the lesson and takes notes using the MCOP^2 observation protocol. The teacher candidate and the MT participate in a debrief session following the lesson that provides insight and feedback on the lesson using the MCOP^2 Observation Protocol to guide their discussion.

Activity 3 serves as the highlight of the clinical experience because it allows teacher candidates to put into action the knowledge and skills that they have learned and refined throughout the module/methods course. Using the MCOP^2 rubric also provides a tangible tool for evaluation of the teaching process. It gives mentor teachers and teacher candidates alike a common language and a common lens through which to see the art of engaging and effective math teaching.

Data and Description of Impact

The implementation of the Lesson Planning Module during and after development cycles has shown promising results across multiple institutions during the 2018–19 and 2019–20 academic years. The module has helped to highlight the important components of lesson planning, while also identifying MTs practices that are aligned/misaligned with these practices. We report on the descriptive data differences we saw cumulatively across the two academic years of implementation.

The pre-assessment of early program beliefs of teacher candidates revealed over 80% believed or strongly believed that drill and practice are essential for developing mathematical understanding. Yet, by the completion of the module activities, there was little to no evidence in teacher candidates' responses on the post-module survey that drill, and practice, were a significant part of the lessons they planned and/or implemented. We consider this one of the significant outcomes discovered during our work as building conceptual fluency in addition to procedural fluency should be a key focus in the teaching and learning of mathematics (NCTM, 2014). On the post-survey, over 90% of the participants reported that the module was effective in developing their ability to create a high-quality lesson plan with their mentor teacher.

Some program faculty implemented the baseline Activity 1, while others bypassed Activity 1 and began with Activity 2. During initial piloting, one methods instructor provided feedback and felt the time devoted to a baseline lesson planning activity made teacher candidates feel uncomfortable in doing an activity or task without prior lesson planning instruction. We concur that this happens, and we defer to the judgement of methods course faculty to make this decision. Our team development weighed this option, but in other methods classes, Activity 2 data was found to have a measurable impact on teacher candidates' beliefs about what a lesson including the SMPs looks like and challenged their beliefs about teaching and learning mathematics when faced with early discomfort in planning about existing beliefs. One teacher candidate survey said, "It was very challenging to do the technical side of lesson planning because I really had to think about what activities effectively produce understanding, which was very difficult."

Comprehensively, we found a few teacher candidates' quotes on the post-module survey that summarize our experiences. Three teacher candidates stated:

> I enjoyed the activities assigned this semester. They gave me insight about classroom experiences, especially while with my mentor teacher. I learned quite a lot from these activities and definitely grew as a future teacher.

> I feel that being able to plan and implement a lesson really helped me see where I could make adjustments during planning. It was a very positive experience, the struggles I faced helped me learn how to be better and the things I still need to focus on. Working with a teacher who understood the [MCOP²] was more beneficial because they were capable of providing very good feedback.

> Lesson [Activity] three was by far the best experience I have had in a classroom to date. I was given the opportunity to teach multiple times and I would have had a hard time knowing where to start working with my MT without it.

Overall, we did find effectiveness of the Module and positive perceptions of teacher candidates; however, we also found that the mentor teacher played a large role in these perceptions with an isolated case or two of the mentor teacher asking to be removed from future consideration of mentoring a teacher candidate during field experiences. However disappointing, we found that to be a positive as it would not place a future teacher candidate in a less than productive field experience.

FEEDBACK MODULE

At the center of any effective teacher education program is the clinical experience. The clinical experience provides an opportunity for teacher candidates to develop a connection between theory and practice. In a supervised learning environment, teacher candidates develop a mastery of teaching skills in context and more practice-based learning than would be possible in a methods classroom. One important teaching skill that promotes student learning is providing meaningful feedback to students (Hattie, 2009). During the clinical field experience, teacher candidates, in collaboration with their mentor teachers, have an opportunity to learn about and engage in the practice of providing feedback to students. However, not all feedback is equally effective and in some cases it can be counterproductive. As such, in preparation for becoming effective classroom teachers, teacher candidates must learn how to provide meaningful feedback that is supportive of students gaining new knowledge, applying prior knowledge, and understanding of mathematics all in an effort to reach a learning goal. Further, teacher candidates need opportunities to practice providing feedback on authentic student work within the context of a classroom under the support and guidance of a mentor teacher.

During mathematics methods coursework that is integrated with a clinical field experience, teacher candidates complete a feedback module of activities designed to guide their learning about the importance of supplying students with meaningful feedback. The purpose of giving feedback is to help students understand what they know, what they can do, and what they still need to work on during learning episodes in pursuance of a defined learning goal. According to research (i.e., Guskey, 2003; Hattie, 2011; Hattie & Timperley, 2007; Wiggins, 2012), effective or constructive feedback promotes learning. Constructive and effective feedback is specific, timely, goal oriented, provides students with guidance on how to improve and information about their performance (Hattie & Timperley, 2007; Wiggins, 2012). Most educator preparation programs do a good job providing practice-based teaching and learning within coursework and the clinical field experience. However, research suggests that teacher candidates, too often, do not receive opportunities to practice providing effective feedback on authentic student work in the context of a real-world classroom (Janssen et al., 2015; Scheeler et al., 2016). Thus, providing teacher candidates with structured applied or practice-based teaching opportunities needed for skill acquisition to deliver appropriate feedback to students that explains what they are doing and encourages student effort and achievement is critical to developing as an effective teacher (Wiggins, 2012).

The Feedback Module was designed for facilitation in a methods course with teacher candidates and their mentor teachers or practicing teachers who might be completing an advanced pedagogy degree. In our case, the Feedback Module was facilitated with teacher candidates and mentor teachers during a mathematics methods course with an integrated clinical field experience. It focused on engaging the standard of mathematical practice *Elicit and Use Evidence of Student Thinking*, primarily because teacher candidates analyze student work, make sense of their understandings, and provide feedback that moves the student closer to understanding and meeting the learning goal. The Feedback Module consists of four main activities that were created using the Hattie and Timperley (2007) Feedback Model, which demonstrates how feedback can be used to enhance teacher classroom effectiveness and student achievement. The module activities consists of (a) introduction to effective feedback through readings and course discussions (b) engaging students in an iterative improvement process (c) rehearsal providing effective feedback after students complete a cognitively demanding mathematics task, and (d) a culminating feedback assignment in the form of letter writing and providing students with feedback, or a feedback observation activity designed to focus on the type of feedback a mentor teacher provides during a lesson.

Teacher candidates were introduced to feedback through readings (*Rough-draft Math: Revising to Learn* (Jansen, 2020), *Effective Feedback for Deeper Learning* (Sarris, 2016), and a video about strategies to promote independent learners). The purpose of the readings and video was to develop teacher candidates' and mentor teachers' understanding of the importance of feedback and assessment to productive mathematics teaching and learning. They learned various ways in which students can be assessed in order to gain information about what students know and understand about mathematics. Then, using the Hattie and Timperley (2007) model for feedback, teacher candidates focused on learning goals, progress that needs to be made to reach stated learning goals, and a selection of tasks and activities that students engaged to support the learning process. Readings and discussions were designed to build on connecting learning, assessment, feedback, and reducing the gap between student understanding and the learning goal.

After the readings and discussions, teacher candidates engaged students in an iterative improvement process (Jansen, 2020) with the support of their mentor teacher while in the field experience classroom. During the facilitation of the iterative improvement process activity, teacher candidates selected a cognitively demanding mathematics task, engaged students in the task, and provided students with an opportunity to share their incomplete solutions within small groups, receive peer feedback and remain open to making changes that might push them forward to understanding the content as opposed to getting a final or right answer (Jansen, 2020). Facilitation of the iterative improvement activity enabled the teacher candidate, as well as the mentor teacher, to shift from an evaluator to making sense of students' ideas and thinking, in support of students who might be struggling to reach a solution.

After engaging students in an iterative improvement process, teacher candidates have an opportunity to rehearse, analyze and provide feedback on student work in the methods course and can make connections between research and practice. The rehearsal and analysis of feedback approximates what practicing teachers do when analyzing student work and providing formative feedback. During this activity, teacher candidates assess student work, share, and discuss feedback type (evaluative, descriptive, or prescriptive) and level of feedback (task, process, self-regulation, or self) and how the type and level of feedback moves learning forward to meeting goals.

There are several culminating activities in the Feedback Module. In this chapter, the focus is on the letter writing assignment. The letter writing process includes the following steps: (a) the teacher candidates select a cognitive demanding mathematics task for students to engage, (b) the teacher candidate writes a letter to a student (or small group of students) that includes a cognitive demanding task for the students to work (c) the student responds with a solution along with a symbolic and written explanation, including any questions they may have (d) the teacher candidate receives the return letter, analyzes the student's explanation and provides written feedback to improve a student's process and self-regulation in a way that helps the student to reach the learning goal and (e) after receiving the second iteration of the student's work, the teacher candidate makes a decision about whether the student has reached the learning goal or if the student needs further instruction.

In his research on language and mathematics learning, Pugalee (2005) found that writing supports mathematics reasoning and problem solving and can be used by teachers to make sense of students' explanations and thinking. The National Council of Teachers of Mathematics (NCTM, 2000) suggests that students write explanations about how they solve problems because as students write and listen to the justifications of solutions, they gain a deeper understanding of mathematics. As such, the purpose of implementing the letter writing assignment within a methods course was to provide teacher candidates with an opportunity to pose a cognitively demanding task to students, analyze student explanations and solutions, provide a level of feedback that would push students' thinking forward, and provide students with an opportunity to revise and resubmit their work. During the letter writing assignment, students were able to ask questions and experience what is valuable about their solution drafts. Further, this process also provides teacher candidates with the opportunity to be a bit more intentional about providing feedback that moves the student closer to the learning goal.

Data and Description of Impact

The Feedback Module enabled teacher candidates and their mentor teachers to collaboratively engage in a series of activities designed to support enhancing teacher effectiveness and student engagement to meet learning goals. The purpose of providing feedback is to decrease the gap between what students understand about specific mathematics content and the learning goal (Hattie, 2009; Hattie & Zierer, 2019). Hattie and Timperley (2007) recommend providing feedback at the process and self-regulation levels because these levels are most effective to decrease the gap between student understanding and the learning goal. Process level feedback targeted students' appropriate use of learned strategies, relationships among ideas, learning from errors, and use of alternative strategies. Self-regulation level feedback targets students' monitoring and regulating their actions towards reaching the learning goal. Feedback at this level addressed the degree to which students use previously given feedback, self-assess, seek additional useful information, and confidence in the correctness of their solution.

We were interested in examining the level of feedback teacher candidates provided to move students forward to increased understanding and learning, not necessarily the correct answer. We were also interested in exploring the teacher candidates' and mentor teachers' experiences engaging in the module activities with specific attention given to their experiences engaging the culminating letter writing activity. The data in this study included teacher candidates' experiences proposing a cognitively demanding mathematics task along with the written feedback they provided students for two iterations of their draft solutions. The data also included the mentor teachers' experiences supporting the teacher candidates to provide process and self-regulating feedback and guiding the students to commitment to responding to the teacher candidates' feedback. All feedback provided was based on content knowledge the students had acquired, all of whom had a minimum degree of proficiency.

Tasks that students engage during class are central to mathematics instruction. Further, the cognitive demand level determines students' level of understanding and learning. Teacher candidates' experiences collaborating with their mentor teacher to select an appropriate task for students to engage were positive. The experience provided an opportunity for the teacher candidate to get an in-depth understanding of students' prior knowledge. One teacher candidate said, "My collaborating teacher shared the students' homework scores from the week before, making the task I picked the perfect level of difficult[y]." Another indicated that "working with a mentor teacher to find a task gave me confidence in knowing that the student would be able to begin the task."

When asked to share their experiences supporting the teacher candidates during the letter writing process, a common theme in the data indicates mentor teachers valued the teacher candidates' focus on the learning goals by "attending to the gaps in students' understandings" and "focusing on the process of understanding as opposed to the correct answer." However, some mentor teachers felt that the letter writing process took "too much time to complete" and suggested the feedback interactions include peer evaluation. The letter writing activity provided teacher candidates an opportunity to simulate a part of teaching that focuses on analyzing student learning and understanding towards meeting a learning goal, within a supportive environment where they too can receive feedback from mentor teachers on their performance (Grossman et al., 2009).

TASK WRITING MODULE

Posing mathematical tasks is an integral part of the practice of teaching, but many teacher candidates do not have opportunities in their teacher preparation program to hone their task writing skills. Too often tasks are provided by the methods instructor for the purpose of conducting math interviews with students (Crespo & Nicol, 2003) and/or to facilitate a quality teaching experience for the teacher candidate—removing the need to focus on developing the task—to allow them to focus on pedagogical delivery. Most educators agree that mathematics teachers should include rich mathematical tasks in their classroom pedagogy (Anderson & Signe, 2011; Slavit & Nelson, 2009; Stein et al., 2008), yet Crespo (2003) noted that posing mathematical tasks is a challenge for teacher candidates who are novices still learning how to teach mathematics. Participation in a mathematical letter writing exchange allows teacher candidates access to real-world experiences of posing useful mathematical tasks and giving feedback to students while having the benefit of time to reflect on their teaching practices (Crespo, 2002). The Task Writing Module is built around a mathematical letter writing exchange (Anderson et al., 2009/2010) between middle and secondary teacher candidates and high school math students. Fennel (1991) indicated that teacher candidates seemed to better understand mathematics and were better able to understand their penpals' interests, attitudes, and learning progression. Additionally, teacher candidates reported that they liked having the freedom to pick the problems they sent to the students based on the content their students were learning at the time. Additionally, teacher candidates gained insight into crucial mathematical communication strategies and debunked some preconceived notions they held concerning student achievement related to student interest in mathematics (Phillips & Crespo, 1996).

So, how do we leverage mathematical letter writing for the purpose of developing teacher candidates' skill set at developing rich mathematical tasks? Logistically, the high school students initiate the letter exchange by writing a letter of introduction to a teacher candidate. The introduction includes general information about the high school student's interests inside and outside of school-related coursework and activities, the student's perceived mathematical abilities, and the individual's attitudes toward mathematics. Introductory letters are delivered to teacher candidates on the first night of their methods course that meets for one three-hour block each week. In that first-class meeting, teacher candidates engage in a Math Task Sorting Activity using the Task Analysis Guide developed by Stein et al. (2000, p. 16) to determine which of 16 tasks fit within the categories of Lower-Level Demands (memorization; procedures without connections) or higher-level demands (procedures with connections; doing mathematics). Teacher candidates are also shown sample tasks and task arcs (https://www.edutoolbox.org/tntools/menu/grade/819/6128) developed by educators in Tennessee and the Institute for Learning (https://ifl.pitt.edu/). The teacher candidates respond the following week with an introduction letter and enclose a grade-appropriate, standards-based mathematical task aligned to the interests shared by the high school students in their introductory letter. Tasks may be adapted and modified from those located in textbooks or online; a key criterion is that the task must be rich enough that it requires an "average" high school student approximately 45 minutes to complete it. Letters and mathematical tasks are alternatively picked up and delivered so that each class receives a response on a biweekly basis. Both teacher candidates and the high school students maintain anonymity by using self-selected pseudonyms.

Throughout the letter exchange, each class receives approximately six letters each, and the teacher candidates send five mathematical tasks during this semester. As the semester progresses, the teacher candidates work in teams to scaffold subsequent tasks based on what they learn about the high school students' abilities and interests. If an original task is too difficult or so poorly written that the high school students cannot successfully complete it, the next task is scaffolded down, and the quality of the instructions are improved. The methods instructor does not preview the tasks each week or offer any substantive feedback on their content or format. Rather, the teacher candidates receive critical feedback from the high school students and the high school teacher. The high school students are asked at the end of each task to rate its quality and to offer feedback to the teacher candidate about the task content, organization, or wording. The high school teacher attends the methods class (in the weeks that letters are delivered from high school students to teacher candidates) and offers general feedback on how the students worked with the tasks. The teacher candidates work together to make decisions for the next task. In this authentic learning experience, in which the teacher candidates learn by trying and failing/succeeding, teacher candidates develop autonomy and confidence in their ability to adapt, modify, and write original mathematics tasks. As a culminating activity in the course, the teacher candidates develop an instructional task (formatted to match those on the edutoolbox platform) and submit it for formal evaluation by the methods instructor. Many of these tasks exhibit such high quality that they are passed along to the Tennessee State Department of Education for review and possible inclusion in the edutoolbox online task database.

Data and Description of Impact

The Task Writing Module has been implemented across seven semesters at Tennessee Tech University with a total of 114 teacher candidates participating in the experience. Each teacher candidate writes a culminating reflection paper at the conclusion of the semester to comment on how they perceived the value of the experience and what they learned from it. Comments are overwhelmingly positive with many citing it as one of the most valuable learning experiences in their TPP. A few excerpts are shared for illustrative purposes:

> My feelings have not changed towards mathematics, but my ideas have changed about how to encourage students to learn and persevere in math"

> [A]s a teacher, I can have such a great influence on my students–even indirectly through letters! My students showed that they really appreciated how my partner and I related the tasks to their interests. My penpal wrote, "I like how you use the things I like in the math problems"

> My student would mention that he thinks math is "very useful." I found that the encouragement I write in the letters truly makes a difference in the students' perceptions of their abilities to do math. My other student wrote, "Thank you for having confidence in me with math. It really helps me try harder."

As these quotes illustrate, teacher candidates' views towards mathematics as a discipline seldom change after participation in the Task Writing Module, but we do see evidence of change with regards to how they view students. By interacting with students in the math letter writing exchange, teacher candidates realize the magnitude of their influence on students' motivation to learn mathematics and the value of encouragement to help students persevere and build confidence.

In fall 2019, a qualitative case study of three of the teacher candidates who participated in the Task Writing Module was conducted (Wilson & Anthony, 2020). The teacher candidates were interviewed, and transcripts were analyzed using inductive analysis. Here we briefly share our findings with specific regards to how the teacher candidates defined and characterized mathematical tasks. When the researcher asked each participant what they initially thought a mathematical task was, the consensus among the participants indicated that a mathematical task was "like a problem or a set of problems that you have to solve." However, as the semester went on, the teacher candidates definition changed to reflect how a math task could be a thematic set of mathematical problems that progressively leads the students into thinking more deeply about mathematics. teacher Ccandidate-1 indicated that a mathematical task could be an activity, and teacher Candidate-2 said it could be a project. Though teacher cCandidate-3 agreed with these ideals, she challenged these concepts by indicating that each mathematical task should start with the activity, project, or the main question, and pertinent questions should follow. Above and beyond this, the three participants characterized mathematical tasks as meeting the unique interests and ability levels of each penpal. Teacher Candidate-1 came up with a creative story about a dragon playing basketball to review rigid motions with her penpals. Teacher Candidate-2 and teacher Candidate-3 focused on including challenge questions that met the varying mathematical abilities of their penpals. These findings contradicted Crespo (2000), who determined that teacher candidates seemed to lower their expectations for lower-performing students and catered to the higher ability students. Teacher candidate-'s description of her penpals addressed a possible reason for this inconsistency.

> Whereas the other guy. He's not so much interested. He also just kind of probably does his work. And like, "Hey, help!" kind of thing. When he can actually do it. He's maybe just, be [sic] like, "Why do it when you can have somebody else show you?" I do, like, really try to understand the students. But—so, yeah. I think they 're—they can both do the work. I think the sporty guy can do the work. If he just saw that it was useful to him. The other penpal, he's pretty good. He's very accurate and precise in his drawings, and he has to be for a guy who draws dragons. So, I think that they're both capable.

Mathematical tasks, as described in this study, had explicit and implicit structures that made the tasks *good*. The intrinsic characteristics of a *good* mathematical task were harder to uncover. However, the implicit structures were concepts that teacher candidates should consider incorporating into their future teaching practices. The participants crafted their mathematical discussions so that their students felt safe to enter and sustain a mathematical conversation without fear of any negative repercussions. Teacher candidate-1 appeared to be better at this since she remembered to keep the mathematical communication going in her letters and her mathematical tasks. Additionally, all three teacher candidates avoided adverse language and tried to incorporate a positive perspective in all of the feedback they gave to their penpals, even when the students were wrong. This positivity helped students change their perspective of their mathematical abilities for the better.

REFLECTIONS AND TAKE-AWAYS

In this chapter, we discussed four different clinical experience modules based on partnerships amongst mentor teachers, teacher candidates, and methods instructors. These modules are integrated into teacher preparation programs by forming a connection between university coursework and teacher candidates' field experiences. Each of the four modules promote partnerships to enhance the teaching preparations of teacher candidates. The Standards for Mathematical Practice Module uses three activities to help teacher candidates and mentor teachers gain a deeper understanding of the SMPs within the Common Core Standards for Mathematics. The Lesson Planning Module uses three modules to gain insight into the preconceived beliefs of teacher candidates in reference to lesson planning. This module guides the teacher candidates to a greater understanding of the components of high-quality lesson plans. The Feedback Module is comprised of four activities that are facilitated by teacher candidates and mentor teachers, or teacher candidates completing advanced pedagogy degrees and are comprised of introducing effective feedback, engaging students in an iterative improvement process, rehearsing task feedback after students complete cognitively demanding tasks, and a feedback assignment or feedback observation activity. The final module is the Task Writing Module, which is aimed to help teacher candidates increase the quality of their task writing.

This work reveals important implications for clinical practice in teacher education programs. Mentor teachers, teacher educators, and prospective teachers need to collaborate with one another to create a positive and productive clinical experience. Our modules organize collaborative efforts among these three stakeholders. In particular, the modules create a space for mentor teachers to take on a more active role in supporting prospective teachers. This is vital since mentor teachers provide a unique perspective of practice that cannot be fully realized in teaching methods courses.

Our authorship team learned from the implementation many valuable takeaways from this work. They include how to best match teacher candidates in the future with teachers who have certain foci in their perspectives from the exit slips or Google Forms that were part of these modules. Additionally, teacher candidates provide methods faculty information during the early activities of the modules that helps identify developmental areas some teacher candidates need more work prior to entering the field experience, while other teacher candidates are ready to focus on clinical practices. While this chapter did not focus on empirical analyses, these reflections were part of our author team's work during the development of these modules.

Further, our study shows the benefit of the Plan, Do, Study, Act (PDSA) Cycle of Knowledge Generation for the development of clinical experience activities. Our CERAC developed these modules through an iterative process wherein we tested modules and refined them using the PDSA cycle. Our process of testing and refining can be replicated to create future modules and lesson plans for other components of mathematics teacher education practice.

Finally, this study shows how collaboration amongst teacher education programs can support prospective teachers and the field of education as a whole. Through our collaboration, we influenced numerous prospective teachers towards better teaching practices and more productive beliefs while simultaneously creating products that can be used at other teacher education programs while engaging mentor teachers. Through collaboration, we can support teacher education both locally and nationally to produce highly qualified mathematics teachers.

We hope this study supports teacher educators and researchers in two ways. First, we hope teacher educators can use the modules we created within clinical experiences at their respective institutions. Second, we hope teacher educators and researchers will build upon our model of collaboration amongst teacher education programs, mentor teachers, and prospective teachers to create new products that support the development of highly qualified mathematics teachers.

Authorship note: All authors have contributed equally to the work of this chapter and advances in clinical practice. Authors are listed in reverse alphabetical order for the listing of the corresponding author first. Graduate students who contributed to this work are listed alphabetically and each shared in their contributions equally.

^ Former doctoral student at The University of Alabama.

ACKNOWLEDGMENTS

Special Recognition: The authors of this chapter wish to thank the exceptional mathematics teachers who have contributed to this chapter's possibility by hosting teacher candidates regularly to complete the triad relationships for preparing tomorrow's mathematics teachers. Their names appear at the end of this chapter.

Funding Acknowledgment: This work was supported in part by the National Science Foundation Grant ID#s: 1726998, 1726362, 1726853, 1849948. Any opinions, findings, and conclusions or recommendations expressed in this chapter are those of the authors and do not necessarily reflect the views of the National Science Foundation.

REFERENCES

American Association of Colleges for Teacher Education. (2018). *A pivot toward clinical practice, its lexicon, and the renewal of educator preparation: A report of the AACTE clinical practice commission.*

Anderson, N., Rutledge, Z., Hall, K., & Norton, R. (2009/2010, December/January). Mathematical letter writing. *Mathematics Teacher, 103*(5), 340–346. http://www.nctm.org/publications/

Anderson, N., & Signe, K. (2011). Learning to pose cognitively demanding tasks through letter writing. *Journal of Mathematics Teacher Education, 15*(2), 109–130. doi:10.1007/s10857-011-9193-9

Association of Mathematics Teacher Educators. (2017). *Standards for preparing teachers of mathematics.* https://amte.net/sites/default/files/SPTM.pdf

Ball, D., Thames, M. H., & Phelps, G. (2008). Content knowledge for teaching: What makes it special? *Journal of Teacher Education, 59*(5), 389–407.

Bryk, A. S., Gomez, L. M., & Grunow, A. (2010). *Getting ideas into action: Building networked improvement communities in education.* Carnegie Foundation for the Advancement of Teaching.

Council for the Accreditation of Educator Preparation. (2012). *The National Council of Teachers of Mathematics specialized professional association standards for mathematics teacher preparation.*

Council for the Accreditation of Educator Preparation. (2020). *The National Council of Teachers of Mathematics specialized professional association standards for mathematics teacher preparation.*

Conference Board of the Mathematical Sciences. (2001). *The mathematical education of teachers (MET).* American Mathematical Society and Mathematical Association of America.

Conference Board of the Mathematical Sciences (CBMS). (2012). *The mathematical education of teachers II (MET II).* American Mathematical Society and Mathematical Association of America.

Crespo, S. (2002). Praising and correcting: Prospective teachers investigate their teacherly talk. *Teaching and Teacher Education, 18*(6), 739–758. https://doi.org/10.1016/S0742-051X(02)00031-8

Crespo, S. (2003). Learning to pose mathematical problems: Exploring changes in preservice teachers' practices. *Educational Studies in Mathematics, 52*(3), 243–270. https://doi.org/10.1023/A:1024364304664

Crespo, S., & Nicol, C. (2003). Learning to investigate students' mathematical thinking: The role of student interviews [Paper presentation]. International Group for the Psychology of Mathematics Education Conference.

Darling-Hammond, L. (2006). Constructing 21st-century teacher education. *Journal of Teacher Education, 57*(3), 300–314.

Darling-Hammond, L. (2012). *Powerful teacher education: Lessons from exemplary programs.* Jossey-Bass.

Darling-Hammond, L. (2014). Strengthening clinical preparation: The holy grail of teacher education. *Peabody Journal of Education, 89*(4), 547–561

Deming, W. E. (1950). *Elementary principles of the statistical control of quality.* Japanese Union of Scientists and Engineers (JUSE).

Deming, W. E. (1993). *The new economics.* MIT Press.

Elementary Mathematics Specialists & Teacher Leader Project. (2012). *Engaging in the mathematical practices* (Look Fors). http://www.nctm.org/Conferences-and-Professional-Development/Principles-to-Actions-Toolkit/Resources/5-SMPLookFors/

Fennel, F. (1991). Diagnostic teaching, writing and mathematics. *Focus on Learning Problems in Mathematics, 13*(3), 39–50. https://www.questia.com/library/p408/focus-on-learning-problems-in-mathematics

Forzani, F.M. (2014). Understanding "core practices" and "practice-based" teacher education: Learning from the past. *Journal of Teacher Education, 65*(4), 357–368.

Gareis, C. R., & Grant, L. W. (2015). Assessment literacy for teacher candidates: A focused approach. *Teacher Educators' Journal, 2015*(1), 4–21.

Gleason, J., Livers, S.D., & Zelkowski, J. (2017). Mathematics Classroom Observation Protocol for Practices (MCOP^2): Validity and reliability. *Investigations in Mathematical Learning, 9*(3), 111–129.

Grossman, P., Hammerness, K., & McDonald, M. (2009). Redefining, redefining teaching, re-imagining teacher education. *Teachers and Teaching: Theory and Practice, 15,* 273–289.

Guskey, T. (2003). How classroom assessments improve learning. *Educational, School, and Counseling Psychology Faculty Publications, 9,* 7–11.

Hattie, J. (2011). Feedback in schools. In R. Sutton, M. J. Hornsey, & K. M. Douglas (Eds.), *Feedback: The communication of praise, criticism, and advice.* Peter Lang.

Hattie, J. (2009). *Teachers make a difference. What is the research evidence?* [Paper presentation]. The Australian Council for Educational Research Annual Conference on Building Teacher Quality, Melbourne.

Hattie, J., & Timperley, H. (2007). The power of feedback. *Review of Educational Research, 77*(1), 81–112.

Hattie, J., & Zierer, K. (2019). *Visible learning insights.* Taylor & Francis.

Hoffman, J. V., Wetzel, M. M., Maloch, B., Greeter, E., Taylor, L., DeJulia, S., & Vlach, S. K. (2015). What can we learn from studying the coaching interactions between cooperating teachers and preservice teachers? A literature review. *Teaching and Teacher Education, 52*(2015), 99–112.

Inside Mathematics. (2017). *9th & 10th grade math—properties of quadrilaterals.* http://www.insidemathematics.org/classroom-videos/public-lessons/9th-10th-grade-math-properties-ofquadrilaterals

Izadinia, M. (2015). A closer look at the role of mentor teachers in shaping preservice teachers' professional identity. *Teaching and Teacher Education, 52*(2015), 1–10.

Izadinia, M. (2016). Student teachers' and mentor teachers' perceptions and expectations of a mentoring relationship: Do they match or clash? *Professional Development in Education, 42*(3), 387–402.

Jansen, M. (2020). *Rough draft math: Revising to learn*. Stenhouse.

Janssen, F., Grossman, P., & Westbroek, H., (2015). Facilitating decomposition and recomposition in practice-based teacher education: The power of modularity. *Teaching and Teacher Education, 51*, 137–146.

Koestler, C., Felton-Koestler, M. D., Bieda, K., & Otten, S. (2013). *Connecting the NCTM process standards and the CCSSM practices*. National Council of Teachers of Mathematics.

Lawley, J., Moore, J., & Smajic, A. (2014). Effective communication between preservice and cooperating teachers, *The New Educator, 10*(2), 153-162.

Maletta, D., Yang, M., & Youssef, M. (2011*). Rubric-implementing Standards for Mathematical Practice*. Park City Mathematics Institute Visualizing Functions. https://projects.ias.edu/pcmi/hstp/resources/rubric/

Martin, W. G., & Gobstein, H. (2015). Generating a networked improvement community to improve secondary mathematics teacher preparation network leadership, organization, and operation. *Journal of Teacher Education, 66*(5), 482–493.

Mathematics Teacher Education Partnership. (2014). *Guiding principles for secondary mathematics teacher preparation programs*. Association of Public & Land-grant Universities.

National Council of Teachers of Mathematics. (2014). *Principles to actions: Ensuring mathematical success for all*.

National Council of Teachers of Mathematics. (2000). *Principles and standards for school mathematics*.

National Governors Association Center for Best Practices & Council of Chief State School Officers. (2010). *Common Core State Standards for Mathematics*. www.corestandards.org/Math

National Council for Accreditation of Teacher Education (NCATE) Blue Ribbon Panel on Clinical Preparation and Partnerships for Improved Student Learning. (2010). *Transforming teacher education through clinical practice: A national strategy to prepare effective teachers*.

Phillips, E., & Crespo, S. (1996, February). Developing written communication in mathematics. *For the Learning of Mathematics, 16*(1), 15–22. https://flm-journal.org

Pugalee, D.K. (2005). *Writing to develop mathematical understanding*. Christopher-Gordon.

Sarris, N. (2016). *Effective feedback for deeper learning*. Retrieved May 11, 2021, from https://www.activelylearn.com/post/effective-feedback-for-deeper-learning

Scheeler, M. C., Budin, S., & Markelz, A. (2016). The role of teacher preparation in promoting evidence-based practice in schools. *Learning Disabilities: A Contemporary Journal, 14*(2), 171–187.

Sears, R., Hopf, F., Torres-Ayala, A., Williams, C., & Skryzpek. L. (2019) Using Plan-Do-Study-Act cycles and interdisciplinary conversations to transform introductory mathematics courses, *PRIMUS, 29*(8), 881–902.

Shakman, K., Wogan, D., Rodriguez, S., Boyce, J., & Shaver, D. (2020). *Continuous improvement in education: A toolkit for schools and districts* (REL 2021–014). U.S. Department of Education, Institute of Education Sciences, Nation-al Center for Education Evaluation and Regional Assistance, Regional Educational Laboratory Northeast & Islands. http://ies.ed.gov/ncee/edlabs

Slavit, D., & Nelson, T. H. (2009). Collaborative teacher inquiry as a tool for building theory on the development and use of rich mathematical tasks. *Journal of Mathematics Teacher Education, 13*(3), 201–221.

Slick, S. K. (1998a). A university supervisor negotiates territory and status. *Journal of Teacher Education*, *49*(4), 306–315.

Slick, S. K. (1998b). The university supervisor: A disenfranchised outsider. *Teaching and Teacher Education*, *14*(8), 821–834.

Stein, M. K., Remillard, J., & Smith, M. S. (2008). How curriculum influences student learning. In F. K. Lester (Ed.), *Second handbook of research on mathematics teaching and learning* (pp. 319–369). Information Age Publishing.

Stein, M. K., Smith, M. S., Henningsen, M., & Silver, E. A. (2000). *Implementing standards-based mathematics instruction*: A casebook for professional development. Teachers College Press.

Strutchens, M. E., Sears, R., & Zelkowski, J. (2020). Improving clinical experiences for secondary mathematics teacher candidates. In W. G. Martin, B. R. Lawler, A. E. Litchka, & W. M. Smith (Eds.). *The Mathematics Teacher Education Partnership: The power of a networked improvement community to transform secondary mathematics teacher preparation* (pp. 199–210). Information Age Publishing.

Tatto, M. T. (1998). The influence of teacher education on teachers' beliefs about purposes of education, roles, and practice. *Journal of Teacher Education, 49*(1), 66–77.

Tatto, M. T. (2018). *The mathematical education of secondary teachers*. In M. T. Tatto, M. Rodriguez, W. Smith, M. Reckase, & K. Bankov (Eds.), *Explore the mathematical education of teachers using TEDS-M Data* (pp. 409–450). Springer.

Tichnor-Wagner, A., Wachen, J., Cannata, M., & Cohen-Vogel, L. (2017). Continuous improvement in the public school context: Understanding how educators respond to plan-do-study-act cycles. *Journal of Educational Change, 18*(4), 465–494.

Wiggins, G. (2012). 7 keys to effective feedback. *Educational Leadership, 70*(1), 11–16.

Wilson, C., & Anthony, H. G. (2020, May). *Preservice math teachers' perceptions of posing geometry problems to rural high school students* [Paper presentation]. The Sixteenth International Congress of Qualitative Inquiry, Urbana-Champaign, IL.

Yow, J. A., Waller, P., & Edwards, B. (2018). A national effort to integrate field experiences into secondary mathematics methods courses. In T. Hodges & A. Baum (Eds.), *The handbook on research of field-based teacher education* (pp. 395–419). IGI Global.

Zelkowski, J., Campbell, T. G., Moldavan, A. M., & Gleason, J. (in press). Maximizing teacher candidate performances based on internal program measures: Program design considerations. *Proceedings of the 10th Annual Mathematics Teacher Education–Partnership Conference*. Association of Public Land-Grant Universities.

Zelkowski, J., Yow, J., Ellis, M. E., & Waller, P. (2020). Engaging mentor teachers with teacher candidates during methods courses in clinical settings. In W. G. Martin, B. R. Lawler, A. E. Litchka, & W. M. Smith (Eds.), *The Mathematics Teacher Education Partnership: The power of a networked improvement community to transform secondary mathematics teacher preparation* (pp. 211–234). Information Age Publishing.

Zeichner, K. (2010). Rethinking the connections between campus courses and field experiences in college- and university-based teacher education. *Journal of Teacher Education, 57*(1), 89–99.

ACKNOWLEDGMENTS

The authors of this chapter wish to thank the following mentor teachers for their mentorship of teacher candidates and participation in this work.

Hannah Adams – McAdory High School

Kim Anderson – Hillcrest High School

Bailey Avina – Alberta School of Arts

Candace Baker – Sipsey Valley Middle School

Jennifer Boyd – Hillcrest Middle School

David Dai – Barton Academy for Advanced World Studies

Andy Hamric – Northside High School

Nathan Kenny – Hillcrest High School

Mariah Simmons – Campbell High School

Melinda Williams – Hillcrest Middle School

CHAPTER 28

PUSHING OUR COMFORT ZONE

A Journey Through
Diverse Clinical Experiences

**Johannah D. Baugher,
Linda Gray Smith, and Joseph P. Haughey**
Northwest Missouri State University

ABSTRACT

Constructed with principles of *The Change Theory*, *The Learning Zone Model*, and *The Mindset Theory*, this book chapter examines a teacher candidate's journey of clinical practice in the School of Education at Northwest Missouri State University. Aligned with *The Guiding Conceptual Model for Clinical Practice* authored by the *American Association of Colleges for Teacher Education* (AACTE), this chapter highlights the value of mutually beneficial school and university partnerships alongside diverse clinical settings. The context of the university is further examined, along with key research findings and implications for future clinical experiences.

Preparing Quality Teachers:
Advances in Clinical Practice, pp. 609–626

INTRODUCTION

United in the common vision to serve as a catalyst for education excellence by preparing P–12 professional educators who apply best practices to positively impact learning, members of the School of Education at Northwest Missouri State University are committed to these ideas (Northwest Missouri State University, 2020c). Northwest's Professional Education Unit (PEU), which includes faculty from Northwest's School of Education as well as content faculty from other schools and departments in the university, further believes in seven guiding principles that all Northwest educators and teacher candidates alike should strive for: (a) exhibiting content knowledge; (b) increasing pedagogical knowledge; (c) using assessment to improve learning outcomes; d) demonstrating professional behaviors; (e) enhancing learning through the effective use of technology; (f) cultivating dispositions; and (g) and embracing diversity (Northwest Missouri State University, 2020c).

In this chapter, we provide a description of clinical practice at Northwest Missouri State University. Efforts to plan and facilitate a range of clinical experiences for our teacher candidates equips them to be career ready from day one and equally prepared to meet the needs of all learners that might cross the door's threshold into their classroom. Just as Northwest is committed to students' success in the university's mission statement, "every student—every day," we desire for our teacher candidates to be richly prepared to meet their individual students' needs every day in a manner that is innovative, growth-oriented, and agile, and the clinical experiences detailed in this chapter foster those practices (Northwest Missouri State University, 2020c).

THEORETICAL FRAMEWORKS

Change Theory

Change theory informed the process used in the redesign of School of Education coursework and clinical practice at Northwest Missouri State University. Michael Fullan (2006) wrote of the foundations needed to support effective change. A focus on motivation over a period of time and the building of knowledge and skills to create the change are fundamental. Meaningful change requires purposeful thinking, persistence, and comfort in seasons of ambiguity (Bolman & Deal, 2008). Furthermore, when navigating times of fluidity, all members of the organization must understand that change is messy and in order to navigate it, an adaptive culture reflective of shared responsibility, critical reflection, authentic leadership, and a commitment to continued learning is paramount (Heifetz et al., 2009; Northouse, 2013; Senge, 1990).

As an organization recognizes the need to change, a thorough knowledge and holistic vision of the change process is essential. Without an understanding of the process of change, the reform is likely to fail (Fullan et al., 2005). Categorized in three stages: unfreezing, moving, and freezing, Burnes and Bargal (2017), further cite the work of Kurt Lewin (Cummings et al., 2016) in his study of social change. Lewin (1947a/b) wrote of three stages of change. The trajectory from *Unfreezing* challenges the organization to rethink the status quo, break from current tradition, and offer a proposal to chart a new course. It is in this stage which most resistance to the change initiative can occur. In the *Moving* stage, the change process is initiated and continues until completion. Lastly, in the *Freezing* stage, the change is institutionalized and slowly becomes the new status quo. As the season of change draws to a close, the new reality within the organization is solidified, catalyzing practice of adaptability among all stakeholders (Heifetz & Laurie, 1997/2011).

THE LEARNING ZONE MODEL

Credited to Tom Senninger, *The Learning Zone Model* further illustrates an individual's transport from their relative comfort zone to their learning zone, as a result of various experiences (ThemPra Social Pedagogy, 2020). This idea, inspired from leaders in the business industry, further extends this model's framework to include four layers: comfort zone, fear zone, learning zone, and growth zone (The Wealth Hike, 2020).

Security and comfortability are the two characteristics most reflective of the *comfort zone*, where situations, experiences, and interactions are of the norm (Levi, 2013). Intrinsic battles of self-confidence and external reliance on others' opinions influence and/or squelch individual behavior in the *fear zone*. Development of new confidence and the tenacity to face problems and related challenges head-on build the *learning zone*. And finally, goal-setting behaviors and heightened levels of motivation and determination are sown deeply in the *growth zone* (The Wealth Hike, 2020).

MINDSET THEORY

Authored by Carol Dweck, *The Mindset Theory* examines mindset principles held by individuals to guide one's actions and behavior. Characteristic of the *growth mindset*, Dweck (2015) closely investigated how students' perception of their own abilities influenced both motivation and achievement, further identifying patterned behaviors among students to seek out new strategies and feedback during times of unsuccess. Dweck (2017) further claims that "when entire [organizations] embrace a growth mindset, their employees report feeling far more empowered and committed; they also receive far greater organizations support for collaboration and innovation" (p. 2).

In an attempt to link theory with practice, programmatic redesign rich in clinical practice enables teacher candidates to navigate ambiguity in new educational contexts and work to move from their relative comfort zones to the growth zone as authentic learning experiences unfold. In the same manner, partnership opportunities that emerge through the scheduling of diverse clinical experiences further support innovative, shared learning initiatives (Bronfenbrenner, 1979). When these principles merge, teacher candidates are fully prepared to teach all learners in a variety of settings, while continuing to draw upon the expertise from those within their eco-logical systems (Bronfenbrenner, 1979). Once committed to the growth mindset, the vision for moving forward is clearer, understanding that is each learning opportunity is a step in the journey.

THEORETICAL SYNTHESIS

Integration of *Change Theory*, the *Learning Zone Model*, and *Mindset Theory* enabled intentional curricular redesign to occur within the School of Education. School leaders and faculty alike were committed to a unified investment in a common vision, and that desire was harvested in action steps that redefined program coursework and clinical practices to benefit teacher candidates. While navigating seasons of change can be an arduous process, redesign efforts began with the end in mind (Covey, 2013) and sought to encourage candidates to move beyond their comfort zones to experience new learning. Just as members of the School of Education embodied a growth mindset, that same expectation was held for our teacher candidates across all programming and clinical practices. Growth is the result of learn-ing, and learning can only occur when we allow ourselves to be changed through thought, action, and practice.

LITERATURE REVIEW

AACTE's Guiding Conceptual Model for Clinical Practice

The *AACTE Clinical Practice Commission Report* (2018) emphasizes the bidirectional relationship between high-quality clinical practice and mutually beneficial partnerships. In our attempt to infuse "clinical preparation throughout every facet of teacher education" (p. 5), the process of curricular redesign parallels *The Guiding Conceptual Model* authored by the *American Association of Colleges for Teacher Education* (AACTE), as well as the teacher preparation standards outlined by the *Council for the Accreditation of Educator Preparation* (CAEP, 2019) and the *Association for Advancing Quality in Educator Preparation* (AAQEP) (2019).

This conceptual model details high-quality clinical practice threaded throughout six steps: *Introductory Courses*, emphasizing pedagogy and human development; *Foundations*, including theoretical lens of philosophical, historical, and social factors; *Human Development*, focusing on developmental stages and cognitive development of PK–12 students; *Methods I*, courses with a focus on instructional strategies with feedback from university- and school-based educators; *Methods II*, which deepens the instructional practices of candidates; and an *Internship*, under the direct supervision of mentor teachers and University supervisors (AACTE Clinical Practice Brief, 2018 p. 10). In the table which follows, university courses are aligned with individual steps of the conceptual model and linked clinical practices are detailed as imbedded throughout programs (Table 28.1).

Across programs within the School of Education, clinical practice opportunities aligned with the model's named steps are afforded across a four-year program to teacher candidates in rural, urban, and suburban settings, reflective of racial, ethnic, economic, and exceptional diversities. Program completers graduate with greater than 550 hours of supervised, clinical practice throughout their program of study. Embedded early throughout candidates' first three academic semesters, teacher candidates

Table 28.1

Crosswalk Between AACTE the Guiding Conceptual Model, University Courses, and Linked Clinical Practices

AACTE The Guiding Conceptual Model Step	University Courses	Linked Clinical Practices
Introductory Courses	Ecology of Teaching and Learning Professional Learning Community I	Education majors at all levels observe a School Board meeting at the local PK–12 school district. Education majors at all levels attend a Poverty Simulation. Education majors at all levels observe a Parent-Teacher Conference.

(Table continued on next page)

Table 28.1 (Continued)

Crosswalk Between AACTE the Guiding Conceptual Model,
University Courses, and Linked Clinical Practices

AACTE The Guiding Conceptual Model Step	University Courses	Linked Clinical Practices
Foundations	Developmental Foundations	Education majors at all levels spend a day in a low-socioeconomic school district visiting elementary, middle and secondary schools.
	Introduction to Curriculum and Instruction	
	Principles of Assessment	Education majors at all levels observe theoretical constructs including: constructivism, behaviorism, and maturationism at a partner PK–12 school.
	Professional Learning Community II	
	Teaching Is Communication	
		Education majors at all levels observe teacher-student communication strategies at a partner PK–12 school.
		Education majors at all levels interview a teacher at a partner PK–12 district about assessment practices.
		Education majors at all levels observe strategies used to engage students at a partner PK–12 school.
Human Development	Developmental Foundations	Education majors at all levels observe developmental characteristics of children and adolescents at a partner PK–12 school.
	Inclusive Classrooms	
	Professional Learning Community III	
		Education majors at all levels teach a mini-lesson to students in the laboratory school on campus.
		Education majors at all levels observe a focus student in a partner PK–12 school and notice accommodations and modifications that are used to meet his/her needs.

(Table continued on next page)

Table 28.1 (Continued)

Crosswalk Between AACTE the Guiding Conceptual Model,
University Courses, and Linked Clinical Practices

AACTE The Guiding Conceptual Model Step	University Courses	Linked Clinical Practices
Methods I	Designing Integrated Curriculum I	Elementary education majors create and implement a "Math Family Night" in which teacher candidates create math activities for elementary students and their families.
	Literacy in the Elementary School	
	Social Studies in the Elementary School	
	Delivering Integrated Curriculum I	Elementary education majors create and implement a "Science Family Night" in which teacher candidates create science activities and their families.
	Professional Learning Community IV	
	Designing Integrated Curriculum II	Elementary education majors teach a lesson in which literacy and social studies are infused with the arts and movement in a partner PK–12 school.
	Math in the Elementary School	
	Science in the Elementary School	Elementary and secondary education and special education students team to teach a lesson in a high-poverty school in an urban area.
	Delivering Integrated Curriculum II	
	Professional Learning Community V	
	Developmental Foundations of Adolescent Literacy	
	Classroom Management Techniques	
Methods II	Designing Intervention and Assessment	Elementary education majors collaborate with teachers in a partner PK-12 school to create and implement a Project-Based Learning Unit.
	Mathematics Assessment and Intervention	
	Literacy Assessment and Intervention	Elementary education majors spend a semester in a residency practicum experience in a partner PK–12 district.

(Table continued on next page)

Table 28.1 (Continued)

Crosswalk Between AACTE the Guiding Conceptual Model, University Courses, and Linked Clinical Practices

AACTE The Guiding Conceptual Model Step	University Courses	Linked Clinical Practices
Methods II	Professional Learning Community VI	Elementary education majors collaborate with teachers in a partner PK–12 school to create and implement a Project-Based Learning Unit.
	Implementing/Practicum I	
	Professional Learning Community VI	Elementary education majors spend a semester in a residency practicum experience in a partner PK–12 district.
	Residency Practicum	
	Professional Learning Community VII	
		Middle and secondary majors spend a semester in a practicum experience observing and teaching in a partner PK–12 school.
Internship	Directed Student Teaching	Elementary, middle and secondary students spend a semester in student teaching.
	Professional Capstone	
	Professional Learning Community VIII	

Adapted from Dimmitt, T., Singleton, E., Gray Smith, L., Wall, T., & Wood, S. (2018). *Redesigned partnerships as a result of redesigned educational preparation programs.* Presented at the meeting of The Teacher Education Council of State Colleges and Universities (TECSCU) and The Renaissance Group (TRG).

actively participate in a range of clinical experiences in coursework which includes: ecology of teaching and learning, developmental foundations of education, introduction to curriculum and instruction, teaching is communication, as well as inclusive classrooms and positive environments. Infusion of such experiences would be impossible without supportive partnerships that exist with PK–12 school districts throughout the Northwest region of Missouri and beyond.

Mutually Beneficial, School and University Partnerships

Through collaborative, intentional design between the School of Education and nine PK–12 school districts, all clinical practice opportunities are defined, allowing the needs of both entities to be successfully met and learning fostered (Bruffee, 1999; Chiariello, 2018; Leslie, 2011; Reischl et al., 2017). Beginning in 2015, advisory council meetings twice a year provided opportunities for input from superintendents of schools, PK–12 educators, university faculty, and teacher candidates. The process remains ongoing as programs evolve. As a result, clinical practice opportunities reflect shared responsibilities between the Educator Preparation Program (EPP) and district partners in the development of teacher candidates, which harvest a mutually beneficial relationship (AACTE Clinical Practice Brief, 2018; Bronfenbrenner, 1979; Hammerness et al., 2017; Zeichner et al., 2015).

In order for such partnerships to persist, the relationship must be viewed not as an isolated event (Zeichner et al., 2015), but instead a "shared sense of culture" (Gill, 2010, p. 5), where learning benefits both institutions (Nobles et al., 2012). When partnerships disadvantage the other, are not fully committed to or invested in the shared experience, they are not likely to continue and frequently dissolve (Holen & Yunk, 2014; Stephens & Boldt, 2004).

Heckman and Mantle-Bromley (2004) further claim that such partnerships have the potential to influence positive change in both institutions, enriching both teaching and learning. Berman (2004) advocates that school district and university partnerships aid recruitment processes, as districts seek to hire teachers who know, understand, and respect the culture of their organization. Similarly, universities desire for their candidates to teach in districts that showcase mutual respect for their institutional culture, too. Through a range of shared, clinical practice opportunities, teacher candidates are better prepared to teach in any diverse, educational setting.

Diverse, Clinical Practice Settings

Experience is an influential teacher for candidates throughout their program. The value of clinical practice in a variety of diverse educational settings is a tool for both teaching and learning (Glassman, 2001; Marchitello & Trinidad, 2019). During the process of clinical practice, teacher candidates can reflect on direct experiences, while transferring that information to clarify and assimilate new knowledge to existing concepts.

Teacher candidates must be prepared to exercise cultural competence in their work with students and families from various backgrounds and experiences (Glassman, 2001). Educator preparation programs must provide candidates with opportunities to better understand the experiences of students from all community contexts and diversities (Banks et al., 2007). Doing so enables candidates to further understand the context of the communities' surrounding schools and the impact that limited resources and other societal challenges present within those communities may have on the internal school environment and student population (Onore & Gildin, 2010).

By participating in the range of diverse clinical practice experiences offered, teacher candidates are prepared to effectively teach in rural, racially homogenous, economically diverse, affluent, suburban, impoverished, and urban settings. At Northwest Missouri State University, the School of Education prepares teacher candidates for their future career immediately, and these diverse, clinical practice settings are one avenue by which that is achieved.

CONTEXTUAL SUMMARY

Northwest is a co-educational, primarily residential four-year state university that enrolls 6,857 students from 44 states: 5,654 undergraduate and 1,197 graduate/specialist (as of fall 2018). The university touts achievements that include a graduation rate in the 89th percentile of its national peer group (Northwest Missouri State University, 2020a). Northwest also boasts career placement rates of 95.6% for undergraduates and 96.4% for graduate students (Northwest Missouri State University, 2020b). As part of the University's retention strategy focused on affordability, Northwest includes textbooks and a laptop in its tuition, which saves students an estimated $7,300 over four years. Northwest also offers 1,200 student employment positions, allowing students to build professional skills through its internationally benchmarked student employment program (Northwest Missouri State University, 2020a).

Though the rural 19 county Northwest Missouri area lacks significant racial and ethnic diversity, the university prides itself, nonetheless, on fostering an increasingly racially and ethnically diverse student body: 1,316 students, or 19% of the student population, identify with underrepresented groups or hail from countries outside the United States. The university established its Office of Diversity, Equity, and Inclusion in spring 2016 to promote racial harmony, campus diversity, and physical and educational accessibility to give all students opportunities for success. Northwest's 219 underrepresented domestic first-time students in the fall of 2018 represented the third-largest total in the university's history and a 14% increase from the previous fall (Northwest Missouri State University, 2020c).

Northwest's total minority enrollment in the fall of 2018 was 879 students, which was up more than six percent from the previous fall and represents almost thirteen percent of the student body. The university's enrollment includes 437 international students, who represent six percent of Northwest's student body. They hail from 37 different countries, the majority from India, Nepal, South Korea, and Nigeria. Northwest also prides itself on being an LGBT-ally campus where students of all sexual orientations and gender identities feel at home (Northwest Missouri State University, 2020c).

Summary of Teacher Candidates and Programs

The School of Education serves approximately 1,500 students primarily from Missouri, Nebraska, and Iowa across a variety of undergraduate and graduate programs. Northwest offers several undergraduate certification programs in early childhood (B–3), elementary (1–6), middle (5–9), secondary (9–12), and K–12. Middle and secondary programs cover a diverse range of content areas, which support area school districts' needs for high-quality teachers: agriculture, art, biology, business, chemistry, English, health, math, music (vocal and instrumental), science, social studies, Spanish, and speech and theatre. Northwest additionally offers numerous graduate-level certification programs; these include programs in educational leadership, school counseling, reading, elementary mathematics specialist, special education, and initial, postbaccalaureate certification programs in middle, secondary and K–12 content areas (Northwest Missouri State University, 2020c).

APPROACHES TO CLINICAL PRACTICE: THE NORTHWEST WAY

Introduction to Clinical Practices at Northwest

Teacher candidates' journey through the School of Education is equitably divided into three phases: Phase I, Phase 2, and Phase 3. Likened in the same way, these phases distinguish early, mid-level, and culminating clinical practices which run parallel to a range of diverse, field experiences which afford candidates with rich opportunities to observe and participate in diverse, educational settings that reflect rural, suburban, and urban contexts. Not only do the teacher candidates participate in field experiences within the 35-mile radius of the university in a rural setting, but they also take part in an additional set of clinical practice opportunities during their third and fourth years of coursework in urban school contexts (Smith et al., 2017).With more than 15 partner school districts, teacher candidates complete clinical experiences in a variety of settings throughout the Northwest region of the state of Missouri, exceeding completion of 550 hours of supervised, clinical practice. In Figure 28.1, the phases are further introduced and briefly described.

Figure 28.1

Phases of Clinical Practice in the School of Education at NWMSU

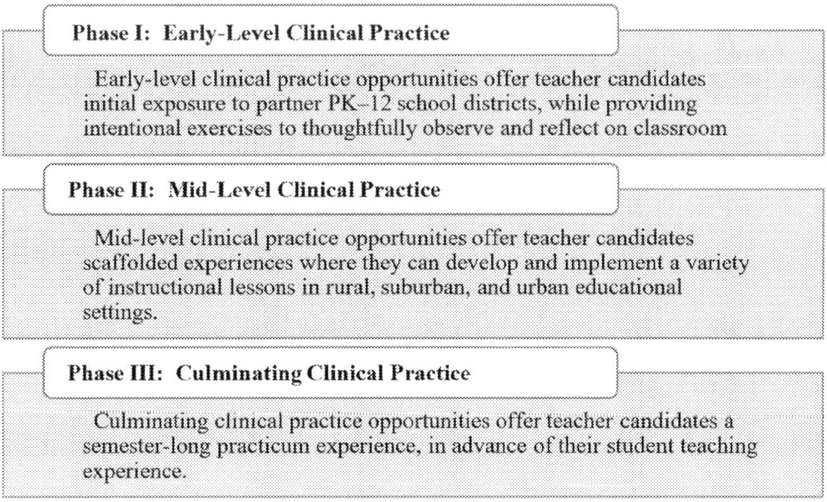

Phase I: Early-Level Clinical Practice

Early-level clinical practice opportunities offer teacher candidates initial exposure to partner PK–12 school districts, while providing intentional exercises to thoughtfully observe and reflect on classroom

Phase II: Mid-Level Clinical Practice

Mid-level clinical practice opportunities offer teacher candidates scaffolded experiences where they can develop and implement a variety of instructional lessons in rural, suburban, and urban educational settings.

Phase III: Culminating Clinical Practice

Culminating clinical practice opportunities offer teacher candidates a semester-long practicum experience, in advance of their student teaching experience.

Early-Level Clinical Practice

Infused within early-level field experiences, all education majors are given the opportunity to observe an official school board meeting at a local, PK–2 school district, participate in an online, poverty simulation exercise (Games for Change, 2020), and witness an authentic, parent-teacher conference. Additional field experiences to further expose candidates to pedagogical concepts, principles of human development, and theoretical constructs include: a day-long observation experience at the elementary, middle, and secondary levels in a low socioeconomic school district; observation of theoretical perspectives to include constructivism, behaviorism, and maturationism at a partner PK-12 school; and observation of teacher-student communication strategies, assessment practices, and engagement strategies at a partner PK–12 school district.

Teacher candidates at all levels further observe developmental characteristics of children and adolescents, identify a focus student alongside appropriate accommodations and modifications implemented to further meet the individual student's needs, and complete a minimum of 15 hours in their work with persons with disabilities. While individual course requirements vary, candidates can expect to participate in a minimum of four, 75-minute clinical experiences at their assigned school district.

Mid-Level Clinical Practice

As teacher candidates are introduced to pedagogical concepts in Phase 1 coursework, an appropriate sequel would be application of those practices. In Phase 2, or mid-level clinical practice, candidates complete a series of methods coursework, along with clinical experiences which dovetail course content. Examples of such experiences could include, but are not limited to: planning and implementing content area-specific activities for area students; development and implementation of interdisciplinary lessons which celebrate infusion of the arts (Duma & Silverstein, 2018; Silverstein & Layne, 2010) with core subject areas; implementation of a secondary lesson in a high-poverty, urban school district; implementation of a collaborative, project-based unit with the partner school district and teacher candidates; and, delivery of a two-day, inquiry-based social justice lesson with elementary-aged students in a rural, school district.

Encouraged to extend their strategy toolbox and guided by professional feedback, teacher candidates participate in additional field experiences which further educate them on the implementation of models such as Multi-Tier Systems of Support (MTSS). Candidates have opportunities to observe those models in an urban setting. Similarly, candidates collaborate with practicing teachers in a partner school district to develop and implement a seven-week project-based learning unit. These experiences effectively scaffold candidates' learning and thus, development in preparation for Phase 3, which encompasses all culminating clinical practice.

Culminating Clinical Practice

As part of Phase 3, culminating clinical practice, teacher candidates apply theory to practice as they are fully immersed in a classroom environment. Mentored by university supervisors and seasoned, classroom teachers, elementary and special education candidates fulfill requirements for a semester-long, on-site residency practicum. On the other hand, early childhood, middle, secondary, and K–12 candidates complete an on-campus practicum. This includes a week-long, 45-hour field experience at, for what many, becomes their culminating student teaching placement. These practicums serve as a prelude to their student teaching experience. Following the practicum, candidates complete student teaching. When placing teacher candidates, placements are organized within four geographic hubs. Organizing it in this way provides timely support to teacher candidates from university-trained supervisors while minimizing travel.

DESCRIPTIVE CASE

In the fall of 2018, Northwest placed 537 first- and second-year education majors in local community districts for clinical observation and early-level clinical practice. Faculty liaisons collaborated with PK–12 teachers in the field experience sites to design experiences aligned with coursework delivered in the Educator Preparation Program. Urban clinical experience sites were identified, and mutually beneficial partnerships were developed with the districts. Teacher candidates boarded university-provided buses for the 110-mile journey to the field experience sites. The experiences provided candidates with opportunities to interact with marginalized, underrepresented populations of individuals from diverse ethnicities, systemic or concentrated poverty, and English-language learners.

Such field experiences can change the perceptions of teacher candidates who participate in them. Involvement in these field experiences produced significant changes in how teacher candidates viewed their ability to make a difference and in their beliefs about diversity (Smith et al., 2017). After the urban field experiences candidates were: (a) more likely to use curricular materials and instructional practices fostering diversity, (b) more aware of students' experiences and cultural backgrounds, and (c) noted diverse schools were "very different" than those they attended (Smith et al., 2017, p. 6).

A review of the teacher candidates' reflections and post-survey responses identified three themes that were used to improve the Educator Preparation Program so candidates would be prepared to teach diverse learners. The themes focused on the importance of relationships between teachers and students; the need for differentiated instruction in response to student experiences; and the acknowledgement that diversity enriches student learning (Smith et al., 2017, p. 7).

A close look at the partnership developed with one school district with multiple buildings provided viewpoints about the university's partnership with the PK–12 district. Multiple themes emerged when examining the qualitative data, but some themes were more predominant:

- Evolution of a mutually beneficial partnership through changes in perception
- Need for intentional, early, authentic, and diverse clinical experiences
- Teacher recruitment opportunities
- Mutually beneficial partnership gains and opportunities

The mutually beneficial partnership is evidenced in the increase of the number of teacher candidates from the university who were hired over a six-year period once the early and mid-level field experiences began in partnership with the PK–12 district (Farnan et al., 2019).

IMPLICATIONS FOR FUTURE, CLINICAL PRACTICE

Clinical practice is an integral piece in the quality preparation of teachers. While extensive planning, effort, and fiscal resources are necessary to implement each field experience, clinical practice is easily justified.

The value of relationships that are cultivated with each new and ongoing partnership cannot be quantified. Supportive partnerships between district teachers and university faculty signify a complete partnership, one where teaching and learning occur in both organizations as a direct result of the paired collaboration. This, in part, enables for deeper and richer partnerships to be sown.

Despite the cost values associated with such clinical experiences, clinical practice is further justified in its impact on teacher candidates and their growth. Exposing teacher candidates to a range of diverse, educational settings throughout early, mid-level, and culminating programmatic phases effectively prepares them to teach in a variety of contexts following graduation.

While journeying through diverse, clinical experiences can often begin as a time of ambiguity, rich learning comes by pushing the comfort zone and embracing the newness during seasons of growth.

RECOMMENDATIONS FOR INITIATING RICH, CLINICAL PRACTICE

Drawing from our collective experience with clinical practice, the following are recommendations we would offer to those cultivating new partnerships, with a like context. First, efforts must be made to intentionally cultivate relationships with PK–12 school districts including both those districts who are geographically close to the university's location, as well as those that would offer diversification from the university's context. Equally important is the exchange of open dialogue between university and district partners. Genuinely seek their input and feedback, while turning those ideas into tangible action steps.

In addition to collaborating with your school district partners, draw upon the knowledge of other educator preparation programs, and learn from their clinical practice experiences. Through seasons of change, commit to periods of dynamic revision, knowing that adjustments will be made as needs change. Engage in data-based decision-making to guide further revision and improvement processes. Take time to collect and analyze multiple forms of data, both qualitative and quantitative, as values are only as effective as the story which they tell, and vice versa. These recommendations require a responsive attitude as you, like your teacher candidates, push your comfort zone.

REFERENCES

American Association of Colleges for Teacher Education. (2018). *A pivot toward clinical practice, its lexicon, and the renewal of educator preparation.* http://www.nysed.gov/common/nysed/files/cpceexecutivesummary-accessible.pdf

Association for Advancing Quality in Educator Preparation. (2018). *AAQEP expectations framework.* https://www.aaqep.org/uploads/1/0/9/3/109302791/aaqep_expectations_framework_posted_january_2018.pdf

Banks, J., Au, K., Ball, A. F., Bell, P., Gordon, E., Gutierrez, K., Brice-Heath, S., Lee, C. Mahiri, D. J., Nasir, N., Valdes, G., & Zhou, M. (2007). *Learning in and out of school in diverse environments: Life-long, life-wide, life-deep.* University of Washington Center for Multicultural Education.

Berman, S. (2004). *Effective recruitment and induction into the school district.* In J. I. Goodlad & T. J. McMannon (Eds.), *The teaching career* (p. 125). Teachers College Press.

Bolman, L. G., & Deal, T. E. (2008). *Reframing organizations: Artistry, choice, and leadership* (4th ed.). Jossey-Bass.

Bronfenbrenner, U. (1979). *The ecology of human development.* Harvard University Press.

Burnes, B., & Bargal, D. (2017). Kurt Lewin: 70 years on. *Journal of Change Management, 17,* 91–100. https://doi.org/10.1080/14697017.2017.1299371

Chiariello, E. (2018). What matters in literacy education: Emerging priorities for 2018. *Literacy Today,* 23–28.

Council for the Accreditation of Educator Preparation. (2019). *Standard 2: Clinical partnerships and practice.* http://caepnet.org/standards/standard-2

Covey, S. R. (2013). *The 7 habits of highly effective people: Powerful lessons in personal change.* Simon & Schuster.

Cummings, S., Bridgman, T., & Brown, K. G. (2016). Unfreezing change as three steps: Rethinking Kurt Lewin's legacy for change management. *Human Relations, 69*(1), 33–60.

Dimmitt, T., Singleton, E., Gray Smith, L., Wall, T., & Wood, S. (2018). *Redesigned partnerships as a result of redesigned educational preparation programs* [Paper Presentation] The meeting of The Teacher Education Council of State Colleges and Universities (TECSCU) and The Renaissance Group (TRG).

Duma, A. L., & Silverstein, L. B. (2018). Arts integration: A creative pathway for teaching. *Educational Leadership,* 55–59.

Dweck, C. (2015). *Carol Dweck revisits the 'growth mindset'*. https://portal.cornerstonesd.ca/group/yyd5jtk/Documents/Carol%20Dweck%20Growth%20Mindsets.pdf

Dweck, C. (2017). *What having a "growth mindset" actually means*. https://leadlocal.global/wp-content/uploads/2016/12/Dweck-What-Having-a-%E2%80%9CGrowth-Mindset%E2%80%9D-Actually-Means-HBR.pdf

Farnan, S., Seeger, V., Smith, L. G., & McBride, M. (2019). "What's in it for us?" How a mutually beneficial partnership changes the landscape of educational practice. *Planning and Changing, 49*(1/2), 20–36.

Fullan, M. (2006). *Change theory a force for school improvement* (Centre for Strategic Education. Seminar Series Paper n. 157). http://michaelfullan.ca/wp-content/uploads/2016/06/13396072630.pdf

Fullan, M., Cuttress, C., & Kilcher, A. (2005). Eight forces for leaders of change: The presence of the core concepts does not guarantee success, but their absence ensures failure. *Journal of Staff Development, 26*(4), 54–58.

Games for Change. (2020). *Spent*. http://www.gamesforchange.org/game/spent/

Glassman, M. (2001). Dewey and Vygotsky: Society, experience, and inquiry in educational practice. *Educational Researcher, 30*(4), 3–14.

Hammerness, K., MacPherson, A., Macdonald, M., Roditi, H., & Curtis-Bey, L. (2017). What does it take to sustain a productive partnership in education? *Phi Delta Kappan, 99*(1), 15–20.

Heckman, P. E., & Mantle-Bromley, C. (2004). *Toward renewal in school-university partnerships*. In J. I. Goodlad & T. J. McMannon (Eds.), *The teaching career* (pp. 82–83). Teachers College Press.

Heifetz, R., Grashow, A., & Linsky, M. (2009). *The practice of adaptive leadership* Harvard Business Press.

Hiefetz, R. A., & Laurie, D. L. (2011). What makes a leader? In *HBR's 10 must reads on leadership*. Harvard Business Review Press. (Originally work published 1997)

Holen, M. C., & Yunk, D. C. (2014). Benefits of 25 years of school district-university partnerships to improve teacher preparation and advance school renewal. *Educational Considerations, 42*(1). https://doi.org/10.4148/0146-9282.1045

Leslie, D. (2011) Seeking symmetry in a school-university partnership: University of Chicago and Chicago Public Schools—a collaborative approach to developing models and tools for professional development and teacher preparation. *Planning and Changing, 42*(1–2), 120–154.

Levi, D. J. (2013). *Group dynamics for teams* (4th ed.). SAGE.

Lewin, K. (1947a). Frontiers in group dynamics. *Human Relations, 1*(1), 5–41.

Lewin, K. (1947b). Frontiers in group dynamics. *Human Relations, 1*(2), 143–153.

Marchitello, M., & Trinidad, J. (2019). *Preparing teachers for diverse schools: Lessons from minority serving institutions*. https://bellwethereducation.org/sites/default/files/Preparing%20Teachers%20for%20Diverse%20Schools_Bellwether.pdf

Nobles, S., Dredger, K., & Gerheart, M. D. (2012). Collaboration beyond the classroom walls: Deepening learning for students, preservice teachers, teachers, and professors. *Contemporary Issues in Technology & Teacher Education, 12*, 343–354.

Northouse, P. G. (2013). *Leadership: Theory and practice* (6th ed.). SAGE.

Northwest Missouri State University. (2020a). *Facts*. https://www.nwmissouri.edu/facts/

Northwest Missouri State University. (2020b). *Career services*. https://www.nwmissouri.edu/career/Post-Grad-Data.htm

Northwest Missouri State University. (2020c). *School of Education*. https://www.nwmissouri.edu/education/

Onore, O., & Gildin, B. (2010). Preparing urban teachers as public professionals through a university-community partnership. *Teacher Education Quarterly* *37*(3), 27–44.

Reischl, C. H., Khasnabis, D. & Karr, K. (2017). Cultivating a school-university partnership for teacher learning. *Phi Delta Kappan, 98*(80), 48–53.

Senge, P. (1990). *The fifth discipline: The art and practice of the learning organization*. Doubleday.

Silverstein, L. B., & Layne, S. (2010). Defining arts integration. *The Kennedy Center Arts Edge*, 1–10.

Smith, L. G., Farnan, S., Seeger, V., Wall, T. J., & Kiene, D. (2017). Teacher candidate perceptions of urban field experiences. *Educational Renaissance, 6*, 1–16.

Stephens, D., & Boldt, G. (2004). School/university partnerships: Rhetoric, reality, and intimacy. *Phi Delta Kappan, 85*(9), 703–707.

The Wealth Hike. (2020). *Helping you grow*. https://www.thewealthhike.com/

ThemPra Social Pedagogy. (2020). *The learning zone model*. http://www.thempra.org.uk/social-pedagogy/key-concepts-in-social-pedagogy/the-learning-zone-model/

Zeichner, K., Payne, K. A., & Brayko, K. (2015). Democratizing teacher education. *Journal of Teacher Education, 66*(2), 122–1

CHAPTER 29

DESIGNING A COHERENT STEM (SCIENCE, TECHNOLOGY, ENGINEERING, AND MATHEMATICS) INITIAL TEACHER EDUCATION PROGRAM

Innovation in Clinical Practice

Karen Goodnough and Mary Stordy
Memorial University

ABSTRACT

Over the last two decades, considerable reform has taken place in initial teacher education (ITE), resulting in many approaches, with varying theoretical orientations, underpinning philosophies, structures, and practices. Furthermore, program revision and reform has shifted ITE to school and community settings, with a stronger emphasis on clinical experiences and practice. In this chapter, we describe the underpinning principles, content,

Preparing Quality Teachers:
Advances in Clinical Practice, pp. 627–649
Copyright © 2022 by Information Age Publishing
www.infoagepub.com
627

structure, and practices of a Canadian primary/elementary Science, Technology, Engineering, and Mathematics (STEM) post-degree ITE program. The notion of coherence is adopted to examine and report on how this innovative program, with strong clinical components such as action research, critical reflection, school-university partnerships, and service learning, to name a few, was designed to prepare future teachers for the complexities of creating inclusive learning environments.

BACKGROUND

Over the last two decades, considerable reform has taken place in initial teacher education (ITE) nationally and internationally (Heng et al., 2019; Hyland, 2018; Rowe & Skourdoumbis, 2019; Yeigh & Lynch, 2017) in response to criticisms of traditional ITE, such as having over packed curricula, weak relationships between theory and practice, and fragmented pedagogy, to name a few (Goodnough et al., 2016; Grossman et al., 2009; Kosnik & Beck, 2011). Feiman-Nemser (2001) also noted a lack of emphasis in traditional ITE on "cultivat[ing] habits of analysis and reflection through focused observation, child analysis, analysis of cases, microteaching, and other laboratory experiences" (p. 1020). This reform has resulted in many approaches to ITE with varying theoretical orientations, underpinning philosophies, structures, and practices. For example, Kitchen and Petrarca (2016) presented a three-dimensional model for ITE based on theory-, practice-, and reflection-oriented continua. While these authors described approaches to ITE that emphasized one or more of these dimensions, they argued that to overcome the limitations of traditional ITE or programs that are more singular in emphasis, the integration of all three components is needed.

From a practical perspective, reform has also resulted in a range of transformations in traditional programs or the creation of new programs that have shifted ITE to school and community settings, with a greater emphasis on clinical experiences and practice (Grossman, 2011; Zeichner & Bier, 2013). While ITE program design and structures vary and there is no one "preferred" approach, an emerging body of literature suggests a number of guidelines that may be adopted to create effective ITE programs, including fostering coherence across program components (Beck & Kosnik, 2006), establishing strong school-university partnerships (Darling-Hammond, 2006), and offering integrated theory-based learning with practice-focused experiences (Allen, 2009; Allen & Wright, 2014).

In this chapter, we describe the underpinning principles, content, structure, and practices of a Canadian primary/elementary STEM teacher preparation post-degree program. The notion of coherence is adopted to examine and report on how this innovative program was designed to prepare future teachers for the complexities of creating inclusive, affirmative learning environments (Goodnough et al., 2016).

Coherence and Integration in Teacher Education

Many studies of ITE programs have reported on the fragmentation and inconsistencies that exist across program structures and experiences (Cochran-Smith et al., 2016; Darling-Hammond, 2014; Feiman-Nemseer, 1990; Zimpher, 1989), often identifying field experiences as a weak component of programs (Guyton & McIntyre, 1990; Wideen et al., 1998). Challenges with creating connection and coherence across program components, especially between university-based course work and field experiences, have been explained in several ways. In some instances, there may be a mismatch between school settings and university programs regarding what constitutes effective teaching and learning and the purposes of initial teacher preparation. Referred to as the "two-worlds pitfall" (Feiman-Nemser & Buchmann, 1989), this disconnect may cause confusion for teacher candidates and hinder their ability to connect theory and practice. Another challenge may be explained by the apprenticeship of observation (Lortie, 1975). Before entering ITE programs, teacher candidates have spent approximately 15,000 hours as K–12 students. The beliefs and perspectives they bring to ITE, based on their extended time as school-based learners, may be at odds with what they are learning as students of teaching. They may have difficulty viewing teaching and learning from the perspective of a teacher after being socialized for many years as K–12 learners (Fitzgerald, 2020; Snow, 2015).

Over the last two decades, there has been a concerted focus on reforming ITE to achieve program coherence and integration, particularly with an emphasis on connecting clinical experiences and other program components (Hammerness, 2006; Hammerness & Darling-Hammond 2002; Russell et al., 2001; Waddell & Vartuli, 2015). Numerous approaches and strategies have been adopted to foster coherence, such as creating collaborative communities, adopting student-centered pedagogies (e.g., action research, service learning, reflection), and establishing school-university partnerships (see Bernay et al., 2020; Chan, 2019; Haddix, 2015; Heggen et al., 2018; Petrilli et al., 2019; Qing-li Tet al., 2019). Furthermore, as a means to gain insight into the nature and creation of program coherence, research is being conducted to examine the views and experiences of teacher candidates as they relate to ITE program coherence (Canrinus et al., 2019; McQuillan et al., 2012; Samaras et al., 2016; Williamson & Warringotn, 2019).

While creating coherence in teacher education programs has been promoted as a means to strengthen ITE, the research in this area is modest (Canrinus et al., 2015; Grossman et al., 2008; Klette & Hammerness, 2016). Moreover, conceptions of coherence have not been discussed extensively

(Buchmann & Floden, 1993; Hammerness, 2006; Tatto, 1996). Generally, coherence in ITE refers to the alignment and integration of ideas and experiences among program components. In adopting coherence as a lens and considering the foundational role clinical practice plays in a new Canadian primary/elementary STEM teacher preparation post-degree program, the authors view coherence as both a characteristic and a process. Their conception aligns with Weston's (2019) perspective, which focuses on three key components: (a) a shared vision of teacher education, (b) consistent, intentional experiences that align with the vision, and (c) evaluation of coherence by teacher candidates. The authors focus on the first two components in this chapter. More specifically, the authors describe the shared vision; the collaborative development by university and community partners of the shared vision; and how program components, experiences, and ideas were aligned with the vision to create coherence.

The Context of Teacher Education at Memorial University

In Canada, education is governed by individual provinces and territories. Newfoundland and Labrador (NL), the context of the program described in this chapter, is one of those jurisdictions, with the NL Department of Education and Early Childhood Development overseeing the organization, delivery, and assessment of education for early childhood and elementary and secondary levels. The province has a population of approximately 520,000 people, including 260 schools with a total enrollment of 63,722 students. Sixty-one percent of schools are classified as rural (Government of Newfoundland and Labrador, 2020). Rural schools are situated in communities that have less than 5,000 people and are not considered to be cities, towns, or larger metropolitan areas. The Faculty of Education of Memorial University of Newfoundland is the sole provider for teacher preparation in the province.

The Faculty of Education offers initial and postgraduate degree and diploma programs for teachers, counsellors and educational psychologists, educational administrators, and adult educators. As part of its mandate, Memorial University has a special obligation to the people of Newfoundland and Labrador for the education of all, especially teachers and education professionals. In terms of primary/elementary education, the faculty offers several options: a five-year Bachelor of Education as a first degree or a Bachelor of Education as a second (post) degree. The first-degree full-time option requires the completion of 150 credit hours (50 university courses of 36 hours each) with 75 credit hours of education courses. Sixty of the 75 are completed prior to admission to the faculty with 15 being required in a focus area such as English, French, history, linguistics, music, religious studies, science, or theatre arts. The first-degree program includes five school-based observation days in each of five semesters before an extended internship is completed in the final year of the program. The post-degree option for the preparation of primary/elementary teachers is a 72-credit hour program, with a four semester, full-time format. In semester one, teacher candidates complete a five-day school-based experience, with a 10-day school practicum being completed in each of semesters two and three. The final 50-day extended internship is completed in the last semester.

In 2018, the faculty implemented a new teacher preparation program, an 85-credit hour Bachelor of Education post degree combined with a certificate in STEM Education. It is designed to prepare teachers of kindergarten through grade six and extends over two years.

DEVELOPING A SHARED VISION

When an opportunity arose, stemming from a substantial financial gift, for the creation of a teacher preparation program with a focus on STEM teaching and learning in the primary/elementary grades, the authors immediately initiated a process to establish a shared vision for the program. Rather than working alone as university scholars in the area of STEM teacher preparation, the authors invited a team of stakeholders to come together regularly as a working group to explore the possibilities for a new program. The members of the working group consisted of a program specialist from a large school district, a science educator from the programs branch of the provincial Newfoundland and Labrador Department of Education and Early Childhood Development, an administrative staff member of the faculty's undergraduate office who understood how to best navigate program creation at the various levels of university governance, a retired mathematics educator as project coordinator, a faculty member specializing in science education, a faculty member specializing in math education, and a faculty member specializing in drama and creativity. The second author acted as the Lead for the working group while the first served as a mentor and advisor to the group. The program Lead had previous teaching experience with a field-oriented program at another Canadian institution, and received helpful guidance from that particular program's creators. Having a shared vision for the STEM program was crucial for the development of a program with coherence. Meeting every two weeks, the group endeavoured to build upon the faculty's prior work in teacher preparation reform over many years. Reflecting on the teaching and learning framework of the University and drawing from the work of Darling-Hammond and Bransford (2005) in particular, the working group developed the principles (see Appendix A) that would eventually guide the program. Over time, and after off-campus and on-campus retreats led by outside facilitators, the working group created detailed drafts of the key principles and components. The program design ideas were shared regularly with an Advisory Board composed of university and community stakeholders. Regularly, the Lead of the working group met with the faculty administrative team, as well as the entire faculty, to gather input and advice and communicate how program development was unfolding. Teachers, school administrators, and university students, while not members of the working group, were consulted.

After this highly collaborative creative process, a unique program was established. Meshed tightly to a set of principles, it was innovative in its design, rich in experiential learning, highly integrated, and grounded in STEM education. The program, commonly referred to as "the STEM Program" is an 85-credit two-year post-degree K–6 Bachelor of Education combined with a Certificate in STEM Education. The certificate aspect cannot be completed outside of the program as it is completely integrated and threaded throughout the program. It is challenging to discuss one element of the STEM program without relating it to the others, as the interconnectedness of the program elements are intertwined. Separating the threads for the purpose of explanation, the authors describe the program using the four descriptors of innovative in design, integration of curriculum, rich in experiential learning, and grounded in STEM education.

INNOVATIVE IN DESIGN

The STEM program is divided into four phases, each with a different theme. There is a sequential progression through each of the phases, building upon and connecting with prior phases (see Table 29.1).

The authors use the term "phases" rather than semesters as phases do not line up perfectly with the institution's semester system, and each phase has a specific focus. As you see from Table 29.1, Phase I and Phase II make up the first year and Phase III and Phase IV comprise the second year. There is a deliberate three-month summer break in program-offering between Phases II and III, providing teacher candidates with time to synthesise and absorb ideas about teaching and learning as they progress through their teacher preparation program.

In general terms, Phase I is focused on disrupting teacher candidates' assumptions about learning, about teaching, and about the purposes of schooling as the program examines the big ideas around learners and learning, and teachers and teaching, what it means to be a teacher in the 21st century, and how these ideas are socially, politically, and culturally

Table 29.1

Program Sequence at a Glance

Year 1	
Phase I (September – December) 12 Weeks	**Phase II** (January – May) 18 Weeks
ED 4100 Learners and Learning – Teachers and Teaching (16 credit hours) **ED 410T** School Field Experience I (3 credit hours)	**ED 4200** Curriculum Content and Curriculum Contexts I (16 credit hours) **ED 420T** School Field Experience II (3 credit hours) **ED 4600** Community Field Experience (4 credit hours) Institutes (4 credit hours) o **ED 4690** Exceptional Learners I o **ED 4691** A Closer Look at the Arts
Year 2	
Phase III (September – December) 12 Weeks	**Phase IV** (January – April) 16 weeks
ED 4400 Curriculum Content and Curriculum Contexts II/ Praxis (8 credit hours) **ED 440T** School Field Experience III (10 credit hours)	**ED 4500** Integration: Diversity and Identity (17 credit hours) **Institutes** (4 credit hours) o **ED 4660** Exceptional Learners II o **ED 4661** Numeracy o **ED 4692** Literacy

contextualized. While teacher candidates at the start of the program often seem most keen to focus on teachers, and in particular the actions of the teacher, the STEM program shifts the gaze of the teacher candidates to the learner, first and foremost. In doing so, they draw their attention inward to themselves as learners as well and are often asked to revisit their own experiences of being a child in primary/elementary school.

The second half of Phase I turns their focus to teaching and to broad issues related to being a teacher. The STEM program helps make teacher candidates aware that they are functioning in the liminal space between being both a learner and a teacher, and they are encouraged to try to become comfortable with the discomfort of this space. In terms of content, the particular focus of the first phase is on learning theories, learner-child development, learner diversity, educational perspectives including ethics, history, and philosophy, relational pedagogy, and the development of teacher professional identity. The theme of Phase II is Curriculum Content and Curriculum Contexts. It is during this phase that teacher candidates inquire and develop their knowledge of and skills with curriculum and associated instructional practices. Extending upon and connecting with the previous theme of *Learners and Learning-Teachers and Teaching*, teacher candidates pay close attention to the political, social, and cultural curricular contexts as they inquire into curriculum content in subject disciplines with a strong emphasis on literacy and numeracy. At the end of Phase II, there is a four-week community field experience, which is discussed in more detail below. Following the community field experience, Phase II concludes back on campus with two-week institutes that focus on the arts, and in particular, music and visual arts. There is also an institute with a focus on the exceptional learner.

The second year of the program begins with Phase III, where the overall theme is *Praxis*. During this phase, teacher candidates have opportunities to connect and integrate the theoretical and practical, which is understood as situationally and ethically appropriate, thoughtful, and intentional action. Teacher candidates continue to broaden their understanding of learners and learning/teachers and teaching, as well as curriculum content and curriculum contexts, and engage in teaching as reflexive action. Worth noting is that both Phase I and Phase III are aligned with the start of the K–6 school year, so teacher candidates can experience how to begin a school year with a new class of children.

The theme of the last phase of the program (Phase IV) is centred on "Integration: Diversity and Identity." It is during this culminating phase that teacher candidates integrate the theoretical and practical understandings from the previous three phases and examine more deeply what it means to be ethically and culturally responsive to diverse students and their communities, while being an inclusive educator with a strong understanding of STEM education. A key aspect of this integration is for teacher candidates to continue to enact their understanding of teaching, and to deepen their understanding of themselves as teachers. In particular, they examine themselves as inclusive educators, as STEM educators, as teacher researchers, and as professionals.

INTEGRATION OF CURRICULUM

A unique feature of the program design is its strongly integrated nature. As explained previously, the theoretical and practical components of the program are explicit in the design. Regarding the on-campus curriculum in particular, in contrast to the often siloed course-based curriculum of many teacher preparation programs, the STEM program functions through large multi-credited course offerings with the curriculum mapped closely to 14 overall program outcomes (refer to Appendix B). The outcomes are the result of three years of meetings by the working group and built upon previous years of work of the faculty during other program reforms.

A team of instructors work together to offer the integrated curriculum through a "block" approach for the first three phases. Such an approach allows for a deep, concentrated focus on one particular topic over a period of time, rather than studying many areas simultaneously or offering multiple courses. During weekly blocks, the program has specific learning structures that allow teacher candidates the opportunity to inquire into becoming a primary/elementary generalist teacher. Being able to focus on one area (e.g., learning to read and attributing that same focus to the field experience in the schools) has allowed teacher candidates to delve deeply into their learning (see Table 29.2).

Table 29.2

Weekly Block Learning Structures

Monday	Tuesday	Wednesday	Thursday	Friday
9:00 – 11:00	9:00 – 12:00			10:00 -12:00
Lecture Series	Case Inquiry	School Field Experience	School Field Experience	Field Seminar
12: - 4:00	1:00 – 4:00			1:00 – 3:00
STEMinar	Workshop			STEMinar

In general terms, there are five learning structures that primarily compose the teacher candidates' experiences on-campus: a Lecture Series, Case Inquiry Tutorial, Workshop, Field Seminar, and STEMinar. Briefly, the Lecture Series frames the specific weekly focus around the theme of the phase. The lecture is an opportunity for teacher candidates to enhance their understanding of the thematic unit by bringing forward provocative ideas, current research, and controversial positions related to the topic under study. Teacher candidates' knowledge of lecture content should be evident in their oral and written work across the other learning structures.

Candidates engage in a case inquiry to experience collaborative inquiry related to various thematic units of study. Cases present issues to be researched, analysed, and debated along with other real-life teaching and learning scenarios. The purpose of case work is to help teacher candidates understand the diverse, often contradictory realities, personal meanings, and multiple identities at play in schools and classrooms in relation to their own emerging positions as teachers and learners. As a participant in casework, teacher candidates are required to explore perspectives, become critically informed from diverse points of view, and see multiple possibilities for practical action in learning and teaching environments.

Workshops require students to be actively involved in a variety of professional skills, activities, and experiences related to the weekly topic. Most of the activities enable students to further develop their professional skills in a particular area of study. For example, during Phase II when the weekly focus is on the teaching of reading, teacher candidates have a workshop on how to do running records with children as a form of assessment.

The weekly Field Seminar is an integral part of the field experience and is structured to provide an immediate bridge between the lived experiences in schools and the on-campus coursework. Dialogue in Field Seminar allows teacher candidates to create meaning and deepen understanding by bringing forward observations, questions, and reflections emerging from their field experiences. Through this, teacher candidates begin to understand how theory and practice are linked, working together to inform learning and teaching. Furthermore, an important aspect of the seminar is formative in nature as it helps prepare teacher candidates for their upcoming time in schools.

The purpose of the STEMinar is to enhance, deepen, and extend teacher candidates' knowledge, understanding, and skills in STEM learning and teaching. In the Monday afternoon session, teacher candidates participate in a variety of highly experiential STEM learning experiences. For example, one week teacher candidates spend time with a biologist as they experience and investigate the intertidal zone of a local river. Another week they examine the connection between mathematics and coding as they explore programming with ball-shaped robots called spheros. During the Friday afternoon session, they examine and frame the weekly learning focus in the broader context of STEM education. Each learning experience is designed to assist in developing a deeper understanding of STEM education in K–6 classrooms and the broader school community. For example, when the focus for the week is on the introduction to the exceptional learner, the STEMinar focuses on the use of digital assistive technologies for the exceptional learner in schools. Another example of a Friday STEMinar is a focus on exploring Indigenous ways of knowing mathematics. This occurs during the weekly block in Phase I that focuses on Indigenous Education.

The STEM program also provides teacher candidates with a particular concentration in the area of inclusive education. In addition to completing coursework in the area of learner diversity, the program has a significant focus on learner exceptionalities. The coursework is purposefully linked to ongoing field experiences both in the classroom and the community-based field placement. Hence, the highly integrated nature of the program provides teacher candidates with a framework to "take up" and reflect upon their beliefs and assumptions of inclusive education across a multitude of learning experiences. In keeping with the Truth and Reconciliation Commission of Canada: Calls to Action (2015), a nationally commissioned report documenting the history and legacy of Canada's residential school system that contains 94 recommendations to repair the harm to Canada's Indigenous peoples and provide ways forward to make systemic change to programs and policies, the curriculum for the STEM program strives to be indigenized to ensure the voices of Indigenous peoples are represented. Where possible, teacher candidates are encouraged to examine and attend to the decolonization of school curriculum and school practices. Injustices are brought to light. Learning experiences such as the Blanket Exercise workshop, which helps participants begin to understand the dark history of residential schools in Canada, are provided. Literature by Indigenous scholars and authors are examined, and time is allotted in various phases of the program for teacher candidates to explore place-based learning. In Phase IV there is a focus on exploring Indigenous education with an instructor who specializes in Indigenous ways of knowing and being. Teacher candidates are encouraged to consider Indigenous perspectives in all their assignments. This work is important and continues to evolve.

RICH IN EXPERIENTIAL LEARNING

School Field Experience (Year 1)

The authors made decisions around the design of the program to reflect the shared vision of the working group regarding the scope and sequence of the curriculum, while embedding experiential learning (Burns & Danyluk, 2017; Harfitt, 2019; Kolb, 1984; Moore, 2010) opportunities in schools from the very beginning and engaging teacher candidates in the theoretical aspects of learning to teach. Drawing from the literature in teacher education, the program creators established strong deliberate connections between theory and practice as a main tenet of the program. By the end of the program, teacher candidates spend over 100 days in classrooms and these field experiences span three of the four phases.

In a cohort model, teacher candidates spend two days on campus with instructors learning the particular topic at hand, and then spend the next two days at one of the program's partner schools, deepening their understanding of the theoretical components. With a strong emphasis on learning in the field from the beginning of the program, the working group felt it was important for schools to be recognized as significant partners in the process of mentoring teacher candidates. The four public schools selected to be partners with the STEM program were carefully chosen as primary/elementary schools, meeting the criteria established by the working group. Some of the criteria for partner school selection included strong leadership teams, school development plans aligned with the principles of the STEM program, and a variety of feeder systems. The fifth and last day of the school week for teacher candidates is spent back on-campus where they unpack the experiences from the school settings and compare their experiences against the theoretical coursework. This is done while situating STEM education within the topic where applicable and appropriate. For the authors, it simply makes sense for teacher candidates to spend time in classrooms with children and teachers while learning about life in schools. The placements last for the entire first year of the program, and program goals and outcomes are laid out regarding the kinds of experiences teacher candidates might have in the schools. During each phase, a field advisor, who also serves as the cohort's instructor for the on-campus Field Seminar component of the program, works closely with the cohort of teacher candidates in the school, along with the school's leadership team, to help teacher candidates make sense of what they are witnessing in the schools. During this phase, they work in pairs as they spend time in multiple classrooms to get a sense of the developmental differences in children, as well as the complexities that exist when working with large groups of children in various contexts. The field advisor, working closely with the on-campus instructors, provides teacher candidates with particular topics for focus, connecting to relevant theoretical components.

During Phase II, the field experience shifts slightly, with teacher candidates being paired with a classroom teacher who is referred to as a partner teacher. The partner teacher's role is that of mentor, much like the role of the field advisor. Together, the partner teacher and field advisor provide a shared mentorship, helping teacher candidates to grow in their understanding and competence of what it means to teach children well. To aid in communication and to make the mentoring relationship most helpful, teacher candidates share online reflective journals with both the partner teacher and the field advisor. Over the course of the semester, all three people write and communicate in the teacher candidate's field journal to reflect, question, offer support, and guide the teacher candidate towards successful completion of the first year of the program. Towards the end of the phase, the field placement contains an immersion week which gives teacher candidates a sense of what it feels like to have a full week in the classroom with children. It is during this time that they may begin to lead a series of well-planned lessons with the approval and support of the partner teacher and field advisor.

Community-Based Field Experience

Near the end of Phase II, teacher candidates have a four-week community-based field experience. The purpose of the community-based field experience is to allow teacher candidates to learn more about an area of teaching where they have self- identified a personal need for growth. For example, some teacher candidates may indicate they want to learn more about science and technology in the real world, so they might spend four weeks learning about ocean mapping technology. This means venturing out on the North Atlantic Ocean with specialists in the field, learning how ocean mapping technology works and functions in the world. Other teacher candidates may feel they have adequate science and mathematics understanding, but require a deeper appreciation of the arts and culture. They can spend four weeks at a provincial art gallery and museum being mentored by an expert archivist. Still others may identify a need to feel more comfortable with people with intellectual or physical challenges and would have their placement at Easter Seals, a provider of programs, services, issues-leadership, and development for the disability community. These experiences from the community help teacher candidates develop a holistic and inclusive view of diverse settings with educational components.

Extended School Field Experience (Year 2)

The second year of the program begins with Phase III where teacher candidates return to the partner schools for an extended field placement and draw on learnings from Phase I and Phase II from both the on-campus and field experiences. They are mentored by a new partner teacher and their Faculty of Education instructor, who also serves as their field advisor. Teacher candidates take a gradual and graduated approach to assuming nearly full responsibilities of a classroom teacher. The purpose of this extended field experience is to bring to life the questions and challenges of learning to teach. In Phase III, in particular, questions and difficulties that arise in the field become possibilities not just for observation, but for learning to exercise sound pedagogic judgement, and thus, taking responsibility for thinking about and practicing decisions that make learning and teaching meaningful and possible. Every attempt is made to provide teacher candidates with a placement different from their first-year field experience. The first month of Phase III involves a similar pattern from Phases I and II where instructors work closely with the cohort on campus for two days and the teacher candidates are then in classrooms for the next two days. Friday sees them back on campus with the field instructor for field seminar as well as case tutorial, which is similar to case tutorial in Phases

I and II with one exception; rather than being presented with cases to deconstruct and wrestle with, teacher candidates are now expected to present rich living cases themselves that intrigue them from their experiences in schools and demonstrate their growing understanding of the complexity of teaching and learning. After the first month of Phase III, time in schools is increased to four days a week with a return to campus for one day for field seminar and case work. For weeks 5–9, the teacher candidates are in schools for five days a week. By the time teacher candidates are in schools full-time, they are doing the majority of teaching and partner teachers, along with the field advisor, provide guidance and feedback orally and in writing through the teacher candidate's field journal. During the final week of Phase III, teacher candidates return to campus to retroactively examine their time in schools and identify their own particular themes of teaching through a major reflective assignment. The field journal provides rich data to draw from, and teacher candidates are encouraged to reflect over the three phases of their time in the partner schools.

Service-Learning Experience

During Phase IV of the program, teacher candidates undertake service learning. While the community field experience is about learning, the service-learning component is about social responsibility and giving back to the community. This component aligns relevant community service with the learning outcomes of the phase. The service-learning experience is an opportunity for teacher candidates to develop civic responsibility and a service orientation. Service learning (Jagla et al., 2013; Meidl & Dowel, 2018) is a powerful form of experiential learning, combining relevant community service experiences with reflective exercises.

GROUNDED IN STEM EDUCATION

The program embraces STEM education as an interdisciplinary approach to learning, where rigorous academic concepts are coupled with real world lessons as students apply science, technology, engineering, and mathematics in context that make connections between school, community, and work, thus enabling the development of STEM literacy. The ultimate goal of this program is to enhance, deepen, and extend teacher candidates' knowledge and skills in STEM teaching and learning by immersing them in the very pedagogic essence of what constitutes STEM itself—the capability to engage in critical inquiry approaches.

The unique design and highly integrated nature of this program reflect how it is hoped practicing teachers engage students in K–6 STEM education settings. Thus, teacher candidates have many and varied opportunities to focus specifically on and to engage in STEM learning experiences. These experiences are intended to broaden teacher candidates' depth of understanding in the STEM areas, and ultimately develop their capacity and confidence as primary/elementary teachers enabling them to foster creativity and curiosity in children. In the context of primary/elementary education, mathematics and science play a different role from technology and engineering in that math and science are school subjects that must be taught well for both a comprehensive education and as a foundation for any STEM activity. As such, this program provides students with enhanced coursework in mathematics and science content and pedagogy.

OTHER UNIQUE PROGRAM FEATURES

Action Research Projects

As stated previously, that last phase of the program pulls all elements together. During this final phase, teacher candidates complete their personal research inquiry into teaching by undertaking data collection for their action research projects. Learning about the nature of action research and how to engage in action research starts in Phase I and continues until they are ready to implement a project in Phase IV. Through these focused action research projects on a STEM-related topic, the teacher candidates go back into classrooms once more to teach a series of lessons and collect data.

Assessment and Evaluation

Assessment for the program is designed to be learner-focused and growth oriented. This approach supports teacher candidates in understanding their learning, growth, and progress. Modeled as an ongoing and continuous feedback loop, assessment occurs primarily while teacher candidates participate and engage individually and collaboratively across all components of the program's learning structures. The program utilizes a pass/fail model of evaluation. Teacher candidates pass the course when they demonstrate a high level of performance within and across the components of the program. The standard for a pass within each assignment, course, and phase of the program is equivalent to a high B performance (75%) in Memorial University's grading system. Achieving an equivalency of 75% is expected if teacher candidates wish to move into the profession as well-informed, knowledgeable, and capable teachers. All courses must be completed at a passing level in order to successfully meet the requirements of a phase. Successful completion of all components for a phase is a prerequisite for advancing to the next phase. If a performance issue arises during a phase, the instructional team works with teacher candidates to develop specific learning plans, based on the program and phase learning outcomes.

Throughout the program, evidence of learning is documented through the development and maintenance of a professional learning portfolio that shows teacher candidates' demonstrable accomplishments across the program phases, and provides evidence of and support for teacher candidates' understandings of their responsibilities, capabilities, capacities, and growth in relation to the learning outcomes of the phase and the overall program outcomes. It includes evidence of learning based upon student engagement across all program learning structures.

Narrative assessments are completed by the instructional team for the on-campus components and by the field advisors and partner teachers for the field experiences. These formal narrative assessments focus on teacher candidates' understandings of their learning, growth, and progress, based on the learning outcomes of the phase and the overall program outcomes. The narratives provide descriptions that include: specific examples of the teacher candidate's strengths, specific examples of areas for improvement, and suggestions for areas in which the student should continue to focus.

Relational Pedagogy

The STEM program attempts to foster a deep awareness of relationships in all work with children, teachers, schools, and the community. From the significance of the pedagogic relationship to the relationship between the various disciplines that constitute STEM education, how people relate to one another and to the earth matters. The learner-teacher relationship is key, as is the partner teacher-teacher candidate relationship, as well as the complex relationship between curriculum content and curriculum contexts. Knowing the social, cultural, political, historical contexts of schools is essential to developing a pedagogy of hope. Understanding diversity and issues of equity are paramount to teacher candidates being able to relate well to children in classrooms.

Cohort Model

Another unique feature is the way the program utilizes a cohort model. While cohort models are not new, the STEM program model, particularly in the field experiences, is different from how most cohorts function in many teacher education programs. Teacher candidates spend all four phases with the same cohort of students during their on-campus experiences. However, during their field experiences, they are broken into two smaller cohorts and spend their time working closely with their teacher candidate peers. During the first year in particular, teacher candidates are often paired up so as to be able to offer peer feedback about their teaching actions. Also, having teacher candidates in pairs gives them a "second set of eyes" for sense-making and dialogue, without putting too much pressure on the busy classroom teacher who may not be readily available to discuss classroom learning episodes. During the first phase, the field advisor meets with the cohort as a group regularly at the school setting to help teacher candidates make sense of classroom activities and to draw connections to on-campus program curricula.

CONCLUSION

In her book, *Powerful Teacher Education*, Darling-Hammond (2006) refers to guided clinical experience as the glue for creating effective teacher preparation programs. She emphasized the importance of the experiences being structured and managed carefully, "tightly tied to simultaneous coursework and seminars that pose problems and tasks to be explored in the clinical setting and that support analysis and further learning about practice" (p. 154). Furthermore, she discussed the need for effective programs to enable teacher candidates to establish strong theory-practice relationships.

In this chapter, the authors describe an ITE program where clinical experiences were the glue for creating a coherent program. Clinical experiences and other program ideas, structures, and practices are highly connected, designed to reflect a shared vision for teacher education. Teacher candidates experience a gradual enculturation into the teaching profession, with a strong reciprocity between university and school/community experiences (Lave & Wenger, 1991).

Faculty, staff, and school-based mentors work collaboratively to support teacher candidates in a co-teaching approach (Rabin, 2020; Tobin & Roth, 2005). The shared vision is embodied in practice as teacher candidates are supported to engage in progressively more intensive and complex work with K–6 students and within university courses, seminars, and experiences. Furthermore, this progression through the program includes the broader sociocultural context of learning and teaching by engaging teacher candidates in community placements and service learning. Teacher inquiry and critical reflection are integral components of the program that encourage teacher candidates to address the challenges of learning to teach such as the apprenticeship of observation.

The chapter describes two components of achieving coherence–a shared vision of teacher education and consistent, intentional experiences that align with the vision. Data are collected from teacher candidates as they progress through the program to further ascertain how and to what extent the program is coherent. Surveys, journal entries, focus groups, and exit interviews are some of the data used. This will be reported elsewhere in the future and used to inform areas where program coherence needs to be strengthened.

REFERENCES

Allen, J. (2009). Valuing practice over theory: How beginning teachers re-orient their practice in the transition from the university to the workplace. *Teaching and Teacher Education, 25*, 647–654. https://doi.org/10.1016/j.tate.2008.11.011

Allen J., & Wright, S. (2014). Integrating theory and practice in the pre-service teacher education practicum. *Teachers and Teaching, (20)*2, 136–151. https://doi.org/10.1080/13540602.2013.848568

Beck, C., & Kosnik, C. (2006). *Innovations in teacher education: A social constructivist approach*. State University of New York Press.

Bernay, R., Stringer, P., Milne, J., & Jhagroo, J. (2020). Three models of effective school–university partnerships. *New Zealand Journal of Educational Studies, 55*(1), 133–148. https://doi.org/10.1007/s40841-020-00171-3

Buchmann, M., & Floden, R. (1993). Coherence: The rebel angel. In M. Buchmann & R. Floden (Eds.), *Detachment and concern: Conversations in the philosophy of teaching and teacher education* (pp. 222–235). Cassell Press. https://doi.org/10.3102/0013189X021009004

Burns, A., & Danyluk, P. (2017). Applying Kolb's model to a nontraditional pre-service teaching practicum. *Journal of Experiential Education, 40*(3), 249–263. https://doi.org/10.1177/1053825917696832

Canrinus, E. T., Bergem, O. K., Klette, K., & Hammerness, K. (2015). Coherent teacher education programmes: taking a student perspective. *Journal of Curriculum Studies, 49*(3), 313–333. https://doi.org/10.1080/00220272.2015.1124145

Canrinus, E. T., Klette, K., & Hammerness, K. (2019). Diversity in coherence: Strengths and opportunities of three programs. *Journal of Teacher Education, 70*(3), 192–205. https://doi.org/10.1177/0022487117737305

Chan, C. (2019). Crossing institutional borders: Exploring pre-service teacher education partnerships through the lens of border theory. *Teaching & Teacher Education, 86*. https://doi.org/10.1016/j.tate.2019.102893

Cochran-Smith, M., Villegas, A. M., Abrams, L., Chavez Moreno, L., Mills, T., & Stern, R. (2016). Research on teacher preparation: Charting the landscape of a sprawling field. In D. Gitomer & C. Bell (Eds.), *Handbook of research on teaching* (5th ed., pp. 439–547). American Educational Research Association.

Darling-Hammond, L. (2006). Constructing 21st-century teacher education. *Journal of Teacher Education, 57*(3), 300–314. https://doi.org/10.1177/0022487105285962

Darling-Hammond, L. (2014). Strengthening clinical preparation: The Holy Grail of teacher education. *Peabody Journal of Education, 89*(4), 547–561. https://doi.org/10.1080/0161956X.2014.939009

Darling-Hammond, L., & Bransford, J. (Eds.). (2005). *Preparing teachers for a changing world: What teachers should learn and be able to do.* Jossey-Bass.

Feiman-Nemser, S. (1989). *Teacher preparation: Structural and conceptual alternatives* (Issue Paper, 89–50). National Center for Research on Teacher Education.

Feiman-Nemser, S. (1990). Teacher preparation: Structural and conceptual alternatives. In W. R. Houston (Ed.), *Handbook of research on teacher education* (pp. 212–233). Macmillan. http://education.msu.edu/ncrtl/pdfs/ncrtl/issuepapers/ip895.pdf

Feiman-Nemser, S. (2001). From preparation to practice: Designing a continuum to strengthen and sustain teaching. *Teachers College Record, 103*(6), 1013–1055. http://hdl.handle.net/10192/33196

Feiman-Nemser, S., & Buchmann, M. (1989). Describing teacher education: A framework and illustrative findings from a longitudinal study of six students. *The Elementary School Journal, 89,* 365–377. http://dx.doi.org/10.1086/461580

Fitzgerald, A. (2020). Out in the field: Examining the role of school-based experiences in preparing primary pre-service teachers as confident and competent teachers of science. *International Journal of Science Education, 42*(2), 290–309. https://doi.org/10.1080/09500693.2019.1710618

Goodnough, K., Falkenberg, T., & MacDonald, R. (2016). Examining the nature of theory–practice relationships in initial teacher education: A Canadian case study. *Canadian Journal of Education, 39*(1), 1–28. http://journals.sfu.ca/cje/index.php/cje-rce/article/download/1964/1827/0

Government of Newfoundland and Labrador (2020). *Education statistics.* https://www.gov.nl.ca/eecd/files/SCH_19_2.pdf

Grossman, P. (2011). A framework for teaching practice: A brief history of an idea. *Teachers College Record, 113*(12), 2836–2843.

Grossman, P., Hammerness, K., McDonald, M., & Ronfeldt, M. (2008). Constructing coherence. *Journal of Teacher Education, 59*(4), 273–287. https://doi.org/10.1177/0022487108322127

Grossman, P., Hammerness, K., & McDonald, M. (2009). Redefining teaching, reimagining teacher education. *Teachers and Teaching: Theory and Practice, 15*(2), 273–289. https://doi.org/10.1080/13540600902875340

Guyton, E., & McIntyre, D. J. (1990). Student teaching and school experiences. In W. R. Houston (Ed.), *Handbook of research on teacher education* (pp. 514–535). Macmillan.

Haddix, M. (2015). Preparing community-engaged teachers. *Theory into Practice, 54*(1), 63–70. https://doi-org.qe2a-proxy.mun.ca/10.1080/00405841.2015.977664

Hammerness, K. (2006). From coherence in theory to coherence in practice. *Teachers College Record, 108*(7), 1241–1265. https://ed.stanford.edu/sites/default/files/from_coherence_in_theory_to_coherence_in_practice.pdf

Hammerness, K., & Darling-Hammond, L. (2002). Meeting old challenges and new demands: The redesign of the Stanford Teacher Education Program. *Issues in Teacher Education, 11*(1), 17–30.

Harfitt, G. (2019). *Community-based experiential learning in teacher education. Oxford Research Encyclopedia of Education.* https://oxfordre.com/education/view/10.1093/acrefore/9780190264093.001.0001/acrefor -9780190264093-e-986.

Heggen, K., Raaen, F. D., & Thorsen, K. E. (2018). Placement schools as professional learning communities in teacher education. *European Journal of Teacher Education, 41*(3), 398–413. https://doi.org/10.1080/02619768.2018.1448779

Heng, L., Quinlivan, K., & du Plessis, R. (2019). Exploring the creation of a new initial teacher education (ITE) programme underpinned by inclusion. *International Journal of Inclusive Education, 23*(10), 1017–1031. https://doi.org/10.1080/13603116.2019.1625454

Hyland, Á. (2018). Teacher education reform in Ireland: Policy and process. *Education Research and Perspectives, 45,* 4–24. https://www.erpjournal.net/wp-content/uploads/2020/01/01_ERPV45_Hyland.pdf

Jagla, V. M., Erickson, J. A., & Tinkler, A. S. (2013). *Transforming teacher education through service-learning.* Information Age Publishing.

Kitchen, J., & Petrarca, D. (2016). Approaches to teacher education. In J. Loughran and M. Lynn Hamilton (Eds.), *International handbook of teacher education research: Initial teacher education* (pp. 137–186). Springer.

Klette, K., & Hammerness, K. (2016). conceptual framework for analyzing qualities in teacher education: Looking at features of teacher education from an international perspective. *Acta Didactica Norge, 10*(2), 26–52. https://doi.org/10.5617/adno.2646

Kolb, D. A. (1984). *Experiential learning: Experience as the source of learning and development.* Prentice-Hall.

Kosnik, C., & Beck, C. (2011). *Teaching in a nutshell: Navigating your teacher education program as a student teacher.* Routledge.

Lave, J., & Wenger, E. (1991). *Situated learning: Legitimate peripheral participation.* University of Cambridge Press.

Lortie, D.C. (1975). *Schoolteacher: A sociological study.* University of Chicago Press.

McQuillan, P., Welch, M., & Barnatt, J. (2012). In search of coherence: 'Inquiring' at multiple levels of a teacher education system. *Educational Action Research, 20*(4), 535–551. https://doi.org/10.1080/09650792.2012.727640

Meidl, T., & Dowell, M., (2018). *Handbook of research on service-learning initiatives in teacher education programs.* IGI Global.

Moore, D. T. (2010). Forms and issues in experiential learning. In D. M. Qualters (Ed.), *New Directions for teaching and learning* (pp. 3–13). Wiley. https://doi.org/10.1002/tl.415

Petrilli, P., Hodge, C., Burns, A., Dantic, J., & Hodge, H. (2019). Clinical practice: Innovative partnership preparing highly effective teachers. *School-University Partnerships, 12*(2), 87–93.

Qing-li, H., Torres, M. N., & Shi-Ji, F. (2019). Collaborative action research for preparing teachers as reflective practitioners. *Systemic Practice & Action Research, 32*(4), 411–427. https://ideas.repec.org/a/spr/syspar/v32y2019i4d10.1007_s11213-018-9461-z.html

Rabin, C. (2020). Co-teaching: Collaborative and caring teacher preparation. *Journal of Teacher Education, 71*(1), 135–147. https://doi.org/10.1177/0022487119872696

Rowe, E. E., & Skourdoumbis, A. (2019). Calling for "urgent national action to improve the quality of initial teacher education": The reification of evidence and accountability in reform agendas. *Journal of Education Policy, 34*(1), 44–60. https://doi.org/10.1080/02680939.2017.1410577

Russell, T., McPherson, S., & Martin, A. K. (2001). Coherence and collaboration in teacher education reform. *Canadian Journal of Education, 26*(1), 37–55. https://journals.sfu.ca/cje/index.php/cje-rce/article/view/2793

Samaras, A. P., Frank, T. J., Williams, M. A., Christopher, E., & Rodick III, W. H. (2016). A collective self-study to improve program coherence of clinical experiences. *Studying Teacher Education: Journal of Self-Study of Teacher Education Practices, 12*(2), 170–187. http://dx.doi.org/10.1080/17425964.2016.1192033

Snow, D. (2015). Professional development school (PDS) evidenced-based claims. Prepared for the membership of the National Association of Professional Development Schools. Retrieved from http://napds.org/wp-content/uploads/2015/03/PDS.Claims.Document.MSUB_.3.8.15.pdf

Tatto, M. (1996). Examining values and beliefs about teaching diverse students: Understanding the challenges for teacher education. *Educational Evaluation and Policy Analysis, 18*(2), 155–180. https://doi.org/10.3102/01623737018002155

Truth and Reconciliation Commission of Canada. (2015). *Truth and reconciliation commission of Canada: Call to action.*

Tobin, K., & Roth, W. M. (2005). Implementing co-teaching and co-generative dialoguing in urban science education. *School Science & Mathematics, 105*(6), 313–321. https://doi.org/10.1111/j.1949-8594.2005.tb18132.x

Waddell, J., & Vartuli, S. (2015). Moving from traditional teacher education to a field-based urban teacher education program: One program's story of reform. *Professional Educator, 39*(1). https://files.eric.ed.gov/fulltext/EJ1084839.pdf

Weston, T. L. (2019). Improving coherence in teacher education: Features of a field-based methods course partnership. In T. E. Hodges & A. C. Baum (Eds.), *Handbook of research on field-based teacher education* (pp. 166–191). IGI Global.

Wideen, M., Mayer-Smith, J., & Moon, B. (1998). A critical analysis of the research on learning to teach: Making the case for an ecological perspective on inquiry. *Review of Educational Research, 68*(2), 130–178. https://journals.sagepub.com/doi/10.3102/00346543068002130

Williamson, T., & Warrington, A. (2019). "Where to take risks and where to lay low": Tensions between preservice teacher learning and program ideological coherence. *Action in Teacher Education, 41*(3), 265–283. http://dx.doi.org/10.1080/01626620.2019.1600598

Yeigh, T., & Lynch, D. (2017). Reforming initial teacher education: A call for innovation. *Australian Journal of Teacher Education, 42*(12), 112–127. https://files.eric.ed.gov/fulltext/EJ1165006.pdf

Zeichner, K., & Bier, M. (2013). The turn toward practice and clinical experiences in U.S. teacher education. *Beitrage Zur Lehrerbildung/Swiss Journal of Teacher Education, 30*(2), 153–170. https://www.academia.edu/25555326/The_Turn_Toward_Practice_and_Clinical_Experience_in_U.S._Teacher_Education

Zimpher, N. L. (1989). The RATE project: A profile of teacher education students. *Journal of Teacher Education, 40*(6), 27–30. http://dx.doi.org/10.1177/002248718904000606

APPENDIX A

STEM Program Guiding Principles

The STEM Bachelor of Education program will:

- Embody the complex, dynamic relationship of teaching and learning that connects skills and knowledge to reflective, research-based practice.
- Engage with and construct dynamic in-depth, integrated knowledge of learning (including assessment, curriculum, evaluation, instruction) and foster optimal learning by all.
- Embrace multiple understandings of knowing and being in the world through studying the nature of learners and learning, human development, and diverse learner needs.
- Prepare learners for a global society, while simultaneously developing knowledge that is unique to the NL educational context.
- Focus on interdisciplinary, interdependent nature of learning, with an emphasis on STEM.
- Commit to improving the human and global condition and potential to effect social and educational change through challenging issues of power, equity, social justice, human rights, inclusion and dignity.
- Ensure learning is supported by early and intensive cohort field experiences in schools, community and university within collaborative relationships.
- Support within and across the semesters, the integrated and interconnected continuous learning across the two-year program.
- Be grounded in strong mutual relationships with partner schools, community, and university.

APPENDIX B

STEM Program Outcomes

Over several years, a dedicated working group of educators from the Newfoundland and Labrador English School District, the Newfoundland and Labrador Department of Education and Early Childhood Development, and the Faculty of Education created the following general program outcomes to guide learning, teaching, and assessment in the STEM Program. Through learning, teaching, curricular and assessment experiences in the field and on-campus, teacher candidates will be immersed in integrated, reflective, research-based praxis.

They will:

Outcome 1: Develop an informed, critical, and justified philosophical view of educational and schooling practices with an awareness of mediating social, political, historical, and cultural contexts;

Outcome 2: Develop an inquiry stance regarding education and schooling that values curiosity, reasoning, imagination, and creativity in learning and teaching;

Outcome 3: Develop a demonstrable commitment to keep each and every child at the centre of all pedagogical decisions and actions;

Outcome 4: Develop praxis knowledge about and skills with curricular content and curricular contexts appropriate for primary/elementary learners with a particular focus on competency regarding literacy and numeracy;

Outcome 5: Develop an understanding of assessment and evaluation practices that are thoughtful and ethical, relevant and appropriate, and are clearly communicable to all stakeholders;

Outcome 6: Develop competence and confidence in the teaching of mathematics to primary/elementary learners;

Outcome 7: Develop an understanding of the integrative nature of STEM Education in the Canadian context;

Outcome 8: Develop an understanding of and appreciation for learner diversity and what it means to be an inclusive educator;

Outcome 9: Develop applicable perspectives and sensitive understandings of indigenous ways of knowing, doing, and being;

Outcome 10: Develop a commitment to uphold principles and practices of relational pedagogy;

Outcome 11: Develop deep, critical, and responsible understandings of the significance of the connective and shared relationships between the earth, its elements, its creatures, and ourselves, and;

Outcome 12: Develop a passionate sense of life-long professionalism as an educator.

CHAPTER 30

WHY WE NEED MORE CLINICAL PRACTICE IN TEACHER EDUCATION

James A. Bernauer
Robert Morris University

ABSTRACT

It is argued in this chapter that teacher preparation programs rely too much on traditional classroom instruction and not enough on guided entry into the teaching profession. Guided entry is defined as a process where students have the opportunity to apprentice with and learn from excellent teachers who have mastered the intricate craft of integrating content and pedagogy. Based upon conversations among both teacher candidates and clinical educators are used to make recommendations regarding how to transform teacher preparation programs based on guided practice.

Preparing Quality Teachers:
Advances in Clinical Practice, pp. 651–665

THE CASE FOR CLINICAL PRACTICE

Perhaps one of the most important takeaways from the AACTE Clinical Practice Commission (2018) report is its emphasis on context and flexibility. Although we are barraged with the need to base any and all of our pedagogical initiatives on "scientifically based research" and "evidence based practices" (see No Child Left Behind [NCLB] Act, 2002), the CPC report makes it clear that quality teaching depends on "the field's own science" (p. 7). As you will see from the conversations with both teacher candidates and clinical educators, complying with federal and state regulations and certification standards does not ensure that our schools of education are adequately preparing students to become quality teachers. It is also quite gratifying to find that the CPC report grounds its findings in the work of enduring exemplars like John Goodlad (1984) and Dan Lortie (1975). I think it would also be appropriate to add additional stalwarts of clinical practice such as John Dewey (1963, 1981) and Eliot Eisner (1998, 2002) since they have argued in different ways and using different perspectives that teaching is as much art as science and requires hands-on as much as brains-on instruction.

As a professor whose teaching responsibilities include pre-service teachers and supervising field experiences in K–12 schools, I have seen my share of students who bloom into fantastic teachers as well as those students who, although they want to become teachers, have simply not been able to pull together that necessary magical combination of content knowledge and pedagogical skill. How many professions demand not only competence in "content" (such as engineering, medicine, or science) but also an equal competence in being able to engage others in learning about content and often to those who are not particularly interested in learning? While there are those who may disparage teaching, the basis of their negative view lies in their own misconceptions of teaching and has little relationship to what we know to comprise quality teaching and the wonders of consequent student learning that extends across not only the cognitive domain but also the emotional, moral, physical, and social domains.

In addition to Dewey (1963, 1981) and Eisner (1998, 2002), Highet (1950) in the very title of his book *The Art of Teaching*" makes it very clear that we simply cannot confine the teaching profession within the straightjacket of the sterility of the current mantra of "evidence-based practices" cited at least 110 times in the NCLB Act especially since teachers are so very-well aware of the great variability among students, times, places, and circumstances and exhibit such varied and rich contexts of opportunities including opportunities cloaked as challenges. We are not a profession dealing with inputs, processes, materials, and outputs but rather with the minds and hearts of individual students who hold the future of our nation and our world. Gardner (2006) argues even more persuasively that because students exhibit multiple types of intelligences, interests, and capacities that we should not continue to prepare teachers along primarily traditional curricular lines while failing to prepare them to facilitate the learning of students who exhibit such a wondrous array of potentialities. And it is a world which we now know only one thing about and that is that we don't know what this future world will look like as we have so painfully learned from the COVID-19 pandemic. We simply cannot prepare students based solely on scientifically based practices that reflect more about what we think we know about the past. The descent of teaching into the strictures of a rigid view of evidence-based practice can be traced to how education research and those who practiced it tried to emulate the scientific approach as perceived in the physical and biological sciences as Lagemann (2000) so skillfully describes. When we look at the medical field, we find an interesting mix of both science and practice where clinical practice is seen as a large part in the education of both doctors and nurses. Here we see theory meeting practice "in the field." However, we also need to remember that doctors and nurses deal primarily with the physical body and the organs within it and while these bodies and organs exhibit great variability, these are nothing like what teachers face when working with the entire person— mind, body, and spirit or perhaps more explicitly across the cognitive, emotional, moral, physical, and social domains—no wonder we need to infuse our own theoretical knowledge with practice!

The implementation of apprenticeships in teacher preparation offers us a basis for reestablishing a more heavily weighted "learning by doing" rationale in teacher education. While there were earlier versions of apprenticeship, we are more familiar with Europe during the Middle Ages with its guilds of silversmiths, blacksmiths, and stonemasons and it was these types of apprenticeships that were introduced here in America during our own founding years (Lorenzo, 2017). Today, formal apprenticeship programs are most apparent in unionized building trades such as carpenters, electricians, ironworkers, and plumbers although companies also employ different variations of apprenticeship programs. Apprenticeships are built on the recognition that, while knowledge and theory are important in building a foundation in a craft, that professions that are heavily skill-based demand that practitioners are given a heavy dose of guided opportunities by more experienced colleagues to transform knowledge into skills within an authentic work setting. I would argue that this includes teaching. It is unfortunate that we continue to label professions as "white collar" and "blue collar" since they carry with them assumptions of superiority of the former over the latter. Becoming proficient in a craft requires the melding of theory and practice and what better way to do that than through a judicious integration of deskwork and field work. However, what we try to do in a classroom amidst the complexity of human interactions among and between students and teachers goes beyond what we find in most other settings. Unfortunately, as Jones (2011) indicates "a significant barrier to the integration of Registered Apprenticeship programs into the postsecondary system is the lack of mechanisms for evaluating student achievement and assigning academic credit for the hands-on portion of an apprentice's training program" (p. 55).

MANAGED AND LEARNING CLASSROOMS

No matter how we might try and get away from identifying our "philosophy of education", it is critical to do so since our philosophy either consciously or unconsciously directs our actions and our practice. We can explore the philosophies as exemplified by Dewey (1981) but perhaps the best way to begin this exploration is to start with what we think our classrooms should look like and what we and future teachers should be doing in them.

Cooper and Garner (2012) recommend creating a "learning classroom" as opposed to a "managed classroom." While they highlight critical differences between these two types of classrooms at the end of each chapter, in essence these differences are captured by the subtitle of the book—"Moving Beyond Management Through Relationships, Relevance, and Rigor" ... in essence, the new "Three R's." Too often when students are taught "classroom management" it is with an eye towards control as exemplified in behavioral learning theory with its emphasis on reinforcement, rewards, and punishment. While there are certainly situations where behavioral learning theory is appropriate, based on what I have observed, excellent teachers are those who inspire student trust and their engagement in learning because they are seen by students as caring teachers who are genuinely interested in their welfare and who make every effort to make learning meaningful and even fun! (see, e.g., Bernauer et al., 2017).

Anecdotally, building principals I have spoken to describe their most effective teachers, as those who are able to seamlessly blend rigor within the context of a safe and caring classroom. It is not those teachers who are popular because they are "cool" that get the nod from principals but rather those who exemplify the new "Three R's" based on their untiring efforts over years of practice to create a classroom experience that is rich with learning amidst an atmosphere of respect and caring. And perhaps what is most important here is that these teachers are not driven primarily by a script or a formula but by a genuine inquisitiveness to learn and continue to grow and learn themselves from continued reading as well as from their students. I like to tell teacher candidates that if they have a classroom of 20 students, there are potentially 21 teachers who can all learn from each other.

Constructivist learning theory is based on the work of several theorists including (Bruner, 1966, 1973, 1996); Piaget (1963, 1964, 1969), and Vygotsky (1978, 1986), as well as philosophers such as John Dewey (1981) and anthropologist Jean Lave (1988, 1997) and is built on the premise that each of us needs to individually as well as socially both construct and reconstruct what we see, hear, and read in order for us to "own" new knowledge; otherwise, it remains simply surface knowledge. It is constructivist theory and the kind of learning that it champions that seems to characterize excellent practitioners. Without the opportunity for our preservice teachers to apprentice with these teachers, how can they ever recognize let alone attain this kind of learning that can more easily blossom into excellent teaching?

It is also instructive to draw upon the lessons learned regarding situated learning. The concept of "positive transfer" is a sought-after goal because it is hoped that what is learned in school transfers to real-life (Perkins & Salomon, 2012). Connected to transfer is the importance of "situated learning" that argues that, in order for transfer to successfully occur, there must be real-world connections between what is learned and what is practiced (Lave, 1988, 1997; Lave & Wenger, 1991). This, of course, supports the importance of clinical practice for teacher candidates.

Sharing Our Model for Field Experiences

As part of our teacher preparation program at my university, in addition to student teaching, we integrate two kinds of "field experiences" into several courses where the focus is on "observing" and "exploring" where observing involves making reflective observations of the clinical educator in practice while "exploring" provides an opportunity for students to get personally and actively involved in the classroom in some capacity. These field experiences begin in their freshman year and are sprinkled throughout their four years of preparation. For the courses that I teach to teacher candidates (*Educational Psychology and Classroom Management* during the first year and *Schools and Society* during the second year), each student is required to write-up a Field Experience Report which includes the following five questions for both observation and exploration:

1. Learning objectives: What were the learning objectives of the class?
2. Instructional methods: What methods were used to achieve these objectives?
3. Learning theories: What learning theories support these instructional methods?

4. Classroom management: What was done to engage students and minimize disruptions?
5. Self-reflection: What went well and what might you do differently?

Each field experience (both observation and exploration) is approximately two hours in duration and instructors strive to help teacher candidates connect these experiences to their academic major—that is integrating content and pedagogy.

LEARNING FROM OUR STUDENTS

Below are the responses of two students from a recent field experience at the same school where "Ron" enacted the lesson at the kindergarten level while "Amy" was in a high school math classroom. These two students were both first-year teacher candidates. Summarized student quotes are offered below to capture the essence of their experiences. I should point out that in my educational psychology class where Ron and Amy were students, I emphasize the overarching need to create a "learning classroom" versus a "managed classroom" (Cooper & Garner, 2012) and recapitulate this when reviewing the field experience report requirements as described above. I selected Ron and Amy to try and capture any differences related to grade level—early childhood education versus high school, but their experiences in the classroom reflected other kind of differences as not only they described here but also many other differences as reported by the other students—there were simply no two experiences that were exactly the same. Of course, this diversity reflects the diversity that teachers encounter in school classrooms every day. Ron and Amy's Field Experience Reports were used as data collection instruments since they were thought to capture their thoughts and perceptions most directly.

What follows is Ron's account of his experiences in the clinical educator's kindergarten classroom as he described on his follow-up Field Experience Report.

Introduction: "In this kindergarten setting, I was able to start the lesson immediately because arrangements had been made beforehand with the classroom teacher. Here are my responses to the five questions."

Learning Objectives: "The objectives that guided my lesson were using the sight words that the children have been working on for the past week. The children had a good understanding of what we were doing because they were familiar with the words. This made the lesson very simple for myself as well as for the children. They were comfortable and easily engaged. I could tell though that the children had specific words that they continuously went over and there was always that little reinforcer. I also think having items like the alphabet, number line, date, weather and so on is a great way to keep the children reminded of their objectives."

Instructional Methods: "With my group, I started out by playing a bingo game that incorporated the sight words they were learning. I was very surprised with their knowledge, as I would hold up the word and they were able to tell me the word as well as recognizing it on the bingo board. They loved this activity because it was very interactive and I also rewarded them at the end. Next, I did an adding math lesson with them. I had a pair of dice and when I rolled them, they had to count the number and then color that number on the worksheet they had. I went around the group and let each child roll the dice and explain the number to me. I think this kept them all engaged in the activity because they knew they would be rewarded for a correct answer. I really enjoyed working in the small groups because it gave me the understanding of where each child was at with what we were working on."

Learning Theories: "I used Piaget's theory and encouraged hands-on experience to serve as building blocks for more complex skills. I was able to let the children actually touch and engage with dice that we used to count with. I used Skinner's theory by saying things like "way to go!", "keep up the hard work!" and giving them high-fives when the students answered something correctly. I really think this helps the children stay motivated because they all want that compliment from their teacher. I also demonstrated this theory by giving the children ring pops and stickers when they completed a task or got an answer right."

Classroom Management: "I minimized disruptions by keeping the children in small groups and using Gardner's techniques in this classroom. For the verbal—linguistic learners, I had the children write out the words they were learning and talked aloud about them. I used Visual-Spatial methods by allowing children to draw, color and do worksheets independently. I tried to keep the children focused by continuously giving them tasks so they did not get distracted. For example, we played the sight word bingo several times until every child won and with that, they wanted to continue to play. For the math lesson, I was able to get them involved in rolling the dice and that kept them focused."

Self-Reflection: "In all, I really enjoyed the classroom. I was really impressed by how the children behaved so there must have been a lot of structure and rules earlier in the year for kindergarteners to be that well behaved. The only thing I think I would do differently would be not giving as much free time. I feel like the children were doing work on their own or were instructed to play with centers instead of being taught. I feel like this could be a problem in the future for the children because they will expect the same amount of free time. I decided to change this and I really think the children were more behaved and excited with some new tasks!"

I was impressed with Ron's report because he took the initiative to coordinate his planned activities beforehand with the clinical educator. The "teaching moment" that I tried to capitalize on was that, while Ron thought that the children were already "well-behaved," because the students "were doing work on their own or were instructed to play with centers instead of being taught" he thought that they were being given too much "free time" and that that their expectations for such free time might carry-over to later grades. I commented on his report as well as in follow-up class discussions, that while Teacher-Candidates are typically quite concerned about classroom management, one of our most important long-term goals is to support the growth of both curiosity and independent learning including play and independent learning in the early grades. We also discussed how achieving a balance between classroom management and student-learning requires both ongoing teacher-learning and professional experience. In fact, I sometimes tell students, "After about three years of teaching, you will be a lot closer to becoming an excellent teacher" in order to stress the need for continual learning. However, I also try to simultaneously motivate and not dampen their enthusiasm for teaching—sometimes a tenuous balance.

Unlike Ron, Amy experienced an entirely different challenge when she arrived at her assigned high-school class as she described on her Field Experience Report.

Introduction: "I walked into this classroom with the idea that I was going to help the students learn in any way that I can. I had emailed the teacher beforehand but received no response where I said I would be willing and able to help with anything needed on that particular day. My student partner and I walked into the classroom completely blind. We were asked to help guide a lesson in a small group setting for the second class which was the 7th grade algebra class."

Learning Objectives: "*My learning objective for this session was to use students' previous knowledge on proportions to help them learn how to solve for discount rates and to provide help solving for absolute values and making tables.*"

Instructional Methods: "*I used examples to help students find patterns in their absolute value tables. During the second period, I used worksheets, calculators, and pieces of paper showing fractions to help students learn discount rates. I used pieces of paper with the equation parts to help them show what information was given and what was not. This helped them realize what they were solving for as well as what pieces of information went where. During the third period, I used a whiteboard and dry erase markers to help the students I was working with to learn how to graph absolute values. By using these tools, it made it easy for the students to graph out their graphs as they went or to wait until they were done with their tables to draw.*"

Learning Theories: "*I used Skinner's operant conditioning. A few of the girls in the group that I was working with wanted to ask me a lot of questions about myself, tattoos, or softball. I told them that I would answer one question for every three problems they got done. This got them to work harder and more quickly to finish their work!*"

Classroom Management: "*In the second class period I struggled at the beginning to keep the students on task. They were excited to have a new person in the classroom and one that "was a cool teacher with tatts". They were asking me lots of questions about who I was, where I was from, what I liked to do, how many piercings I had and other things along those lines. As the class period went on, I got my group under control and they actually ended up finishing a lot of their school work. I got the girls without calculators and told them that I would only answer a question every time they finished three problems. This got them working pretty quickly. I had a new student in my group and we were covering a topic that she had never seen before so I spent a lot of my time working one-on- one with her. One of her group mates was really good at discount rates so I paired them up together so they could work together. This kept two of them busy so I could focus on another girl who was the most outspoken of the group. She knew what she was doing but she wanted me to approve every step before she would go to the next one. On her scratch paper, I drew sections so I could check off each one quickly so she could move on. In the third class period, the students were very much on task and needed little to no prompting to stay on topic and stay engaged.*"

One student was staring at his phone and not doing his work on the white board. I walked over to him and told him that the faster that he finished his problems correctly, the faster he could get back to creating his music playlist. He smiled and put his phone away."

Self-Reflection: "I think a lot went well in these class periods. I think that creating the question system is a short-term fix to a problem that would likely continue once the new exciting person fades. Someone that is off task and creating a disturbance in a classroom one day isn't necessarily going to be content with a few answers. I would have liked to get to spend a little more time with the students in that class so I could help them understand the concepts better. The periods were so short that I felt like just as soon as they started to understand, they were leaving to go to their next period. One thing that I would love to have changed was the policy about how students can be on their phones as soon as they finish their work. I think this wastes a lot of valuable learning time and allows bad habits to form. Before I even got to check if students' problems were all right, they had their phones out and were texting, on social media, and playing games. This shows me that they don't care about their answers and much as they care about their phones. However, overall I had a great experience and can't wait to become a teacher!"

Like Ron, I was also impressed by the insights that Amy shared especially in her self-reflection. I also commented on her classroom management section regarding her student-centered approach for learning and emphasized that classroom management is about 90% engaged learning and 10% techniques such as motion management, eye contact, overlapping, and so forth. It is also important to note however that the lack of communication between the teacher-candidate and the clinical educator underscores the challenges inherent in fostering and coordinating university-school partnerships especially if staff and resources are already stretched thin trying to cope with existing demands. Although we take pride in the relationships we have developed with our K–12 partners, we only have one staff member working with these schools to arrange and manage the myriad of field experiences that are required each year. In addition, at the K–12 end, while we have had overwhelmingly positive experiences with superintendents, principals, and teachers, as anyone knows who has worked in schools, they tend to be "messy." This messiness can result in sidetracking even well-laid plans due to assemblies, fire drills, sickness, parent issues, teacher issues, student issues, and a whole gamut of other things. In addition, the reflections by Ron and Amy as well as my other students offer us insights into how we might go about restructuring our clinical experiences in cooperation with our host schools to create a more coherent program.

Based on both their written narratives and my follow-up conversations with these two students, I was gratified to see that they indeed had begun to enact the triumvirate of *relationships-relevance-rigor* while recognizing that while relationships are the necessary starting point, all three components must be integrated and seen as a whole-cloth that cements the connections between learning and classroom management. The other critical perspective that I try to instill in our preservice teachers is that in any classroom we should always recognize the roles of both student-teachers and teacher-students that give substance to the oft cited need for lifetime learning and condensed to its roots is the expression noted earlier "that if you have 20 students in a classroom, there are 21 potential teachers." By emphasizing the equal importance of teacher learning and student learning, my goal is to help students envision a vibrant learning classroom for both student and teacher learning which serves to prevent "teacher burnout."

While Ron and Amy are undergraduate pre-service teachers, I also had the opportunity to "listen in" to an online conversation among some of my doctoral students who are also experienced practicing teachers—"Mary, "Jane" and Elaine." Here is a brief synopsis of their discussion:

Mary: "I was thinking about collegiate prep for teachers. Although student teaching is a great concept, and we all had to do it, I often feel as though they do not get to see the real picture of what it is all about. Our student teachers "play" with the kids and make friends with them. Then they are surprised when they start working and it's not about pretty bulletin boards and binders but those phone calls with parents that were not expected ... sorry for the rant :) I would love to know if more/different prep could lead to more consistency in the field of education in general and special education in particular."

Jane: "Mary, you make a great point and none of that seemed like a rant to me! So much of our student teaching experience is sheltered from the realities of actually doing the job. I'm sure that is especially true for special educators, where the paperwork and frustrating phone calls are abundant. Maybe more realistic experiences would help to better prepare educators for the difficulties of the job. Your discussion here has me thinking back to my topic of using student data in planning/instruction. I've wondered if there isn't enough collegiate prep for this as well. This is another piece that student teachers really don't see or get involved in. Then it can be overwhelming when they're required to update a data wall, attend data analysis meetings, and somehow make use of all this information as they plan. If this is going to be such a big part of education, I feel like pre-service educators need more experience with it. Ok, now I'm ranting. :)"

Elaine: "Mary and Jane, as a regular education teacher, I was ill prepared for anything regarding special education. I couldn't even answer questions in my first interview because I did not receive adequate preparation on that topic. I still have teachers, many teachers, who do not understand the difference between modifications and adaptations, they do not read the SDI sections of the IEP and leave the special education teachers to make all of them. I am constantly providing training and additional information about their role in the child's education and how they are liable for their actions, or lack thereof."

Readers may find it surprising that this interchange was part of a discussion in a course in statistical procedures. I had asked these students to share their thoughts about the realities of teaching and how their preparation connected to teaching practice—including the usefulness of statistics! I found that these insights offered by certified teachers made a great case for the need for both more and better-designed clinical experiences in teacher education. Might it not be the case that even though schools of education try their best to prepare students to become excellent teachers, that we fail to offer the right balance between theory and practice?

GUIDED ENTRY INTO TEACHING

So, what can we do to educate teachers in ways that prepare them to create learning classrooms?

First, we must proclaim loudly and persistently that quality teachers and teaching entail a lot more than a record of academic scholarship! They also require a concomitant ability to create the kind of classroom environment that transcends "scientific" teaching approaches and whose success cannot be "measured" based solely on the results of standardized tests. Rather, if we believe that growth and attitudes towards lifelong learning are more important than "achievement," then it is time that we start redesigning teacher education to reflect these goals. We also must remember that we do not demean the teaching profession by thinking of it as a craft requiring the integration of theory and practice; rather, this recognition will enable us to create a mindset as we redesign teacher preparation programs that is more authentic to the realities of the classroom and thus to enable teachers to transform our classrooms into genuine places of learning.

Second, we must work to free the teaching profession from its need to devote so much valuable teaching time to accreditations, certifications, and high stakes standardized tests. Rather, we need to embrace our larger calling and view ourselves as lifetime adventurers whose primary goal is to view our students as fellow adventurers in learning and growth along all areas of development—cognitive, emotional, moral, physical, and social. This mindset is a requirement for enabling teachers to make remarkable and lasting impacts on the lives of all of our students. Of course, this will also require that teachers and administrators make strong efforts to help reshape educational policy.

Third, as a consequence of the first two admonitions we should strive to develop well-articulated ongoing apprenticeships grounded in the Three R's of Relationships, Relevance, and Rigor as described by Cooper and Garner (2012). As noted earlier, while apprenticeships are associated more with the "blue collar" trades, the concept underlying apprenticeships is that they provide a real-world or authentic setting where knowledge, skills, and attitudes can be integrated and nurtured under the tutelage of experienced teachers. While student teaching is supposed to fulfill this role, as Mary, Jane, and Elaine as practicing teachers described in their conversation, in too many cases this requirement does not allow future teachers to experience the kind of deep learning that results from the honing of theory by extended practice. The experiences of pre-service teachers Ron and Amy show that there are still a lot of nuts and bolts that must be tightened to create the kind of K–12 University partnerships that work in a coherent manner.

Fourth, we need to reexamine the kind of coursework that we require in teacher education. I have seen too often how we continue to try and superimpose the legacy of a flawed conception of quantitative and psychological research view on education research that is grounded in a flawed conception of the applicability of the scientific method (Lagemann, 2000). I can still recall quite vividly seeing an elementary school student with his backpack getting off the bus after school when I was a full-time doctoral student at a research university. Being a newly-minted member of the American Educational Research Association (AERA) and excitedly preparing to attend my first conference a question struck me—"what will we discuss and learn that will positively impact the life of this student?"—this question still haunts me. Why do we continue to spend so much time trying to foster a mindset where skill with standardized assessments and quantitative research is given great importance while the art of teaching demands that we nurture individuals with an environment where the hierarchy of relationships, relevance, and rigor offers us a much more fertile way to guide teachers into the profession? Our goal needs to be fostering scholar-practitioners who understand and appreciate that not only does learning inform practice but also that practice also informs learning. Amidst all of the continuing calls to make teaching and learning more scientific, there are some signs within this research community that point to the need to look at teaching and learning from a more pragmatic and practitioner-based perspective. For example, Yurkofsky et al. (2020) describe *continuous improvement* as a way to view research as grounded in both the individual school context and also dependent on the active involvement of practitioners. Hopefully, this type of thinking will begin to permeate our research efforts and thus serve to help us make teacher education more aligned with the realities of the classroom.

Overall, we must creatively explore ways to restructure teacher education in ways that result in the elevation of both the profession and teachers themselves. We also need to freely share our successes and challenges among ourselves as different school districts and universities work to shape teacher preparation programs whose cornerstone is some type of clinical practice so that teacher-candidates are provided with ongoing opportunities to hone their knowledge and skills within the context of the classroom. Perhaps we can learn new ideas from our colleagues in nursing and other professions where "clinicals" are a vital part of their preparation programs. There is one thing for certain and that is that we need to boldly proclaim that teaching is one of the most important professions and as both an art and a science, we have the right and the obligation to teach those kinds of practices that our best teachers have discovered that promotes exciting and profound learning and growth among our students. We need to remember that we need to see ourselves as lifetime adventurers whose primary mission is to help nurture the same kind of adventure among our students.

REFERENCES

American Association of Colleges for Teacher Education (2018). *A pivot toward clinical practice, its lexicon, and the renewal of educator preparation: A report of the AACTE clinical practice commission*.

Bernauer, J. A., Bernauer, M. P., & Bernauer, P. J. (2017). A family affair: Caring in teaching and implications for teacher and researcher preparation. *Brock Education Journal, 26*(2), 4–15.

Bruner, J. S. (1966). *Toward a theory of instruction*. Norton.

Bruner, J. S. (1973). *Beyond the information given: Studies in the psychology of knowing*. Norton.

Bruner, J. S. (1996). *The culture of education*. Harvard University Press.

Cooper, N., & Garner, B. K. (2012). *Developing a learning classroom: Moving beyond management through relationships, relevance, and rigor*. Corwin.

Dewey, J. (1963). *The child and the curriculum; The school and society*. The University of Chicago Press.

Dewey, J. (1981). *The philosophy of John Dewey*. The University of Chicago Press.

Eisner, E. W. (1998). *The enlightened eye*. Prentice Hall.

Eisner, E. W. (2002). *The educational imagination*. Merrill Prentice Hall.

Gardner, H. (2006). *Multiple intelligences*. Basic Books.

Goodlad, J. I. (1984). *A place called school*. McGraw-Hill Book Company

Highet, G. (1950). *The art of teaching*. Vintage Books.

Jones, D. A. (2011). Apprenticeships back to the future. *Issues in Science & Technology*, 27(4), 51–56.

Lagemann, P. (2000). *An elusive science. The troubling history of educational research*. University of Chicago Press.

Lave, J. (1988). *Cognition in practice: Mind, mathematics, and culture in everyday life*. Cambridge University Press.

Lave, J. (1997). The culture of acquisition and the practice of understanding. In D. Kirshner & J. A. Whitson (Eds.), *Situated cognition: Social, semiotic, and psychological perspectives* (pp. 17–35). Erlbaum.

Lave, J., & Wenger, E. (1991). *Situated learning: Legitimate peripheral participation*. Cambridge University Press.

Lorenzo, J. (2017). *The rise of the modern American apprenticeship*. Public Policy Initiative. https://publicpolicy.wharton.upenn.edu/live/news/2196-the-rise-of-the-modern-american-apprenticeship#_edn10

Lortie, D. C. 1975). *Schoolteacher*. The University of Chicago Press.

No Child Left Behind Act. (2002). P.L. 107-110, Title IX, Part A, Section 9101 (22), p. 544, 20 U.S.C. 7802.

Perkins, D. N., & Salomon, G. (2012). Knowledge to go: A motivational and dispositional view of transfer. *Educational Psychologist, 47*, 248–258. https://doi.org/10.1080/00461520.2012.693354.

Piaget, J. (1963). *Origins of intelligence in children*. Norton.

Piaget, J. (1964). Development and learning. In R. Ripple & V. Rockcastle (Eds.), *Piaget rediscovered* (pp. 7–20). Cornell University Press.

Piaget, J. (1969). *Science of education and the psychology of the child*. Viking.

Vygotsky, L. S. (1978). Mind in society. *The development of higher mental process*. Harvard University Press.

Vygotsky, L. S. (1986). *Thought and language*. MIT Press.

Yurkofsky, M. M., Peterson, A. J., Mehta, J. D., Willis, R. H., & Frumin K. M. (2020). Research on continuous improvement: Exploring the complexities of managing educational change. *Review of Research in Education, 44*(1), 403–433. https://doi.org/10.3102/0091732X20907363

CHAPTER 31

EDUCATION AND CULTURE

One University's Experience Placing Teacher Candidates in Classrooms in the Cotswold Region of England

Tracy Mulvaney and Kathryn Lubniewski
Monmouth University

Wendy Morales
Middletown Township Public Schools

ABSTRACT

In 2010, the National Council for Accreditation of Teacher Education (NCATE) published the Blue Ribbon Report focusing on expanding and improving clinical education. This report was then operationalized by the Association for Colleges for Teacher Education's (AACTE) Clinical Practice Commission's (CPC) report in 2018. Both documents place an emphasis on clinical education as the primary structure in which teacher preparation stands. As a result, educator preparation programs (EPPs) have been given guidance on defining clinical practice (CP), creating a common lexicon for CP concepts, improving research-based CP experiences, and designing pathways

Preparing Quality Teachers:
Advances in Clinical Practice, pp. 667–684
Copyright © 2022 by Information Age Publishing
www.infoagepub.com
667

in which EPPs can implement CP strategies. This chapter aims to describe a unique program and partnership with an International\Teacher Preparation Touring Program based in Winchcombe, England that includes a full-time two-week clinical component. The clinical practice experience places students in elementary and secondary schools, and schools for students with disabilities in the Cotswold region of England. Although the travel abroad component of the program is over approximately three weeks, the program spans almost an entire academic year and further enriches the relationship between Monmouth University University's educator preparation program and the CPC proclamations outlined in the 2018 report (AACTE, 2018).

INTRODUCTION

The Monmouth University School of Education Study Abroad Program is unlike most others offered throughout the United States. This unique academic experience marries immersive cultural learning to a two-week full-time clinical practice, placing teacher candidates in P–12 schools in international settings. Candidates prepare the semester prior to the study abroad and participate in the actual course the semester after. In the United States, all teacher preparation candidates are required to complete some form of clinical practice, however how many candidates can say they have completed an additional 75 hours teaching outside of the United States in another country? This unique three-credit course provides students with a three-pronged approach (see Figure 31.1) to maximize the study abroad experience: pre-travel preparation (academic and cultural awareness), immersive cultural experience, and post-travel reflection and scholarship.

All candidates in their sophomore year or above are eligible to participate in the program. Although the program spans a full academic year, the travel occurs in the winter intersession, and the course for credit occurs in the spring. In brief, prior to their travel abroad, candidates participate in pre-travel seminars that assist them in preparing to travel and teach abroad in the fall semester. These seminars focus on topics related to the host culture, education differences and similarities between the host country and the United States, professionalism (dispositions), and travel essentials (e.g., passport, health/safety). Then during January, they spend approximately three weeks traveling through London and various regions of England while interning for two full weeks in P–12 schools. The travel component of this program occurs during winter recess when students have no other course or clinical obligations on or around campus. Throughout their travel, they participate in seminars and complete reflections about their experience. Upon return in the spring semester, students engage in activities that support reflection and scholarship while being enrolled in the actual course. This year-long timeline allows for the maximization of

Figure 31.1

Monmouth University Teacher Preparation Study Abroad Framework

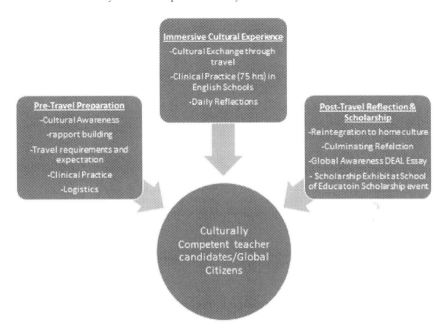

the experience by providing students with extensive preparation activities, cultural immersion, and reflection and scholarship opportunities.

BACKGROUND AND CONTEXT

This program began over 30 years ago at an institution in Illinois. It has since developed and been duplicated at Monmouth University in New Jersey. The foundations of the program were based on Levinson's (1978) theory of adult learning, where he describes an early adult transition from the ages of 17–22, where individuals leave home and make their first choices about career and education. During this time, individuals are making decisions based on the need to want to "be seen" as an adult. By choosing to enroll in this course, teacher candidates are taking on the role of a teacher's assistant in another country and holding the responsibilities of that "job" during the two-week time period that they are there. They quickly find out whether this is a field that they are interested in, or if they want to transition out based on the experience that they have. In turn helping them in the next transition phase of entering the adult world (ages 22–28), which one of the main goals is committing to an occupation.

Arnett's (2000) theory of emerging adulthood is also a foundation to this course because he describes young adults as roughly the ages of 18 to 25 years old, and that they have five distinctive features: (1) identify exploration, (2) instability, (3) self-focus, (4) feeling in-between adolescence and adulthood, and (5) a sense of broad possibilities for the future. One of the purposes of the development of this course was also to support the feature of exploration. Through the design of projects within the course like the stakeholder interview, or the daily reflective journals, teacher candidates are challenged to explore their thoughts. The course also embedded the feature of self-focus by using reflection to help guide young adults through their daily perceptions and experiences in the classroom. The foundations of Levinson and Arnett's theories helped with the creation of the learning goals for the course, and to support the development of teacher candidates within the program.

PROGRAM GOALS

The academic programming and learning goals are central to the experience for students. The course goals (see Figure 31.2) focus on elements resulting in an improved cultural competence within teaching and an overall improved knowledge and practice of global citizenship. The goals span the entirety of the program and mastery is measured throughout. The embedded nature of this course allows instructors to gage progress on goal achievement using a holistic assessment approach.

The program goals are broadly written to encompass those covered under our university general education requirements for global understanding credit. Woven into the coursework are course goals that include high leverage teaching practices, pedagogical theory and practice, and clinical practice preparation and support. These goals are taught, assessed, and reported through the university's established processes. Some examples of the types of assessment are later discussed in this chapter under program design.

Review of the Literature

Countless studies have detailed the many benefits of study abroad programs. For example, the Institute for the International Education of Students (IES), examined survey data from more than 3,400 alumni of study abroad programs from 1950–1999 and found a positive impact on participants' personal growth, intercultural development, academic commitment, and career development (Dwyer & Peters, 2004). Ungar (2016)

Figure 31.2

Monmouth University School of Education Study Abroad Goals

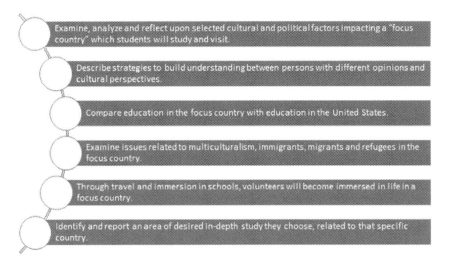

claimed that the solution to Americans knowing and understanding others in today's global society is to "massively increase the number of U.S. college and university students who go abroad for some part of their education and bring home essential knowledge and new perspectives" (p. 112). The National Association of Foreign Student Advisers (NAFSA) reiterated Ungar's argument by stating that those who study abroad are, "better prepared for the demands of the twenty-first century" and develop skills that improve United States foreign policy, as well as national and economic security (NAFSA, 2021).

More specifically, Gardner et al. (2008) found that employers identified certain positive traits in their employees who had engaged in a study abroad experience. These included the employees' ability to adapt to change, gain new knowledge from experiences, understand cultural differences, and interact with people who possess different interests, values, or perspectives. A study by Smith and Miltry (2008) confirmed that even short-term programs, "enhance students' cross-cultural skills and global understanding" (p. 240). Research has demonstrated that engaging in study abroad experiences improve students' cognitive processes related to creative thinking (Lee et al., 2012). Despite these benefits, most postsecondary students do not engage in study abroad opportunities.

The Commission on the Abraham Lincoln Study Abroad Fellowship Program, formed in 2005, established a goal that 1 million American students would participate in a study abroad program by the 2016–17 academic year. The commission argued that students who studied overseas, "enhanced their interest in academic work, helped them acquire important career 'skill sets,' and continued for decades to influence their perspective on world events" (p. vi). Unfortunately, the commission did not reach its goal. According to the Institute of International Education (IIE), only 341,751 of the nation's students participated in study abroad programs in the 2017–18 academic year. While this number reflected a 2.7% increase from the year before, it does not come close to the goal set by the commission in 2004 (IIE, 2019).

Research has demonstrated that participating in study abroad is especially important to students in teacher preparation programs. In today's globalized world, teachers must prepare their students to succeed in an increasingly connected, culturally diverse society. In 2018, the Program for International Student Assessment (PISA) assessed students' global competence for the first time since it was first administered in 2000. The Organisation for Economic Co-operation and Development (OECD, 2020) defines globally competent individuals as those who can, "examine local, global and intercultural issues … understand and appreciate different perspectives and worldviews and interact successfully and respectfully with others … [and] take responsible action toward sustainability and collective well-being." Although the United States did not participate in the global competence assessment in 2018, numerous world-renowned organizations such as UNESCO, Asia Society, and the Longview Foundation call for an increased focus on global education in all grade levels and subject areas (Morales, 2020).

Due to the fact that there are few opportunities for in-service teachers to develop their own global competence (Morales, 2020), the responsibility predominantly falls on postsecondary teacher education programs. In 1992, Merryfield and Harris pointed out the lack of global studies in teacher education programs. They provided recommendations for how to increase teacher candidates' global perspectives including creating "cross-campus ties" that "internationalize the campus" (Merryfield & Harris, 1992, pp. 60–61). Kahn et al. (2014) argued that teacher preparation programs need to increase their students' cultural competence by providing them with multicultural education courses, as well as opportunities to work with diverse groups of students and participate in a variety of field experiences to increase their cultural competence. The research supports this claim. A study by Poole and Russell (2015) found a "significant positive relationship" between preservice teachers' global perspectives and their exposure to "global content courses and co-curricular cross-cultural experiences" (p. 50).

Many institutes of higher education have dedicated significant resources to increasing their preservice teachers' global competence through different types of structured international experiences. These programs have yielded other significant results as well. DeVillar and Jiang (2012) shared the positive impact an international student teaching experience had on preservice teachers' self-efficacy. Not only did the participants find value in the cultural and language experiences in their host classrooms, but they were also able to successfully transfer instructional techniques they learned abroad into their U.S. classrooms. Similarly, Chao et al. (2019) discovered an increase in preservice teachers cross-cultural understanding and critical awareness after studying abroad. These competencies were also successfully integrated into the participants' pedagogical practices when they started teaching in the United States.

Cushner (2007) stressed the importance of experiential learning in developing preservice teachers' global perspectives. He stated:

> Experiential learning, which engages both the right and left hemispheres of the brain, links an experience with cognition. The international immersion experience plays a major role in the success of this effort—there is just no substitute for the real thing. (p. 35)

While national organizations dedicated to teacher preparation and practice do not specify that experiential learning must take place abroad, their expectations certainly confirm the belief that preservice teachers should engage in more than the traditional student teacher experience. In 2010, the National Council for Accreditation of Teacher Education (NCATE) published the Blue Ribbon Panel report that promoted clinical practice as the foundation for all teacher preparation. The American Association of Colleges for Teacher Education (AACTE) operationalized the Blue Ribbon Panel report by developing its Clinical Practice Commission report, which served to define ten essential proclamations to define essential, research based practice for effective clinical preparation (AACTE, 2018). The Monmouth University School of Education has aligned those 10 essential proclamations to study abroad program experience (see Table 31.1).

The program aligns directly to each of the 10 components. Each proclamation is seamlessly stitched into the program implementation. Additionally, the program goals are aligned not only to the CPC report proclamations, but supports the appropriate standards outlined by the Council for the Accreditation of Educator Preparation (CAEP), the main accrediting body for educator preparation.

In their 2022 standards, CAEP stated that partnerships and clinical practices should offer candidates experiences in, "different settings and modalities, as well as with diverse P–12 students, schools, families, and

Table 31.1

Monmouth University University Teacher Education International Clinical Program Alignment to AACTE Clinical Practice Commission Proclamations

CPC Proclamation	MU Alignment to Proclamation
Central Proclamation	Two-week full-time clinical practice (CP) in P–12 international classrooms promotes the value of CP as central to high-quality teacher preparation.
Pedagogy Proclamation	Candidates provide support in international schools and teach high impact lessons in collaboration and under the guidance of host school-based clinical educators.
Skills Proclamation	Candidates utilize and are assessed by their international clinical educator on high leverage teaching practices.
Partnership Proclamation	The international partnership between Monmouth University University and our P–12 partners in England and Hong Kong are well established, have been vetted through faculty staff and administrative processes and continue to thrive.
Infrastructure Proclamation	The study abroad infrastructure is built through the university approval process, Office of International Studies, and our partners in the international school settings. A course is offered as a three-credit Global Understandings course that has been approved for all education majors.
Developmental Proclamation	The partnership continues to develop based on the assessment of each experience by all stakeholders. Due to this approach, participation by candidates continues to grow.
Empowerment Proclamation	Candidates complete reflections throughout the program that show growth in empowerment. They present their experiences at SOE staff meetings, scholarship night, and to others interested in the program.
Mutual Benefit Proclamation	Collaboration between candidates, school- and university-based clinical educators and international tour liaisons work together to ensure success of candidates.
Common Language Proclamation	AACTE language is strengthened throughout the CP experience. In additions, candidates learn language common in international schools to ensure an understanding when engaged in the CP.
Expertise Proclamation	This offers teacher candidates experiences that can inform the process and vision for renewing educator preparation.

communities" (CAEP, 2021, Standard 2). Furthermore, the National Board for Professional Teaching Standards (NBPTS, 2016) stresses the importance of teachers building a global learning community and developing an "understanding of multiculturalism" (p. 39). These expectations solidify the claim that exposure to diverse settings and people benefit teachers and their students. Participating in a study abroad opportunity is certainly one-way preservice teachers can work toward increasing their own global competence and eventually that of their students.

PROGRAM CONTEXT AND DESIGN

Design

The foundation and design of the program is what is critical to the in-depth experiences that are reported by the teacher candidates who have attended the study abroad course. The key components are ongoing seminars, focused reflections, immersive clinical experiences, and reflective practitioners to lifelong scholars.

Ongoing Seminars

Seminars begin the semester prior to travel and continue throughout the program. There are four pretravel seminars and are conducted at the university in the states. During these seminars, the faculty build a rapport and supportive community with the group. The teacher candidates learn about the host culture, cultural norms, and their potential biases. There is an in-depth examination of the host culture's educational system with comparisons between the United States and the host country. During the seminars, they also prepare for international travel by completing specific documents that are needed, learning about the requirements of travel, and the expectations while traveling within the course.

Seven seminars occur during travel. During these seminars, the teacher candidates share their experience, learn from each other, and from guest speakers who are invited to share and build on the cultural experience in England. The faculty guide the discussion to include key ideas or misconceptions that were discussed in their daily individual journals (see below under focused reflections).

After traveling during the spring semester, there are three seminars. During these seminars, the teacher candidates debrief and reflect on their experiences now that they have returned. They discuss how this is going to affect their teaching and prepare how they are going to professionally share the information that they have learned.

Focused Reflections

Throughout the experience, the teacher candidates are required to reflect in individual journals that are only shared with the faculty teaching the course. The reflections are focused and have specific questions that build on each other as the course continues. For example, the first reflection journal is, "What is something you are excited about? What are you the most nervous about?" When they are abroad, they get to pick from a list of prompts to answer. So, one of the prompts may be, "What was the biggest challenge today? What would you do differently? What did you learn from it?" Then when they return from the study abroad experience an example prompt is, "Now that you are home, what have you noticed? How has this impacted you?"

An important component of these reflections is that the questions focus on where they are at that point of their cultural journey. It is important to provide them with choices of the prompts because depending on the day, feelings, and other factors some prompts are more appropriate than others are. The reflections occur three times pre-travel, then every day when they are teaching in schools (see more about immersive clinical experiences), and then two times post-travel.

Immersive Clinical Experiences

The main feature of this program is that the individual teacher candidates from the United States are placed in an immersive experience for two weeks. As we stated above, Alan interviews current certified teachers in England to evaluate and identify teachers to support teacher candidates from the United States. When teacher candidate's sign up for the course, they are asked to identify their content areas for certification and preferred grade levels of teaching. They identify three choices of settings and have options for specific schools in England that focus on students with disabilities. Then Alan and the faculty from the United States work together to partner the teacher from England with the teacher candidate from the United States.

Teacher candidates begin the two-week immersive experience on the first day after the winter break. The faculty go with the teacher candidate on the first day and arrive a little bit earlier than the teacher arrives. Some of the placements set up a scheduled meeting for the teacher candidates to learn about the school, while others just work individually with the cooperating teacher. The first day is a full day of observing and working with their cooperating teacher. The teacher candidate is prepared to enter this setting because of the ongoing seminars and support. The first day for the teacher candidate is typically doing a lot of observing and asking questions to become familiar in the classroom; however, observations are not encouraged to last too many days because the goal of the program is to gain as much hands-on-experience as possible.

Within the second or third day, the teacher candidates are encouraged to support the teacher as much as possible. Some responsibilities include walking around while the teacher is teaching and answering questions, making copies, creating bulletin boards, or working with students one-on-one or in small groups. As the two-week experience builds, the teacher candidate should become more involved in the classroom by co-teaching with the cooperating teacher and eventually teaching a lesson or a few!

One of the assignments that is built into the immersive experience during the first week is for the teacher candidates to identify key stakeholders (within the school) that their cooperating teacher communicates with on a daily basis. The teacher candidates then identify and set up a time during the site visit to meet with one of these individuals to gain insight on education in England. During their interview they ask a set of specific questions like, "What is your role in the school?", "Why did you become a teacher?", and "What are the benefits of working at this school?" to name a few questions. They also need to add in at least two additional questions that they created on their own based on their understanding and experiences. Finally, the teacher candidates write up a reflection about what they learned answering some questions like, "What is something you have been looking forward to doing at this placement?", "What is something you have been nervous about doing at this placement?", and "Describe your collaboration and plans to collaborate to improve student learning."

During the immersive experience, cooperating teachers and teacher candidates are encouraged to have the faculty come to observe them in the classroom. The open communication with the school or cooperating teacher as well as the teacher candidate are critical in the success of the program. At the end of the experience, the cooperating teacher provides feedback evaluating the performance of the teacher candidate (see Appendix). The cooperating teacher is asked to complete the evaluation of their performance based on a 0–5 ranking scale, with 0 meaning major improvement up to five meaning exceptional. The cooperating teacher is requested to put this in a sealed envelope and return it to the faculty member, teacher candidate or to mail it back to the United States so that the evaluation can be as authentic as possible.

Reflective Practitioners to Lifelong Scholars

Once the teacher candidates return to the states, it is critical that cultural exploration and work continues throughout not only the course but also their lives. There are two ways that this is assigned through the course (along with their post-seminar reflections) is through a research-based model of clinical reflection. It begins where the students describe an experiential learning related experience (D), then they examine experience from personal, academic, and civic engagement perspectives (E), and finally they articulate their learning (AL). This type of critical reflective essay is called a DEAL essay (Ash, Clayton, & Moses, 2009). Along with the DEAL essay, the teacher candidates are also required to complete and participate in a poster presentation at scholarship week.

For the DEAL essay (adapted from Ash & Clayton, 2009), teacher candidates write a critical essay, using a variety of sources that provides a detailed analysis of education in England compared to the United States. This assignment is built on the premise that understanding of interconnectedness and interdependence within a particular culture and the larger world will help us to better appreciate and comprehend that culture's educational practices.

The poster presentation that the teacher candidates complete for scholarship week includes a reflection on the site (context), description of the students, their specific assignments/role, what the teacher candidate learned through the experience, and a reflection. In the reflection, the teacher candidate addresses the strengths and problems in education facing other countries, solutions, obstacles, ethics, the personal relevance of the issues, and how these issues shape global phenomena, and the impact on globalization. They also include how they influenced the site based on knowing this information.

Finally, as part of ongoing personal development, the faculty who hosted the trip also organize activities outside of the university classroom where the group can get together to catch up and continue to build their relationships. Some examples of this could be going to a park, meeting for ice cream or lunch, or meeting at an on-campus activity. The teacher candidates are also offered opportunities to help in the recruitment process for the upcoming study abroad course. During these opportunities, they are invited to share their experiences and answer questions about the course to potential teacher candidates who are interested in attending the course in the future. The teacher candidates will often discuss that they love sharing their experience and helping others make the decision to study abroad because it is something that has made such an impact on their lives. Throughout each of these culminating experiences, it is important that teacher candidates realize that the relationships that they formed while abroad can last a lifetime and create opportunities that they may not have had otherwise.

Assessment of Learning

Student success in respect to achieving course goals is measured throughout the experience. Informal and formal assessments that are both formative and summative in nature are utilized to capture the whole experience from start to finish. Informal assessments include observations, quizzes, checklist of tasks completed, reflections, seminar participation, and university based clinical educator observation of classroom performance/engagement. The two main formative assessments include the DEAL essay and the Scholarship Night Poster Presentation. Figure 31.3 shares some sample forms of formative and summative assessments used to evaluate each candidate's mastery of program and course goals through the framework.

IMPLICATIONS FOR FUTURE WORK

The Monmouth University School of Education is committed to furthering the work on study abroad programming. A committee has been formed to discuss international education, and part of their charge is to create, support, and approve study abroad programs within the School of Education, prior to submitting it through the university process. The committee meets monthly and presents regularly at the School of Education. The

Figure 31.3

Assessing Student Learning in the School of Education Study Abroad Program

Assessments Used throughout the Study Abroad Experience		
Pre-Travel Preparation	**Immersive Cultural Experience**	**Post-Travel Reflection and Scholarship**
- Formitive Quizzes	- Reflections	- Reflections
-Task completion (travel documents, course documents)	-Nightly Seminar participation	- DEAL Essay
-participation in five seminars	- University Observation of candidate	-Scholarship Night Poster Presentation
	-Formal cooperating teacher evaluation	- Participation in Faculty Development (optional)
		-Recruitment for future travel

committee often works in collaboration with the Social Justice Committee and creates professional development opportunities for faculty and staff to grow. Additionally, students who have participated in the study abroad programs have come to present their experiences to the School of Education.

Growing the Program

The foundations of the program in England (i.e., ongoing seminars, focused reflections, immersive clinical experiences, and reflective practitioners to lifelong scholars) can be created in other areas around the world. The School of Education at Monmouth University felt that it was important to provide a variety of cultural experiences for the teacher candidates. Therefore, after two successful events in England, a new program was designed to place students in schools for approximately two weeks in Hong Kong. The inaugural trip was scheduled for January of 2020; however, political unrest diverted the trip to China on relatively short notice. Although the teacher candidates were able to visit primary, secondary and postsecondary schools, they were not able to work consistently in classrooms. The trip to Hong Kong, we hope, will continue to run every other year opposite England. Faculty have been encouraged to explore other partnerships for both initial and advanced educator preparation programs.

One such advanced opportunity the School of Education is exploring is connecting the Educational Leadership Program with schools in Europe. The doctoral program in Educational Leadership has a course titled "International Leadership Styles." This course is designed to study P–12 school and leadership models and structures. The course has been presented in either online or hybrid form, but really lends itself well to a study abroad course design. The program has initiated conversations regarding this opportunity and will continue to explore it.

Research and Scholarship

The School of Education faculty has also discussed researching this study abroad model in the following ways: impacts on candidates, impacts on students in the host country, strength of the partnership, and effectiveness of the program model/framework. Long and short-term impacts on candidates should be studied and measured using prompts stemming from the CPC Proclamations, most specifically the empowerment, central, pedagogy, skills, and expertise proclamations. Some examples are to collect data from the pre, during, and post reflective journals to compare how the teacher candidate's perceptions have changed throughout the experience. Another idea for research is to create a presurvey and administer it prior to their experience in the course, and then administer it after they return to the states. Even, use this survey a year after they have returned to compare the data to see the long-term impacts of the experience. Data gained from this research could be shared in multiple ways including journals, books, conference presentations, webinars, and more.

To evaluate the effectiveness of the partnership, prompts can be drawn from the Partnership and Mutual Benefit Proclamations of the AACTE Clinical Practice Commission Report. Such research could include interviews of stakeholders from the involved Monmouth University faculty, host country P–12 administrators and clinical educators, and program level administrators from both Monmouth University and the England administrative sides. A grounded theory approach to data analysis would be beneficial to determine themes. Another consideration would be to conduct a case study evaluation of the whole program to be used to compare to other subsequent international partnerships of the same model within the Monmouth University School of Education.

Finally, to ensure the program continues to align with the AACTE's Clinical Practice Commission's Infrastructure and Developmental Proclamations, the university is considering a thorough investigation into the effectiveness of the program. That investigation would consider data gleaned from that obtained through the candidate/student and partnership studies. It would also include an evaluation of the operations including budget, administrative effectiveness and efficiency, ability to replicate, and the development of a system of continuous program improvement.

CONCLUSION

The Monmouth University School of Education study abroad program provides students with clinical experiences in school placements in England. Following the research provided in the literature review, along with the AACTE Clinical Practice Commission Report, the program boasts a dynamic opportunity to engage in clinical practice. The full-time immersive two-week clinical practice is supplemented with opportunities to learn about and explore culture in both the city of London and the small towns of the Cotswold region. Given the success of the program, the faculty continues to strengthen the partnership, while exploring other possibilities. The School of Education is committed to providing students with increased opportunities for immersive learning both in the United States and abroad.

APPENDIX

Evaluation of Performance (to be completed by Cooperating Teacher or Professional)

The following evaluation and information should be completed by a Certified Teacher or Licensed Professional, who supervised this field experience. Please circle the number that best applies (5 = exceptional to 0 = needs major improvement).

Professional Behavior as a Future Teacher	Professional Behavior With Students
Goes "above and beyond" and strives to attain excellence. 5 4 3 2 1 0	Demonstrates a positive attitude. 5 4 3 2 1 0
Demonstrates great interest in learning about school/students. 5 4 3 2 1 0	Asks thoughtful questions to enhance student learning. 5 4 3 2 1 0
Behavior shown to faculty, staff, classmates, and/or those we serve. 5 4 3 2 1 0	Seeks opportunities to help. 5 4 3 2 1 0
Is consistently on-time. 5 4 3 2 1 0	Communicates appropriately with students. 5 4 3 2 1 0
Dresses appropriately. 5 4 3 2 1 0	Aptitude for teaching. 5 4 3 2 1 0
Additional Comments:	

REFERENCES

American Association of Colleges for Teacher Education. (2018). *A pivot toward clinical practice, it's lexicon, and the renewal of educator preparation: A report of the AACTE Clinical Practice Commission.*

Arnett, J. J. (2000). Emerging adulthood: A theory of development from the late teens through the twenties. *American Psychologist, 55*, 469–480.

Ash, S. L., & Clayton, P. H. (2009). Generating, deepening, and documenting learning: The power of critical reflection in applied learning. *Journal of Applied Learning in Higher Education, 1*(1), 25–48.

Chao, X., Xue, M., Jetmore, R., Fritsch, R., Kang, B., & Xu, M. (2019). Organic learning. *Teacher Education Quarterly, 46*(2), 7–29.

Commission on the Abraham Lincoln Study Abroad Fellowship Program. (2005). *Global competence & national needs. One million Americans studying abroad.* http://www.nafsa.org/_/Document/_/lincoln_commission_report.pdf

Council for the Accreditation of Educator Preparation. (2021). *2022 initial levelstandards.* http://www.ncate.org/~/media/Files/caep/standards/2022-initial-standards-1-pager-final.pdf?la=en

Cushner, K. (2007). The role of experience in the making of internationally-minded teachers. *Teacher Education Quarterly, 34*(1), 27–39.

DeVillar, R. A., & Jiang, B. (2012). From student teaching abroad to teaching in the US classroom: Effects of global experiences on local instructional practice. *Teacher Education Quarterly, 39*(3), 7–24.

Dwyer, M. M., & Peters, C. K. (2004). The benefits of study abroad. *Transitions Abroad, 37*(5), 56–58.

Gardner, P., Gross, L., & Steglitz, I. (2008). Unpacking your study abroad experience: Critical reflection for workplace competencies. *CERI, 1*(1), 1-2008.

Institute of International Education. (2019). *Number of international students in the United States hits all-time high.* https://www.iie.org/Why-IIE/Announcements/2019/11/Number-of-International-Students-in-the-United-States-Hits-All-Time-High.

Kahn, L. G., Lindstrom, L., & Murray, C. (2014). Factors contributing to preservice teachers' beliefs about diversity. *Teacher Education Quarterly, 41*(4), 53–70.

Lee, C. S., Therriault, D. J., & Linderholm, T. (2012). On the cognitive benefits of cultural experience: Exploring the relationship between studying abroad and creative thinking. *Applied Cognitive Psychology, 26*(5), 768–778.

Levinson, D. (1978). *The seasons of a man's life.* Alfred A. Knopf.

Merryfield, M. M., & Harris, J. (1992). Getting started in global education: Essential literature, essential linkages for teacher educators. *School of Education Review, 4*(1), 56–66.

Morales, W. G. (2020). *The impact of global citizenship education on select Grades 35 teachersin a New Jersey public school district* [Unpublished doctoral dissertation]. Monmouth University University.

National Association of Foreign Student Advisers. (2021). *Public policy benefits of study abroad.* https://www.nafsa.org/policy-and-advocacy/what-we-stand-for/public-policy-benefits-study-abroad

National Board for Professional Teaching Standards. (2016). *What teachers should know and be able to do*. http://accomplishedteacher.org/wp-content/uploads/2016/12/NBPTS-What-Teachers-Should-Know-and-Be-Able-to-Do-.pdf

Organisation for Economic Co-operation and Development. (2020). *PISA 2018 global competence*. https://www.oecd.org/pisa/pisa-2018-global-competence.htm

Poole, C. M., & Russell, W. B. (2015). Educating for global perspectives: A study of teacher preparation programs. *Journal of Education, 195*(3), 41–52.

Smith, D. E., & Mitry, D. J. (2008). Benefits of study abroad and creating opportunities: The case for short-term programs. *Journal of Research in Innovative Teaching, 1*(1), 236–246.

Ungar, S. J. (2016). The study-abroad solution: How to open the American mind. *Foreign Affairs, 95*(2), 111–123.

ABOUT THE AUTHORS

James A. Bernauer, Robert Morris University teaches undergrad, masters, and doctoral students in the School of Nursing, Education, and Human Studies primarily in the areas of educational psychology, learning theory, qualitative research, and statistical procedures. His primary interest is to better understand and improve both teaching and learning.

Esther M. H. Billings, PhD, is a Professor in the Department of Mathematics at Grand Valley State University, focusing on the mathematical preparation of elementary teachers. Her research interests include: supporting and preparing prospective teachers to teach via mediated field experiences, examining the ways job-embedded professional development impacts teachers' instruction, and ways to support and develop learners' algebraic thinking.

Melinda C. Knapp, PhD, is a Senior Instructor in the College of Education at Oregon State University-Cascades. She is particularly interested in how novice and expert teachers attend to students' mathematical thinking through discourse with other students. Her research has focused on examining the learning potential of mediated field experiences and identifying practice-based approaches in learning to teach and in professional development.

Charlotte J. D. Sharpe, PhD, is an Assistant Professor of Mathematics Education at Syracuse University. She studies how teachers develop productive beliefs about and practices for working with diverse learners. Her research foci include mediated field experiences, school and district supports for teacher learning, and design-based research methods for studying student and teacher learning.

Barbara A. Swartz, PhD, is an assistant professor of Mathematics Education at West Chester University of Pennsylvania. She integrates her research and teaching efforts to prepare effective teachers of mathematics at all levels and has a passion for designing learning opportunities that support all learners in making sense of mathematics. Her research interests revolve around investigating effective ways to develop current and future teachers' knowledge, skills, and dispositions to implement equity-based teaching practices, including the eight teaching practices recommended by the National Council of Teachers of Mathematics.

Sararose D. Lynch is an associate professor of education at Westminster College in New Wilmington, PA where she primarily teaches mathematics and special education methods courses. Her research lies at the intersection of math education and special education. She is interested in how teachers develop productive beliefs about and practices for designing learning opportunities that support all learners in conceptually-based mathematics classrooms.

Virginia McCormack, is a Professor of Education. She works with diverse students in all of the Education programs. She is a certified/licensed P–12 classroom teacher and administrator with experiences in early childhood, middle childhood, and adult and young adult classrooms in rural, suburban, and urban locations. Dr. McCormack has served as chair of Ohio Dominican University's Education Division and Director of the MEd program. She participates on university committees; has received several grants for course development, reading and teacher preparation; and develops curricular programs and endorsements for undergraduate and graduate studies.

Lesley J. Shapiro, EdD, is a science teacher at Classical High School in Providence, RI where she teaches biology, chemistry, and various science electives. Lesley has been a cooperating teacher for Rhode Island College since 2012 and has worked with seven student teachers. Her research interests include the development of preservice and early career teachers pedagogical practice and professional engagement through intentional mentoring.

Rudolf V. Kraus is an assistant professor of secondary education at Rhode Island College in Providence, RI where he is the coordinator of science education, teaches methods courses, and supervises secondary science teacher candidates. His research interests include the development of relationships in clinical practice experiences and integration of inquiry-based pedagogy in science classes.

Holly Henderson Pinter, PhD, is an associate professor of middle grades education at Western Carolina University. Pinter completed a PhD in 2013 at the University of Virginia. Dr. Pinter's teaching and research center on the implementation of standards-based mathematical teaching practices, preservice teacher education policy and practice, and developmentally responsive teaching at the middle level. Pinter teaches methods and pedagogy courses in the elementary and middle grades department as well as serving as the Math 1 teacher and instructional liaison at the university's laboratory school, The Catamount School, and serves as program coordinator for elementary and middle grades education.

Amanda L. Rose, EdD, is a secondary-level assistant principal and instructional coach in Lee County, Florida. Her research interests include the professional development needs of alternatively certified teachers in Florida and methods to support novice teachers to ensure quality teaching and retention in the profession.

Jennifer A. Sughrue, PhD, is a professor of educational leadership and the coordinator of the EdD in Education program at Florida Gulf Coast University. Her research interests span K–20 education law and policy, with an emphasis on law- and policy-to-practice.

Amber G. Candela is an associate professor of mathematics education at the University of Missouri–St. Louis where she primarily teaches mathematics methods courses. Her research interests include the professional development of mathematics teachers.

April Regester is an associate professor of inclusive education at the University of Missouri–St. Louis. April's introduction to inclusive education was in high school, where she had the privilege of participating in programs designed to include and support students with and without disabilities. The benefits of inclusive experiences led to her own career pathway and research interests to improve access and equity for all students, including those with disabilities.

Nancy Robb Singer is an associate professor and associate dean at the University of Missouri–St. Louis. Her research interests include teacher preparation and induction, composition theory and research, and writing assessment.

Jennifer Fisher is an assistant teaching professor of art education at the University of Missouri–St. Louis where she primarily teaches visual art methods courses. Her research interests focus on high ability visual artists.

Julie Smith Sodey is an assistant teaching professor at the University of Missouri–St. Louis. Her teaching is focused on educator preparation, and she designs and supervises early clinical experiences in P–12 schools and community agencies.

Stephanie Koscielski is the Director of Clinical Experience and School Partnerships at the University of Missouri–St. Louis where she oversees clinical experiences and related certification requirements for the university's teacher candidates.

Nicolle von der Heyde is a science educator who primarily teaches science methods courses. Her research interests include the professional development of science teachers

Karin Sprow Forté, DEd, is an Assistant Teaching Professor of Teacher and Lifelong Learning and Adult Education. She is the Professor-in-Charge of the ESL certificate program and was the Co-PI on the Pennsylvania Department of Education grant, "Teacher Residency Collaborative Project."

Jane M. Wilburne, EdD, is a Professor of Mathematics Education and Chair of the Teacher Education Division at Penn State Harrisburg. She was the PI on the grant funded by the Pennsylvania Department of Education, "Teacher Residency Collaborative Project."

Michael J. Swogger is an Assistant Teaching Professor of Education at Penn State Harrisburg. He is the Coordinator of the Secondary Education Social Studies degree program as well as the Secondary Education Coordinator. He has been an educator for 22 years.

Tina Wagle is a Professor and MEd Coordinator in the Education Division of the School for Graduate Studies at SUNY Empire State College. Her areas of interest include teacher education, issues of social justice, languages other than English, and has given many presentations and written publications in this area. She has been teaching in higher education for twenty years and prior to that taught high school Spanish. She was the recipient of a SUNY Chancellor's Award for Excellence in Faculty Service in 2008, named a SUNY Online Teaching Ambassador in 2018, was named the Susan H. Turben Chair in Mentoring, 2019–2021, and was awarded the SUNY Chancellor's Award for Excellence in Teaching in 2021.

Michelle R. Eades-Baird, SUNY Empire State College Michelle Eades-Baird is an assistant professor of science education in the Master of Arts in Teaching program at SUNY Empire State College. Prior to entering academia, she was a classroom science teacher for 17 years and earned her PhD from SUNY Buffalo. Her research interests include: preservice and in-service teacher pedagogical content knowledge (PCK) development, disciplinary practices and literacies in science education, science inquiry, teaching for social justice, and reform-based teaching practices.

Donna Mahar is an Emeritus Professor of education at SUNY Empire State College. For over a decade, Dr. Mahar's research has focused on creating virtual professional development spaces for pre- and in-service teachers, Since 2017 she has been presenting workshops on using literacy to create trauma sensitive classrooms. Mahar has National Board Certification in Early Adolescent English Language Arts and has been actively involved in writing elementary literacy and learning standards for the National Board of Professional Teaching Standards and the Council for the Accreditation of Educator Preparation.

Jeremy Zelkowski, Associate Professor of Secondary Mathematics Education at The University of Alabama, is the program coordinator for secondary mathematics teacher education programs. He has directed the programs since 2008. His research is focused on mathematics education policy, programmatic design, measurement validation, and teacher education program outcomes. Teaching mathematics with technological tools and engaging students in mathematical practices has centered his teaching philosophy. He has engaged teacher candidates and inservice teachers in professional learning opportunities in many federally funded grant programs. Previously, he taught high school mathematics in Louisiana before earning his PhD in Mathematics Education in the NSF-funded AC-CLAIM doctoral program at Ohio University.

Jan A. Yow, Professor of Secondary Mathematics Education at the University of South Carolina, is the program coordinator for secondary mathematics teacher education programs. Her research is focused on mathematics teaching and learning and teacher leadership. Teaching mathematics to each and every student at high levels guides her teaching philosophy. Most recently, Dr. Yow has worked with developing mathematics and science teacher leaders in rural communities and investigating how STEM teacher leadership is enacted nationally. Previously, she taught high school mathematics before earning her PhD at the University of North Carolina. Dr. Yow maintains both her 6–12 teaching license and National Board Certification to keep her grounded in her work with classroom teachers.

Patrice Parker Waller is an Associate Professor of Mathematics Secondary Education at California State University, Fullerton where she coordinates the Foundational Level Math Credential program. Dr. Waller has helped to prepare over 60 secondary mathematics teachers in Virginia and California. She holds a Doctor of Philosophy in Teaching and Learning with a concentration in Mathematics Education from Georgia State University. Her research interests include culturally responsive mathematics teaching in secondary mathematics and teaching and learning mathematics abroad. Dr. Waller is committed to the continuous improvement of mathematics instruction in the secondary and post-secondary education.

Belinda P. Edwards, PhD is a Professor of Mathematics Education in the Department of Secondary and Middle Grades Education at Kennesaw State University. Her scholarship and teaching focuses on Mathematics Methods and Clinical Practice & Partnerships with specific focus on preparing culturally responsive mathematics teachers using the learning cycle and approximations of practice during the clinical field experience. She has served as Co-PI on NSF Noyce and Teacher Quality grants and has experience planning and facilitating professional learning that seeks to develop culturally responsive mathematics teachers at both the practicing and induction levels.

Holly G. Anthony is Professor of Mathematics Education at Tennessee Tech University. Her research interests include STEM education, the professional development of teachers, and integrated mathematics curricula. She teaches mathematics content courses for preservice elementary/middle school teachers and mathematics methods courses for preservice secondary teachers. She leads numerous professional development workshops for inservice K–12 mathematics teachers each year.

Tye Campbell is an Assistant Professor of Education at Crandall University in Moncton, New Brunswick. He studies small group collaboration in mathematics and teaches a range of education courses. He previously taught middle school and high school mathematics in Alabama and Colorado before earning his PhD at The University of Alabama in 2021.

Anna Keefe is a doctoral candidate in the Mathematics Department at The University of Alabama. Her research interests include psychometric properties of undergraduate mathematics exams, teacher education programs, and modes of mathematics instruction. She is a part of the leadership team for a collaborative project that aims for teachers in underserved school districts to become mathematics teacher leaders. Her teaching philosophy is rooted in teaching for all and encouraging student engagement.

Carey Wilson is a research assistant at the Millard Oakley STEM Center at Tennessee Tech University and is pursuing her doctorate in STEM education full-time. She has taught Algebra I, geometry, Algebra II, Bridge mathematics, RTI, and personal finance classes at the public high schools she worked at for the past seven years. Finally, Carey is interested in integrating STEM subjects to help secondary level students arrive at deeper understandings of mathematics and its practical real-world applications especially within the context of science, technology, and engineering.

Marilyn E. Strutchens is an Emily R. and Gerald S. Leischuck Endowed Professor, Mildred Cheshire Fraley Distinguished Professor, and Interim Department Head of Curriculum and Teaching Auburn University, AL. Her research focuses on equity issues in mathematics education, clinical experiences for secondary teacher candidates, professional development for mathematics teachers, and growth and development of teacher leaders in mathematics education.

Basil Conway IV is an Associate Professor of Mathematics Education in the College of Education and Health Professions at Columbus State University and serves as the online mathematics education graduate program director. He researches and publishes in the areas and intersections of statistics education, equity, opportunity, access, social justice, and clinical experiences.

Charmaine Mangram is an Associate Professor in the Institute for Teacher Education (Secondary) program at University of Hawai'i at Mānoa. She studies professional development for future and current secondary mathematics teachers and parental engagement focused on mathematical practices.

David R. Erickson is a retired Professor of Mathematics Education in the Phyllis J. Washington College of Education at the University of Montana-Missoula. He was a founding partner in the paired placement Clinical Experiences Research Action Cluster of the Mathematics Teacher Education Partnership and continues to advocate for professional growth of teachers in the teaching and learning of mathematics and serves as a university supervisor for student teachers.

Brea Ratliff is currently pursuing a PhD in secondary mathematics education at Auburn University. Her research interests include equity in mathematics education, teacher education and leadership, and community/youth development.

Karen Goodnough, is the Dean of the College of Education at Memorial University. Her work focuses on action research, inclusive science education, preservice teacher education, problem-based learning, and STEM (Science, Technology, Engineering, and Mathematics) education.

Mary Stordy, is an associate professor on the education faculty at Memorial University. Her work focuses on mathematics education, the ontology of elementary mathematics educators; the ecological nature of mathematics, and interpretive research—particularly hermeneutics and phenomenology.

Amy J. Good is an associate professor in the Department of Reading and Elementary Education in the Cato College of Education at UNC Charlotte. She teaches undergraduate, graduate, and doctoral level courses in education. Her research interests include elementary social studies, National Board for Professional Teaching Standards, and professional development for teachers.

Daniel Mason Alston is an assistant professor of Elementary Science Education at the University of North Carolina at Charlotte and a graduate of Clemson University. His scholarship examines the development and impact of student-centered teaching methods such as, inquiry-based and STEM instruction. He also seeks to better understand the various person variables (e.g., emotions, motivations, beliefs) which impact the instructional choices teachers make in the classroom and how these person variables impact the learning environment.

Jean Payne Vintinner is a clinical assistant professor in the Department of Reading and Elementary Education at the University of North Carolina at Charlotte. A former high school English and reading teacher, her academic interests include adolescent literacy, content-area reading, and motivating struggling readers.

Ian C. Binns, PhD, is an associate professor of elementary science education in the Department of Reading and Elementary Education at the Cato College of Education at the University of North Carolina at Charlotte. His research focuses on the interaction between science and religion with the goal of helping people understand science and religion, what makes them unique, and how they both benefit society. Ian is also a host of the podcast Down the Wormhole, a show exploring the "strange and fascinating relationship between science and religion."

Tracy C. Rock, PhD, is a professor in the Department of Reading and Elementary Education in the Cato College of Education at UNC Charlotte. Her teaching and research interests include inquiry models of teacher professional development, elementary social studies education, and service learning.

S. Michael Putman is a professor and the department chair in the Department of Reading and Elementary Education at UNC Charlotte. His research interests are focused on the development of teacher self-efficacy and intercultural competencies through field experiences, local and international, and the relationship of affective variables on literacy outcomes, including those associated with online inquiry.

Cheryl R. Ellerbrock, PhD, is an associate professor of Social Science, Middle Grades, and General Secondary Education at the University of South Florida. At USF, she teaches a variety of undergraduate and graduate courses in middle level and general secondary education and serves as program co-coordinator of both an undergraduate residency-based middle school teacher preparation program and a doctoral program in teacher education. Dr. Ellerbrock has authored numerous articles and book chapters that center on ways to promote responsive school experiences for young adolescent learners. Specifically, she explores the ways adolescent learners' needs are supported in secondary schools and examines ways to prepare middle and high school teachers as well as teacher educators to be responsive to the needs of their students.

Rachelle Curcio, PhD, is a clinical assistant professor for Elementary Education and the Director of the University of South Carolina Professional Development Schools Network. Her research focuses on clinically centered teacher preparation for diverse 21st century classroom context with an explicit emphasis on school-university partnerships, practitioner inquiry, and coaching.

Eliza G. Braden is an associate professor of elementary education in the Instruction and Teacher Education at the University of South Carolina. Her research interests include critical literacy and language practices of Black and Latinx children and families, culturally relevant pedagogies, and critical multicultural children's literature. Eliza teaches courses in elementary literacy methods, reading assessment, and culturally relevant pedagogy. Eliza's work is published in *Journal of Children's Literature, Teachers College Record, Talking Points, and Journal of Language and Literacy Education*.

Catherine Compton-Lilly is the John C. Hungerpiller Professor at the University of South Carolina where she teaches courses in literacy studies and works with local educators. Her past research followed eight of her former first grade students through high school. In a current study, now in its 12th year, she is exploring the longitudinal school experiences of children from immigrant families. Dr. Compton-Lilly has authored several books and articles including the *Reading Research Quarterly, Research in the Teaching of English, Written Communication,* and *The Journal of Literacy Research.* Her interests include examining how time operates as a contextual factor in children's lives as they progress through school.

Michele Myers is a clinical associate professor at the University of South Carolina (UofSC) and Master of Arts in Teaching degree program Coordinator. She has over 26 years of experience in education and has served in the capacity of early childhood teacher, curriculum coordinator, and principal. Currently she teaches embedded literacy methods, reading assessment, classroom management, and culturally sustaining pedagogy courses for undergraduate and master level preservice teachers at UofSC. Her research focuses on culturally sustaining pedagogy and familial networks of support in children's literacy development. Myers is the president elect for Literacies and Languages for All Institute (LLA) and past president of the Early Childhood Education Association (ECEA).

Beth White is a senior lecturer in the College of Education in the Department of Instruction and Teacher Education at the University of South Carolina. She has over 31 years of experience in education and has served as a middle school teacher and elementary literacy coach. Her specialty areas are teaching literacy methods and reading assessment courses for elementary education teacher candidates, coaching teachers of readers and writers and serving as a PDS liaison for Irmo Elementary School in Columbia, SC. She also serves as an administrative program coordinator for the BA in Elementary Education at the University of South Carolina.

Carol Rees, PhD, is a professor at Thompson Rivers University in Kamloops, British Columbia in Canada. She is the coordinator of teacher education programs. Her area of research spans K–12 and postsecondary science education, including science teacher education.

Rupinder Deol Kaur is a master's of education graduate and a research assistant at Thompson Rivers University.

Beverly Ruberg is a faculty mentor, supervising teacher candidates on practicum at Thompson Rivers University. She has also been a sessional lecturer, coordinator and consultant at the university, and she is a retired school principal.

Magdalena Maslowski, Thompson Rivers University is a graduate from the BEd STEM program at Thompson Rivers University. She is currently a teacher in Princeton, British Columbia, Canada.

Brendon Bauhuis, Thompson Rivers University is a graduate from from the BEd STEM program at Thompson Rivers University. He is currently a teacher in Kamloops British Columbia Canada.

Grady Sjokvist is a science teacher in Kamloops Thompson School District in British Columbia, Canada. He is currently the science coordinator at NorKam Senior Secondary School.

Danielle Livingstone is a science and math teacher in Kamloops Thompson School District in British Columbia, Canada currently teaching at NorKam Secondary School.

Mary-Kate Sableski is an associate professor in the Department of Teacher Education at the University of Dayton. She teaches undergraduate and graduate courses in children's literature, literacy assessment and intervention, and reading methods. Her research interests include diversity in children's literature and struggling readers. She can be reached at msableski1@udayton.edu.

R. Lennon Audrain graduated from the Harvard Graduate School of Education with a master's degree in technology, innovation, and education at age 21. Currently, he is a PhD student in educational policy and evaluation in the Mary Lou Fulton Teachers College at Arizona State University. A former Latin and Spanish teacher in both Arizona and Massachusetts, his research interests explore how precollegiate, grow-your-own teacher programs and community colleges are mechanisms for teacher recruitment and teacher education and how these programs can be enhanced with educational technology. He earned his bachelor's degree in classics, concentrating in Latin and first master's degree in curriculum and instruction, both from Arizona State University at age 19.

Jody Googins is an assistant professor of Secondary Education in the School of Education at Xavier University. Dr. Googins received her PhD in Educational Leadership, with a focus in Leadership, Culture, and Curriculum, at Miami University, in Oxford, OH. She has a BS in political science from Xavier University, an MEd in Secondary Education from Miami University, and an MEd in Athletic Administration from Xavier University. Her research interests include teacher and curriculum stories, equity, and culturally responsive teaching. Previous to her time at Xavier

University, Dr. Googins was a high school teacher in Southwest Ohio for 18 years, and she served as a visiting assistant professor at Miami University.

Paula E. Egelson, EdD, recently retired as the Divisional Director of Research and Accountability at the Southern Regional Education Board in Atlanta. Dr. Egelson has also worked as a community organizer, classroom teacher, professional developer, and director of school improvement. Areas of research interest besides student teaching effectiveness include formative assessment, student equity, and students of poverty.

Jacob Hardesty is the Dean of the College of Social Science, Commerce, and Education and associate professor of Education at Rockford University, where he teaches courses in the foundations of education. In addition to his research on student teaching, his primary research interest involves the historical connections and tensions between popular culture and public education. He completed his PhD in 2013 at Indiana University in educational history.

Johannah D. Baugher, EdD, is an assistant professor and the Graduate Reading Program Coordinator in the School of Education at Northwest Missouri State University in Maryville, Missouri, where she teaches undergraduate and graduate-level literacy methods coursework. Prior to her career in higher education, Dr. Baugher taught several elementary grades. Dr. Baugher received her BSEd in Elementary Education with a Concentration in Language Arts, as well as her MSEd in Reading from Northwest Missouri State University. She completed her EdD at the University of Missouri–Columbia in Educational Leadership and Policy Analysis. Dr. Baugher resides in Spickard, Missouri, with her husband where they operate Iron B Ranch, a Registered Angus cow-calf operation in rural Grundy and Mercer counties.

Linda Gray Smith is an associate professor of education at Northwest Missouri State University, where she designs and teaches courses in the On-line Professionals Educational Leadership Program for both master's degree and specialists students. As coordinator of the undergraduate K–12 and secondary programs, Dr. Smith teaches courses taken by students in those program areas. Her research interests include intentional field experiences and coursework focusing on diversity and equity to prepare undergraduates to meet the needs of each learner. Prior to joining the faculty at Northwest Missouri State University, Dr. Smith served as a school superintendent, principal, and teacher in K–12 districts.

Joseph P. Haughey is an associate professor of English education and assistant director of teacher education at Northwest Missouri State University, where he teaches classes in literature and pedagogy, including courses in Shakespeare and young adult literature. His research interests include the historical analysis of Shakespeare's evolving role in American education, the use of graphic adaptations in the teaching of challenging and canonical texts, and general issues more broadly in teacher preparation, critical literacy, antiracism in education, and rural education.

Zora Wolfe is an associate professor and Program Director of the K–12 Educational Leadership and Instructional Technology Programs at Widener University (Chester, PA). Her areas of expertise include developing teacher practice in inquiry based pedagogy, collaborative inquiry communities, and teacher leadership.

Patricia Newman is the Director of Teacher Education and Certification at Widener University (Chester, PA). Her areas of research interest include special education, K–12 educational leadership, professional development, teacher certification, and teacher retention.

Sarah W. Sharpe, PhD, is an assistant professor of elementary education at Columbus State University, where she teaches in the teacher education program. Prior to entering higher education, she taught for five years in public schools as an elementary teacher.

David T. Marshall, PhD, is an assistant professor of educational research at Auburn University. He has eight years of experience working with urban teacher residency programs and has conducted research and evaluation with an alternative certification program for the past three years. Previously he taught middle and high school social studies in traditional public and public charter schools in Philadelphia, Pennsylvania.

Parinita Shetty is a School Based Mental Health Clinician working in collaboration with the Anchorage School District to provide integrated mental health treatment and guidance to teachers to help students overcome behavioral, emotional, and social problems that interfere with success at school and home. Parinita completed her Master's in Clinical Mental Health Counseling from Auburn University.

John E. Henning, Dean of the School of Education, is an experienced educational practitioner, researcher, and leader. He has a MED in Vocational Education and a PhD in Educational Psychology from Kent State University. His primary research interests include practice-based teacher education, teacher development, instructional decision-making, and classroom discourse. These interests developed from more than 20 years of experience as a high school teacher. Dr. Henning is an active scholar and researcher, with more than 50 publications.

Tracy Mulvaney is assistant dean in the School of Education at Monmouth University. She has a BS in Rehabilitation and an MA in Special Education both from the University of Arizona. She also holds an EdD in Educational Leadership from Northern Arizona University. Her research interests include clinical based teacher preparation models, teacher burnout, and various topics of special education.

Bernard F. Bragen, Jr., is serving as the Superintendent of the Edison Township Public Schools. He earned his doctorate in educational leadership from Nova Southeastern University, an MA in urban school leadership from New Jersey City University, an MA in special education, and a BS in management science/finance from Kean University. Most recently, Dr. Bragen was assistant professor and program director for the Monmouth EdD Program in Educational Leadership.

William O. George III is serving as the Superintendent of Schools for the Middletown Township Public Schools. He earned a doctorate degree in Educational Leadership from Seton Hall University, a Master of Science degree in Educational Leadership and Administration from Monmouth University, a Master of Arts degree in physical education from Ohio State University and a Bachelor of Science degree in health and physical education from Michigan State University. Dr. George has been honored with the Monmouth County Superintendent of the Year award, the New Jersey Governor's Educational Services Professionals Award, and the Distinguished Citizen Award by the YMCA.

Michelle Cook is a professor of Science Education and Associate Dean for Undergraduate Studies in the College of Education at Clemson University. In her current role, she provides leadership for all aspects of teacher preparation programs in the college. She earned a doctoral degree from North Carolina State University and undergraduate and master's degrees from the University of North Carolina at Chapel Hill. Prior to joining Clemson University, she taught high school science in North Carolina.

Laura Eicher is the Director of the Teacher Residency Program at Clemson University. She earned a PhD in Curriculum and Instruction from Clemson University and a Master of Arts in Education degree in biology from The Citadel. Prior to joining Clemson University, she taught high school science for 18 years in public schools in South Carolina.

Leigh Martin is the Executive Director of the Office of Field and Clinical Partnerships and Outreach at Clemson University. In this role, she provides leadership for College partnerships and for all aspects of candidates' field placements. She earned a PhD from Clemson in Curriculum and Instruction in 2016. Prior to working at Clemson, she taught middle school and high school mathematics and worked with math and science instructional coaches throughout the state of South Carolina.

Dan Hanley is the Director of STEM Education Research and Evaluation at Western Washington University. He received his PhD from the University of Colorado-Boulder in Educational Psychology and Research/Evaluation Methodology. Over the past 20 years, he has developed and conducted numerous evaluations and studies for the National Science Foundation, Department of Education, the Navy, Colorado's Department of Education, and Washington State's Department of Education (OSPI). As a Fulbright Scholar to Norway in 2001, he examined Norway's system of school-based evaluation. Dr. Hanley's research interests include STEM educational reform in P–12 and higher education settings, as well as inservice and preservice STEM teacher preparation.

Matthew Miller, PhD, is a faculty member in the department of Elementary Education at WWU. For the past 20 years, Dr. Miller's research and practice have focused on preservice teacher education program design, clinical residencies, teacher education partnerships, new teacher mentoring, and clinical practice. Recently, Dr. Miller co-designed and now co-leads Preservice Mentoring Academies for the Washington Office of Superintendent of Public Instruction (OSPI) and currently co-directs the local "Prepared To Teach" initiative, a national project sponsored by the Bank Street College of Education that is focused on partnership development for co-designed, financially supportive, and sustainable clinical residencies.

Jennifer Sorensen, PhD, is assistant professor of chemistry and liaison to teacher education at Seattle University. She pursued graduate training in both theoretical chemistry and science education with the intent to work across boundaries between colleges of science and education, secondary schools, and informal science environments. Dr. Sorensen was a Science Team Leader for the Washington State College Readiness Project, and PI on an NSF-funded project that adapted teacher professional development pedagogies to train community volunteers to engage youth in science inquiry. Her teaching and research interests include equity strategies in STEM classrooms and practice-based science teacher education.

Allyson Rogan-Klyve, PhD, is an assistant professor of science education in the science and mathematics education department at Central Washington

University. She also serves as the field placement coordinator for the TeachSTEM program at CWU. Her primary research interests include high-leverage teaching practices and teacher education pedagogies that help new teachers enact these practices.

Robin Hands is the Director of Clinical Practice at the Farrington College of Education, Sacred Heart University (SHU), Fairfield, CT. She began her career as an elementary school teacher and administrator. Before coming to SHU, she was the Director of School-University Partnerships at the University of Connecticut. Her scholarship focuses on teacher education, clinical practice, and school-university partnerships. She was recently appointed to the Board of Directors for the National Center for Clinical Practice and Education Preparation (NCCEP) and is a member of the National Association for Professional Development Schools (NAPDS) and the National Network for Educational Renewal (NNER).

René Roselle is an associate professor, the Director of Teacher Preparation, and co-directs the Bridgeport Residency Program at Sacred Heart University's Farrington College of Education. Dr. Roselle's scholarship focuses on teacher education, clinical practice, and school-university partnerships. René served on the American Association of Colleges of Teacher Education's (AACTE) Clinical Practice Commission (CPC) and was appointed to the Board of Directors for the National Center for Clinical Practice and Education Preparation (NCCEP). Before joining the faculty at Sacred Heart, René was an Associate Clinical Professor at the University of Connecticut and a high school special education teacher.

Annie Kuhn has been an educator for 25 years and is currently teaching fifth grade in Glastonbury, Connecticut. In addition to being a classroom teacher, Annie has served as liaison between her district and the University of Connecticut for the past 10 years, providing a clinical perspective. She mentors preservice and first-year teachers, and most recently began teaching as an adjunct professor at Sacred Heart University.

June L. Cahill is currently serving in the role of Principal at E. B. Kennelly School in Hartford, Connecticut. June has 17 years of classroom teaching experience, three years as an Instructional Coach and seven years in her role as a school administrator, including Academic Dean and Principal.

Luke Hands holds an MEd in urban education from the University of Massachusetts, Amherst. He is currently a social studies teacher at Edwin O. Smith high school in Storrs, CT. Before teaching at E. O. Smith, Luke taught at Central and Commerce High schools in Springfield, MA. Luke serves as a mentor in the state of CT and works with students from the University of Connecticut, Central Connecticut State University, and Eastern Connecticut State University. He has also taught as an adjunct in UConn's teacher education program.

Rebecca Hines is an associate professor at the University of Central Florida and is the Principal Investigator on the OSEP personnel preparation project, LEAD-PREP: Leadership preparation through residencies and enhanced partnerships. She currently oversees the undergraduate Exceptional Student Education program in the College of Community Innovation and Education at UCF, and created the new Exceptional Student Education Learning and Language track to provide more opportunities for students interested in working with students with disabilities. In addition to teacher preparation, her research interests include working with students with emotional/behavioral disorders, inclusion, and technology integration.

Eileen M. Glavey, PhD, is currently an assistant professor of Inclusive & Special Education at Western Carolina University. She recently served as the Project Director of an OSEP Stepping-Up Technology grant-funded project researching the use of a robotics and artificial intelligence to increase the social and emotional skills of students with Autism Spectrum Disorder. Dr. Glavey has extensive experience teaching in pre-K–12 classrooms. She currently mentors teacher candidates to prepare them for inclusive classrooms. Her professional interests include school and community inclusion, teacher preparation and the effects of emotional regulation and emotional expression of teachers on student behavior.

Whitney Hanley, PhD, motivated by the role the educational system can play in developing critically conscious educators, Whitney Hanley studies the qualitative ways in which schools and communities support the success of culturally and linguistically diverse females with disabilities and their peers. Dr. Hanley's teaching experience of 8 years includes Elementary and Middle School special education as well as Undergraduate Special Education Teacher Preparation. She is currently a Special Education Teacher in Gwinnett County Public Schools in Lilburn, GA.

Annette Romualdo, PhD, is currently an assistant professor in Special Education and Special Education Program Coordinator at the University of Minnesota, Duluth. She earned a PhD in Special Education at the University of Central Florida, as a Project LEAD scholar. Dr. Romualdo has a Bachelor's degree in Biology from North Park University and a Master's degree in Secondary Education, mathematics emphasis from the Hawai'i Pacific University. Dr. Romualdo's passion is to increase the equity and access for students with intellectual disabilities in inclusive post-secondary settings. Dr. Romualdo's research interests also include the academic achievement of persons born late-preterm, with a focus on adolescence and transition.

Matthew Ohlson, PhD, is the Director of the Taylor Leadership Institute and Associate Professor of Leadership at the University of North Florida. A former teacher and administrator in the Boston Public Schools, Dr. Ohlson earned his PhD in Organizational Leadership from the University of Florida and has serves as a Leadership Coach to 7 Olympians, 12 professional athletes and more than 400 educational leaders throughout the nation. Dr. Ohlson has been focused on collaborating with rural schools, athletic teams, nonprofits and businesses to increase recruitment, retention and achievement using leadership development as a catalyst for increased outcomes. Dr. Ohlson has been awarded the Florida College Access Network (FCAN) Innovator Award, NPR American Graduate Champion, National Jefferson Award for Public Service and the Work of Heart Award from the United Way.

Lauren J. Gibbs, EdD, is the executive director at the Tiger Academy in Jacksonville, Florida. Prior to working at Tiger Academy, she was the director of Professional Development Schools and associate director for the Center for Urban Education and Policy at the University of North Florida's College of Education. A majority of Lauren's career was spent at the University of Florida's Lastinger Center for Learning. In this position, Lauren was the designer, coordinator, project manager, and lead facilitator for multiple district coaching initiatives across the state of Florida. I Most recently, Lauren has taken on the role of school leader in a PDS on the Northeast side of Jacksonville. Lauren has published multiple articles on coaching and has presented at various conferences around the country on the PDS and coaching work she has helped to design and lead. Lauren also coordinated an alternative Educator Preparation Institute through the University of Florida where she trained alternatively certified teachers in high-need schools. Before working with the Lastinger Center, she was an inclusion teacher in second, fourth, and fifth grades at P. K. Yonge Developmental Research School. Lauren holds a doctorate in curriculum and instruction from the University of Florida.

Easter Brown was as Resident Clinical Faculty (RCF) member where she served as supervisor, mentor, and coach of preservice and in-service teachers. Easter recently completed her first year as assistant principal at Argyle Elementary in Orange Park, FL. She is also a UNF doctoral student, beginning her third year this fall.

Shelley Lester served a pivotal role in fostering the partnership between UNF and the Clay County Schools (FL) including supporting the development of pre/in-service teachers as well as fostering learning and communication throughout this K20 PDS partnership.

Justin Faulkner brings 14 years of experience in Clay County District Schools as the new principal of Green Cove Junior High School. His previous leadership experience includes a three-year principalship at Orange Park Junior High School and four years as an assistant principal of Orange Park High School where he fostered new partnerships with the University of North Florida and the National Association of Professional Development Schools. In 2017, he was selected as Clay County's Assistant Principal of the Year. Mr. Faulkner is also a member of Leadership Florida as well as works with the FLDOE and Wallace Foundation on the revision of the state of Florida's Level 1 and 2 leadership pathways. Along with several other leaders in Clay County, he is pursuing his doctorate in Educational Leadership at the University of North Florida.

Stephanie Gomez-Jackson is a doctoral student pursuing a degree in Educational Leadership at the University of North Florida. She is an educator with over 16 years of experience and currently serves as the owner of two preschools where she oversees curriculum implementation and professional learning initiatives. Prior to becoming an entrepreneur, she has served as an elementary school principal for six years. Stephanie's experiences in culturally diverse schools with a lack of culturally responsive learning environments has led to her vested interest in developing teachers and educational leaders and facilitating professional learning that focuses on using students' cultural and ethnic backgrounds to cultivate their academic mindsets.

Clayton Anderson serves the Clay County School District as a Supervisor of Maintenance. In this capacity he infuses his "all means all" approach and is working to create a system wide lift through empowerment of the team at the foundational level. Prior to the Supervisor position, Mr. Anderson had the opportunity to serve in Clay County for 17 years with 16 of them serving in various capacities at Orange Park High School. Under his leadership at OPHS, they saw a significant change in climate/culture through sweeping facilities improvement, increased student expectations in learning and a stronger focus on instruction. These significant improvements allowed OPHS to increase as a "B" graded school and grow 14% in graduation rate over the past six years.

Ruthmae Sears, is an associate professor at the University of South Florida. She is the coordinator for developmental mathematics courses, and the bachelors and master's program in secondary mathematics education. Dr. Sears is also the lead faculty facilitator for the university's inclusive and equitable pedagogy program. Her research focuses on curriculum issues, the development of reasoning and proof skills, clinical experiences in secondary mathematics, and the integration of technology in the teaching and learning of mathematics. Dr. Sears is a principal and co-principal investigator for multiple NSF funded grants. Addititionally, Dr. Sears is the associate editor for the NCTM journal, Mathematics Teacher: Learning and Teaching PreK-12 (MTLT), the co-chair for the Accelerating Systemic Change Network (ASCN) in STEM Higher Education Working group for Equity, and Inclusion and the Florida Department of Education's State Course Numbering System (SCNS) Discipline Coordinator in the field of Mathematics Education.

Patricia Brosnan, is an associate professor of Mathematics Education and associate chairin the Department of Teaching and Learning at Ohio State University. Dr. Brosnan's research interests are in improving struggling students' mathematics learning as well as improving teachers' mathematics content and pedagogical knowledge.

Cynthia Castro-Minnehan, University of South Florida. Mrs. Castro-Minnehan is a doctoral candidate in Mathematics education at the University of South Florida. Her research interest focuses on clinical experiences and technology integration in mathematics.

Pier Junor Clarke, Georgia State University. Dr. Junor Clarke is a clinical professor in the Department of Middle and Secondary Education at the College of Education & Human Development, Georgia State University. She is the Mathematics Education Unit Leader and Lead coordinator and faculty of the Master of Arts in Teaching and Certification program for secondary mathematics education. Her research focuses on the development, retention, and sustainability of effective professional learning communities that support high quality secondary mathematics teachers in urban settings.

Jamalee Stone, Black Hill State University. Dr. Stone is an associate professor of mathematics education in the College of Education and Behavioral Sciences at Black Hills State University (BHSU) in Spearfish, SD. Her research interests include equity and mathematics education, and preservice teachers' use of co-planning and co-teaching during their clinical experiences.

Meghan Shaughnessy is an assistant professor of mathematics education at Boston University's Wheelock College of Education and Human

Development. Her research focuses on the design and study of practice-intensive approaches to the professional preparation and ongoing learning of teachers and approaches to formatively assessing developing skills with teaching practice.

Sarah Kate Selling, PhD, is a medical student at Stanford University. Her current research focuses on relationship-centered communication training for pediatric residents and the role of coaching programs in residency education. Previously she was an Assistant Professor of Mathematics Education at the University of Utah, where she studied mathematics classroom discourse and pedagogies of practice-based teacher education.

Nicole Garcia is a mathematics teacher educator at the University of Michigan and associate director of TeachingWorks. Her research interests focus on the development and learning of mathematics teachers from pre-service education throughout their professional career.

Deborah Loewenberg Ball is the William H. Payne Collegiate Professor of education at the University of Michigan, an Arthur F. Thurnau Professor, and the director of TeachingWorks. She taught elementary school for more than 15 years, and continues to teach mathematics to elementary students every year. Ball's research focuses on the practice of teaching, using elementary mathematics as a critical context for investigating the challenges of building relationships with children and helping children develop agency and understanding, and on leveraging the power of teaching to disrupt patterns of racism and to contribute to building a just society.

Austin Kureethara Manuel is an assistant professor in Curriculum and Learning Department in the West College of Education at Midwestern State University. His research interests are student responses and feedback, learning and teaching mathematics, cognitive aspects of learning mathematics, human services, and professional development schools.

Christina Janise McIntyre is an associate professor in the Curriculum and Learning Department of the Gordon T. and Ellen West College of Education and is the graduate program coordinator for Curriculum and Instruction. She currently holds the designation of the West College of Education Distinguished Professor. She has a BA in English, an MEd in Counseling, and a PhD in Instructional Leadership and Academic Curriculum from the University of Oklahoma. Her research interests include preservice teacher education, culturally responsive pedagogy and teacher professional development.

Emily Kate Reeves is an associate professor in the Curriculum and Learning Department of the West College of Education and the Chair of Human Subjects and Review Committee (IRB). She has a BSIS in Interdisciplinary studies, an MA in Educational Leadership, and a PhD in Curriculum and Instruction from Texas Tech University. Her research interests include literacy, culturally responsive pedagogy, professional development, and both in-service and preservice teacher education.

Daphney L. Curry is an associate professor and Interim Dean of the West College of Education at Midwestern State University. Dr. Curry is also chair of the Curriculum and Learning Department and is the 2020 recipient of the Hardin Professor Award. Her research interests focus on literacy, culturally responsive pedagogy, in-service and preservice professional development, and professional development schools.

Tracy Mulvaney is the Assistant Dean for the School of Education at Monmouth University. She holds an EdD in Educational Leadership from Northern Arizona University. Her BS in Rehabilitation and MA in Special Education were achieved at the University of Arizona.

Kathryn Lubniewski is currently an associate professor at Monmouth University and the Director of the Master of Art's in Teaching program. She earned a doctorate from West Virginia University in special education as well as her BS in multidisciplinary studies and MA in elementary education. Her current scholarship focuses on teacher training and technology.

Wendy Gray Morales serves as the assistant superintendent of a New Jersey public school district, as well as an adjunct professor at Monmouth University. Dr. Morales earned a BA in Radio & Television from The George Washington University, a MA in History from American Public University, and an EdD in Educational Leadership from Monmouth University.

Printed in the United States
by Baker & Taylor Publisher Services